MAN THE HUNTER

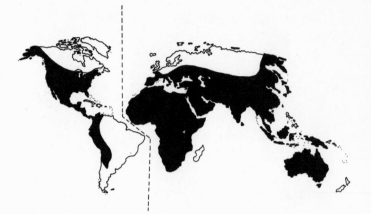

World Population: 10 million
Per Cent Hunters: 100

(10,000 B.C.)

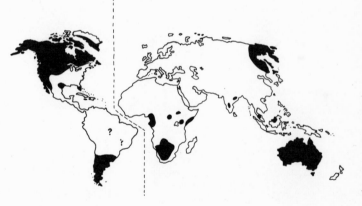

World Population: 350 million
Per Cent Hunters: 1.0

(1500 A.D)

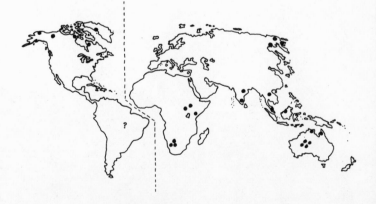

World Population: 3 billion
Per Cent Hunters: 0.001

(present

MAN THE HUNTER

Edited by
Richard B. Lee
and
Irven DeVore
with the assistance of
Jill Nash

ALDINE PUBLISHING COMPANY/CHICAGO

First published 1968 by
ALDINE PUBLISHING COMPANY
529 South Wabash Avenue
Chicago, Illinois 60605

Library of Congress Catalog Card Number 67–17603
Designed by Chestnut House
Printed in the United States of America

To Claude Lévi-Strauss

Preface

In November, 1965, Sol Tax asked us to organize a symposium on current research among the hunting and gathering peoples of the world. This meeting was conceived to follow logically from an earlier symposium on the Origin of Man held at the University of Chicago in April, 1965. There were a number of reasons why we felt a conference devoted exclusively to the hunting way of life would be appropriate at this time. Current ethnographic studies have contributed substantial amounts of new data on hunter-gatherers and are rapidly changing our concept of Man the Hunter. Social anthropologists generally have been reappraising the basic concepts of descent, filiation, residence, and group structure. In archeology the recent excavation of early living floors has led to a renewed interest in and reliance on hunter-gatherer data for reconstruction, and current theories of society and social evolution must inevitably take into account these new data on the hunter-gatherer groups. Finally, hunting and gathering, as a way of life, is rapidly disappearing and it was hoped that the symposium would serve to stimulate further research while there were still viable groups to study.

It was clear, however, that the first order of business was to present the new data on hunters and to clarify a series of conceptual issues among social anthropologists as a necessary background to broader discussions with archeologists, biologists, and students of human evolution. A preliminary canvass was made in January, 1966, of seventeen younger anthropologists who had recently completed field work among hunting peoples, and their enthusiastic response led us to contact an additional fifty scientists in social anthropology, human biology, archeology, demography, and ecology, particularly those who in their writings had shown an interest in hunter-gatherer data and theory. The positive response of this larger group insured the success of the symposium, and the Wenner-Gren Foundation for Anthropological Research generously agreed to sponsor the meeting and to cover traveling and living expenses for the participants.

The symposium on Man the Hunter was held at the Center for Continuing Education at the University of Chicago, April 6–9, 1966. In attendance were some 75 scholars from as far afield as India, Japan, Australia, Uganda, Kenya, and the German Democratic Republic, as well as from centers in France, England, Canada, Latin America, and the United States. In an intensive four-day meeting, those present heard 28 background papers and twelve formal discussions, and participated in over ten hours of open debate. Since most of the papers had been distributed in advance, it was possible to limit formal presentations to ten minutes each in order to leave time for discussion. Our impression is that most participants found this intensive format exhausting but rewarding.

With three exceptions, all of the original papers presented at the symposium are published here. The majority have been substantially revised in the light of our discussions in Chicago. In addition, two new papers, one by Yengoyan and the other by Washburn and Lancaster, are included in the book although they were not presented at the meeting.

The format of this book follows closely that of the symposium. The introductory section contains a general statement by the editors of the problems and issues to be discussed and an inventory by Professor G. P. Murdock of the current status of the world's hunting and gathering peoples. Each of the remaining sections corresponds to one of the topical sessions of the symposium, and each section contains the relevant papers as well as the edited transcript of the symposium discussion. As editors we are aware that publishing verbatim material from symposia does not always work out successfully; we hope that our attempt at editing has eliminated redundancy and inconsequential material while still conveying some of the excitement and the confrontation of different viewpoints that characterized the symposium itself.

On behalf of all the participants we want to thank the Wenner-Gren Foundation for Anthropological Research for providing the financial support that made possible the symposium and the preparation of this volume. Mrs. Lita Osmundsen and the excellent staff of the Foundation in New York solved the complex problems of travel, visas, and financing with their usual efficient dispatch, enabling all of us to converge miraculously on Chicago on the appointed day.

Sol Tax conceived the idea of a symposium on Man the Hunter and brought it to fruition. As chairman of the meetings he brought us together on time and skillfully kept speakers within their time limits; on behalf of a group of anthropologists who had a great deal to say, we offer Sol our affectionate resentment. The staff of *Current Anthropology* worked to distribute advance papers, to compile accurate transcripts and address lists, and generally to keep the symposium running smoothly.

Our thanks go as well to Lee Pravatiner and the staff of the Center for Continuing Education. With accommodations, food service, press, duplicating facilities, and meeting rooms all under one roof, the Center was an ideal place for a symposium of this size and complexity. Few of the participants realized the contribution that Mr. Pravatiner made to the success of the meeting; he attended to countless details of seating arrangements, reservations,

messages, transcription, and mimeographing, and did so tactfully and unobtrusively. Personally we were struck by the contrast between the complex social and technological system that enabled us to meet and the much simpler systems of the hunting and gathering peoples we were discussing.

In addition we should mention the pleasant evening that many of us spent at the American Indian Center in north Chicago. Our thanks go to members of the Center and to its director Robert Rietz, for their hospitality.

The transcription and editing of the twenty hours of tapes from the sessions proved to be a formidable job; we are particularly grateful to Paul L. DeVore of the University of Chicago for the 180 pages of transcription and to Jill Nash of Harvard University for her aid in editing the transcript and for many other editorial services. Miss Nash also read through the entire manuscript and made many helpful suggestions which have been incorporated in the final version. Dr. David A. Horr of Harvard undertook the compilation of the references and handled many editorial details in the latter half of the book.

The drawings were executed by Judith Tempkin and Jane Britton; the former also assisted in the final preparation of the bibliography. Mrs. Marcia Harding Anderson, Mrs. Elizabeth Burnham, and Mrs. Linda Moseley, all of the staff of the Department of Social Relations of Harvard University, typed portions of the manuscript; the final version was produced by Mrs. Nellie Miller.

Richard Lee offers a special vote of thanks to the students in Social Relations 251 and 252, graduate seminars at Harvard in the spring semesters of 1966 and 1967, respectively. The members of these seminars read most of the preliminary manuscripts and their lively discussions did much to clarify the core issues presented in the book.

Both of us wish to thank our colleagues in the Department of Social Relations at Harvard for providing a congenial intellectual atmosphere and for making a number of useful suggestions on specific portions of the manuscript; we appreciate particularly the help of John W. M. Whiting, A. Kimball Romney, Evon Z. Vogt and David H. P. Maybury-Lewis. We also want to thank our publisher,

Alexander J. Morin, for his patience and forbearance while we labored to complete the manuscript before our departure for further field work among the Bushmen.

Finally we acknowledge our major debt to our contributors, many of whom are hunter-gatherers in spirit as well as in professional interest. No two anthropological field workers share exactly the same motivations and world-view, except perhaps a common interest in understanding the human condition. We cannot avoid the suspicion that many of us were led to live and work among the hunters because of a feeling that the human condition was likely to be more clearly drawn here than among other kinds of societies.

RICHARD B. LEE
IRVEN DEVORE

Contents

Bushm

WENNER-GREN FOUNDATION FOR ANTHROPOLOGICAL RESEARCH

Symposium on Man the Hunter

PARTICIPANTS

Sol Tax, Chairman
University of Chicago

Alexander A. Alland
Columbia University

James N. Anderson
University of California, Berkeley

Asen Balikci
Université de Montréal

Marco Bicchieri
Beloit College

Lewis R. Binford
University of California, Los Angeles

Sally R. Binford
University of California, Los Angeles

Joseph B. Birdsell
University of California, Los Angeles

Jean Briggs
Memorial University of Newfoundland

Ralph Bulmer
University of Auckland

Napoleon A. Chagnon
University of Michigan

✳ J. Desmond Clark
University of California, Berkeley

Georges Condominas
École Pratique des Hautes Études, Paris

William Crocker
Smithsonian Institution

Ralph Crocombe
Australian National University

David Damas
National Museum of Canada, Ottawa

James Deetz
Brown University

Edward Deevey, Jr.
Yale University

P. E. de Josselin de Jong
Leiden University

Irven DeVore
Harvard University

A. Jorge Dias
Lisbon

Frederick L. Dunn
Hooper Foundation
University of California, San Francisco

Fred Eggan
University of Chicago

Leslie G. Freeman, Jr.
University of Chicago

Peter M. Gardner
University of Texas

David M. Hamburg
Stanford University

June Helm
University of Iowa

L. R. Hiatt
University of Sydney

F. Clark Howell
University of Chicago

Glynn L. Isaac
University of California, Berkeley

Irawati Karvé
University of Poona

C. S. Lancaster
University of California, Berkeley

Donald W. Lathrap
University of Illinois

William S. Laughlin
University of Wisconsin

Duhyan Lee
Seoul National University

Richard B. Lee
Harvard University

Claude Lévi-Strauss
College de France

Toichi Mabuchi
Tokyo Metropolitan University

Lorna Marshall
Peabody Museum, Cambridge, Mass.

M. J. Meggitt
Queens College, New York

George Peter Murdock
University of Pittsburgh

Chie Nakane
University of Tokyo

Roger C. Owen
Queens College, New York

Angel Palerm
Pan American Union, Mexico

Arnold R. Pilling
Wayne State University

Merrick Posnansky
Makerere University College, Uganda

Edward S. Rogers
Royal Ontario Museum, Toronto

Frederick G. G. Rose
Institut für Völkerkunde, Berlin

James R. Sackett
University of California, Los Angeles

Marshall D. Sahlins
University of Michigan

Edward Schieffelin
University of Chicago

David M. Schneider
University of Chicago

William Shack
University of Chicago

Lauriston Sharp
Cornell University

Surajit Sinha
Indian Institute of Management, Calcutta

Richard Slobodin
McMaster University

Julian H. Steward
University of Illinois

Stuart Struever
Northwestern University

Wayne Suttles
Portland State College

Reina Torres de Arauz
Universidad de Panama

Colin M. Turnbull
American Museum of Natural History

Sherwood L. Washburn
University of California, Berkeley

Hitoshi Watanabe
University of Tokyo

John W. M. Whiting
Harvard University

B. J. Williams
University of California, Los Angeles

James Woodburn
London School of Economics

Aram A. Yengoyan
University of Michigan

PART I

Introduction

I.

Problems in the Study of Hunters and Gatherers

RICHARD B. LEE AND IRVEN DEVORE

Cultural Man has been on earth for some 2,000,000 years; for over 99 per cent of this period he has lived as a hunter-gatherer. Only in the last 10,000 years has man begun to domesticate plants and animals, to use metals, and to harness energy sources other than the human body. *Homo sapiens* assumed an essentially modern form at least 50,000 years before he managed to do anything about improving his means of production. Of the estimated 80,000,000,000 men who have ever lived out a life span on earth, over 90 per cent have lived as hunters and gatherers; about 6 per cent have lived by agriculture and the remaining few per cent have lived in industrial societies.

To date, the hunting way of life has been the most successful and persistent adaptation man has ever achieved. Nor does this evaluation exclude the present precarious existence under the threat of nuclear annihilation and the population explosion. It is still an open question whether man will be able to survive the exceedingly complex and unstable ecological conditions he has created for himself. If he fails in this task, interplanetary archeologists of the future will classify our planet as one in which a very long and stable period of small-scale hunting and gathering was followed by an apparently instantaneous efflorescence of technology and society leading rapidly to extinction.

"Stratigraphically," the origin of agriculture and thermonuclear destruction will appear as essentially simultaneous.

On the other hand, if we succeed in establishing a sane and workable world order, the long evolution of man as a hunter in the past and the (hopefully) much longer era of technical civilization in the future will bracket an incredibly brief transitional phase of human history—a phase which included the rise of agriculture, animal domestication, tribes, states, cities, empires, nations, and the industrial revolution. These transitional stages are what cultural and social anthropologists have chosen as their particular sphere of study. We devote almost all of our professional attention to organizational forms that have emerged within the last 10,000 years and that are rapidly disappearing in the face of modernization.

It is appropriate that anthropologists take stock of the much older way of life of the hunters. This is not simply a study of biological evolution, since zoologists have come to regard behavior as central to the adaptation and evolution of all species. The emergence of economic, social, and ideological forms are as much a part of human evolution as are the developments in human anatomy and physiology.

The time is rapidly approaching when there

will be no hunters left to study. Our aim in convening the symposium on Man the Hunter was to bring together those who had recently done field work among the surviving hunters with other anthropologists, archeologists, and evolutionists who are interested in the results of these studies. But it was also clear that there were a series of issues among social anthropologists that required clarification before a dialogue with others could become meaningful. Therefore, the first half of this book is devoted to the presentation of new data on contemporary hunters, along with discussion and evaluation of current issues. The later chapters consider the relevance of these data to the reconstruction of life in the past.

A number of divergent viewpoints are represented in this volume and many of the issues to be raised remain unsolved. As both editors and partisans, it is our task to point out areas of general agreement while trying to avoid glossing over real differences where they occur. Considering the many points of view presented at the symposium, it would be impossible to touch on all of the interesting material. We make no apologies for our selection but offer it as a partial guide to the papers and discussions.

DEFINING HUNTERS

The symposium considered the definition of "hunters" but did not succeed in satisfying everyone. An evolutionary definition would have been ideal; this would confine hunters to those populations with strictly Pleistocene economies—no metal, firearms, dogs, or contact with non-hunting cultures. Unfortunately such a definition would effectively eliminate most, if not all, of the peoples reported at the symposium since, as Marshall Sahlins pointed out, nowhere today do we find hunters living in a world of hunters.

Murdock (Chapter 2, this volume) and others took an organizational view which equated hunting and gathering with the "band" level of social organization. However, not all hunters live in bands. Suttles, for example (Chapter 6), documents the quite substantial non-agricultural tribal societies of the Northwest coast of North America. Judging from recent archeological evidence from the

Paleolithic of France and of European Russia, a number of ancient hunting societies may have operated on a similar scale.

A further consideration was introduced by Lathrap (Chapter 3) and others who cited a number of hunting peoples who were "failed" agriculturalists. This *readaptation* to hunting, or "devolution" as it has been called, characterized such classic "hunters" as the Siriono of South America and the Veddas of Ceylon.

It was clear that there was much to be learned even from the ambiguous cases of tribal hunters, "devolved" hunters, and reformed hunters. To throw out impure cases was to lose the chance of gaining any significant understanding of modes of adaptation, group structure, social control, and settlement patterns. The symposium agreed to consider as hunters all cases presented, at least in the first instance. It was also generally agreed to use the term "hunters" as a convenient shorthand, despite the fact that the majority of peoples considered subsisted primarily on sources *other than meat*—mainly wild plants and fish.

THE REPRESENTATIVENESS OF OUR SAMPLE OF HUNTERS

There has been a burst of field research on hunting peoples in the last ten years, and this symposium was the first opportunity to bring together this diverse group of field workers.

The Australian contingent included L. R. Hiatt (Arnhem Land), M. J. Meggitt (Walbiri), Arnold Pilling (Tiwi), and Aram Yengoyan, all of whom have done field work in the 1950's and 1960's, as well as Birdsell, Rose, and Sharp whose field work dates to the 1930's and 1940's. Workers from Africa included Bicchieri, Turnbull (Mbuti), Woodburn (Hadza), and Marshall, Lee, and DeVore on the !Kung Bushmen. Field work in Asia was reported by Dunn, Gardner, Sinha, Watanabe, and Williams. Lathrap and Crocker presented data on the part-time hunters of tropical South America. The largest group had done field work in North America: Balikci, Damas, and Laughlin on the Eskimos; Helm, Rogers, and Slobodin on subarctic Indians; and Owen and Suttles on Indians of the Pacific coast. Julian H. Steward, in many ways the founder of modern hunter-gatherer studies, submitted a paper, but was prevented by illness from attending the conference itself.

One of the first questions considered at the symposium was whether the sample currently available to ethnographers is representative of the range of habitats which hunters occupied in the past. Ever since the origin of agriculture, Neolithic peoples have been steadily expanding at the expense of the hunters. Today the latter are often found in unattractive environments, in lands which are of no use to their neighbors and which pose difficult and dramatic problems of survival. The more favorable habitats have long ago been appropriated by peoples with stronger, more aggressive social systems.

Taking hunters as they are found, anthropologists have naturally been led to the conclusion that their life (and by implication the life of our ancestors) was a constant struggle for survival. The three maps presented in the frontispiece show a radically different picture. In 10,000 B.C., on the eve of agriculture, hunters covered most of the habitable globe, and appeared to be generally most successful in those areas which later supported the densest populations of agricultural peoples. By A.D. 1500 the area left to hunters had shrunk drastically and their distribution fell largely at the peripheries of the continents and in the inaccessible interiors. However, even at this late date, hunting peoples occupied all of Australia, most of western and northern North America, and large portions of South America and Africa. This situation rapidly changed with the era of colonial expansion, and by 1900, when serious ethnographic research got under way, much of this way of life had been destroyed. As a result, our notion of unacculturated hunter-gatherer life has been largely drawn from peoples no longer living in the optimum portion of their traditional range.

To mention a few examples, the Netsilik Eskimos, the Arunta, and the !Kung Bushmen are now classic cases in ethnography. However, the majority of the precontact Eskimos, Australian aborigines, and Bushmen lived in much better environments. Two-thirds of the Eskimos, according to Laughlin, lived *south* of the Arctic circle, and the populations in the Australian and Kalahari deserts were but a frac-

tion of the populations living in the well-watered regions of southeast Australia and the Cape Province of Africa. Thus, within a given region the "classic cases" may, in fact, be precisely the opposite: namely, the most isolated peoples who managed to avoid contact until the arrival of the ethnographers. In order to understand hunters better it may be more profitable to consider the few hunters in rich environments, since it is likely that these peoples will be more representative of the ecological conditions under which man evolved than are the dramatic and unusual cases that illustrate extreme environmental pressure. Such a perspective may better help us to understand the extraordinary persistence and success of the human adaptation.

ETHNOGRAPHIC RECONSTRUCTION

Many of the best-known studies of hunter-gatherers have relied on ethnographic reconstructions of situations that were no longer intact. In the early years of field anthropology, Kroeber in California, Boas on the Northwest coast, and Radcliffe-Brown in the Andaman islands and Australia compiled the recollections of older informants to produce a picture of the culture and society. The "facts" of the case were thought to include the verbalized cultural tradition—language, myths, folktales, and kin terms—and concrete expressions—rituals, house types, tools, dress, and religious objects. As anthropology developed, however, a different view emerged about what constituted the ethnographic facts. More attention was paid to the study of individuals and groups in ongoing social systems. The interest in ideology was retained, but this was tempered by the task of comparing stated norms with observed behavior. When discrepancies between "real" and "ideal" came to light, the ethnographer could then make further inquiries and observations and attempt to explain "how the system really works."

The shortcoming of the reconstructive method is that there is no means of testing and rechecking hypotheses. After the socio-economic system ceases to function, the only check available is the test of internal consistency, and the early ethnographers were more or less successful in constructing models of social systems that were self-consistent.

The controversy on this question is very much alive in current social anthropology and the issue forms a central theme in this volume (Chapters 10, 17a, 17c, 17h, 18, 19, 22b, and 22c). The relevance for methodology hinges on the question of how much of an ongoing system can be reconstructed 25–50 years after the event, solely on the basis of informants' accounts. Birdsell and others take the pessimistic view that such important features as group structure and territorial relations vanish with contact (Chapter 17a). Williams, in the same vein, reports that he was unable to reconstruct the residence arrangements of a Birhor group whose campsite had been mapped in detail by another anthropologist only six years previously. Woodburn notes that the Hadza present themselves as having a matrilineal descent system, when in fact the kinship and the group structure are bilateral; the fiction is used by the Hadza to emulate their agricultural, matrilineal neighbors. This fact is significant in itself, but more important, it would make impossible an accurate reconstruction of Hadza social organization at a later date, if one had to rely solely on the memory of informants.

On the other hand, several participants were more sanguine about the persistence of cultural traditions into the postcontact period. Lévi-Strauss cited the example of the retention of marriage ideology by Australian aborigines in the face of acculturation and demographic reverses (Chapter 17b, 17c). In addition, careful reconstructions of precontact ecological situations were presented by Watanabe, for the Ainu of the 1880's (Chapter 7), and by Balikci, for the Netsilik Eskimos in 1919–20 (Chapter 8).

Finally, June Helm pointed out that the group structure of such diverse peoples as the Dogrib Indians, the !Kung Bushmen, and the Nambikwara showed striking similarities in spite of widely differing social ideologies (Chapter 13). This suggests that small-scale societies may arrive independently at similar solutions to similar demographic and ecological problems. Without the opportunity of observing behavior, however, such an important point would be impossible to establish. This problem is discussed further by Anderson (Chapter 17c).

THE SUBSISTENCE BASE

Strictly speaking, hunting and gathering refers to a mode of subsistence, and many of the conference papers discussed problems of ecology and economic organization. Several field workers pointed out that the subsistence base of hunters was much more substantial than had been previously supposed. It came as a surprise to some that even the "marginal" hunters studied by ethnographers actually work short hours and exploit abundant food sources. Several hunting peoples lived well on two to four hours of subsistence effort per day and were not observed to undergo the periodic crises that have been commonly attributed to hunters in general (Chapters 4, 5, and 9b). Other peoples for whom detailed activity data were unavailable were nevertheless reported to show a "lack of concern" about the problem of finding food. This led the conference participants to speculate whether lack of "future orientation" brought happiness to the members of hunting societies, an idyllic attitude that faded when changing subsistence patterns forced men to amass food surpluses to bank against future shortages (Chapter 9c).

Dissenting views were reported. Balikci spoke of a "constant ecological pressure" which caused real hardship and anxiety among the Netsilik Eskimos (Chapter 8). Williams (Chapter 9c) found that the Birhor of India not only worked hard for their food but often went hungry. It was clear that Sahlins' characterization of the hunters (Chapter 9b) as the "original affluent society" would not apply in all cases. However Sahlins' argument served to underline the point that anthropologists have tended to view the hunters from the vantage point of the economics of scarcity. Viewed on their own terms, the hunters appear to know the food resources of their habitats and are quite capable of taking the necessary steps to feed themselves. It is unlikely that hunters would have deliberately chosen the catch-as-catch-can existence that has been ascribed to them. Since a routine and reliable food base appears to be a common feature among modern hunter-gatherers, we suspect that the ancient hunters living in much better environments would have enjoyed an even more substantial food supply.

HUNTING VS. GATHERING

The hunting of mammals has been considered the characteristic feature of the subsistence of early man, and two chapters in this volume explore the implications of hunting for human evolution (Washburn and Lancaster, Chapter 32; and Laughlin, Chapter 33). Modern hunters, however, depend for most of their subsistence on sources other than meat, mainly vegetable foods, fish, and shell fish. Only in the arctic and subarctic areas where vegetable foods are unavailable do we find the textbook examples of mammal hunters. Over the rest of the world, hunting appears to provide only 20 to 40 per cent of the diet (Lee, Chapter 4).

Binford, Washburn and Lancaster, and others expressed the view that fishing, seed-grinding, and hunting with dogs are late adaptations, dating from the Mesolithic and therefore not characteristic of Pleistocene conditions. Thus, the eclectic diet of the modern hunters may tell us little about the food habits of early man. Our own view is that vegetable foods in the form of nuts, berries, and roots were always available to early man and were easily exploited by even the simplest of technologies. It is also likely that early woman would not have remained idle during the Pleistocene and that plant foods which are so important in the diet of inland hunter-gatherers today would have played a similar role in the diet of early peoples. We agree, however, that hunting would become increasingly important as populations migrated out of the tropics into areas where plant foods are scarce. In addition, hunting is so universal and is so consistently a male activity that it must have been a basic part of the early cultural adaptation, even if it provided only a modest proportion of the food supplies.

SOCIAL AND TERRITORIAL ORGANIZATION

The analysis of the social structure of the hunting and gathering peoples proved to be a particularly difficult area of investigation because of the ambiguous conditions in which hunters are currently found. Fluidity of band composition appeared to be the most characteristic feature of the modern hunters, but participants disagreed on whether this flexibility was basic to the hunting way of life or whether it was a product of recent acculturation. We will briefly outline the history of band theory from Radcliffe-Brown, through Steward to Service and then go on to consider the evidence from recent field research.

THE PATRILOCAL BAND

Radcliffe-Brown gave this concept its modern expression in "Social Organization of Australian Tribes," where he described the patrilineal, patrilocal, territorial, exogamous horde as "the important local group throughout Australia" (1931, p. 35). The horde was a group of patrilaterally related males who lived and worked within their totemic estate and exchanged women with other such male-centered groups. Steward, in a general review of hunter-gatherers, admitted the horde or "patrilineal band" as one of three types of group structure, but he added the composite bands of the Northern Athapaskans and the family bands of Great Basin Shoshoneans (1936, 1955). This three-part division was later called into question by Elman Service (1962), who took the view that the "patrilocal band," as he called it, was not only the characteristic form of local organization in Australia but was also the basic form for *all* hunter-gatherers in the past (1962, pp. 65–67, 107–109). The composite and family bands, in Service's view, were artifacts of recent acculturation and breakdown.

Recent research has cast doubt on the model of the patrilocal band. Hiatt, reviewing the literature on Australian local organization (1962), failed to find a single indisputable example of Radcliffe-Brown's horde. The existence of patrilineal totemic clans has been well documented, but these functioned in ritual contexts and not as residential or economic units. Hiatt concludes:

> It is now clear that over a great deal of the continent the male members of totemic descent groups did not live together on separate pieces of land. They commonly lived in communities that contained male members of several totemic descent groups and regularly sought food over

areas that included totemic sites other than their own. Investigators that failed to find the horde in particular tribes were not (as some of them thought) observing aberrant forms of local organization. They were probably looking for something that never existed in any tribe (1962, p. 286).

Other ethnographers who had worked among "patrilocal band" peoples also failed to find this form of organization operating now or at any discoverable period in the past. Turnbull among the Mbuti Pygmies (Chapter 15), Lee and Marshall among the Bushmen (Chapters 4 and 17c) and Meggitt (Chapter 19) all report the occurrence of composite and flexible local groups. Others have studied the ethnohistoric record of peoples that Service claimed had patrilocal organization in the past. Helm on the Athapaskans (Chapter 13), Damas on the Eskimo (Chapter 12), and Pilling on the southeastern Australians (Chapter 16) present evidence that the composite bands observed in the present were characteristic of the earliest contact periods as well.

The patrilocal band, however, is not an empty category; cases are presented in which a patrilocal organization was in evidence, including the Ona of South America (Bridges, 1949, cited by Lathrap in Chapter 9d), the Kaiadilt of Australia (Tindale, 1962b, cited by Birdsell in Chapter 17a) and the Birhor of India (Williams in Chapter 14).

On the basis of present evidence, it appears that the patrilocal band is certainly not the universal form of hunter group structure that Service thought it was. Anderson (Chapter 17c), Turnbull (Chapter 15), Eggan (Chapter 17i), and others pointed out that the fluid organization of recent hunters has certain adaptive advantages, including the adjustment of group size to resources, the leveling out of demographic variance, and the resolution of conflict by fission. These features are independent of the effects of acculturation and would have been no less adaptive in precontact situations. Given these advantages, few of the conferees would endorse Service's view that the patrilocal band "seems almost an inevitable kind of organization" or that "the composite band . . . is obviously a product of the near destruction of aboriginal bands after contact

with civilization" (1962, p. 108). In fact Service himself has recently revised his opinion that the patrilocal band is inevitable.

Service has correctly drawn attention to the effects of contact on hunter-gatherer social organization, and this remains a difficult problem for the ethnographers. Although fluid organization makes ecological sense for many hunters, and could be shown to be more adaptive than patrilocal organization, in itself this is not evidence for aboriginal conditions. Since all hunting societies have suffered to some extent from contact, we may never be able to prove conclusively that one form or another was typical of the past in any specific case.

THE PROBLEM OF CORPORATION

Sharp (Chapter 17h) warns against the use of "prefabricated constructs" in the study of band organization. The prevalence of such constructs may derive from the application of concepts developed in tribal societies to the study of simpler and smaller-scale societies. The social units of tribal societies are based on the control and husbandry of real property usually in the form of agricultural land or livestock (Fortes, 1953). In addition, the formal political institutions such as courts, councils, and chieftainships lends a distinctive character to social relations of tribesmen that is lacking in the smaller-scale societies of hunters and gatherers. Radcliffe-Brown's well-known views on the universal importance of lineal descent and corporation (1952) may have led him to impose a corporate unilineal model on Australian local groups.

However, the reports in this volume make it clear that the hunter-gatherer band is not a corporation of persons who are bound together by the necessity of maintaining property. A corporation requires two conditions: a group of people must have some resource to incorporate about and there must be some means of defining who is to have rights over this resource. Among most hunter-gatherers one or both of these conditions are lacking. In Australia and among the Birhor, the patrilineal descent groups are present but these groups do not maintain exclusive rights to territorial resources (Hiatt in Chapter 10, Williams in

Service
really??

fission

Chapter 14). Among the Mbuti Pygmies the territories are well-defined but the membership in the resource-using group is open and changes frequently (Turnbull in Chapter 15). Among the Dogrib (Helm in Chapter 13), the Bushmen (Lee in Chapter 4), the central Eskimo (Damas in Chapter 12 and Balikci in Chapter 8) and the Hadza (Woodburn in Chapter 11), both the composition of the group and the range they exploit may vary from season to season. The existence of this variety makes it difficult to accept a model of hunter local groups that encapsulates each group of males within a territory, with exchange of women as the primary mode of communication between groups.

FLEXIBILITY AND THE
RESOLUTION OF CONFLICT BY FISSION

Turnbull (1965b and Chapter 15) has defined an important means of social control among the Mbuti Pygmies. When disputes arise within the band, the principals simply part company rather than allow the argument to cross the threshold of violence. By this seemingly simple device, harmony is maintained within the co-operating group without recourse to fighting or to formal modes of litigation. The essential condition seems to be the lack of exclusive rights to resources; thus it is a relatively simple matter for individuals and groups to separate when harmony is threatened. The effect of this practice is to keep the population circulating between band territories. Such a form of conflict resolution would not be possible in situations where social units are strictly defined and firmly attached to parcels of real estate. Woodburn and Lee reported a similar mode of conflict resolution among the Hadza and !Kung Bushmen; judging from their generally flexible group structure, resolution of conflict by fission may well be a common property of nomadic hunting societies.

ORDER AND CHAOS IN
HUNTER-GATHERER SOCIETY

One of the attractions of the patrilocal band model is the neatness of its formulation. In such a model the society is structured by the opera-

tion of a small number of fundamental jural rules: territorial ownership by males, band exogamy, and viripatrilocal postmarital residence. However, the model leaves scant room either for local and seasonal variations in food supply or for variance in sex ratios and family size within and between local groups. Nor does the model, in many cases, accord with the observed facts, and in this light it appears to be more a convenience for the analyst than a workable socioeconomic system.

Flexibility of living arrangements presents at first a confusing and disorderly picture. Brothers may be united or divided, marriage may take place within or outside the local group, and local groups may vary in numbers from one week to the next. Helm (1965a and Chapter 13) has made a valuable contribution to the methodology of band-composition analysis. By tabulating the primary relative linkages within Athapaskan groups, she has been able to show that married couples always join groups in which a sibling, parent, or child of one of the spouses is already resident. This produces a local group whose members are joined by a series of links through brothers, sisters, and spouses, often centered around a strong core of male siblings. However, the orientation is bilateral rather than lineal and serves to unite persons into effective work groups regardless of whether the kinship ties are patrilateral, matrilateral, or affinal. Application of this method to other hunters reveals a similar mode of affiliation among the Nambikwara, Bushmen, Hadza, and Arnhem Land aborigines. The bilateral nature of hunter local groups is not simply a matter of people failing to conform to their stated jural rules; several of the peoples just mentioned do not express an ideology of fixed membership groups. There is order in hunter-gatherer society, although not necessarily an order imposed by the operation of residence and descent rules.

MARRIAGE ARRANGEMENTS IN AUSTRALIA

The way Australian aborigines marry has held a central place in the anthropological study of kinship. The articulation between kin terms and cross-cousin marriage on the one hand, and moieties, sections and subsections on the other, have provided materials for a number of analysts, including Radcliffe-Brown, Leach, Murdock, Needham, and Lévi-Strauss. Since the symposium was concerned with the hunting way of life and not with the study of marriage *per se*, the several papers on the subject attempted to place Australian marriage and section systems into the general context of hunter-gatherer ecology and demography. Hiatt, for example (Chapter 18) presents a model of the operation of an eight-section system and then goes on to show that, given the small population of the Gidjingali of Arnhem Land, only a fraction of the marriages can be contracted between the cross-cousins specified by the model. The lack of women of the appropriate kin position makes it necessary for most men to seek a spouse elsewhere. Although over 90 per cent of the marriages are "morally proper," in other words contracted between persons of the correct subsections, the net result is that women do not function as a medium of exchange between descent groups. In his comment (Chapter 22b) Lévi-Strauss acknowledges the importance of relating stated norms to demographic variables but he goes on to say that his work in Australian kinship has been "concerned with a different problem: to ascertain what was the meaning of the rules, whether they be applied or not." He expresses the view that the evidence of a "collapsing Australian tribe" is not sufficient to make us discard the earlier formulations of Radcliffe-Brown and others which demonstrated that marriage was indeed regarded by the natives as an exchange of women between descent groups.

Meggitt (Chapter 19) and Yengoyan (Chapter 20) both bring demographic data to bear on the study of section systems, but they arrive at different conclusions. Meggitt notes that a series of fifteen central Australian tribes all exhibit a division into eight subsections, despite the fact that the populations of several of the tribes are less than 200 persons, too small for marriages to be contracted only between the members of appropriate subsections. This fact leads Meggitt to conclude that "among the Australian aborigines, subsections are not necessarily concerned in . . . the regulation of marriage" (Chapter 19). Yengoyan argues that subsections do regulate marriage, but only very

large tribes can successfully operate an eight-section system. A tribe of 1,100 persons, for example, would have no difficulty in arranging "proper" marriages since each of the eight divisions would contain about 25 eligible mates. On the other hand, a tribe numbering 200 persons or less would not be able to arrange marriages without considerable deviation from the stated rules and, in fact, few of the small tribes in Yengoyan's sample exhibited an eight-section organization.

Rose (1960b and Chapter 21) adds a further demographic variable by demonstrating that among the Australians, men tended to marry women a generation younger than themselves. In combination with polygyny, this practice allows men in their forties and fifties to monopolize the majority of women of marriagable age. The function of this "gerontocracy" as Rose calls it, is to combine the women into effective food-producing units, centered around a male at the peak of his "political" career.

Recent demographic research has added a new dimension to the study of Australian systems. Aboriginal marriage now appears to be more explicable in terms of the economic conditions under which the people actually lived. Yet the basic question raised by Lévi-Strauss remains: How are the stated rules of social life articulated into a meaningful whole? It is clear that more work is urgently required in Australia, although we suspect that it may already be too late to establish the relation of ideological forms to the behavior of persons on the ground.

DEMOGRAPHY AND POPULATION ECOLOGY

Many of the peoples discussed at the symposium live in small-scale societies in which the total population numbers a thousand persons or less. The social and ecological consequences of "smallness" were considered in several papers. Dunn (Chapter 23) made the interesting point that small groups of nomadic peoples living at low population densities would be much more resistant to epidemic diseases than farming peoples who live at higher densities in settled villages. Others speculated on the ideal sizes of hunter local groups and breeding populations, and two figures in particular came to be called the "magic numbers" of hunter-gatherer demography (Chapter 25c). Birdsell (Chapter 24) cites a figure of 500 as the modal size of tribes in aboriginal Australia; such a population was large enough to insure an adequate recruitment of mates and yet small enough for everyone to know everyone else. There was some evidence that tribes of larger size tended to subdivide into smaller and more manageable units. Twenty-five to fifty persons were the figures most frequently reported for the size of local groups or bands among modern hunter-gatherers, although we failed to arrive at any satisfactory explanation for this central tendency.

Perhaps the most important demographic issue was the question of what are the factors that keep the populations of hunters in check. Throughout the world hunter densities rarely exceed one person per square mile; most of the accurate figures reported at the conference ranged between one and 25 persons per hundred square miles. We feel that the one-per-square-mile figure is a useful estimate of Pleistocene carrying capacity. It was not until the development of agriculture that human populations were able to break this limit for the first time, while present agricultural densities in most parts of the world exceed the highest hunter densities by a factor of ten to one thousand.

Disease, malnutrition, and infanticide were each considered as possible control mechanisms for hunter-gatherer populations. Since food supply appears to be abundant in modern cases, the constant threat of famine has probably been overestimated as a population control. On the other hand, the management of fertility by means of long lactation, birth control, the killing of twins, and systematic infanticide may have been as frequent in early populations as they are among hunters today. Birdsell and Deevey (Chapters 22b, 22d) went so far as to suggest that a 15–50 per cent incidence of infanticide may have existed throughout the preagricultural history of man.

Helm and Washburn (Chapter 9a) following Bartholomew and Birdsell (1953) suggested that we consider what works in the long run. A population may thrive for several generations and give every appearance of being successfully adapted, only to be cut back severely by an ecological reverse once in a hundred years. Probably the most successful long-term situation is for a population to become stabilized at 20 or 30 per cent of carrying capacity, but at the present it is not possible to determine how such an equilibrium may be achieved. Fortunately, it is still possible to gather the necessary demographic data among some of the modern hunter-gatherers, and we hope that these data, plus computer simulation of population models, will yield exceptionally useful results.

"NOMADIC STYLE": A TRIAL FORMULATION

Although the conference on Man the Hunter raised more questions than it answered, there seemed to be a widespread feeling among the participants that a useful beginning had been made in understanding the hunters better. A number of older theories were corrected in light of new data and, where issues were unresolved, we came away at least with a clearer appreciation of our differences, To attempt to draw a general picture of the hunters at this time would certainly be premature; we would, however, like to offer a trial formulation of our views to serve as a starting point for future research and discussion.

We make two basic assumptions about hunters and gatherers: (1) they live in small groups and (2) they move around a lot. Each local group is associated with a geographical range but these groups do not function as closed social systems. Probably from the very beginning there was communication between groups, including reciprocal visiting and marriage alliances, so that the basic hunting society consisted of a series of local "bands" which were part of a larger breeding and linguistic community. The economic system is based on several core features including a home base or camp, a division of labor—with males hunting and females gathering—and, most important, a pattern of sharing out the collected food resources.

These few broadly defined features provide an organizational base line of the small-scale society from which subsequent developments can be derived. We visualize a social system with the following characteristics. First, if individuals and groups have to move around in order to get food there is an important implication: the amount of personal property has to be kept to a very low level. Constraints on the possession of property also serve to keep wealth differences between individuals to a minimum and we postulate a generally egalitarian system for the hunters.

Second, the nature of the food supply keeps the living groups small, usually under fifty persons. Large concentrations of population would rapidly exhaust the immediate resources, and members would be forced to disperse into smaller foraging units. It is likely, as Mauss observed (1906), that several bands would come together on a seasonal basis, resulting in a division of the year into "public" and "private" periods. Because of the small size of the living groups and the wide variance of family size, bands wax and wane in numbers. It is probably necessary to continually redistribute the population between bands in order to maintain food-gathering units at an effective level.

Third, the local groups as groups do not ordinarily maintain exclusive rights to resources. Variations in food supply from region to region and from year to year create a fluid situation that can best be met by flexible organizations that allow people to move from one area to another. The visiting patterns create intergroup obligations, so that the hosts in one season become the guests in another. We think that reciprocal access to food resources would rank as equal in importance with exchange of spouses as a means of communication between groups. It is likely that food may antedate women as the original medium of exchange (cf. Lévi-Strauss, 1949).

Fourth, food surpluses are not a prominent feature of the small-scale society. If inventories of food on hand are minimal, then a fairly constant work effort has to be kept up throughout the year. Since everyone knows where the food is, in effect the environment itself is the storehouse; and since everyone knows the movements of everyone else, there is a lack of concern that food resources will fail or be appropriated by others.

Fifth, frequent visiting between resource areas prevents any one group from becoming too strongly attached to any single area. Ritual

sites are commonly associated with specific groups, but the livelihood of the people does not depend on such sites. Further, the lack of impediments in the form of personal and collective property allows a considerable degree of freedom of movement. Individuals and groups can change residence without relinquishing vital interests in land or goods, and when arguments break out it is a simple matter to part company in order to avoid serious conflict. This is not to say that violence is unknown; both homicide and sorcery are found among a number of current hunter-gatherers. The resolution of conflict by fission, however, may help to explain how order can be maintained in a society without superordinate means of social control.

At the symposium we presented some of these ideas under the general heading of the "Nomadic Style." Several others found this view plausible and suggested ways in which specific cases might have developed out of this baseline. L. Binford noted that northern adaptations required a more elaborate material basis, including fixed facilities such as fish weirs and game fences, and more substantial dwellings, clothing, and tool kits. Steward pointed out that the development of traction and water transport would allow northern peoples to own more and yet still retain mobility (Chapter 34). And Suttles (Chapter 6) showed how the fisherman of the Northwest coast may have originally started out in small nomadic bands, but were subsequently led into surplus accumulation, heavy facilities, and ceremonial exchange by the necessity to bank against vagaries in salmon supply.

It seems clear that when the means of production come to depend upon the exclusive control of resources and facilities, then the loose non-corporate nature of the small-scale society cannot be maintained. If this view is correct, then a major trend in human affairs has been the transformations of social relations as advanced technologies and formal institutions have come to play a more and more dominant role in the human adaptation. The institutions of property, of clan organization, of government, and of the state did not spring full-blown in a divine creation. The study of the hunters may help to understand how these things came into being.

2.

The Current Status
of the World's Hunting and Gathering Peoples

GEORGE PETER MURDOCK

Ten thousand years ago the entire population of the earth subsisted by hunting and gathering, as their ancestors had done since the dawn of culture. By the time of Christ, eight thousand years later, tillers and herders had replaced them over at least half of the earth. At the time of the discovery of the New World, only perhaps 15 per cent of the earth's surface was still occupied by hunters and gatherers, and this area has continued to decline at a progressive rate until the present day, when only a few isolated pockets survive.

Many of the peoples who subsisted by hunting and gathering at the time of Columbus ìave disappeared entirely and been replaced by stronger peoples. Others have been reduced to dependency—on reservations or as servants or outcaste groups. Still others have made a transition, in some form or other, to modes of subsistence based on agriculture, animal husbandry, or industrial employment. Only a handful still live an independent life of hunting and gathering, nearly all of them under markedly altered conditions. It is time—indeed, long past time—that we took stock of these dwindling remnants, for it is only among them that we can still study at first hand the modes of life and types of cultural adjustments that prevailed throughout most of human history.

In this paper I shall attempt to enumérate and briefly characterize the regions of the world where peoples with hunting and gathering economies survived long enough to be studied by modern ethnographers, with special reference to those groups amongst whom fundamental field research may still be possible.

The definition of hunting and gathering economies was the subject of considerable discussion at the symposium. For the sake of simplicity in presentation, I shall adopt a strict definition and merely allude here, by way of introduction, to three marginal subsistence categories which some would include with hunting and gathering and others would differentiate.

MOUNTED HUNTERS

Several groups of peoples who subsist primarily by hunting depend largely on domestic animals which they ride in pursuing or surrounding their game. Notable among them are the North American Indians of the Plains and the adjacent sections of the Plateau and Great Basin and the South American Indians of Patagonia and the adjacent Gran Chaco, both of which groups hunted with horses during the period of their ethnographic description. Comparable to

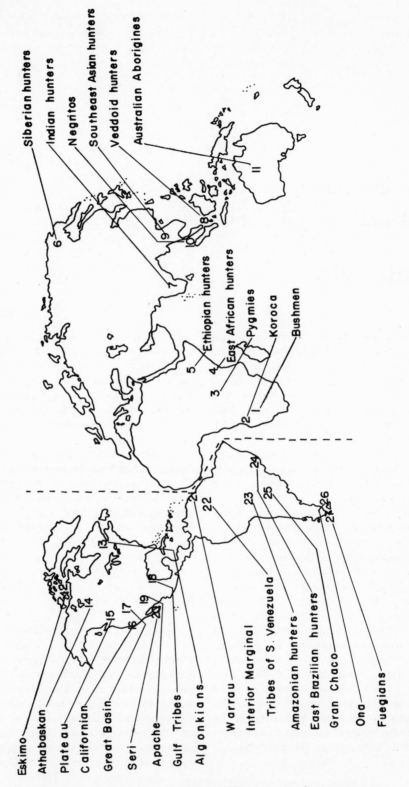

Siberian hunters
Indian hunters
Negritos
Southeast Asian hunters
Veddoid hunters
Australian Aborigines

Ethiopian hunters
East African hunters
Pygmies
Koroca
Bushmen

Eskimo
Athabaskan
Plateau
Californian
Great Basin
Seri
Apache
Gulf Tribes
Algonkians
Warrau
Interior Marginal
Tribes of S. Venezuela
Amazonian hunters
East Brazilian hunters
Gran Chaco
Ona
Fuegians

FIGURE 1. DISTRIBUTION OF RECENT HUNTERS AND GATHERERS.

them are several hunting peoples in Mauritania, including the Nemadi described by Gabus (1951–52), who employ camels in the chase. Mounted hunters approximate pastoral nomads in a number of respects, the chief difference, perhaps, being the fact that their domestic animals do not provide a major part of their food supply.

SEDENTARY FISHERMEN

Various other peoples who lack both agriculture and large domestic animals depend not so much on hunting and gathering as on fishing, shellfishing, or the pursuit of aquatic animals. Where they lead an essentially nomadic mode of life, I classify them with hunters and gatherers. Sometimes, however, their marine food supply is so plentiful and stable that they have been able to adopt an exclusively or predominantly sedentary mode of life. Such conditions offer the possibility of attaining a considerable degree of cultural complexity otherwise achievable only with intensive agriculture. The Indians of the North Pacific coast, for example, seem to me to fall well beyond the range of cultural variation of any known hunting and gathering people. The Calusa, a sedentary fishing people of southern Florida, as Goggin and Sturtevant (1964) have shown, had even elaborated a political system with fairly sizable states. Along the Niger and Congo rivers in Africa, numerous societies which subsist primarily by fishing and trade have cultures in no way inferior in complexity to those of their agricultural neighbors. In northeastern Asia the Ainu, Maritime Chukchee, Gilyak, Kamchadal or Italmen, and Maritime Koryak possibly, though less certainly, fall into the same category.

INCIPIENT TILLERS

Not a few peoples, especially though not exclusively in lowland South America, practice agriculture but obtain more of their food supply from hunting, fishing, and gathering and show a clear preference for hunting over tillage. Several participants in the symposium, notably Crocker with reference to the Gê, characterized

such incipient agriculturists as having a hunting-gathering ideology. While I freely grant their point, I have preferred to exclude such groups from my survey. After all, I know many American farmers who till the soil for a living but derive considerably more personal gratification from their subsidiary hunting and fishing activities.

In the listing of hunting and gathering peoples below, consequently, I omit all groups which I would categorize as mounted hunters, sedentary fishermen, or incipient tillers. I gratefully acknowledge the many suggestions made by participants in the symposium which have enabled me substantially to amplify and revise the original draft of this paper. Twenty-seven surviving groups of hunter-gatherers are enumerated in this survey. The geographical distribution of these peoples is plotted in Figure 1.

AFRICA

1. *Bushmen*

I shall begin my enumeration with the Bushmen of south and southwest Africa, of whom about 45,000 are reported to survive today (Tobias, 1956; Silberbauer, 1965). The vast majority of these, however, are attached to the Tswana as serfs or to Europeans as servants or laborers and have undergone intensive acculturation. Nevertheless, about 5,000 of them still pursue essentially their aboriginal nomadic mode of life. Lorna Marshall (1957, 1959, 1960), in particular, has demonstrated that field work of the highest quality is still possible among them. They are dealt with in greater detail by Richard B. Lee (Chapter 4, this volume).

2. *Koroca*

On the desert coast and adjacent foothills of southwestern Angola live the Koroca and the related Kwepe and Kwise, who practice no agriculture. From very fragmentary reports, they appear to resemble the Bushmen in culture and the Bergdama in physique (Almeida, 1965). Remarks by Jorge Dias suggest that they merit more intensive study.

Desmond Clark believes that there may also be Bantu hunting tribes in the same general area.

3. *Pygmies*

About 170,000 Pygmies are reported to survive in the tropical forest region of central Africa, nearly all in a dependent symbiotic relationship with the neighboring Negro tribes. The majority, especially those in Rwanda, Burundi, and the central portion of the Republic of the Congo, have either adopted agriculture or otherwise become strongly acculturated. In the Ituri Forest region of the northeast, however, the Aka, Efe, and Mbuti groups still preserve large portions of their indigenous culture. For the Mbuti, in particular, we have a substantial monograph by Schebesta (1938–50) and the more intimate and revealing studies by Turnbull (1961, 1965b). There is certainly room for further field work here, and probably also among the inadequately described Pygmies of Cameroon and Gabon.

4. *East African Hunters*

Until very recently, available information on the surviving hunting populations of east Africa has been exceedingly scanty. Now, however, we have a series of substantial accounts of the Dorobo from Huntingford (1951, 1954, 1955) and the still more recent field work among the Hadza or Kindiga by James Woodburn (Chapter 3, this volume). The Teuso or Ik described by Colin Turnbull, though possibly related to the Dorobo, are not a hunting people in the strict sense adopted here. It is doubtless too late to expect new information on the Asa or Aramaic beyond the scraps contained in Merker (1904), but it still may be possible to conduct rewarding field work among the Ariangulo, the Boni, or the Sanye.

5. *Ethiopian Hunters*

William Shack reminded the symposium that there are half a dozen groups of hunters and gatherers in central Ethiopia, extending from the lakes of the Rift valley on the east to the edge of the plateau in the west. He called particular attention to the Fuga, whom he found still flourishing in the Gurage country. I omit-

ted these peoples in my original survey because, from the scanty references available to me, they seemed more like despised outcaste groups than independent tribes. If they do in fact lead independent lives, they certainly deserve early and intensive study.

EAST ASIA

6. *Siberian Hunters*

The non-agricultural peoples of Siberia have long since been largely converted to a pastoral mode of life in the interior or, on the coast, have come to depend primarily upon fishing and have adopted a relatively sedentary settlement pattern. The only two Siberian peoples who seem to meet our strict definition of hunters and gatherers are the Ket or Yenisei Ostyak, on whom we have a brief sketch by Shimkin (1940), and the Yukaghir, on whom we have a full monograph by Jochelseon (1926). Both tribes have doubtless been so altered by Soviet acculturation policies that further field work among them is unlikely to yield rewarding results.

7. *Indian Hunters*

There are in India a number of hunting societies, mostly dependent and often approximating the status of specialized castes. The fullest ethnographic account is probably that by Fürer-Haimendorf (1943) on the Dravidian-speaking Chenchu, but Majumdar (1944) has contributed a brief account of the Korwa of Uttar Pradesh. B. J. Williams describes the Munda-speaking Birhor in this symposium (Chapter 14), and there is fragmentary information on the Irula and Kurumba of the Nilgiri Hills. Peter Gardner has provided me with a list of additional Indian hunting groups: the Kadar, Malapandaram, Paliyan, and Yanadi, all of whom have been studied, and the still undescribed Allar, Aranadan, Eravallar, Mala Vedan, and Vettuvan.

8. *Veddoid Hunters*

It is almost certain that no further ethnographic information of consequence is obtainable from the Rock Vedda of Ceylon, who had already practically disappeared when the Seligmans (1911) made their classic study. I agree with Gardner that the Vedda are probably a case of "devolution." The Senoi or Sakai of Malaya, according to a personal communication from Robert Dentan on the basis of his recent field work among them, have everywhere adopted a substantial dependence upon agriculture. I have no recent information on the peoples of Indonesia who have been called Veddoid, very probably incorrectly, and who have been reported to practice very little agriculture, such as the Kubu of Sumatra (Hagen, 1908; Schebesta, 1928) and the Punan of Borneo (Furness, 1902; Hose and McDougall, 1911; Roth, 1896).

9. *Southeast Asian Hunters*

Participants at the symposium have called my attention to several hunting and gathering peoples in Southeast Asia of whom I had previously been unaware. Thus Georges Condominias cites the Ruc of central Vietnam, Peter Gardner the Penang and Phi Tong Luang, and Lauriston Sharp the Mrabri or Yumbri of northern Thailand. The References at the end of this volume include the following supplied by Sharp on the Mrabri: Bodes (1963), Flatz (1963, 1964), Kraisri and Hartland-Swann (1962), Velder (1963, 1964).

10. *Negritos*

Most of the Negrito tribes of the Philippines practice at least a modicum of agriculture and thus fall outside the range of our discussion. We do, however, possess substantial accounts of two non-agricultural Negrito groups—the Andamanese by Man (1883) and Radcliffe-Brown (1933) and the Semang of Malaya by Evans (1937) and Schebesta (1929). I suspect that further field work may still be possible among both of them.

OCEANIA

11. *Australian Aborigines*

The Tasmanians are long since extinct (although new ethnohistoric materials have

appeared: Plomley, 1966), and the peoples of Melanesia, Micronesia, and Polynesia who lack large domestic animals and depend only minimally on agriculture are sedentary in consequence of their dependence on fishing, sago gathering, or trade, so that they fall outside our definition. This leaves the Australian aborigines as the sole surviving representatives of hunters and gatherers in Oceania. Most of them have either disappeared or have become strongly acculturated. Recent work among the Tiwi, in Arnhem Land, on Groote Eylandt, and elsewhere, however, demonstrates that the possibilities for productive field work have by no means been yet exhausted. Substantial additional information on the Australian indigenes is presented by Frederick Rose (Chapter 21), Aram Yengoyan (Chapter 20), L. R. Hiatt (Chapters 10 and 18), Mervyn Meggitt (Chapter 19), and Arnold Pilling (Chapter 16) in this volume.

NORTH AMERICA

12. *Eskimo*

Field research among the Eskimo has exhibited a remarkable spurt in recent years. Asen Balikci (Chapter 8) and David Damas (Chapter 12, this volume) present some of the results, which are perhaps especially illuminating in the field of social organization. Some Eskimo groups have long approximated a sedentary mode of life because of primary dependence upon the products of the sea, and others have recently been approaching this status because of acculturative influences. The majority, however, are still migratory for at least a part of the year, and a few inland groups are completely divorced from the sea. Among the latter are the Nunamiut of northern Alaska, on whom we have a recent substantial monograph by Gubser (1965).

13. *Northeastern Algonkians*

The hunting patterns of the Algonkian tribes of eastern Canada were clearly modified considerably with the development of the fur trade. The available information is relatively good, though the input of new information appears to be dwindling. Whenever I begin to suspect that the law of diminishing returns is setting in, however, I am reassured by some significant new publication from the pen of Dunning (1959), Honigmann (1962a, 1962b), or Leacock (1954).

14. *Northwestern Athapaskans*

A few years ago it appeared that the potential ethnographic crop for the Athapaskan tribes of northwestern Canada and interior Alaska had been almost completely harvested by Osgood, Honigmann, and McKennan. Appearances were deceptive, for recently we have had a succession of monographs and articles of the very highest quality from June Helm (1961, 1965a, Helm and Lurie, 1961). The prospects for further productive research in this area thus seem by no means closed.

15. *Plateau Indians*

The Indians of the Plateau area resemble those of the adjacent Northwest coast in many respects, notably in the widespread dependence upon salmon fishing, but they devoted considerably more time and energy to seasonal migrations in search of roots, berries, and game. New information is still appearing in a fairly steady stream, though much of it is perhaps supplementary rather than fundamental. For the northern tribes of the area, notably the Lillooet and Shuswap, I suspect that basic field work of a quality comparable to that of Helm on the Northern Athapaskans may still be possible for a number of years to come.

16. *California Indians*

Alfred Kroeber and his students, both through intensive field work and the Culture Element Survey, have probably exhausted most of the possibilities for fundamental ethnographic research among the tribes of the California area, so that only fragmentary information remains to be recovered, except perhaps across the border in Baja California.

17. *The Great Basin*

The prospects seem somewhat better for the Shoshonean, Yuman, and other tribes of the

Great Basin. My basis for this judgment is the surprising amount of new and valuable data which eight of my own graduate students have brought back from a summer each with the field training program conducted for the past two years by the University of Nevada.

18. *Gulf Indians*

On the Indian tribes who formerly inhabited coastal Texas and adjacent northeastern Mexico—the Karankawa, Tonkawa, Coahuilteco, etc.—we possess only fragmentary data, and it is much too late to obtain any new information. It is interesting to note, however, that fairly substantial archival material is beginning to come to light from sixteenth-century Spanish missionaries. The Drivers (1963) have recently summarized the information on the Chichimeca-Jonaz, and Kimball Romney informs me that he has unearthed remarkably full kinship data on the Coahuilteco.

19. *Apache*

Thirty years ago Morris Opler was able to obtain full ethnographic data on most of the Apache tribes of the Southwest, by no means all of which has yet been published. Field work continues in this area, with results that are by no means always disappointing.

20. *Seri*

The Seri Indians of the coast of Sonora on the Gulf of California are known from a famous but partly fanciful monograph by McGee (1898) and from a more sober sketch by Kroeber (1931), both unfortunately based on extremely brief field trips. During the symposium Roger Owen characterized the Seri as "one of the black marks on American ethnography" and expressed the opinion that field work of good quality is still possible among them.

SOUTH AMERICA

21. *Warrau*

As Wilbert (1958a) has demonstrated in a recent monograph, the Warrau Indians of the delta of the Orinoco River still adhere in large measure to an essentially aboriginal mode of life, and fundamental field work of high quality is still possible among them.

22. *Interior Marginal Tribes of Southern Venezuela*

The so-called "interior marginal" peoples of southern Venezuela and adjacent Colombia and Brazil have until recently remained practically unknown, but in the last few years preliminary reports have appeared on such tribes as the Guahibo, Piaroa, Sanema, and Shiriana, among at least some groups of which agriculture is absent or virtually so (Wilbert, 1958b, 1966; Migliazza, 1964). These reports indicate that fundamental field research is still possible, and, as a matter of fact, three of my own graduate students have been working recently among the Guahibo (Morey, 1967).

23. *Amazonian Hunters*

As regards the "interior marginal" tribes of southwestern Amazonia, we already possess substantial accounts by Holmberg (1950) on the Siriono and by Lévi-Strauss (1936, 1940) on the Bororo and Nambicuara, and the Guato have been well described by Schmidt (1905, 1942). I understand, too, that new material of high quality has recently become available on the Guayaki (Lévi-Strauss, this volume; cf. Bertoni, 1941; Vellard, 1939).

24. *East Brazilian Hunters*

The non-agricultural peoples of eastern Brazil, of whom the Botocudo, Caingang, and Puri are perhaps the best known, are today either extinct or shattered. The last major ethnographic report from this area, that by Henry (1941) on the Aweikoma, makes it clear that fundamental field work is no longer possible here.

25. *Gran Chaco*

A fair amount of information, though not always of the highest quality, is available on the tribes of the Gran Chaco—the Chamacoco, Choroti, Mataco, Mocovi, Toba, etc. Though good field work is certainly still possible in this area, the aboriginal situation has altered substantially through the adoption of agriculture, domestic animals, and an increasingly sedentary mode of life (Baldus, 1931; Boggiani, 1894; Karsten, 1932; Métraux, 1937; Nordenskiöld, 1919).

26. *Ona*

The Indians of the Argentinian steppe, like those of the Plains of North America, early adopted the horse and are thus as mounted hunters excluded from our consideration. However, their kinsmen in the extreme south, the Ona, never became independent on the horse and thus qualify for inclusion. We are fortunate in having a fairly recent and extremely comprehensive account of the Ona by Gusinde (1931–39).

27. *Fuegians*

Finally, we must list the Indians of the extreme southwestern tip of South America—the Alacaluf, Chono, and Yahgan—for they lived a migratory life despite their primary dependence on shellfish, aquatic mammals, and other products of the sea. The Chono are ill described and extinct. There is fuller information on the Alacaluf and especially the Yahgan, but both tribes are now reduced to tiny remnants, and the prospects of obtaining further fundamental descriptive material are therefore extremely slim.

By way of concluding this rapid survey of the world's hunting and gathering peoples who have survived long enough to be studied by modern anthropologists, I should like to stress the fact that their largest concentration is found in aboriginal North America, where they have been studied mainly by American and Canadian anthropologists. The publications of these scholars are thus especially crucial for any general or comparative study of the material culture and subsistence economy of hunting and gathering peoples.

Second, the great majority of these North American societies are characterized by social systems of a bilateral rather than unilineal type, and indeed constitute well over half of the known bilateral societies of the entire world, so that they are equally crucial for the comparative study of this rapidly expanding aspect of social organization. It is thus entirely understandable why people like Damas, Dunning, and Helm have recently been concentrating on this range of problems in their North American researches.

Finally, owing to the influence of Lewis Henry Morgan, North American ethnographers have paid special attention to kinship terminology and its social concomitants for several generations. As a consequence, we possess reasonably adequate kinship information on perhaps 85 per cent of all the North American tribes whom the white man has ever encountered, as contrasted with a comparable figure of not more than 15 per cent for the known tribes of Africa. Thus, future field research in this continent, despite the steadily decreasing range of its geographical possibilities, can be based on an exceptionally solid background of past accomplishment.

PART II
Ecology and Economics

3.

The "Hunting" Economies
of the Tropical Forest Zone of South America:
An Attempt at Historical Perspective

DONALD W. LATHRAP

The Amazon Basin contains the largest block of tropical rain forest in the world. The patterns of human utilization of this region and the history of how these patterns evolved through time is of considerable interest as a major chapter in the progressive expansion of human populations, and in the adaptation of such populations to diverse ecological settings.[1]

At the time of the first European contact, the Amazon Basin showed a considerable range of cultural pattern in terms of size and complexity of social units, complexity of material culture, and even in basic patterns of subsistence activity. The flood plain of the main stream of the Amazon and of its major tributaries sustained large, sedentary populations engaged in intensive root-crop farming combined with fishing and the hunting of aquatic mammals and reptiles. The exact size and complexity of sociopolitical units attained by these riverine societies, as of A.D. 1500, continues to be a matter of controversy since all such societies were very early disrupted by the effects of slave

1. This paper is a somewhat expanded version of the presentation given at the symposium. It has benefited from the symposium discussions, and through advice given by my wife Joan W. Lathrap and Dr. Frederic K. Lehman.

raiding, missionization, and diseases introduced by the Europeans. While it is clear that none of these societies rivaled the kind of sociopolitical unit which had been typical of the central Andes for the last 500 to 1,000 years before Columbus, it is equally clear from the various reviews of the early sources (Métraux, 1948a; Nimuendajú, 1952a; Palmatary, 1960, 1965; Rowe, 1952) that such riverine groups were far larger and more complex than the presently surviving remnant groups representing tropical forest culture. An even greater discrepancy exists between our knowledge of the contact period riverine societies of the Amazon Basin and the generalized notion of "tropical forest culture" or "tropical forest stage" which has been developed by Meggers and Evans (Meggers, 1954, 1957a, 1957b; Meggers and Evans, 1956).

The demographic and cultural situation in the slightly elevated regions between the major rivers was in sharp contrast to that of the flood plains. The interfluve areas were characterized by scant populations organized into small, widely dispersed and mobile social units. These groups typically showed simple and relatively unproductive agricultural systems and relied heavily on the hunting of terrestrial and

23

arboreal game for their sustenance. Unlike the groups inhabiting the more accessible and economically more valuable floodplains, the simple, dispersed Indian societies of the interfluve have in many instances survived until recently without major modifications in culture (Carneiro, 1964, p. 9).[2]

The presentation of a full, composite ethnographic picture of all such simple non-riverine groups is far beyond the scope of this paper, but certain key points in the above generalizations should be documented. In the area with which I am most familiar, the Peruvian Montaña, groups such as the Cashibo, Amahuaca, Remo, and Mayoruna are completely characteristic. A recent comparison of the agricultural practices of the Isconahua group of Remo, with those of the Shipibo, a riverine Panoan group, has shown the relative inefficiency of the Remo system and suggested that this inefficiency was an adjustment to the poorer agricultural potential of the interfluvial zone, the Remo's accustomed habitat (Momsen, 1964, pp. 76–77). Carneiro's excellent discussion of Amahuaca agriculture indicates equally rudimentary practices. For instance, he says: "At best, the Amahuaca are reluctant weeders" (1964, p. 14). The Shipibo on the other hand appear to be rather systematic and finicky on these matters.

Points which are crucial to the present discussion are the great importance which the hunting of terrestrial and arboreal game had for these interfluvial groups, and the degree to which the dependence on such game affected all other aspects of their culture. Carneiro has repeatedly demonstrated (1960, 1961, 1964) that it is not agricultural potential which directly controls the size and mobility of tropical forest social groups. In the Amahuaca case he gives a clear demonstration that the agriculture system, rudimentary as it is, is still capable of producing far more vegetable foods than the people are able to use (1964, pp. 17–18). It is the absence of significant aquatic resources (1964, p. 10) leading to a dependence on terrestrial hunting for the protein

necessary to the diet which largely controls the nature of the social group. Carneiro is worth quoting at length on this point:

> First of all, it should be kept in mind that the Amahuaca are still hunters almost as much as they are gardeners. Consequently, considerations having to do with the availability of game are very important to them. Even though three or four families settled in one locale for a year do not hunt out the game animals within the usual hunting radius of the settlement, they nevertheless probably make a noticeable inroad in their numbers. By the end of a year it has become necessary to walk farther to find game, and this is a decided inconvenience. If this inconvenience were counterbalanced by an equal or greater inconvenience in building a new settlement each year, the Amahuaca might not move so frequently. But Amahuaca houses can be built in three days and Amahuaca families are independent units perfectly free to pick up and move when and where they want to. Thus the Amahuaca, in deciding to move their settlements, do not have to overcome the inertia that would face a society which had a large village, substantial houses, and centralized political authority. In short, since the resistance to moving is small, the forces required to bring it about can likewise be small (1964, p. 16).

Holmberg (1950) paints a far bleaker picture of the results of the necessary dependence on terrestrial hunting by such interfluvial groups. While probably somewhat extreme in terms of the average situation for such groups throughout the Amazon Basin, his description of hunger and life among the Sirionó still stands as the most detailed coverage of the kind of economic patterns shared by such groups.

A final factor which characterized the primitive groups on the interriverine uplands is that they were typically denied access to the flood plain environment by the warlike activities of the riverine groups. It was the continual threat of slave raiding, head taking, and in some instances cannibalism which held the non-riverine groups in their less favorable environment. Nimuendajú's discussion of the territory of the Tukuna illustrates the point admirably:

> The Tukuna did not then inhabit the banks of the Amazon-Solimões, for fear of the Omágua,

2. In view of the discussion which followed the presentation of this paper, it is perhaps advisable to make explicit that the Gê and Bororo groups of the east Brazil highlands fall outside the territorial and ecological limits set for this paper.

who occupied the islands of that river throughout its course in Tukuna territory and even far beyond, while the banks of the Putumayo-Içá were held by Aruak tribes—the Mariaté, Yumána, and Pasé (1952b, p. 8).

The most feared enemies of the ancient Tukuna —one might say their only enemies—were the Omágua. [The Omágua] attacked by canoe, with great spears. They captured many: some of them were sacrificed to their idols and the rest served as slaves in their husbandary (1952b, p. 65).

Marcoy's general discussion of the attitude of the riverine Shipibo toward the non-riverine Cashibo is equally telling, and his description of the crucifixion of a Cashibo unfortunate enough to fall into Shipibo hands is even more graphic (1873, vol. 2, pp. 162–63).

Concerning the relation between the riverine Arawakan and Tucanoan tribes of southeastern Colombia and the interfluvial Macú, Métraux says:

The *Arawakan* and *Tucanoan* tribes of the upper Rio Negro, Caiarí-Uaupes, and Tiquié Rivers have since time immemorial waged merciless war against the *Macú*, whom they enslave or reduce to serfdom. Some small groups of *Macú* come to work for the sedentary *Uanana* and *Desana* and, after a few months, disappear again into the bush. The *Tucano* of the Tiquié River subjected a large group of *Macú* to their rule, but on the slightest suspicion of sorcery, they were prompt to attack them and sell their captives to the Whites (1948b, p. 866).

Carneiro also alludes to the constant hostility between the Amahuaca and their riverine neighbors as a factor tending to maintain their small, highly mobile, social units (1964, p. 16).

It is the culturally simple groups of the slightly elevated interfluvial regions of the Amazon Basin who are of possible interest to this symposium. It is clear from the foregoing discussion that they are typically dependent on the hunting of terrestrial and arboreal game for the essential protein complement of their diet, and arguments have been presented suggesting that the hunting practices of such people are a more important factor in conditioning their total way of life than are their relatively rudimentary and inefficient agricultural systems.

There has been a tendency to treat these people as unmodified representatives of a very early and primitive stage of tropical forest culture. Thus in a recent description of the Isconahua group of Remo, we find the authors, Whiton, Greene, and Momsen saying: "Their culture was that of incipient tropical forest slash-and-burn and close to neolithic man" (1964, p. 123). The suggestion has also been made that some, perhaps most, of these peoples represent groups of primitive hunters only slightly modified by trait-unit diffusion from their more advanced agricultural neighbors, and thus show a large degree of cultural continuity from a pre-Neolithic period or stage. Métraux is explicit about such an interpretation (1948b, p. 861), while such a view appears implicit in most of Steward's discussion of the same problem (1948b, pp. 896–99). Some such view would also appear to be implicit in Needham's emphasis on the anomaly of a system of asymmetric prescriptive alliances occurring in a "small-scale, hunting and collecting society" such as the Sirionó (1961, p. 252).

There is reason to question both of these interpretations and to suggest that many, perhaps all, of these simpler and less sedentary groups are the degraded descendants of peoples who at one time maintained an advanced form of tropical forest culture. In the remainder of this paper I hope to develop a simplified model of the historical background of such peoples.

I will assume that man entered South America with an economy oriented toward the hunting of big game, the large grazing animals typical of the grasslands and savannah. If the earliest inhabitants of South America indeed did function as predators on the grazing fauna, it is unlikely that they initially would have extended their range beyond that of the major element of their subsistence.

Such hunting groups appear to have entered South America before 15,000 B.C. (Rouse and Cruxent, 1963a, p. 537) and to have extended their range to the Straits of Magellen by 9000 B.C. (Lanning and Hammel, 1961, p. 147). There is insufficient space to review the distribution of Late Pleistocene and Early

Post-Pleistocene sites in South America, but the available evidence is compatible with the hypothesis that the earlier occupations were confined to areas of relatively open vegetation: seasonal grasslands, high grasslands, open thorn forest, etc.

For groups with a technology and social system well adapted to cooperative hunting on the grassland, the tropical forest would not have been an attractive environment for permanent occupation or intensive utilization. The more common forms of game, both animals and birds, had as their typical habitat the upper levels of the forest canopy or were semi-aquatic to aquatic. In terms of mammalian fauna, the floor of the tropical forest away from the rivers supported a poverty of species and a low density of individuals. Gilmore comments on the generally unfavorable nature of the tropical forest as a hunting territory (1950, p. 354), and information on groups such as the Sirionó suggests that even for a people with a technology specifically adapted to the problems of hunting within the tropical forest, the tropical forest is far from prime hunting territory.

One would expect that most of the areas of more open vegetation including the east Brazil highlands, the llanos of Venezuela and Colombia, and parts of the Guiana highlands would have been occupied before groups with a specifically hunting orientation would have attempted a direct penetration of the central block of tropical forest within the Amazon Basin. Indeed, there is no direct archeological evidence that such penetration ever took place. The earliest demonstrable penetration of the tropical forest of the Amazon Basin is oriented to the far richer riverine resources.

The more astute students of tropical forest culture, such as Sauer, Lowie, Steward, and Goldman, have all observed that tropical forest culture is less an adaptation to the forest as such, than to the riverine environment within the tropical forest. Since this point has been consistently ignored by those who tend to see the tropical forest as a uniform environment, it may be well to offer extensive documentation. Sauer's emphasis on the importance of riverine resources suffuses his whole discussion of the origin of the tropical forest pattern of cultivation (1952, pp. 40–49). And Lowie comments:

At the core of the area the diagnostic features are: the cultivation of tropical root crops, especially bitter manioc; effective river craft; the use of hammocks as beds; and the manufacture of pottery.

The very wide distribution of certain traits in the area is correlated with navigation. Thanks to their mobility, the canoeing tribes were able to maintain themselves in the midst of boatless populations, to travel with ease over periodically inundated tracts, and to diffuse their arts and customs over enormous distances (1948, p. 1).

Steward makes the same points even more strongly:

The distribution of culture elements and complexes reveals at least one broad pattern. The basic Tropical Forest cultures occur mainly in the areas accessible by water routes, both the coast and the great rivers. ... The inference is clear that what is thought of as a typical Tropical Forest or selvan culture—a developed agriculture and a technology manifest in twilled and woven baskets, loom weaving, cotton hammocks, ceramics, and other material traits—flowed along the coast and up the main waterways stopping where streams were less navigable ... (1948b, p. 883).

Goldman's statement of the Cubeos' view of their ecological setting has an almost poetic force:

The river forms a wider community of related sibs. With some exceptions the sibs have aligned themselves along a river on the basis of degree of closeness and of rank. Sibs that have segmented from a parental sib ordinarily occupy an adjacent site. The river is the most important territory. It is a highway and a link between related sibs, the source of ancestral power, and the economic zone of the men, fish being the main source of animal protein. Even most land animals are hunted along the river banks.

The orientation of the Cubeo is toward the river and not toward the forest. Whereas the forest is undifferentiated terrain, the rivers are known to every turn and outcrop of rock or other feature. The river is the source of the ancestral powers, of benefits as well as of dangers. The forest is a source mainly of dangers (1963, p. 44).

The advantages of the riverine environment over the slightly elevated interriverine zone include not only the greater availability of animal protein, but also a much higher agricultural potential. Sauer discusses the difference between the two zones in terms of land form (1950, p. 324), while Sternberg stresses the very real difference in agricultural potential of the lands lying within the Amazon Basin:

> Or take the prospect of an unlimited extent of rich crop land. The luxurious forest which mantles most of the region has commonly been interpreted as an unconditional promise of inexhaustible fertility. The very real productivity of bottomlands, periodically flooded and rejuvenated with silt-laden waters, has thus been ascribed to the enormous area corresponding to the generally acid and poor soils of the terras firmas, or uplands (1964, p. 13).

Thus it cannot be too strongly emphasized that the deep alluvial soils within the active flood plains have a far greater agricultural potential than the laterized and heavily eroded soils on the slightly elevated uplands back from the rivers. My Shipibo friends inform me that such deep, alluvial soils in certain parts of the central Ucayali flood plain will support continuous root-crop agriculture for up to fifteen or twenty years.

Sauer has stressed that the tropical forest agricultural pattern is essentially one of carbohydrate production, with the fat and protein requirements of the diet supplied by a technologically sophisticated utilization of the prodigious fish, aquatic mammal, and aquatic reptile resources of the flood plain (1952). Evolved tropical forest culture involves not just developed root-crop agriculture, but a developed set of fishing practices, including fish poisoning and effective water craft. Archeological manifestations suggesting all of these accomplishments appear early along the major rivers within the Amazon Basin.

Along the flood plain of the central Ucayali River in the Montaña of eastern Peru we find remains of such cultures as early as 2000 B.C. (Lathrap, 1958; 1962; 1965a, pp. 797–98; 1965b, p. 12). The elaborate and technologically sophisticated ceramic style designated Early Tutishcainyo cannot be derived from any early central Andean ceramic style. It does, however, show certain basic similarities to the earliest examples of tropical forest culture known from the flood plains of the Lower Orinoco in Venezuela, suggesting that both ceramic styles may have derived from some common source along the intermediate network of rivers (Cruxent and Rouse, 1959; Lathrap, 1963; Rouse and Cruxent, 1963b). The geographical setting in the central Ucayali presents the grossest kinds of obstacles to a meaningful estimate of settlement pattern and density of occupation for the earliest complexes. Given the degree to which jungle litter tends to camouflage all land surfaces, given the fact that the activity of the more numerous colonial ants tends to bury all ancient land surfaces under three to six inches of culturally sterile deposit, and most importantly given the destructive power of the continually meandering river which erases all traces of early settlements not located at the precise edge of the flood plain, the available evidence suggests that Early Tutishcainyo already represents a dense occupation of the suitable ecological niche.

In the course of the long cultural sequence which follows Early Tutishcainyo on the central Ucayali there exists evidence for at least three instances of complete ethnic replacement; two of the intrusive ceramic styles, so strongly suggesting the entrance of new ethnic groups, are clearly derived from the central Amazon. The long archeological sequence on the central Ucayali fully substantiates the picture of cultural development which Steward sketched on the basis of ethnographic distribution alone:

> Culturally, the *Chuncho* (the Indians of the Montaña) belong with the Tropical Forest peoples. They appear to represent a series of migratory waves that had spent their force against the barrier of the Andes, where representatives of many widely distributed linguistic families ... subsided into comparative isolation (1948a, p. 507).

A series of waves of migration, basically in an upstream direction, is also suggested by the distribution of languages in two of the more fully studied South American linguistic stocks, Macro-Arawak and Tupí-Guaraní. Noble

(1965) has presented a detailed reconstruction of the proto-language of Macro-Arawak including estimates of the degree of relationship among the various languages within Macro-Arawak. Rodrigues (1956) has presented a brief statement as to the classification of the various Tupí-Guaraní languages. A full treatment of the significance of these classifications for the understanding of South American culture history is beyond the scope of this paper, but I am at present engaged in preparing a manuscript which will attempt to evaluate the distribution of the languages of these two stocks in terms of past population movements. In attempting to summarize what is a complex picture, one might say that the more divergent, and presumably more anciently dispersed branches of Macro-Arawak tend to be near the headwaters of the major western tributaries of the Amazon, while the more closely related Maipuran languages within Arawak tend to dominate the mainstreams of the western segment of the Amazon, the Rio Negro, and the Orinoco. Likewise the more divergent branches of Tupí-Guaraní are ranged near the headwaters of the various major southern tributaries of the Amazon, while the more closely related languages within the family dominate the broader flood plains of the lower reaches of these rivers, much of the mainstream of the Lower Amazon, the Atlantic coast of Brazil, and much of the flood plain of the Paraná. The most economical explanation for these observations (especially when they are coupled with Noble's demonstration of an ultimate relationship between Proto-Arawak and Proto-Tupí-Guaraní, relating to a period before the dispersal of these two stocks) would be that the proto-languages of the two stocks occupied adjacent stretches of the Central Amazon between 3000 and 2000 B.C. with Proto-Arawak on the upstream side. From this hearth, colonization spread outward, mainly in an upstream direction, along all available waterways. Certain marked congruences between the distribution of ceramic styles and the distributions of particular linguistic families or subfamilies suggest the possibility of indicating the archeological concomitants of these major migrations demonstrable on linguistic grounds, and I hope fully to explore this possibility in the aforementioned forthcoming paper.[3]

The pattern of outward migration suggested by all of these converging lines of evidence could best be explained by intense and continuing population pressures of the flood plain of the Central Amazon, the most favorable environment for the support of tropical forest culture. Such continuous expansion by groups moving out to colonize further areas of flood plain progressively pushed smaller or militarily weaker groups farther upstream or off the flood plains entirely. In presenting this view I am, of course, in complete accord with Vayda's argument that warfare among tropical forest farmers has profound economic and demographic effects even though it may have a religious or recreational rationale (Vayda, 1961b).

This extreme and continuing competition for territory is understandable, if one realizes the limited amount of flood plain—the only ecological niche really suitable to tropical forest culture—available in the Amazon Basin. Sternberg summarizes the point nicely:

> It has been seen how the uplands are generally poor, and it must be granted that they occupy the major part of the Amazon region, comprising more than a million square miles and leaving only a slight fraction of the area to the fertile *várzeas*, or floodplains. Nevertheless, one is dealing with lands of continental dimensions and this small fraction represents no insignificant area: the *várzeas*, rejuvenated every year by the silt brought down by the river, occupy some twenty-five thousand square miles . . . (1964, p. 324).

Considering that these processes have been continuous from about 2500 B.C. up to the time of the contact, it is clear that a large number of

3. Readers familiar with the literature on South American archeology will know that Meggers and Evans have presented a markedly different model of demography and population movements in the Amazon Basin (1961). Other archeologists who have worked under their close supervision have followed the Meggers-Evans hypotheses rather slavishly (for example, Hilbert, 1962a, 1962b). That the Meggers-Evans model is not mentioned in the text of this paper does not indicate that I am ignorant of its existence. Rather I find that all of the data presented by Meggers, Evans, and Hilbert, as opposed to their speculation about the data, can be accommodated quite easily in my own model.

ethnic groups were forced off the flood plains into less favorable environments.

Most of the primitive groups inhabiting the tropical forest uplands away from the major flood plains can be interpreted as the wreckage of evolved agricultural societies forced into an environment unsuitable to the basic economic pattern. Deprived of the riverine resources, such groups had to rely on the hunting of forest game to provide the protein and fat essential to the diet. A more intense orientation to hunting the relatively scarce game available led to more nomadism, a decline in agricultural productivity, and a still greater dependence on wild food.

I am convinced that this picture accounts for all of the simpler groups within the Tupí-Guaraní, Arawak, and Panoan linguistic stocks.

As we gain more knowledge the interpretation may be extendable to other groups, whose cultural and linguistic affiliations are less clear, such as the Tukuna, Mura, and Macú. The speed with which this kind of cultural devolution can take place is suggested by the relatively minor linguistic differences between the riverine Panoans such as the Shipibo and Conibo and the very "primitive" interfluvial Panoan groups such as the Cashibo and Remo.

While the "hunting" cultures of the tropical forest zone of South America offer highly explicit examples of the cultural and demographic effects of a dependence on hunting in an area where hunting is neither profitable or easy, they probably instruct us not at all about the nature of pre-Neolithic hunting cultures.

4.

What Hunters Do for a Living,
or, How to Make Out on Scarce Resources

RICHARD B. LEE

The current anthropological view of hunter-gatherer subsistence rests on two questionable assumptions. First is the notion that these peoples are primarily dependent on the hunting of game animals, and second is the assumption that their way of life is generally a precarious and arduous struggle for existence.

Recent data on living hunter-gatherers (Meggitt, 1964b; Service, 1966; and papers in this volume) show a radically different picture. We have learned that in many societies, plant and marine resources are far more important than are game animals in the diet. More important, it is becoming clear that, with a few conspicuous exceptions, the hunter-gatherer subsistence base is at least routine and reliable and at best surprisingly abundant. Anthropologists have consistently tended to underestimate the viability of even those "marginal isolates" of hunting peoples that have been available to ethnographers.

The purpose of this paper is to analyze the food getting activities of one such "marginal" people, the !Kung Bushmen of the Kalahari Desert. Three related questions are posed: How do the Bushmen make a living? How easy or difficult is it for them to do this? What kinds of evidence are necessary to measure and evaluate the precariousness or security of a way of life? And after the relevant data are presented, two further questions are asked: What makes this security of life possible? To what extent are the Bushmen typical of hunter-gatherers in general?

BUSHMAN SUBSISTENCE

The !Kung Bushmen of Botswana are an apt case for analysis.[1] They inhabit the semi-arid northwest region of the Kalahari Desert. With only six to nine inches of rainfall per year, this is, by any account, a marginal environment for human habitation. In fact, it is precisely the unattractiveness of their homeland that has kept the !Kung isolated from extensive contact with their agricultural and pastoral neighbors.

Field work was carried out in the Dobe area, a line of eight permanent waterholes near the South-West Africa border and 125 miles south of the Okavango River. The population of the Dobe area consists of 466 Bushmen, including 379 permanent residents living in independent camps or associated with Bantu cattle posts,

1. These data are based on fifteen months of field research from October, 1963, to January, 1965. I would like to thank the National Science Foundation (U.S.) for its generous financial support. This paper has been substantially revised since being presented at the symposium on Man the Hunter.

Table 1   Numbers and Distribution of Resident Bushmen and Bantu by Waterhole*

Name of Waterhole	No. of Camps	Population of Camps	Other Bushmen	Total Bushmen	Bantu
Dobe	2	37	—	37	—
!angwa	1	16	23	39	84
Bate	2	30	12	42	21
!ubi	1	19	—	19	65
!gose	3	52	9	61	18
/ai/ai	5	94	13	107	67
!xabe	—	—	8	8	12
Mahopa	—	—	23	23	73
Total	14	248	88	336	340

* Figures do not include 130 Bushmen outside area on the date of census.

as well as 87 seasonal visitors. The Bushmen share the area with some 340 Bantu pastoralists largely of the Herero and Tswana tribes. The ethnographic present refers to the period of field work: October, 1963–January, 1965.

The Bushmen living in independent camps lack firearms, livestock, and agriculture. Apart from occasional visits to the Herero for milk, these !Kung are entirely dependent upon hunting and gathering for their subsistence. Politically they are under the nominal authority of the Tswana headman, although they pay no taxes and receive very few government services. European presence amounts to one overnight government patrol every six to eight weeks. Although Dobe-area !Kung have had some contact with outsiders since the 1880's, the majority of them continue to hunt and gather because there is no viable alternative locally available to them.[2]

Each of the fourteen independent camps is associated with one of the permanent waterholes. During the dry season (May–October) the entire population is clustered around these wells. Table 1 shows the numbers at each well at the end of the 1964 dry season. Two wells

2. The Nyae Nyae !Kung Bushmen studied by Lorna Marshall (1957, 1960, 1965) have been involved in a settlement scheme instituted by the South African government. Although closely related to the Nyae Nyae !Kung, the Dobe !Kung across the border in Botswana have not participated in the scheme.

3. Bushman group structure is discussed in more detail in Lee (1965, pp. 38–53; and Chapter 17c, this volume).

had no camp resident and one large well supported five camps. The number of camps at each well and the size of each camp changed frequently during the course of the year. The "camp" is an open aggregate of cooperating persons which changes in size and composition from day to day. Therefore, I have avoided the term "band" in describing the !Kung Bushman living groups.[3]

Each waterhole has a hinterland lying within a six-mile radius which is regularly exploited for vegetable and animal foods. These areas are not territories in the zoological sense, since they are not defended against outsiders. Rather they constitute the resources that lie within a convenient walking distance of a waterhole. The camp is a self-sufficient subsistence unit. The members move out each day to hunt and gather, and return in the evening to pool the collected foods in such a way that every person present receives an equitable share. Trade in foodstuffs between camps is minimal; personnel do move freely from camp to camp, however. The net effect is of a population constantly in motion. On the average, an individual spends a third of his time living only with close relatives, a third visiting other camps, and a third entertaining visitors from other camps.

Because of the strong emphasis on sharing, and the frequency of movement, surplus accumulation of storable plant foods and dried meat is kept to a minimum. There is rarely more than two or three days' supply of food on

Table 2   The Bushman Annual Round

	Jan.	Feb. SUMMER RAINS	Mar.	April	May AUTUMN DRY	June	July WINTER DRY	Aug.	Sept.	Oct. SPRING DRY	Nov.	Dec. FIRST RAINS
SEASON		SUMMER RAINS			AUTUMN DRY		WINTER DRY			SPRING DRY		FIRST RAINS
Availability of Water		Temporary summer pools everywhere		Large summer pools			Permanent waterholes only					Summer pools developing
Group Moves		Widely dispersed at summer pools		At large summer pools			All population restricted to permanent waterholes					Moving out to summer pools
Men's Subsistence Activities 1.	Hunting with bow, arrows, and dogs (Year-round)											
2.		Running down immatures					Trapping small game in snares				Running down newborn animals	
3.	Some gathering (Year-round)											
Women's Subsistence Activities 1.	Gathering of mongongo nuts (Year-round)											
2.			Fruits, berries, melons				Roots, bulbs, resins			Roots, leafy greens		
Ritual Activities	Dancing, trance performances, and ritual curing (Year-round)					Boys' initiation*						†
Relative Subsistence Hardship			Water-food distance minimal				Increasing distance from water to food				Water-food distance minimal	

* Held once every five years; none in 1963–64.
† New Year's: Bushmen join the celebrations of their missionized Bantu neighbors.

are bypassed, so that gathering never exhausts *all* the available plant foods of an area. During the dry season the diet becomes much more eclectic and the many species of roots, bulbs, and edible resins make an important contribution. It is this broad base that provides an essential margin of safety during the end of the dry season when the mongongo nut forests are difficult to reach. In addition, it is likely that these rarely utilized species provide important nutritional and mineral trace elements that may be lacking in the more popular foods.

Diet Selectivity

If the Bushmen were living close to the "starvation" level, then one would expect them to exploit every available source of nutrition. That their life is well above this level is indicated by the data in Table 3. Here all the edible plant species are arranged in classes according to the frequency with which they were observed to be eaten. It should be noted, that although there are some 85 species available, about 90 per cent of the vegetable diet by weight is drawn from only 23 species. In other words, 75 per cent of the listed species provide only 10 per cent of the food value.

In their meat-eating habits, the Bushmen show a similar selectivity. Of the 223 local species of animals known and named by the Bushmen, 54 species are classified as edible, and of these only 17 species were hunted on a regular basis.[4] Only a handful of the dozens of edible species of small mammals, birds, reptiles, and insects that occur locally are regarded as food. Such animals as rodents, snakes, lizards, termites, and grasshoppers, which in the literature are included in the Bushman dietary (Schapera, 1930), are despised by the Bushmen of the Dobe area.

Range Size and Population Density

The necessity to travel long distances, the high frequency of moves, and the maintenance of

4. Listed in order of their importance, the principal species in the diet are: wart hog, kudu, duiker, steenbok, gemsbok, wildebeeste, springhare, porcupine, ant bear, hare, guinea fowl, francolin (two species), korhaan, tortoise, and python.

populations at low densities are also features commonly associated with the hunting and gathering way of life. Density estimates for hunters in western North America and Australia have ranged from 3 persons/square mile to as low as 1 person/100 square miles (Kroeber, 1939; Radcliffe-Brown, 1930). In 1963–65, the resident and visiting Bushmen were observed to utilize an area of about 1,000 square miles during the course of the annual round for an effective population density of 41 persons/100 square miles. Within this area, however, the amount of ground covered by members of an individual camp was surprisingly small. A day's round-trip of twelve miles serves to define a "core" area six miles in radius surrounding each water point. By fanning out in all directions from their well, the members of a camp can gain access to the food resources of well over 100 square miles of territory within a two-hour hike. Except for a few weeks each year, areas lying beyond this six-mile radius are rarely utilized, even though they are no less rich in plants and game than are the core areas.

Although the Bushmen move their camps frequently (five or six times a year) they do not move them very far. A rainy season camp in the nut forests is rarely more than ten or twelve miles from the home waterhole, and often new campsites are occupied only a few hundred yards away from the previous one. By these criteria, the Bushmen do not lead a free-ranging nomadic way of life. For example, they do not undertake long marches of 30 to 100 miles to get food, since this task can be readily fulfilled within a day's walk of home base. When such long marches do occur they are invariably for visiting, trading, and marriage arrangements, and should not be confused with the normal routine of subsistence.

Demographic Factors

Another indicator of the harshness of a way of life is the age at which people die. Ever since Hobbes characterized life in the state of nature as "nasty, brutish and short," the assumption has been that hunting and gathering is so rigorous that members of such societies are rapidly worn out and meet an early death. Silberbauer, for example, says of the Gwi

Bushmen of the central Kalahari that "life expectancy . . . is difficult to calculate, but I do not believe that many live beyond 45" (1965, p. 17). And Coon has said of the hunters in general:

> The practice of abandoning the hopelessly ill and aged has been observed in many parts of the world. It is always done by people living in poor environments where it is necessary to move about frequently to obtain food, where food is scarce, and transportation difficult. . . . Among peoples who are forced to live in this way the oldest generation, the generation of individuals who have passed their physical peak is reduced in numbers and influence. There is no body of elders to hand on tradition and control the affairs of younger men and women, and no formal system of age grading (1948, p. 55).

The !Kung Bushmen of the Dobe area flatly contradict this view. In a total population of 466, no fewer than 46 individuals (17 men and 29 women) were determined to be over 60 years of age, a proportion that compares favorably to the percentage of elderly in industralized populations.

The aged hold a respected position in Bushman society and are the effective leaders of the camps. Senilicide is extremely rare. Long after their productive years have passed, the old people are fed and cared for by their children and grandchildren. The blind, the senile, and the crippled are respected for the special ritual and technical skills they possess. For instance, the four elders at !gose waterhole were totally or partially blind, but this handicap did not prevent their active participation in decision-making and ritual curing.

Another significant feature of the composition of the work force is the late assumption of adult responsibility by the adolescents. Young people are not expected to provide food regularly until they are married. Girls typically marry between the ages of 15 and 20, and boys about five years later, so that it is not unusual to find healthy, active teenagers visiting from camp to camp while their older relatives provide food for them.

As a result, the people in the age group 20–60 support a surprisingly large percentage of non-productive young and old people. About 40 per cent of the population in camps contribute little to the food supplies. This allocation of work to young and middle-aged adults allows for a relatively carefree childhood and adolescence and a relatively unstrenuous old age.

Leisure and Work

Another important index of ease or difficulty of subsistence is the amount of time devoted to the food quest.[5] Hunting has usually been regarded by social scientists as a way of life in which merely keeping alive is so formidable a task that members of such societies lack the leisure time necessary to "build culture."[6] The !Kung Bushmen would appear to conform to the rule, for as Lorna Marshall says:

> It is vividly apparent that among the !Kung Bushmen, ethos, or "the spirit which actuates manners and customs," is survival. Their time and energies are almost wholly given to this task, for life in their environment requires that they spend their days mainly in procuring food (1965, p. 247).

It is certainly true that getting food is the most important single activity in Bushman life. However this statement would apply equally well to small-scale agricultural and pastoral societies too. How much time is *actually* devoted to the food quest is fortunately an empirical question. And an analysis of the work effort of the Dobe Bushmen shows some unexpected results. From July 6 to August 2, 1964, I recorded all the daily activities of the Bushmen living at the Dobe waterhole. Because of the coming and going of visitors, the camp population fluctuated in size day by day, from a low

5. This and the following topic are discussed in greater detail in Lee, "!Kung Bushman Subsistence: An Input-Output Analysis" (in press).

6. Lenski, for example, in a recent review of the subject, states: "Unlike the members of hunting and gathering societies [the horticulturalists] are not compelled to spend most of their working hours in the search for food and other necessities of life, but are able to use more of their time in other ways" (1966, p. 121). Sahlins (Chap. 9b, this volume) offers a counter-argument to this view.

of 23 to a high of 40, with a mean of 31.8 persons. Each day some of the adult members of the camp went out to hunt and/or gather while others stayed home or went visiting. The daily recording of all personnel on hand made it possible to calculate the number of man-days of work as a percentage of total number of man-days of consumption.

Although the Bushmen do not organize their activities on the basis of a seven-day week, I have divided the data this way to make them more intelligible. The work-week was calculated to show how many days out of seven each adult spent in subsistence activities (Table 4, Column 7). Week II has been eliminated from the totals since the investigator contributed food. In week I, the people spent an average of 2.3 days in subsistence activities, in week III, 1.9 days, and in week IV, 3.2 days. In all, the adults of the Dobe camp worked about two and a half days a week. Since the average working day was about six hours long, the fact emerges that !Kung Bushmen of Dobe, despite their harsh environment, devote from twelve to nineteen hours a week to getting food. Even the hardest working individual in the camp, a man named ≠oma who went out hunting on sixteen of the 28 days, spent a maximum of 32 hours a week in the food quest.

Because the Bushmen do not amass a surplus of foods, there are no seasons of exceptionally intensive activities such as planting and harvesting, and no seasons of unemployment. The level of work observed is an accurate reflection of the effort required to meet the immediate caloric needs of the group. This work diary covers the mid-winter dry season, a period when food is neither at its most plentiful nor at its scarcest levels, and the diary documents the transition from better to worse conditions (see Table 2). During the fourth week the gatherers were making overnight trips to camps in the mongongo nut forests seven to ten miles distant from the waterhole. These longer trips account for the rise in the level of work, from twelve or thirteen to nineteen hours per week.

If food getting occupies such a small proportion of a Bushman's waking hours, then how *do* people allocate their time? A woman gathers on one day enough food to feed her family for three days, and spends the rest of her time resting in camp, doing embroidery, visiting other camps, or entertaining visitors from other camps. For each day at home, kitchen routines, such as cooking, nut cracking, collecting firewood, and fetching water, occupy one to three hours of her time. This rhythm of steady work and steady leisure is maintained throughout the year.

The hunters tend to work more frequently than the women, but their schedule is uneven. It is not unusual for a man to hunt avidly for a week and then do no hunting at all for two or three weeks. Since hunting is an unpredictable business and subject to magical control, hunters sometimes experience a run of bad luck and stop hunting for a month or longer. During these periods, visiting, entertaining, and especially dancing are the primary activities of men. (Unlike the Hadza, gambling is only a minor leisure activity.)

The trance-dance is the focus of Bushman ritual life; over 50 per cent of the men have trained as trance-performers and regularly enter trance during the course of the all-night dances. At some camps, trance-dances occur as frequently as two or three times a week and those who have entered trances the night before rarely go out hunting the following day. Accounts of Bushman trance performances have been published in Lorna Marshall (1962) and Lee (1967). In a camp with five or more hunters, there are usually two or three who are actively hunting and several others who are inactive. The net effect is to phase the hunting and non-hunting so that a fairly steady supply of meat is brought into a camp.

Caloric Returns

Is the modest work effort of the Bushmen sufficient to provide the calories necessary to maintain the health of the population? Or have the !Kung, in common with some agricultural peoples (see Richards, 1939), adjusted to a permanently substandard nutritional level?

During my field work I did not encounter any cases of kwashiorkor, the most common nutritional disease in the children of African agricultural societies. However, without medical examinations, it is impossible to exclude

Table 4   Summary of Dobe Work Diary

Week	(1) mean group size	(2) adult-days	(3) child-days	(4) total man-days of consumption	(5) man-days of work	(6) meat (lbs.)	(7) average work week/adult	(8) Index of Subsistence Effort
I (July 6-12)	25.6 (23-29)	114	65	179	37	104	2.3	.21
II (July 13-19)	28.3 (23-27)	125	73	198	22	80	1.2	.11
III (July 20-26)	34.3 (29-40)	156	84	240	42	177	1.9	.18
IV (July 27-Aug. 2)	35.6 (32-40)	167	82	249	77	129	3.2	.31
4-wk. Total	30.9	562	304	866	178	490	2.2	.21
Adjusted Total*	31.8	437	231	668	156	410	2.5	.23

* See text.

KEY: Column 1: Mean group size = $\dfrac{\text{total man-days of consumption}}{7}$.

Column 7: Work week = the number of work days per adult per week.

Column 8: Index of Subsistence Effort = $\dfrac{\text{man-days of work}}{\text{man-days of consumption}}$ (e.g., in Week I, the value of "S" = .21, i.e., 21 days of work/100

days of consumption or 1 work day produces food for 5 consumption days).

Table 5   Caloric and Protein Levels in the !Kung Bushman Dietary, July–August, 1964

Class of Food	Percentage Contribution to Diet by Weight	Per Capita Consumption		Calories per person per day	Percentage Caloric Contribution of Meat and Vegetables
		Weight in grams	Protein in grams		
Meat	37	230	34.5	690	33
Mongongo Nuts	33	210	56.7	1,260	
Other Vegetable					67
Foods	30	190	1.9	190	
Total All Sources	100	630	93.1	2,140	100

the possibility that subclinical signs of malnutrition existed.[7]

Another measure of nutritional adequacy is the average consumption of calories and proteins per person per day. The estimate for the Bushmen is based on observations of the weights of foods of known composition that were brought into Dobe camp on each day of the study period. The per-capita figure is obtained by dividing the total weight of foodstuffs by the total number of persons in the camp. These results are set out in detail elsewhere (Lee, in press) and can only be summarized here. During the study period 410 pounds of meat were brought in by the hunters of the Dobe camp, for a daily share of nine ounces of meat per person. About 700 pounds of vegetable foods were gathered and consumed during the same period. Table 5 sets out the calories and proteins available per capita in the !Kung Bushman dietary from meat, mongongo nuts, and other vegetable sources.

This output of 2,140 calories and 93.1 grams of protein per person per day may be compared with the Recommended Daily Allowances (RDA) for persons of the small size and stature but vigorous activity regime of the !Kung Bushmen. The RDA for Bushmen can be estimated at 1,975 calories and 60 grams of

7. During future field work with the !Kung Bushmen, a professional pediatrician and nutritionist are planning to examine children and adults as part of a general study of hunter-gatherer health and nutrition sponsored by the U.S. National Institutes of Health and the Wenner-Gren Foundation for Anthropological Research.

protein per person per day. (Taylor and Pye, 1965, pp. 45–48, 463). Thus it is apparent that food output exceeds energy requirements by 165 calories and 33 grams of protein. One can tentatively conclude that even a modest subsistence effort of two or three days work per week is enough to provide an adequate diet for the !Kung Bushmen.

THE SECURITY OF BUSHMAN LIFE

I have attempted to evaluate the subsistence base of one contemporary hunter-gatherer society living in a marginal environment. The !Kung Bushmen have available to them some relatively abundant high-quality foods, and they do not have to walk very far or work very hard to get them. Furthermore this modest work effort provides sufficient calories to support not only the active adults, but also a large number of middle-aged and elderly people. The Bushmen do not have to press their youngsters into the service of the food quest, nor do they have to dispose of the oldsters after they have ceased to be productive.

The evidence presented assumes an added significance because this security of life was observed during the third year of one of the most severe droughts in South Africa's history. Most of the 576,000 people of Botswana are pastoralists and agriculturalists. After the crops had failed three years in succession and over 100,000 head of cattle had died on the range for lack of water, the World Food Program of the United Nations instituted a famine relief program which has grown to include 180,000 people, over 30 per cent of the population (Government of Botswana, 1966). This program did not touch the Dobe area in the isolated northwest corner of the country and the Herero and Tswana women there were able to feed their families only by joining the Bushman women to forage for wild foods. Thus the natural plant resources of the Dobe area were carrying a higher proportion of population than would be the case in years when the Bantu harvested crops. Yet this added pressure on the land did not seem to adversely affect the Bushmen.

In one sense it was unfortunate that the period of my field work happened to coincide with the drought, since I was unable to witness a "typical" annual subsistence cycle. However, in another sense, the coincidence was a lucky one, for the drought put the Bushmen and their subsistence system to the acid test and, in terms of adaptation to scarce resources, they passed with flying colors. One can postulate that their subsistence base would be even more substantial during years of higher rainfall.

What are the crucial factors that make this way of life possible? I suggest that the primary factor is the Bushmen's strong emphasis on vegetable food sources. Although hunting involves a great deal of effort and prestige, plant foods provide from 60–80 per cent of the annual diet by weight. Meat has come to be regarded as a special treat; when available, it is welcomed as a break from the routine of vegetable foods, but it is never depended upon as a staple. No one ever goes hungry when hunting fails.

The reason for this emphasis is not hard to find. Vegetable foods are abundant, sedentary, and predictable. They grow in the same place year after year, and the gatherer is guaranteed a day's return of food for a day's expenditure of energy. Game animals, by contrast, are scarce, mobile, unpredictable, and difficult to catch. A hunter has no guarantee of success and may in fact go for days or weeks without killing a large mammal. During the study period, there were eleven men in the Dobe camp, of whom four did no hunting at all. The seven active men spent a total of 78 man-days hunting, and this work input yielded eighteen

animals killed, or one kill for every four man-days of hunting. The probability of any one hunter making a kill on a given days was 0.23. By contrast, the probability of a woman finding plant food on a given day was 1.00. In other words, hunting and gathering are not equally felicitous subsistence alternatives.

Consider the productivity per man-hour of the two kinds of subsistence activities. One man-hour of hunting produces about 100 edible calories, and of gathering, 240 calories. Gathering is thus seen to be 2.4 times more productive than hunting. In short, hunting is a *high-risk, low-return* subsistence activity, while gathering is a *low-risk, high-return* subsistence activity.

It is not at all contradictory that the hunting complex holds a central place in the Bushman ethos and that meat is valued more highly than vegetable foods (Marshall, 1960). Analogously, steak is valued more highly than potatoes in the food preferences of our own society. In both situations the meat is more "costly" than the vegetable food. In the Bushman case, the cost of food can be measured in terms of time and energy expended. By this standard, 1,000 calories of meat "costs" ten man-hours, while the "cost" of 1,000 calories of vegetable foods is only four man-hours. Further, it is to be expected that the less predictable, more expensive food source would have a greater accretion of myth and ritual built up around it than would the routine staples of life, which rarely if ever fail.

Eskimo-Bushman Comparisons

Were the Bushmen to be deprived of their vegetable food sources, their life would become much more arduous and precarious. This lack of plant foods, in fact, is precisely the situation among the Netsilik Eskimo, reported by Balikci (Chapter 8, this volume). The Netsilik and other Central Arctic peoples are perhaps unique in the almost total absence of vegetable foods in their diet. This factor, in combination with the great cyclical variation in the numbers and distribution of Arctic fauna, makes Eskimo life the most precarious human adaptation on earth. In effect, *the kinds of animals that are "luxury goods" to many hunters and gatherers, are to the Eskimos, the absolute necessities of life*. However, even this view should not be exaggerated, since most of the Eskimos in historic times have lived south of the Arctic Circle (Laughlin, Chapter 25a this volume) and many of the Eskimos at all latitudes have depended primarily on fishing, which is a much more reliable source of food than is the hunting of land and sea mammals.

WHAT HUNTERS DO FOR A LIVING: A COMPARATIVE STUDY

I have discussed how the !Kung Bushmen are able to manage on the scarce resources of their inhospitable environment. The essence of their successful strategy seems to be that while they depend primarily on the more stable and abundant food sources (vegetables in their case), they are nevertheless willing to devote considerable energy to the less reliable and more highly valued food sources such as medium and large mammals. The steady but modest input of work by the women provides the former, and the more intensive labors of the men provide the latter. It would be theoretically possible for the Bushmen to survive entirely on vegetable foods, but life would be boring indeed without the excitement of meat feasts. The totality of their subsistence activities thus represents an outcome of two individual goals; the first is the desire to live well with adequate leisure time, and the second is the desire to enjoy the rewards, both social and nutritional, afforded by the killing of game. In short, *the Bushmen of the Dobe area eat as much vegetable food as they need, and as much meat as they can*.

It seems reasonable that a similar kind of subsistence strategy would be characteristic of hunters and gatherers in general. Wherever two or more kinds of natural foods are available, one would predict that the population exploiting them would emphasize the more reliable source. We would also expect, however, that the people would not neglect the alternative means of subsistence. The general view offered here is that gathering activities, for plants and shellfish, should be the most productive of food for hunting and gathering man, followed by fishing, where this source is available. The hunting of mammals is the least re-liable source of food and should be generally less important than either gathering or fishing.

In order to test this hypothesis, a sample of 58 societies was drawn from the *Ethnographic Atlas* (Murdock, 1967). The basis for inclusion in the sample was a 100 per cent dependence on hunting, gathering and fishing for subsistence as rated in Column 7–11 of the Atlas (Murdock, 1967, pp. 154–55). These 58 societies are plotted in Figures 1 and 2 and are listed in Tables 7 and 8 of the Appendix to this Article.[8,9]

The *Ethnographic Atlas* coding discusses "Subsistence Economy" as follows:

A set of five digits indicates the estimated relative dependence of the society on each of the five major types of subsistence activity. The first digit refers to the gathering of wild plants and small land fauna; the second, to hunting, including trapping and fowling; the third, to fishing, including shell fishing and the pursuit of large aquatic animals; the fourth, to animal husbandry; the fifth, to agriculture (Murdock, 1967, pp. 154–55).

Two changes have been made in the definitions of subsistence. First, the participants at the symposium on Man the Hunter agreed that the "pursuit of large aquatic animals" is more properly classified under hunting than under fishing. Similarly, it was recommended that shellfishing should be classified under gathering, not fishing. These suggestions have been followed and the definitions now read: *Gathering*—collecting of wild plant, small land

8. Two societies, the Gwi Bushmen and the Walbiri of Australia, were not coded by the *Ethnographic Atlas*. Their subsistence base was scored after consulting the original ethnographies (for the Gwi, Silberbauer, 1965; for the Walbiri, Meggitt, 1962, 1964).

9. In order to make more valid comparisons, I have excluded from the sample mounted hunters with guns such as the Plains Indians, and casual agriculturalists such as the Gê and Siriono. Twenty-four societies are drawn from Africa, Asia, Australia and South America. This number includes practically all of the cases that fit the definition. North America alone, with 137 hunting societies, contains over 80 per cent of the 165 hunting societies listed in the *Ethnographic Atlas*. The sampling procedure used here was to choose randomly one case from each of the 34 "clusters" of North American hunter-gatherers.

fauna and shellfish; *Hunting*—pursuit of land and sea mammals; *Fishing*—obtaining of fish by any technique. In 25 cases, the subsistence scores have been changed in light of these definitions and after consulting ethnographic sources.[10]

In Tables 9 and 10 of the Appendix to this article, the percentage dependence on gathering, hunting, and fishing, and the most important single source of food for each society are presented. Such scores can be at best only rough approximations; however, the results are so striking that the use of these scores seems justified. In the Old World and South American sample of 24 societies, sixteen depend on gathering, five on fishing, while only three depend primarily on mammal hunting: the Yukaghir of northeast Asia, and the Ona and Shiriana of South America. In the North American sample, thirteen societies have primary dependence on gathering, thirteen on fishing, and eight on hunting. Thus for the world as a whole, half of the societies (29 cases) emphasize gathering, one-third (18 cases) fishing, and the remaining one-sixth (11 cases) hunting.

On this evidence, the "hunting" way of life appears to be in the minority. The result serves to underline the point made earlier that mammal hunting is the least reliable of the subsistence sources, and one would expect few societies to place primary dependence on it. As will be shown, most of the societies that rely primarily on mammals do so because their particular habitats offer no viable alternative subsistence strategy.

The Relation of Latitude to Subsistence

The peoples we have classified as "hunters" apparently depend for most of their subsistence on sources *other* than meat, namely, wild plants, shellfish and fish. In fact the present sample over-emphasizes the incidence of hunting and fishing since some three-fifths of the cases (34/58) are drawn from North America (north of the Rio Grande) a region which lies entirely within the temperate and arctic zones. Since the abundance and species variety of edible plants decreases as one moves out of the tropical and temperate zones, and approaches zero in the arctic, it is essential that the incidence of hunting, gathering, and fishing be related to latitude.

Table 6 shows the relative importance of gathering, hunting, and fishing within each of seven latitude divisions. Hunting appears as the dominant mode of subsistence *only* in the highest latitudes (60 or more degrees from the equator). In the arctic, hunting is primary in six of the eight societies. In the cool to cold temperate latitudes, 40 to 59 degrees from the equator, fishing is the dominant mode, appearing as primary in 14 out of 22 cases. In the warm-temperate, subtropical, and tropical latitudes, zero to 39 degrees from the equator, gathering is by far the dominant mode of subsistence, appearing as primary in 25 of the 28 cases.

For modern hunters, at any rate, it seems legitimate to predict a hunting emphasis only in the arctic, a fishing emphasis in the mid-high latitudes, and a gathering emphasis in the rest of the world.[11]

The Importance of Hunting

Although hunting is rarely the primary source of food, it does make a remarkably stable contribution to the diet. Fishing appears to be dispensable in the tropics, and a number of northern peoples manage to do without gathered foods, but, with a single exception, *all* societies at all latitudes derive at least 20 per cent of their diet from the hunting of mammals. Latitude appears to make little difference in the amount of hunting that people do. Except for the highest latitudes, where hunting contributes over half of the diet in many cases, hunted foods almost everywhere else constitute 20 to 45 per cent of the diet. In fact, the mean, the median, and the mode for hunting all converge on a figure of 35 per cent for hunter-gatherers at all latitudes. This percentage of

10. For their useful suggestions, my thanks go to Donald Lathrap, Robin Ridington, George Silberbauer, Hitoshi Watanabe, and James Woodburn. Special thanks are due to Wayne Suttles for his advice on Pacific coast subsistence.

11. When severity of winter is plotted against subsistence choices, a similar picture emerges. Hunting is primary in three of the five societies in very cold climates (annual temperature less than 32° F.); fishing is primary in 10 of the 17 societies in cold climinates (32°–50° F.); and gathering is primary in 27 of the 36 societies in mild to hot climates (over 50° F.).

Table 6   *Primary Subsistence Source by Latitude*

Degrees from the Equator	Primary Subsistence Source			
	Gathering	Hunting	Fishing	Total
More than 60°	—	6	2	8
50°–59°	—	1	9	10
40°–49°	4	3	5	12
30°–39°	9	—	—	9
20°–29°	7	—	1	8
10°–19°	5	—	1	6
0°–9°	4	1	—	5
World	29	11	18	58

meat corresponds closely to the 37 per cent noted in the diet of the !Kung Bushmen of the Dobe area. It is evident that the !Kung, far from being an aberrant case, are entirely typical of the hunters in general in the amount of meat they consume.

Conclusions

Three points ought to be stressed. First, life in the state of nature is not necessarily nasty, brutish, and short. The Dobe-area Bushmen live well today on wild plants and meat, in spite of the fact that they are confined to the least productive portion of the range in which Bushman peoples were formerly found. It is likely that an even more substantial subsistence base would have been characteristic of these hunters and gatherers in the past, when they had the pick of African habitats to choose from.

Second, the basis of Bushman diet is derived from sources other than meat. This emphasis makes good ecological sense to the !Kung Bushmen and appears to be a common feature among hunters and gatherers in general. Since a 30 to 40 per cent input of meat is such a con-

sistent target for modern hunters in a variety of habitats, is it not reasonable to postulate a similar percentage for prehistoric hunters? Certainly the absence of plant remains on archeological sites is by itself not sufficient evidence for the absence of gathering. Recently-abandoned Bushman campsites show a similar absence of vegetable remains, although this paper has clearly shown that plant foods comprise over 60 per cent of the actual diet.

Finally, one gets the impression that hunting societies have been chosen by ethnologists to illustrate a dominant theme, such as the extreme importance of environment in the molding of certain cultures. Such a theme can be best exemplified by cases in which the technology is simple and/or the environment is harsh. This emphasis on the dramatic may have been pedagogically useful, but unfortunately it has led to the assumption that a precarious hunting subsistence base was characteristic of all cultures in the Pleistocene. This view of both modern and ancient hunters ought to be reconsidered. Specifically I am suggesting a shift in focus away from the dramatic and unusual cases, and toward a consideration of hunting and gathering as a persistent and well-adapted way of life.

Appendix

Table 7 The Sample of Hunter-Gatherers (excluding North America)		Table 8 The North American Sample	

People (Atlas No.)	Latitude and Longitvde (Degrees)
Africa n = 5	
1. !Kung Bushmen (Aa1) ...	20S, 21E
2. Dorobo (Aa2)	2S, 36E
3. Mbuti Pygmies (Aa5) ...	2N, 28E
4. Hadza (Aa9)	3S, 35E
5. Gwi Bushmen (1)	22S, 23E
Asia n = 5	
6. Gilyak (Ec1)	53N, 142E
7. Yukaghir (Ec6)	70N, 145E
8. Ainu (Ec7)	44N, 144E
9. Andamanese (Eh1)	12N, 93E
10. Semang (Ej3)	6N, 101E
Australia n = 6	
11. Aranda (Id1)	24S, 134E
12. Murngin (Id2)	12S, 136E
13. Tiwi (Id3)	12S, 131E
14. Dieri (Id4)	28S, 138E
15. Wikmunkan (Id6)	14S, 142E
16. Walbiri (2)	22S, 133E
South America n = 8	
17. Paraujano (Sb5)	11N, 72W
18. Shiriana (Sd6)	4N, 63W
19. Yahgan (Sg1)	55S, 69W
20. Ona (Sg3)	54S, 69W
21. Alacaluf (Sg5)	52S, 74W
22. Chamacoco (Sh6)	20S, 59W
23. Aweikoma (Sj3)	28S, 50W
24. Botocudo (Sj5)	18S, 42W

People (Atlas No.)	Latitude and Longitude (Degrees)
1. Copper Eskimo (Na3)	69N, 110W
2. Kaska (Na4)	59N, 128W
3. Ingalik (Na8)	62N, 160W
4. Chugach (Na10)	60N, 166W
5. Nunamiut (Na12)	68N, 152W
6. Kutchin (Na20)	66N, 135W
7. Chipewyan (Na30)	60N, 105W
8. Montagnais (Na32)	48N, 72W
9. Northern Saulteaux (Na33) ...	52N, 98W
10. Eyak (Nb5)	60N, 145W
11. Tsimshian (Nb7)	55N, 130W
12. Quileute (Nb18)	48N, 125W
13. Chinook (Nb19)	46N, 124W
14. Tlingit (Nb22)	58N, 134W
15. Bellabella (Nb23)	52N, 128W
16. Cowichan (Nb26)	49N, 123W
17. Tututni (Nb31)	42N, 124W
18. Chimariko (Nb33)	41N, 123W
19. Tubatulabal (Nc2)	36N, 118W
20. Diegueno (Nc6)	32N, 116W
21. Modoc (Nc9)	43N, 122W
22. Achomawi (Nc10)	41N, 121W
23. Wintu (Nc14)	41N, 122W
24. Coast Yuki (Nc15)	39N, 124W
25. Lake Yokuts (Nc24)	36N, 120W
26. Cahuilla (Nc31)	33N, 116W
27. Washo (Nd6)	39N, 120W
28. Chilcotin (Nd8)	52N, 122W
29. Flathead (Nd12)	46N, 113W
30. Umatilla (Nd19)	46N, 119W
31. Panamint (Nd32)	36N, 117W
32. Kaibab (Nd53)	36N, 113W
33. Yavapai (Nd66)	35N, 112W
34. Seri (Ni4)	29N, 112W

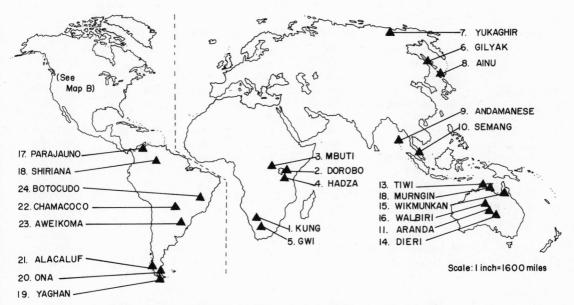

FIGURE 1. OLD WORLD AND SOUTH AMERICAN HUNTER-GATHERERS

Table 9   Subsistence Base of Hunter-Gatherers
(Old World and South America)

People	Gathering	Hunting	Fishing	Primary Subsistence Source		
1. !Kung Bushman*	70	30	0	G		
2. Dorobo*	60	40	0	G		
3. Mbuti	60	30	10	G		
4. Hadza*	80	20	0	G		
5. Gwi Bushmen	70	30	0	G		
6. Gilyak*	30	30	40			F
7. Yukaghir*	10	60	30		H	
8. Ainu*	30	30	40			F
9. Andamanese*	50	20	30	G		
10. Semang	40	30	30	G		
11. Aranda*	70	30	0	G		
12. Murngin*	60	30	10	G		
13. Tiwi*	60	30	10	G		
14. Dieri	70	30	0	G		
15. Wikmunkan*	60	30	10	G		
16. Walbiri	70	30	0	G		
17. Paraujano*	40	10	50			F
18. Shiriana	30	40	30		H	
19. Yahgan*	30	20	50			F
20. Ona	20	60	20		H	
21. Alacaluf*	30	20	50			F
22. Chamacoco	60	40	0	G		
23. Aweikoma*	60	40	0	G		
24. Botocudo	50	40	10	G		
Total				16	3	5

* In some of the cases marked, the subsistence percentages have been changed from those published in the *Ethnographic Atlas*. The categories have been redefined so that shell fishing is included under "Gathering," and pursuit of sea-mammals under "Hunting." In the *Atlas*, both are included under "Fishing."

FIGURE 2. NORTH AMERICAN HUNTER-GATHERERS.

Table 10   Subsistence Base of Hunter-Gatherers
(North America)

People	Percentage Dependence on:			Primary Subsistence Source		
	Gathering	Hunting	Fishing			
1. Copper Eskimo*	0	55	45		H	
2. Kaska	10	40	50			F
3. Ingalik	10	40	50			F
4. Chugach*	10	60	30		H	
5. Nunamiut	10	70	20		H	
6. Kutchin	10	40	50			F
7. Chipewyan	0	60	40		H	
8. Montagnais	20	60	20		H	
9. Saulteaux	20	35	45			F
10. Eyak*	20	45	35		H	
11. Tsimshian*	20	30	50			F
12. Quileute*	30	30	40			F
13. Chinook*	30	20	50			F
14. Tlingit*	10	40	50			F
15. Bellabella	20	30	50			F
16. Cowichan*	40	30	30	G		
17. Tututni*	45	20	35	G		
18. Chimariko	40	30	30	G		
19. Tubatulabal	50	30	20	G		
20. Diegueno	50	40	10	G		
21. Modoc	50	30	20	G		
22. Achomawi	30	40	30		H	
23. Wintu	30	30	40			F
24. Coast Yuki*	60	20	20	G		
25. Lake Yokuts	50	20	30	G		
26. Cahuilla	60	40	0	G		
27. Washo	40	30	30	G		
28. Chilcotin	20	30	50			F
29. Flathead	30	40	30		H	
30. Umatilla	30	30	40			F
31. Panamint	60	40	0	G		
32. Kaibab	70	30	0	G		
33. Yavapai	60	40	0	G		
34. Seri*	30	20	50			F
Total (North America)				13	8	13
Total (World)				29	11	18

* In some of the cases marked, the subsistence percentages have been changed from those published in the *Ethnographic Atlas*. The categories have been redefined so that shell fishing is included under "Gathering," and pursuit of sea-mammals under "Hunting." In the *Atlas*, both are included under "Fishing."

5.

An Introduction to Hadza Ecology

JAMES WOODBURN

The Hadza (also known as Hadzapi, Tindiga, Kindiga, and Kangeju) are a small group of nomadic hunters and gatherers living in the vicinity of Lake Eyasi, a salt, rift-valley lake not far south of the equator in Tanzania.[1]

Their language contains click consonants and several authorities have claimed that it may be related to Bushman languages in southern Africa (for example, Bleek, 1931a, 1931b, 1956; Greenberg, 1950; Westphal, 1956). My own work on the language[2] suggests that the material put forward as evidence for such a link is unsatisfactory and some research now in progress indicates that Hadza may possibly have distant affinities with languages of the Erythraic (Hamito-Semitic) group (A. N. Tucker, personal communication). Work carried out in 1966 and 1967 with N. A. Barnicot

and F. J. Bennett on Hadza anthropometry and blood-grouping has not yet shown any evidence for a physical link with Bushmen, but only preliminary results are so far available. There is no satisfactory evidence for a cultural tie with Bushmen.

If we treat as Hadza all those who speak the Hadza language as their first language, there are three separate groupings of Hadza. In the tsetse bush to the east of Lake Eyasi, an area of, until recently, well over a thousand square miles, are some four hundred nomadic hunters and gatherers whom I shall refer to as the Eastern Hadza. South of these are more than a hundred settled Hadza who live, and have lived at least since the first Europeans visited the area in the 1890's, by agriculture and by hunting, and who have intermarried intensively with the neighboring Bantu-speaking Isanzu tribe. The third group of Hadza, the great majority of whom live by hunting and gathering, are to be found in the neighborhood of Kimali to the west of Lake Eyasi and number about 250 people. Little contact occurs between the Eastern and the Western Hadza: only very occasionally have individuals moved temporarily or, more rarely, permanently from one of these areas to another. Almost all my field research,[3] carried out continuously from 1958 until 1960, and again for short periods in 1961, 1965, 1966, and 1967, was done among the nomadic Eastern Hadza, and in this paper

1. This account consists of a simplified version of part of my unpublished Ph.D. thesis at the University of Cambridge (1964) which is currently being revised for publication. Adequate factual data in support of the argument cannot be presented here but will appear in due course in the monograph.

2. I am preparing material on the language for publication.

3. I would like to thank the following bodies which provided funds for field research: The Royal Society; the World Health Organization; the Wenner-Gren Foundation for Anthropological Research; the East African Institute of Social Research; the Goldsmiths' Company; the Smuts Memorial Fund; the Sir Bartle Frere Fund; the Mary Euphrasia Mosley Fund.

49

I shall refer almost exclusively to them.[4]

Unlike most other East African hunters and gatherers, the Eastern Hadza are relatively independent of their agricultural and pastoral neighbors. Although they rely on trade and begging to obtain tobacco, cloth, beads, iron, and other goods, they have not entered into an elaborate dependence on, or interdependence with their neighbors. In this respect they stand in marked contrast to the Mbuti Pygmies of the Congo (Turnbull, 1965b and Chapter 15, this volume) and the Kenya Dorobo described by Huntingford (1954).

The small numbers of the Eastern Hadza should not be taken as evidence that they are a broken down remnant of some much larger group. Their numbers have been quite adequate to maintain their language, their culture, and their social organization; there is no evidence to indicate that their numbers were either much greater or much smaller in the past. No very serious epidemic, no large-scale war, no time of famine is remembered.

Environment

The country of the Eastern Hadza, dry, rocky savanna, dominated by thorn scrub and acacia trees and infested with tsetse flies, has been described by a traveler who walked through it in 1921 as "a barren land . . . to all intents and purposes a desert" (Barns, 1923, pp. 71–72). Barren though it may be in places, the country is rich in wild foods. Animals are exceptionally numerous and were certainly even commoner at the beginning of the century. Elephant, rhinoceros, buffalo, giraffe, eland, zebra, wildebeeste, hartebeeste, waterbuck, impala, Thomson's gazelle, warthog, baboon, lion, leopard, and hyena are all common, as are smaller animals such as anteater, porcupine, hare, hyrax, dik-dik, klipspringer, jackal, tortoise, and many others. All of these animals, apart from the elephant, are hunted and eaten by the Hadza. The amount of meat that could be regularly harvested without endangering the future of the game in the area is probably as great or greater than anywhere else in the world where hunters and gatherers live or have lived in the recent past.

Vegetable food—roots, berries, the fruit of

the baobab tree, etc.—though not often obvious to the casual observer, is always abundant even at the height of the dry season in a year of drought. The type of vegetable food available is different in the six-month wet season from the dry season[5] but there is no period of shortage. The honey and grubs of seven species of wild bee are eaten; supplies of these vary widely from season to season and from year to year.

Sources of water are widely distributed over the country in the wet season but are very few in the dry season. The Hadza consider that about three or four miles is the maximum distance over which water can reasonably be carried and camps are normally sited within a mile of a water source.

Part of the country consists of open grass plains but the Hadza never build camps there. Camps are invariably sited among trees or rocks and, by preference, among both.

Subsistence

The Eastern Hadza assert no rights over land and its ungarnered resources.[6] Any individual may live wherever he likes and may hunt animals, collect roots, berries, and honey and draw water anywhere in Hadza country without any sort of restriction. Not only do the Hadza not parcel out their land and its resources among themselves, they do not even seek to restrict the use of the land they occupy to members of their own tribe. For at least the last fifty years outsiders have been steadily encroaching on land traditionally occupied by

4. The ethnographic information given in this paper refers to the position in 1960 at the end of my main period of field research. Recently most of the nomadic Hadza have been encouraged to settle by the Tanzanian government.

5. The rainfall of, on average, 22.61 inches a year (at Yaida) falls almost exclusively during the period December to May with peaks in December and March (East African Meteorological Department—Summary of Rainfall for the Year 1955).

6. Hadza subsistence is described in an ethnographic film, *The Hadza*, produced in 1966. Camera Director: Sean Hudson; Anthropological Director: James Woodburn. (16mm, 40 minutes, black and white with sound.) Copies are available from the author, Department of Anthropology, London School of Economics, Aldwych, London, WC 2, England.

the Hadza, and by eliminating most of the game and destroying much of the vegetation in the areas they have occupied, they have denied the use of most of these areas to Hadza living by their traditional means of subsistence. However, in 1960 the Hadza still had plenty of land and abundant resources.[7]

In spite of the exceptional numbers of game animals in their area, the Hadza rely mainly on wild vegetable matter for their food. Probably as much as 80 per cent of their food by weight is vegetable, while meat and honey together account for the remaining 20 per cent.[8] In terms of calories, however, meat and honey represent far more than 20 per cent of the total.[9] Although a large number of species of plant food are eaten, only a few are systematically gathered and provide important quantities of food. The bulk of the vegetable food eaten by the Hadza is in fact obtained from only ten species of plant. The edible part of four of these plants is the root,[10] of five others the berry,[11] and of the remaining one its large fruit which contains edible pulp and seeds with edible kernels.[12]

Vegetable food is collected almost every day by the women of the camp who go out as a group or groups with their children. They make their way leisurely to the place where the vegetable food is to be found, which is usually

7. A potentially serious situation was developing (Woodburn, 1962), however, in that the annual rate of encroachment had increased enormously as a result of a very large, government-sponsored, tsetse-clearance scheme. If encroachment continued at this rate, serious pressures were likely to develop within a few years. The pressures were eased, though, by the cessation of the clearance scheme in about 1963 and by the settlement of the majority of the Eastern Hadza in 1964 and 1965.

8. These figures are very approximate as they are based on observation but not on measurement. During field work in 1967 detailed measurements will, if possible, be made.

9. The calorific values of Hadza foods are at present under investigation.

10. *Ipomoea transvaalensis* Meeuse, *Coccinea aurantiaca* C. Jeffrey, *Vigna esculenta* (De Wild.) De Wild. ex Th. et H. Dur, and *Vigna macrorhyncha* (Herms) Milne-Redh.

11. *Cordia gharaf* Ehrehb, *Salvadora persica* L., *Grewia pachycalyx* K. Schum, *Grewia bicolor* Juss, and *Grewia similis* K. Schum.

12. *Adansonia digitata* (Baobab tree).

within an hour's walk of the camp. Whatever the type of vegetable food, a large proportion is eaten where it is gathered. Berries are quickly and easily collected and are eaten raw. Roots are obtained with rather more difficulty; they are dug up with a simple, sharpened wooden digging stick and are, in most cases, lightly roasted on an open fire. Only the food which remains after the women and children have satisfied their hunger is brought back to camp and, even of the food brought back to camp, less than half is given to the men.

Men do not rely on the women to supply them with all the vegetable food that they need. They wander off into the bush individually for a while almost every day to satisfy their hunger. They gather vegetable food only for their own needs and normally bring none back to camp.

Hunting is done exclusively by men and boys and is an essentially individual pursuit. A man hunts only with bow and arrow; no guns, spears, traps, nets, or snares are now in use. Hunting procedure is simple and differs very little whether the target is a lion, a zebra, or a guinea fowl. Once he has sighted his quarry the solitary hunter stalks it slowly and with care until he is, if possible, 25 yards or less away and then attempts a shot. For any animal larger than, say, a jackal, a poisoned arrow will be used. An animal hit with a poisoned arrow will usually be tracked down only after an interval of a couple of hours to allow the poison to kill the animal near the place where it is shot. To track it earlier might cause it to run for many miles before collapsing from the effect of the poison. Occasionally animals are shot at night from hides over water and are tracked the following morning. The large animals which are most frequently killed are impala, zebra, eland, and giraffe.

The men, like the women, satisfy their hunger at the place where food is obtained. A man on his own will normally light a fire, cook, and eat on the spot any small animal he kills, and only after he is satisfied will he bring meat back to camp and, even there, a small animal is as likely to be eaten by the men as by the women and children. Men and women are thus unusually independent of each other in obtaining food. This arrangement has important implications for Hadza social structure which will be discussed in detail in my forth-coming monograph.

Although vegetable foods form the bulk of their diet, the Hadza attach very little value to them. They think of themselves and describe themselves as hunters. From informants' assertions, one would gather that little but meat is eaten. In addition to being the preferred food, meat is also intimately connected with rituals to which Hadza men attach great importance.

Honey, although highly valued as a food, is especially important as a trading commodity. Neighboring tribesmen use honey for making beer and are eager to obtain it in trade.

The foods which Hadza eat, the size and the positioning of their camps, the activities within the camps differ markedly between the dry and wet seasons. These differences are not a simple product of ecological factors. In Hadza culture seasonal polarity is stressed. Activities which are characteristic of the wet season tend to be avoided during the dry season and vice versa. In the wet season the emphasis is on root gathering and hunting small game especially hyrax; in the dry season the emphasis is on gathering berries and hunting large animals. Camps are commonly small and widely dispersed in the wet season, large and concentrated near the few available sources of water in the dry season. In the small camps of the wet season men and women are not segregated to any great extent and live together relatively harmoniously, but in the large camps of the dry season sexually segregated activities (such as gambling) are stressed and the opposition, even hostility, between men as a group and women as a group is reiterated.

EASE OF SUBSISTENCE

Hunting and gathering tribes are often described as living on the verge of starvation. It is easy to gain such an impression after living for a short while with the Hadza; often by night-fall every scrap of food in the camp has been eaten unless a large animal happens to have been killed recently. Moreover the Hadza place such emphasis on meat as proper food and treat vegetable foods as so thoroughly unsatisfactory in comparison that they are apt to

describe themselves as suffering from hunger when they have less meat than they would like. In fact, there is never any general shortage of food even in time of drought. The range of foods in the bush is so great, if one knows what these are and how to obtain them, that if weather conditions should cause the failure of some type of root or berry, or the migration of some of the game, some other type of food is always available. For a Hadza to die of hunger, or even to fail to satisfy his hunger for more than a day or two, is almost inconceivable.

I have already mentioned the exceptional abundance of game animals in this area. Although Hadza, in common probably with all other human societies, do not eat all the types of animal available to them—they reject civet, monitor, lizard, snake, terrapin among others—they do eat an unusually wide range of animals including predators such as lion, leopard, serval, wild cat and scavengers such as hyena, jackal, vulture.[13] With their very powerful bows and their poisoned arrows they are able to kill without any great difficulty all the animals in the area with the sole exception of elephant, which are too large to be killed by the type of poison they use. In spite of the large number of species which they are both able to hunt and regard as edible, the Hadza do not kill very many animals and it is probable that even in the radically reduced area they occupied in 1960 more animals could have been killed of every species without endangering the survival of any species in the area.

The low opinion which Hadza have of the vegetable food which makes up the bulk of their diet is not surprising when its unpalatability is taken into account. Roots are, in general, tough, fibrous, and have little taste; many of the berries are hard and dry and contain large stones which are swallowed whole; *undushi* berries leave a dry, sticky residuum in the mouth; *k'alahai* berries split the lips and tongue if eaten in quantity. Very little of the vegetable food is eaten with much enthusiasm. But the advantage of vegetable food over meat (or honey), and the basic reason why it constitutes the bulk of the diet of the Hadza, is that

13. Some individuals will not eat some of these animals especially when strangers are present.

it can be obtained quickly and, above all, predictably. When they go out to look for vegetable food, the women can be sure that they will find some type without undue effort. Hunting, even by a highly skilled hunter, on the other hand, is always an unpredictable pursuit and therefore one which is less suitable as a basis for day-to-day subsistence.

With food of some sort always available, the Hadza give little attention to the conservation of their food resources. When women dig up roots, they do not attempt to replace any portion of the plant to grow again. When they gather berries, heavily laden branches are often torn from the trees and carried back to camp. When a woman is building the framework of her grass hut, she is as likely to use branches from berry trees as from any other type of tree that happens to be near at hand. The Hadza may inadvertently assist in propagating berry trees in their locality by their practice of swallowing the berry stones which pass intact through the digestive tract, but they make no deliberate effort to conserve the trees and other food-producing plants.

When a nest of wild bees is found and raided for its honey, no portion of the comb is left to encourage the bees to stay on. Moreover, little effort is made to leave the nest suitable for reoccupation. If the nest is in a hollow tree and the entrance has been cut open with an axe to extract the comb, the hollow will not again be used by bees unless the hole through which the comb has been extracted is partially blocked. When there happens to be a stone of suitable size near at hand, this may be wedged into the hole in the hope that the bees will later return and reoccupy the hollow. As often as not, though, the hole will be left unblocked; people do not feel obliged to attend to this task and do not bother about it unless they can do so very easily.

In hunting no attempt is made at systematic cropping. A man out hunting will shoot any animal he comes across. There are no inhibitions about shooting females (even pregnant females) or immature animals. Adult males are preferred but only because they are generally larger. Hadza do not often kill more animals than they need but this is only because hunting requires effort and they see no virtue in hunting unless they are hungry for meat.

Meat may sometimes be wasted: if a large animal is killed by a man of a small camp, some of the less palatable portions may be left behind for the vultures and hyenas. If two animals are killed on the same day, the more distant one may be abandoned. When tracking an animal wounded by a poisoned arrow, it will commonly be abandoned if it is not found in one day's tracking.

In camp meat is widely distributed and rapidly consumed.[14] The Hadza are familiar with techniques for drying meat in the sun and could, if they wished, preserve stocks for months, at least in the dry season. But in practice meat is rarely preserved: it is eaten in large quantities until it is finished. Meat should be shared with those who ask for it. In particular pregnant women have the right to eat meat belonging to anybody.[15] To eat meat slowly, to preserve it and store it would be largely wasted effort, other people would simply demand meat when their own was finished and it would be wrong to refuse them.

Hunting is not a coordinated activity. Men hunt individually and decide for themselves where and when they will go hunting. When a man goes off into the bush with his bow and arrows, his main interest is usually to satisfy his hunger. Once he has satisfied his hunger by eating berries or by shooting and catching some small animal, he is unlikely to make much effort to shoot a large animal. Of course, if he sees an animal close by which can easily be hunted, he will almost always take the opportunity. Men most often return from the bush empty-handed but with their hunger satisfied.

During the dry season Hadza men spend much more time gambling than hunting. The gambling game, played with bark disks, is a game of chance in which skill plays hardly any part. The most usual and most acceptable stake is a metal-headed arrow, preferably of the poisoned type. In the course of a day arrows (and other possessions which are staked) will change hands hundreds of times. In practice,

14. The system of distribution will be described in my forthcoming monograph.

15. Except for certain portions known as *epeme* meat which are reserved for the initiated men.

the majority of men in dry season camps where gambling is being carried on will often have lost all their metal-headed arrows and will therefore be unable to hunt big game. Arrows without metal heads which are suitable for hunting birds and small animals are not used as gambling stakes. Men are, then, able to satisfy their hunger easily enough during the dry season when gambling is going on, but they spend little time hunting big game due to their lack of suitable arrows or their desire to conserve whatever arrows they possess for gambling purposes.

Many men are, in any case, quite unprepared or unable to hunt big game even when they possess the necessary arrows. Large animals are killed by a small minority of the adult men. Perhaps as many as half of the adult men fail to kill even one large animal a year. The active hunters are usually men in their late teens, or in their twenties or thirties; few men continue to hunt large game actively after the age of 45. There are some men who have killed scarcely a single large animal during their entire adult lives. Whether a man hunts is his own affair. Other men will not put pressure on him. He may, though, find it more difficult to marry a wife, or, once married, to keep a wife, if he is unsuccessful in hunting big game.

In spite of the fact that the Hadza make scarcely any attempt to conserve the food resources of their area, that they rapidly eat all the food which comes into camp without preserving it, that they do not cooperate very much or coordinate their food gathering activities with each other, that they make hunting difficult for themselves by using their arrows for gambling, that a high proportion of men are failures at hunting, they nonetheless obtain sufficient food without undue effort. Over the year as a whole probably an average of less than two hours a day is spent obtaining food.[16] There are seasonal variations and variations from year to year but not very considerable ones.

We have good evidence that the food they eat is adequate nutritionally. In 1960 I was

visited in the field by D. B. Jelliffe and F. J. Bennett of Makerere College Medical School, and they examined 62 Hadza children. According to their report, "the clinical nutritional status of all the children was good by tropical standards; in particular, the syndromes of kwashiorkor and nutritional marasmus, rickets, infantile scurvy, and vitamin B deficiency syndromes were not seen." In 1966 and 1967 Dr. Bennett, this time in cooperation with N. A. Barnicot and myself, did further work on Hadza nutrition. More than 450 Hadza were examined in detail; some of these were resident in settlements, others were still living in the bush by their traditional means of subsistence. The nutritional status of those who were resident in the bush was again found to be good by tropical standards.

My impression is that, over the year as a whole, the Hadza spend less energy (and probably less time) obtaining their subsistence than do neighboring agricultural tribes, but until detailed comparative research is done the matter must remain in doubt. From a nutritional point of view the Hadza again appear to be better off than their agricultural neighbors although to establish this, too, more research is needed. It is clear that agriculturalists are liable to suffer from recurrent famine in this area while hunters and gatherers are not. In the early years of this century, before the colonial government provided effective famine relief measures, numerous Isanzu took to the bush from time to time and lived like the Hadza on bush produce until the famine eased and the were able to return to cultivation. Some stayed on and intermarried with the Hadza. In general the bush plants on which the Hadza mainly rely yield with great regularity; failure is far rarer than it is with vulnerable, introduced cultivated plants such as maize and other cereals grown by neighboring peoples. In comparison with their agricultural neighbors the Hadza are well protected against the dangers of famine. They are doubly protected by the diversity of the food supplies available and by the lesser vulnerability of wild plants to such natural hazards as drought, insects, and birds. Hadza prefer maize and millet meal porridge to their own unappetizing berries and roots but, until the recent settlement schemes were initiated in

16. This figure is a very rough approximation and will probably have to be altered when adequate measurements are made.

1964, they did not in general think these foods were worth all the effort and uncertainty of cultivation.

Perhaps largely because of the temporal priority of hunting and gathering, there has been a widespread tendency to see it as a hard and demanding way of life in which the necessities of the food quest dominate people's lives. With the Hadza this is clearly not the case and judging from some of the other papers in this volume, they may not be exceptional. I have sought to show that the Hadza meet their nutritional needs easily without much effort, much forethought, much equipment, or much organization. The social implications are important and will be discussed partly in a second paper in this volume and partly in my forthcoming monograph.

6.

Coping with Abundance:
Subsistence on the Northwest Coast

WAYNE SUTTLES

Although the aboriginal peoples of the Northwest coast of North America were not hunters so much as fishermen, they seem especially worth including in a survey of Man the Hunter for two reasons: First, their rich, maritime, temperate-zone habitat is a type in which few food-gathering peoples survived until historic times, partly because this very type of habitat elsewhere saw the growth of more advanced forms of subsistence.[1] Second, the Northwest coast peoples seem to have attained the highest known levels of cultural complexity achieved on a food-gathering base and among the highest known levels of population density. The Northwest coast refutes many seemingly easy generalizations about people without horticulture or herds. Here were people with permanent houses in villages of more than a thousand; social stratification, including a hereditary caste of slaves and ranked nobility; specialization in several kinds of hunting and fishing, crafts, and curing; social units larger than villages; elaborate ceremonies; and one of the world's great art styles. The area appears to have been matched in population density, among food-gathering areas, by only two or three areas adjacent to it—California and parts of the Arctic and Plateau culture areas. (Kroeber, 1939; but it would be good to have comparable data for the Ainu

and the Lower Amur peoples.) These feature of Northwest coast culture and demography are generally thought to have been made possible, or even inevitably produced, by the richness of the habitat of the area and the efficiency of the subsistence techniques of its peoples. Perhaps, then, the study of Northwest coast subsistence can offer some guidance in estimating the possibilities of cultural development under comparable conditions in prehistoric times. (See Chapter 1, this volume.)

In a short paper I cannot hope to do justice to the variety and complexity of Northwest coast culture and its historic relations (for a general survey, see Drucker, 1955, 1965),[2] nor to go into the problem of aboriginal population sizes and densities except to comment that Mooney's and Kroeber's figures (Kroeber, 1939, pp. 131 ff.) have generally been revised upwards (Baumhoff, 1963, pp. 157–61; Duff, 1964, pp. 38–46; H. Taylor, 1963). I shall simply take the cultural complexity and population density as proven, and discuss our

1. The Ainu, described in this volume by Watanabe, Chap. 7, are perhaps the food-gathering people in the most similar habitat, but northwestern North America is climatically more like northwestern Europe than like northeastern Asia.

2. A complete bibliography of the area may be found in Murdock, 1960.

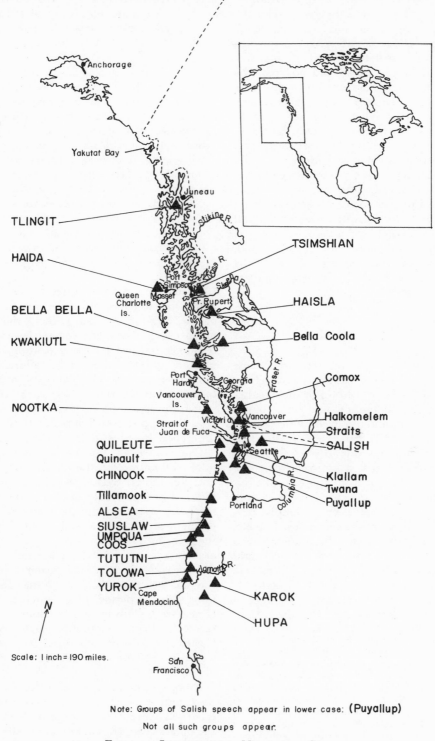

Note: Groups of Salish speech appear in lower case: **(Puyallup)**

Not all such groups appear.

FIGURE 1. INDIANS OF THE NORTHWEST COAST.

knowledge of subsistence and its relationship to them. But as you will see, I do not consider the relationship a simple one and so I must range through several sorts of phenomena. In general, my thesis is that while the habitat was undeniably rich, abundance did not exist the year round but only here and there and now and then and that such temporary abundances —though they may well be a necessary condition for population density and cultural development of the sort seen on the Northwest coast —are not sufficient to create them. Equally necessary conditions were the presence of good though limited food-getting techniques, food-storing techniques, a social system providing the organization for subsistence activities and permitting exchanges, and a value system that provided the motivation for getting food, storing food, and participating fully in the social system. I shall deal with each of these conditions in succession.

Habitat

The Northwest coast was an area where one could find, on a single occasion, quite literally tons of food. Salmon ran into the smaller streams by the thousands and into larger streams by the tens and hundreds of thousands. Waterfowl came to the marshes by the tens and hudnreds of thousands. A single sturgeon can weigh nearly a ton, a bull sea lion more than a ton, a whale up to thirty tons. But this aspect of the Northwest coast habitat is only too well known. It has been so emphasized that the implications of the phrase used above, "on a single occasion," have been ignored and the habitat has been presented as a constant source of plenty. But as I have said elsewhere (Suttles, 1960, 1962), it was not constant. It did not provide an ever-reliable abundance of natural resources simply there for the taking. Abundance there consisted only of certain

3. The coast Salish groups with whom I have worked on and off for a number of years are the speakers of the Halkomelem and Straits languages, whose territory includes the lower Fraser valley, the southern end of Georgia Strait, and the northern shores of the Strait of Juan de Fuca. Since they are roughly at the center of the total coast Salish area, I call them the central coast Salish.

things at certain places at certain times and always with some possibility of failure. Describing the central coast Salish[3] habitat, I wrote:

The environmental setting of native culture was characterized by four significant features: 1) *variety of types of food*, including sprouts, roots, berries, shellfish, fishes, waterfowl, land and sea mammals; 2) *local variation* in the occurrence of these types, due to irregular shorelines, broken topography, differences between fresh and salt water, local differences in temperature and precipitation; 3) *seasonal variation*, especially in vegetable foods and in anadromous fishes; 4) *fluctuation from year to year*, in part due to the regular cycles of the different populations of fish, in part to less predictable changes, as in weather (1960, p. 302; see also Suttles, 1962, pp. 527–29).

In their subsistence activities, the central coast Salish had to cope with these variable features of the habitat. It seems likely that farther north on the coast there were fewer types of resources but greater concentrations and thus possibly greater dangers in failure, through human error or natural calamity, of resources to appear at the right place at the right time (1962, pp. 530–33). Farther south I would expect the opposite to hold. But these subareal differences have yet to be worked out.

One cause of unexpected hardship was purely climatic. Because of the Japan Current and prevailingly westerly winds from the ocean, the weather is usually mild and damp. Summers are cool and during many winters the temperature only now and again drops below the freezing point. In the central coast Salish area, winters without frost are not unknown. But occasionally masses of extremely cold continental air break out through the coast mountains to bring periods of as much as ten days of near-zero (Fahrenheit) weather to the outer coast. In British Columbia such severe outbreaks have been recorded at twelve- to eighteen-year intervals (Young, 1943, pp. xli–xlii).

From a number of places along the coast we have indications that there were times when food was scarce. For groups dependent upon the open ocean, the cause was usually a stretch of bad weather; for groups on rivers, it was tardiness or failure in a fish run. In both situations it was of course also a matter of human failure to have accumulated enough food for the emergency.

For the Haida of the Queen Charlotte islands we have a statement by an early observer, Poole, quoted by Niblack, who writes:

> Some of these berries are collected and dried for winter's use, forming, with dried fish, the principal winter's supply. Poole, (1863) says of the Haida, that they often, through feasting or improvidence, eat up all the dried berries before spring, and "were it not for a few bulbs which they dig out of the soil in the early spring-time, while awaiting the halibut season, numbers of Indians really would starve to death" (Niblack, 1890, pp. 276–77).

For the Tsimshian of the Nass and Skeena rivers we have Boas's statement, derived from his analysis of Tsimshian mythology, that "sometimes when the olachen were late in coming, there would be a famine on Nass River" (Boas, 1916, p. 399). In his comparison of Tsimshian data with Kwakiutl data in *Kwakiutl Culture as Reflected in Mythology*, Boas writes:

> The difficulties of obtaining an adequate food supply must have been much more serious among the Tsimshian than among the Kwakiutl, for starvation and the rescue of the tribe by the deeds of a great hunter or by supernatural help are an ever-recurring theme which, among the Kwakiutl, is rather rare. One story of this type is clearly a Tsimshian story retold. . . . Starvation stories of the Kwakiutl occur particularly among the tribes living at the heads of the inlets of the mainland, not among those who dwell near the open sea, where seals, sealions, salmon and halibut are plentiful (Boas, 1935, p. 171; see other references in Piddocke, 1965, p. 247).

For the Nootka, who occupy the west coast of Vancouver Island in less sheltered waters than the Kwakiutl, we have Drucker's statement that a poor dog salmon or herring run followed by weather bad enough to prevent people from going out for cod or halibut "quickly brought privation" when people sought foods they ordinarily disdained. He cites

Father Brabant's report of "two successive springs at Hesquiat when pickings were lean and children cried out with hunger, until the weather abated enough for the fishermen to go out." He also cites family traditions of the hardships of winters on the outer coast before alliances had been made with groups with salmon streams (Drucker, 1951, pp. 36–37).

Swan says of the Makah at Cape Flattery:

> The ease with which these Indians can obtain their subsistence from the ocean makes them improvident in laying in supplies for winter use, except of halibut; for, on any day in the year when the weather will permit, they can procure, in a few hours, provisions enough to last them for several days (1870, p. 30).

Yet he later (p. 76) describes a period in April of 1864 when the weather did not permit going out fishing or whaling and how the Ozette were concerned enough about this to accuse an old man of sorcery and threaten to kill him if he didn't stop his incantations and make fair weather. The Quileute, Swan was told, had killed an alleged sorcerer for bringing bad weather during the halibut season only a few summers earlier.

Discussing relations between the upper and lower classes among the Chinook of the mouth of the Columbia River, Ray (1938, p. 56) says that his principal informant "declared that the upper class could infringe as much as it pleased upon the lower classes and added that famine was unknown to the former since the food of the latter was appropriated in such a circumstance." Ray adds that the informant's specific examples were the acts of chiefs. In the context of Ray's other statements, it appears that the Chinook village chief received, or seized, tribute and redistributed food to his people, favoring the upper class. My point in citing this is simply to indicate that shortages were conceivable.

Finally, we have Gould's (1966) recent re-analysis of the wealth quest among the Tolowa, an Athapaskan-speaking people on the Oregon-California border. This is the group described by DuBois (1936) as having distinctly separate "subsistence" and "prestige" economies in the paper that first introduced these terms into the study of primitive economies. According to

DuBois, subsistence was not a problem; scarcity existed only in "treasures" (dentalia shells, obsidian blades, and woodpecker scalps); food circulated freely in a "subsistence economy," while men bent their efforts in gaining prestige through amassing wealth in the "prestige economy." But Gould has found no separate "subsistence economy" in that there is no evidence for specialization in subsistence or the exchange of foods. There do appear, however, to have been differences in the productivity of households due in part to differences in the number of women available to process foods in season. It is true that "treasure" items were not constantly used to buy food, nor ideally nor publicly so used, but they were commonly used to buy food during periods of shortage. In fact, storing food to sell to others was recognized as an important method of acquiring wealth; hence, the interest the Tolowa show in acquiring women, the processors of food. Wealth is converted into prestige by its use in ceremonial displays and in payment of bride price, which establishes the social status of children to the marriage (Gould, 1966, pp. 70, 77, 86). Thus recognition of the existence of periods of shortage and of problems in subsistence has made possible a reinterpretation of the data that give them a greater coherence than in the earlier analyses.[4] There is really only one Tolowa economy; in it food is converted into wealth and wealth is converted into prestige. Occasional shortages of food provided the occasions for converting wealth into food. Hungry people wanted food; greedy people wanted wealth. Why did the greedy want wealth? Because wealth brought prestige. Gould does not ask why the Tolowa sought prestige. But it seems likely that it was because indirectly prestige-seeking enabled hungry people to obtain food. Or, if this seems to imply

conscious purposiveness, we may say it is because populations that have unconsciously stumbled on ways of feeding hungry members survive better than those who let them starve.

I have dwelt at length on the existence of times of scarcity on the Northwest coast precisely because recognizing their existence may be essential to our understanding of the complexities of Northwest coast culture. Some years ago Bartholomew and Birdsell pointed out that it is a firmly established ecological generalization, known as "Liebig's law of the minimum," that the size of a population is determined not by the mean condition but by the extremes. "A semi-arid area may have many fruitful years in succession, but a single drought year occurring once in a human generation may restrict the population to an otherwise inexplicably low density" (Bartholomew and Birdsell, 1953, pp. 487–88; see also comment by Sherwood L. Washburn and June Helm, Chapter 9a, this volume). Perhaps, also, a single, once-a-generation failure of a major fish run or prolonged period of severe weather may explain an otherwise inexplicable practice such as the Northwest coast search for prestige.

What we need to know for the whole coast is not merely what resources were present and when and where they were found under ordinary conditions, but also the *minimal* occurrences in space, time, and quantity. This means we should pay special attention to what foods are, or were, available in winter, even though winter was culturally defined by most peoples of the area as the ceremonial season during which people lived on stored food. As we have seen from the quotations given, stored food was not always available. It also appears that there were differences between inland river environments, sheltered saltwater bays, and the open ocean shores. There were probably also differences from south to north. None of these has been worked out in detail, but I am confident, that, with the growing body of biological and climatological data on the area, we shall one day be able to state fairly accurately what the resource base of each people's territory were.

Of course it is necessary to distinguish between what foods *could* have been hunted, fished, and gathered, and those foods actually obtained in practice. The difference between

4. The fact of shortages in the Tolowa area was not just recently discovered. Driver, in his element list for northwestern California, under "Slaves," shows that "Starving person gives self for keep" was affirmed by his Tolowa informant, one of his two Karok informants, and both Yurok, while "Girls traded for food in time of famine" was affirmed by the Tolowa and both Yurok (Driver, 1939, p. 357). But Gould (1966) has indicated the relevance of the fact to the Tolowa socioeconomic system. For a suggestion regarding the relevance of the exchange of girls for food to residence rules, see the last section of this paper.

potential and actual is in part a function of the efficiency of food-getting methods.

FOOD-GETTING METHODS

The state of our knowledge in this respect, too, is certainly not as good as we would want it. We do not have and probably shall never have any figures on the quantities of food actually collected and consumed per capita, on the ratio of meat, fish, and vegetable food in the diet,[5] on the number of man-hours spent in the food quest, and on percent of the population supported in leisure or other non-subsistence activities. Moreover, for much of the area we do not even have the facts in the form of good ethnographic accounts of just how food was obtained. This is not to say there are no good works at all. Boas's material on Kwakiutl subsistence activities, mainly in the form of native texts with translations (Boas, 1909, pp. 461–516; 1921, part 1), gives the native view of a number of food-getting and food-storing techniques and a great many recipes. In these texts we see what was important to the informant, but do not always find the answers to questions the ethnographer would ask. From some, however, we can make inferences about quantities of food taken and consumed. Among the ethnographies of the area, Drucker's (1951) on the Nootka (see also Drucker, 1965, chap. 7, for a dramatic account of Nootka whaling) and Elmendorf's (1960) on the Twana (a coast

5. While going through central coast Salish material for the symposium, I guessed that in the diet of adults, vegetable foods would have amounted to less than 10 per cent of volume but might have been higher for children, who probably foraged for such things as cat-tail roots and thimble berries that adults would be less likely to bother with. I assume that in the diet of all, even small amounts of certain vegetable foods may have been very important to health. I was surprised then to note, in Murdock's *Ethnographic Atlas*, estimates of 20 per cent dependence on gathering for the Nootka and 30 per cent for the Kwakiutl (cf. Lee, chap. 4, this volume). As Lee notes, the *Atlas* defines "gathering" as the "gathering of wild plants and small land fauna," while "shellfishing" is included with "fishing" as is sea mammal hunting. Since small land fauna were almost wholly ignored on the Northwest coast, the figures must refer to vegetable foods alone.

I am willing to admit that my guess of 10 per cent dependence on vegetable foods for the central coast Salish may be too low, but the Kwakiutl figure given in the *Atlas* is surely too high. The *Atlas* gives estimates for twenty Northwest coast "societies." In the extreme south, the Yurok and the Tolowa proportions of gathering/hunting/fishing are 40/10/50 per cent and 40/20/40 per cent, respectively. This is an area where acorns were used and naturally the proportion for gathering is greater. From here northward the most common figure for gathering is 20 per cent; only the Puyallup and Kwakiutl have 30 per cent, while the Coos, Quileute, Twana, and Klallam have 10 per cent. The Puyallup are a coast Salish group living inland from Puget Sound who quite likely did depend more on roots and bulbs than did their salt-water neighbors, though with the complex exchange systems of the area we cannot be sure. But there seems no reason at all to give the Kwakiutl a higher figure than the Nootka, Bella Coola, and coast Salish of northern Georgia Strait, all of them adjacent to Kwakiutl and all given 20 per cent. It is true that George Hunt recorded 44 recipes for preparing vegetable foods and instructions for preserving some fifteen of them (Boas, 1921, part 1). But the texts indicate that some of these foods were quite restricted in where they grew and the small quantities served to feast a village. Some too were described as emergency foods and evidently dangerous if eaten in quantity. Most of the roots were in fact so small that it is hard to imagine gathering large amounts of them. Altogether it does not seem to me that the Kwakiutl would have been very different from the Nootka, of whom Drucker writes:

> There was a tremendous emphasis on fats—oils and greases—in the dietary pattern. Probably the fats made up for the virtual lack of starch and sugar forms of carbohydrates. Prior to the introduction of potatoes, flour, and pilot bread in historic times, starch foods were limited to the very occasional meals of clover and fern roots, and the few other roots. It is obviously impossible to judge at this late date, but one receives the impression from informants that if the average person ate a dozen or two meals of roots in the course of a year, it was a lot. Berries provided the only sugar prior to the introduction of molasses, and were highly prized. But the berry season was rather short, except for that of *salal* berries, and the few baskets of them women picked seem to have adorned rather than materially augmented the diet. Instead of these things, one hears constantly of fats and oils (1951, pp. 62–63).

To me this statement hardly implies the 20 per cent gathering given the Nootka by the *Atlas*. On the other hand, some of the coast Salish groups probably did have more vegetable food in their diet than the Nootka and Kwakiutl, yet two of them (Klallam and Twana) were assigned only 10 per cent—my original guess for those I am calling the "central" groups, which include the Lummi, who are given 20 per cent by the *Atlas*. I can only conclude that the question should be left open.

I agree with Lee that shellfish gathering has more in common with the gathering of plant foods than with fishing. Both plants and shellfish are immobile and were collected (on the Northwest coast) mainly by women using digging sticks and baskets. They differ only in food value. But sea-mammal hunting and fishing can

Salish group) are outstanding. The only specialized monograph is Kroeber and Barrett (1960) on fishing in northwestern California. But for much of the area between the Klamath and the Columbia and north of the Kwakiutl, we have only very sketchy accounts.

The reason for the deficiency in figures on subsistence is not hard to find. The purely aboriginal way of life had been greatly altered in most parts of the Northwest coast by the end of the last century and quantitative data are, as Kroeber pointed out (1939, p. 3), not ordinarily recoverable by the method of ethnographic reconstruction we must use in western North America. The reasons for the scant attention often paid to subsistence techniques are also easy to find. Some of the techniques had disappeared by the beginning of this century or had survived in forms altered by the introduction of European goods. But, also, the very complexity of social forms and richness of art and ceremony that draw attention to the area are likely to draw attention away from mere subsistence. Thus when McIlwraith (1948) had the opportunity to play a part himself in the Bella Coola winter ceremonies, he did so and the results form a good part of his two-volume work on that people. I find this quite understandable, but still wish we had more on Bella Coola salmon fishing than the pluses and minuses in Drucker's (1950) element list. Another reason for the neglect of subsistence probably lies in the assumption that the habitat was so rich that subsistence simply was not a problem. Finally, an understanding of just how any given subsistence technique works requires moving outside of culture and

present a similar case. The difference between catching a 5-pound salmon in a net and harpooning a 20-ton whale seems clear enough, but what do we do when we find the same coast Salish "sea-food producer" (a native category) harpooning at one time a 200-pound seal and at another a 1,000-pound sturgeon? The difference, as it was with roots and shellfish, is simply a matter of food value, and not a very great one at that. The coast Salish also harpooned salmon and netted seals, ducks, and deer. If we base our taxonomy on implements and activities, we have to ignore the taxonomy of biology, and vice versa. If we set up a category of activity based on either type of implement (as "net") or biological taxon (as "fish"), we will still be ignoring two other variables, specialization and cooperation, which may be more pertinent to the questions we are asking than are types of implements or animals.

seeing the technique as part of an ecosystem; this is not easily done if one is unfamiliar with the natural history of the area and has only a few summer months to spend in it.

But the situation is by no means hopeless. In spite of the fact that year by year the purely aboriginal way of life recedes into the past, I fully expect that a few years hence we shall know much more about Northwest coast subsistence than we know today. I have several reasons for this optimism. First, contrary to gloomy predictions by colleagues that I'd find all was lost, when I began working with the coast Salish I discovered that it was still possible to do ethnography and to get much new data on subsistence. I am sure that my experience could still be duplicated in other areas, if for no other reason than that some activities survive yet in modified form. Second, data from the related fields of linguistics, archeology, and ethnohistory and from the ethnography of other areas can be increasingly used in interpreting the ethnography of one's own area. For example, some of my informants and the informants of others have believed that the gill net is not aboriginal in the Salish area. However, a comparison of native terms for the gill net and the record of an earlier observer suggest that it probably was, in fact, aboriginal. I expect that further probing will settle the matter. Third, the growing body of biological and climatological knowledge can be used to interpret the ethnographic data. For example, the testimony of informants that their ancestors fished by trolling in winter as well as spring is supported by the work of researchers in fisheries (for example, Rounsefell and Kelez, 1938, pp. 749–50). Their work indicates not only that spring salmon are present in winter but that Indians did troll for them. Also, other biological work shows that herring spawn in this area in winter and early spring (Clemens and Wilby, 1946, pp. 79–80) and would therefore be available during times of the month when tides are low. Finally, meteorological data could undoubtedly be obtained indicating average number of days during winter months when weather would permit trolling in each of several areas.

When I express this optimism about the possibility of increasing our knowledge of Northwest coast subsistence, I do not mean to imply that we shall surely be able to reconstruct the quantitative data. But what we surely can do is define more narrowly the requisites and limits of each technique so that we can make some estimates of the relative effectiveness of the different techniques under similar conditions and the same technique under different conditions.

FOOD-STORING METHODS

The techniques for preserving food are certainly as important as those for getting food. Thousands of salmon swimming upstream in September would not make winter a time of ceremonial activity if people lacked the means of preserving them, nor would several tons of blubber on the beach. No doubt some people would not have survived some winters without storage methods.

A few foods do not keep well at all. Mussels and salmonberries, for example, seem to be too soft and watery. But most fishes and meats, some shellfishes, and some berries can be preserved by drying, either with or without smoke. Clams and some meats were steamed and *salal* berries were sometimes cooked before drying.

Whether fish or meat can be dried outside in the sun or must be smoked indoors depends of course upon the season of the catch and the climate of the area. In the central coast Salish area, where summers are relatively dry and sunny, summer catches of sockeye and humpback salmon, as well as halibut, lingcod, and other fish, were generally dried on outdoor racks at summer fishing camps, where the fishermen could live in mat shelters. Fall runs of springs, cohoes, and dog salmon, however, usually had to be smoked indoors because of the danger of rain. Occasionally separate structures may have been built for smoking fish, but evidently the usual "smokehouse" was the ordinary winter plank house and in local English usage this is what it is still called. The importance of this difference in preserving methods for social relations is easily seen. In the drier season a nuclear family, on its own, could store up a considerable amount of food with a minimum of shelter, but in the wetter season it would be bound to the plank house of its extended family. Because of its use as a smokehouse, the plank house is thus an important instrument of production, and the ownership or control of a house at the site of a fish weir used in the fall may have had as important social and economic consequences as ownership or control of the weir itself. In the Salish area, weirs were in fact usually public property but houses were not.

In many other parts of the coast, climatic conditions probably did not permit as much preserving of food outside as in the Salish area. During the three months of summer, Victoria (in the Salish area) gets an average of 14 days of rain (out of an annual total of 133) while Port Hardy (in Kwakiutl country) gets 38 (out of a total of 204), Masset (Haida) 41 (out of 210), and Prince Rupert (Tsimshian) 46 (out of 215). During an average year Victoria gets a total of 2,092 hours of sunshine while Prince Rupert gets 1,019, or roughly half (figures from Kendrew and Kerr, 1955). Precipitation is also greater on the outer coast to the south than in the central coast Salish area. These differences certainly have implications for food preserving and possibly for social relations.

It should be noted that not all species of salmon, perhaps not even all populations of the same species, keep equally well. My Salish informants say that fatter fish last longer and thus sockeye and dog salmon are their favorites. Other species may not last through the winter months.

Another very important method of storage is the rendering of fat into oil, which can then be kept in such containers as seal bladders (in the Salish area), kelp bulbs (Kwakiutl), or wooden boxes (Chinook). Throughout most of the coast, dried fish or meat was eaten after being dipped in oil; sea-mammal oil was used from the Salish and Nootka southward, and eulachon oil was used from the Kwakiutl northward. On the Fraser, where seal oil was less plentiful, salmon oil was also used (Duff, 1952, p. 66). This constant use of oil seemed excessive to Europeans but it may have compensated for the scarcity of carbohydrates (Drucker, 1951, p. 62; Rivera 1949, p. 34; see also note 5 of the present paper).

In the north, oil was also used for preserving some kinds of berries. From the Chinook southward, meat was preserved by pulverizing it and mixing it with grease. Salmon eggs were first allowed to get "high" and to form a kind of cheese-like substance, and eulachon were also allowed to decay before rendering; however there was evidently no general practice of allowing fish to decay. Storage pits are reported for a few areas and so are raised caches, but probably throughout most of the area preserved food was stored in boxes, baskets, and bags placed on racks inside the dwelling house.

A number of foods, such as dog salmon, must have required far more effort in the storing than in the taking. Thus limits in the exploitation of times of abundance may have been set less by people's capacity to *get* food than by their capacity to *store* it. How much of a very heavy fall run of dog salmon could be stored must have depended on the number of hands available for the work of cutting and skewering, the drying-rack capacity of the houses at the site, fuel for smoke, and finally the number of containers available. As Gould has stressed, preserving food was largely the work of women a ' for this reason rights over women and bri ṣ prices were so important in the economy of the Tolowa. The role of women in subsistence no doubt deserves reappraisal elsewhere on the Northwest coast. But it must be remembered that women need not be wives; they may also be slaves.

VALUES AND SOCIAL ORGANIZATION

Of course the possibilities offered by the environment and the techniques of food-getting and food-storing could be realized only through the work of people, organized by their social systems and motivated by their value system. To survive that occasional period of scarcity, people had to have not only the earlier periods of abundance; the weirs, nets, etc., to take the food with; and the drying racks, houses, etc., to preserve and store it with; but they also had to have a reason for doing it and the ability to mobilize the labor for it.

Probably the knowledge that there is an occasional period of scarcity is not reason enough to make most people store up food for every winter. But the Northwest coast peoples had "better" reasons. From the Yurok and Tolowa northward there was the ultimate goal of prestige, into which food was eventually converted. From the Chinook northward there was also the cultural definition of winter as a ceremonial season, when people should not have to seek food. (This last reason for storing food was also found through much of the Plateau as well.) Swan's account of sorcery among the Makah (1870) suggests that some people did not expect random variation in their environment anyway; they attributed bad weather to human malice and coped with it by threatening the supposed sorcerer. If people stored food for "cultural" reasons rather than rational recognition of possible failure in the environment, this may explain why they sometimes did improvidently eat up all their stores in feasting, as Poole reported for the Haida. Nevertheless, the "cultural" reasons may have enabled larger populations to survive in this habitat than rational planning alone would have done.

In social organization, there seems to have been a rough sort of south-to-north gradient of increasing tightness of structure and size of social unit. Kroeber found the Yurok so individualistic that he declared:

> Property and rights pertain to the realm of the individual, and the Yurok recognizes no public claim and the existence of no community. His world is wholly an aggregation of individuals. There being no society as such, there is no social organization. Clans, exogamic groups, chiefs or governors, political units are unrepresented even by traces in northwestern California (1952, p. 3).

Nevertheless, Kroeber's data suggest possibly three kinds of social groups engaging in subsistence activities: the members of the household, the joint owners of a fishing place, and the large group from several villages that built the *Kepel* weir. This last group is an example of what Anastasio (1955) has called a "task grouping," in which members of social units defined by other criteria come together for a particular purpose at a particular time and place. These task groupings are generally under the leadership of a person who has the requisite technical and/or ritual knowledge. Treide (1965) has recently analyzed the function of such "salmon chiefs" as the ritual director of the Kepel weir for much of western North America.

Northward, on the Oregon coast the village seems to have consisted of an unnamed patrilineal kin group formed by patrilocal residence and to have functioned as a unit under some circumstances (Barnett, 1937, elements 1345, 1400). Among the Chinook at the mouth of the Columbia, there was a village chief (who may have been simply the head of a patrilocal kin group) who evidently exacted tribute from his villagers and redistributed it (Ray, 1938, p. 56).

The central coast Salish social organization was seemingly looser than that of the Chinook. Village exogamy was preferred but residence was ambilocal so neither the household nor the village formed any kind of definable kin group. There were, however, cognatic kin groups perhaps best understood as "stem kindreds," that is, the personal kindreds of successive generations of "owners" of certain ceremonial rights and one or more of the more productive natural resources. One of these men might tend to dominate a village but there was no village chief as such. The village was recognized as a unit when it came to certain types of sharing and certain ceremonial activities, but in general the household was autonomous. Task groups were directed by the "owners" of resources, such as fishing sites and clam beds; by owners of special gear, as the net for a deer drive; or simply by skilled specialists in the activity. Such subsistence activities and also ceremonial activities often brought together people from several villages over areas which crossed dialect and even language boundaries, but there were no structural principles that allowed for the definition of discrete social units.

Wakashan (Nootka and Kwakiutl) social structure seems to have been similar to that of the Salish in that both lacked rules of unilocal residence and unilinear descent. The Nootka and Kwakiutl, however, were much more structured through the principle of ranking of titles in series. Within the cognatic kin group, individuals, at least the more important ones, held positions ranked in relation to one another. Within the village (or "tribe"), kin groups were so ranked. In a few areas "tribes" formed confederacies through the same principle. Among the Wakashans, as among the Chinook, "chiefs" (in fact, kin group heads)

evidently received tribute and acted as redistributers. (For the Nootka, see Drucker, 1951, especially pp. 220–21, 251–57.)

The highest development of formal organization with permanent discrete social units was that found among the northern peoples. The Tsimshian, Tlingit, Haida, together with the Haisla (the northernmost Kwakiutl), had a system of matrilineages, sibs, and phratries or moieties. The largest of these kin groups were the phratries of the Haisla and Tsimshian and the moieties of the Tlingit and Haida. These were simply exogamous units and served to classify every person in the whole northern area for marriageability. Except for the Tsimshian, the largest unit with economic and political functions was the lineage. But the Tsimshian of the lower Skeena and Nass rivers went farther and acknowledged the chief of the leading lineage of a village as the village chief. Garfield believes that this probably occurred early in the eighteenth century. Then, early in the nineteenth century, villages up the Skeena established colonies near its mouth and these each remained under the authority of the chief of the mother village, who in some cases also moved to the colony. "At this stage," writes Garfield, "tribal chieftainship emerged and the tribal chief was regarded as the active leader of his tribesmen regardless of where they lived." The village chief and the tribal chief, like the earlier lineage chief, received tribute and made decisions regarding moves to fishing sites and other subsistence activities (Garfield, 1951, pp. 34–35).

The greater development of formal organization in the north was probably accompanied by more effective control of larger labor forces. This difference in turn may account for the remarkably different views we find on the economic importance of slavery on the Northwest coast.

Barnett, writing primarily of the Kwakiutl and coast Salish, suggests that slaves were "in bondage . . . as much a liability as an asset and . . . useful primarily as overt demonstration of the ability to possess them" (1938, p. 352). Drucker writing about the area in general says:

It is difficult to estimate the slave population of the area, but if was certainly never very large, for slave mortality was high. Slaves' economic utility was negligible. They gathered firewood, dug clams, and fished, but so did their masters (1965, p. 52).

Kroeber, listing exchange values among the Yurok, expressed mainly in strings of dentalia, writes:

> A slave was rated at only one or two strings. Evidently the Yurok did not know how to exact full value from the labor of their bondsmen, not because the latter could not be held to work, but because industry was too little organized (1925, p. 27).

The Yurok did not take slaves in war nor buy them from other peoples; all Yurok slaves were fellow Yurok enslaved by debt. The greatest number of slaves held by one man did not exceed three (p. 32).

On the other hand, Garfield (1945, p. 628; 1951, p. 30) has strongly opposed the view that slaves were kept merely for prestige value and argued that their contribution must have increased the productivity of their owners' households. A potlatching Tsimshian chief was not expected to mention what his slaves contributed in labor, but if he gave them away he boasted of what he had paid for them. During the nineteenth century a slave was worth from two hundred to a thousand dollars. They were mainly war captives and their descendants. The numbers held were much higher than among the southern tribes.

> Ten to twenty slaves are reported as belonging to each of the nine tribal chiefs of Port Simpson in the middle nineteenth century. Each of approximately fifty Port Simpson lineage heads is also reported to have owned from two to as many as ten slaves (Garfield, 1951, p. 30).

It does seem that the mere fact that slaves performed the same task as their masters does not rule out their being of economic importance. If adding a wife or daughter-in-law can increase the productivtiy of a Tolowa household and give additional economic advantage, as Gould reports, why not adding a slave to a Tsimshian household? Kroeber may have been correct regarding the organization of labor

among the Yurok, but can't we expect more from the Tsimshian? Driver (1961, pp. 245–46, 387–38) has pointed out that at the southern end of the Northwest coast a master could not kill a slave nor did he have sexual rights over a female slave, while in the north he held both these rights. This too suggests the possibility of greater control over their labor in the north.

Slavery may also be seen as one of several possible ways of making the human population fit the resources. The most drastic of these is infanticide in times of scarcity. As far as we know this was not practiced on the Northwest coast. The least drastic is fluidity of social groupings, allowing "surplus" people at a place with poor resources to move in with those at more favored places. This fluidity was a prominent feature of the coast Salish social system. With local exogamy, a man's four grandparents were likely to have been from four different villages; at each of these he had residence rights and he also had the option of living with his wife's people. For men of property it was certainly preferable to stay in one's father's village, but no rule required it. The Wakashans also seem to have been flexible in the residence of lower-ranking people. For the northerners, the sib system may have facilitated the mobility of sib-identified groups. But for northwestern California and the Oregon coast we get consistent reports of patrilocal residence and also of impoverished parents selling their children into slavery. Perhaps if residence rules are rigid, selling "surplus" children is the only peaceful alternative to infanticide.

Finally, in looking at social organization in relation to subsistence we should note that the local group was not simply a task force for the exploitation of resources. In one season it could function as a producer and distributor of surplus *and* in another season as an absorber of surplus produced by other groups. Elsewhere (Suttles, 1960, 1962) in discussing the central coast Salish socioeconomic system, I have pointed out how the preference for local exogamy and the exchanges that occured between affines in different villages may have been adaptive under conditions of variable occurence of natural resources. A man with a temporary abundance of any food had three choices: (1) he could share it with his fellow villagers, if they could consume it (which they could not if they too had the same abundance); (2) he could preserve it, if it was preservable and he had the labor force and time before the next harvest of fish, berries, etc., was due; or (3) he could take it to his in-laws in another village (where this particular food might be scarce) and receive in return a gift of wealth, which he might give later to in-laws bringing food to him. If he got more wealth than he gave, he could always potlatch and convert the wealth into glory, which of course might attract more prosperous in-laws. Thus, exchange between affines made it possible for a household *not* to store food and still take advantage of times of abundance.[6]

Vayda (1961a) and Piddocke (1965) have suggested that the Kwakiutl potlatch system may also be seen as an adaptation to a fluctuating environment rather than the "absurdly wasteful" epiphenomenon it had sometimes been labeled. From Piddocke's review of the data, it appears that the Kwakiutl converted food into wealth by selling it to those in need (somewhat as Gould reports the Tolowa having done) and then (unlike the Tolowa) converted the wealth into prestige through competitive potlatching. Piddocke argues that the entry of new wealth into the system and the reduction of the population through disease increased the size and frequency of potlatches to the "fantastic" level of the classic descriptions.

Weinberg (1965) has criticized and expanded on Vayda's suggestion and worked out a model of Kwakiutl culture as a self-regulating adaptive system in which the stability of culture is dependent on fluctuation in the environment within certain limits. When, in the nineteenth century, the limits were exceeded in the direction of surplus, the spectacular growth of the potlatch that followed was essentially an effort to maintain the stability of the culture (cf. "Romer's Rule" of Hockett and Ascher, 1964).

It has been implicit in the previous discussion of the coast Salish that items of "wealth" (blankets, canoes, hide shirts, etc.) did not constitute all-purpose money. As in several other parts of the world, there were restrictions on the occasions when wealth items could properly change hands. These restrictions seem to have been less severe among the Tolowa, but still present in that only exchanges that related to marriage and litigation were publicized, while those that were purely commercial were not, hence the appearance of a separate "prestige economy." Among the Kwakiutl, too, giving was certainly more honorable than selling. The areas where commercial transactions were most open and honorable seem to have been the north and, most especially, the lower Columbia. But even here commerce was not wholly free for it is reported that chiefs (lineage heads?) held monopolies over trade in their territories. It seems possible that such monopolies may have had their origins in exchanges between affines in areas of different resources. In both cases the most important trade was between the coast and interior—the Tlingit with the Athapaskan hinterland and the Chinookans with the Plateau Sahaptins. Perhaps the most important question, at present unanswerable, is: *Why didn't* a market economy develop and spread out from these areas? Or were these commercial developments so recent that there was no time left for further growth? This may be, yet archeological evidence suggests that some form of trade goes back to the early occupation of the area.

CONCLUSIONS

I am afraid I have raised more questions about the Northwest coast than I have been able to answer. If I can offer any conclusion it can only be this: The Northwest coast material suggests that where people are faced with great seasonal and local variations in the amount of food offered by their habitat, their success in exploiting the abundance depends on more than technology alone. They must also have: (1) the organization of labor for getting and

6. Exchange between affines may also have served simply to keep more people busy. Woodburn states (Chapter 17c, this volume) that a skilled Hadza hunter could not control the number of his hangers-on. I suspect that a good provider among the coast Salish had the same problem, an increased number of less productive resident kin. But this was offset by his obligation to take food to his in-laws, who were honor-bound to repay him with wealth, which he did not have to redistribute. A man's affines in other villages may have been his covert allies against potential spongers at home.

storing food (marital rights? kin obligations? property rights? monopoly of technical and/or ritual knowledge?); (2) some means of redistributing population on the habitat (wide kin ties and fluidity of residence? slavery?) and/or of redistributing the bounty of the habitat among the population (barter in food? exchange of food for durable goods? markets?); and (3) some motivating value (prestige?). It seems to me that these factors together with an adequate technology, are necessary conditions for coping with abundance, regardless of whether it appears in the form of fish, sea mammals, land game, or even vegetable food.

From the data presented on the "simpler" hunters by other members of the symposium, it appears that those hunters often are capable of organizing drives and other activities that would take quantities of animals if available. They also seem to have, and necessarily so, a fluidity of organization that permits redistribution of population and at least rudimentary trade. Perhaps the greatest point of contrast is that the simpler hunters lacked the characteristic Northwest coast feature of motivation to achieve and maintain superior status through production of surplus. For this reason it seems to me that the "hunting ideology" or nomadic style (Lee and DeVore, Chapter 1, this volume) may turn out to be well worth the attention it seems to have attracted. Finally, I would ask, when we find archeological evidence of unexpected cultural complexity and population density, is it altogether hopeless to seek ethnographic parallels from the Northwest coast? This is not to say that I believe the Upper Paleolithic Europeans held slaves and gave potlatches. But I expect that some day we will be in a position to say whether they possessed the functional equivalents.

7.

Subsistence and Ecology of Northern Food Gatherers with Special Reference to the Ainu

HITOSHI WATANABE

INTRODUCTION

The symposium on Man the Hunter devoted a great deal of attention to problems of analyzing group structure and subsistence activities. The relations between these two areas and their spatial correlates, however, did not receive the attention they deserve. The purpose of this paper is to consider these two questions in more detail. First, I discuss the arrangement of settlements with reference to resources and attempt to clarify the concepts of nomadism and sedentarism. Second, I discuss the allocation of subsistence activities by sex and age, in order to reconsider the issue of division of labor and how it evolved. For documentation I draw upon field research among the Ainu (Watanabe, 1964a, 1964b, 1964c) and other ethnographic data on Arctic and subarctic food gatherers.

THE PROBLEM OF "SEMI-NOMADISM"

Residential Shifts and the Food-quest

Gjessing (1944) introduced the concept of a "semi-nomadism" in contemporary Arctic and subarctic food gatherers in his study of house and settlement types of the Circumpolar Stone Age. The so-called semi-nomadism of those peoples, however, shows such remarkable variation that it is difficult to apply the concept. A simple typology of three terms (nomadic, semi-nomadic, and sedentary) is not sufficient to describe the wide variety observed in patterns of residential shift. To make a systematic investigation of semi-nomadism, I have attempted a classification of the residential shift patterns of northern food gatherers (Table 1).

This classification shows that the residential shift patterns of those peoples termed semi-nomadic actually vary across the spectrum. A feature common to all such people is settled life in winter. Thus, the variation in residential shift pattern is, in a large measure, brought about by the differences in the residence arrangements in summer. Such peoples as the Ainu (Watanabe, 1964a, 1946b, 1964c), the Koryak (Jochelson, 1905–08), and the Bering Strait Eskimo (Nelson, 1899), attained the highest stability of residence in the sense that they occupied one and the same permanent dwelling all the year round. Of these peoples only the Ainu subsisted largely on land mammals, the rest chiefly subsisting on sea mammals

Table 1   A Tentative Classification of Residential Shift Patterns

Pattern of Residence		Ethnographic Examples	
Winter	Summer	Northern	Southern
I			
Wandering	Wandering	?	Semang
II			
Settled; Temporary Shelter	Wandering	Caribou Eskimo Copper Eskimo	Bushmen Siriono
IIIa			
Settled; Quasi-permanent Shelter	Wandering	Nunatarmiut	?
IIIb			
Settled; Permanent Shelter	Wandering	Kuchin Yukaghir (Upper Kolyma)	Forest-Andamanese
IVa			
Settled; Permanent Shelter	Periodical Expeditions to Definite Sites; Temporary Shelter	Tareumiut Klallam	?
IVb			
Settled; Permanent Shelter	Periodical Expeditions to Definite Sites; Permanent Shelter	Nootka	?
V			
Settled; Permanent Shelter (Among northern peoples often in the same locality)	Settled; Permanent Shelter	Eskimo (Bering Strait) Ingalik Koryak Gilyak	Vedda
VI			
Settled; Permanent Shelter	Periodical Expeditions to Definite Sites; Quasi-permanent Shelter	Eskimo (Bering Strait) Koryak Ainu (Hokkaido)	Paiute (Owens Valley)
		(Tentative Classification)	

(Left margin, vertical: Increasing Stability, with downward arrow)

and/or fish. Other northern gatherers living largely on land mammals are all nomadic wanderers in the summer. The period of the longest inhabitation at the same place, however, varies greatly in different groups. The Nunatarmiut (Larsen and Rainey, 1948), for instance, stay in winter villages for as long as nine months, although younger group members wander about and live in temporary camps even in winter. On the other hand, the Copper Eskimo (Jenness, 1922) lives in the winter settlements for only about three months.

The classification presented here may also be applied to southern food gatherers, provided the division of the seasons is replaced by dry and rainy seasons. It is almost certain that

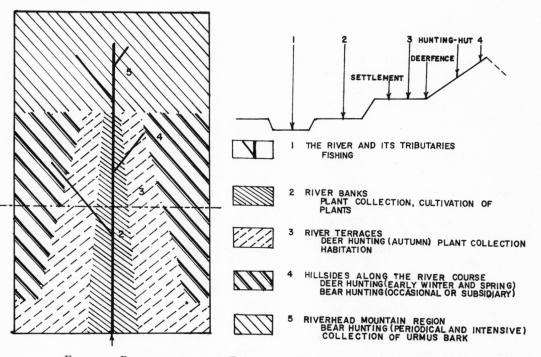

1 THE RIVER AND ITS TRIBUTARIES
FISHING

2 RIVER BANKS
PLANT COLLECTION, CULTIVATION OF PLANTS

3 RIVER TERRACES
DEER HUNTING (AUTUMN) PLANT COLLECTION
HABITATION

4 HILLSIDES ALONG THE RIVER COURSE
DEER HUNTING (EARLY WINTER AND SPRING)
BEAR HUNTING (OCCASIONAL OR SUBSIDIARY)

5 RIVERHEAD MOUNTAIN REGION
BEAR HUNTING (PERIODICAL AND INTENSIVE)
COLLECTION OF URMUS BARK

FIGURE 1. REPRESENTATION OF ECOLOGICAL ZONES OF A RIVER VALLEY AS THE TERRITORY OF AN AINU GROUP.

among food gatherers outside the Arctic and subarctic regions there also exists a wide variation of the residential-shift pattern. One extreme of the variation is represented by the Semang who move about throughout the year (Forde, 1934, 1954) and the other by the Owens Valley Paiute who inhabited permanent villages more or less year round (Steward, 1938). Significant here is the fact that both extremes represent groups subsisting on plant collecting. Other southern hunter-gatherers show considerable variation in the residential pattern. The case of the Vedda (Seligmann and Seligmann, 1911) demonstrates that the residential shifting can be restricted to only two sites occupied alternately. On the other hand, the Forest Andamanese (Radcliffe-Brown, 1933) are a good example of southern hunter-gatherers with a permanent settlement as a base for seasonal hunting and collecting.

In southern regions, however, it is difficult to find any hunter-gatherers who maintain as permanent a year-round residence as do the Ainu. Is the high residential stability of the Ainu a result of their subsistence on salmon? The economic importance of this fish for the Ainu is certainly great. But the deer also had an important place in their diet, and there is evidence to suggest that in some areas more than half of their animal food supply was derived from deer alone. In a settlement on the upper Tokapchi, for instance, the annual catch of the deer per family was not less than 300 while the annual store of fish per family consisted of 500–600 dog salmon and 600–800 cherry salmon. The figures are not likely to be exaggerated. The deer was hunted not only for the meat but also for the skin which was an important item of trade. The meat was consumed both by the Ainu themselves and by their hunting dogs. They also habitually prepared extra stores of food as insurance against the year when resources failed. The Tushipet valley in Tokapchi had no runs of dog salmon and the Ainu there lived chiefly on deer. In spite of their dependence on deer, even the Tushipet Ainu maintained perennially inhabited settlements.

Residential Stability, Ecological Zones, and Habitat

One of the fundamental factors relevant to the high stability of residence among the Ainu may have been the distribution of the ecological zones within narrow river valleys they inhabited (Fig. 1). Ecological zones refer to the zones of exploitative activities classified in terms of physiography and biota. The subsistence activities of the Ainu were conducted in the following ecological zones, each of which yielded specific resources in specific seasons: (1) The river: cherry salmon fishing (summer, in the main stream and some tributaries); dog salmon fishing (autumn, in the main stream); (2) The river banks: collecting of wild plants (spring to autumn); (3) The river terraces: deer hunting (autumn); plant collecting (spring to autumn); human habitation (all year); (4) The hillsides along the river course: deer hunting (early winter, at or near the animals' winter quarters); (5) The mountain region around the source of the river: bear hunting, specialized (spring and autumn); collection of elm bark for clothing (usually spring).

Zones 1–3 were exploited from a single center, namely the permanent settlement which is usually situated on the edge of the river terrace. The outermost zones 4 and 5 were hunting areas, each exploited from a different hunting hut. Some Ainu, especially those living downstream, did not engage in bear hunts and consequently had no hunting hut in zone 5. Such a settlement group as Tonnika of the Azuma valley exploited the zone 4 directly from their permanent settlement since the Azuma valley is so narrow that zone 4 was within easy walking distance of the base camp.

Seasonal migrations to the hunting huts were generally undertaken by the male members of each household in the settlement. When men moved, their wives and children were left behind; the remaining family members had various tasks, of which the collection of edible plants in zones 2 and 3 was the most important. The periodic migration occurred each spring and autumn; men moved to the same hut to stay for about one month during each hunting season. Thus men shifted residence usually twice every year; however, the total period of their stay away from their homes was only about two or three months per year. The permanent houses in the settlement were occupied by the entire family for nine to ten months of the year and by housewives and their children nearly all the year.

From 1884 onward, the Japanese government encouraged the Ainu to take up agriculture. Each Ainu household was granted a plot of land, was given agricultural implements and seeds, and received technical instructions from official Japanese specialists. Consequently, they were suddenly transformed from a gathering life to a farming life. Even before this change, however, the coastal Ainu and part of the interior Ainu, probably under Japanese influence, had farmed by shifting cultivation, although on a very small scale. The old techniques were simpler and the farm work was usually performed by women. There are concrete data (Watanabe, 1964a) showing that those groups who practiced farming gathered wild roots with less frequency and in smaller quantity than those who did not. But there is no evidence that the introduction of the primitive (pre-1884) agriculture significantly increased the stability of residence among them.

A similar distribution pattern of ecological zones and a high stability of residence are found among the Northern Paiute in Owens Valley (Steward, 1938). In both Hokkaido and Owens Valley, it is the presence of narrow valleys that permitted the maintenance of year-round residence.

The residential shift pattern depends upon

ecology, that is, the relationship between habitat and subsistence technology. The ecological study of the Basin-Plateau tribes by Julian Steward (1938) clearly indicates that even within the same cultural group the residential shift pattern may vary a considerable degree according to the variation of habitat. Among the Upper Tanana of the Yukon, the pattern of residential moves varied even from band to band (McKennan, 1959).

If the variation of habitat can affect the residential shift pattern, there may be a possibility that some form of the residential shift pattern can be defined for populations of early man. Karl Butzer (1964) pointed out the existence in southwestern France of Mousterian and late Paleolithic caves which he interpreted as perennially inhabited dwellings, and suggested that the Neanderthalers of the less severe forest-tundra environments were able to maintain settlements based on permanently available animal resources. This is an indication that under certain favorable conditions even early man may have been able to inhabit certain sites with little shifting of residence. In this connection it is noteworthy that the mountain valleys of inland Alaska described by William Irving (1953) provide a set of biotic zones compactly arranged within small territories which suggest suitable conditions for Arctic hunters to maintain stable residence. Modern Alaskan groups have no year-round residence, but at least some of the Nunatarmiut maintained their quasi-permanent villages for the greater part of the year, perhaps nine months (Larsen and Rainey, 1948).

Variability of the Residential Stability at the Level of the Individual

An aspect of the complexity of the northern semi-nomadism is the fact that a residential shift does not always mean movement of the entire social group, since settlements are not always completely deserted. In other words, there is the variability in residential stability at the level of the individual as well as of the family and band.

An analysis of ethnographic reports would reveal that among many of the northern hunters there are some non-moving, sedentary individuals or families who occupy the same

dwelling all year, while there are others who shift their residence. Such variation of residential stability is correlated with differentiation in subsistence activity at the level of the individual or the family, which will be mentioned below. Peoples who maintain some sedentary members at the base camp are those who make, instead of nomadic wanderings, seasonal expeditions from the permanent dwelling to other sites. Such definite evidence is found among the Ainu (Watanabe, 1964a), the Northwest coast Indians (Drucker, 1951; Gunther, 1927) the Ingalik (Osgood, 1958), the Tareumiut (R. Spencer, 1959), and the Bering Strait Eskimo (Nelson, 1899). Indirect evidence suggests that perhaps other peoples, such as the Koryak (Jochelson, 1905-08), belong to this category. Groups without such sedentary members are those who make nomadic wanderings whether they have a permanent winter dwelling or not. The examples are the Copper Eskimo (Jenness, 1922) and the Upper Kolyma Yukaghir (Jochelson, 1926).

As far as evidence is available, the sedentary persons appear to be the less able-bodied, the aged, women, and children. These persons among the Ainu and Ingalik (Osgood, 1940) were engaged in collecting and/or fishing in areas near their settlement while others were away from the settlements hunting and/or fishing at distant localities. But among the Ainu and Tareumiut (R. Spencer, 1959, 1965), at least, even some able-bodied men would remain perennially in their permanent settlements owing to the circumstances of gathering. Among the Ainu, some male members of a nuclear family seasonally moved to a mountain hut for bear hunting, while others remained in their settlement, engaged on fishing and deer hunting. Among the North Alaskan coastal Eskimo (R. Spencer, 1959, 1965), some nuclear families moved to the summer camps for fishing and hunting land mammals, while others remained in the winter villages hunting sea mammals. Even among nomadic wanderers such as the Nunamiut (R. Spencer, 1959) and the Chipewyan (Birkett-Smith, 1930), there is a considerable degree of occupational differentiation at the level of the individual or the family. R. F. Spencer (1965) pointed out the Tareumiut's freedom to choose the summer work best suited to their needs or their skills. To what extent such differentiation and the freedom of choice in subsistence activity exists among other food gatherers, is a problem worthy of further exploration.

Among some northern food gatherers, as previously mentioned, there is a tendency for some individuals or families to remain in the same permanent dwelling all the year although the proportion of the moving population to the sedentary one is yet to be investigated. The non-moving members are less able-bodied persons or the aged, women, and children. Among nomadic food gatherers abandonment of the aged as well as the sick is a common practice (Simmons, 1945; Watanabe, 1966). Possibilities for the aged, the sick, and the infirm to survive or live longer may be greater among sedentary food gatherers than among nomadic ones. This implies that opportunities for such persons to remain perennially settled may have had adaptive significance (Watanabe, 1966). One of the possible effects is greater life span, which, in turn, would influence the age composition of the population. Another possible effect is in selective pressure. Sedentary life may give greater possibilities of survival to the sick and infirm or pregnant. These effects may vary and change according to the variation and change in residential stability as well as other ecological conditions inside and outside the dwelling. S. L. Washburn and I. DeVore (1961a) pointed out the importance of the home base for populations of early man, and its evolutionary implication concerning hominisation. During the Pleistocene, variation in the residential shift pattern must have had some effects on the stability of the home base in both its earlier and later stages and consequently must have influenced human evolution (Watanabe, 1966).

Hunting as an Occupation of Males

The development of meat-eating and the establishment of a hunting way of life are regarded as important ecological factors in hominid evolution (Washburn and Avis, 1958; Washburn and Lancaster, Chapter 32, this volume; Zuckermann, 1933). A related problem is the consistent allocation of hunting to

males and collecting to females. Sex differences in psychology and physiology alone would not be sufficient to explain this division of labor. The problem will be further pursued by making reference to data from modern hunter-gatherers.

Individualistic or Noncommunal Hunting of Larger Mammals

Hunting of small animals by women is not a rare phenomenon. Among such peoples as the Shoshoni (Steward, 1938) and the aboriginal Australians (Berndt and Berndt, 1964; Spencer and Gillin, 1927), it is, in fact, a woman's occupation.

In case of relatively large mammals there is information from various peoples that women take part in communal hunts (Turnbull, 1965a, 1965b). Occasional cases are not unknown of women hunting large mammals alone. Some Copper Eskimo women (Jenness, 1922) hunted seal and the caribou occasionally; Ainu women and children (Watanabe, 1964a) sometimes hunted deer with sticks, ropes, and/or dogs when they had opportunities. But there is no society in which individualistic or noncommunal hunting of larger mammals is the socially recognized regular occupation of women. It is this individualistic hunting of larger mammals that is invariably the task of males. Communal hunts, however, do not always exclude females.

Among modern hunter-gatherers, exclusion of females from the individualistic hunting of larger mammals seems to be closely related to the making and using of hunting weapons and associated economic and/or religious ideas. Women have no weapons of their own which are specially made to hunt animals. If they want to hunt they must do so without weapons or otherwise with some provisional weapons such as sticks. Rarely do they use specially made hunting weapons such as harpoons or spears, although these might be borrowed temporarily from males. Under these restrictions women's hunting activities are confined to small animal hunts, communal hunts in which they take part in driving, and, very rarely, individual hunts of larger mammals.

Ethnographic data suggest that perhaps the development of hunting weapons and ideas

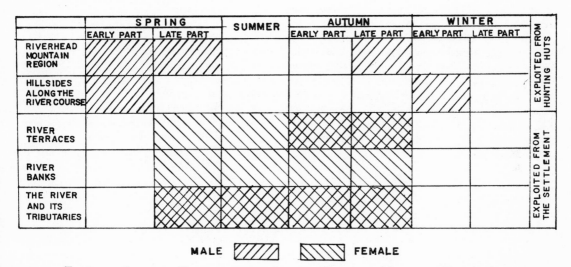

MALE ▨   ▨ FEMALE

FIGURE 2. SEASONAL CHANGES IN THE ACTIVITY FIELDS OF MALE AND FEMALE AINU.

associated with them is one of the factors relevant to the tendency towards the exclusion of females from hunting.

Differentiation of the Activity Field according to Sex

Another possible factor pertinent to the allocation of hunting to males is the differentiation of the activity field according to sex. The activity field means the area of land covered by each individual in his subsistence activities.

Among the Ainu (Watanabe, 1964a, 1964b), the male's activity field is clearly and markedly differentiated from the female's (Fig. 2). The male's field extends far beyond that of the female and the two fields have little overlap. The extension of the male's field is the result of hunting, while most of the female's activity field is the area near the base camp covered in her collecting activities.

The degree of the differentiation of the two fields seems to vary from people to people. Among the Semang (Forde, 1934, 1954), who are mostly vegetarian and whose hunting is sporadic and confined to smaller game, the differentiation seems to be much less marked than among the Ainu. But among the Kuchin (Osgood, 1936a), men are active full-time hunters of large game, and the activity field of males markedly deviates from that of females even in the way in which camps are moved. A Kuchin woman trudges slowly on with her burden, following the direct line from one camp to another, while her husband carrying only a gun circles widely through the hills and covers many more miles in transit.

It seems to be certain that the differentiation of the activity field according to sex is a universal phenomenon among modern food gatherers. It may be one of the ecological characteristics of man. Owing to this

Table 2   Allocation of Hunting Tasks by Age

Tribe	Age Division	
Ainu (Watanabe, 1964a)	Younger men: Bear hunting in areas distant from the settlement	Older men: Deer hunting in areas nearer to the settlement
	Younger men: Spearing fish (cold season)	Older men: Peep-hut fishing (cold season)
Chukchee (Bogoras, 1904–09)	Son: Long expeditions for sea mammals	Elderly father: Shorter trips for sea mammals
	—Communal reindeer hunting—	
	Younger men: Stabbing the animals in canoe	Older men (with women and children): Interception of the wounded animals carried away by the stream
Tikerarmiut (Larsen and Rainey, 1948)	Able-bodied men: Winter seal hunting	Old people (and children: Fishing crabs through ice holes
Nunatarmiut (Larsen and Rainey, 1948)	Younger people: Winter hunting in the mountains	Aged (and some women and children): Left in semi-permanent villages in winter
Iglulimiut (Damas, 1963)	Younger men: Roaming inland after caribou (August–September)	Older men: Hunting sea mammals (August–September)
Dogrib and Yellowknife (R. Spencer, 1965)	—Located by the Hunt Leader—	
	Younger men: Far afield for trapping	Older people (and women and children): Berry picking or at a fish camp
Paiute (Steward, 1938)	—Communal Deer Hunts—	
	Young men: Driving of deer	Older men: Hiding by game trails to shoot deer
	—Communal Buffalo Hunts—	
	Young men: Sent out to find the game	Old Men: Butchering of the kill

differentiation the structure of man's home range differs from that of nonhuman primates.

Plants stand still, but animals move; the distribution of specific plants does not always coincide with that of specific animal species. Owing to the ecology of biotic species it is usually difficult to get edible plants and large mammals in the same place at the same time. Consequently hunting ground for the animals and collecting fields for the plant food are not identical. Synchronous exploitations of both resources by one and the same group necessitates the splitting of the unit.

Data from the Ainu and other food gatherers imply the possibility of an interpretation of the process of the allocation of hunting to males in the following way: (1) long and active pursuit of larger mammals brought about the differentiation of the activity field into the collecting and the hunting fields; (2) the necessity of synchronous exploitation of these spatially separated fields forced the group to split; (3) this splitting and the selection for hunting ability on the basis of physical and psychological differences resulted in the allocation of hunting to males and collecting to females.

It may be assumed that the selection for hunting skills began when early man took up long and active pursuits of larger mammals. The Yukaghir (Jochelson, 1926) and Ingalik (Osgood, 1958), for instance, clearly exhibit the importance for larger mammal hunters of physical and psychological capacities such as the ability of continuous running and endurance. The sexual division of labor might be reversible in work other than individualistic

hunting of larger mammals, but in this kind of hunting no reverse case is found at all.

Tendency toward Age Division of Labor

One of the most neglected phases of the economic life of food gatherers is age division of labor. Careful examination of ethnographic data reveals that among food gatherers there is a tendency for the more strenuous work to be allocated to younger members of the population study, although this division of labor is not so striking as the sexual division of labor. However, it is know that in hunting, at least, some northern food gatherers practice division of labor between the younger and the older. It is sometimes division of tasks within an occupation and sometimes a division of whole occupations. Although it is uncertain to what extent the division is rigid and fixed, it is apparent that the division of labor crosscuts the sexual division of labor to form an important part of the organization of food getting. In Table 2, the allocation of hunting tasks by age is cited for seven northern groups.

The age division of labor shows a tendency towards the differentiation of the activity field in which the younger men exploit more distant fields and the older men fields nearer to base camp.

Age division of labor must have some relationships to the age composition of the society concerned. In view of the shorter life span of early man (Vallois, 1962), here is an interesting problem on the history of that division of labor.

The Netsilik Eskimos:
Adaptive Processes

ASEN BALIKCI

The Netsilik Eskimos inhabit a vast area over 300 miles in length and over 100 miles in depth north and west of Hudson Bay.[1] The region is barren, covered with innumerable rocky hills, lakes, sea inlets, and vast stretches of flat tundra. The climate is arctic, characterized by extremely cold winters and short cool summers. The local tundra bears no trees and its vegetation consists of creeping shrubs, tufted grass-like plants, lichens, and mosses. When traveling through this cold desert in 1923, Knud Rasmussen counted 259 Eskimos of whom 150 were males and only 109 females. They lived a nearly traditional life, having had only minimal contact with Europeans up to that time and having obtained guns only a few years before. The Netsilingmiut hunted the caribou, the musk-ox, and the seal, they fished the salmon trout and, with the exception of some berry picking in August, did no gathering. The question asked in this paper is: What were the adaptive processes and survival strategies utilized by the Netsilik Eskimos in this extremely harsh environment? It is assumed here that adaptation can be analyzed

at three distinct levels: (1) the technological, (2) the socioecological, and (3) the demographic.

TECHNOLOGICAL ADAPTATION

Netsilik technology consists of four major complexes, on the basis of the raw materials utilized: the snow-ice complex (snowhouses, ice-houses, ice-caches, etc.), the skin complex (clothing, kayaks, sledges, tents, etc.), the bone complex (tools and weapons), and the stone complex (cooking utensils). Netsilik technology is thus adaptive in two ways: first, through the ingenious manufacture of a large number of specialized artifacts from a small number of locally available raw materials; and second, in reference to the adaptive features of the finished artifacts related to specific environmental conditions. It is primarily these forms of easily visible technological adaptation that drew the admiration of ethnographers.

ECOLOGICAL ADAPTATION

Order and Predictability in the Annual Round

Among the four socioecological processes of adaptation to be considered is the predictability

1. The data summarized here refer to the second and third decade of our century. They were collected in the field in 1960 from elderly informants as part of a general reconstruction of Netsilik traditional culture (Balikci, 1964).

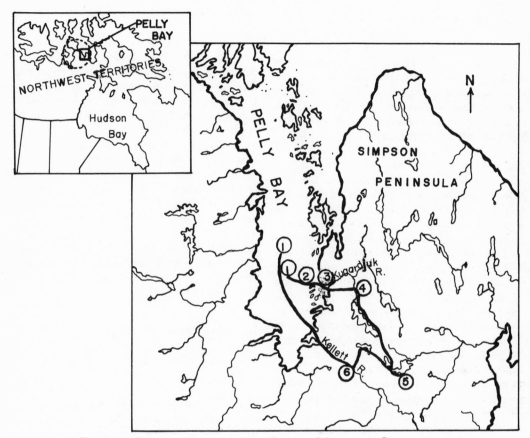

FIGURE 1. RECONSTRUCTION OF THE ANNUAL MIGRATION CYCLE OF THE
ARVILIGJUARMIUT, A NETSILIK SUBGROUP, FOR THE YEAR 1919.

Camp No.	Season	Subsistence Activity
Camp 1 } Camp 2	Midwinter	Seal hunting at the breathing holes
Camp 3	Spring	Seal hunting at the large breathing holes
Camp 4	Midsummer	Fishing at the stone weir
Camp 5	Early fall	Caribou hunting inland
Camp 6	Late fall	Fishing through the thin river ice

and order implicit in the annual migration circuit (see map, Fig. 1). In winter, after the caribou had left the country, the Netsilingmuit had to rely almost exclusively on the seal for survival. Since the seal keeps open a large number of breathing holes, it was advantageous to have numerous hunters, with harpoons in hand, to control an equal number of holes. Large hunting parties had maximal chances for a speedy catch. Hence the rationale for extended igloo communities consisting of over sixty people and comprising several distantly related extended families. Winter was the season of intense social life, spectacular shamanizing and other ceremonial activity (Fig. 1, Camps 1 and 2).

Early in June when the seals came lying on the ice, the large winter camp broke up into smaller social units having usually an extended family as a core. Tents were set up on the shore and group sealing continued at the large breathing holes (Camp 3). In July, the restricted groups moved inland, fishing with the fishing harpoon and occasionally hunting caribou with the bow and arrow. After the first week of August, the stone weirs were built across rivers and the salmon trout running upstream were caught in large amounts with leisters (Camp 4). At the end of August began the vitally important caribou hunts from kayaks at the caribou crossing place (Camp 5). This was a collaborative activity involving a division of tasks between beaters and spearers. Early in October the restricted groups moved camp to some larger river and fished salmon trout with leisters through the thin river ice (Camp 6). As winter came on the larger groups re-formed for sealing through the breathing holes (Camps 1 and 2).

During spring, summer, and autumn the restricted social units were isolated in the tundra and social life was markedly less intense. The Netsilik migration route thus reveals a basic winter-marine and summer-inland dichotomy involving a dual pattern in social morphology in harmony with the classic analysis of Marcel Mauss on the seasonal variations of Eskimo society (Mauss, 1906). There is thus a clear correlation between the movements of society and the known distribution of game, permitting the exercise of prediction (Balikci, 1964). It clearly indicates an adaptive pattern,

the migrating groups taking advantage of particular game concentrations through the different seasons.

Alternatives and Substitutions in Subsistence Strategy

The endless search for alternatives, the practices of substitution and *ad hoc* inventiveness constitute another class of adaptive strategies. Each seasonal hunt knows of some alternative. If the fall caribou hunts with spears from kayaks failed, the bow and arrow was used. In winter, musk-ox hunting could be substituted for sealing. In summer, if fishing with the leister was unrewarding, the fishing harpoon or the sleeping hooks were employed. There always seems to have been a way out of a difficult situation. The alert hunter had to take advantage of any changes in game availability and specific local conditions such as wind direction and topography and adapt his hunting strategy with ingenuity. In hunting, no conditions are static and quick *ad hoc* decisions were necessary.

Flexibility of Group Structure

Constantly changing opportunities and pressures favored flexibility in residence and determined temporary fission of co-residential groups. At all seasons the co-residential groups functioned as production and distribution units, yet in various stress situations the community would split, separating extended families. Or a nuclear family would go on extensive fishing or trading trips. Or two brothers would hunt temporarily in different areas and thus maximize game returns, the possible failure of the first being compensated for by the success of the second. Later the original group would reassemble. Clearly such fissive practices are adaptive in character and appear to be common to many of the hunting peoples discussed at the symposium.

Sharing

Delayed consumption involving elaborate caching techniques and various sharing patterns equalized food distribution both through time and within the community. Sharing patterns ranged from informal gift giving and occasional or regular commensality to rigidly structured, community-wide division of seal meat. Such rigorous sharing was based upon a system of named dyadic partnerships involving all hunters in camp and cutting across kinship alignments. Thus an unlucky hunter was always certain by right to obtain a portion of the daily catch secured by any one of his partners (Van de Velde, 1956). Clearly such a system is adaptive. Camp fellows share together or starve together.

The adaptive processes described here can be best understood in relation to the almost continuous ecological pressure to which the Netsilik were subjected. Traveling and moving camps was a very arduous task. Lack of dog feed severely limited the keeping of dogs to only one or two per family. The heavy sledges had to be pulled or pushed by both men and women. Only very small children were allowed to sit on the sledge. Old people had to drag themselves behind, and were often left behind to sleep out on the ice if they had not caught up with the others. Seal hunting involved a motionless watch on the flat ice under intense cold maintained for many hours. In order to build the stone weir, the stones had to be carried in the ice-cold water for several days. Beating the fast-running caribou over great distances in the tundra was an exhausting task. Stalking the caribou with the bow and arrow also involved endless pursuits across the tundra, the hunters lying on the wet grass and trying to approach the game while hiding behind tufts of moss. The nomadism of the hunting life in this extremely rigorous climate imposed a constant strain on the humans. Hunting was a never-ceasing pursuit, the game had to be brought to camp at all cost, and the hunter had to stay out until a successful kill: "The man that is wise never lolls about idle when the weather is good; he can never know when bad days may eat up his meat caches and drive him and his family into starvation" (Rasmussen, 1931, p. 134). At a camp of Kugguppamiut, Rasmussen observed that for the whole of the winter twelve hunters caught about 150 seals: "this may well be said to have been dearly bought food."

DEMOGRAPHIC ADAPTATION

Such continuous pressures and hardships necessitated internal, sociodemographic controls. The most rigorous was female infanticide (Balikci, MS.). On King William Island, Rasmussen counted 38 girls killed out of 96 births, in a genealogical sample of eighteen marriages. He concluded: "Despite the high birth rate the tribe is moving towards extinction if girl children are to be constantly suppressed" (1931, p. 141). The Netsilingmuit considered life as harsh and short, and girls were thought to be less productive than boys who were the future hunters. An informant said to Rasmussen, "Parents often consider that they cannot afford to waste several years nursing a girl. We get old so quickly and so we must be quick and get a son" (1931, p. 140). In the same context, a Pelly Bay Eskimo pointed to his dog team and added, "Bitches simply don't pull as hard as the dogs do." This high rate of female infanticide generated the sex imbalance noted by Rasmussen and resulted in great difficulties in finding a wife. So anxious were the parents to secure future wives for their little boys that they betrothed them to any one of their female cousins (Balikci, 1963). Cousins, both cross and parallel, were preferred because the parents of the promised couple were closely related, trusted each other, and kept their word; their children thus had maximal chances to become husband and wife. Furthermore, suicide in crisis situations, invalidicide and senilicide were additional responses to harsh pressures (Balikci, 1960). We may consider these forms of demographic controls as adaptive, in the sense that unproductive members of society were eliminated, the size of the family adjusted to the capacity of the provider, and the survival chances of future hunters were maximized.

DISCUSSION

It is assumed here that the combination of adaptive processes and controls functioned successfully under conditions of optimal ecological pressure. Of course we admit with Rasmussen that: "Everything is naturally focussed entirely and absolutely upon the requirements

that the increasing search for the daily meat
necessitates" (1931, p. 142). Yet with peak
ecological pressure, disaster occurred. For the
two years preceeding his journey of 1923, Rasmussen counted 25 deaths due to starvation,
equivalent to 10 per cent of the tribal population. Order and predictability, together with
flexibility, certainly existed, yet they did not
leave the Netsilik with much leisure and evidently failed on some occasions to assure his
survival.

A brief comment may be necessary concerning the notions of harsh environment and
ecological adaptation and pressure. Harsh
environment refers more closely to objective
geographic realities. In the case of the Netsilik
area, it includes primarily a long winter
characterized by intense cold, lack of timber,
and shifting and occasionally unpredictable
game concentrations. The term ecological
adaptation is the effect of the most striking features of environment on human life, as evi-
denced in subsistence techniques, economic
organization, and settlement patterns. It is
obviously a dynamic process and relative to the
technical equipment of a society. Ecological
pressure is but one phase of the general adaptive process and implies diminution of food
availability, and increased difficulty in securing a livelihood. Such periods of hardship were
consciously recognized by the Netsilik who reacted accordingly by trying alternative strategies. The work/leisure time ratio may be
considered as one objective criterion for measuring the degree of ecological pressure. Food
availability over prolonged periods expressed
in quantitative terms may be another such
measure. Depending on a multiplicity of
factors, pressure phases may be of greatly varying irregular occurrence, or they may be cyclical and seasonal. They may attain a critical
level which results in starvation for productive
members of society.

Now within the vast Eskimo area there are
great regional differences in the processes of
ecological adaptation. For instance, both
northern Alaska and the Netsilik country may
be considered to have harsh environments, yet
the abundance of larger sea mammals in
Alaska has allowed a much denser population
to develop relatively sedentary patterns.
Greater food availability seems to have reduced prolonged ecological pressure among the
Alaskan Eskimos and made possible the growth
of complex ceremonialism. In the Netsilik area,
on the other hand, prolonged pressure phases
appear to have been much more frequent and
severe. The relatively low seal availability and
the erratic character of caribou migrations
seem to have been mainly responsible for this
state of affairs. The Caribou Eskimos dwelling
inland illustrate another case of precarious
ecological adaptation with frequent pressure
phases.

The Bushmen (Lee, Chapter 4, this volume)
seem to enjoy a regular availability of resources
allowing for considerable leisure time. The
Bushmen are primarily collectors of plant
foods and only secondarily hunters. In their
region, pressure phases seem infrequent.
Clearly the Netsilik Eskimos stand in sharp
contrast to the Bushmen. The Netsilik case
can be considered as an extreme example of
human adaptation to a harsh environment. In
our opinion, both Bushmen and Netsilik
constitute extreme cases, and neither can be
considered as typical as far as ecological
adaptation of hunters-gatherers is concerned.
It is rather obvious that in each geographic
zone inhabited by hunters-gatherers, different
adaptive forms are going to be found with
different qualities of pressures. A regional typology should have a greater heuristic value
than blunt assumptions about global lack or
presence of ecological pressure in hunting and
gathering societies.

9.

Discussions, Part II

9a. THE CENTRAL ESKIMO: A MARGINAL CASE?

Speakers: *Balikci, Damas, Eggan, Helm, Washburn.*

DAMAS: I would like to question one or two points in Dr. Balikci's paper. I think that he is right in indicating that winter communities comprise several extended families. But from the group charts that I have been able to reconstruct for the early 1920's, the families were connected by primary ties. And in an earlier period, the Netsilik winter groups were considerably larger, probably averaging 100–150, implying a more substantial subsistence base. Between 1900–20, about 150 people moved down to trade at Repulse Bay, and the Chesterfield area, which accounts for the smaller band size of the later period.

Dr. Balikci's treatment of alternative means of food procural seems to imply that they may all be equally fortunate choices. I suggest instead that in the winter, hunting through the breathing hole was the only practical way for the group to survive. At times, the Netsilik made long trips for polar bear, and in extreme cases they jigged for tomcod. But these were not reliable means of survival.

I think that the quotation from Rasmussen in Balikci's paper regarding the harried existence of the Kuggup is not altogether typical of the Central Eskimo. There seems to be quite a variation within the Netsilik area in the game potential. The Tom Bay, Bellot Strait, and Queen Maud Gulf areas were probably better endowed than the area in which Rasmussen found the Kuggup.

Finally, apropos of the deaths from starvation mentioned in Dr. Balikci's paper, it might be interesting to note that starvation was usually related to bad weather. In the particular case cited, there was a late freezing of the sea accompanied by storms, which made the ice rough and unsuitable for normal winter hunting.

BALIKCI: Concerning the first point in reference to the primary ties linking extended families, I am in agreement with Dr. Damas. This is to be expected for small, bilaterally organized communities. My aim was to emphasize that on many occasions extended families among the eastern Netsilik behaved as discrete social units, independent of the close ties between particular members of different extended families. As for the restricted size of winter settlements in the early 1920's, emigration may probably account for this, at least partially. Yet a figure as high as 150 individuals seems difficult to accept in view of the limited subsistence base. More probably, large groups occupying an area were divided into two or three camps located close by to allow visiting. It seems reasonable to assume that there was considerable flexibility in the size and duration of winter settlements. As for my data, I took the four or five years before Rasmussen's journey of 1923 as baseline.

I did not imply that alternative means of food procural were as good as the main subsistence technique for a particular season and site. My point is that substitutes were available as a temporary device to avoid disaster. The effectiveness of the alternatives depended on particular local conditions. The very use of the terms of alternatives and substitutes implies their quality as "second-best" choices.

In reference to regional variation in game availability within the Netsilik area, I agree with Dr. Damas' comment. Of course there was considerable variation: Pelly Bay was good for fish, Tom Bay was good for seals, the area behind Tksiaktorvik was good for caribou, and the western Netsilik could obtain a good deal of tomcod. But I wished to produce a global scale for the Netsilik and did not have place for regional variations.

HELM: I refer to a paper published some years ago in which Bartholomew and Birdsell (1953) said, in effect, that it does not matter how well you eat during eleven months of the year if you have no food during the twelfth month. I think that this holds true in terms of generations. If a group maintains or increases its population for, say, three generations, but there is then a severe population loss, there is apt to be a cutback in incipient development and even the continuity of cultural forms. Has this happened among the Central Eskimo?

BALIKCI: It is difficult to answer this for very long time depths. However, with the exception of occasional cases of people getting lost in traveling or getting caught in bad weather—as in the example from Rasmussen—widespread starvation of a magnitude required to induce culture loss, is a very rare phenomenon.

WASHBURN: Dr. Balikci has shown that there can be a real struggle for existence in some extremely marginal areas, while, on the other hand, others have spoken about hunters that were not living marginally and who did not harvest all the food they might. I would like to suggest that these are not necessarily contradictory notions. If we look at what happened to the idea of the struggle for existence in genetics, we find that it started in the con-

ception of an all-out tooth-and-claw struggle and then changed to a consideration of what works in the long run.

I think this is the kind of shift that we need to make when we look at human economies. It is not so important to worry whether people are going to die tomorrow or whether they are eating to their maximum capacity. What we want to know and understand is the kind of system that works and keeps on working. For a quantitative example, Bourlière (1963) estimated the amount of meat on the hoof both in the Congo forest and in the savanna on the edge of the forest. The amount in the forest proved to be only about 5 per cent as great as that in the savanna. So objectively speaking, there is a great deal more to be harvested in the savanna.

I would like to shift for a moment to Paul K. Anderson's study (a seminar given to the Zoology Department, Berkeley, in 1965) of mice in Canada living near great grain depots. Now, from the point of view of mice, these depots represent an infinite supply of food, so there is no reason why the mouse population should not soar to infinity. But this is not what happens at all. The mice build up a group of about twenty, then subadult and young adult males migrate *away from* the food supply. Here is a built-in genetic system devised, so to speak, to keep these animals moving out. They have not been evolved to eat tons and tons of grain and are, therefore, completely unable to adjust to the presence of it. I think that the lesson of this is that an economy may be completely adaptive when those involved are eating only 20–30 per cent of the available food. It is *not* adaptive to eat the complete food supply, since—aside from the troubles brought on even by a minor variation in supply—anything like a major seasonal variation will break down the system. So if through warfare the Pygmy group occupies twice the area that it needs for its normal food supply, this may actually be an adaptive situation in the long run. We have, then, to abandon the notion of an immediate struggle—even though it shows up among groups like the Eskimo—in favor of a far more subtle approach, in which we try to determine just what percentages of the food supply would be used in a good adaptation by a particular group.

EGGAN: I want to follow up one of Washburn's points on adaptation versus flexibility. There is a series of norms or sanctions with regard to the sharing of food. It seems to me that they often differ with the kind of food—meat, fish, or vegetable—with the size of the animals involved, and with the latitude of the location. I remember looking at the Siberian-central Asian data, and in that area food-sharing increases to the north and decreases to the south. I wonder whether these patterns of sharing, if we worked them out, might not give us something relevant to the problem of adaptation, even an index to it.

9b. NOTES ON THE ORIGINAL AFFLUENT SOCIETY

Speaker: *Sahlins*

SAHLINS: I should like to pick a point that is embedded in Colin Turnbull's discussion, implied in Suttles', elaborated in Lee's, and given ultimate explanation I think in Washburn's comments, particularly his suggestion that a 20–30 per cent use of productive capacity may prove quite adaptive over the long run. What I want to talk about is, as it were, the inner meaning of running below capacity, the consequences for the quality of hunting-gathering economical life.

If economics is the dismal science, the study of hunting-gathering economies must be its most advanced branch. Almost totally committed to the argument that life was hard in the Paleolithic, our textbooks compete to convey a sense of impending doom, leaving the student to wonder not only how hunters managed to make a living, but whether, after all, this was living? The specter of starvation stalks the stalker in these pages. His technical incompetence is said to enjoin continuous work just to survive, leaving him without respite from the food quest and without the leisure to "build culture." Even so, for his efforts he pulls the lowest grades in thermo-dynamics—less energy harnessed per capita per year than any other mode of production. And in treatises on economic development, he is condemned to play the role of bad example, the so-called "subsistence economy."

It will be extremely difficult to correct this traditional wisdom. Perhaps then we should phrase the necessary revisions in the most shocking terms possible: that this was, when you come to think of it, the original affluent society. By common understanding an affluent society is one in which all the people's wants are easily satisfied; and though we are pleased to consider this happy condition the unique achievement of industrial civilization, a better case can be made for hunters and gatherers, even many of the marginal ones spared to ethnography. For wants are "easily satisfied," either by producing much or desiring little, and there are, accordingly, two possible roads to affluence. The Galbraithean course makes assumptions peculiarly appropriate to market economies, that man's wants are great, not to say infinite, whereas his means are limited, although improvable. Thus the gap between means and ends can eventually be narrowed by industrial productivity, at least to the extent that "urgent" goods became abundant. But there is also a Zen solution to scarcity and affluence, beginning from premises opposite from our own, that human material ends are few and finite and technical means unchanging but on the whole adequate. Adopting the Zen strategy, a people can enjoy an unparalleled material plenty, though perhaps only a low standard of living. That I think describes the hunters.[1]

The traditional dismal view of the hunter's fix is pre-anthropological. It goes back to the time Adam Smith was writing, and maybe to a time before anyone was writing. But anthropology, especially evolutionary enthropology, found it congenial, even necessary theoretically, to adopt the same tone of reproach. Archeologists and ethnologists had become Neolithic revolutionaries, and in their enthusiasm for the revolution found serious shortcomings in the Old (Stone Age) Regime. Scholars extolled a Neolithic Great Leap Forward. Some spoke of a changeover from human effort to domesticated energy sources, as if people had been liberated by a new labor-saving device, although in fact the basic power

1. I realize that the Netsilik Eskimo as described by Balikci constitute an exception in point. I shall not speak to this case here, but second Richard Lee's explanation (or disposition) of it (Chapter 4, this volume).

resources remained exactly the same, plants and animals, the development occurring rather in techniques of appropriation (i.e., domestication. Moreover, archeological research was beginning to suggest that the decisive gains came in stability of settlement and gross economic product, rather than productivity of labor.)

But evolutionary theory is not entirely to blame. The larger economic context in which it operates, "as if by an invisible hand," promotes the same dim conclusions about the hunting life. Scarcity is the peculiar obsession of a business economy, the calculable condition of all who participate in it. The market makes freely available a dazzling array of products all these "good things" within a man's reach—but never his grasp, for one never has enough to buy everything. To exist in a market economy is to live out a double tragedy, beginning in inadequacy and ending in deprivation. All economic activity starts from a position of shortage: whether as producer, consumer, or seller of labor, one's resources are insufficient to the possible uses and satisfactions. So one comes to a conclusion—"you pays your money and you takes your choice." But then, every acquisition is simultaneously a deprivation, for every purchase of something is a denial of something else that could have been had instead. (The point is that if you buy one kind of automobile, say a Plymouth fastback, you cannot also have a Ford Mustang—and I judge from the TV commercials that the deprivation involved is more than material.) Inadequacy is the judgment decreeed by our economy, and thus the axiom of our economics: the application of scarce means against alternate ends. We stand sentenced to life at hard labor. It is from this anxious vantage that we look back on the hunter. But if modern man, with all his technical advantages, still hasn't got the wherewithal, what chance has this naked savage with his puny bow and arrow? Having equipped the hunter with bourgeois impulses and Paleolithic tools, we judge his situation hopeless in advance.

Scarcity is not an intrinsic property of technical means. It is a relation between means and ends. We might entertain the empirical possibility that hunters are in business for their health, a finite objective, and bow and arrow are adequate to that end. A fair case can be made that hunters often work much less than we do, and rather than a grind the food quest is intermittent, leisure is abundant, and there is more sleep in the daytime per capita than in any other conditions of society. (Perhaps certain traditional formulae are better inverted: the amount of work per capita increases with the evolution of culture and the amount of leisure per capita decreases.) Moreover, hunters seem neither harassed nor anxious. A certain confidence, at least in many cases. attends their economic attitudes and diecsions. The way they dispose of food on hand, for example—as if they had it made.

This is the case even among many present marginal hunters—who hardly constitute a fair test of Paleolithic economy but something of a supreme test. Considering the poverty in which hunter and gatherers live in theory, it comes as a surprise that Bushmen who live in the Kalahari enjoy "a kind of material plenty" (Marshall, 1961, p. 243). Marshall is speaking of non-subsistence production; in this context her explication seems applicable beyond the Bushmen. She draws attention to the technical simplicity of the non-subsistence sector: the simple and readily available raw materials, skills, and tools. But most important, wants are restricted: a few people are happy to consider few things their good fortune. The restraint is imposed by nomadism. Of the hunter, it is truly said that this wealth is a burden (at least for his wife). Goods and mobility are therefore soon brought into contradiction, and to take liberties with a line of Lattimore's, the pure nomad remains a poor nomad. It is only consistent with their mobility, as many accounts directly say, that among hunters needs are limited, avarice inhibited, and—Warner (1937 [1958], p. 137) makes this very clear for the Murngin—portability is a main value in the economic scheme of things.

A similar case of affluence without abundance can be made for the subsistence sector. McCarthy and McArthur's time-motion study in Arnhem Land (1960) indicates the food quest is episodic and discontinuous, and per capita commitment to it averages less than four hours a day (see accompanying Figs. 1 and 2). The amount of daytime sleep and rest is unconscionable: clearly, the aborigines fail to "build culture" not from lack of time but from

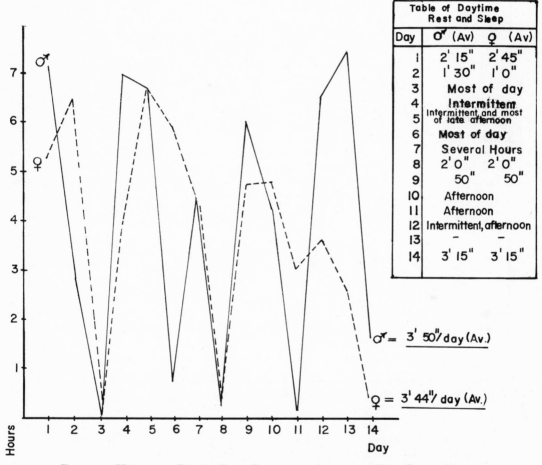

Table of Daytime Rest and Sleep		
Day	♂ (Av)	♀ (Av)
1	2' 15"	2' 45"
2	1' 30"	1' 0"
3	Most of day	
4	Intermittent	
5	Intermittent, and most of late afternoon	
6	Most of day	
7	Several Hours	
8	2' 0"	2' 0"
9	50"	50"
10	Afternoon	
11	Afternoon	
12	Intermittent, afternoon	
13	–	–
14	3' 15"	3' 15"

♂ = 3' 50"/ day (Av.)

♀ = 3' 44"/ day (Av.)

FIGURE I. HOURS PER DAY IN FOOD-CONNECTED ACTIVITIES: FISH CREEK GROUP (CONSTRUCTED FROM McCARTHY AND McARTHUR, 1960, p. 190).

idle hands. McCarthy and McArthur also suggest that the people are working under capacity—they might have easily procured more food; that they are able to support unproductive adults—who may, however, do some craft work; and that getting food was not strenuous or exhausting. The Arnhem Land study, made under artificial conditions and based only on short-run observations, is plainly inconclusive in itself. Nevertheless, the Arnhem Land data are echoed in reports of other Australians and other hunters. Two famous explorers of the

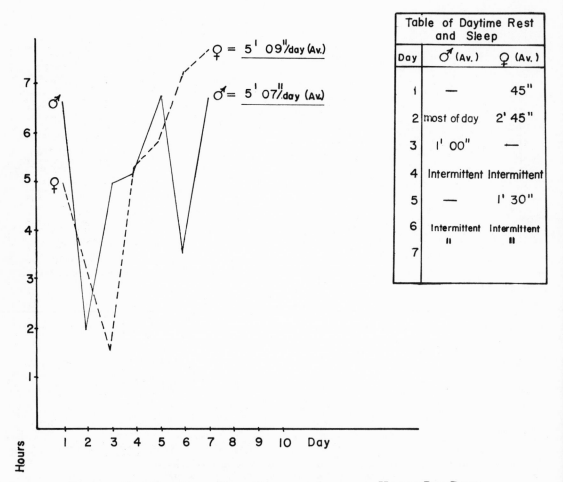

FIGURE 2. HOURS PER DAY IN FOOD-CONNECTED ACTIVITIES: HEMPLE BAY GROUP
(CONSTRUCTED FROM MCCARTHY AND MCARTHUR, 1960, p. 191).

earlier nineteenth century made estimates of
the same magnitude for the aborigines' subsistence activities: two to four hours a day
(Eyre, 1845, 2, pp. 252, 255; Grey, 1841, 2,
pp. 261–63). Slash-and-burn agriculture, incidentally, may be more labor-intensive: Conklin, for example, figures that 1,200 man hours
per adult per year are given among the

Hanunóo simply to agriculture (Conklin, 1957
p. 151: this figure excludes other food-connected activities, whereas the Australian data
include time spent in the preparation of food
as well as its acquisition). The Arnhem
Landers' punctuation of steady work with sustained idleness is also widely attested in
Australia and beyond. In Lee's paper he

reported that productive members of !Kung Bushman camps spend two to three days per week in subsistence. We have heard similar comments in other papers at the symposium. Hadza women were said to work two hours per day on the average in gathering food, and one concludes from James Woodburn's excellent film that Hadza men are much more preoccupied with games of chance than with chances of game.

In addition, evidence on hunter-gatherers' economic attitudes and decisions should be brought to bear. Harrassment is not implied in the descriptions of their nonchalant movements from camp to camp, nor indeed is the familiar condemnations of their laziness. A certain issue is posed by exasperated comments on the prodigality of hunters, their inclination to make a feast of everything on hand; as if, one Jesuit said of the Montagnais, "the game they were to hunt was shut up in a stable" (Le Jeune's *Relation* of 1634, in Kenton, 1927, 1, p. 182). "Not the slightest thought of, or care for, what the morrow may bring forth," wrote Spencer and Gillen (1899, p. 53). Two interpretations of this supposed lack of foresight are possible: either they are fools, or they are not worried—that is, as far as they are concerned, the morrow will bring more of the same. Rather than anxiety, it would seem the hunters have a confidence born of affluence, of a condition in which all the people's wants (such as they are) are generally easily satisfied. This confidence does not desert them during hardship. It can carry them laughing through periods that would try even a Jesuit's soul, and worry him so that—as the Indians warn—he could become sick:

> I saw them [the Montagnais] in their hardships and their labors, suffer with cheerfulness. . . . I found myself, with them, threatened with great suffering; they said to me, "We shall be sometimes two days, sometimes three, without eating, for lack of food; take courage, *Chihine*, let thy soul be strong to endure suffering and hardship; keep thyself from being sad, otherwise thou will be sick; see how we do not cease to laugh, although we have little to eat" (Le Jeune's *Relation* of 1634, in Kenton, 1927, 1, p. 129).

Again on another occasion Le Jeune's host said to him: "Do not let thyself be cast down, take courage; when the snow comes, we shall eat" (Le Jeune's *Relation* of 1634, in Kenton, 1927, 1, p. 171). Which is something like the philosophy of the Penan of Borneo: "If there is no food today there will be tomorrow"—expressing, according to Needham, "a confidence in the capacity of the environment to support them, and in their own ability to extract their livelihood from it" (1954, p. 230).

9c. Does Hunting Bring Happiness?

Speakers: *Alland, L. Binford, Crocker, Helm, Hiatt, Marshall, Owen, Suttles, Turnbull, Williams, Woodburn.*

HIATT: I think one may follow even further the point of Marshall Sahlins' paper and raise a question about the mentality of hunter-gatherers. Lee and DeVore have said that one of the points that we might consider would be "nomadic style." In light of what Sahlins said, I wonder whether we ought also to talk about the "parasitic mentality." What he said certainly fits the aborigines; they are, so to speak, a happy-go-lucky people. I wonder whether this description applies to the other hunters and gatherers that we have heard about during this conference.

WILLIAMS: I think I may have an aberrant group in many senses; they seem not to be so well off as some of the groups described here; they hunt and are hungry most of the time; and they really do not laugh a lot. However, I will give Marshall Sahlins the point that they do not worry much about it or try to change the situation.

HELM: I do not think the thesis of confidence in the yield of tomorrow holds for the boreal forest peoples. Rather, my reading of northern Indian equanimity is that it is fatalistic rather than optimistic: If either the day or the morrow does not provide for itself, there is little one can do about it.

OWEN: No one has ever accused the Yuman-speaking nomads of being especially jolly. The group that I worked with in Baja California are now deculturated and are peasant farmers in a certain sense. Perhaps their concern with farming has some relevance to what June Helm has just suggested, because it is precisely to-morrow that they are unconcerned about, since they have no real control over it. They muster enough energy to plow a field and sow it, but then their uncertainty about the future creeps in and they let it go. The cattle eat the crops, and that's God's will, by God. Now, this would suggest to me that these populations—who have never known any great abundance—are unconcerned with tomorrow because they cannot control it, rather than because they expect that it will take care of itself.

SUTTLES: In response, again, to Hiatt's question, the Northwest coast Indians have never been called happy-go-lucky, so far as I know. Of course, they do plan for the future and may have been trapped into this, in Sahlins' terms. It is this, I think, that makes them different from others that we have discussed.

ALLAND: As I understand it, the Naskapi also worry and care about the morrow, and they handle this in a magical way by throwing a scapula into the fire and thus determining the direction to be taken in future hunts. And Omar Moore (1957) has suggested that this incidentally helps them to maximize hunting, since it randomizes the hunting territories they exploit so that the animals do not become accustomed to being hunted in a particular place. At any rate, whether or not this model works, there is evidence again that a hunting group may be anxious about the future and *will* try to do something about the morrow.

BINFORD: It might be interesting to speculate about the "happiness" of the people responsible for the archeological remains recently uncovered by R. S. MacNeish (1964) in the Tehuacán Valley. These people were coping with their environment during the period of initial use of domesticated plants. Judging from the archeology, they lived in an arid area which did not compare favorably with the Bushman habitat, particularly in regard to the availability of native tuberous roots and other dependable wild plant sources. The impetus to invest in the development of storage technology and in the horticultural perfection of certain plants must have occurred in the context of "some concern" for the future. I was pleased to hear Dr. Suttles say that the hunters of the Northwest coast also showed concern, since they depended heavily on resources

which were exploited for limited periods and stored for future consumption. The Tehuacá-nos' similarly increased the time utility of their resources through storage and preservation techniques. I suspect that the people of the Tehuacán Valley were not very "happy" in the sense suggested earlier.

The happiness factor may not, after all, be so much a direct function of hunting; happiness should vary directly with the degree to which subsistence input levels are maintained in a steady state despite seasonal fluctuations in yield from the standing crop of available resources. Increased sedentism together with storage and preservation techniques, as in the cases of the Tehuacános and the Northwest coast Indians, was, at least initially, a response to the failure to maintain such a steady state. It is expectable that such adaptations would be coupled with "concern for tomorrow."

In contrast, one might expect to find a more happy-go-lucky attitude among groups which have achieved a homeostatic relationship with regard to food resources. Such a group might move from one resource area to another, consuming immediately available products; or a group might gain time utility from resources through storage and preservation techniques and stabilize population below the point at which exploitation of the standing crop would threaten productivity. The point here is that "happiness" in the sense of little care for tomorrow would be more a function of homeostasis than of hunting *per se*.

If we can judge from the tremendous conservatism and stability of many Pleistocene hunting adaptations and from the stability and tenacity of some groups of modern hunters, there are many hunting groups which have achieved a balanced equilibrium with their environment. I am suggesting that it is this tendency of hunting adaptations to reach homeostasis which makes for the "happy hunter."

CROCKER: I thought we had buried the Gê-speaking peoples today with our emphasis on pure hunting subsistence, but I find that the hunter's mentality now being described fits the Canella. Yet they have a great deal of agriculture and may, in earlier times, have had even more. This raises a problem. If we are going to talk about the hunter's mentality, maybe we have to talk about peoples who have other modes of subsistence—even, perhaps, fully agricultural peoples. It is a question of the yardstick that we use and the purposes we are pursuing.

WOODBURN: It may be worth mentioning a lack of commitment different from the lack of commitment to the morrow and yet, perhaps related to it. The Hadza are strikingly uncommitted to each other; what happens to other individual Hadza, even close relatives, does not really matter very much. People are often very affectionate to each other, but the affection is generally not accompanied by much sense of responsibility. If someone becomes ill, he is likely to be tended only so long as this is convenient.

Now, in the literature on hunters and gatherers, abandonment of the sick is quite frequently mentioned and is almost invariably interpreted as deriving directly from ecological pressures. The notion is that an individual is abandoned only through necessity, when the survival of other people is at stake. But this explanation does not make sense of the case material I collected among the Hadza and I strongly suspect that it also does not adequately explain the incidence of abandonment in most other societies from which the custom is recorded. In one of the cases of which I have records, a boy became paralyzed below the waist, probably from poliomyelitis. He was carried for quite a number of camp moves. Then, on one occasion, the people of the camp moved to a site where they had expected to find water and found none. They were perhaps only about four or five miles from water, but they had reached the point at which it had become rather tedious to carry him for the unexpected additional move when they were rather tired and rather thirsty. So they left him behind with food and water and with his bow and arrows—not that these were of much use to him—and he did not survive. Those who abandoned him included his own mother and certain other close relatives. A similar lack of commitment to other people is apparent in many other contexts.

For an explanation, I think we should look beyond the obvious ecological factors. We should give far more attention to the consis-

tency of this behavior with the degree to which social relationships bind individuals to each other. With a few exceptions, a Hadza does not depend on specific individuals standing in particular relationships to him for access to property or to adult status, or for assistance in cooperative activities. In this respect the Hadza and similar hunters and gatherers differ very fundamentally from most other tribal societies.

I would suggest that much of the sort of behavior which Marshall Sahlins has described—the listlessness, the apathy, the merry squandering of windfalls, the lack of concern for the morrow—is intimately bound up with this relative lack of responsibility to specific other individuals, the relative absence of binding obligations to them. I am not suggesting for one moment that this applies to all hunters and gatherers but I certainly do think that it may apply to many of them. It may also have applied to many ancient hunters and we ought to bear this in mind when considering why their populations apparently remained stable over so vast a period.

TURNBULL: I would like to support Woodburn's observations with data on the Ik. There is an almost exact parallel, and I have seen abandonment without any kind of emotion whatsoever. One person was shot in the stomach in a raid at about one o'clock in the morning and was still conscious when I was first told about it at six o'clock in the morning, and people had done nothing about him except to fold him into the death position. They only began to take an interest in him when I began to wonder what I should do about it.

I think this also bears on what Hiatt said about the mentality of the hunter. Both the Pygmies and the Ik laugh a lot; in fact, they get quite hysterical. But this does not mean that they do not also cry. At any rate, they are violently emotional. They fight continuously, although the fighting is without malice. In some cases, a Pygmy camp may be characterized by innumerable disputes, many of which are almost deliberately created. They are created with the specific objective of concealing a real dispute.

One last point, not previously mentioned, is that both these hunting communities are characterized by an almost complete lack of magic, witchcraft, or sorcery. I would like to hear more about this from students of other societies.

MARSHALL: In response to Colin Turnbull's last remark, I would like to say that the !Kung we worked with were free from a belief that there were witches among them. They had an apparently vague idea of a sorcery-like power, but spoke of other people far away having such power and using it for evil. !Kung informants insisted that their "medicine men" only tried to cure and protect with their "medicine."

9d. HUNTING *vs.* GATHERING AS FACTORS IN SUBSISTENCE

Speakers: *Alland, Bicchieri, L. Binford, Lathrap, Laughlin, R. Lee, Marshall, Struever, Washburn*

BICCHIERI: I would like to point out that in my doctoral dissertation on the ecology of food-gathering peoples (1965) I utilized a sample of thirty societies very similar, in the choice of units, to the one used by Lee. My analysis also emphasized the need for determining the actual dependence of a specified group on hunting versus gathering. It appears to me that it is essential, for meaningful cross-cultural comparison, that the relative amount of a group's dependence on hunting as contrasted to gathering to be specified. The term "hunters"—as used by J. H. Steward—tends to obscure the actual exploitative condition, and, as a consequence, inhibits inferences regarding socio-economic covariations. One basic implication, for example, lies in the fact that the chances of productive failure, everything else being equal, are halved by a mixed hunting-gathering exploitation. Practicing such mixed exploitation, a group can, more often than not, fall back on the alternative technique when necessary. Thus the Kalahari Bushmen, with a hunting *and* gathering subsistence base are likely to resist environmental failures more readily than, for instance, the Copper Eskimo who have to rely solely on hunting.

STRUEVER: This distinction between hunting and gathering interests me. It may be useful for solving some problems, but irrelevant to others. For example, if our object is to understand the considerable complexity of a particular collecting group, this is a problem of productive potential of their environment vis-à-vis plants and/or animals and of the efficiency of their exploitative and maintenance technology. A hunting-gathering distinction has no value for solving this particular problem.

Also, we have not really defined what we mean by the hunting-gathering distinction. Are we talking about differences in the food substances themselves—plant materials *vs.* flesh, or is the distinction a technological one, i.e., hunting and gathering technologies can be distinguished from each other? If the distinction is technological, would you call the collecting of migratory waterfowl by means of traps or cast nets gathering or hunting? Would you call herding fish onto mud flats or draining lakes and then collecting the fish population, gathering or fishing?

But the problem of distinguishing hunting from gathering seems peripheral to our major interests which center more on the productivity of an environment vis-à-vis non-domesticant resources and how human groups structure themselves socially and demographically to use a technology of measurable efficiency to exploit this environment.

LAUGHLIN: It is interesting to notice the kinds of information that are discarded if the catching of sea mammals is classified as fishing, rather than hunting. One of these losses is in our understanding of the development of some kinds of technology. Now, most of the sea mammals are hunted from kayaks, which have enormous advantages over open boats like umiaks (which, in turn, have great advantages over intertidal zone collecting). When it comes to input-output analysis, we must count the extensive training of a child to become a kayak hunter. A second major time investment is in the scanning operation; though this is still quicker and more efficient from a kayak than, say, scanning on foot along a coastline.

BINFORD: While I am in complete sympathy with obtaining quantitative data on subsistence, I think that the emphasis on the percentage contribution of gathering versus hunting to total subsistence may divert us from a major point of ecological studies—the dynamics of human adaptations in various environments. For example, if we are concerned with trying to understand human radiations from a relatively limited range in the basal Pleistocene, it becomes critical to understand variations in the structuring of subsistence resources through the phasing of an annual cycle among the major environmental zones which man successively penetrated. We might reasonably expect that hunting played very different roles in particular habitats. Man's radiation was, in general, from a relatively dry semitropical park savanna through zones of increasing year-'round dampness and annual cold. In environments of the latter type permanent resident fauna include a relatively high proportion of predators; herbivores are either seasonal residents, or are very rare in species numbers, or they are represented by species which hibernate during the months when plants are dormant or blanketed with snow. In penetrating the more northerly environmental zones, man must have put greater reliance on hunting (predation) and on the development of storage and preservation techniques. A small amount of available meat during periods of plant food scarcity might have been more crucial to survival than the vast quantities of plant foods available during times of plenty.

To point out that non-agriculturalists living in relatively arid and sub-tropical environments are heavily dependent on plant foods tells us little about the importance of hunting in the evolutionary history of man and culture, nor does it provide a basis for generalizing about the role of hunting in adaptations to different environments.

ALLAND: I agree with Lee's input-output model, and I think it makes sense in terms of nutritional requirements. People require a rather large number of calories in order to subsist, but they require only a rather small amount of protein—45–50 grams per day of animal protein and perhaps a bit more in vegetable protein. These things should also be measured. It seems to me that the investment of calories in getting animals may be greater than the output in calories; yet if the caloric output of gathering vegetables shows a surplus, you find a surviving society.

LEE: To carry on the points made by Binford and Alland, I might say that when we think of man the *hunter*, we generally think of the higher latitudes: the temperate and arctic zones; while the concept of man the eclectic

subsister calls to mind the middle and low latitudes, i.e., the tropical zones. This eclecticism and emphasis on vegetable foods appears even in the game-rich environments, as the Hadza case shows.

To take up a physiological point: eating a lot of meat just does not make physiological sense in the Bushmen case, because it takes five times as much energy (with heat generated in proportion) to process by digestion a unit of meat as it takes to process a unit of vegetable food (Bourlière, 1964, p. 336). So in a cold area, it makes good sense to eat a lot of meat; but in a hot area, the reverse is true.

WASHBURN: Another nutritional point is that man the animal is adapted to certain kinds of food. He has to have certain things in his food supply, and this makes measurements by quantity tricky. We are dealing with an animal that has relied on meat as part of his diet for at least a couple of million years, so 20 per cent, or even a smaller quantity of meat, may be a very important constituent of the total diet.

LATHRAP: I would like to inject a word of caution here. Most of the hunters whom we have been discussing so far during this conference are peoples who live in environments not particularly favorable to hunting, or who share their territory with more complex groups. The Ona bands of northern Tierra del Fuego survived into the first decade of the present century in an unacculturated condition. Here we find people with good hunting territories which they jealously defended from all outsiders. The larger part of their caloric intake was from game (the guanaco being the prime source), and only minimal use was made of vegetable foods.

Interestingly enough, all of the classic stigmata of "hunting peoples," which have been brought into question at this symposium, were strongly developed among the several Ona bands, which were in fact patrilineal. Patrilineages were clearly defined and strictly exogamous. Each held a sharply delineated territory with absolute rights over the included economic resources. The facts of the case are reasonably clear since we have a good account of the culture written by Bridges (1949) who actually lived with Ona bands while the culture was still flourishing. There are also more formal and detailed ethnographies culled from the memories of Ona informants who had participated in the aboriginal situation (Gusinde, 1931–39; Lothrop, 1928).

With regard to the question of the "hunter's mentality" the Ona are particularly instructive. Ona culture stressed emotional control, and Bridges' account makes it clear that this particular ethical imperative was observed far more often than it was breached. There were a number of ingenious institutions which were effective in minimizing intraband hostilities and in channeling agression toward outsiders or toward wives, who in strict sense were outsiders. The Ona both preached and practiced the support of the aged.

When we consider projecting cultural traits and modal personality structures backward to a time when most hunters presumably found themselves in favorable circumstances, we might find the example of the Ona more instructive than that of the handful of still extant hunting groups who are scarcely making a go of it *as hunters*.

MARSHALL: I hope that there will be more discussion about the attitudes of hunting-gathering peoples toward gathering. Assuming that there is more food to be gathered, why do they not gather more at a time? The Hadza gather for only two or three hours a day, the !Kung, perhaps more hours, but only on an average every other day, or sometimes one in three days. It has been suggested that because they do not have to work every day they can be said to have an "affluent society." This is a *bon mot*, but does not add to the understanding of the reasons. I have pointed out that the !Kung we worked with are all thin and that they constantly expressed concern and anxiety about food. There must be reasons why they do not gather and eat more. I think that energy for digging runs out and the daylight hours come to an end, for one thing. It has been suggested that they cannot eat more roots, berries, and seeds than they do, because the roughage is too much. Also, I believe we might look more into a possible social reason. If a woman gathered very much more than her family needed at a given time, would it turn out that she was working for others? Would she draw envious attention upon herself and be blamed for not being more generous if she had an ex-

cess of food and kept it for herself? (!Kung custom required that meat be shared, but not veldkos.)

9e. MEASURING RESOURCES AND SUBSISTENCE STRATEGY

Speakers: *Alland, L. Binford, Birdsell, Deevey, Eggan, Gardner, Sahlins.*

BIRDSELL: There has been a great deal of discussion about carrying capacity and productive potential and about how much of a given food source could be reaped or killed. I suggest that we really do not know this in any specific case. I do not think that ecologists know what the combined human/predator load would be for a given animal in a given situation. But, against this, there is considerable evidence that as one food source is overstrained, people turn to another in compensation. This is particularly true of shellfish in certain cases where one species is over-reaped and there is a change to a less favored species. In other words, the empirical proof is testable, but the theoretical description of what constitutes overdraft would be difficult. We would have to know the total ecology of the total biota to come to a specific statement, a task which probably would not be worth the trouble.

DEEVEY: By way of poking a little fun, let me note as an ecologist that it is refreshing to find that anthropologists have now discovered for themselves that the Arctic tundra, the temperate deciduous forest, the tropical savanna, and the tropical rainforest are not all the same kinds of environment, even from the point of view of subsistence. That they are different seems self evident to an ecologist, although certainly we have had trouble quantifying these differences. It is difficult to measure what we call productivity, and even when we measure with modest success the caloric content of the vegetation, the apportionment of the caloric content among the various species is *not* easy to measure. So we have no clear idea ecologically as to what we mean by the change in diversity between arctic, temperate, and tropical conditions. It is refreshing, then, to see anthropologists now measuring quantities that bear on this.

Let me frame a question for ecologically minded anthropologists to answer. A few years ago I naively thought it might be good to total up the measured animal productivity in a temperate deciduous forest, just by way of seeing in theory how much human protoplasm a given area of the forest could support on a hunting and gathering economy. Not being professionally a terrestrial ecologist, I was surprised to find that the animal productivity that goes into deer and other such "catchable" animals is a negligible fraction of what goes into songbirds, which, in turn, is a negligible fraction of what goes into insects. And then I looked at mice and found that—although they too are less productive as an ongoing portion of the ecosystem than are insects—mice are considerably more productive than either deer or songbirds. And I calculated that if men were capable of utilizing the annual yield of mice, there ought to be population densities of the order of 100 times as great as those that there actually were in such forests.

It is known that in a closely regulated predator-prey situation, the more the predator takes, the more he can get (up to a cẽrtain point, naturally). This is because the predator presses down the demographic structure of the prey population, so that it is in its maximum productive stage. The predator can then take the annual yield, which otherwise would be lost to natural mortality. So I ask the ethnographic experts whether there is any evidence that people anywhere have lived the year round solely on mice.

EGGAN: Some well-meaning group of whites tried to move a group of Shöshone out of a desolate valley, and the Shoshone answered, in effect: "What? Leave all these wonderful mice around here?"

GARDNER: I have wondered how the South Indian Paliyans managed to maintain a population density that must be nearly two persons per square mile. Deevey gives us an answer—because they catch mice, rats, bats, . . . and let the big game go!

BINFORD: In light of Dr. Deevey's statement, we may be able to restore the Tehuacan people to the list of happy natives. A Canadian by the name of Callen (Callen and Cameron, 1960) has studied the human feces recovered from the Tehuacan excavations and was able to get quantitative information on the diet of the people—a rare thing indeed. One of the more common inclusions in the coprolites was undigested bone and hair of mice and other small rodents.

ALLAND: A simple example from psychology might be applicable here. If rats are presented with a learning situation in which two stimuli are rewarded randomly—one 30 per cent and the other 70 per cent of the time—they soon learn that it is a better strategy to press the 70 per cent bar all of the time than to try to figure out the game. Unfortunately, humans do not do this; they try to beat the game. So, when there are alternate resources of deer and mice, I suspect that they will always take the deer and leave the mice for emergencies.

SAHLINS: With regard to Professor Birdsell's remarks made at the outset about carrying capacity, we do have for slash-and-burn agriculturists a whole series of estimates of their relation to critical capacities, as measured by their agricultural needs—land in use at a particular time, land that they need to have available, etc. These techniques, of course, were developed in Africa and applied to native reserves, where it was almost always discovered that the people were over capacity. But they have since been applied to peoples not on reserves, for instance in the South American tropical forests and the results nearly everywhere indicate that population densities are about 20–50 per cent of capacity—in other words, in the range mentioned earlier by Dr. Washburn.

PART III

Social and Territorial Organization

IO.

Ownership and Use
of Land among the Australian Aborigines

L. R. HIATT

Aboriginal territorial organization is currently a subject of controversy (Hiatt, 1962, 1966; Stanner, 1965). I shall first present the classical description, then indicate the different picture at present emerging, and finally raise some speculative issues suggested by modern ethological research.

THE CLASSICAL DESCRIPTION

Radcliffe-Brown (1931) distinguished three kinds of grouping—tribe, clan, and horde. A tribe consisted of people who spoke the same language and occupied a continuous tract of land. It was divided into patriclans, each owning a defined territory that included a number of totemic sites. A horde consisted of the male members of a patriclan, their wives, and unmarried female members. It was independent and autonomous, managing its own affairs and acting as a unit in its relations with other hordes.

THE RECENT PICTURE

Elkin (1950, pp. 17–18) stated that "the local organization in many tribes was not the clear-cut patrilineal patrilocal exogamous group occupying a definite territory which some textbooks imply." Meggitt (1962) was the first to assert specifically and in detail that some of Radcliffe-Brown's generalizations did not hold for at least one tribe (the Walbiri). My own field investigations between 1958 and 1960 (Hiatt, 1965) among the Gidjingali of Arnhem Land also failed to confirm Radcliffe-Brown's view; and subsequently I drew attention to similar material in reports of earlier workers who merely thought they had discovered isolated aberrant forms (Hiatt, 1962).

There is no quarrel with Radcliffe-Brown's statements about the tribe as a linguistic division or the patriclan as a land-owning unit. The argument is about the horde—more precisely, about residential associations, exploitation of resources, and group movements. What follows is a summary of my earlier paper (1962).

Composition of Communities

Radcliffe-Brown asserted that the local unit was based on a single patriclan. Yet at least seven observers since 1930 have described more or less stable communities that included members from two to twelve patriclans. Several writers mention dispersal and reunion according to seasonal conditions, visiting, and occasional joint participation of several communities in the same ceremony. The aborigines themselves saw these events as temporary separations from the main group or temporary amalgamations with other groups.

Exploitation of Resources

Radcliffe-Brown stated that each horde had to obtain most of its foods and water from its own territory. He also wrote: "Acts of trespass against this exclusive right of a horde to its territory seem to have been very rare in the social life of the aborigines but it appears to have been generally held that anyone committing such a trespass could justifiably be killed" (1952, pp. 33–34). Yet eight observers since 1930 have reported that unrestricted movement of foodseekers over broad regions that included the totemic sites of many patriclans. This does not mean that all comers had free access to every locality. A Walbiri community, for example, included members of from six to twelve patriclans who habitually ranged over a defined area that included the totemic estates of the constituent clans. But they entered the territories of other communities on invitation (Meggitt, 1962, chap. 5).

Territorial Boundaries

Radcliffe-Brown said that known boundaries defined each patriclan's territory, on which were situated its totemic sites. Some later observers have reported such boundaries, others have described them as uncertain or ill defined, and others again have denied their existence. The subject is important mainly in relation to Radcliffe-Brown's assertion that a patriclan exercised an exclusive right to the natural resources of its territory. In tribes like the Walbiri and Gidjingali, patriclans did not claim such rights and accordingly did not establish demarcations around their totemic estates for the purpose of controlling access.

I should make it clear that I do not regard these empirical refutations of Radcliffe-Brown's generalizations as somehow adding up to a new generalization. In view of the wide range of ecological variation in Australia, it seems unlikely that aboriginal local organization conformed to a single type, though now it is

probably too late to establish with confidence the main varieties.

To anticipate the objection that Radcliffe-Brown was in a better position than later investigators to observe the real thing, I would remark that the main studies of local organization in Australia have been carried out on the frontier, not beyond it, and that Radcliffe-Brown's research was no exception. We have all faced the problem of reconstructing a nomadic past from a mission-, station-, or town-based present. Elsewhere I have suggested that Radcliffe-Brown's "cell-like" account of local organization was based on his unverified assumption that an acknowledged ritual relationship between a patriclan and its estate implied an exclusive economic and residential connection as well (1962). Here, in support of the kind of account given by Meggitt and myself, I mention Elkin's view (as yet unpublished) that the congregation of aborigines around European settlements was, in terms of local organization, a change not of kind (as commonly supposed) but of degree. At least in the early phase of contact the natives regarded these establishments as "super-water-holes."

ETHOLOGY AND PRIMITIVE HUNTERS

Carpenter wrote that: "It would seem that possession and defense of territory which is found so widely among the vertebrates, including both the human and subhuman primates, may be a fundamental biologic need" (1941, p. 158). It is now evident that there are important exceptions. Schaller (1965) reports that groups of mountain gorillas restricted their activities to home ranges, but these areas were not exclusively occupied by one group. He concludes: "The almost complete overlap of some ranges and observations on peaceful interactions between groups indicate that gorillas have no territory in the sense of an exclusive area defended against others of the same species" (p. 342). Reynolds and Reynolds (1965) state that chimpanzee groups in the Budongo Forest were constantly changing membership, splitting apart, meeting others and joining them, congregating, or dispersing. And Goodall (1965) says that because chimpanzee groups in the Gombe Stream Reserve freely united from time to time, they could not be divided into separate communities. Even baboon territorial organization seems less rigid than previously supposed. Whereas Ardrey (1961, p. 77) spoke of the troop as a society which "demonstrates all those hostile traits normal to the individual territorial proprietor," DeVore and Hall (1965) in a recent report describe cases of close daily contact between different baboon groups without displays of intergroup aggression.

Modern ethology thus raises no difficulty for an account of aborigines which implies that they lacked territorial instincts. Nevertheless, patriclans did have inalienable rights to pieces of land. Given the evidence that they did not also exercise exclusive rights of use over these properties, it seems legitimate to ask why tribal areas embraced a number of separate clan estates. I shall approach the problem by selecting a Gidjingali patriclan as an example and discussing two questions: (1) What did a clan estate look like to its owners?; and (2) What did it feel like?

1. The Mararagidj patriclan (which I shall abbreviate to "Mara") in 1960 comprised 25 members. It owned seven named sites distributed over roughly one square mile of coastal flat. Five sites were totemic (several shell middens and parts of a tidal creek, all connected with a mythological Dingo), two were non-totemic (a mud flat formed by tidal inundation, and a place called "Where-the-plum-tree-died"). Only one site was a camping place.

The Mara belonged to a community of about 135 people called the Anbara, whose home range comprised six contiguous estates owned by the constituent clans. They usually camped together at one or other of two, possibly three, places suitable for a group of this size. In other words, the local community consisted of members of six different patriclans, and at any given camp the majority of members were living *outside* their estates.

The men fished with spears along the coast and tidal creeks and also hunted land animals, while women gathered plant foods and shell fish. Men often built fish traps across creeks running through their own estates. But there were no restrictions on movement, and the camp seems to have been a base from which

people might range anywhere over the entire Anbara region (about twenty square miles), returning at dusk with the day's catch. The Mara estate itself did not have a site suitable for such a large encampment, but from time to time clan members temporarily left the Anbara community to spend a period on their homeland. I should add that folk always said they had been born on their estates, though further questioning often indicated that they were not certain.

2. Each clan owned a number of designs representing its totemic sites and the mythological creators supposed to be living beneath or near them. The designs were used in initiation and mortuary rites, which were not necessarily held on the clan's estate.

It is thus true to say that there was a ritual tie between a clan and its estate. But there was also an emotional bond with the land itself that seems to some extent independent of mythological associations. Totems were regarded with awe rather than affection, and when an aborigine spoke lovingly of his clan estate, he described its natural features, not its supernatural underworld.

We have now reached the core of the problem. Given that the aboriginal owners of a piece of land were not solely or even largely dependent on it for their survival, and that they often spent more time away from it than on it, how do we account for the strength of their emotional attachment? I do not pretend to know the answer. The only relevant facts I can bring forward are that members of a Gidjingali clan thought of their estate as their birthplace and the birthplace of their forefathers (though they did not believe, as some other tribes did, that their totemic sites were repositories of spirit-children); and as a home to which they periodically wished to return. The evidence is clearly against the existence in aboriginal clansmen of an instinct to occupy and defend their territory. But it points to a strong impulse to establish and maintain territorial ownership.

An easier question to answer is why Gidjingali clans did not confine themselves to their estates. There are clearly adaptive advantages to having access to a broader subsistence range. Centripetal forces in communities such as the Anbara included desires for variety in diet and human company, the safety of larger numbers, and the economic security against poor seasons afforded by a bigger hunting expanse. The operation of these forces was facilitated by an ethic of generosity and hospitality which defined the good man as the generous man. But the persistence of small clan estates in the face of communities of clans and communal use of land indicates the presence of a counterforce. Ritual responsibility was undoubtedly a factor, but another component was an emotional bond with the land itself. The source of this emotion is not clear.

11.

Stability and Flexibility
in Hadza Residential Groupings

JAMES WOODBURN

In another paper in this volume (Chapter 5) I describe how the Eastern Hadza obtain their food relatively easily by hunting and gathering. Their nutritional needs are met quickly and without much effort, coordination, or cooperation.

In this paper the characteristics of Hadza residential groupings are briefly described. This account is only an introduction; a full description with the necessary supporting numerical date will be given in my forthcoming monograph on the Hadza.

Hadza residential groupings are open, flexible, and highly variable in composition. They have no institutionalized leadership and, indeed, no corporate identity. They do not own territory and clear-cut jurally defined modes of affiliation of individuals to residential groupings do not exist. The use of the term "band," with its connotations of territorial ownership, leadership, corporateness, and fixed membership is inappropriate for Hadza residential entities and I prefer to use the term "camp," meaning simply the set of persons who happen to be living together at one place at one time (Woodburn, 1964).

I consider first the area in which the Hadza live and the geographical regions into which they divide it. The nature of the camps, their composition and their flexibility are then examined. Synchronic and diachronic census material is presented to show the way in which groupings change through time and to demonstrate that in spite of their flexibility and variability, important underlying regularities persist.

The principal purpose of the paper is simply descriptive, but my intention is also to stress that we cannot hope to understand the residential arrangements of hunters and gatherers, especially those with flexible residential arrangements, unless we make use of numerical data, in particular diachronic numerical data.

THE GEOGRAPHICAL DIVISIONS OF THE COUNTRY OF THE EASTERN HADZA

The area the Eastern Hadza occupy consisted in the recent past of well over 1,000 square miles of land. Until the 1930s the Hadza had this country to themselves, but then two villages of outsiders were founded at fertile places right inside Hadza country and within a few years their population far outnumbered that of the Hadza. At the same time there has been constant loss of land on the edge of their country to neighboring tribes and more especially to the Iraqw. But the serious incursions are all relatively recent and had not had any effect on the Hadza system of land tenure until the Hadza were settled in 1964 and 1965.

The Hadza commonly use certain terms to refer to regions of their country and for the people associated with these regions. For example, *Mangola* is used for an area around the Mangola River. This area cannot be precisely defined, for the use of the term depends partly on context. If one asks a Hadza living far from Mangola about the whereabouts of some person and is told that he lives at Mangola, this means that he is living somewhere within an area of some hundreds of square miles around the Mangola River. On the other hand, if one is told by a man living only five miles away from the Mangola River that some person is living at Mangola, this normally means that the persons is living within a mile or two of the lower reaches of the river.

The word *Sipunga*, meaning the region around Sipunga Mountain, has similar variations in meaning according to context. A third term *Tli'ika* (literally "the west") is commonly used to refer to a stretch of high ground running northeast from Isanzu between the Yaida Valley and Lake Eyasi to about half way above the lake where the fourth and final region, *Han!abi* (literally "the rocks"), begins. Han!abi, which is, as its name suggests, a mountainous, rocky area, extends along the same ridge between Lake Eyasi and the Yaida plains up to the mountains overlooking the Mangola River which are generally considered to be part of the Mangola region. Unlike Mangola and Sipunga, neither Tli'ika nor Han!abi have a focal point in a single geographical feature, but all four regions resemble each other in having no clearcut boundary. To draw boundaries would be quite artificial; the regions grade into each other.[1]

On the other hand, no part of the country in which the Hadza live to the east of Lake Eyasi lies outside the areas to which these terms may be applied when used with their widest connotations. We cannot separate them off from each other, but between them they cover the whole country. Only the extensive open Yaida plains are outside the classifications, but this is not country in which people live. Hadza never live in the open plain, but only in the bordering thickets and hills which fall within the named areas.

The division of Hadza country into four named, roughly defined localities bears some relation to Hadza social arrangements. At any one time each of these areas is likely to contain between 50 and 150 Hadza. One commonly talks of the *Sipunganebe* (people of Sipunga), *Mangolanebe* (people of Mangola), *Tli'ikanebe* (people of the west) and *Han!abi-cebe* (people of the rocks). These names do not refer to a fixed body of people in each area but simply to the aggregate of individuals who at any particular time or in any particular context are associated with one locality rather than another.

Each of these areas contains sufficient sources of food and water to maintain its inhabitants throughout the year and many people, especially the elderly, restrict their nomadic movements for years at a stretch largely to a single one of these four areas. At the peak of the dry season, when water is scarce and when the berries of *Cordia gharaf*. Ehrenb. and *Salvadora persica* L. ripen in huge quantities near to these few sources of water, the majority of the inhabitants in each of these areas may be found concentrated in a few large camps within perhaps two or three miles or less of each other and close to the berries and water supplies of their area.[2] I have never heard of any occasion on which all the inhabitants of one of these areas joined together to form a single camp, although their mode of subsistence would not of itself make this impossible.

In one of the four areas, Sipunga, there is a marked cleavage into two divisions, one lying close to the Sipunga mountains and the other centering on Yaida River. For much of the

1. In earlier formulations (Woodburn, 1962, 1964, and the conference draft of this paper) I defined only three regions and omitted Han!abi. Although Mangola and Tli'ika could, when used with their widest possible connotations, be said to include most, if not all of Han!abi, further field work in 1967 has convinced me that the term "Han!abi" is used sufficiently often to define the area lying in the southern borderlands of Mangola and the northern borderlands of Tli'ika to demand separate consideration. I hope that this alteration may help to stress the vagueness and the lack of precision with which these terms are used by the Hadza.

2. In Tli'ika, and especially in Han!abi, these two popular berries are less numerous and less concentrated than in Mangola and Sipunga and the people there usually remain more dispersed at the height of the dry season.

year the camps of the Yaida division are far from those of the Sipunga division, but at the peak of the dry season most of the people living near Yaida usually come to live in camps in close association with the camps of the Sipunga division among the berry trees under Sipunga Mountain. The division of the country into four areas is conspicuously linked with the fact that, wherever they may be in the wet season, camps are reasonably clearly grouped into four widely separated clusters at the peak of the dry season.

People, singly and in groups, move freely from region to region. Any individual Hadza may live, hunt, and gather anywhere he or she likes without any sort of restriction and without asking permission from anyone. Neither individuals nor groups hold exclusive rights over natural resources, over land and its ungarnered produce, and there is never any question of people who have long been associated with a particular area having exclusive or even prior rights there. Even the expansion of neighboring agricultural and pastoral tribes into Hadza country is not opposed, and each year much land is lost.

The inhabitants at any particular time of each of these regions do not share a joint estate; nor do they unite to perform any activity; nor do they acknowledge any bond uniting them in opposition to other areas. They cannot be described as constituting a group and to use the term "band" or "horde" to describe them would be completely inappropriate.

CAMP SIZE, COMPOSITION AND NOMADIC MOVEMENT

At any time, the 400 or so Hadza who lead a nomadic hunting and gathering life to the east of Lake Eyasi are living in camps containing very varied numbers of people—from a single person to almost a hundred people. The average camp contains about eighteen adults. But the members of a camp do not constitute a stable unit, either in place, in numbers, or in composition. People do not camp continuously at a particular site for more than a few weeks and they usually move much more often. At the time members of a camp all move, they may go together to a new site; they may split

up and form camps at two or more new sites; they may go as a body to join some existing camp, or they may divide, some joining an existing camp and others building a camp at a new site. Even while people are living together in a camp at a particular site, the composition of the camp changes: some people move in and some move out. In spite of this flexibility, there are interesting consistencies in the composition of camps which will be described later.

The individual members of a camp at a particular time are not present on account of their common attachment to a body of resources; nor does a camp have an acknowledged leader to whom common allegiance is owed. A camp at any particular time is often known by the name of a well-known man living in it at that time (for example, /ets'a ma Durugida—Durugida's camp). But this indicates only that the man is well enough known for his name to be a useful label, and not that he acts either as a leader or as a representative of the camp. At any particular time a camp is an agglomeration of individual members tied to each other by a variety of kinship and affinal ties.

In my doctoral thesis I use data derived from two censuses, which I describe as my synchronic and diachronic censuses, to establish which relationships of kinship and affinity are important in residential arrangements. For the synchronic census, I took down particulars of the membership of ten camps in the Sipunga and Mangola regions in June and July, 1960. These camps contained approximately 60 per cent of the Eastern Hadza. The diachronic census consists of a record of the changes and consistencies in the composition of a series of camps. Taking one particular old widow named Bunga, the mother of two married sons and two married daughters, I recorded, on 25 separate occasions spread over more than three years, the people who were living in the same camp as she was.

Bunga was, in the estimation of the Hadza, a respectable and conventional women who lived regularly, by Hadza standards, with her close kin and affines and who moved camp less frequently than many other people, especially younger people. On all 25 occasions, the camps were in the Sipunga region. The particulars of the members of these camps tend therefore to stress the continuities rather than the discontinuities in Hadza residential groups. Yet even with this emphasis on continuity, there were radical differences in the size and composition of these camps. The minimum number of adults present was 3 and the maximum was 37. There were less than 10 adults present on four occasions, between 10 and 19 adults present on twelve occasions, between 20 and 29 adults present on seven occasions and between 30 and 39 adults present on the remaining two occasions. A total of 67 adults, more than a quarter of the entire Eastern Hadza adult population, lived with Bunga in at least one of these camps. The Hadza apply the word *huyeti* (visitor) freely to anyone living in an area in which he does not normally live or living with people with whom he does not normally associate. But the use of the term differs according to the speaker and to the context, and it is quite impossible to divide up the members of a camp into those that are residents and those that are *huyeti*. However, an examination of the diachronic census does permit the isolation of a set of people who were regularly associated through time, and the nature of the bonds linking these persons will be mentioned in a later section of this paper.

With the rich food resources of their country and their knowledge of how to exploit these resources, it may seem hard to understand why the Hadza live in small, unstable nomadic groups which move at frequent intervals and constantly change in size and composition. In my monograph on the Hadza I shall discuss the way in which individuals and groups move from place to place far more frequently than is strictly necessary if movement is seen simply as a means of providing the best possible access to supplies of food and water. We ourselves are so tied down by, among other things, the sheer quantity of our possessions, that we with justification regard the movement of a household from one place to another as difficult and not to be attempted without substantial reason. But we must be careful not to allow our ethnocentrism to creep into our ethnography. The Hadza, like many other nomadic people, value movement highly and individuals and groups move to satisfy the slightest whim. Their possessions are so few and are so easily carried that movement is no prob-

lem. Indeed people often find it easier to move to the place where a game animal has been killed than to carry the meat back to their camp. The Hadza may move camp to get away from a site where illness has broken out, to obtain raw materials—stone for smoking pipes, wood for arrow shafts, poison for arrows, herbal medicines and so on, to trade, to gamble (see Chapter 5, this volume), to allow the realignment of the huts in a camp after changes in camp composition, to segregate themselves from those with whom they are in conflict, and for many other reasons. People do often move primarily because food and water are less readily available than they would like; and even where some other motive is present, they will of course at the same time try to improve their access to food and water. However, movement normally takes place long before it is essential, long before shortages have become in any way serious.

The variations in the size and in the composition of camps again cannot be interpreted in simple ecological terms. There are no grounds for suggesting that the constant and considerable changes in camp size and composition neatly parallel similarly frequent and substantial fluctuations in the available sources of food or in the arrangements used to procure food. At any season a wide variety of sizes of camp is ecologically viable. During the wet season, camps are, on average, smaller than in the dry season, but not, I think, because of any important difference in the rigor of the environmental pressures in the two seasons. Perhaps the most important single factor creating the larger camps of the dry season is that at this time of the year more large game is being killed. The meat of a large animal is by custom widely distributed through the camp and people tend to congregate in camps where there are skilled and successful hunters. The optimum size, considering this factor alone, will be the largest number of persons who can share an average-sized game animal and feel that they have had an acceptable quantity of meat. In the wet season, when few large animals are killed, there is less incentive for people to congregate in large camps and the divisive effects of quarrels tend to keep the size of the camps small. The general emphasis on seasonal polarity, mentioned briefly in Chapter

5, this volume, is also relevant. Many other factors, some ecological, some not, affect camp size, but cannot be discussed here. The limits on camp size set by the availability of food and water and the techniques used to obtain them are very broad and permit wide fluctuations; wide fluctuations in fact occur.

We must beware of any tendency to treat fixed, permanent ties linking together aggregates of people as normal, and loose, impermanent bonds as abnormal and requiring special explanation. Because the Hadza do not join in groups to assert exclusive rights over portions of land, or other property, because they do not unite to defend either resources or their own persons, because they cooperate very little with each other in their subsistence tasks, there is little to bind individuals to specific other individuals. People do depend on obtaining meat from other people, but they are entitled to a share of meat simply by being in a particular camp at a time when a large animal is killed there and do not have to rely on specific categories of kin or other specific individuals to supply them. With a few important exceptions, which will be described below, people depend simply on living with *any* other Hadza and not on living with a particular set of people standing in specific relationships towards them. They range widely, associating themselves now with one collection of people, now with another according to their desires and whims of the moment.

Regularities in Camp Composition

I cannot here give much of the detail which is set out at length in my doctoral thesis and which will be published in my forthcoming monograph about the regularities that occur in camp composition. But the more important regularities are as follows:

Married Couples

The Hadza refer to any man and woman who cohabit and who publicly acknowledge their cohabitation as being husband and wife, whether or not any ceremony of marriage had taken place, and whether or not the man and the woman accept the obligations which hus-

bands and wives normally accept towards each other and each other's kin. This is not to say that these obligations are of little consequence: they are, in fact, exceedingly important and a marriage is most unlikely to last unless they are accepted.

Ceasing to live together, even for a matter of a few weeks, puts a marriage in jeopardy. A husband goes away on a visit to some other part of the country without his wife at his peril. He may well find that when he returns she has either married someone else or that she has repudiated him by putting on the dress of an unmarried girl to indicate her availability for marriage. People who are stated by informants to be married are therefore almost always co-resident with their spouses. In the synchronic census I encountered 115 spouses of monogamous marriages and of these 112 were living with their spouses. The remaining three were married according to Hadza informants; that is, informants believed that the separations were temporary and that the couples would resume cohabitation. All three of the marriages were, however, demonstrably unstable. Separation, even for short periods, may be both an indication that the marriage is not entirely successful and a contributory factor to its eventual breakdown. At the same time, not all separations are necessarily either symptomatic or damaging; spouses of successful marriages do occasionally live apart for a while, but they risk their marriages by doing so.

Compared with many other societies, marriage is relatively unstable. The calculated divorce rate[3] is 49 per 1,000 years of marriage, though this is only a very rough approximation. Few figures for other East African societies are available in this form. The Amba have a rate of 31.5 (Winter, 1956, p. 39) but no figures are available for tribes near to the Hadza. The rate for England and Wales, 1950–52 was 2.8 and for the United States, 1949–51, it was 10.4 (*Demographic Yearbook*, 1968).

In comparison with other Hadza relationships, the noteworthy aspect of the marital relationship is not its instability, but on the contrary its stability and strength. A marriage is

---

3. I am using the term "divorce" loosely to refer to separation stated by the Hadza to be permanent.

broken by divorce on average only about once in twenty years of married life. In general, most Hadza men settle down and live for many years with a particular wife; to sustain the marriage they do not leave her for long on her own and they fulfill onerous obligations, described below, to her and also to her mother.

Once they marry for the first time, usually by their early twenties, very few men live for long unmarried. After the death of a wife or permanent separation from her, the husband will soon remarry. In the ten camps of the synchronic census, there was only one man who had previously been married who then lacked a wife. On the other hand there were thirteen previously married women who at the time of the synchronic census were unmarried. Of these, eight were past the menopause.

A few men have more than one wife. This complicates their residential arrangements and their position cannot be discussed here.

Parents and Children

My census data shows that children whose parents are separated almost invariably live with their mother. In adult life both men and women often live with their parents, but the emphasis is on residence with the mother. If the parents are separated or the mother is dead, it is unusual to find a man or a woman living in the same camp as the father.

Both husband and wife value co-residence with their mothers. However, residence with the wife's mother is considerably more frequent. Considering only monogamous marriages in which the spouses were living together, there were in the synchronic census 28 husbands and 34 wives with mothers alive. Twelve (that is, 43 per cent) of these husbands and 23 (68 per cent) of the wives were living with their mothers. But the emphasis on residence with the wife's mother is greater than might appear from these figures.

Let us examine the residence of those monogamous individuals who are co-resident with their spouses and who have *both* a living mother and a living mother-in-law. In the synchronic census there were 42 such people (that is, 21 couples):

> 15 couples were living with the wife's mother

> 7 couples were living with the husband's mother

> 4 couples were not living with either mother

But five of these couples were living in camps containing both mother and mother-in-law. From these five cases, no indication can be gained of any difference between the attraction of living with the wife's mother and the attraction of living with the husband's mother. If these cases are omitted, the figures are as follows:

> 10 couples were living with the wife's mother alone

> 2 couples were living with the husband's mother alone

> 4 couples were not living with either mother

In other words the monogamous couples of the synchronic census who were faced with a choice between living with the husband's mother and living with the wife's mother, had exercised their choice in favor of the wife's mother five times as often as in favor of the husband's mother.[4]

A high valuation is placed on residence with the mothers of husband and wife, yet four couples were found living in camps in which neither mother was present. As it happens, in each of these four cases, there are unusual circumstances[5] and in quite a high proportion of cases observed at other times in which a couple is living away from both mothers, there is an obvious reason to account for their behavior.

The diachronic census data support the findings from the synchronic census and allow the matter to be taken an important step further. It enables us to see whether decisions about which mother to live with are lasting. In my diachronic census, only one couple among those with both mothers alive who lived for a time with the husband's mother did not at

4. Taken alone, these figures are so small as to be worth very little. I quote them here because they are consistent with observations and figures collected at other times and because they illustrate, I think, the sort of data on residence which we need (in a more detailed form) if we are to compare the residential arrangements of hunters and gatherers.

5. The circumstances are described in Woodburn, 1964, pp. 142–44.

some other period live with the wife's mother. In this one case the wife's mother was living not among the Hadza but with a neighboring tribe.

Marriage involves an obligation, and one which is observed, to live with the wife's mother and, except in special circumstances, the only time a couple with both mothers alive will live for long away from the wife's mother is when they are living with the husband's mother. For a marriage to survive, a husband must live regularly not merely with his wife but also in the same camp as her mother. If his own mother is alive he and his wife will usually (but not always) visit her from time to time. There is no question of any obligation to live with her.

A man has important property obligations toward his wife and his mother-in-law. Long strings of bridewealth beads should be, and usually are, given by the bridegroom to his parents-in-law. They are taken and worn by the mother-in-law around her waist. Thereafter, throughout his life of the marriage, the husband should keep his wife and mother-in-law supplied with meat and with trade goods. Almost all trade is carried on by men; women rely mainly for access to these goods not on their own kin but on their husbands and sons-in-law. Beads, tobacco, and cloth are especially keenly desired and demanded. Husbands cannot afford to fail too often if they wish to preserve their marriages.

The pattern of dyadic ties that I have described links persons into a grouping which has the same genealogical composition as a matrilineal or matrilocal extended family, that is a woman and her married daughter (or daughters), together with their husbands, and their unmarried offspring of both sexes. In a few cases in which women have survived to a great age, the grouping will contain three generations of married women: the apical woman will have both married daughter(s) and married granddaughter(s) in her grouping. These groupings are not joint or extended families since they are not corporate groups and do not have a recognized head.[6] I prefer to use a neutral term and to refer to them as "simple residential units."

6. Cf. Richards (1950, p. 210), Murdock (1949, p. 33 f.), and *Notes and Queries in Anthropology* (1951, p. 72).

By stating that a simple residential unit has no recognized head, I mean that there is no institutionalized position of head of the unit, no person who exercises authority over other members of the unit whether by virtue of his or her genealogical position or by any other qualification. In some units one or more individuals may stand out as influential persons, but in other units this is not the case. However, the unit does have a genealogical focus in the person of the apical women. We might, therefore, describe the units as matrifocal, but even this is, in some cases and contexts, misleading. Sometimes, especially if the wife's mother is old or of weak character, has no husband, and has only one married daughter, it can be seen that the mother is aligning herself residentially with her married daughter and her son-in-law, rather than they with her. But usually it is the mother who, more than any other person, serves as the genealogical focus around which a simple residential unit clusters. At any particular time a camp will usually contain one or more simple residential units together with a very few people who are not members of these units. When two or more units are present in a single camp, they may be linked by kinship and affinal ties or they may not. If no tie links them, they are most unlikely to stay together long. Units which are regularly residentially associated are usually bound together by a number of close kinship or affinal ties. Not even the more important ties linking together units—such as the tie between a woman and her married son or the tie between a pair of siblings—are very highly valued or involve significant property obligations. The kinship and affinal ties of the apical woman are temporarily prior to those of the junior members of the unit and they tend to be more often used in establishing links between the component units of the camp.

Conclusion

The flexibility and variability of Hadza residential arrangements are fundamental; the regularities within the flux that is Hadza society emerge clearly only from an examination of residential arrangements through time. Such regularities as do exist are linked with the continuing property obligations of certain pairs of persons to each other, above all husband and wife, and mother-in-law and son-in-law. In Hadza society, individuals are bound to each other by dyadic property ties between relatively few categories of persons, and the type of unit that is a simple product of these ties must be distinguished from the corporate domestic and other groups, whose members cooperate, possess important joint interests, and accept authority within the group, which are characteristic of most small-scale societies.

The highly flexible social arrangements of the Hadza are by no means unique among hunters and gatherers. At this symposium, data has been presented on a number of peoples whose residential arrangements show some striking similarities to the Hadza. For instance, the !Kung Bushmen, the Mbuti, the Ik, the Dogrib, the Netsilik Eskimos, and even the Gidjingali of northern Australia all live in groupings that change frequently in size and composition.

The widespread occurrence of this flexibility brings us back to the problem of field method. The analysis of group structure is a crucial area of research, and, if comparative studies are to be of any value, it is essential that the field workers concerned develop a common body of techniques. One of the most important results to come out of the symposium on Man the Hunter may be the development of measures of general use for describing and analyzing the open and fluid social groups of hunting and gathering peoples.

12.

The Diversity of Eskimo Societies

DAVID DAMAS

SURVEY OF ESKIMO SOCIETIES

It is not necessary for the student of hunting societies to extend his survey further than the Eskimo area to gain an appreciation of their diversity.[1] The large permanent villages of the North Alaskan and Bering Sea whale hunters and the fragmented mobile groups of the Caribou Eskimo represent extremes of settlement and community types occurring within an area of considerable cultural and linguistic uniformity (Fig. 1).

Two important characteristics of social groups are the size and the duration of aggregates. Aggregations exceeding 50 and often 100 persons formed at one time or other during the year in almost all Eskimo regions. The maximal aggregates of the Caribou Eskimo which occurred at caribou drives appear to have been smaller units (Birket-Smith, 1929, p. 74). Spencer (1959, p. 132) feels that caribou drives of the similarly adapted Nunamiut attracted as many as 200 or 300 individuals, but Gubser (1965, p. 167) thinks that 50 to 150

1. The time level used in this paper is "aboriginal" since it refers to the earliest accounts or to reconstructions made by ethnographers (including the author's). My statements regarding Netsilik, Copper, and Iglulik Eskimo also rely heavily on data from societies contemporary with the Fifth Thule Expedition of 1921–24. These represent basically aboriginal groups in most important features of social organization (Damas, in press).

was the usual range. These short-lived aggregates generally lasted only a few weeks. The snowhouse encampments of most Central Eskimo groups appear to have often included more than 100 persons and at times as many as 200 (Boas, 1888, p. 425) for a usual duration of two to four months.

Considerable variation can be noted in the duration of occupancy and the size of villages composed of permanent structures (cf. Watanabe, this volume). The North Alaskan villages of up to 300 inhabitants (R. Spencer, 1959; Van Stone, 1962) were occupied for about ten months of the year, with some individuals remaining at the sites during the entire year. Villages of the stone and sod house dwelling Polar Eskimo (Ekblaw, 1948), Coast of Labrador Eskimo (G. J. Taylor, 1965), and East Greenlanders (Holm, 1914; Thalbitzer, 1914) generally averaged fewer than fifty inhabitants and were occupied for four to seven months. In these cases the Eskimo merged into larger groups at some time during the year's cycle. Economic, social, and ceremonial motives were probably all involved in this tendency to aggregate.

Kinship plays an important role in Eskimo social organization, just as it does in the organization of other hunting groups. Central Eskimo groupings reveal extensive linking of overlapping kindreds (Damas, in press a). In the absence of adequate data from other regions, continuity of kinship ties within most local groups might be expected to exist in consistency with the apparent general absence of rules of local exogamy. Matri-patrilocal residence has been reported for the Nunivak Eskimo (Lantis, 1946) and St. Lawrence Eskimo (Hughes, 1960) while matrilocality is attributed to the Nunamiut (Pospisil, 1964) and neolocality to the Copper Eskimo (Jenness,

in the case of the Eskimo of the Coast of Labrador, the polygamous joint family (G. J. Taylor, 1965). Throughout the Eskimo area spouse exchange and adoption provided a growing edge to the network of kinship.

Other structural features were peripheral to or independent from kinship. In North Alaska (R. Spencer, 1959) and in the MacKenzie delta (Stefansson, 1914) the voluntary

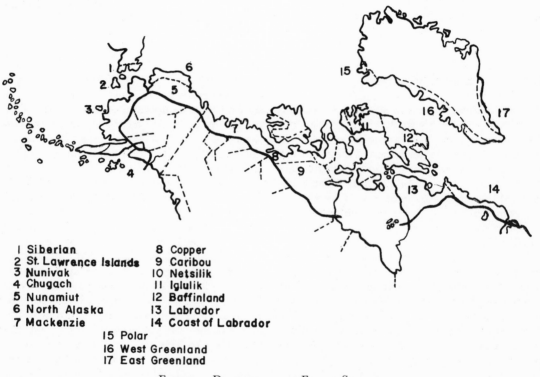

I Siberian	8 Copper
2 St. Lawrence Islands	9 Caribou
3 Nunivak	10 Netsilik
4 Chugach	11 Iglulik
5 Nunamiut	12 Baffinland
6 North Alaska	13 Labrador
7 Mackenzie	14 Coast of Labrador
	15 Polar
	16 West Greenland
	17 East Greenland

FIGURE 1. DISTRIBUTION OF ESKIMO SOCIETIES.

1922). Patrilineages occur in the Bering Sea region (Hughes, 1960; Lantis, 1946) and the patrilineal principle is projected to the clan level on St. Lawrence Island and among the Siberian Eskimo (Menovshchikov, 1964; Hughes, 1965). Elsewhere the chief kinship based segments within the community were the nuclear family, which seldom operated as an independent unit, the extended family, and

units of the whaling crew and the *karigi* or associated men's house segmented the communities. The *karigi* existed without association with boat crews on Nunivak (Lantis, 1946), but, on the other hand, the boat crew was organized according to lineages on St. Lawrence Island (Hughes, 1960) and among the Siberian Eskimo (Menovshchikov, 1964). Whaling crews were recruited from the members of adjacent villages in the case of the Chugach Eskimo (Birket-Smith, 1953).

Partnerships of various sorts were important social features in much of the Eskimo area. Trading partnerships crossed the ecological boundary between coastal and inland groups in North Alaska (R. Spencer, 1959). Seal sharing practices provided essential elements to Netsilik (Balikci, 1964, pp. 36–37; Van de Velde, 1956), and Copper Eskimo (Damas, in press b) social structures. Partnerships in dancing were also prominent in Central Eskimo society (Damas, in press b).

Whatever the chief segments or sorts of relationships that may have existed within Eskimo local groups, they were always identified by name with a territory. The postbase *-miut* or *-meit* together with a base which indicated a region, was a designation applied to major and minor local groupings among the more nomadic Eskimo as well as to permanent villages. This identification with territory seldom, if ever, implied a defense of hunting area.

THREE CENTRAL ESKIMO SOCIETIES

Table 1 has been included in order to make possible more detailed comparison with other hunting societies. It covers the general social and economic features of three major Eskimo groups studied by the writer.[2] Each of the groups represented genealogical bodies with extensive linkage within and sharp separation from each of the others. These factors together with differences in dialect and culture justify separation of the groups for purposes of analysis. The term "tribe" has been usefully applied (Helm, 1965a, p. 384) to such entities without implying political aspects of the term.

Aboriginally the 450 to 500 Netsilik (Boas, 1888, p. 454; Damas, in press a), 500 to 550 Iglulik (Damas, 1963, p. 23; Manning, 1943, p. 103) and 800 Copper Eskimo (Jenness, 1922, p. 42; Rasmussen, 1923, p. 70) were divided into groups averaging 100 members who lived part of each winter in villages established on the sea ice. These were the largest yearly aggregates and appear to have been strongly

2. Field work was carried out in the Iglulik Eskimo area in 1960–61, in the Copper Eskimo area in 1962–63, and in the Netsilik Eskimo area in 1965.

associated with the ecology of the ringed seal. However, ceremonial and social motives for assemblage probably were also important.

Fluidity in membership occured among the groups of each tribal region but the winter aggregations of two successive years were comprised of a stable core of 60 to 70 per cent of the members. I have indicated (Damas, in press a) that the hunting groups that merged in such winter camps formed the "band" and that the aggregation itself was the "band assemblage." These designations seem consistent with accepted ethnological usage. It would probably weaken the typological value of the band concept to extend its application to large permanent settlements like those found in West Greenland or the Alaskan and Bering Sea areas.

The seasonal economic cycles of the Copper and Netsilik Eskimo were identical in main features (see Table 1). The Iglulik Eskimo cycle differed in that there was greater emphasis on sea mammal hunting and less on fishing.

Band composition appears to have been uniform in the three regions. Table 1 refers to composition as "bilateral with prominence of male relevant ties." This generalization has been abstracted from charts of primary kin ties based on censuses of the Fifth Thule Expedition of 1921–24 (Mathiassen, 1928; Rasmussen, 1931, 1932). These charts reveal the predominance of male-male primary kin ties over female-male or female-female ties. Enough of of the latter two types of links occur to inject considerable bilaterality into the genealogical shape of the band (Damas, in press a).

Criteria for family type used in the table are those of residential arrangement and minimal sharing units. Among the Netsilik and Iglulik tribes the families are characterized as "virioriented extended." These groups occupied multi-family dwelling or compounds of single dwellings. They were indivisible sharing units. Usually one or more of the nuclear family heads in these units was attached uxorilocally. Factors of population structure, especially isolation through death of agnates, and bride service appear to account for such cases (Damas, 1963). The Copper Eskimo are one of the few Eskimo groups whose family structure exemplifies the nuclearity usually represented for the Eskimo in interpretive writing (Linton,

Table 1   Central Eskimo Social and Economic Features

	Copper	Netsilik	Iglulik
Seasonal Economic Cycle	Winter: Breathing hole sealing Spring: Summer: Caribou and fish Autumn:	Winter: Breathing hole sealing Spring: Summer: Caribou and fish	Winter: Breathing hole sealing Thin ice walrus hunting (secondary) Spring: *Utuq* sealing Summer: Caribou and sea mammals from kayaks Autumn: Caribou
Band Composition	Bilateral with prominence of male relevant ties	Bilateral with prominence of male relevant ties	Bilateral with prominence of male relevant ties
Family Organization	Nuclear	Extended (viri-oriented)	Extended (viri-oriented)
Composition of Hunting Groups	Variable—larger groups at caribou drives, fish runs, sewing places: (a) kin (b) spouse exchange partners (c) non-kin	Extended family, (ideal) combine with others at sewing places, caribou drives, fishing runs	Extended family, split during part of summer—larger at sewing places
Leadership	Ephemeral	*Ihumataq* heads extended family	*Isumataq* over extended family, also band *Isumataq*
Basis of Sharing Practices	Partnerships	Partnerships and kinship	Kinship—sharing among extended families regulated by band *Isumataq*
Commensal Units	Village-wide communal eating	(1) Men of extended family (2) Women of extended family	Variable—(1) Individual (2) Nuclear family (3) Extended family

1936, p. 163; Murdock, 1949, p. 227; Service, 1962, p. 99).

The structure of the family is reflected in the makeup of the hunting groups which comprised the chief local groupings during a large part of the year's cycle. In the spring the Iglulik and Netsilik winter band aggregates split into extended family clusters averaging perhaps fifteen to twenty persons each. The Iglulik split further during part of the summer when the younger men roamed inland after caribou while pairs of older men hunted from kayaks in the sea. The nucleation of the Copper Eskimo family was expressed in the irregular composition of summer hunting groups. Lacking the high degree of cohesiveness of extended family structure found in the other two regions, the Copper Eskimo hunting groups were made up either of a core of siblings, or of spouse exchange partners, or of actually unrelated or distantly related persons. In all three areas aggregations of an intermediate size in relation to the winter sealing village and summer hunting groups gathered for short periods at the sites of caribou drives or fish runs.

The diversity in the organization of hunting groups is apparent in the other features shown in the table: leadership, sharing practices, and commensal units.

Leadership was weakly developed among the Copper Eskimo and personal qualities alone appear to have been responsible for whatever authority certain individuals enjoyed. The Netsilik extended family was headed by the oldest male member, the *ihumataq*, but there appears to have been no overall band leader. This family leadership pattern was extended to cover the entire band in the Iglulik Eskimo region. The band *isumataq* was usually the head of the largest extended family unit in that area (Damas, 1963).

Sharing practices and commensal practices together formed complementary systems of distributing the catch in each area. Among the Copper Eskimo, individual nuclear family heads formed partnerships which determined the sharing of specific parts of the seal. The network of distribution was extended in the area of consumption by the practice of communal eating on a village-wide basis. In the Netsilik region, seal-sharing partnerships also existed between individuals, but the meat

thereby acquired became the property of the extended family. The two commensal units, the men and the women, ate separately in adjoining domes of the family's snowhouse compound. The catch of the Iglulik Eskimo was distributed by the band *isumataq* among the lesser *isumatat*. Their commensal units were variable and based on expediency. Sometimes the returning hunter ate alone; other meals were restricted to the nuclear family, and some were shared by the entire extended family.

The character and magnitude of variation within these three regions may not seem significant when viewed in worldwide perspective, but certainly they are important enough to require explanation.

There is an apparent integration or co-ordination of social features that can support the contention that the three societies were balanced, internally consistent units. The nucleation of Copper Eskimo families is compensated for in economic matters by highly structured sharing and communal eating. The need for communal eating appears less urgent among the Netsilik since the extended family acts as a pool for resources. Partnerships in sharing appear to be largely unnecessary among the Iglulik since the distribution of food among extended families throughout the band was provided for by the band *isumataq*.

Looking beyond the internal arrangement of these social and economic features to external explanations, an examination of the table lends little support to facile correlations. If one assumes that the chief source of regional variation of societies will be ultimately related to variations in ecology, two hypotheses could be posited for the Central Eskimo regions discussed here: (1) Uniformity of resources and exploitative patterns in the three regions are so similar that one would expect great similarity in social features. I have argued against such social uniformity. (2) Similarity in the economic life of the Copper Eskimo and Netsilik in contrast to the somewhat divergent economy of the Iglulik Eskimo should be reflected in social features. This correlation cannot be strongly supported by the table.

While a closer examination of ecological factors may reveal correlations with social structure, in the opinion of the writer that approach will fall far short of total explanation of regional variations in the Central Arctic. Historical factors of common heritage, diffusion, and cultural drift will have to be considered in this context.

This summary of some of the important social features in three Central Eskimo regions indicates that, in addition to the general diversity found among the major Eskimo areas, variability in patterns of community organization occurs within an area exhibiting highly similar or even identical patterns in the dispersal of people.

Variability provides the raw material for studies of "concomitant variation" (Nadel, 1951) or "controlled comparison" (Eggan, 1954), approaches which will be rewarding if applied in the Eskimo area. This discussion of three Eskimo groups is only a beginning to more detailed comparative studies. To extend useful comparative studies throughout the entire Eskimo area requires more detailed information about a number of groups than is available at present. However, even such a casual review of social diversity as I have given suggests further channels for enlarging the understanding of hunting societies in general.

RELATIONSHIP TO OTHER STUDIES OF HUNTING SOCIETIES

As indicated above, the concept of the band does not seem to be applicable in all Eskimo regions. Certainly within the realm of hunting societies there are peoples similar in their sedentary existence to the North Alaskan or Bering Sea Eskimo who fall outside the scope of a useful application of "band." Even if one restricts comparison to nomadic groups, difficulties arise in the use of the term "band." During a recent conference on band organization[3] it was found that the term "band" had

3. The Conference on Band Organization sponsored by the National Museum of Canada held in Ottawa, Ontario, August 30 to September 2, 1965, dealt with a number of problems that are relevant to studies of the social organization of hunting societies. The proceedings of that conference will be published in the National Museum of Canada Bulletin Series. A more complete analysis of the band composition of the Central Eskimo together with implications for the study of band societies will be found in the paper "Characteristics of Central Eskimo Band Structure" (Damas, in press) which is included in the proceedings of the band conference.

been applied to such widely variant groups as the Birhor of India with average size groups of 25 and the Peel River Kutchin group of 300 to 400 members. In trying to establish common criteria for usage, it was generally agreed that two major types of units could be subsumed under "band," those that aggregated at some point in the year's cycle and those that comprised only a conceptual unity.

A number of other factors which complicate attempts to isolate the band in nomadic hunting societies were also revealed during that conference. A careful examination of a larger sample of these societies is needed before such problems of band organization can be resolved.

Whatever term is assigned to groups that comprise a society, certain bases for comparison can be posited. Helm (in press a) states the following regarding such comparisons:

> By anthropological convention, band societies are set apart from non-band societies of all kinds. But I do not believe the features conventionally used to identify a band society—nomadism, lack of central tribal authority, and hunting-gathering pursuits ... make the problems of methodology in the analysis and classification of community composition inherently different from those encountered by perceptive ethnologists working in non-band societies.

It is possible to compare the kinship makeup and the family organization of the permanent winter villages of North Alaska with the band assemblages and family organization in the Central Eskimo regions. On a larger scale, units showing useful bases for comparison will certainly be found throughout much of the hunting and gathering world.

Reference to voluntary relationships such as Central Eskimo seal sharing partnerships or North Alaskan whaling crews or *karigi* organization suggest that classifications of the social structures of hunting groups have perhaps placed too much emphasis on kinship factors. Classifications or typologies of hunting societies should be enlarged to include features that lie outside kinship considerations. Residence and marriage practices have generally been the chief criteria for classifying bands but perhaps these features are not always the chief distinguishing attributes of band societies.

Classification of bands in the Central Eskimo area based only on kinship composition, which is uniform, tends to obscure important differences in the family organization, the patterns of leadership and food distribution practices. The selection of criteria for band types from such diverse features requires considerable care.

In addition, classifications can be meaningful only if the ethnography of individual groups is sound and approaches completeness. Just as there is no great uniformity in the quality or completeness of information about all Eskimo societies, there is no great uniformity in the data on hunting peoples throughout the world. Considerable additional research is needed before statistical comparisons of hunting groups can be highly reliable. The rapid disappearance of such groups places the problems of salvage foremost. In many cases a closer examination of ethnohistoric sources will be the chief means available for reconstructing clear pictures of such societies.

Problems of function also appear to be compounded by the variability that has been noted here. The integration of such features as *karigi* organization or seal sharing practices into societies differing in a number of other features suggests that possibly in the world at large alternate features will be integrated into similar systems and similar features integrated into otherwise contrasting systems.

Finally, problems of the adaptation of society to environment seem to become more complex when the diversity noted here is taken into account.[4] This diversity did not always conform to a concomitant variation in subsistence or ecology. Although strong arguments can be advanced for a close harmony existing between the pattern of exploitation and certain features of the settlement pattern in the Eskimo area and probably in the world of hunters as a whole, the relationships that exist between these settlement patterns and variable community patterns appear to be less rigid and perhaps will allow alternatives in every conceivable case.[5]

While the diversity of the social forms found within hunting and gathering societies may comprise only a narrow segment of the total spectrum of social types, a proper appreciation of this diversity will be an important step toward their proper classification and eventually toward an understanding of the problems of process or evolution.

4. A more detailed appraisal of ecological factors in Central Eskimo society will be forthcoming in an article by the author in the proceedings of the Conference on Cultural Ecology, Ottawa, Ontario, August 3–6, 1966.

5. Chang (1962) has applied the concepts "settlement pattern" and "community pattern" to circumpolar societies, but in doing so he assumes a closer relationship between the two systems than is espoused in this paper.

13.

The Nature of Dogrib Socioterritorial Groups

JUNE HELM

This is an attempt to characterize and categorize socioterritorial groups among the Athapaskan Dogrib Indians of the northwestern Canadian subarctic.[1] By socioterritorial, I specify those kinds of groups which conjoin settlement pattern with community pattern (Helm, in press a). That is, I am concerned both with "any form of human occupation . . . over a particular locale" or range (Chang, 1962), and with the nature of the social group constituted by the occupants of the locale or range.

The three kinds of socioterritorial groups which I identify among the Dogrib[2] I have termed the *regional band* (comparable to the "macrocosmic unit of social organization" identified by Honigmann [1946, p. 64] for the inland Northern Athapaskans), the *local band* (equivalent to Honigmann's "microcosmic unit"), and the *task group*.

Membership in these three kinds of socioterritorial entities is in no wise mutually exclusive. An individual may at the same time have social identity as a member of a regional band and of a local band, and, by the simple fact of his presence, also be a member of a task group. Segments of the local band and regional band operate as task groups (as defined below). These three kinds of groups, however, may be segregated analytically by time-and-space dimensions—namely, temporal duration and spatial (settlement) cohesion—and by

three foci around which membership revolves.

The foci of membership identification and recruitment are (1) territorial range, (2) specific resources and resource locales within the range, and (3) kinship. I see the ecological-subsistence complex of range and resources conjoined with an ego-based kinship network as the basic forces in the creation and structuring of the three sorts of socioterritorial groups. Range, resources, and kinship not only affect, but *effect*, socioterritorial organization. Furthermore, each in turn serves as the prime focus of identity and affiliation for regional band, for

1. I present the discussion in terms of the Dogribs, on whom I have the most data. I have, however, drawn on material from neighboring Arctic Drainage Athapaskan peoples to build the broad characterization which I believe to be generally applicable to the Mackenzie Drainage Athapaskans or Dene. All data are, of course, postcontact. I deal with what I judge to be the more traditional social and demographic arrangements (not treating of the trading-for settlement, for example), but the extent to which these match truly aboriginal arrangements must always remain problematical. Some of the major postcontact shifts in exploitative and demographic patterns, such as increasing sedentarization, are discussed in Helm and Damas, 1963.

2. For the purposes of brevity, I shall ignore the difficult problem of what, if anything, constitutes a "tribe" in such a simple society as the Dogrib. I suggest that in structural terms the "tribe" may be defined as the greatest extension of population throughout which is sufficient intermarriage to maintain many-sided social communication.

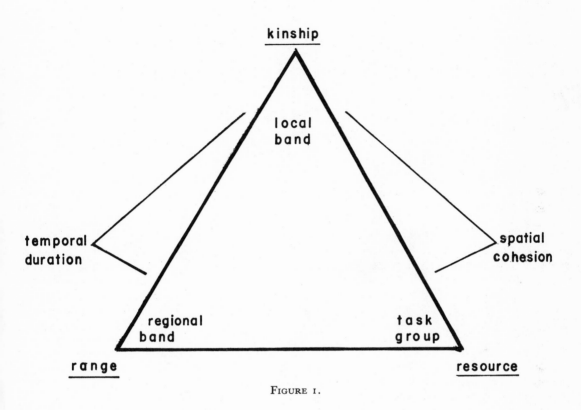

FIGURE I.

the task group, and for the local band, respectively. For the regional band, the prime focus of identity is the territorial range; a task group forms in response to a specific and localized[3] resource; the strength of primary kin bonds holds the local band together in space and through time.

The varying weight of these three factors affects the temporal and spatial dimensions

3. In this paper, the usage of "local" and "localized" in regard to human groups and resources should not necessarily to taken to mean immobility. "Local" and "localized" here refer to the spatially compacted condition of the group (e.g., a local band) or of the resource (e.g., a caribou herd), whether the group or resource is "on the move" or not.

of the three kinds of socioterritorial groups.

The triangle diagram (Fig. 1) attempts a visual construction of the interplay of the specifying and discriminating features of regional bands, local bands, and task groups. The size of these kinds of socioterritorial groups is a function of the identity-affiliation factors and the time-space dimensions. Table 1 presents a chart of the main features differentiating the three kinds of groups.

In the persons exploiting the various and variable resources within a recognized range or territory, the regional band has its social identity as a "people." The total territory yields sufficient materials for the necessities of life (famine periods excepted) so that within its

Table 1   Diagnostic Features of Dogrib Socio-Territorial Groups

	Regional Band	Local Band	Task Group
FOCI OF IDENTITY AND MEMBERSHIP			
TERRITORIAL RANGE	*Prime focus of identity.* Total range as identified by tradition and use.	Tendency to concentrate activities and movement within own range (often segment of a total regional band range) but with freedom to exploit greater range.	Specific route and/or resource locale.
RESOURCES	General exploitation of all resources within range.	General exploitation of all resources within range.	*Prime focus of identity.* Specific resource (caribou, fish, fur bearers, poitn-of-trade, etc.).
KINSHIP	Bilateral primary consanguine linkage between conjugal pairs.	*Prime focus of identity.* Bilateral primary linkage between constituent conjugal pairs, with a core sibling set as the focus of affiliation.	Relatively flexible? Apparently involving friendship and special abilities as factors in recruitment as well as the kind of kinship directives operative in band membership.
TIME-SPACE DIMENSIONS			
TEMPORAL DURATION	Several (many?) generations.	A few years to a generation or two.	Overnight* (e.g., moosehunt) to several weeks (e.g., linked-family winter trapping party).
SPATIAL COHESION	No (i.e., scattered "settlement").	Yes, most of the time (i.e., nucleated "settlement").	Yes, by its nature.
ADDITIONAL FEATURES			
SIZE (dependent variable of above features)	*Est. range:* 12–50 conjugal pairs plus dependents.	*Est. range:* 2–12† conjugal pairs plus dependents. *Est. mode:* 4	*Range variable.* *small size:* e.g., trapping party—2 or 3 men, or one or a few families; moosehunt party—2 or 3 men. *large size:* multifamily fishing camp—est. 5–15 families; fall caribou hunt—"crews" of c. 10 males each.
CONSTITUENT UNITS	Conjugal pairs and dependents; local bands.	Conjugal pairs and dependents.	Of two sorts: (a) conjugal pairs and dependents (e.g., linked-family trapping party, fish camp); (b) able-bodied males (e.g., present-day fall caribou hunt, trapping partnership, spring beaver hunt, trading party, extinct war party).

* Overnight by definition. This excludes a women's daytime berrying party away from camp-settlement, one or two persons gathering firewood, tending rabbit snares or fish nets for a few hours, etc. In other words, a task group, as defined, involves a "settlement" in the sense of Campbell's definition: "A settlement is any place occupied by one or more individuals for one or more nights, for any purpose that falls within the ordinary, expected, and predictable round of activities for the society in question."

† It is my guess that more than fifty years ago, (before extensive cabin-building) composition was less stable and the size of local bands did not attain the higher figure.

domain the regional band can endure as an identity for generations. (Table 2 presents documentation identifying and placing Dogrib regional bands.) Characteristically, the total constituency of the regional band is not physically together. The families that make up the regional band are most apt to all come together when operating as a task group exploiting a resource which allows large assembly, as at a fall fishing camp. Most of the time, physical co-presence and social communication is shifting, intermittent, and piecemeal. Within the regional band there is kin-connectedness in the form of a network of primary affinal and consanguineal ties between members.[4] But neither kinship nor a single specific resource is the focus of total group identity *per se*.

The local band also exploits a range, often as a subunit within a regional band, and, like the regional band, is "concerned with the total problem of living within its territory" (Slobodin, 1962, p. 75). But it is distinctive as a spatial grouping-together of kinsmen, characteristically structured around a core sibling set, including females as well as males, with their spouses. To nucleated-settlement pattern and core-kin focus must be added some degree of temporal duration to set the local band apart from a kind of task group.

The task group is pre-eminently a grouping-together of persons concentrating upon the exploitation of a specific seasonal resource, ordinarily at some locale or along some route within the total range of a regional band. Whether activities are coordinated and/or produce shared depend upon the particular purpose of the task group (Helm, 1965a). By definition, the task group lacks temporal duration beyond a few weeks. The social composition of the task group may either be based on the basic social building block, the family, composed of a conjugal pair with dependents, or it may be all male. It is apparent that kin linkages serve as a mechanism of affiliation in forming a task group, but there is also evidence

that friendships and special aptitudes sometimes play a role.

Task groups vary in size and in sex-age composition, depending largely upon the nature of the resource which is the focus of task group creation. Today, two or three nuclear families (usually linked by sibling and/or parent-child ties) may join together for periods of two weeks to two months of trapping, combined with general subsistence activities. The distinction between such a seasonal, linked-family task group and what I identify as a local band can be made only on the sliding scale of duration. I have suggested elsewhere that the aboriginal equivalent of today's local band may have been a relatively short-lived small grouping of this sort (Helm, 1965a, p. 379).

At the appropriate season, a task group may also be formed of many nuclear families around a fishing locale or along the route of a caribou migration. But task groups need not always be constituted of family units. Today, most hunting expeditions, for example, are all male, with the women and children left behind in camp or village.

CONCLUSIONS AND THEORETICAL CONSIDERATIONS

In conclusion, I must make some effort to clarify the nature of the kinship principle which I see operative in Athapaskan band affiliation —specifically, in post-nuptial band residence. I believe the same principle also to be, if not critical, significant in task-group assemblages.

From the Dogribs, as with other Mackenzie Drainage Athapaskans, it is impossible to elicit "rules" regarding preferential marriage or local or regional band endogamy or exogamy. So also, with post-nuptial residence, except for the traditional understanding that the young husband should "work for" (and thereby reside with or by) his father-in-law until the birth of the first child. Add to all this the fact that the people move around the land "visiting" and that occasionally some do not return from whence they came.

The results of a search for residential pattern in this seeming flux have been presented in an earlier paper (Helm, 1965a). From inspection of the kinship connections between conjugal

4. Analysis of one Dogrib regional band, the Marten Lake People, over a 50-year period reveals that every resident in three generational horizons had as fellow member of the band one or more primary consanguines (siblings and/or parents) or held the primary affinal tie of marriage to an already consanguineally linked member of the band (Helm, 1965a).

FIGURE 2. RANGES (APPROXIMATE) OF DOGRIB REGIONAL BANDS (AFTER PETITOT,
1891; OSGOOD, 1932, 1936; AND HELM, 1962 FIELD NOTES).

Some local band-hamlets are indicated by numerals (for identification, see
Table 2). The eastern reaches of Band C, Edge-of-the-Woods People, are barren
grounds, exploited only for brief seasonal caribou hunts (and, in the past, musk-ox
hunts).

Table 2   Dogrib Regional Bands: Documentation over a 70-year period

(Regional Band designations are underlined. Local group designations are not complete, but are included when noted in the literature. Designations of local bands are not underlined.)

Petitot (1891)

(A) *Klin-tchanpe:* Flancs-de-Chien, Plats-Côtés-de-Chien proprement dits-Le long de la baie du Nord du grand lac des Esclaves.

(B) *Tsan-tpie-pottinè:* gens du lac Excrementiel—Autour du lac la Martre et le long de la riviere de même nom.

(C) *Tpa-kfwèlè-pottinè:* gens de l'Anus-de-l'Eau, gens du large—Au sudest du grand lac des Ours, et à la source du fleuve Copper-mine.

(D–E) *Ttsè-pottinè:* gens des Canots en écorce, gens du Lac—Autour des rivages méridionaux du grand lac des Ours.

Est. Total Pop.: 1864—Petitot (1884–85) records 788 Dogribs trading into Old Fort Rae, plus 47 in Forts Norman and Franklin area at Great Bear Lake. Total = 835.

Osgood (1932)

(A) *Band 1:* inhabits the country close to Rae. A subdivision . . . hunts in the country west of the N. arm of Great Slave Lake to within 75 miles of Mackenzie River.

(B) *Band 2:* inhabits the country around lac la Martre and lac Grandin . . .

(C) *Band 4:* lives east of band 3.

(D) *Band 3:* occupies the country on both sides of the canoe route between Great Slave Lake and McTavish Bay. It does not come closer to Great Bear lake than lake Clut, south of Conjuror bay.

(E) *Band 5:* emigrated from band 3. Has become disassociated, living in Satudene country and trading into Norman since 1914.

Oblate Census (1911); with number of family heads (f h)

(A) (1) Les Pêches (11 f h)
     (2) "Famille Bruno"—Rivière aux Saules, aux Fort (19 f h)
     (3) Fond du Lac (23 f h)

(B) *Lac la Martre* (17 f h)

(C) *Camp Germain* (13 f h) [V.T.: main group of the Edge-of-the-Woods People.]
     (6) Maisons de Befwo (4 f h);
     (7) Kfwekat'inlin (5 f h);
     (8) Camp Gallu (9 f h);
     [Cabin sites en route to the "edge of the woods." V.T. remembers these as hamlets abandoned as a generation died.]

(D–E) *Le Lac d'Ours* Brigade Jeremie (19 r h)
     Brigade du Chef du Lac d'Ours (12 f h) [The "Brigades" probably refer to the followers of two trading chiefs. V.T.'s memory of the affiliations of men listed in each brigade does not separate the two brigades into Bands D and E respectively. Several men listed under the Bear Lake Chief's brigade V.T. assigns to the *et'at'i*ⁿ proper and vice versa. This probably reflects the shifting affiliations of families through time.]

Est. Total Pop.: 1911—Total of 132 family household units. At 1959 ratio of 6.24 persons per household unit, a total population estimate of 823 persons is arrived at. This estimate may be too high (before medical services).

[*continued*

Table 2 continued]

Vital Thomas, Dogrib informant (*1962**) plus other field data	(A)	*tagahot'i^n* : "Follow-the-Shore-People." People inhabiting the shore of the North Arm of Great Slave Lake between the settlements of Rae and Yellowknife.

    (1) Many formerly lived at Trout Rock. Many have moved. Some are now at enotah, so known as enotahot'i^n.

    (2) betcoko^{n}t'i^n: Fort People ("Big-Knife-House People.") Indians who stay at the Fort. "All the rest, couldn't say they are really Fort People, because sometimes they move out for hunting and fishing."

    (3) kareli^{n}hot'i^n: The present Marion River Village. "They came there because of good fishing there and good shelter from the wind. And everybody followed the rivers, summer and winter."

(B)   *tso^{n}tihot'i^n* : "Feces Lake People." Marten Lake People. Between 1925–52 there were two local band clusters, at (4) egak'i^{n}li^n and at (5) mi^{n}got'i^n (site of the "People of the Nets"). All have now settled around the government schoolhouse at the mi^{n}got'i^n site.

(C)   *wekwitihot'i^n* (Snare Lake People), or *detsi^{n}lahot'i^n* ("Edge-of-the-Woods People"), or *xozihot'i^n* ("Barrens People"), "depending on where they go" Until 1962–63 these people had been for some years based in the Fort. About twenty families have since started a settlement at (9) Snare Lake. The site of (7) kwekateli^n is still occupied seasonally.

(D)   *et'at'i^n* : "Next-to-Another-Tribe-People." Many frequented Faber Lake. Some now residing in bush hamlets at (10) Rae Lake and (11) Hislop Lake.

(E)   *satihot'i^n* : "Bear Lake People," beyond the *et'at'i^n*, "mostly along the south side of Great Bear Lake." Recognized by V.T. as "mostly Dogribs." Now, a few descendants in the Rae area, most at Great Bear Lake trading into Fort Norman.

Est. Total Pop.: 1959—Government count (mimeo band rolls) of Dogribs (including those in Yellowknife) = 1,023, with 164 family-household (hu-wi-ch) units, yielding 6.24 persons per unit.

* During a return to the field in 1967, it was possible to check with Vital Thomas the summary compiled from the 1962 data. Several minor emendations based on the 1967 data have been incorporated here. Data on Dogrib peopulations presently near the town of Yellowknife and others formerly south of Yellowknife are not included.

pairs in a sample of Athapaskan bands, I adduce the covert directive of primary relative relationship serving as a determinate limit on local and regional band residence-affiliation of the conjugal pair after marriage. Almost without exception, no married pair is residing with a local band or within a regional band domain unless at least one spouse of that pair, male or female, had at time of entry a primary consanguine, of either sex, already resident within the band.

In practice, this bilateral primary linkage principle allows multiple residence alternatives for the conjugal pair. From the position of male Ego, for example, the man may marry *within* the local[5] and/or regional band where he resides with his parents. Or he may, after bride-service, bring an "alien" wife back to his band. Or he and his wife may, early or later in conjugal life, elect to live with the band where his wife's parents or one or more siblings are established. Or he and his wife may link into a band where his brother or sister, married to a member of that band, resides. In later years, the man and his wife may "join" the band where a married child resides. And so on.

I have recently begun to look at other hunting societies for which ethnologists have provided data on the kin-composition of actual

5. Requisite age, unmarried status and kinship distance of the co-resident female permitting. The small size and closely kin-linked composition of the local band usually forces a man to look for a bride beyond his local band.

local groupings, short-lived or long-lived.[6] I find that Professor Lévi-Strauss' (1940) fluctuating Nambikwara bands (*a* 1 and *b* 1) display primary bilateral linkage by conjugal unit around a sibling set with a brother-leader, comparable to the Northern Athapaskan local band. The pattern of kin-composition of a sample of !Kung Bushman bands (Marshall 1960, pp. 323–33) is indistinguishable from that of Athapaskan local bands, as is Marshall's description of the chain-like residential linkage through bilateral primary ties (pp. 344–45). From Australia, the information provided by McCarthy and McArthur (1960) on the kin-composition of two Arnhem Land task groups reveals bilateral linkages between constituent conjugal pairs (with the result that men of different "country," totem, and moiety are in co-residence). Hiatt has recently specified a

6. I am indebted to Beryl C. Gillespie for her search for cases in the literature.

number of Australian aborigine societies in which the "usual common residence groups," as constrasted with the patri-line land-owning units, were composed of men of several patrilineal descent groups and in which the "small food-seeking units [task groups] commonly contained agnatic kinsmen" (1962, p. 285). In terms of who is actually "in community" with whom—for example, brother-in-law with brother-in-law rather than brother with brother—the picture of *de facto* residence association and economic interaction is quite different from that to be deduced from attributions of *de jure* patrilocality.

From these few cases alone, I submit that, for full comprehension of the economic and social dynamics of hunting societies and for cross-societal comparisons, the empirical patterns of post-nuptial co-residence, stable or shifting, demand as much attention as do formal "rules" of kin alliance and residence assignment.

14.

The Birhor of India
and Some Comments on Band Organization

B. J. WILLIAMS

This paper falls into roughly three sections. The first is a preface explaining a particular approach to the study of hunting-gathering groups and why this is used by a person whose primary interests are in physical anthropology. The second part constitutes data on a particular group, the Birhor of India, who became a subject of investigation in the pursuit of these interests. The third part explores some implications of such a view of hunting-gathering society.

My interests are those of a physical anthropologist, using, primarily, the approaches of population genetics in the study of human evolution. Some areas in which these interests are closely allied to interests of ethnology are (1) social organization as it effects mating patterns and (2) the extent to which a single model of hunting-gathering society might apply to Paleolithic groups. The problem is not whether it is possible to have more or less complex societies based on a hunting economy, but what is the modal form and how extensive might such a form have been at a given time in the past. The question is one of whether or not the findings of the ethnologist can potentially be useful in making statements about past social structures and population demography which have a bearing on genetic parameters such as total mating population size, degree of isolation, rate of gene flow, and rate of inbreeding.

Not being an ethnologist, I have proceeded in what may seem to the ethnologist a slightly cavalier fashion—to set up a model of hunting society based on certain assumptions, then to seek evidence on certain points of the model. Field investigations among the Birhor of India were a part of this endeavor. Some of the assumptions are sketched in the following paragraphs.

The broader assumptions are as follows:

1 (a). Most animals will exhibit either sexual or economic territoriality—or both.

1 (b). Animals whose variation in population numbers is strongly influenced by variation in food supply or other economic variables will exhibit economic territoriality.

1 (c). Such territoriality implies spatial aggregation.

2. Counter to the above is the ecological-economic desideratum of distributing the population homogeneously with respect to the distribution of food supply or other vital resources.

The optimal resolution of these two forces is a local organization whose size is the minimum necessary to exploit the collected foods, maintain territorial integrity and absorb or accommodate all but the rarest kinds of chance fluctuation in resources, sex ratio, and so forth.

To state a conclusion in advance of the argument, I feel that what was called the patrilocal horde by Radcliffe-Brown (1931), the patrilineal band by Steward (1938b, 1955) or the patrilocal band by Service (1962) represents such an optimal solution for hunting-gathering economies over a very broad range of environmental diversity. To what extent this kind of local organization was realized is what was debated at the symposium and in the ethnographic literature today.

This is not to agree entirely with the conceptualization of the hunting-gathering band as presented by Radcliffe-Brown, Steward, and Service, nor is it to say that the patrilocal band is the only possibility. As one interested in population genetics I am interested in the existence of a predominant form—not the full range of possibilities that might be realized, as perhaps would be the interest of the ethnologist. And I believe that what I call the lineage-band, a local group whose central members are of a single lineage, represents such a structure for hunting-gathering economics. The argument leading to this conclusion, based on the preceding assumptions, runs as follows: To go back to the concept of territoriality for a moment, we find that only among the Canidae and the Primates can multiple, sexually mature adult males be accommodated within the same, territorially autonomous, social group. This phenomenon reaches its highest development in the Primates. This has occurred in both cases through the evolution of a dominance hierarchy which can be learned by individual males and which is strong enough to override, with a certain effectiveness, sexual impulses.

In the genus *Homo* alone this system is extended to permit greater cooperation among males by the assignation of defined sexual rights which are relatively exclusive between a male and one or more females. The stable emotional ties engendered.permit cooperative behavior on a scale not found in other Primate societies. These affective ties are further extended outward in all contemporary human societies by means of what we term a kinship system, that is, symbols are attached to certain affective emotions early in the life of the child

which can then be extended by extending the symbols to a group larger than the immediately co-resident household.

Furthermore, in contemporary societies in which kinship systems provide an important part of the jural structure of society, marriage bonds are channeled in such a way as to extend these affective ties between suprafamilial social units permitting cooperative or collaborative interactions which could not otherwise be maintained and which we recognize as forms of affiliation.

I suggest that the most efficient form of local organization for hunting-gathering societies, in terms of the criteria set forth previously, is one in which marriage rules lead to exogamic marriage practices between territorially autonomous groups. This makes possible a smaller territorial group, that is, a population whose distribution is more closely correlated with the distribution of resources than if all matings had to be contracted within the group and if marriage alliances were not maintained with all surrounding such groups.

These marriage alliances serve a number of functions leading to demographic stability: (1) they reduce conflict between territorially autonomous groups (in a sense they reduce autonomy); (2) they can provide access to "windfalls" for all the affiliated bands at certain times of the year, for example, beached whales, fish run sites, passes used by migratory herds, etc.; (3) they provide a form of insurance in that matrilateral connections can be utilized (assuming patrilocal residence) in seeking haven in times of hardship, that is, the population can temporarily redistribute itself.

I suggest, therefore, that the territorial social unit most often to be expected in societies with hunting economies is an exogamous band of the minimum size necessary to maintain continuing marriage relations with all surrounding such bands. This criterion is met by a band size of 35–75 individuals. The criterion of exogamy is met in unilineal bands by unilateral cross-cousin marriage. This form of marriage was not the case among the Birhor, as will be shown below. Other practices detailed in the ethnographic literature seem to serve also to extend affiliation to surrounding groups. Among the Andamanese an unusual elaboration of adoption practices seems to have fulfilled this function. This may also have been the case to a certain extent among Eskimo groups.

The bonds of alliance created by marriage exchange are reinforced by the annual aggregation of some or all of the bands so affiliated, at a season when such gatherings are economically feasible, and under circumstances hedged by ceremony. Assuming that the autonomous local groups are patrilocal lineage-bands, the major ideological thrust of such gatherings would be to reinforce, symbolically objectify, and ceremonialize the matrilateral bonds affiliating the lineage-bands whose *de facto* existence needs little symbolic mediation.

It is for this reason that when the impact of Western civilization is such as to disrupt the normal dispersal of hunting populations—collecting them around trading posts, mission stations, cattle stations or schools—the local band organization disappears almost completely and very quickly. The matrilateral connections, enshrined in ideology, remain. They remain in some cases to organize the part-society then existing; they remain for the salvage ethnographer to retrieve. As Radcliffe-Brown said with respect to Australian groups "the local organization is the first part of the social system to be destroyed by the advent of the Europeans" (1931, p. 35).

What has been presented above is a model of hunting society, perhaps sketched so briefly as to be cryptic, which is not quite the inflexible band which seemed implicit in Steward's formulation. The territorial group, hence the group with primary autonomy, is the patrilocal lineage-band. It is capable of splitting into even smaller, non-territorial family bands in response to seasonal scarcity. It is, on the other hand, allied with a larger group of bands which permits and even requires larger aggregates for at least short periods of time. This larger grouping, because of the circulation of females and the visiting patterns involved in marriage affiliations, tends to form a cultural unity, linguistically and otherwise.

Implicit in such a model is the idea that the size of the basic social unit (or units) is not a function of environmental richness, but instead a function of the system of filiation. Corollary to this, geographic variation in environmental richness is met by variation in the size of the territory occupied by the lineage-band.

Investigations were carried on among the Birhor of Hazaribagh District, South Bihar, India, during 1961–62. The Birhor of this region are still engaged in hunting-gathering activities and provide some information on the hypotheses proposed. In some important ways the Birhor do not meet the conditions assumed in the model of hunting-gathering society. They are neither politically autonomous nor are they economically autonomous.

They live in an area that has been inhabited by tribal agriculturalists for a very long period of time. During the past 100-plus years, the area has also seen a large influx and growth of population of Hindu and Muslim agriculturalists who now far outnumber the tribal population.

The Birhor trade hunted and collected items to the villagers in exchange for rice. This exchange does not usually take place in markets. The principal game animal netted and traded by the Birhor is the hare. These, if they are to be traded, have to be traded on the same day they are caught, before they die. This necessity rules out the normal village market as an outlet. The Birhor also spend some time making rope from the inner-bark fiber of certain vines. These they also trade for rice. Many bands take such ropes to village markets; others still prefer to avoid markets.

Not only do the Birhor live in a form of economic parabiosis with the agriculturalists, but they are in some ways a politically subjugated minority. Their primary political defense, vis-à-vis villagers, is a carefully cultivated anonymity. This is a modus vivendi which fits quite well the migratory hunting pattern of the Birhor.

These conditions which are a result of intensive interaction with dominant groups makes the Birhor less than ideal as a basis for inferences about possible forms of social organization in hunting groups living only among other hunters. On the other hand, they have the great advantage of being hunters now. Therefore, the data on the Birhor is not a reconstruction from the memory of informants. The difficulties inherent in working with "memory cultures" have, I believe, been particularly important in discussions of local organization among former hunting groups and this has not been sufficiently emphasized in the literature (cf. Chapter 17a).

The Birhor band is composed of relatives, and an individual can normally visit other bands only in which he has relatives. The ability to visit another band also implies the potential of being able to join that band on a more permanent basis. Most of the males of a given band will be members of a single patrilineal descent group. These descent groups are differentiated in having slightly different pantheons, slightly different ceremonies concerning these deities, and different sacred mountains.

In a field census of 25 bands it was found that thirteen bands had only one lineage represented; eight had two lineages; three had three lineages; and one band had four lineages represented. The latter band was atypically large and semi-settled. In terms of number of individuals, even multi-lineage bands are predominantly of a single lineage. Also, since this is census data, it includes families who are involved in extended visits or who otherwise do not feel themselves permanently attached to the group in which they were censused.

The residence arrangements found in these bands often do not fit simple descriptive categories such as patrilocal, matrilocal, or the more esoteric compounds. A brief description of the composition of four bands with which the author worked most intensively is given below.

Band one: At its usual maximum, this band contained nine households. Three household heads were brothers. One was the widow of a fourth brother. One was the husband of a sister of these brothers. The seventh household head was a classificatory "brother" of the core sibling group, but his genealogy and theirs could not be traced reliably to a common ancestor. The eighth was a "son" of the classificatory brother. The ninth, who joined this band in 1961, was the brother-in-law of the eighth.

Band two: This band consisted of four households. The two elder household heads were brothers. One household head was a son of these brothers. The fourth head was a son-in-law of these brothers.

Band three: This was an unusual case in that the head of this group had been orphaned when very young and raised in a band not of his father's lineage. It is difficult, under such circumstances, for a man to secure a bride and even more unusual that he can form a band around himself. This band consisted of six households. The household heads included the old man, two of his married sons, two sons of his first wife (by an earlier husband of hers), and the son of one of the latter men.

Band four: Structurally, this was the simplest band. If consisted of the household of an old man and the six households of his married sons, the offspring of his two co-wives.

Although the genealogical connections between families in some of the bands varies widely, and in some cases could not be traced, the situation is not viewed as being this complex by the Birhor. For them, the bands were made up almost entirely of brothers and fathers and sons with their families. Of the 25 families involved, 22 fit this pattern, given the Birhor kinship system. The only three household heads who could not be fitted into a brother-brother or father-son relation were kinds of brothers-in-law. And these three, it should be noted, were not living with their wife's mother's natal band but with their wife's father's natal band. In sum, I believe that the category "patrilocal" is, at least, less misleading as a description of the residence system than any other rubric we might apply.

In a previous paper (Williams, in press), I presented evidence that extended familiarity with a local hunting area does not appear to be a factor favoring patrilocality by virtue of increasing hunting efficiency. Among the Birhor, a person who is a better-than-average hunter tends to be so whether he is in familiar or unfamiliar territory.

The Birhor do try to remain in a familiar area and, as this is by band, this takes on aspects of what could be called a "home range." These ranges overlap extensively and if territoriality is defined in terms of boundary defense, there is no territoriality. Because of their subordinate position the Birhor are in no position to exclude anyone from any area. One suspects that if they were not subordinate in this way, the situation might be different. There is some resentment towards a band which moves outside its traditional area and encroaches closely on another band. Also, there is occasionally considerably hostility toward the agricultural Santhal who sweep through on their annual "big hunt" which can remove quite a bit of game in one day.

In my earlier paper (in press) major portions of which were circulated prior to this symposium, two other points were made of interest in the present context. The first was that the descent unit characterizing the band is best termed a lineage. The second point was that the band, which has as its core a patrilineage, is extremely flexible in size and therefore not disrupted by seasonal variability in resources. By this, I mean that each lineage-bound splits into smaller band units during a part of the year and reaggregates, as the hunting improves, to again attain maximal size in May.

Marriage practices among the Birhor are fairly simple. There is only one clearly stated rule: a person does not marry a relative. Of course there is more to the situation in practice. A person also does not marry a non-relative if raised in the same band. Brother's wife's "sister" is marriageable, and in fact is almost inevitably chosen when available. Although a number of forms of marriage are named and can be described by the Birhor, only one kind commonly occurs; this is sister exchange. Often a lineage "sister" will be used.

The prevalence of this practice seems to be connected with the difficulty of arranging marriage. Most bands in the near vicinity are ruled out as they are related by marriages in the previous one or two generations. The primary interest of the elder males is to provide a wife for a son in order to keep him in the band. Therefore, daughters become important in an exchange for daughters-in-law. Since the bands between whom the marriage is being arranged are at least semi-strangers, and thus not too well trusted, the equivalence of the exchange is assured by immediate exchange of "sisters" between two men who are seeking spouses. Once this has been successful, other marriages are easily arranged by similar exchanges between these bands for the remainder of the generation. This practice is also encouraged by the fact that women are less likely to run away from a band if they have "sisters" who are also residing there.

Marriage arrangement is also rendered difficult by the fact that market items such as cloth and perhaps cheap jewelry are required as wedding gifts. In these exchanges, there is a reasonable equivalence, but the fact that they must be made seems to insure that a man without support from several families cannot arrange a marriage. For this reason, orphans often marry older widows, where such exchanges are not required. Such men will also accept residence in the wife's father's band in return for a wife, although such instances are not common.

Such marriage practices deviate from those set out in the model given in the introductory paragraphs of this material. But they deviate in predictable ways. A strong tendency toward unilocal residence is present and exogamy is present. The model, however, requires unilocal residence and exogamy by means of cross-cousin marriage to maintain ties of affiliation where stable territorial relations are present.

Among the Birhor the possibility of territoriality is completely ruled out as mentioned earlier. Therefore, for various reasons, bands do tend to "drift" over long periods of time, although they prefer to remain in a familiar area. Given these circumstances, the rule that one does not marry a relative maximizes the probability of developing kin ties with any new band encountered in the course of migration. This means that the marriage rule in practice among the Birhor effects the maintenance of marriage affiliation with surrounding groups in a long-standing situation of some territorial fluidity, much as does the rule of cross-cousin marriage in a situation of territorial stability.

Similar marriage rules whose effect is to produce obligate exogamy between territorially autonomous groups have been recorded for many hunting societies. It must be emphasized that this practice has to be viewed as different in some respects from exogamic practices between clans or other social units which exist within the context of a supraordinate political organization.

Were it not for its widespread ethnographic documentation, such a system of territorial exogamy would seem intuitively not very likely, precisely because the units involved in the exchange are territorially autonomous. One would expect marriages *between* such units to be more difficult to arrange than marriages *within* such units. In effect, the participants are sending daughters to, and are expecting daughters-in-law from, groups over which they have no control except that via sentiments which might exist as a result of prior exchanges of this kind. Further, such obligate exogamy, to my knowledge, is not found operating between territorially exogamous societies except in hunting bands. In the smallest tribal societies such as those of highland New Guinea, we find a certain, perhaps sizable, percentage of marriage between territorial groups; in royal lineages we find a great deal of marriage between territorial groups. This may be functionally equivalent in many ways to exogamy in hunting bands; that is, it serves to filiate otherwise autonomous groups.

If such is the function of marriage at the band level of social organization, we can draw further inferences concerning band organization. In human society it is not always possible to locate a strictly endogamous group. But, on the other hand, an exogamous unit can always be located. It may be exogamic in both prescription and practice, or it may be so only in practice. A further implication of marriage as filiation is that the exogamous unit must be able to maintain cohesion indefinitely without the necessity of reinforcing this cohesion by marriages within the unit. From this point, two questions immediately suggest themselves: First, what is the *largest* group in a kinship-based society having a hunting economy in which social cohesion can be maintained indefinitely without internally contracted marriages? Second, what is the *minimum* size of the exogamous group which can maintain such a system indefinitely?

The answer to the latter question can be given by considering a simple demographic requirement. That is, the exogamous group must, on the average, provide marriage connections with the average number of territorially contiguous groups—as a minimum. This must also take into account vagaries of the sex ratio and other stochastic processes which will raise the minimum size above that required on the basis of a strictly mechanical model of man. Since the number of nearest neighbors, considering a large area, will be between 5-6 groups, this sets a fairly uniform

minimum size, a size I suggested earlier as being 35-75 individuals.

With regard to the question of maximum exogamic band size, I would guess from reading ethnographic accounts and from my own work that this average maximum size will not be far from the average minimum size. The suggestion is that this band grouping which is exogamic readily tends to fission when it is of such a size as to be able to operate as two separate bands, given the minimum size criterion.

If this is the case, it is of great interest to the archeologist and the physical anthropologist as well as to the ethnologist. Since the number of nearest neighbors is a geometrical "given," it is the same for 25,000 years ago as today—the same for a rich environment as for a poor environment. If there is not a great difference between the maximum and minimum size of such groups, then the archeologist, with an estimate of population density, should be able to say what minimum distance between sites would be expected to show culturally differentiated elements. If such predictions can be confirmed archeologically, the next question will be to ask how far back they can be confirmed.

For the physical anthropologist, the implications are clear. If such a system existed in Paleolithic populations, the rate of inbreeding and of gene flow are given directly from such a model. Inbreeding and gene flow are important factors in determining the rate at which populations can become physically differentiated and the ability of populations to maintain genetic polymorphisms.

This rather simplified hypothesis of factors determining band size in such groups can be, if it is a part of the story at all, only a part. The Birhor, as I have indicated, are patrilocal and exogamous but not territorial, and they do not practice cousin marriage. Yet the Birhor clearly strive to maintain their groups above a certain size. The critical minimum seems to be somewhere just below 25 individuals. At such a level, factors other than the demography of marriage exchange apparently come into play. These may be ecological, they may even be psychological factors. In any event they seem to need fuller exploration in the studies of ethnologists.

15.

The Importance
of Flux in Two Hunting Societies

COLIN M. TURNBULL

INTRODUCTION

This paper examines the flexibility of social organization characteristic of two East African small-scale societies, the Mbuti Pygmies of the tropical rain forest of the northeast Congo and the Ik of the dry, open mountains near the borders of Uganda, Kenya, and Sudan. Both the Ik and Mbuti, as hunters and gatherers, work within their respective environments rather than attempting to alter them. Because neither is under the rigid control a truly marginal economy might impose, each is able to maintain a fluid band composition, a loose form of social structure, and to utilize flux as a highly effective social mechanism.

By flux I mean the constant changeover of personnel between local groups and the frequent shifts of campsites through the seasons. This apparent instability is, in fact, the very mechanism that gives these societies their cohesion. Both the Mbuti and the Ik are composed of many constantly shifting elements forming established patterns. Flux is expressed as recurrent fission and fusion which affects the composition of local bands. A similar state of flux is found in a number of hunting and gathering societies, such as the Hadza and Bushmen, and may be characteristic of the majority of peoples described at the sym-

posium. Before undertaking a comparison of flux in Mbuti and Ik society, a brief ethnographic sketch of each will be given.

MBUTI

The Mbuti Pygmies have been previously described by Schebesta (1938–50), Putnam (1948), and Turnbull (1961, 1965a, 1965b, 1965c). They live by hunting and gathering in the interior of the Ituri forest. There are two economic divisions: the net-hunters who live in large camps of seven to thirty families, based on communal or cooperative hunting, and the archers, who live in much smaller groups, and who hunt individually with bow and arrow. The residential units of both net-hunters and archers constantly change in composition as individuals and families circulate between the territorially based bands.

The total population of Mbuti appears to stand at about 40,000 and all of these are more or less closely associated with their Sudanic and Bantu neighbors, the Lese, Mangbetu, and Bira. This association has existed for at least several hundred years and as a consequence all pygmies speak only the languages of the village cultivators adjacent to them. What makes the continuation of their hunting life possible is the existence of the forest itself, which their neighbors fear to penetrate and to which the pygmies have become closely adapted. Their adaptation to the forest is conspicuously expressed in their technology and subsistence but is also deeply rooted in their ideology.

The Mbuti of the Epulu area, with whom I did field work in 1954 and 1957–58, practiced no agriculture, although they did engage in trade with the villagers, and spent brief periods living with these neighbors and eating their foods.

The villagers regard the Pygmies as their vassals, but, as I have argued elsewhere, the Pygmies manipulate this relationship to their advantage and maintain their primary orientation to the forest.

Ik

Very little is known about the Ik (Gullivers, 1953; Wayland, 1931), and to all outward appearances, they are predominantly cultivators. Yet, because one year out of every four or five brings a drought which destroys all crops, the Ik periodically abandon cultivation and revert to hunting. Thus, although they are cultivators for 75 per cent of the time, for the remaining 25 per cent they are 100 per cent hunters and gatherers.

The Ik, who number somewhat over 1,500, have previously been known as Teuso or Teuth, a name they reject as being applied to them only by the Dodos. They distinguish themselves from all pastoral tribes, such as Dodos, Turkana, and Karimojong, and they associate themselves with nearby hunting tribes, such as the Niangea and Napore, and even the more distant Tepes. They do so, despite a mutual unintelligibility of languages, by describing themselves and their fellow hunters as *kwarikik*, meaning "mountain people"; but they claim no closer connection with the other "kwarikik" than the common mountain environment. There is no thought of common origin. Neverthless, though separated by hundreds of miles, the environmental factor seems important enough to all kwarikik for them to recognize and feel a unity, against all others who are not mountain people.

The Ik live during the agricultural cycle in small, isolated, heavily stockaded villages that are almost as discrete as their hunting bands. Even within each village there are numerous divisions that prevent any solidification into effective corporate units much larger than the nuclear family. The divisions and subdivisions do not necessarily follow any lines of kinship, nor are they permanent. The groups may not even last the maximum duration of any one village site, namely, two years. Clan membership is only significant as a convenience for a rough reckoning of whether or not a proposed marriage is allowable. Marriage within the clan, however, does occasionally take place, and then the clan is said to have divided. One side of the dividing line is called "big," and the other "small." These features are all directly comparable to the Mbuti band, and when the Ik village converts itself into a hunting and gathering band, the same principles of organization operate with equal effectiveness, and equal fluidity.

Comparisons

Environment

The environments of the Mbuti and Ik contrast sharply. The forest of the Mbuti, for the most part, is flat with occasional hilly regions. Its climate varies scarcely at all throughout the year. The maximum annual temperature range is 20°, and the normal daily variation is usually far less, perhaps 5° (between 75° and 80°F.). Rain falls evenly over the entire area, and is evenly spread throughout the year. Game and vegetable supplies are similarly uniform in distribution, and are abundant throughout the area. There is nothing that makes one part of the forest more or less desirable than any other part at any time of the year.

On the other hand, the mountain territory of the Ik is for the most part arid, though studded with richly wooded valleys and gorges. Some areas are much more wooded while others may verge on desert. Far from the absence of seasons characteristic of the Ituri forest, the Ik habitat is one of violent climatic extremes. During the summer, the sun scorches the ground dry with its fierce intensity, while in the winter, the clouds obscure the sun, making the air cold and damp. Violent gales blow up and down the valleys, sweeping the torrential rains with them. Dry gorges become swollen rivers in minutes and, as quickly, become dry again. Small, tightly localized areas can become devastated by wind and flood, while all around these areas, it may be calm and dry. A region that fares well one year may fare badly the next. The game population is seasonally nomadic and edible vegetable supplies are tightly localized rather than evenly distributed.

In light of this contrast between the Mbuti and the Ik environments, a curious feature emerges. The Mbuti treat their stable environment as though it were unstable, creating imaginary seasons of plenty and scarcity, while the Ik treat their highly unstable environment as though it were stable, and consequently bring upon themselves alternating periods of real plenty and scarcity.

However, it should be stressed that the usual notion that hunters live a marginal existence does not apply in either case. The economies, at first glance, may give the impression of being precarious, but in fact this is not the case. Famine or anything approaching it is utterly unknown to the Mbuti who have an axiom that "the only hungry Mbuti is a lazy Mbuti."

The same axiom would have applied to the Ik, up to the drastic encroachments of both the central administration and the neighboring pastoral tribes in recent years which have hemmed them in, confined them, and hampered their traditional economy in every possible way. Yet even now it would be true to say that the only hungry Ik is one who is unable or unwilling to run the gauntlet of the various armed forces that forbid them access to major portions of their former subsistence range.

Land Use and Group Size

Naturally, the methods of exploitation of the resources vary according to the environment, as does the hunting organization and the gathering pattern. Both Mbuti and Ik hunting bands fluctuate in size from seven to thirty

nuclear families, but whereas an Mbuti band is territorially circumscribed, and is so defined, it is much less so with the Ik. An Mbuti band can comfortably confine its movements from one year to the next within 100 square miles, due to the uniform distribution of the game in the forest. An Ik band is forced by climatic fluctuations to undertake seasonal movements over large areas, up to about 10,000 square miles.

Differences due to migration patterns of game and to seasonal differences in the availability of vegetable foods have social consequences as well. The Mbuti band, as a territorial unit, retains independence for most of the year and rarely needs to share its territory with another band, while the Ik bands often come together in larger concentrations in order to exploit the localized resources.

Subsistence Techniques

What is more remarkable than the differences between these two areas is the range of subsistence organization *within* each area. Among both the Mbuti and the Ik, two styles of hunting organization are in use. The Mbuti are divided into net-hunters and archers, and the Ik into net-hunters and spear-hunters.

Regarding the Mbuti, there is no environmental reason why half of them should be net-hunters and the other half archers, although there may be some historical explanation. Nonetheless, the forest is so divided and each division regards the other as somewhat quaint and wonders how the other can survive. Yet on investigation it became clear that each half is well versed in the other's hunting technique; visitors from one division to the other have no difficulty at all in adapting to the different hunting methods. And it is strange indeed that in the same environment and with equally adequate technologies, the net-hunters regard the brief honey season as a time of plenty, while the archers see it as a time of scarcity. Each group takes appropriate measures to meet the perceived situation, the net-hunters splitting into small units, and the archers congregating into larger ones!

Among the Ik, it is equally difficult to discern why some should hold to the net-hunt (of the Acholi type) while others say that hunting with spears is more effective. Again, there appears to be no discernible differences in habitat which would explain the different styles of hunting.

Part of the explanation may lie in the fact that in both cases, the environment is generous enough to allow alternative hunting techniques. In common with other tropical hunter-gatherers discussed at the symposium, gathering of vegetable foods is fully as important a factor in diet as is hunting. Although hunting is a more prestigious activity, gathering strategies play a large part in determining the band's daily and seasonal movements. Even in the direction of their all-male spear hunt, the Ik take the distribution of vegetable foods into consideration and women are called on for advice. Thus a common basis of abundant vegetable food sources may make possible alternate and equally felicitious styles of hunting.

THE IMPORTANCE OF FLUX

Among the Mbuti, the constant process of fission and fusion that characterizes every band, is more predictable than among the Ik. The flux appears as a systematic pattern which I have analyzed elsewhere (1965a, 1965b, 1965c). The focal point of the process is the honey season, during which the net-hunters spread out into fragmented subbands, sometimes uniting siblings, sometimes dividing them, but always separating antagonistic elements. At the end of the honey season, the band begins to re-form, carefully avoiding any lines of fracture that remain unhealed. The net-hunters normally form bands larger than those of the archers, for a net-hunt demands cooperation between a minimum of six or seven nuclear families, and allows a maximum of thirty. The honey season, they say, is a time of such plenty that the game can easily be caught by hand, and so there is no need for the large cooperative net-hunt. During the previous ten months, the necessity of constant cooperation, and the proximity and intimacy in which all band members must live with one another, invariably gives rise to numerous latent antagonisms and even a few open hostilities. If hostilities were to go unchecked, it would destroy the essential unity of the band

and consequently ruin the success of the hunt. Thus the honey season is an important safety-valve, allowing for the radical reconstitution of face-to-face groups.

The archers, in exactly the same environment, do precisely the reverse. They hunt in maximal bands *only* during the honey season, and for the rest of the year split up into minor and ultimately minimal segments. Their stated rationale is that the honey season is a time of poor hunting, and thus, maximum cooperation is demanded. The reality is that whereas the net-hunting band is of necessity united throughout the bulk of the year, the archer band is splintered into tiny segments, sometimes only two or three families, each independent of others. The ideal number of archers for either tracking or ambushing game is three; five would already be felt as unwieldy. The composition of these small segments does not remain constant throughout the year, anymore than does the composition of the net-hunting band, but the net-hunters must endure close association with much greater numbers of people than do the archers.

When hostilities come into the open, the solution is for one or the other disputant to pack up and leave. But the very size of the minimal archer segments means that the healing of internal disputes is of much less concern to them during the honey season than it is to the net-hunters. The problem for the archers is how to maintain any semblance of band unity under such conditions, and band unity must be expressed, for territory is defined by bands, just as bands are defined by territory. It is essential that territorial boundaries should be known so as to avoid any conflicts that might arise due to allegations of trespass or poaching. The need, then, is for each band to draw together all its scattered segments and to act as a band, within its territory, for at least some part of the annual cycle. On the excuse that hunting is poor at the honey season (I could find no justification for the excuse, though I prefer to leave it an open issue), the archers of each band gather together and participate in the *begbe*, or communal beat, which in technique is similar to the net-hunt.

The Ik band is similarly in a constant state of flux, and again, its composition is determined primarily by non-economic factors.

The process, though less predictable than that of the Mbuti, clearly does not follow any unilinear descent pattern in fission. Age and territoriality are prime factors in the regulation and definition of the band, and the conflict-resolving aspects of its shifting composition are predominant. The Ik also have a honey season, which comes at a time of general abundance. Communal activity breaks down, even during the agricultural cycle, and major changes in band composition are likely to take place in adjustment to political factors by separating antagonistic segments. The honey season is followed by a termite season which breaks the band into its minimal segments and takes these far afield—during the hunting year. At the end of this season, the bands gradually re-form into agricultural units, if rain promises well, and cooperate in the building of new villages and the hoeing of new fields. However, each village retains the internal divisions of the hunting bands, though, as with the Mbuti, the Ik seldom revert to previous groupings.

POLITICAL AUTHORITY

There is no form of centralized authority in either society, apart from the nominal authority vested by the European administrations in their appointed headmen. This lack is perhaps at first surprising, considering that both Mbuti and Ik are divided into virtually autonomous bands with no formal system of interrelationship, and that each band is constituted in such a way as to create the minimum of cohesion within itself. Even nuclear families are not the solid social entities we might expect them to be. It is difficult to see what are the threads that hold each society together as such, for despite the apparent lack of cohesion, both the Ik and the Mbuti are strongly united, as peoples, in opposition to their neighbors.

On the contrary, in each case there is a strong hostility felt towards any individual who aspires to a position of authority or leadership. Hostility is even shown towards those who, without any such aspirations, are plainly better fitted to lead than others by virtue of sheer ability.

Part of the answer lies again in the environment, for while it determines certain aspects of the mode of economic exploitation, within that general framework it leaves a large margin of latitude and always allows the certainty of, at the very least, a sufficiency of food, if not a surplus. This assurance of food is clearly seen in the unpredictability of the daily hunt. Even when game is known to be close, a band (in either society) may well at the last moment decide not to go hunting at all. It may find an excuse, such as a trivial dispute, or it may not bother to find any. The result may even be hunger on that day. Yet when already sated with successive days of good hunting and feasting, a band may decide to set off in the most unlikely direction and return, at the end of a long and arduous day, with nothing to show for it. Sometimes rain will make hunting impractical, and again hunger might ensue since neither society (the Ik considered in their hunting cycle, here) will store or keep anything for the morrow. After two or three consecutive rainy days, which is about the maximum that can be expected, a fine day may dawn and find the band still determined to stay in camp and attend to unimportant chores.

A band may hunt as a single unit, or it can split up and hunt as several independent units. There is no predicting which it will do among the Ik, where seasonal variations are strongly marked, yet among the Mbuti where there are virtually no seasons (except for the two months of the years during which honey is available in addition to all the usual food supplies) the process of fission and fusion is clearly predictable.

It all seems to be a rather topsy-turvy world for both Mbuti and Ik, where the things that happen are those that could least reasonably be expected. I am perhaps somewhat over-emphasizing the lack of organization, but here that seems important, for all too often hunters and gatherers are expected to set a shining example of social organization at its simplest and its clearest, and to illustrate with crystalline lucidity the fundamental principles upon which all respectable social systems are based.

The fact is that both the Mbuti and the Ik work within their permissive environments rather than attempting to control them. They are unencumbered by the rigid imperatives that would be imposed by a truly harsh environment. Thus they are able to maintain a fluid band composition and a loose social structure; and are able to utilize this flux as a highly effective social mechanism, providing scope for action in all aspects of social life.

CONCLUSIONS

In summing up, I want to stress three points. First it seems clear that it is environmental permissiveness and not environmental rigor that makes possible the system of flux. Second, the major function of flux is not ecological adaptation but what could be called political adaptation. And third, the fission and fusion of individuals and groups does not follow lines of kinship.

The relative abundance of food that obtains in both traditional situation permits the system of flux. It allows for the fluidity of composition that affords a simple means of averting disruption without imposing a legal mechanism that would in itself be even more disruptive to the total society. The predictability of food supplies allows for neighboring bands to plan their movements so as to avoid conflict.

It is plain that in each case the process of fission and fusion follows lines of dissent rather than those of descent, and that the major function is conflict-resolving. At no time during the process can any trace of the concept of unilinear descent or affiliation be found. The band can only be defined as that group of individuals living and hunting within recognized territorial boundaries at a given time. A cross-cutting loyalty is formed by attachment and cooperation between age-mates, age being the vital bond that takes clear precedence over kinship, among both the Mbuti and the Ik.

Another function of flux might be said to be religious, for, by deemphasizing stability in interpersonal relations, the process throws the people into closer recognition of the one constant in their lives, the environment and its life-giving qualities. Under such conditions of flux where band and even family relations are often brittle and fragmentary, the environment, in general, and one's own hunting territory in particular, become for each individual the one reliable and rewarding focus of his attention, his loyalty, and his devotion.

16.

Southeastern Australia:
Level of Social Organization

ARNOLD R. PILLING

In 1889, when only those aboriginal tribes in the eastern half of Australia were well known, Alfred William Howitt, one of the great pioneers of Australian ethnology, proposed that the well-watered coastal areas of Australia had an "advanced social development." Howitt's nineteenth-century evolutionary reasoning is best expressed in his own words:

> With the exception of that part of North-Eastern Queensland where the Kamilaroi type touches the coast, the whole of the coast tracts, speaking broadly, between the Great Dividing Range and the sea, both in Queensland and New South Wales, and between the Murray River and the sea in Victoria and South Australia, were occupied by communities having abnormal types of class system which in most cases count descent through the male line. These coast tracts, taken as a whole, are the best watered and the most fertile parts of Australia, and moreover, the richest in animals and plant food for an aboriginal population.
>
> This coincidence of advanced social development with fertility of country is not without some significance. The most backward-standing types of social organization, having descent through the mother and an archaic communal marriage, exist in the dry and desert country, the more developed Kamilaroi type, having descent through the mother, but a general absence of the Pirauru

marriage practice is found in the better watered tracts which are the sources of all the great rivers of East Australia; while the most developed types having individual marriage and in which, in almost all cases, descent is counted through the father, are found along the coasts where there is the most permanent supply of water and most food (Howitt, 1889a, pp. 33–34).

For those unfamiliar with the ethnographic descriptions available in 1889, it should be stated that the "Pirauru marriage practice" is a variety of ceremonial sexual license reported for the Dieri of the arid Lake Eyre area of northeastern South Australia, which Howitt and others in that era interpreted as the only occurrence, surviving into modern times, of the hypothetical original form of human mating, so-called "group marriage," in which a group of males was alleged to be married to a group of females.

Today most anthropologists reject the Dieri *pirauru* as evidence of group marriage; in fact, during the twentieth century, group marriage has been rejected by the majority of social anthropologists as an ancestral form of marriage. Likewise dismissed as invalid is any assertion that either matrilineal descent or patrilineal descent, by itself, may be taken as evidence of an advanced social stage.

Yet there still lingers on the suggestion that southeast Australia, the area specified by Howitt, in some way represents a unique level of social development.

Some of the writers on aborigines claim as features of the aboriginal social structure of the Southeast such traits as powerful chieftainships, social stratification as exemplified by hereditary chieftainships, and "a more advanced type of political organization" and, by reporting such occurrences, appear to validate for the Southeast a level of social organization not known elsewhere in Australia. To be specific, powerful "chiefs" or "kings" were noted by several early chroniclers; for instance, Howitt (1904, p. 337) cites William Thomas, a Guardian of Aborigines in the Colony of Victoria in the 1850's (W. Thomas, 1878, p. 118), as the author of such statements. Howitt, himself, alleged an emergent variety of social stratification when he suggested that the chieftainships of southeastern Australia tended to be hereditary. In 1940, Norman B. Tindale (p. 150) specified the Kamilaroi and Wiradjuri tribes of southeastern Australia as having "the beginnings of a more advanced type of political organization"; while, in 1953, Tindale's assertion was accepted by Joseph B. Birdsell, who attributed this advance to "matrilineal descent" (pp. 175, 193).

Southeastern Australia includes a relatively well-watered coastal area. Therefore, a proposition made by Elman Service becomes significant when the social and political level of this region is discussed. Service writes:

> [An] interesting characteristic of Australia is that a regular progression from the rich, rainy, coastal areas with their large and relatively sedentary local groups to the desert interior with its widely scattered, small, wandering population is equally a progression from *least* formality and complication in the former to *greatest* in the latter area (1962, p. 74).

This assertion of less formality and complication for rich, rainy, coastal areas is in apparent contradiction to any claim of a more advanced social level for coastal southeastern Australia. However, both are claims of a special social and/or political level for this area. In contrast to such suggestions of a unique variety of social organization for all or a part of the southeast, in 1950, Birdsell (p. 279) stated that "the low level of social organization attained in Australia was constant and nowhere permitted the successful governing of large groups of people."

Clearly, there is need for a review of the data on social and/or political level in southeastern Australia. The question which the present paper will try to answer is: Are the social and political patterns known for any of the aboriginal tribes of southeastern Australia sufficiently distinct to warrant a placement of these hunters at a different social level than other Australian aboriginals?

In answering this question it is relevant to consider (1) the data on powerful chieftainships, (2) the material concerning social stratification and hereditary chieftainships, (3) problems relating to the complexity of social organization in southeastern Australia, and (4) the evidence for a more advanced political organization among the Kamilaroi and Wiradjuri tribes.

LIMITATIONS

Before turning to the major topics, two serious limitations of the present paper should be made explicit.

1. I have not been in a position to carry out actual on-the-spot ethnographic investigation of problems prior to preparation of this paper. In fact, probably no investigator working in the last fifty years could have collected much meaningful data in southeastern Australia on the subjects under consideration, for our interest is in the pre-European patterns as they existed in the Australian state of Victoria primarily, prior to 1835. Any field worker undertaking the present study in 1966 would suffer from the same lack of firsthand experience with the pre-European societies being considered, for as early as 1880 Howitt (p. 224) stated that the information he could collect on Kurnai local groups was "imperfect," but was "all that . . . [could then be] rescued from oblivion, and must suffice."

2. The number of primary sources available to me is to a degree inadequate for the study at hand; some of the rarer published sources

have not been accessible. Only by months of touring local libraries, archives, and newspaper offices can one collect the data for detailed ethnohistorical analysis such as should properly be the foundation of the present paper. But even with the references available, tentative conclusions about the social level of the Southeast can be reached.

POWERFUL CHIEFTAINSHIPS

Some early writers on southeastern Australia stressed the power of native leaders by using labels such as "king" (Howitt, 1904, p. 307, citing William Thomas). For instance, Thomas Honery writing about the Wailwun tribes of western New South Wales in 1878 (p. 250) refers to their headmen as "kings"; while R. H. Mathews (1896c, p. 296), reporting events of the same tribe about fifteen years later, notes that the local whites use the "king" designation for a native local leader. Mathews (1894, pp. 110–11) also mentions the use of the "king" label by a Kamilaroi for a headman during a ceremony in 1894; while a northwestern New South Wales half-caste informant of Beckett (1958, p. 104) still retained the usage in the 1950's.

Howitt discusses the use of the terms "king" and "chief" by early writers and states:

> I have chosen the term Headman as being less likely to be misunderstood than that of Chief, which has associations not applicable to the Australian savage. But if we must use the word Chief to imply a person having power to direct the people of his class or tribe, and that his directions or orders are obeyed by them I say . . . [there] are Chiefs. Although when compared with those of well-known tribes in other parts of the world, their power is limited, yet it is an actual power command, coupled with a certain measure of ability to compel obedience (1904, p. 320).

Similarly, Le Souëf states, concerning the tribes of Victoria:

> A good deal has been written and said about chieftainship, but nothing of the kind exists; there are certainly a few men—generally the

boldest and strongest and very often the most mischievous—who acquire some ascendency in their tribe, but they have not recognized authority as the American Indian chiefs have (1878, p. 295).

It would appear that any assertions of powerful chieftainship for Victoria are overstatements of the type of leadership present; leadership was essentially of the same type in southeastern Australia as elsewhere on the continent.

SOCIAL STRATIFICATION

The assertion by Howitt (1904, p. 319) that in some tribes the local group leadership passed from father to son might be taken as a suggestion of a kind of minimal occurrence of social stratification. Howitt, indeed, states:

> Most of the Headmen were related to each other by marriage, and thus in a family . . . where there was a tendency for authority to become hereditary, there was a germ of a practice which, under favourable circumstances, might have established a privileged family, such as some of my correspondents have spoken of (1904, pp. 310–11).

However, I would suggest two possible circumstances under which transmission of local group leadership from father to son should not be taken as the emergence of social stratification as an occurrence in the aboiginal Southeast. The first of these explanations would acknowledge the existence of such transmission, but would question its presence in the pre-European era. Beckett (1958, p. 104) notes that in some parts of Australia local cattle and/or sheep station owners formerly appointed a special local tribal elder as "king." It would seem possible that the station-owning family would also impose English primogeniture as it applies to titles when the office of "king" was again vacant; indeed, the aboriginal group may have borrowed the British pattern of inheritance for kingships in imitation of English royal pattern without any overt statement by the station owners as to how the kingship should pass on to the next generation. As Howitt's data were collected at least thirty years after the initial settling of the

Southeast by Europeans, it seems that such a European pattern may have, by then, become accepted pattern in some tribal groups, without it necessarily reflecting pre-European patterns.

A second possible explanation rests in part upon the general presence in Australia of "gerontocracy/polygyny," as discussed by F. G. G. Rose (1960b) for Arnhem Land and other Australian groups. Le Souëf reports gerontocracy/polygyny, apparently for all Victorian Aboriginal groups, when he writes:

> Polygamy is universal; but it is generally the old men of the tribe who have the greatest number of wives. The reason of this is that they exchange their young daughters for young wives for themselves (1878, p. 291).

Rose (1960b, p. 119) notes the same pattern for the Kurnai.

A survey of the pre-European data for Tiwi (Pilling, 1961, Table 1) showed that five "big men" (or headmen) allegedly sired 76 children; while 14 "ordinary married men" allegedly sired 42 children, meaning, in this instance, that about two-thirds of the children born were sired by headmen. That is, a man with several wives and many children was more likely to become a leader, a leader had the prestige which brought him more wives, and more wives produced more children. On an average, such a headman, at his death, had more adult sons; there would be more votes cast by these sons than by all other men in the group; and this feature alone would favor one of these sons, usually the eldest, being chosen as the next leader. That is, in southeastern Australia, as well as elsewhere on the continent, a son may inherit his father's headmanship, without such an occurrence being a suggestion of social stratification, when the majority of men are the sons of headmen, as was probably often the case in aboriginal local groups.

COMPLEXITY OF SOCIAL ORGANIZATION

Elman Service's statement (1962, p. 74) that there is "a regular progression from the rich, rainy, coastal areas with their large and relatively sedentary local groups to the desert interior with its widely scattered, small, wandering population is equally a progression from *least* formality and complication in the former to *greatest* in the latter area" needs detailed evaluation. Yet such a task is hampered by an uncertainty as to what is meant by "formality" and "complication" in his statement. The way in which one is to measure the complexity of social organization in hunting and collecting groups needs explicit statement. Does Service mean that there is a larger number of status terms, as he implies at one point (1962, p. 73)? Does he mean there are more non-kinship status terms?

What Service means by "formality" and "complication" becomes obvious by reference to his page 74, where he states that his criterion is "more kinds of sodalities," which he seems to define as *non-residential special-purpose groups* (1962, p. 21).

To test Service's generalization, let us compare the number of "kinds of" "non-residential special-purpose groups" (1962, pp. 74, 21) for several coastal areas with those for the desert tribes. Service lists for desert tribes three kinds of non-residential special-purpose groups: (1) initiation-centered sodalities, (2) totemic "clans," and (3) blood-brotherhoods (Service, 1962, p. 74). Reference to the Kurnai for southeastern Australia shows at least two, and probably three, varieties: (1) initiation-centered sodalities (Howitt, 1904, p. 616–38), (2) totemic sex moieties (Howitt, 1904, pp. 148–50), and (3) totemic "clans" (Howitt, 1904, p. 135). The Gournditchmara tribe of western Victoria also has two, and possibly three, types of sodalities: (1) totemic matri-moieties, (2) totemic matriclans (Howitt, 1904, pp. 124–25), and (3) initiation-centered sodalities (Howitt, 1940, p. 690). Clearly, one cannot say that the number of "kinds of . . . non-residential special-purpose groups" is dramatically higher for the arid parts of Australia than for the two southeast Australian groups noted.

However, the invalidity of Service's generalization becomes even more conspicuous when one lists the number of kinds of sodalities for the Tiwi, a north coastal group: (1) "one-grandfather" or *aminiyati* groups, (2) patrilineal dance groups, (3) totemic matriclans,

(4) totemic supermatriclans, (5) totemic matri-phratries, (6) unnamed matrimoieties, (7) named subdivisions of matriclans, dependent upon recognized alternating genealogical generations, and (8) initiation-centered sodalities (Pilling, 1958, pp. 43–73).

Let the preceding suffice to illustrate that there is no justification for claiming that Australian desert groups have a significantly more complex social structure than every Australian coastal group, including those of the Southeast. In fact, I would stress that we are very far from knowing how to measure complexity of social organization among Australian, as well as other, hunting groups.

KAMILAROI AND WIRADJURI

The assertions of Tindale (1940, p. 150) and Birdsell (1953, pp. 175, 193) that the Kamilaroi and Wiradjuri tribes have "a more advanced type of political organization" are worthy of evaluation. It should be noted initially that these recent assertions of an advanced type of political organization relate not to coastal tribes in southeastern Australia, but to the tribes of the headwaters of the great Murray-Darling river system. Tindale states that a general positive correlation between amount of rainfall and density of population does not seem to hold

> among the Kamilaroi and Wiradjuri, where especially widespread communities seem to have developed in relatively fertile country (1940, p. 150).

Birdsell writes:

> Consolidation among tribal groups seems to have occurred in the central interior of New South Wales, among such tribes as the Kamilaroi and Wiradjuri. This trend appears to reflect the development of a more advanced type of political organization based upon matrilineal descent (1953, p. 175).

The statement of Tindale above does not indicate why he believes the Kamilaroi and Wiradjuri may be said to have "the beginnings of a more advanced type of political organiza-

tion." We must, therefore, attempt to test the validity of his claim without any hint as to the basis he used to determine the political level of these tribes. The relative power of the headmen, the existence of hereditary headmanships, and the number of kinds of sodalities (as defined by Service) will be our measures.

Powerful Headmen

In regard to the power of headmen, it is noteworthy that the term "king" was used by a native in 1894 for an image of a Kamilaroi headman, but in a context which seemed to disclaim that such a "king" was then viewed as awesome by young aboriginal males (Mathews, 1894, pp. 110–11). Mathews' (1897b, p. 151) description of a northern Kamilaroi Bora, or initiation, ceremony in the 1890's states that at one point during the ceremony "one or more of the head men of each tribe stand out in their turn." Mathews (1894, p. 106) also reports the Kunopia local group of the northern Kamilaroi as having two leaders in 1894, while the Gundabloui group of the same tribe had but one headman. Elsewhere, Howitt writes of the northern Kamilaroi:

> Mr. Cyril E. Doyle, writing to me of the Kamilaroi blacks of the Gwydir River, says that the old men of the tribe formed a council which managed all matters of importance. It was they who sent messengers to distant places (1889b, p. 322).

Concerning the southern Kamilaroi, Howitt states:

> As to the southern tribes of the Kamilaroi, situated to the northward of Maitland, I have evidence dating back to about 1830. There might be two or three Headmen in each division of the tribe. Their position was one of influence and authority, and depended on the valour of the individual (Howitt, 1904, p. 302).

In regard to the statements above, it should be noted that both Mathews and Doyle seem to use the term "tribe" for local group; while Howitt employs "division of the tribe" to designate such a unit. If these interpretations of terms are correct, close analysis reveals new information. The early reports on the Kamilaroi, that of Doyle and that for the area north of Maitland, do not mention supreme local group leaders, but only a kind of council of several elders; the occasional occurrence of a single local headman is not mentioned until the 1890's, more than fifty years after the area was first settled by Europeans.

Apparently somewhat in contrast to the above opinion, Howitt writes:

> The oldest Headman would be the chief or principal man in the council of elders. He could carry a measure by his own voice, as the Kamilaroi have great respect for age. The Headman had a great amount of authority, and all the disputes among the members of his division of the tribe would be settled by him (1904, pp. 302–303).

The context of this statement becomes clearer when one refers to other of Howitt's words:

> The greatest *Bora* of all the Kamilaroi tribes was always held at Terryhaihai. All the Headmen were there, and the oldest was the principal, or president of them, and he could carry some decisions by his own voice (1904, p. 594).

Howitt's reference to the power of the oldest or principal headman may easily be no more than a statement in relation to his functioning at the time of Bora ceremonies, and probably relates to the era after the provision of government rations during Boras allowed greater attendance at Bora ceremonies.

The concentration of power in the hands of the oldest headman at a Bora suggests that in this context a single male became the Kamilaroi leader. However, in contrast to Howitt's statement suggesting that all Kamilaroi assembled for Boras, Mathews' accounts (1894, 1895, 1896c, 1897b) of Boras in the 1890's make it clear that such ceremonies did not bring together males from all Kamilaroi local groups, so that such a ceremonial leader did not become even temporarily *the* Kamilaroi leader.

In summary, it appears that Kamilaroi local groups may never have been led by a single senior male in the pre-European era, but were occasionally considered to be so controlled in the era after the Europeans appointed "kings." At Kamilaroi Bora ceremonies, the oldest headman present assumed the leadership of the whole assembled group, at least by the late nineteenth century. Such a pattern of leadership is not especially complex or elaborate for aboriginal Australia, nor does it suggest an especially powerful occurrence of leadership for the Kamilaroi. For instance, Howitt (1904, pp. 297–98) notes that among the Dieri of the arid interior in the 1880's that "some one [of the headmen] is superior to the others" of the tribe, and by then had become essentially *the* tribal leader; while Howitt (1904, pp. 314, 526) suggests for the Yuin of the southern coast of New South Wales that each local group had only one leader, one of whom assumed the headship of the Yuin tribal Kuringal ceremony.

What little is known of local group leadership for the Wiradjuri suggests that this tribal group had no more powerful local leaders than the Kamilaroi. Howitt says:

> In the southern Wiradjuri a Headman is called Bidjabidja, and, as I have heard him described, is one who "gives orders to people," there being a Headman of this sort in each local division. . . . If, for instance, he were the oldest Yibai [one of the four intertribal sections—A.R.P.] . . . he would be the head of the Yibai sub-class; but, assuming that he also became the Headman of the local group, then all the people of that division, not only of this "Budjan" (sub-class), would obey him. Each totem also had its Headman. I have heard the *Bidja-bidja* spoken of by a term equivalent to "master," this being the analogue of the *Biamban* of the Yuin (1904, p. 303).

Another passage by Howitt causes one to realize that there were usually several headmen in a Wiradjuri local group:

> In each locality the oldest man of any totem [named division of the four intertribal sections—A.R.P.] is the head of the totem there, and the oldest man of any totem is the head of that as a whole. Important messages, such as those relating to the initiation ceremony . . . are sent by a headman. The messenger must be of the same totem as the sender, and the messenger is sent to the oldest man of the same totem in the locality to which the message is sent. This oldest man is the head of the totem there (1889b, p. 321).

Mathews (1897d, p. 118) in his discussion of the Burbung initiation ceremonies of the Wiradjuri indicates that the local headman of the host locality acts as the "initiator," that is the person who initiates arrangements for the Burbung ceremony. Beyond this minor office, no single individual seems to have held a special role during Wiradjuri initiations.

In general, we may say that the role of the headman among neither the Kamilaroi or the Wiradjuri seems outside of the range of political power found elsewhere in southeastern Australia and seems somewhat less powerful than that held by the Dieri tribal headman.

Hereditary Chieftains

The existence of families which have produced many chiefs or a strong tendency for hereditary chieftainships might have caused Tindale and Birdsell to assert the existence of a more advanced political organization for the Kamilaroi and Wiradjuri. However, the evidence does not support an unusual development of hereditary leadership for either group. Howitt says of the Kamilaroi office of headman:

> It was not hereditary, but a man who distinguished himself as a warrior or orator would become a leader by mere force of character, and his son, if valiant, would be very highly thought of (1904, p. 302).

Of the Wiradjuri, Howitt writes:

> The office of Headman was in a sense hereditary, for a son would inherit the position of his father, if he possessed any oratorical or other eminent ability. But if not, then the son of the brother of the deceased Headman would probably hold the position, and failing him some qualified relative of the same sub-class. But this was with the consent of the community, for the office went in fact by election in each division (1904, p. 303).

Quite obviously, neither the Kamilaroi or Wiradjuri had sufficiently hereditary chieftainships to mark them as distinct from other Australian groups.

Number of Kinds of Sodalities

Service's suggestion that social complexity should be judged in terms of the number of kinds of non-residential special-purpose groups causes one to turn to this topic in order to measure the sociopolitical level of the Kamilaroi and the Wiradjuri. This area is well documented for the two tribal groups. The Kamilaroi have five varieties: (1) matrimoieties; (2) four sections, with determination of membership based on the maternal section (Radcliffe-Brown, 1931, p. 230; Mathews, 1897e, p. 160; 1904, p. 214); (3) totemic matriclans (Mathews, 1897e, p. 159; Radcliffe-Brown, 1931, p. 230); (4) a second matrimoiety system, which was probably reflected in the residential pattern, and consisted of the "blood" and "shade" divisions (Mathews, 1904, p. 209; Radcliffe-Brown, 1931, p. 232); and (5) Bora-centered sodalities (Mathews, 1894, 1895, 1896c, 1897b). The Wiradjuri of the upper portion of the Murrumbidgee River (Mathews, 1897e, p. 175), likewise, had four, or possibly five, kinds of sodalities: (1) matrimoieties; (2) four sections, with determination as among the Kamilaroi (Mathews, 1896a, 1897a, 1897e, pp. 173–74; Radcliffe-Brown, 1931, p. 230), (3) named, totemic subdivisions of these sections (Mathews, 1897f, pp. 173–74), (4) Burbung-centered sodalities (Howitt, 1884, pp. 438, 443, 445, 447, 452, 455, 456, 458; Mathews, 1896b, pp. 38, 39; 1896d; 1897c; 1897d), and possibly (5) "blood" and "shade" matrimoieties (Radcliffe-Brown, 1931, p. 232). The remainder of the Wiradjuri tribal area is alleged to have the Kamilaroi pattern of organization (Mathews, 1897e, p. 175).

If one rates societies in terms of the number of kinds of non-residential special-purpose groups, the interior Kamilaroi and Wiradjuri tribes show an incidence of a couple of more types of units than either the desert Aranda or the coastal Kurnai; they have fewer types of sodalities than the north coastal Tiwi. The Kamilaroi and Wiradjuri are not significantly outside of the range of other Australian groups, if one measures political advancement in terms of the number of kinds of sodalities.

Matrilineal Descent

Birdsell asserts as mentioned before that the alleged Kamilaroi and Wiradjuri political advance is "based upon matrilineal descent" (1953, p. 175). His phrasing suggests two possible interpretations: (1) the occurrence of matrilineal descent among these tribes caused Birdsell to classify them as more advanced, or (2) the allegedly "more advanced type of political organization" was the product of some aspect of the matriliny of the social patterns of these tribes. Few modern anthropologists would accept as meaningful the classification of a tribe as more advanced simply because it had matrilineal descent, so we may safely exclude the first possibility, and limit our discussion to the second.

Can the existence of matrilineal descent have been the sole cause of whatever feature of Kamilaroi and Wiradjuri society is taken by Tindale and Birdsell as indication of "the beginnings of a more advanced political system" among these two tribes? A negative response would seem to be the only one which would be given by a person familiar with the social patterns of the tribes of eastern Australia. At least half of the present states of South Australia, New South Wales, and Queensland were occupied by aboriginal groups having matrilineal descent (Howitt, 1889a, opp. p. 31; 1904, opp. p. 90; Radcliffe-Brown, 1931, opp. p. 42). Within this area, many of the tribes adjacent to the Kamilaroi and most of the tribes of Queensland have the "Kamilaroi Type" of matrilineal descent (Howitt, 1889a, opp. p. 31). Yet neither Tindale nor Birdsell suggest that the other tribes in this area have a social structure with an advanced political organization. Clearly the Kamilaroi type matrilineal social organization was not viewed by Tindale and Birdsell as sufficient grounds for classifying all these tribes as more advanced.

Conclusion

Only one conclusion seems possible about any assertion that singles out the Kamilaroi and Wiradjuri as especially advanced compared to other Australian tribes, especially the Queensland tribes to their north. A review of the major ethnographic accounts of these two tribes does not suggest that "the development of a more advanced type of political organization" was sufficiently under way in these groups to have been noted by the ethnographers and other chroniclers who considered these tribes during the last century when many informants were alive whose parents, if not themselves, had known the pre-European social patterns. Whatever political development has occurred to cause these tribes to be classified as "more advanced" must, indeed, be very recent.

Summary

A review of sources on southeastern Australia, an area where the environment was clearly richer than in many other parts of Australia, strongly suggests that the aboriginal tribes of this area did not have any especially advanced, or simple, type of social organization. Schemes proposing that, throughout, this area had either a significantly elaborate or especially simple social and/or political structure seem not to be based upon a detailed and careful analyses of the best available sources.

The most nearly accurate previously-published statement on the actual social level of southeast Australia is to be found in a 1950 paper by Joseph B. Birdsell (p. 279); "The low level of social organization attained in Australia was constant."

17.

Discussions, Part III

17a. On Ethnographic Reconstruction

Speakers: *Birdsell, Gardner, Hiatt, R. Lee, Meggitt, Rose, Williams, Woodburn*

LEE: A central theme in the papers we have been hearing today concerns the reconstruction of ethnographic situations that are no longer intact. We can take off from Hiatt's paper (1962 and Chapter 10, this volume) in which he points out that Radcliffe-Brown among the Kariera was working with a detribalized situation. This field situation undoubtedly contributed to Radcliffe-Brown's excessive emphasis on formal rules. The fact is that formal rules are a residuum in a memory culture, where the local organization has broken down. Naturally, the kind of material they feed the anthropologist will be their ideology, not the description of day-to-day movements. However, we have heard of a number of cases at this conference in which ethnographers have observed the local organization still functioning, and these observations—as distinguished from interviewing informants in a memory situation—show that groups in Australia, Africa, North America and India, are flexible and composite, and one sees people exercising options according to a number of variables—not only kinship connection, but also personal associations, and ecology. This is quite a different picture from the simple model of the patri-local, territorial, exogamous, band that has come to us via Service (1962), out of Radcliffe-Brown (1931). What we are actually observing is the work group, and it is important for us to distinguish, as Leach suggests, between the conscious models of ideal group structure and statistical models derived from the real choices of real people. No one would deny that the conscious model is also a part of reality; it is. But it is equally dangerous to assume, as Radcliffe-Brown did, that the conscious model alone was an accurate or even approximate reflection of group structure.

BIRDSELL: I think Dr. Hiatt has raised a very important point, which I would like to discuss both indirectly and directly. The question is not so much his quarrel with Radcliffe-Brown —which Stanner answered last year (Stanner, 1965) although he left it hanging on this note: "All the large communities that have been quoted in the 1962 paper by Dr. Hiatt, are indeed, modern ones and post-acculturational and, in fact, tied—to one degree or another— to European economy."

Now, before approaching that, let me say that my own belief is that precontact Australians can have lived in as large a group as that for which we can define a subsistence base. Reconstruction is a tricky business, and I would like to present and discuss three recent examples of this approach.

1. One is the very elegant reconstruction of

Ainu social organization and local grouping by Dr. Watanabe (1964 and Chapter 7, this volume). It is a very careful reconstruction going back almost a century in time. In it he has used ecological data and genealogies to provide the demographic variables.

2. Ted Strehlow in a recent publication (1965), rather strikingly reinvents Radcliffe-Brown's geometrical pattern of patrilineal local groups. I should note that Strehlow was born in Aranda territory, grew up speaking as much Aranda as he did English and German, and he has devoted his life to the study of the Western Aranda. In short, I think his data are as impeccable as data collected this late could be. He does find rigorous territoriality, defined in terms of people and totem associations and having definite boundaries.

3. Recently Norman Tindale (1962b) published a reconstruction of the Kaiadilt people and their country. This is a group of (originally) 120 people living on Bentinck Island in the Gulf of Carpentaria. He found them about four years after they were removed from the island; previously, they had been totally isolated and, therefore, were still within four years of precontact structure. Interestingly enough, as far as you can define marine densities by terrestrial areas (which is not a good measure), these are as densely situated a people as any in Australia; they come to about three persons per square land mile. Among them, he could reconstruct eight bands, each territorially resident in a fixed area—even to the detail of discovering one disputed interband territory. Band size, ranging from something like 8 to 35, is interesting, since they lived by generalized food resources. These, then, were small bands in enormous density. Though, perhaps, the most advantaged of tropical island peoples, they show the same rigorous territorial pattern projected by earlier modelists.

Now, I think no one will quarrel with the Sydney workers in terms of the reconstruction of social organization; they have done it superbly. But, as Stanner also points out (1965), there are almost no workers in Australia who have fitted real men into real country. So I suggest that what we need is the insertion of significant ecological analyses, based upon significant demographic data. I would say, then, that one cannot go to a modern mission station, government station, or mining town and—without inserting demography and ecology—reconstruct previously functioning local group structure, or, for that matter, territoriality. These things vanish with contact.

HIATT: I would like to deal with several of the points raised by Dr. Birdsell. It is at least questionable that Stanner (1965) has "answered" my 1962 paper; it was more an exegetical attempt to show that Radcliffe-Brown had not said the things I attributed to him. In one part of his paper, he does say—as Birdsell noted—that the modern studies have dealt with postcontact communities. This is a curious assertion, since, as far as I know, all the studies of local organization in Australia have involved communities that have been seriously affected by European contact. Radcliffe-Brown was in no better position to study territoriality than the rest of us.

I do not think that my rebuttals of Radcliffe-Brown's ideas add up to a new generalization. Given the ecological diversity in Australia, it is unlikely that there was a single type of local organization. And I suspect that it is too late now to establish the main varieties. However, if Tindale has shown that there is a horde in the Gulf of Carpentaria, I am quite happy about it. I did not say categorically that there was not one, but only that so far no one has ever seen one.

Concerning Strehlow's work—the Hermannsburg Mission was established a long time ago, about 1875 (Strehlow, 1965, p. 142), and his father's notes refer to a period twenty years after contact. As far as I have been able to make out from Strehlow's written material, he provides no empirical support for Radcliffe-Brown's model. In fact, I quote him in my 1962 paper as giving evidence that is inconsistent with the model.

No one, I think, is satisfied with our methods for reconstructing the past. The people that I worked with in Arnhem Land had been living a nomadic life until a year before I arrived. I do not suggest that they were completely unaffected by European contact; some of them had been wandering to neighboring missions or even walking 200 miles into Darwin. In 1957, the government established a settlement in their home country and, once the word got around, they all moved in very quickly, so that it was not possible for me actually to see an indigenous, nomadic, ongoing economy. But I did live for a month away from the settlement with a group of about fifty people, plotted totemic sites carefully, asked about boundaries (there were none), asked about use of resources around totemic sites, and, in general, observed about fifty people from several different patriclans living harmoniously together— specifically, not arguing about the fact that some members of the group were living on totemic estates that did not belong to them. Similarly, I recorded many disputes that had occurred, roughly, between 1940 and 1957— when the people were still living in the area largely unaffected by European settlement. These disputes were narrated in great detail, and I found that one of their favorite mnemonic devices for recalling disputes was the memory of the places where the disputes happened and the people who were there. So in the course of describing a dispute, an informant would name a dozen or so characters; and this makes it possible to say of a particular waterhole belonging to a particular clan at a particular time, there were many people present who did not belong to that particular clan. All in all, I don't think my opportunities and methods were vastly inferior to Tindale's on Bentinck Island.

MEGGITT: I should point out in passing that Stanner's 1965 paper fails to rebut Hiatt's paper (1962). It might be better construed as an exercise in ancestor worship.

ROSE: I also wish to address myself to Birdsell's remarks. I think one should realize that Strehlow was dealing with the Western Aranda in the early part of the century, and they had in fact been in contact with a white settlement since about 1875 (an area to the west of them was settled about that time). He also used the genealogical method, which I, at least, try to avoid.

I must confess that I have not yet read Tindale's paper on Bentinck Island, but I would like to comment on Tindale's reports on the Groote Eylandt people, who were in a pristine state when he investigated them in 1922 (Tindale, 1925). Tindale took photographs of groups of aboriginals whom he describes as belonging to a particular patrilineal totemic

group, and I had these photographs identified in 1948. The identifications entirely confirmed Hiatt's and Meggitt's conclusions, for it turned out that each of the photographed groups belonged to several totemic groups.

WILLIAMS: I want to return to Birdsell's ideas about reconstructing local residence arrangements, about which I take a pessimistic view. B. K. Sen published a paper in 1955 (Sen and Sen, 1955) in which he mapped the site of a group of Birhor and specified the membership of each household. Working with the same people, only six years later I was unable to reconstruct the situation Sen had described. Furthermore, after keeping track of every move over a fourteen-month period, I tested again by walking around old sites with the men and asking them where the houses had been and who had occupied them, and could not get consistent answers from man to man. The lack of ideological reification of the patrilocal group is such that I suspect that if the Birhor were put all in one place, fifty years from now, no one would know that he had occupied a patrilocal group. Therefore, I have no confidence in our ability to reconstruct these things, once the *de facto* arrangement has ceased to exist.

WOODBURN: I also want to talk about formal rules and problems of reconstruction. I think that with the Hadza it would be quite impossible to get an accurate idea of their system, even in the present, if one were to rely merely on informants. Their ideas about what they do differ very substantially from what they actually do. One (and only one) of the factors that influences this is the fact that the Hadza are very eager to gain the esteem of members of other tribes. A great deal of what they say is affected by this desire, especially when they are talking through interpreters. When asked about aspects of their own amorphous and elusive social organization, which they with some justification fear would be ridiculed by most outsiders, they commonly take refuge in describing the formal rules of neighboring tribes and particularly of the Isanzu, whom they know best. The Isanzu have a matrilineal system which is only imperfectly understood by most of the Hadza and the sort of description that one is likely to get as a result of questioning rather than observation is of a decidedly odd and rather incoherent form of matrilineal organization, whereas in fact they have a non-unilineal system.

GARDNER: Several papers have raised the question of whether devolution, detribalization, or cultural simplification has led to retention of formal structures (clan names, formal rules, and so on) for which there are no ongoing practices that can be observed. Other discussants have noted the very frequently occurring situation in which discrepancy between rule and practice can be ascribed to *additions* rather than losses. The Paliyans of South India are another case in point. They told me that they were patrilocal, when by Helm's procedure (in press a) for determining *de facto* bilaterality they are 53 per cent virilocal and 47 per cent uxorilocal. They say that they universally marry cross-cousins and cross-nieces, which 21 per cent of them actually do, but 19 per cent marry parallel-cousins and parallel-nieces, which according to the "rules" would be classificatory incest. They claim to use Iroquois kin terminology, which in fact they do use in front of outsiders—including anthropologists—but by hearing "mistakes" and conversations where my presence was not noted I found that they use Hawaiian terms among themselves. In order to appear respectable in culture contact situations, they attempt to be orthoprax, in terms of the culture of their neighbors; but this is all very superficial and recent, the "rules" are not a residue of old, abandoned institutions. This same situation apparently obtains among the Mbuti Pygmies, and among the Yanadi and Chenchu of India.

17b. THE PROBLEM OF LINEAGE ORGANIZATION

Speakers: *Damas, Deetz, Sinha, Williams*

DAMAS: In deciding the issue of the presence or absence of lineal organization in hunting people, we ought to consider further the question of acculturative influences. For instance, among the Birhor there seems to be some evidence that the lineages themselves may be borrowed from surrounding agricultural peoples—who have the same name for the

lineage. This raises a question in regard to Williams's model as to how essential the lineage is. Specifically, one wonders whether the Birhor would have worked out some alternative solution to this adaptive problem if they had not had an opportunity to borrow a solution from their neighbors.

WILLIAMS: I think we agreed at the 1965 conference on Band Organization[1] that patrilocal and patrilineal bands should be separated, and specifically over the matter of lineage. Perhaps, we can leave aside the terminological questions and discuss specifically what has been borrowed. The Munda and the Santal have named clans, and these are the names that the Birhor have borrowed. I can assign no function to the names themselves; they do not regulate marriage. That is, they are not exogamic units, because one finds marriages within named clans. These are supposedly patrilineal, but I also found men who were agnatically related but gave themselves different names. These, then, are borrowed and do not fit the model.

On the other hand, this is not what I call a lineage. What I do call a lineage—rightly or perhaps wrongly, as I discover from talks with Woodburn—is a group of males who inherit property. There is very little symbolic objectification of a lineage, so to distinguish a lineage required a lot of looking. It is true, however, that each group of males inherits a pantheon, and each learns a different way of treating it. Also, members of a lineage band behave differently towards one another than they do in their interactions with people outside the lineage. For example, if they are patrilineally related males and another group of patrilineally related males come to visit, they move in directly; while if the visiting group is related in any other way—e.g., in-laws through the wife—they first establish a camp several hundred yards away and then feel out the social situation before moving in. The distance of their camp from the resident group is a function of the distance of their kinship relation.

SINHA: I want to draw upon the earlier reports by Roy on the Birhor of the Ranchi

---

1. Held at the National Museum of Canada, Ottawa, under the chairmanship of David Damas.

district, the district neighboring on Hazaribagh. It appears in Roy's report (1925) that the totemic clans, rather than the lineages, seem to be quite important as exogamous units. Of course, we cannot be very sure how specific his information was. But if we go back to our previous idea of devolution, it could possibly be the case that the Birhor at some time in the past, like many of the other Munda-speaking group of tribes, had totemic clans with a greater depth of lineages when they were practicing shifting cultivation. Then we would suppose that only the symbolic names persist; while the operational units have become lower-depth lineages with bilateral compromises. Does this sound feasible?

WILLIAMS: It does sound feasible, at least. Dr. Sinha has already cited evidence on some east-central hunting groups which, thirty years ago, were not hunting as much as they do today; they were shifting agriculturalists. This raises a suspicion that this condition has been prevalent throughout India. Also, there is a general feeling that one simply should not find hunters in an area in which there has been a high civilization for thousands of years. In any case, if they were agriculturalists in the past, I was not able to find any evidence for it beyond the names already mentioned.

Now, as to Roy's data: I did not work in his area, nor do I know what techniques he used. I can say, however, that I did ask the Birhor for these clan names and when I sat down with an informant and asked him into which of these groups he would marry, he would give me a definite answer, an answer which, however, bore no relation to actual marriage choices.

DEETZ: I would like to comment on the distinction between patrilocal and patrilineal bands. It occurs to me that a territorially based single patrilocal extended family is a *de facto* patrilineage or, at any rate, is so perceived by us. If, however, we compare this to a Nuer patrilineage, we should look at the type of corporate ownership that we are dealing with. In the case of the Nuer, the ownership is of cattle, or of something else tangible. But in most cases in which we speak of corporate ownership on the part of hunting-type patrilocal bands, the thing that is owned and shared is something infinitely expandable. For example, if I have eight boys and sixteen cattle,

I can give each boy two cows; while if I have sixteen gods, I can give all sixteen to each of the eight boys. Therefore, we should distinguish carefully between what we might call corporate property as opposed to corporate ideology. The real need for sharing tangible material that cannot be split down and is passed on unilineally is of a different order from the treatment of something like totems, pantheons, legends, or far-distant geographical places, which can be diffused in all directions and do not demand the same sort of corporate action.

17c. ANALYSIS OF GROUP COMPOSITION

Speakers: *Anderson, Balikci, Helm, Laughlin, R. Lee, Marshall, Slobodin, Woodburn*

SLOBODIN: I have a question for Dr. Helm. I wonder if kinship is talked about in two senses in her paper—kinship *in posse* and kinship *in esse*: i.e., the range of possible kinship, as distinguished from kinship actualized in activities. When a couple or family moves into a group (and it turns out that there is almost always a sibling of one of the spouses in the group), they are actualizing one of many possibilities. Among the Kutchin—for whom I present data (Slobodin, 1962) similar to that used by Dr. Helm—first cousins are equated with siblings, and it is in fact very difficult for a couple to move into a group where neither spouse has a sibling. So it has been enlightening to me for her to emphasize the importance of this sibling relationship. Pehrson (1957) did this for a northern pastoral group. But in both cases, the relationship is specific to a purpose actualized there. It is not a principle of kinship in general; there is kinship involved in other kinds of groups, too.

HELM: I do not see the distinction made by Slobodin between the range of possible kinship as distinguished from kinship actualized in activities as being a point of confusion in my paper. I have used the generic term "kinship" in the same way that I have used the generic terms "resource" and "range." These are merely the most convenient and simple designations that I could muster to project the broadest perspective. I have taken pains in this paper and others (e.g., Helm 1965a, 1965b) to specify the particular kinds of kin relationships that are "actualized in activities," the activity in question being co-residence or contiguous residence as a socioterritorial identity. The "actualized" kind of kinship connection is the primary bond of sibling-to-sibling or child-to-parent as it is "activated" bilaterally, from either spouse of the conjugal pair, to allow residence entree of that pair into one or another of the groups where primary consanguines reside.

One non-sociological variable that I see to be quite as important in the creation and duration of Dene local bands as Pilling sees it in his Australian material is progenitiveness and the physical survival of the resultant sibling set. Three or four or more siblings who survive into adulthood along with a forceful father or brother tend to stay together around that figure, and they are apt to pull in male affines as co-resident group members, as well. Thereby, the group tends to endure in time and space, focused around the bilateral primary linkages between the conjugal pairs that result from marriages by the sibling set, including the females as well as males of the set among the Dene. Herein lies the bilaterality of the Dene system.

As to the fact that cousins are called "siblings" among the Kutchin, this is equally true of the kinship terminology system of the Dogribs (and three out of every four Slave Indians give this nomenclature as well). But, like the Kutchin, every Dogrib knows his cousins from his siblings. Dr. Slobodin makes that same point I do when he says that "it is, in fact, very difficult for a [Kutchin] couple to move into a group where neither spouse has a sibling." In my paper, I deal with real siblings, not terminological "siblings." It is true that sometimes the "effective sibling set" (as discussed in Helm, 1965a) may include more than uterine siblings. I have cases of an adopted sibling and of a parallel cousin becoming the leader of a uterine sibling set. I think these cases simply demonstrate that the basic two-sex sibling unit may be socially extended for the uses and purposes of a dominant male. The fact that the kinship terminology allows cousins to be termed as siblings may indeed aid in the extension of the fraternal sentiment, when it is socially or economically advantageous to do so.

WOODBURN: I have been asked to describe the place of sibling ties in Hadza residential arrangements and also to specify their system of cousin terminology.

In my second paper in this volume (Chapter 11) I have described how the most important bonds in the composition of Hadza camps are those between husband and wife and those between mother-in-law and son-in-law. These two types of dyadic bond in combination give rise to a non-corporate unit which has the genealogical form of a matrilineal extended family and which I describe as a simple residential unit.

As a consequence of the two types of tie that make up the simple residential unit, young married sisters commonly live together while their mother is still alive, although they do not have important property obligations to each other. After the death of their mother they may well have married daughters of their own, and residentially their focus of interest will be on these daughters rather than on their sisters. Two sisters each of whom is at the apex of a simple residential unit will often live together from time to time but are unlikely to live together regularly unless their units are additionally linked by other ties. If the son of a woman at the apex of a unit marries, the unit he marries into is unlikely to live regularly with the unit of his mother and sisters unless, again, there are multiple ties between the units. Quite often two or more brothers marry into the same unit or a brother and a sister marry a brother and a sister. In one instance two sisters and two brothers had married two sisters, a brother, and a half-brother. In cases of this sort, where multiple bonds link a pair of units, they are to be found together much more frequently than would otherwise be the case.

Since a man normally lives with his wife's mother, he will not find it easy to maintain two marriages simultaneously unless he marries two sisters, which is possible but disapproved. When a man does have two wives, it is very often a transitory stage between two monogamous marriages. This is apt to happen when the first marriage is not going well: the man marries another wife and eventually chooses to maintain one or the other of the marriages.

Rather surprisingly, the cousin terms of the Hadza are of Crow type, although in other respects the system is not Crow. The Hadza say that a man should not marry a first cousin of any sort, but one occasionally finds cases of marriage with either the parallel or the cross-cousin. The preferred marriage is a cross-generational one with the classificatory sister's daughter, though, as with any cross-generational marriage, it is rare in practice.

LEE: I shall be speaking about the Dobe-area !Kung Bushmen of Botswana (Lee, 1965) and their neighbors, the Nyae Nyae !Kung of South-West Africa, studied by Lorna Marshall (1957, 1959, 1960). Unlike the Hadza, among whom marriage seems to be a transitory union, marriage among !Kung Bushmen is very stable, and the nuclear family is the basic cohesive unit that stays together throughout the year. This does not mean the !Kung have a family level of organization. They live in multifamily groups of 10–50 individuals with modes at 15 and 25 persons.

One must realize that censuses of a camp will show different totals from day to day; the 15–25 figure, however, is a consistent central tendency. Thus the two basic units of !Kung society are the nuclear family, and the multi-family living group which I prefer to call the *camp*, although others may want to call it a *band*.

When one tabulates the links within the camp using the method developed by June Helm (in press a), one finds male-male, male-female, and female-female sibling links, as well as affinal links of both sexes. Thus in terms of genealogical composition, the Dobe !Kung camp looks very much like the northern Athapaskan microband.

Helm also pointed out that among the Dog-rib, a strong group of siblings will tend to attract male affines to the task group. This is a prominent feature of !Kung groupings and such a mode of affiliation may be character-istic of other hunter-gatherer peoples as well. Among the !Kung, demographic factors such as family size and survivorship account for much of the variance observed in social groupings. Large families tend to attract others, and small families attach themselves where they can; with people moving as often as they do, it is impossible to discern the opera-tion of jural rules of residence. The !Kung camp does not constitute in any way a patri-local band. Following the suggestion of Knight on the Naskapi (1965), I prefer to call their residence arrangements "pragmaticolocal."

We should not be surprised to find that where jural rules do occur, they have built-in options. Consider the Bushman name relation, first described by Lorna Marshall (1957). The ascription of personal name is ambilateral, with a patrilateral emphasis. The Bushmen say that the first child of each sex should be named after the paternal grandparents and subsequent children after the maternal grandparents; in practice, half of the people have patri-names and half matri-names. Since each sibling group is split by the name relationship, no unilineal corporate entity can emerge. What is more important is the fact that the name relationship restructures kinship terminology. If you share a name with another individual, then the kinship terms that you use radiate from the fact of the common name, and these name partnerships leapfrog genealogical con-nections. This makes it difficult to talk about kin term typologies since Ego's cousin terms will be Eskimo, or Crow, or Omaha, depend-ing on his name relationship!

In addition to the !Kung, name sharing is found among the Eskimo (Guemple, 1965) and among the Kaingang of South America (Henry, 1941 [1964]). It might be interesting to determine whether name sharing is com-mon to other hunter-gatherer groups.

MARSHALL: The Nyae Nyae !Kung and Dobe-Area !Kung have much in common. I found that among the people we worked with, the ideal naming pattern stated by Richard Lee was followed consistently. After using the names of all the grandparents in proper order, a further child was usually named after one of the father's siblings or a sibling's spouse. I might note, regarding the effect of common naming upon kinship terminology, that the perspective that a person adopts is primarily that of the specific individual after whom he is named. Since there are relatively few names to go around, the chance sharing of a name with several people does not involve quite the same number of rules and patterns in the use of kinship terms. The people we worked with claimed that they did not marry lineal kin or collaterals up through first cousins, and this seemed to be quite consistently maintained. However, they did frequently break another stated marriage rule to the effect that one should not take a spouse having the same name as one's own parent.

BALIKCI: With reference to the Netsilik Eskimos of the Arctic coast, I have asked myself the question: What keeps these people together in a band? And I have found several reasons for it. There are, of course, such things involved as kinship ties, the vital necessity of cooperative acquisitive activities, and some ceremonial activities. But there is another class of social facts that tie people together; namely, patterned dyadic relationships, which seem to be pretty important in this area of the Arctic coast. One can enumerate a number of these dyadic partnerships—wife-exchange, meat-sharing (which are extremely rigorous and involve named dyads), joking, avoidance, trading, drumming-singing (which sometimes go together with wife-exchange partnerships), wrestling, old-friend, and name-sharing. All these partnerships are reciprocal, and most of the time they are contractual; although meat partners are given to children soon after birth. These are peace-making devices in the camp that both cut across kinship lines and tie extended families together. Sometimes such dyadic relationships are ambivalent, especially in the case of wife-exchange partnership. After exchanging wives over a period of months, husbands are likely to begin disliking one another and wind up as enemies instead of friends. This is manifest in the songs sung at the drum dances. I wonder whether dyadic relationships play as important a role in other hunter-gatherer bilateral societies.

LAUGHLIN: I think it is interesting that dyadic and name relationships have survived in rather robust form in the Aleutian islands, where the population has been severely limited and where there have been some serious changes. One of the most common practices is that of naming after a common event. There is also a reciprocal use of single kinship terms, so that two persons may be calling each other uncle. Another important relationship that shows up occasionally among the Eskimo is called *anakiisak*. When a person is born, an older persons is named his *anakiisak* or pro-tector. The older person is supposed to protect the infant through all the stages of life and in embarrassing circumstances (hence, if a child wets on the floor, an old woman may do the same thing, in order to partake in the shame). When the young person gets older and his *anakiisak* gets very old, the younger one helps the older one out of this world. This seems to function to a considerable degree today, more, perhaps, in the Aleutians than in Kodiak or in western Alaska. There are other such relationships. The two men that went out in the two-hatched kayak were "partners"; they had to get along. Some magic was possible there, and some deaths resulted.

ANDERSON: Concerning the analysis of group composition, the issues which I wish to emphasize represent the other side of the coin of arguments presented by Sahlins (1965) on the relationship of group ideology and group composition. Of course, this is not an either/or matter. Deriving structure from ideology or composition involves different activities but both have value. These analytical activities are complementary. Acknowledging this, I will emphasize the group composition side in order to relate a number of points which have emerged in the papers and discussions.

One of the quite general findings concerns what has been termed fluidity in group composition and group size over time. Though shifting group affiliations do not surprise us, the high frequency of their occurrence among hunters and collectors does warrant further investigation. From the examples we have been presented, they appear to occur (though probably with differing frequency) among relatively settled as well as nomadic peoples, where orientation is lineal as well as bilateral, where territorial attachment of groups is tight or loose, and where the habitat is relatively richly or poorly endowed. Indeed, if fluidity of group affiliation is as general as it seems, then hunting and gathering peoples would appear to be not only what Sahlins terms the "original affluent society" but also the "original mobile society," at least in terms of residence arrangements. And if in the original affluent society wants are restricted, then in the original mobile society shifting alignments permit individuals and families to maximize fulfillment of their wants (material and non-material).

By "fluidity" in the composition of social units and "residential mobility," I am summarizing an apparently widespread but not universal feature of hunting and gathering societies which is to be distinguished from strictly seasonal fragmentation or shifts. The Ainu have seasonal residential shifts as do all hunters and gatherers, but Dr. Watanabe's reports do not indicate fluidity in camp composition. Neither Hiatt nor Williams report it either, though Balikci, Damas, Helm, Lee, Marshall, Slobodin, Suttles, Turnbull, and Woodburn have reported a situation of fairly continuous realignments of individuals or families. In fact, a number of the latter indicate that fluidity of alignments is so great that the entities formed do not meet the usual definition of band or group. Balikci, Laughlin, Sharp, Turnbull, and Woodburn have emphasized the relative importance of various patterned reciprocal dyadic relationships over groups integrated by normative or functional ties. This is more than merely semantics. The use of the term "group" or "band" for local or task units among *some* of the cases may even lead to a faulty conception of observed social interactions. The terms "aggregate," "unit," or "network" would seem to be more appropriate in describing certain local or activity-oriented units. On reexamination, some units identified as "bands" could turn out to be what Dr. Sharp has characterized as overlapping "ego-centered sets of societies." And even where groups are established, reciprocal dyadic ties which frequently reinforce or provide additional bases of alliance are worthy of fuller investigation (cf. Chapter 17h).

Three other corrective findings are provided from the papers and discussions. First, exclusive territoriality with territorial defense by a fixed group of people is rare at best. However, association between a named land area and a fairly stable social unit is common, whether the centripetal factor is a totemic spot, a resource place, a water hole, or a "home base," i.e., a relatively limited range within a wider area to which the activities of aged, young, sick and reproducing persons are restricted. Second, in a number of hunting and gathering peoples it is difficult to elicit norms of residence, descent, or marriage, the commonly signifi-

cant rules in group structure. Third, there appears to be more specialization for certain tasks among hunters than has been stressed up to now.

With these findings in mind, I wish to return to the question of why fluidity in group composition may be such a common feature for hunters and gatherers. It has already been mentioned that chance demographic factors may impose difficulties on those peoples having well-defined norms of group structure to follow. Among hunters whose rules are less precisely stated, certain patterned but less formal practices confer a degree of constancy in group composition. With the Dogrib, the !Kung, and the Tiwi, sibling and affinal bonds are of primary importance in affiliating families. With the Hadza, sibling ties are of less importance than those uniting a mother and her married offspring (especially mother-daughter) and those between spouses. Age ties and sibling ties are factors among the Mbuti Pygmies. Among other hunting peoples, spouse exchange, adoption, ritual obligations, and friendship provide some continuity. I find especially intriguing Dr. Woodburn's and Dr. Turnbull's remarks on the one hand about the lack of commitment or loyalty of hunter to one another, and on the other hand that interpersonal bonds are purely expedient. If such a lack of commitment to others and a view of relationships as expedient has wider currency among hunters, then the importance of dyadic ties and of fluidity of group composition are more easily understood. I think that we can reject Dr. Woodburn's lead that lack of commitment is related to lack of dependence on others for access to things. The fact that the majority of Hadza men are "hangers on" as regards kills of meat belies a lack of independence, especially since size of meat portion distributed is a factor in budding off. Maintenance of a broad series of reciprocally validated exchange bonds with kinsmen, affines, friends, partners, etc., certainly provides fullest security in circumstances which are apt to be rather constantly changing. Where alternatives for access to wants change not only with fluctuations in resources but also with fluctuations in demography of the social unit, it *is* difficult to plan ahead. But what better security is there for the future than to keep a wide range of strategic social ties "warm"?

The emphasis on informal and dyadic alignments and the fluidity of many hunter and gatherer peoples can thus be seen to have some advantageous consequences. The presence of a range of options by which individuals and families pursue their best interests at any time may be viewed as a workable, if imperfect, cybernetic system. Shifting arrangements based upon best options within the guidelines of social rules or preferences (as far as is possible) may most effectively relate a hunting population to short-term fluctuations in resources and conditions of life, as Lee, Alland, and others suggest. Social flexibility allows for optimal exploitation of the preferred effective resources by the total population, including ill and aged as well as the able. And, as a number of conferees have suggested, fission may be the principal means of regulating interpersonal conflict. On the other hand, as Dr. Balikci suggests, reciprocal dyadic relationships—which croscut social bonds established on kinship or family ties—are peacemaking devices. Clearly more data on these relationships are needed.

Finally, that the above is possible does not militate against the suggestion by Sahlins and others (e.g., Rappaport, 1966) that ideology and rules may have adaptive advantages over longer term fluctuations.

17d. Social Determinants of Group Size

Speakers: *L. Binford, Helm, Williams, Woodburn*

BINFORD: I would like to ask Bob Williams to elaborate on his comment that there may be size limitations to various organizational features of society. For example, what are the maximum sizes of groups that may cooperate without having affinal ties or other articulations which arise not out of face-to-face interaction but out of some symbolic partitioning of society? It seems that many of the people who have presented material on composite bands have mentioned the size range of 15–25 people. What factors would operate to limit local group size? What factors seem to lead to an optimum size of 15–25?

WILLIAMS: In my own group, it is difficult to tell what is cause and what is effect. For instance, the marriage requirements are such that a man cannot arrange to bring a bride for his son without help. He cannot get the needed help unless he is co-resident with the people who are to help him. And I have seen people move back in with others of their patri-line in order to get this kind of help. This would suggest that such a type of cooperation is necessary, but one can see the causality in two possible ways. This might be a device that ensures a certain group size, or—taking a functionalist point of view—one might say that the bride's family is ensuring that there is a kinship group of adequate size to take care of their daughters. This, like many other things, regulates the size of the band, but it is always hard to distinguish cause and effect. But the very presence of such non-economic factors—as mentioned also by Turnbull—assures us that group size is not determined merely by ecology and economy.

WOODBURN: I argue that the environment and technology of the Hadza set only very broad limits to the possible sizes of camps. In practice, one finds camps containing from one to a hundred people; the average camp contains about eighteen adults. One factor that seems to set a rough upper limit on the number of people in a camp is the size, and not the number, of animals killed. By custom the meat of an animal is divided widely among the members of a camp. Hadza have a fairly definite notion of what constitutes a reasonable individual portion of meat and if they do not get this amount, people may begin to move out. The good hunters are especially likely to leave.

HELM: Is there any way in which a good hunter can control a large group of strangers following him?

WOODBURN: None at all. It is striking that among the Hadza most of the hunting is done by a small proportion of the men. As I have mentioned earlier, perhaps as many as half of the adult Hadza men kill fewer than one large animal per head per year. Many men eat more meat than they contribute and the good hunters just put up with this situation.

17e. RESOLVING CONFLICTS BY FISSION

Speakers: *Hamburg, Hiatt, Turnbull, Woodburn*

HAMBURG: Dr. Turnbull has put considerable emphasis on the utilization of fluid band composition for the resolution or avoidance of conflict. Can you say something more about the sources of such conflict?

TURNBULL: Among the Mbuti, conflicts usually involve anxiety over marital problems. Perhaps due to the composite nature of the band, there is a good deal of sister exchange, and this leads to obvious conflicts of loyalty between brothers or between a man and his wife. Occasionally, there is conflict over food but very little over property—sometimes a minor theft, perhaps. The sources of conflict seem rather trivial and sometimes are even invented. I think they represent simply the great internal tensions that build up during a period of hunting under very close conditions.

HIATT: I wonder whether Dr. Turnbull could identify the cohesive factors—both of ideology and self-interest.

TURNBULL: Among the Mbuti—where practically all the tendencies seem to be towards fission—the one really strong cohesive factor is simply the forest itself. This is where the religious aspect comes in. The forest is the only constant in their lives; there are no allegiances among themselves as individuals or as families to which they can look for a feeling of constancy. As I said before, a band can only be defined as that group of individuals who are living and hunting in a certain territory at a certain time. The composition of the band is always changing, but the band as an ideal continues to exist within a given territory. So there is a feeling of loyalty towards the territory. In times of fission, the Mbuti are thrown upon themselves and upon this relationship to the forest. Their activities become less and less communal until finally, at the height of the honey season, individual men, women, and even children go out alone and live off the forest. There is a clear idea of the enormous generosity of the forest, and the structural importance of this recognition is seen in the fact that the bounty and benevolence of the forest form the major topics of discussion in times of

crisis, just as they form the basis of the great religious songs, which more than anything bind Mbuti society together.

Although I am not yet sure, I strongly suspect that the Ik have a similar feeling about their environment. In their own lives there is no room for affection as we understand it; couples and families break up, and women abandon children to decrepit grandparents—apparently without remorse. They are a rather cold and calculating people, and relationships are seen in terms of expediency. But one does sense a feeling of affection and of a unifying bond when one sees them sitting at the band's sitting place—a rocky outcrop, chosen for its view. In times of anxiety, they will sit there and gaze across the mountains and valleys and seem to feel affection for them. Like the Mbuti, the Ik also recognize that the environment provides them the necessities of life.

WOODBURN: Among the Hadza a very similar situation occurs; movement and division of camps because of conflict is extremely common. When people do move or leave a camp because of conflict, they very often give an ecological reason for their movements. They suddenly discover that the berries somewhere else are better. By giving such a neutral ecological explanation, they solve disputes simply by refusing to acknowledge them.

17f. TERRITORIAL BOUNDARIES

Speakers: *Hiatt, R. Lee, Pilling*

PILLING: Regarding territoriality, to say that boundaries are totally absent among hunters is an oversimplification. Let me draw examples from my knowledge of the Tiwi of North Australia. Certain sectors of the boundaries of territories belonging to some of their local groups are fairly exact; however, this is true primarily where the boundaries coincide with wide bodies of water, and even in these instances—I should note—I never heard of boundaries having a fixed location on the surface (or bottom) of such a body of water.

To understand the location of boundaries on land, it should be noted that among the Tiwi the countryside is covered by a large number of small named localities with only vaguely defined limits, somewhat in the way that a farmer in America or England has names for localities on the land he owns or works. In most instances, these Tiwi-named localities were within the territory of one local group. However, a few were neutral, or buffer, localities between the territories of different local groups; in such areas members of either local group could camp, even when members of the other local group were also camped there.

On one occasion, I was traveling with some men near the center of Melville Island, and one said: "This is where (so-and-so named locality) ends, and this is where (so-and-so other named locality) begins." I already knew that one of these localities was a netural area, and the other was considered to be in the territory of a specific local group. Therefore, I was hearing a statement that in this one instance the land boundary was a sharp boundary. When I asked my Tiwi traveling companions about the sharpness of this boundary, they showed their impatience at my ignorance; for the name of the neutral area was ecologically specific, meaning "the area where (so-and-so tree) grows," and that grove happened to have a sharp edge. Therefore, the application of the specific local geographical term meant that there was a sharp boundary. Thus, there are few instances among the Tiwi where there is a very precise edge to the territory of a local group.

But it should be stressed that in Tiwi thinking these boundaries seem to be a by-product of application of an ecologically related word, and not the product of the presence of a concept of precise, fence or line-like boundaries.

HIATT: I found something similar to this. The typical situation, I think, is one in which there is a cluster of named totemic or non-totemic sites that form what Stanner (1965) has called a "heartland." Between one heartland and the next, there is usually no sharp boundary; there is an area between the two about which no one cares much. But I did find one or two cases of the sort of thing that Dr. Pilling was talking about. One totemic site was a sand ridge which was said to have been formed by a totemic sea monster. The people in talking of this site could say quite explicitly, "This is the end of Yiridja and the beginning of Dua." But this situation is very uncommon.

LEE: Culturally defined boundaries do not necessarily imply sanctions against trespass. You can achieve the same ecological and social effect by having rules for accommodating people across boundaries as when there are no boundaries at all. All of the hunting peoples we have been discussing have the institutionalized means for moving from group to group. So if we find boundaries in a given case, we should not commit the frequent error of assuming that they enclose a defended and exclusive territory.

17g. PREDATION AND WARFARE

Speakers: *Chagnon, Hiatt, R. Lee, Owen, Pilling, Woodburn*

OWEN: One of the factors in the reduction of the western North American hunters and gatherers has been the attrition on them from surrounding agriculturalists. No one has mentioned yet that hunters and gatherers sometimes hunt domestic animals, which often results in the domestic people hunting the wild ones, so to speak. I wonder whether anyone else has observations to make about population control exerted by neighbors.

LEE: The 425 !Kung Bushmen of the Dobe area share their range amicably with 340 Herero and Tswana pastoralists. This situation has not developed into the "patron-client" relationship of the Mbuti, but neither is it one of constant warfare. They have reached a *modus vivendi* over a period of forty years, and cattle theft by Bushmen occurs now on an average of only once in several years. The last case of a Bushman murdering a Mutswana occurred in 1946, and this dispute involved women, not livestock.

WOODBURN: The Hadza do not often come into conflict with their neighbors. There have been a few violent encounters with the pastoral Tatoga, who gain the esteem of their fellow tribesmen by killing members of other tribes. As many Tatoga as Hadza seem to have died in these encounters, but they are not an important cause of mortality for either tribe.

The Hadza talk of a time before the arrival of Europeans when they had to conceal their camps more than they do today and when they built their fires in holes in the ground to avoid detection at night. They say they had many enemies then. But it is now impossible to judge whether many people were killed by enemies. In recent years there have been one or two cases of Hadza hunting domesticated animals and in one of these a Hadza was murdered.

CHAGNON: So far, we have concerned ourselves with settlement patterns and distribution of peoples largely in terms of economics. Now it seems that we have drifted into the context of conflict and warfare of hunters in a world of non-hunters, as Sahlins puts it. I would like to hear from those who have studied the Australian aborigines about the effects of warfare between bands on the distribution of the groups. By "warfare" I mean any hostile relationship between autonomous groups that may alter their seasonal pattern. For example, while the distribution of food might make it advisable for them to split up during the year, perhaps fear of night attack or of witchcraft from a neighboring group might preclude their breaking up into indefensible collecting groups.

PILLING: On the question of warfare and feud, I would like to draw on material from the very vivid memory culture of Tiwi informants who had lived this way of life in their early adulthood. The night raids were effectively terminated, about 1912, when Sir Baldwin Spencer was inadvertently injured by a Tiwi during a spear-throwing demonstration. It was apparently made very clear at that time that the continuation of spear-throwing and the use of guns (which had come into use for night raiding) would no longer be tolerated by the Europeans. This Spencer incident was correlated with the end of night raiding and sneak attacks and it *appeared* to have stopped pitch battles producing death. But, in fact, as late as 1948 death-causing battles with clubs were still occurring. My chief informant, the major leader of one faction, survived this 1948 battle only by having nearly all the doctors in the Darwin Hospital in attendance upon him for many hours, performing brain surgery. (It appears that the administrators were fearful that the Tiwi, armed with guns, might cause a major stir, if this leader died. National and international news releases of such a story might reflect unfavorably upon the administrators.) Club battles lasted, although without

death-causing injuries, until at least 1953, even in the face of the threat of strong sanctions against them from Europeans.

Under the old pattern, sneak attack was sufficiently common that informants spoke of special ecological adjustments to it. When local group A managed in a raid to kill a man in opposing local group B, retaliation was to be expected. Normally, a female intermediary—living in local group B, but born in the territory of local group A—came to A to warn them of future planned retaliation by B. At this, the threatened group A was likely to move to the mangroves, a very specialized and unpleasant ecological niche with, among other things, crocodiles and a sloshy mud floor. Some of my older informants, who had lived under these conditions, considered it a blessing when the pattern of sneak attack was terminated in 1912. Apparently, camps in the mangroves were never larger than that of a married couple with children, and they might have to live in this manner for as long as several months. The hiding in mangroves ended when an adult male of the group hiding was apprehended and killed by the enemy, or when an exchange of messages indicated another means than sneak attack would be used to even the score. These alternative means of evening the score included pitched spear-battles or a planned context for counter-injury, but in either of these cases deaths would have been considered improper.

It is important to note the incidence of fatalities associated with the old pattern of sneak attacks and the way of life with which it was correlated. In one decade (1893–1903), at least sixteen males in the 25-to-45 age group were killed in feuding; either during sneak attacks or in arranged pitch battles. Those killed represented over 10 per cent of all males in that age category, which was the age group of the young fathers.

17h. HUNTER SOCIAL ORGANIZATION: SOME PROBLEMS OF METHOD

Speaker: *Sharp*

SHARP: Let me continue to try to sum up some of the issues that have been raised here.

One thing that strikes and humbles me is the smallness of our sample, both in the number of peoples studied by those present here and, even more generally, as shown by Professor Murdock's paper. And for many of the tribes that we do know about, we still have only very fragmentary data, which points up the urgency of ethnographic research to increase the sample upon which we can draw in considering such a problem as the nature of the social unit.

A second major defect in our data is the lack of situational material, material in context. This lack raised a number of problems earlier, for example, the problems of ethnographic reconstruction. Should we try to limit ourselves to pure forms, and reject material that comes to us only in complex and acculturative situations? These questions arise in any ethnographic research and have to be dealt with as they arise. For the future, I am fairly sanguine about the help that we can get from our archeological, ethnohistorical, and historical colleagues if we leave the channels open for collaboration and communication—which, of course, is one of the prime reasons for this symposium.

The Importance of Longer Field Studies

To overcome the evils of the old hit-and-run ethnography of which many of us have been guilty, we need longer-term field studies and follow-up studies to get descriptions of process. This is necessary also to give us longer runs for statistical handling. For example, I have never discovered whether there is any validity to the fascinating statistic that I drew from two censuses, three years apart, of the Yir Yoront on Cape York, which showed a birth ratio of 125 males to every 100 females (a ratio that was corrected in later age as males died from snakes, sharks, fighting, etc.). Do the anxieties of hunting life somehow affect the chemistry of conception, or is it simply the accidental result of a two-year census, as opposed to a longer one? The dangers of extrapolating from our few data are great.

Longer-term studies will tell us something more about the matter of devolution. Societies that seem to be going downhill have all the greater claim to be studied. Dr. Gardner mentioned the Phi Tong Luang in northern Thailand (Bernatzik, 1938 [1958]), who are undoubtedly hunters. But, apparently, they are the survivors of a domestic slave group freed by a prince of Nan and sent into the bush. They had no technical knowledge beyond sweeping floors and arranging flowers, and, presumably, fell back to a hunting subsistence level. They are being studied, but only inadequately; yet we know that they were reported very early, long before Bernatzik first published on them. Aside from the matter of their presumed origin, we should be interested by the perseverance of this group in the midst of the rice culture and court civilization of Siam.

Definition of Social Units

The question of units still needs a good bit of work, both in the study and in the field. Family and kin structures appear to be manageable; we can build band units, hunting groups, etc., either in terms of an aggregation of family units or as segments of family groups. But we still have trouble with the suprafamily or the reconstituted subcommunity units. Again, this problem is not limited in ethnographic studies to hunters alone; Leach (1943, 1961), Lehman (1963), and others have worried about it with regard to tribal studies. It is even a problem—at least, in Southeast Asia—in regard to states; we Europeans come in with a conception of states with fixed boundaries and find that in precontact times there was a much more flexible and overlapping system in effect. The whole matter is still biased by the imposition of prefabricated constructs—the patriclan, the horde, and the band—which we go looking for.

The construct of the society has given me trouble, and I do not know whether we can talk about this in all cases. In studying the aboriginal population on Cape York Peninsula, I simply could not find a society. I would have to describe it in terms of an ego-centered *set* of societies; no one individual was the center of a system of networks that overlapped isotypically with anyone else's. Not only were there networks and chains, but these were also institutionally divided. A man might participate in a trade network or chain that went southward; whereas his ritual networks might go northward, and with no overlap between the members of the two groups. The same would be true for symbolic and even for some technological behaviors. All of these, incidentally, were phrased in terms of kinship, which gave the basis for moving outward from the series of individuals with which one started.

The Application of Role Theory

These problems all point to deficiencies in our descriptive methods and the resulting content of our descriptions; some participants have called for development of sociometric techniques. Given my bias toward roles as useful descriptive units, and since we have to look at the interaction of *something*, I suggest that a further elaboration of role constructs would allow us to go into any society—whether highly structured, like the Australian societies, or less structured, like Eskimo groups—and, by an inductive process, build up the networks of roles. We should not only include masculine roles, feminine roles, children's roles, totemic leaders' roles, etc.; but we should also see roles in terms of behavioral activity, including ideational and emotional aspects. This might help us get really comparative information.

The roles would have to be seen in spatial and temporal, as well as in social contexts. There are diurnal and seasonal patterns. When a woman is out with her children and with other women digging yams during the daytime, is she a wife, or is the role of wife latent then? What are the possibilities for the manifestation and latency of roles, especially of children engaged in anticipatory learning? I think that the role approach forces us to look at contexts—the setting, duration, and frequency of behaviors. We would find that a certain woman is the head of a matrifocal family eight or twelve hours a day and head of a nuclear family during the rest of the time. Most of the ethnographic accounts do not give us that kind of information. If we break up the 24-hour day and 365-day year in terms of roles and networks of roles, we will come up with more realistic and exact descriptions for comparative use. This would allow us to tackle a number of the problems that have merely been touched upon at the symposium—problems of definition, correlations, criteria of nomadism ("nomadic style"), territoriality, descent, and devolution.

The Study of Ritual

It seems to me that the main gap in the material presented so far—and I suppose that this is true of a great deal of the material being collected today—occurs in the area of symbolic or ritual behavior. I could re-emphasize the point made by Dr. Helm that we must deal with *socio*-territorial groups. This is partly a matter of having enough personnel in the field to be in about eight places at once and enough time to remain through several seasonal cycles. We have to get at the socio-symbolic or ritual aspects of behavior, the idea categories that are imposed on the land and the people, thus linking specific people with specific bits of land—as in the totemic complexes that Dr. Hiatt mentioned. So far as I know, the Eskimos do not have land ideologies and rituals of this type, but one wonders if this may be because those who have described them had too narrow a conception of symbolic and ritual behavior. The character of the idea system is, of course, of vital importance in the survival of these groups. Given a universal rigid kind of system, as in Australia, a change in one part of the system is likely to bring about change elsewhere, notwithstanding Dr. Drucker's recent statement about the Haida (1965). On the other hand, one gets the impression that the Alaskan groups, and band groups in general, have a much more elastic ideological system. And, as Dr. Deetz pointed out, the ideological elements are manageable and provide a major means of adjustment if they are of importance to the social behavior of the group. Myth can be adjusted to reality, and to a certain extent reality can be adjusted to myth.

These considerations relate to a whole series of more specific problems. I do not see, for example, how once can claim to have found corporate structures without the names or symbols of corporateness that provide for stability and maintenance. (Only "he who thinks that he'll be the same tomorrow does not need a name.") Names furnish ideas about land ownership and boundaries. Apropos of this last, I do not quite understand how Dr. Hiatt's groups can have named plots of land and yet not have boundaries, however wide or vague. It is difficult to say when corporateness is needed by a group. What conditions would require a group to take on corporate character-istics, and what are the ideological correlates of such corporate structures?

17i. Typology and
Reconstruction: A Shoshoni Example

Speakers: *Eggan, Hiatt*

Eggan: I have several comments, beginning with some brief remarks, on typology. Julian Steward was the first to bring some typological order out of the chaos of band organization (1936, 1955). You will recall that he set up three types, partly empirical and partly ideal: the patrilineal band, the composite band, and the matrilineal band. And he attempted to relate them to one another and to cultural ecology. Elman Service more recently remodeled Steward's band typology (1962); he keeps Steward's two main types but sees the composite as an acculturative product of the patrilocal or patrilineal band, and he adds an "anomalous band" to take care of the Shoshoni and Eskimo.

I think it is clear that our sessions have demonstrated that Service is going in the wrong direction. Bands show a much greater variety than either Steward or Service allow. If social organization is adaptive, then this variety is exactly what we would expect. We have heard about a great variety of bands and will probably hear of more in the future. However, I think there will prove to be a limited number of viable combinations; although this is still to be determined.

In contradiction to Service, I think that patrilineal bands are a specialization on the more flexible, amorphous base than most of us have been describing. That is, I do not think that it is some sort of primary unit that has degenerated in late times.

Another aspect of this problem has been raised a number of times for North America and other areas. There is seasonal alternation between regional or macrobands and local or microbands, and we need to sort these out systematically. This offers us an opportunity to do better comparative work than we normally have done, since, after all, one has the same people under different ecological or seasonal differences rearranging themselves in different groupings. We should have some closer control on such situations, so that we can specify more clearly the factors operative in them.

I would like to make some remarks on the Shoshoni of the Great Basin, since they have been mentioned by several people and might cast a little more light on what has happened in Australia. I might say that the Shoshoni, in relation to their neighbors to the north and south, are in a peaceful situation like that described by Dr. Turnbull. This is true both within linguistic groups and, for the most part, across the linguistic boundaries, as well. The Shoshoni and their linguistic neighbors, the Ute and the Northern and Southern Paiute, throw some light on the development of band organization under extreme ecological conditions. This is an area of long occupation by what archeologists call the Desert Culture, a combination of hunting of small game on the part of men and gathering by women. This has gone on since at least 8,000 B.C., perhaps even earlier. There has been a nearly continuous cultural record; even though there is evidence of movements into and out of the area.

The Great Basin area itself is quite different from most other culture areas. It is dish-shaped with a culture of bare essentials in the center and a series of specializations at the margins, including incipient agriculture or use of the horse, according to the opportunities offered by the local habitat. Basic social structure is essentially a loose network of ties based on kinship and marriage. It is completely bilateral and runs across linguistic boundaries, and it functions both to supply spouses and to spread information about the sporadic appearance of new food supplies.

The winter group was made up of two to five families or ten to twenty people, who were almost invariably kin. There might be a different kin composition from one year to the next, but the size of the group was fairly stable. The basic ties were sibling bonds, parent-child bonds, and marriage ties. Residence throughout the area was generally matrilocal, at least initially. Brother-sister exchange was universal and was accompanied by polygyny (usually sororal) and fraternal polyandry (sometimes temporary, sometimes institutionalized). Brother-sister exchange gave double bonds or "knots" at certain places in the network.

In a few central regions along the Humboldt River, one found a more stable food supply, which made it possible for groups of two to five families to remain in the same place year after year. In summer, they made a circular trip of 25 to 150 miles, each group stopping at a series of places known to them. In these localities it was possible for parents and children to remain together for more than one generation, and in the second generation the normal process of brother-sister exchange made for the institutionalization of cross-cousin marriage. This trend was strong enough to affect the kinship system, resulting in a Dakota pattern for the terminology and a joking and permissive relation between cross-cousins. This marriage was thought to be of value, since children reared there learned the area thoroughly.

In areas to the north and east, there were areas of rather more stable food supplies. Salmon came up the Snake River, and the introduction of the horse made possible larger groupings. Interestingly enough, cross-cousin marriage here gave way to what Steward calls "pseudo-cross-cousin" marriage, where one marries a step-cross-cousin, a sociological cross-cousin, rather than a real one. This makes possible integration on a broader scale and allows for, say, the assimiliation of a mother with a daughter coming into a band. This dates back before 1700, as shown by the fact that the Comanche had pseudo-cross-cousin marriage too.

Now, around the margins of this area there is another set of specializations. In the Owens Valley, where seed resources and other resources were more abundant, the density was increased from one person per twenty square miles to one person per two square miles. And due to the matrilocal residence of the women concerned with seed-gathering, there was a development of matrilocal bands which—as Steward says somewhere—are almost, but not quite matrilineal clans, as he defined them.

Toward the south, the Southern Paiute, with incipient agriculture, also had relatively large bands. And I predict that when we get the archeological sequences worked out for proto-Hopi and the Tusayan Area, we will find that in Basketmaker I there is a transition from the Basin-type Desert culture to incipient matrilocal bands and, probably, matrilineal clans in association with agriculture.

I happen to have grown up, anthropologically, on Australia. And I am somewhat surprised to find that many of the same straw men are being demolished, and in some cases by slightly dubious statistics. I am also surprised at the cavalier dismissal of the work of earlier scholars. Given the state of knowledge of Australian social organization in 1930, it seems to me that Radcliffe-Brown's contribution was a very considerable one. It was too narrow and did not take into account the systems of Arnhem Land, nor did it treat technology and religion. But it seems to me a base upon which to build and elaborate, rather than something to be destroyed.

HIATT: To reply to Dr. Eggan's comment about our knocking down Radcliffe-Brown's straw men, which is very nearly what Stanner says, I want to say for the record that the horde and the subsections are, at the very least, very sturdy straw men. I make no quarrel with the fact that Radcliffe-Brown was a worthy pioneer in aboriginal studies, but this does not mean that one should not take issue with him on particular points.

EGGAN: Just for the record, I was referring to the last paragraph in Dr. Meggitt's paper.

PART IV

Marriage and Models in Australia

18.

Gidjingali Marriage Arrangements

L. R. HIATT

Lévi-Strauss, whose distinguished contribution to anthropology we honor at this conference, has paid a good deal of attention to the Australian aborigines. In this paper I shall discuss some of his views by relating them to the Gidjingali tribe of northern Arnhem Land.[1]

"Gidjingali" is the term for the language spoken by people who, until recently, lived south of Cape Stewart and around the mouth of the Blyth River. When I carried out my field work between 1958 and 1960, most of them were living about thirty miles from their homelands at Maningrida, a government settlement established in 1957 at the mouth of the Liverpool River. Elsewhere in this volume I have described some aspects of their traditional local organization.[2]

People of northeastern Arnhem Land referred to the Gidjingali as the "Burera," whom Warner (1937, pp. 15, 36) included as one of the eight tribes he designated collectively as the

"Murngin." Although he admitted that they had a very different language from the rest and were affiliated linguistically with tribes further to the west (p. 37), he apparently believed that they shared with other of his "Murngin" tribes a kinship system based on matrilateral cross-cousin marriage. This was not so. The Gidjingali had an Aranda-type kinship system which was based on marriage between certain kinds of second cousins (e.g., MFZDS–MMBDD).[3] A total of four categories of male relatives were distinguished in Ego's grandparental generation.[4]

Lévi-Strauss (1949, 1963 [1958]) attaches fundamental importance to mechanisms of reciprocity. He believes that marriage regulations and kinship systems can best be understood by regarding them as "a kind of language, a set of processes permitting the establishment, between individuals and groups, of a certain type of communication" (1963, p. 61). The mediating factors in this case are not words but women, who are circulated between clans, lineages, or families.

Gidjingali kinship terminology and marriage rules can be adequately described within the limits of a hypothetical system of exchange-marriage among four patriclans. The model bears little relation to marriage arrangements in contemporary practice, and so I shall use the method of conjectural history in presenting it. I shall leave till later the question whether

1. I have made substantial alterations in this paper since presenting it at Man the Hunter Symposium in Chicago.

2. Chapter 10, "Ownership and Use of Land Among the Australian Aborigines."

3. I shall use the following abbreviations: B = brother; D = daughter; F = father; M = mother; S = son; Z = sister.

4. For main characteristics of Aranda-type systems, see Elkin (1964, pp. 99–103).

it has any explanatory, as distinct from ex-
pository, value and, in particular, whether
there is any evidence for supposing it to represent a communication system that uses women
as units.

The Model

Suppose that on some past occasion on aboriginal law-maker named Plato[5] proclaimed the
following constitution:

Section 1 : *Kinship groups and terminology*

a) Descendants in the male line of four men in
Plato's grandparental generation—his FF,
MF, FMB, and MMB—henceforth belong to
four separate clans, named p, q, r, and s
(Fig. 1).

b) A person should apply a different kinship
term to his FF, MF, FMB, and MMB; and to
their respective sisters, sons, and daughters
(Fig. 2).

c) Everyone should abide by the principle
of the equivalence of siblings of the same sex.
For example, a man should apply the same
term to both his F and FB; another term to
both his M and MZ.

d) Everyone should abide by the principle
of the combination of alternate generations.
For example, within his own clan a man should
apply the terms "FF" or "FFZ" to all members of his FF's genealogical generation and
generations alternating with it; and the terms
"F" or "FZ" to all members of other generations. The same principle should be applied
to the other three clans, giving a total of sixteen
terms as indicated in Figure 2.

5. In the original version of this paper, I called the
imaginary law-maker "Moses." Lévi-Strauss, in the
course of his speech accepting the Viking Fund Medal
and Award, spoke of the possible past existence of an
aboriginal Socrates with mental powers capable of
formulating the kind of model I had presented earlier in
the conference. He did not say what he had against my
choice of Moses, but I agree that on the evidence available Socrates would seem to have had the higher I.Q.
Lévi-Strauss might also tend to favor a mind capable of
conceiving perfect Forms and imperfect Particulars. Yet
Socrates was a social critic rather than a law-maker, and
so, as a compromise, I have substituted Plato for Moses.
(Plato's later dialogues, including *The Laws*, present his
own rather than Socrates' views.)

Section 2 : *Marriage rules*

a) Men should not marry within their own
clans.

b) The right to dispose of a girl in marriage
is vested equally in her M and MB. She may
be bestowed an infant but should not live with
her husband till puberty.

c) Men should abide by the principle of
niece-exchange. That is, when a man receives
a woman in marriage, he should subsequently
bestow his own ZD on his WMB.

d) Sons should follow in the same tradition
of exchange as their fathers. Thus, as Plato's
MMB gave a niece to Plato's F (Fig. 1), so
Plato's MMBS should give a niece to Plato;
and Plato's F and Plato should in return give
nieces to their respective WMBs. Figure 3
illustrates the results of such exchanges. Arthur
and Jack have exchanged their nieces, Jill and
Ada. Jack has married his MMBDD, Arthur
his FZDDD. Arthur's DD, Laura, is related to
Jack's son, Simon, as both MMBDD and
FZDD. By extending the diagram further it
can be shown that all niece-exchanges between
the patrilineal descendants of Arthur and Jack
ad infinitum result in marriages to women related to their husbands as both MMBDD and
FZDDD.

e) The rule that sons should follow in the
same tradition of niece-exchange as their
fathers should be interpreted broadly in terms
of clan affiliation, not solely in terms of actual
F–S connections. Thus, clans p and s should
exchange nieces; and, likewise, clans q and r
should exchange nieces.

f) It follows from the two previous rules that
a man has rights to the daughters not only of
his true MMBD but also of all the other
women in her patriclan classified as her sister;
conversely, he has rights to the daughters
not only of his true FZDD but also of all the
other women whose MMs belong to his own
clan.

g) The oldest of a group of men sharing
rights to women as defined in the previous
clause has priority, the second oldest second
priority, and so on. Polygyny is permitted, but
an older man should not take additional wives
by insisting on his prior right if to do so means
subjecting a younger unmarried man to
unreasonable hardship.

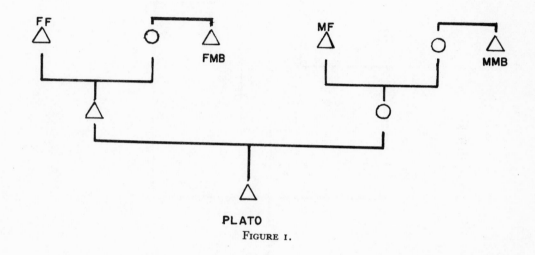

PLATO

FIGURE 1.

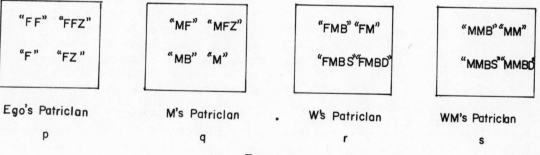

FIGURE 2.

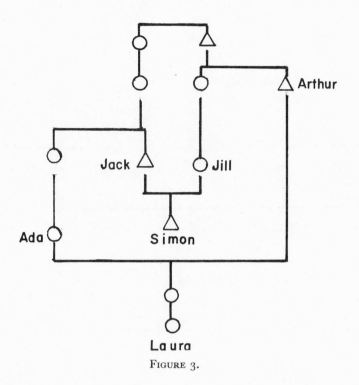

FIGURE 3.

h) No one should marry a person who is not a member of p, q, r, or s. If all the principles set out in this and the previous section of the constitution are obeyed, a closed system of niece-exchange will be set in motion along the lines indicated in Figure 4.

THE FACTS

If Gidjingali marriages once conformed to the principles of this system, they were no longer doing so when I arrived in 1958. The basic kinship terms and the definition of marriage rights were as described. But there was no rule stating that marriages should occur within closed systems of four patriclans. In fact they did not. More important, only a small per-

centage of men managed to marry women to whom they had rights. In this section I shall try to explain why.

In 1960 the Gidjingali numbered about 300. They were divided into four communites and 28 patriclans (mean 10.6, range 2 to 29). Marriages occurred both within and between communities, and, indeed, between Gidjingali and members of neighboring tribes. A person applied one of the four sets of kinship terms (Fig. 2) to members of every patriclan he encountered.

I shall limit my analysis to the Anbara community, which contained a total of 48 adult males and 47 adult females (by "adult" I mean over the age of about 14). I shall use the expressions MMBDD and FZDDD to mean the women to whom Ego had marriage rights, not just his true MMBDD and FZDDD (see Fig. 5).

At the time of observation 25 men were without wives (56 per cent were under 25 years of age). The remaining 23 men (practically all of them aged over 25) were married to a total of 35 wives, only six of whom were related to their husbands as MMBDD or FZDDD. Two questions arise: (1) why were there so few unions consistent with the exercise of marriage rights (only 17 per cent)? and (b) how did the other unions come about? The answers are relevant to a general question raised by Firth (1954, p. 12) when he asked

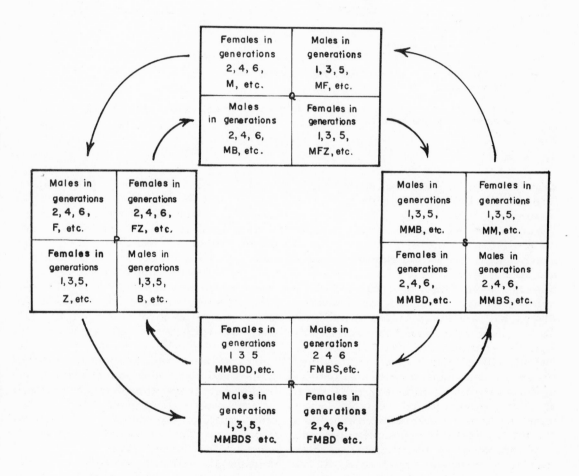

Arrows indicate niece exchange. Thus men of generations 2,4,6 in P and Q marry each other's sisters, receiving them from bestowers in generations 1,3,5 in S and R respectively.

FIGURE 4.

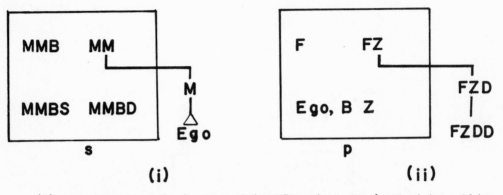

(i) Ego had rights to the daughters of his MMBD and all other females in her patriclan classified as her sister.

(ii) Ego also had rights to the daughters of any other woman classified with his MMBD whose MM belonged to his own patriclan.

FIGURE 5.

what happened in Australian systems when individuals lacked relatives of the kind they were expected to marry.

Examination of genealogical and age data disclosed that, when 18 of the 35 women married, adult males with rights to them were nonexistent. That is, in order to marry upon reaching puberty, these 18 women had to wed men without rights to them. A similar analysis showed that 19 of the 48 Anbara men did not have a MMBDD or FZDDD of marriageable age. The remaining 29 had a total of 27 mature relatives of these kinds, but the distribution of relationships was such that only 21 male-female pairs could be formed. In short, at the time of observation demographic factors alone limited the number of men married to a MMBDD or FZDDD to a possible 44 per cent.

Now in cases where there was no one with a right to a particular female child, it was accepted that her M and MB could without delay choose a man with no right to her. The only formal requirement was that he should belong to the same terminological category as would a man with a right (that is, the girl

should be his classificatory MMBDD); or, alternatively, he should be an actual or classificatory cross-cousin of the girl. The advantage to bestowers in making an early promise to a mature male was that they could from that moment expect him regularly to send them presents, support them in quarrels, and eventually give a niece to his WMB.

Sometimes men with no rights to any women acquired as wives females to whom no other men had rights. Sometimes men with rights waived them in a display of generosity in favor of men without rights. But sometimes interests clashed and fights broke out. It is impossible in this short paper to analyze these conflicts (which occurred more frequently than any other type), or even to outline the opportunism with which bestowers and seekers of wives tried to advance their own interests. I must simply assert that, in a context in which there was a chronic disproportion between the demand for wives and the supply of female relatives specified by the rule defining marriage rights, the rule was often ignored. These breaches, in combination with demographic factors already described, helped to reduce the percentage of men married to a MMBDD or FZDDD even further. I did not observe anything remotely approaching a closed system of exchange-marriage among four patriclans of the type postulated in Figure 4.[6]

MODELS, FACTS, AND FEELING CHEATED

It is not clear from Lévi-Strauss' writings whether he would regard these facts as of any significance for his theory on kinship and marriage. He stated in his inaugural lecture at the Collège de France in 1960: "In admitting the symbolic nature of its object, social anthropology does not thus intend to cut itself off from *realia*. . . . One cannot study . . . social rules independently of the things which correspond to them" (1966, p. 115). Although the word "correspond" might be interpreted narrowly to mean only behavior that conforms with the rules, the context suggests that he was referring to the relationship between rules and what actually happens. In the same year, however, he described Maybury-Lewis as a "prisoner of the naturalistic misconceptions which have so long pervaded the British school," because "when he is presented a structural model which departs from empirical reality, he feels cheated in some devious way" (1960, p. 52). The two statements are not contradictory, but they leave us wondering how much trust Lévi-Strauss is seeking. After suggesting that the different aspects of social life may constitute phenomena whose inmost nature is the same as that of language, he raised the question: "How can this hypothesis be verified?" (1963, p. 62). Before being led into the non-empirical wilderness, we might also like to know how it can be falsified. Or if the theory is merely a heuristic model, in which case normal criteria of falsifiability might properly be regarded as inappropriate, we might still reasonably ask how we are to tell whether or not we are being misguided.

6. For a fuller account, see Hiatt, 1965.

7. Here is an appropriate place to say that I completed this paper before reading Sahlins' review (1966) of *Structural Anthropology*. I shall have the dubious distinction of being among the first to fulfill his prophecies.

8. See Jones, 1925; Malinowski, 1960.

It is at least of passing interest to note that Lévi-Strauss' theoretical approach to social phenomena bears some striking resemblances to that of Freud.[7] First, both writers treat social institutions as manifestations in some degree of certain unconscious properties of the human mind. Lévi-Strauss has written: "The road will then be open for a comparative structural analysis of customs, institutions, and accepted patterns of behavior . . . the so-called 'collective unconscious' would, in the final analysis, be no more than the expression, on the level of individual thought and behaviour, of certain time and space modalities of the universal laws which make up the unconscious activity of the mind" (1963, p. 65). The difference is that the unconscious processes postulated by Freud are conative and affective, whereas those postulated by Lévi-Strauss are cognitive.

Second, in dealing with empirical material both Lévi-Strauss and Freud distinguish between manifest and latent content. Lévi-Strauss has argued that "a theoretical hypothesis which deviates from the manifest content of the ethnographical data is substantially upheld, if we are able to discover, in the latent content supplied by the myths, the religious representations, etc., some data showing a remarkable parallelism between the native categories, and those arrived at by the way of theoretical reconstruction" (1960, p. 50). To grant such conditions is (as well-known from the psychoanalytic debate) at least to give verification the inside-running; and when special hypothesis-saving devices are introduced as well (such as those used by Ernest Jones with the Trobriand material),[8] falsification is left hobbled at the starting-gate. Lévi-Strauss has not, as far as I know, resorted to psychoanalytic devices when informants have failed to give the required answers. Instead, he has postulated an interference with their cognitive processes. In his reply to Maybury-Lewis, he explained a discrepancy between the structural model and ethnographic reality by asserting that the natives had "let themselves be mystified by their own system" (1960, p. 51).

I shall try to anticipate how Lévi-Strauss might deal with the assertion that, among contemporary Gidjingali, women did not circulate between groups in systems of marriage-exchanges. One possibility would be to argue that this fact in itself does not disprove the hypothesis that the kinship terminology and marriage rules constituted an apparatus originally set up for the purposes of communication and used as such. It merely indicates that the apparatus had fallen into disuse. In 1958–60 the lines of communication were still there as an integral part of the kinship system, but, for demographic and other reasons, messages were no longer being sent.

The hypothesis would thus be saved by making it refer to an unobserved state of affairs in the past. In that case my presentation of the model in Figure 4 as an imaginary historical event might have been apt, though whether Lévi-Strauss would accept such a concrete account is another matter (but see note 5). That he is prepared in principle to use the method of conjectural history is indicated clearly by his statement: "One may well ask oneself, then, if Radcliffe-Brown's mistrust of historical reconstruction did not correspond to a stage of scientific development which will soon have passed" (1966, p. 115). This allows us to add yet another similarity between Lévi-Strauss and Freud.

Another defense of the theory might be to say that the postulated communication apparatus is a latent or unrealized aspect of the kinship system, created and perpetuated by unconscious mental structures present in all Gidjingali, but prevented from functioning by demographic and other factors. In this view there would be no critical difference between past states and present, and hence no need to postulate a conception once perfectly realized but now barely acknowledged. To put this another way, the first version of the theory would represent contemporary Gidjingali kinship terminology and marriage rules as "survivals" from a past period when the "true" meaning or purpose of the system was realized in actual behavior (see "The Concept of Archaism in Anthropology," Lévi-Strauss, 1963, p. 117). The second version would postulate the "true" meaning or purpose of the system as a chronically unrealized unconscious ideal.

Explanations of the observed in terms of the unobserved are notoriously susceptible to charges of circularity (e.g., "There is a present in my stocking because Santa Claus came last night; Santa Claus exists because there is a present in my stocking"). We could not place much faith in an explanation of Australian kinship systems in which the effect is the only evidence for the occurrence of the alleged cause. The absence of independent evidence has always been the difficulty for conjectural history, and (as far as the evolution of kinship systems is concerned) I fail to see how such evidence might be provided by "stratigraphic excavations, the introduction of statistics into archaeology, the analysis of pollens, and the use of carbon-14, and above all the closer and closer collaboration between ethnologists and sociologists, on the one hand and archaeologists and prehistorians, on the other" (Lévi-Strauss, 1966, p. 115).

Lévi-Strauss has provided more substantial instructions for discovering independent evidence of unconscious causal factors by directing us to myth, ritual, and religious symbolism (1960, pp. 50, 53). I did not detect such material during my investigations, but perhaps I was not looking for it. The only data that appear to support Lévi-Strauss' theory were undisguised.

First, the people had in relation to marriage arrangements a definite notion of reciprocity between individuals: namely, that if X gives a niece to Y, then Y should subsequently give a niece to X (Fig. 3). Second, marriage rights were defined partly in terms of clan membership (Fig. 5). Third, occasionally men spoke of traditional exchange relationships between clans. Do these three facts indicate that at least some Gidjingali consciously harbored an ideal image of marriage arrangements of the sort represented in Figure 4?

A full discussion of the question would require an analysis of the corporate functions of Gidjingali patriclans. Elsewhere I have argued that they were neither local nor political units and that their main functions were ritual (Hiatt, 1965). But here I shall confine myself to marriage.

The Gidjingali were polygynous, and the ratio of men to women was about equal. This meant that the demand for wives always exceeded the supply. Bachelors worried about their chances of acquiring spouses, married men of losing them. Men and women with girls to dispose in marriage used them to further their own interests. In this context, the system of kinship and marriage to some extent regulated the distribution of scarce resources. Marriage rights stated in terms of specific genealogical links (Fig. 5) located for a man a few women to whose daughters he could make strong claims. Only 17 per cent of unions in the sample I discussed under the heading "The Facts" were consistent with the exercise of such rights. But, as well as narrow rules defining marriage rights, there were also broad rules stated in terms of kin categories. These located for a man a much larger number of women (all those classified with his MMBDD and with his FZD) with whom marriage would be morally proper (or "straight," as it has often been expressed). His difficulty here was that other men had genealogically defined rights to many of these women, and he was accordingly at a jural disadvantage.

Because some confusion has arisen from a failure to distinguish between genealogically defined marriage rights and moral attitudes to marriages stated in terms of kin categories, I shall restate the position in a different way. If a man acquired as a wife (e.g., by elopement) a women belonging to one of the following six categories—Z, FZ, M, MM, MMBD, FMBD—the marriage was regarded as immoral, whether or not the husband had in the process infringed the genealogically defined right of another man. If he married a woman belonging to one of the remaining two categories—MMBDD, FZD—the marriage was regarded as morally proper, again whether or not he had infringed the marriage right of another man. About 90 per cent of Gidjingali marriages were "straight" in this sense. Occasionally, as a result of previous irregularities, a man had a genealogically defined right to a woman who belonged to a category of female relatives with whom marriage was immoral. If he married her, people said that, strictly speaking, the union was improper, but they admitted that the situation was a mix-up.

Given the struggle for wives, it is not surprising that bestowers tended to be hardheaded. Sometimes they bestowed nieces in response to a legitimate claim, sometimes in defiance of it; but usually they aimed at placing the recipient under an obligation. In these circumstances niece-exchange appeared as a contractual arrangement between individuals rather than a symbolic transaction between groups.

I said that marriage rights were defined partly in terms of clan membership. This meant that a man might regard all women of a specified category within a specified patriclan as his potential mothers-in-law and that he might legitimately make a claim on any one of them. It did not mean that the clan as a whole had a joint responsibility to provide him with a wife, and I never saw clansmen speak or act in these terms. I also said that occasionally men spoke of traditional exchange relationships between two patriclans (though never four, as in the system represented in Fig. 4). Analysis of genealogies failed to bear out such assertions, and the people did not take them seriously. Possibly we have here, emerging from the unconscious, a half-formed ideal of how the system should work. Another possibility (which might put the previous one in a different light) is that such assertions were instances of special pleading voiced during disputes in order to bolster dubious marriage claims. Of this I have evidence.

The discussion would be incomplete without some mention of moieties and subsections (indeed, Lévi-Strauss might consider that without them it has not started). The Gidjingali were divided into two exogamous patrimoieties, but the people had no notion of marriage-exchange between them. In view of the facts that a man's ZD belonged to the opposite patrimoiety, and that the system ruled out both daughter-exchange and sister-exchange (to which I shall return later), this is not surprising.

The eight Gidjingali subsections were named divisions corresponding to the eight "brother-sister" terminological categories indicated in Figures 2 and 4. They apparently diffused into the area within the last century (Elkin, 1950); and they have significance mainly in ceremonies of recent adoption. They are neither more nor less significant for marriage regulations than the terminological categories to which they gave objectivity (i.e., in principle it means the same to say "I and everyone I call 'B' may marry anyone we call 'MMBDD' or 'FZD' " as to say "I am in WAMUD subsection, and WAMUD men may marry either

BANGADI or GODJOG women"). The men of a subsection belonged to many different patriclans and tribes over a large area of Arnhem Land.

I must point out that informants were able to indicate the give-and-take of women in subsection terms. In order to relate the following example to Figure 4, I shall put the appropriate kin category in brackets after the subsection: BALANG (MMBS) gives Bangadidjan (MMBDD) to WAMUD (B), and WAMUD (B) gives Ngaridjan (ZD) to BALANG (MMBS). People demonstrated with blocks of wood representing individual men and women. I should point out that folk regularly used subsection terms to address or refer to particular individuals. They knew that men of one subsection did not have corporate rights of disposal over all the women of another, and they did not think of the subsections as solidary groups exchanging nieces, sisters, or any other female kin in marriage (Meggitt, 1962, Ch. 10; also Meggitt, Chapter 19, this volume).

CONCLUSION:
COMMUNICATION OR COMPETITION?

I have demonstrated the possibility of constructing from Gidjingali kinship terminology and marriage rules a hypothetical model of marriage-exchange that verifies Lévi-Strauss' theory that systems of kinship and marriage are really communication systems with women as the mediators. I argued that, among contemporary Gidjingali, women did not circulate in marriage along lines set out in the model, that the people were not using their kinship system as a communication apparatus of the kind postulated, and that they gave little indication of recognizing this as a possibility or of holding it as an ideal. The discrepancy between the model and the facts is wide. Here I concur with Firth: "I am in sympathy with the view that the nature of the evidence, the ethnographic fact, is often less important for the development of our subject than the inference, the generalization, the theoretical argument presented. This can be treated as a 'model,' an heuristic instrument not meant to depict or mirror social reality. But at a certain point, if the argument is not meant as a purely

intellectual exercise, it must apply to some set of demonstrated facts" (1966, p. 2).

I said that, in some degree, the Gidjingali system of kinship and marriage regulated the distribution of scarce resources in women. The question that interests Lévi-Strauss is why the distribution should have taken its characteristic Australian form. His faith in reciprocity as the key to the problem may well be justified. But substantial modifications to his theory would have to be made before it would apply even roughly to the Gidjingali. Here two main points would need to be taken into account. First, the right to give a girl in marriage was vested in her M and MB.[9] Patriclans, subsections, and patrimoieties as corporate groups had nothing to do with the decision, and there was no rule or ideal saying that they ought to. A model of marriage-exchange using these groups as units departs seriously from reality. Second, the Gidjingali had a clear notion of reciprocity in marriage. I have referred to this as "niece-exchange," by which I mean that a bestowal placed the receiver under an obligation to return in kind. Gidjingali men did not have rights to give their sisters or their daughters in marriage.

The second fact is incompatible with Lévi-Strauss' generalization that "in human society a man must obtain a woman from another man who gives him a daughter or a sister" (1962, p. 46). It also raises a question of some significance for all Aranda-type systems (the most widespread kind in Australia). They cannot be accounted for in terms of daughter-exchange because a man's DD belongs to the category of his cross-cousins. An explanation in terms of sister-exchange, on the other hand, is likely to be at variance with the facts of bestowal. Typically, females are promised in marriage as infants by relatives in a senior generation, not by their male siblings. Hypotheses about sister-exchange drawn as inferences from anthropological kinship charts or subsection diagrams are unlikely to have any counterpart in attitudes of the aborigines themselves.

9. A woman's interests and her brother's did not always coincide, but I cannot discuss here what happened when conflict arose (see Hiatt, 1965, pp. 44, 89).

The recent work of Rose on age relationships has an important bearing on this subject.[10] Starting with Lévi-Strauss' view that reciprocity is the keystone of the kinship structure, it is possible by following Rose's method to demonstrate a number of interesting consequences relevant to Australian systems. Aboriginal girls usually married at about 15 years of age, whereas men were lucky to have a wife by the age of 25. The discrepancy was largely a product of polygyny in communities where the sex ratio was about equal. Let us examine the significance of this state of affairs for three possible types of marriage-exchange, regardless of the formal features of the kinship system —(1) sister, (2) daughter, (3) niece.

1. A reasonable working assumption is that few women would be more than ten years younger than their oldest brother and that few men would be more than ten years older than their youngest sister. It would be uncommon, therefore, for a man married at 25 to have a sister aged 15 and his 15-year-old wife to have

10. Rose, 1960. See also discussion between Rose (1965a), Leach (1965a), and Fox (1965).

11. I have belatedly read Barbara Lane's two papers, "Structural Contrasts between Symmetric and Asymmetric Marriage Systems: A Fallacy," *Southwestern Journal of Anthropology*, 17 (1), 1961; and "Jural Authority and Affinal Exchange," *Southwestern Journal of Anthropology*, 18 (2), 1962. Her remarks on niece-exchange are clearly relevant to my analysis of Aranda-type systems, and I apologize for not having given them the attention they deserve.

a brother aged at least 25. These would be the conditions necessary for a sister-exchange to take place in accordance with the minimal age difference between a girl married at puberty and her husband. In most cases the sisters of a man married at 25 to a pubertal girl would be either older than the bride's brothers or, at any rate, not much younger.

2. If a man married at 25, he could not expect to receive a DD in return for his D until he was at least 57 (25 plus 16 plus 16).

3. Suppose a man has a twin sister who marries at 15. By the time he is 31, he might have a 15-year-old ZD. If she marries a man aged 25, also with a twin sister who has married at 15, her husband might have a ZD aged 9. If he fulfills his obligation, her father will acquire a second wife by the age of about 37. (I have used the unlikely example of twin sisters to strike a rough mean between older and younger sisters.)

If it is fair to say that Australian marriage systems were characterized both by a demand for plural wives by dominant older men and by individual reciprocity for mutual advantage (and this I believe to be true), then it might be argued that niece-exchange would have satisfied the requirements better than other possible exchanges.[11] This suggestion, based more on man's animal nature than his spirit, might in the long run provide a better starting-point for an exercise in conjectural history than the view that kinship and marriage are best understood as systems of communication.

19.

"Marriage Classes" and Demography in Central Australia

M. J. MEGGITT

In comparative studies of primitive peoples the Australian aborigines have long held a special place and, perhaps for this very reason, a number of misconceptions concerning their society and culture have entered the anthropological literature. This paper, which is essentially negative in tone, aims at attacking one of these propositions.

Anthropologists and others, writing in general terms about the aborigines, commonly emphasize one or other of two points. Either they single out aborigines as the prime example of simple hunters and gatherers whose way of life is effectively and completely adapted to their environment, or they remark on the complexity of aboriginal social organization.

Thus, from the nineteenth century onward there have been many statements such as the following:

> The Australian . . . who never thinks of the day to come and does not possess other sources of food than those offered him by the bush in the shape of game and of scanty fruit, develops an eminent skill in obtaining his prey at any moment without the help of others and without any complex contrivance. . . . This mode of living makes him the most independent of men, but it also stands in the way of all progress, forcing him to roam restlessly over wide areas (Semon, 1899, p. 154).

What is disconcerting is the way in which assertions about the efficiency of the aboriginal hunter early achieved the status of stereotypes; the same few literary references have been cited many times, with no real understanding of the need to take even the broadest ecological factors into account when generalizing about aboriginal custom. In particular, failure to specify environmental, demographic, economic, and technological differences has led to the acceptance of a picture of the Australian aboriginal everywhere as a highly nomadic, desert-dwelling kangaroo-hunter, with all that such exotic features imply in characterizing a culture. For instance Basedow says:

> The aboriginal's ideal of life is attained when he finds himself in hot pursuit of the game which shares with him the wilds of his ancient haunts. . . . The love of the sport, the keenness of the senses, and the astounding powers of endurance are natural attributes, which the aboriginal alone knows how to use to their fullest. These are the hereditary gifts of man which characterize the primitive hunter (1925, p. 2).

And it is of interest that, in an otherwise excellent description of aboriginal culture, Basedow devotes to an account of men's hunting more than five times the space that he gives to women's food-gathering, whereas recent studies indicate that women's contribution to the daily diet is usually far greater than that of the men (see, for instance, references cited by Meggitt, 1964a, 1964b).

Ashley-Montagu goes even further in fixing this stereotype of the Australian as the desert hunter. In Chapter 2 of *Coming into Being among the Australian Aborigines* (1937), entitled "The Arunta, the type pattern of Australian culture," he says that, because of the common origin of Australian cultures, "any particular culture may in a general way be taken to represent the pattern of Australian culture, the type of which is represented by the culture of the Arunta."

Only in the last two decades have anthropologists demonstrated any great sophistication in recognizing and analyzing regional variations in demographic and environmental factors in Australia and their effects on technological, economic, and social practices. It is unfortunate that, because of the effects of European contacts, this insight has come too late.

In the same way, there has developed through the years a series of stereotypes as early speculations, later hypotheses, and subsequent models concerning aboriginal social organization have been hypostatized into elements of a society that never was.

Perhaps the most obvious example of this process has been the way in which the notion of the horde became accepted as the statement of a great truth (Radcliffe-Brown, 1930, 1951). Ignoring the caveats entered long ago by such investigators as Elkin (1938, p. 40; 1953) and Piddington and Piddington (1932), anthropologists, especially those unacquainted with aboriginal society at first hand, simply assumed that the patrilineal, patrilocal horde was a real entity to be found everywhere in Australia. It is only in the light of recent statements to the contrary by field workers such as Berndt (1959), Hiatt (1962), and Meggitt (1962) that

1. Stanner (1965), for instance, still cleaves to the Radcliffe-Brown model; however, I do not find his arguments in this case persuasive.

2. Sharp's pioneering work (1940) should not be overlooked, although he did not try then to answer such questions as how the age and sex distribution in an aboriginal community affects marriage choices.

this neat but misleading picture is being replaced—albeit reluctantly[1]—by an acceptance of the great variability that actually existed in aboriginal local organization.

A similar sequence of conceptual hardening, followed by slow recognition of the need for empirical studies, has occurred in the investigation of systems of kinship and marriage among the aborigines. Although field workers such as Elkin (1932, 1938, 1938–40) and Kaberry (1939) urged that clear statements be made of the actual degree of variation or choice incorporated in these systems, once again anthropologists abroad simply reified the schematic statements of kin terms and of marriage prescriptions into concrete elements of social behavior and assumed that this was somehow the essential nature of aboriginal societies, that is, that they were in constant equilibrium.

In particular there has been a failure to appreciate the significance of demographic differences within and among these small-scale societies and their importance in conditioning marriage arrangements. Only in the last few years have fieldworkers published quantified data that bear directly on these problems (Rose, 1960a, 1960b; Goodale, 1962; Meggitt, 1962, 1965b; Hiatt, 1965).[2]

But, while the results of empirical research in these several areas have slowly broken through the accretion of reifications that has grown out of former misconceptions, there remains a set of social phenomena about which many anthropologists have been firmly in error. The phenomena are the modes of classifying the world in social and ritual terms which take the form of moiety, section, and subsection systems; the mistake is to regard these schematic categories of cosmic classification as substantive or causally effective "marriage classes," to see them as the primary determinants of marriage arrangements.

The confusion clearly stems from an earlier anthropological preoccupation with the derivation of monogamy from putative group marriage. For exponents of such hypothetical schemes the discovery in the nineteenth century that certain aboriginal tribes were divided in halves, quarters, or eighths, and that these divisions were in some sense exogamous, was of great moment. Here, at a stroke, they could add the missing rungs to their evolutionary ladders. Thus, from an initial stage of group marriage in which all males of the group (= "tribe"?) might mate indiscriminately with any of the females, there developed (for unknown reasons) a situation in which half the women (= that half including mothers and sisters?) were excluded as mates. The presence of moieties among some aborigines was taken to be a survival of that period. Similarly, the existence of sections among other tribes attested to an earlier extension of the prohibitions on mating to three-quarters of the women of the tribe, just as subsections reflected an extension to seven-eighths of the women.

After this, various specifications of mates in terms of classificatory kinship reduced mating to limited polygyny and finally, although not in aboriginal societies, one and only one woman at a time could be the mate of a given man.

Obviously such a simple explanatory scheme was unlikely to survive long but, even though it succumbed to reason, it had significant effects in that subsequently most anthropologists, whatever their theoretical orientation, continued to assume that moieties, sections, and subsections were "marriage classes" in substantially the sense intended by writers such

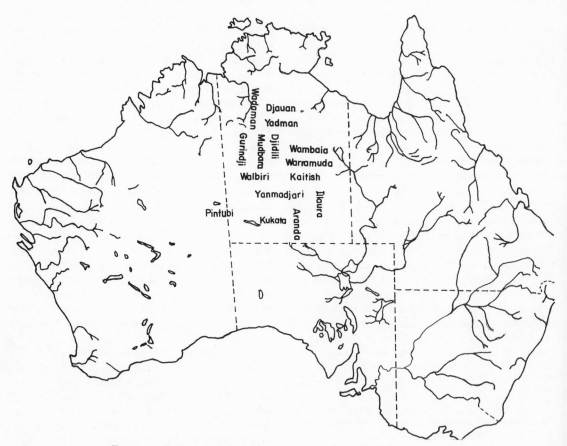

FIGURE 1. LOCATIONS OF ABORIGINAL TRIBES IN CENTRAL AUSTRALIA.

as Frazer, Fison, and Morgan. Thus this assumption not only importantly conditioned the early attempts of men such as N. W. Thomas (1906) to treat Australian data from the armchair; it also significantly biased the observations made in the field by investigators and travelers as varied as Howitt (1889a, 1904), Spencer and Gillen (1899, 1904, 1927), Basedow (1925), and Chewings (1936).

But even as the speculation that moieties, etc., were "marriage classes" was congealing into received dogma, several anthropologists engaged in intensive field research among aborigines were discovering data that led them to express serious doubts about the proposition. Elkin, guided by his usual meticulous concern for the facts of field work, was one of the first to suggest the need for a reassessment. Thus in 1933 he said:

> too much emphasis has been placed on (sections and subsections) as methods of regulating marriage and of classifying kin at the expense of understanding their totemic significance and function . . . though their number and incidence is in ideal intimately related to social behavior (marriage and kinship), they are just as much concerned with the ordering of man's relationship with nature. The latter function, indeed, may be primary (1933, p. 66; see also his comments in *The Australian Aborigines*, 1938).

Considerable support for Elkin also came from the observations of Kaberry (1937, 1939), Stanner (1936), and Warner (1937). All three offered firsthand evidence to show that there is no necessary connection between the presence of sections, etc., and the regulation of marriage in aboriginal society. Especially relevant was

3. Service (1960) is an exception, although I do not think his alternative "environmental" account is adequate.

4. I must emphasize that I am not categorically denying *any* connection between moiety, section, or subsection membership and the selection of spouses. Reay's (1962) data, for instance, make it clear that in some circumstances (as when several remnant tribes live together today) subsection membership may be an additional and even an important factor in the arrangement of marriages. Indeed, it may be that, in situations of European contact or declining population, the greater the failure of kinship-phrased marriage prescriptions to work, the more likely are the people to rely on the broadly based sections or subsections to define spouses.

the demonstration that a tribe such as the Kariera, the Murngin, or the Murinbata could readily adopt a section or subsection system that was incompatible with its prescriptive rules of marriage, and that nevertheless both usages could be maintained. Subsequent field work by Falkenberg (1962), Meggitt (1962), and Hiatt (1965) confirmed these kinds of conclusions.

Despite presentation of such evidence in the 1930's, however, the view persisted in some quarters (and apparently is still held today) that among aborigines moieties, sections, and subsections are groupings, membership in which crucially determines marriage arrangements or choices.[3] Thus Lawrence (1937) argued this at some length and with much ingenuity, although it is difficult to see what he proposed as evidence for his assertions. Later Murdock (1949) took Lawrence's position as being in some way conclusive, but again it is hard to discern the empirical basis for this.

In the light of the history I have so briefly sketched, I want to devote the rest of this paper to presenting further evidence (albeit of a negative sort) to support the view that subsection systems are not primarily concerned to regulate marriage.[4]

The argument is simple. As I have already remarked, data published by Rose, Goodale, Hiatt, and myself indicate that demographic factors, or variations in them, may in particular cases exert considerable and fairly direct influence on patterns of marriage in aboriginal society. But, as I shall show, demographic differences have little or no effect on the presence or even on the functioning of subsection systems. The reason seems clear—marriages, as well as marriage prescription, concern finite numbers of real people in interaction; if, as can easily happen in a situation of change, there are not enough individuals to fill or to exemplify the pertinent statuses or categories, the system simply fails and soon ceases to be. On the other hand subsections, like moieties and sections, are fundamentally conceptual schemata for the classification, not merely of spouses or even of people at large, but of the entire world that the aboriginal knows. That is to say, as long as that universe exists, or substantial parts of it persist, all categories can be occupied (although not necessarily all by

Table 1   Central Australian Tribes—Statistical Summary

Tribe	N	$\bar{X}e$	$\Sigma/D/$	Id	C%	F%
Walbiri	1570	98.1	146.0	1.48	35	50
Aranda	758*	47.4	363.6	7.66	27	47
Yanmadjari	506	31.6	98.0	3.10	27	50
Illiaura	430	26.9	179.6	6.67	36	50
Warramunga	256	16.0	84.0	5.25	39	48
Gurindji	251	15.7	69.6	4.43	22	45
Kaitish	235	14.7	55.6	3.78	32	56
Pintubi	227	14.2	95.0	6.69	41	51
Djauan	227	14.2	80.6	5.67	18	40
Mudbara	194	12.1	52.6	4.34	32	40
Djingili	142	8.9	56.2	6.31	21	44
Wadaman	137	8.5	47.0	5.53	17	49
Wambaia	88	5.5	33.0	6.00	34	59
Kukata	69	4.3	40.8	9.49	46	56
Yangman	54	3.4	20.8	6.12	20	44
Mean	343	21.4				

*not including 197 Aranda for whom the relevant information was not available.

people) and the system can continue. It follows then that demographic changes and changes in local and economic organization (even though considerable) of the kind that have commonly been associated with European contacts need not entail a breakdown in the subsection system of a particular tribe.

The sample of tribes from which I draw my data is fairly small—fifteen tribes in all. They are all located in the Northern Territory, and all are hinterland groups that normally reside in arid to semi-arid country (see Fig. 1). Thus these tribes are reasonably comparable in terms of important environmental variables and in terms of population densities. I deliberately avoided using groups from the more richly endowed coastal regions. Perhaps the easiest way to locate the sample is to note that these people are all immediate or close neighbors of the Walbiri, the tribe with which I have worked intensively and which I know best.[5]

Another point, relevant to my argument, is that members of this sample have experienced different degrees and kinds of contact with Europeans, ranging from mildly to markedly disruptive. But whatever the effects that these

changes have had on local organization, economic conditions, or marriage arrangements, none of the tribes in the sample has abandoned its subsection system.

The population figures I use here derive from the 1957 Register of Wards compiled by the Welfare Branch of the Northern Territory Administration, which indicates—where appropriate—section, subsection, or clan affiliation as well as tribal membership. Comparison of the Walbiri figures given there with my own suggests (to me at any rate) that the census as a whole is tolerably accurate. If anything, it tends to overestimate some tribal numbers because the mobility of the aborigines may lead to double counting.

I summarize the relevant figures in Table 1. The symbols I use have the following meanings:

N = the number of members of the tribe.

$\bar{X}e = N/16 =$ the number of males or the number of females expected in each subsection if they were evenly distributed; that is, $N/8 =$ the number of people ideally in each subsection.

$/D/ = \bar{X}e - \bar{X}o =$ the difference (ignoring arithmetical sign) between the expected and the

5. I worked with the Walbiri in 1953–54, 1954–55, and 1959–60. I thank the University of Sydney for its financial support during this time.

observed number of males or of females in each subsection of the tribe.

$\Sigma/D/$ = the sum of the deviations, ignoring arithmetical sign.

Id = $\Sigma/D/\bar{X}e$ = the sum of the deviations divided by the expected mean.

= the Index of Deviation for the tribe.

C% = the ratio of children under the apparent age of 14 years to the total size of the tribe.

F% = the ratio of females of all ages to the total size of the tribe.

The first point to note is the range of tribal size in the sample—from a mere 54 members to 1,570 members. But despite these differences in size (which in some cases at least are directly connected with different kinds of encounters with Europeans), every one of these tribes still has a subsection system. Indeed, the names of the categories are cognate from tribe to tribe, and tribesmen are able to employ this resemblance when visiting each other.

The second important point is that in every tribe the observed distribution of males and females (both adults and children) through

the subsection system differs appreciably from the expected mean. Although I am not convinced of the propriety of utilizing the Chi-squared test of significance in such an inquiry,[6] application of the test indicates that probably only in one case (that of the Kaitish) is the difference between the observed and expected distributions not statistically significant. I can given no reason for the one exception.

Third, when Indices of Deviation are computed for all fifteen tribes and are correlated with the actual size (N) of the tribes in terms of the Rank Difference coefficient, the result $Rho_{Id, N} = -.37$ is *not* statistically significant. That is to say, there appears to be no significant relationship, positive or negative, between simple size of the tribe and the distribution of tribal members through the subsections.

Fourth, when the Indices of Deviation are correlated with the ratios of children (C%) in the fifteen tribes, the result $Rho_{Id, C\%} = +.20$ is also not statistically significant.

Fifth, when the Indices of Deviation are correlated with the ratios of females (F%) in the fifteen tribes, the result $Rho_{Id, F\%} = +.11$ is again not statistically significant.

These seem to me to be the only calculations that may safely be made on the basis of the specifications of the available sample of tribes, but I am persuaded that they enable us to say confidently that, for these hinterland tribes at any rate, intertribal demographic differences have no discernible effects on the presence or absence of subsection systems. A fortiori, then, these results may be taken to support empirically the proposition that, among the Australian aborigines, subsections are not necessarily concerned in a substantive manner in the regulation of marriage.[7]

---

6. Because subsections are by definition correlated categories (through indirect matrilineal descent).

7. Naturally this conclusion would benefit from a definitive demonstration that the deviation of the specifications of actual unions from ideal marriage prescriptions in a tribe varies inversely with its numerical size. Although the relevant data are not available for all the tribes in the sample used here, it is the case that in the largest tribe, the Walbiri, adherence to marriage rules is clearly marked—some 92 per cent of unions do in fact conform (see Meggitt, 1962, p. 86; 1965).

APPENDIX

Examples of actual distributions of individuals through subsections and moieties.

Walbiri

Matrimoiety I		*Matrimoiety II*	
(Djabaldjari) ×		(Nagamara)	
109 (68 men+41 boys)		(24 women+41 girls) 65	
(Nabaldjari) ×		(Djagamara)	
107 (75 w+32 g)		(49 m+58 b) 107	
(Djabangari) ×		(Nambidjimba)	
85 (48 m+37 b)		(62 w+29 g) 91	
(Nabangari) ×		(Djambidjimba)	
104 (72 w+32 g)		(52 m+37 b) 89	
(Djangala) ×		(Nungarai)	
95 (72 m+23 b)		(66 w+39 g) 105	
(Nangala) ×		(Djungarai)	
98 (73 w+25 g)		(68 m+33 b) 101	
(Djuburula) ×		(Nabanangga)	
100 (67 m+33 b)		(68 w+28 g) 96	
(Naburula) ×		(Djabanangga)	
125 (95 w+30 g)		(58 m+35 b) 93	

MM I = 823   N = 1,570   MM II = 747

Matrimoiety I
255 men+134 boys = 389 males
315 women+119 girls = 434 females

Matrimoiety II
227 men+163 boys   = 390 males
220 women+137 girls = 357 females

= 779 males+791 females

men = 482		boys = 297	
women = 535		girls = 256	
adults = 1017		children = 553	

	Pintubi	

Matrimoiety I		Matrimoiety II	
(Djabaldjari) 23 (8 m+15 b)	×	(Nagamara) (4 w+4 g)	8
(Nabaldjari) 28 (18 w+10 g)	×	(Djagamara) (5 m+1 b)	6
(Djabangari) 4 (3 m+1 b)	×	(Nambidjimba) (8 w+7 g)	15
(Nabangari) 9 (8 w+1 g)	×	(Djambidjimba) (9 m+8 b)	17
(Djangala) 22 (8 m+14 b)	×	(Nungarai) (12 w+1 g)	13
(Nangala) 21 (14 w+7 g)	×	(Djungarai) (13 m+3 b)	16
(Djuburula) 19 (10 m+9 b)	×	(Nabanangga) (7 w+3 g)	10
(Naburula) 13 (4 w+9 g)	×	(Djabanangga) (2 m+1 b)	3
MM I = 139	N = 227	MM II = 88	

Matrimoiety I
29 men+39 boys   = 68 males
44 women+27 girls = 71 females

Matrimoiety II
29 men+13 boys   = 42 males
31 women+15 girls = 46 females

= 110 males + 117 females

men	=	58	boys	=	52
women	=	75	girls	=	42
adults	=	133	children	=	94

Yangman

Matrimoiety I		*Matrimoiety II*	
(Djabaldjari) 4 (3 m+1 b)	×	(Nagamara) (3 w+0 g) 3	
(Nabaldjari) 4 (3 w+1 g)	×	(Djagamara) (3 m+0 b) 3	
(Djabangari) 1 (1 m+0 b)	×	(Nambidjimba) (2 w+1 g) 3	
(Nabangari) 2 (1 w+1 g)	×	(Djambidjimba) (2 m+0 b) 2	
(Djangala) 5 (5 m+0 b)	×	(Nungarai) (1 w+3 g) 4	
(Nangala) 4 (4 w+0 g)	×	(Djungarai) (4 m+4 b) 8	
(Djuburula) 2 (2 m+0 b)	×	(Nabanangga) (1 w+0 g) 1	
(Naburula) 3 (3 w+0 g)	×	(Djabanangga) (5 m+0 b) 5	

MM I = 25   N = 54   MM II = 29

Matrimoiety I
11 men+1 boy   = 12 males
11 women+2 girls = 13 females

Matrimoiety II
14 men+4 boys   = 18 males
7 women+4 girls = 11 females

= 30 males + 24 females

Men = 25	boys = 5
women = 18	girls = 6
adults = 43	children = 11

20.

Demographic and Ecological Influences on Aboriginal Australian Marriage Sections

ARAM A. YENGOYAN

Aboriginal Australian social structure has been traditionally regarded as a complex cultural elaboration which integrates whole societies or "tribes." Most sociological interpretations have stressed the formal aspects of structure, although Kroeber (1938, p. 217) has attempted to demonstrate that formal aspects of Australian social organization (such as clans, moieties, descent groups, and totemism) are secondary structural patterns which rely on primary patterns such as subsistence and locality. In summary, Kroeber (1938, p. 218) concluded that the elaborate system of Australian marriages takes the form of unconscious experiment in the manner of fads and fashions. Though there is no disagreement with Kroeber's distinction between primary and secondary structures, one can examine the functions and interrelationship between section systems and environmental and demographic factors.

The specific purpose of this paper is to examine the ecological and demographic factors which regulate different section systems.[1] The following points will be investigated:

1. A correlation between different section systems and certain environmental conditions is present and empirically observable.

2. Population size is an important feature in the operation of section systems and in part determines their ideal functioning.

3. Section systems may also function in regulating interaction over a delimited area, thus serving as a means of "insuring" utilizable resources.

The analysis of such problems is always limited due to the scarcity of reliable quantified data on population structure, areas of exploitation, etc. Population models, which are constructed from a generalized knowledge of hunting and collecting groups, may be utilized as an operational device to illuminate certain problems and areas of investigation. The population pyramid in this paper represents such a device, since accounts of precontact aboriginal population structure were unobtainable.

METHOD

The population parameter (population size, area, and density) represents the primary unit in relating environmental factors to section

1. I wish to thank the following individuals for their assistance, comments, and criticism of the original and revised versions of this paper: J. A. Barnes, J. B. Birdsell, Fred Eggan, Clifford Geertz, Ernest Goldschmidt, L. R. Hiatt, M. J. Meggitt, David M. Schneider, Elman R. Service, H. Clyde Wilson, and Eric R. Wolf.

systems, and also the pivotal point in the ideal operation of section systems as regards their function in marriage regulation. Birdsell (1953, pp. 205–206) has demonstrated a .8 correlation between mean annual rainfall and population density for 123 ecologically homogeneous tribes. Since water is the most important environmental variable, it has a direct influence on the type of local biota and cultural variables which regulate a group's extractive efficiency and population structure.

Population size, area, and density are then correlated with different section systems. The population pyramid is utilized to demonstrate how tribal size may set specific limitations on the functioning of any marriage system. Population area figures are not always available nor reliable. However, one readily notices from Tindale's (1940) map that the largest tribal areas are located in extreme arid conditions and are commonly characterized by the occurrence of subsection systems.

ENVIRONMENT AND SUBSISTENCE

Rainfall represents the determining variable for the existence of different vegetation belts in Australia. Mean annual rainfall varies from 2–3 inches to 150 inches per year. Highest aridity occurs in the center of the continent; as one moves outward toward the coastal regions rainfall increases reaching a maximum in the Cairns rain forest of Queensland (G. Taylor, 1943, p. 83).

Mean annual rainfall is not always an adequate criterion for available surface waters. For example, unearned or secondary waters may fall in one tribal area but are utilized in another. This phenomenon is present where one finds large rivers with substantial seasonal drainages. An example of how secondary waters affect assumed population densities occurs in the region of the Murray and Darling river drainages. The mean rainfall in this area is 5–10 inches per year; however, population densities are exceedingly high on the riverine frontages. Both rivers have their sources in the high dividing ranges to the east which are characterized by a 30–50 inches of rainfall. The runoff from these drainage systems is sufficient enough to produce a flourishing biota

and a relatively high population density downstream (Commonwealth of Australia, 1953).

Even in areas with an adequate rainfall, deserts may be common. This phenomenon occurs in regions lacking zinc and copper as trace elements, thus making any type of vegetation quite sparse (Anderson and Underwood, 1959, p. 97).

The mapping of surface water supplies represents a difficult task. Johnston (1940) marked available water supplies along aboriginal routes for the western portion of South Australia. Although this account is quite limited, it does provide an adequate description of routes and names dealing with water supplies. Routes in the Ooldea region are from one water source to the next, thus the utilization of a route varies with seasonal differences in water supplies. Water is derived from rock holes, soaks, wells, claypans, dams, roots of the desert oak, and the *mallee* tree. The more important water supplies have some totemic significance and play an important part in aboriginal ceremonial and social life (Johnston 1940, pp. 34–35).

Since water supply distribution are unavailable for the remainder of the continent and mean annual rainfall data are not precise enough, effective annual rainfall may be utilized. Effective annual rainfall is the amount of rain utilized after evaporation is excluded. Hence, in the Australian case, rain in excess of one-third of the evaporation is termed effective rainfall. Evaporation in most areas is high and in the central regions it may exceed 100 inches per annum. Approximately 76 per cent of Australia has a growing period of four months or less (Commonwealth Scientific and Industrial Research Organization, 1960, p. 30). Australian vegetation patterns are directly related with effective annual rainfall. Rainforests exist in coastal Queensland, eastern New South Wales, southern Victoria, and the southwestern portions of West Australia, while spinifex desert areas are located in the central and western parts of the continent.

The diet of the Australian aborigine is basically vegetarian (Meggitt, 1964b), though nearly all edible animals and plant foods are consumed. Diets vary from desert areas to coastal regions, yet in both cases the samples substantiate the claim that the aborigines exploit practically all sources of available energy and cover the full range of foods which may be economically utilized. The Walbiri of central Australia represent a good example of how a desert group has extensively utilized the spinifex environment (Sweeney, 1947, p. 289). Native plant foods are divided into three groups: bush fruits, root foods, and seeds. Bush fruits consist of wild oranges, wild figs, desert plums, berries, desert tomatoes, desert raisins, desert yams, and onion grass, while seeds consist of pod seeds, grasses, and wild herbage. The dominant animal foods are kangaroos, euros, desert marsupials, rock wallabies, lizards, carpet snakes, and rabbits. Honey, eggs, gall insects, and grubs are other miscellaneous foods (Cleland and Johnston, 1933, p. 114). Annual precipitation is about eight inches, thus the growing period is quite short though it is longer than in the Lake Eyre region to the south.

Even in high precipitation areas such as southeast Australia, no single grain is obtainable in vast quantitites. All forms of life compete for available resources, yet one notes a regulation of activities among animals and man which to a certain extent are mutually interdependent relationships. As one moves from the center to the well-watered fringe areas, resources are more abundant and seasonal availability is longer. Utilized resources increase in quantity and quality on the coastal regions where a new biota is exploited. Coastal tribes have access to marine resources such as fish, whales, dugong, turtles, and shellfish, as well as different plant foods such as coastal yams, lilies, pandanus, cycad nuts, and numerous varieties of roots and grasses.

For a relatively dry continent such as Australia, ranging from tropical to desert habitats, the variation in flora will be dependent to a large degree on rainfall. The biomass of the flora will be expected to vary directly with the intensity of annual rainfall. Since man stands at the peak of the food chain, exploiting all lower trophic levels (animals *and* plants) population densities must also respond to rainfall variation.

All technological implements and skills revolve around the primary subsistence patterns of hunting and food collecting. Wood, bone, and stone are the most commonly utilized materials, with the proportion of utilization varying with the habitat. The two most important extractive devices are the stone axe or chopper and the digging stick. Sharp (1952, p. 69) stated that among the Yir Yiront, the stone axe was not only an important male implement, but also possessed a high degree of ritual value since it symbolized masculinity and age. Tindale and Noone (1941, p. 122) observed similar conditions in central and western Australia. Stone is used for flakes, scrapers, bulbs, and adzes; however, in most cases each of these tools may be remanufactured from one type to another (Tindale, 1957, p. 40). The adze is a crucial tool since it is used to make boomerangs, spearheads, sacred objects, water bowls, winnowing troughs, etc. Women's tools are digging sticks, clubs, and occasionally stone implements.

Both sexes are fully involved in extracting daily food supplies. Hunting activities are predominantly men's work, while women collect plant foods, seeds, eggs, and occasionally hunt rabbits. Women are often better "trackers" than men, although if large game is seen or water is located, the women will tell the men who, in turn, will decide what course of action to follow. Females will collect foods up to four or five miles from a campsite, while men will go nearly seven or eight miles from a camp in order to hunt large game. When foods are exploited within a 6- to 8-mile radius from a camp, the local group will shift to another site. Collecting is generally foreign to men's work, although hunters will gather plant foods to fill immediate needs while away from the camp.

All food is distributed among the local group and promptly consumed. Ideally the local group claims everything in their own territory; however, if certain foods are abundant, any individual may partake in it.

TRIBES AND SECTIONS

The population unit employed in this paper is the tribe. Though there is much controversy about definitions and formal aspects of aboriginal local organization (Birdsell, 1958; Hiatt, 1962; Stanner, 1965) and about the concept of the tribe (Berndt, 1959; Davidson, 1938a), the use of the term *tribe* is primarily arbitrary. Since the majority of trained anthropological field workers as well as other observers have presented demographic and cultural data under this or that "named" tribe, the problem of defining a tribe to fit all particular cases is not necessary. However, a tribe may be considered as a reference group by which individuals identify with each other either through common language, ritual and legend, kinship and marriage, or locality.

The Australian tribe possesses no effective political and economic control. Although tribal functions are minimal as regards sociocultural factors, it does represent an effective breeding unit. Intratribal marriages constitute from 80–90 per cent of all unions (Tindale, 1953), and it may be suggested that rates of intertribal marriages may vary with demographic factors. Whereas the local group possesses mechanisms for socioeconomic activity and social control, the tribe as an "ideally" endogamous unit, though not always, would designate a genetic and demographic unit.

Sections and subsections should not be fully equated with marriage classes, nor do sections only function in the regulation of marriage choices (Meggitt, Chapter 19, this volume). The same author (1964a) has noted that sections and subsections "were essentially ritual categories," while Elkin has stated that "what the [sections] do is to summarize relations into four groups, in one of which a possible spouse is normally found; but in the same group various other types of relations are also included." The determination of marriage mates is based on kinship relationships.

Thus, the section system is a shorthand index for combining kin relations into categories for multiple purposes, be it possible marriage mates, ritual, or economic activity. Finer distinctions within each section category are left to genealogical connections and locality. Meggitt (1962, p. 169) also recognized sections as simplified combinations of individuals when he stated that "basically, [the Walbiri] regard subsections as a summary expression of social relationships that may sometimes be practically useful but just as often is dangerously ambiguous." Hiatt's (1965, p. 50) interpretation of Gidjingali subsections followed Meggitt's analysis.

While marriages are based on kinship relations and locality, the analysis of marriages is commonly summarized in terms of sections or subsections. Thus, preferred, alternative, and wrong marriages stem from the kinship system but are presented within a section-subsection framework. In this paper, sections and subsections are utilized as a summary index of marriages, and not as the determining factor in regulating marriage choices.

THE POPULATION PARAMETER

For operational purposes, a parameter is defined as all key quantifiable variables that structure a population. Furthermore, a parameter not only designates the population of a particular unit but also circumscribes one unit from other comparable ones. Thus, to a geneticist, the parameter delimits effective breeding units which may be compared to one another for the demarcation of clines. In utilizing the tribe as a unit of comparison, the governing variables which characterize the demographic structure are population size, area, and density. Size and area co-vary with environmental factors, while density is the function of both variables.

Since Birdsell (1953) has demonstrated a correlation between population density and mean annual rainfall for ecologically homogeneous tribes, a relationship may also exist between population size and area, and rainfall. Tindale (1940, p. 150) noted that the size of tribal areas was inversely proportional to rainfall. In regions where tribal areas were large, the annual rainfall was remarkably low. There was also a high degree of correlation between tribal limits and ecological-geographical boundaries. Lines of communication and migration tended to follow natural lines of least resistance across the continent, often clinging to open plains, creeks, rivers, and lines of water along ranges, and avoiding dense forests and rugged mountains. Tindale's (1940) tribal map reveals that the largest tribal areas occur in the central and western deserts, while the small, more fragmented areas are along the coast and in other favorable habitats.

The average Australian tribal size is given by Krzwicki (1934, p. 305) as 500, with a range from 150 to 2,500. Elkin's (1964, p. 25) figure for the tribal average is 500 to 600, with a range from 100 to 1,500. Tindale (1940) also recognized an average tribal size of 500, though he noted that it may be high. Lumholtz regarded tribal size as about 200 members in regions adjoining rain forests (Wheeler, 1910, p. 33). In general, one would expect to find tribes whose sizes are lower than the continental average on the coastal and interior coastal areas. Although the coastal tribes have less area and fewer individuals, they still possess the highest population densities.

In order to observe variations in population size and density, different environmental areas will be briefly discussed. In West Australia, from the Kimberleys, southwest to Eighty Mile Beach, a number of tribal groups on the coast and interior coastal area utilize both marine and terrestrial resources. The coastal Kariera are one of the best reported groups (Radcliffe-Brown, 1931). The Kariera occupied an area of 3,750 square miles with an estimated population of 750. The tribe was divided into 20 to 25 local groups, each occupying a defined area. Band size varied from 30 to 40 individuals. Population density in this relatively favorable environment was one person per five square miles. Elkin estimated that the well-watered portion of the Kimberley district may have had an overall population of 10,000 living on 65,000 square miles, or one person per six or seven square miles (Meggitt, 1964, p. 166). Reports by Hernandez (1941), Stanner (1932), and Webb (1933) for other coastal and interior coastal groups indicated similar population conditions.

Further southwest, near the Swan River, Stirling estimated one native per two square miles during the early years of the settlement, while Radcliffe-Brown (1930, p. 689) calculated one person per four square miles. Population densities become progressively lower in the eastern portion of West Australia (that is, Great Sandy Desert, Gibson Desert). The Rawlinson Ranges area, from Lake Christopher east to the western edge of the Petermann

Ranges, may have had a density of one person per 30 to 40 square miles. This area of approximately 5,400 square miles contained a population of 172 persons.[2] For the whole of West Australia, Radcliffe-Brown (1930, p. 695) estimated a former aboriginal population of 52,000 and an overall population density of one person per 18.8 square miles.

The northern section of the state of South Australia (that is, north of Port Augusta) represents one of the lowest rainfall areas in Australia. This area is approximately 300,000 square miles and has a rainfall average of less than ten inches per year. Tribes with higher population densities occupied the area of the Murray drainage. Radcliffe-Brown (1930, p. 690) estimated an aboriginal population of 6,000 for the southern portion while the northern part of the state may have had population densities as low as one person per eighty square miles. The Musgrave Ranges in the northeast had a population density of one person per 30–35 square miles, though variations between the ranges and plains alter this estimate. The Ooldea groups in western South Australia were tribally fragmented due to conflicts over trade routes and sacred waters. From Berndt's (1942) account, one deduces that the Ooldea area may have supported a relatively large population though the overall density was exceedingly low. Howitt (1891, p. 33) estimated the Dieri of the eastern lakes region at 1,100 members with a density of one person per twenty square miles; however, this density figure may be too high due to the exceedingly poor environmental conditions. A total population of approximately 3,000 for the whole of the lakes region may have been reasonable enough (Elkin, 1931, pp. 51–52).

Southeast Australia (Victoria and eastern New South Wales) represents the most extensive cultural elaboration and highest population densities in Australia. Curr (1886–87) estimated the total Gippsland population at 1,500, and Howitt's (1904, p. 23) figures for whole Gippsland area yielded a population density of one person per 9–10 square miles. Radcliffe-Brown (1930, p. 691) assumed an irreducible minimum figure of one person per fifteen square miles for the Gippsland area. For the Mt. Burr and Mt. Gambier areas, Campbell (1939, p. 35) concluded that 2,000 abori-

2. These figures, as well as those for the Musgrave area of N. W. South Australia, were obtained in discussion with W. McDougall, the native patrol officer for South Australia, who is employed by the Department of Supply and attached to the Weapons Research Establishment, Woomera, South Australia. Population data for the Rawlinsons was collected in 1955–56.

gines lived in this region in 1895 though they were being exterminated at a rate of 50 per cent every five years. On the southern frontage of the Murray and Darling rivers, Howitt (1904, p. 53) designated an area of 2,500 square miles occupied by ten tribes totaling 1,200 individuals. Population density in this area was approximately one person per two square miles. For the same area, Curr estimated one person per 2.3 to 3 square miles (Radcliffe-Brown, 1930, p. 691) and Wallace in the 1870's reported that local groups along the Murray drainage consisted of 60 to 100 people (Campbell, 1934, p. 28).

Coastal New South Wales had an estimated population of 25,000 with a denser population on the north coast (Radcliffe-Brown, 1930, p. 695). Megitt (1964, p. 165) noted that early observations of the Sydney district from Botany Bay to Broken Bay suggested a population range of 1,500 to 3,000 occupying a narrow coastal strip of 400 to 500 square miles.

The Queensland coastal area was generally similar in tribal densities to the southern coastal regions. From Broad Sound to the Clarence River, the population density was one person per three to four square miles (Radcliffe-Brown, 1930, p. 694). On the Cape York Peninsula, the Yir Yiront had an average density of one person per 4.8 square miles, but then density was twice as high (one person per 2.4 square miles) if only utilized land is considered (Sharp, 1940, p. 486).

In general, Arnhem Land population densities were unusually high and are comparable to the coastal tribes of Victoria, New South Wales, and Queensland. The Groote Eylandt inhabitants in 1939 numbered 300 to 350, with a density of one person per three square miles (Rose, 1960b, p. 12). Hiatt (1965, p. 17) reported Gidjingali population density at two persons per square mile on an occupied area of 150 square miles. The Carpentarian Gulf tribes also had an overall density of two persons per square mile according to Thomson (1934a). The Kaiadilt of Bentinck Island showed comparable and even higher population densities. Tindale (1962b, p. 304) stated that

The density of population for the whole of Bentinck Island area in 1940 (the last year when all were present) was 1.7 persons per square mile

of total land and reef surface, or over 6.8 persons for each square mile of reef. Since part of the total area is inaccessible, and only used at some risk (as indicated by two tragic episodes accompanying efforts to reach Allen Island in 1940 and 1947) only about 14 square miles of reef were in constant use, i.e., over 8 persons obtained their food on each square mile of reef (1962b, p. 304).

Murngin population density was about one person per eight or nine square miles (Warner, 1937, p. 16). On the Daly River, 100 to 150 Murinbata occupied 500–700 square miles (Stanner, 1936, p. 187).

As one moves into the more rigorous environments of central Australia, densities become lower since desert populations need more land to support themselves. The Aranda, who occupied the more productive portions of central Australia, numbered less than 2,000 and occupied over 25,000 square miles (Spencer and Gillen, 1899). For the Walbiri, Meggitt (1962, p. 32) concluded that the precontact population ranged from 1,000 to 1,200 in an area of 35,000 square miles. The average population density was one person per 35 square miles. These low densities are comparable to other desert areas such as the Rawlinson Ranges and the Pitjandjara of the Musgrave-Mann-Tomkinson Ranges.

The total aboriginal population of Australia had an overall average density of one person per twelve square miles. Radcliffe-Brown's (1930) enumeration of the aboriginal population by states is as follows:

District	Est. No. of Aborigines	Area (sq. mi.)	Density
Western Australia	52,000	975,920	One per 18.8
South Australia	10,000	380,070	One per 38.0
Victoria	11,500	87,884	One per 7.6
Queensland	100,000	670,500	One per 6.7
New South Wales	40,000	310,372	One per 7.8
Northern Territory	35,000	523,620	One per 15.0
Tasmania	2,500	26,215	One per 10.5
	251,000	2,974,581	One per 11.9

The remainder of the population data, which has been extracted from Curr (1886–87), Krzwicki (1934) and other sources, is listed in Tables 1, 2, and 3.

From the variation in population size and densities, one notices how ecological factors interplay in limiting and preserving environments. "Primitive" man's territoriality is not only limited by cultural factors, but also by environmental and demographic components which regulate population size and tribal interaction.

Section Systems and the Population Parameter

The correlation between section systems and each component of the population parameter is listed in Tables 1, 2, and 3. In each table, the absence of sections, which is labeled "0," the moiety organization ("2"), sections ("4"), and subsections "(8)" are horizontally demarcated. Table 1 lists tribal areas by square miles, while Tables 2 and 3 deal with population size and density respectively. Since the samples are relatively small, the median rather than the average or mean has been utilized in each case. From Table 1, note that with an increase in tribal area, there is a complementary change in the number of sections, except from "0" to "2."

Tribal sizes also increase with the number of sections. With a sample of 76 cases, this correlation may represent a higher degree of assurance. However, the subsection systems are represented by only seven cases, thus limiting the quantitative base of our statements. Further investigation on the relation of tribal size to number of sections follows in the Discussion.

In the plotting of median points for tribal area and size (Tables 1 and 2), the same pattern emerges in each case. With a corresponding increase in tribal area and size, one notes an increase in tribes with sections and subsections. However, this relationship may not hold true for those tribal groups where the most important marriage restriction is local group exogamy. Since the "0" tribes occupy the environmentally favorable coastal areas, the hypothesis as stated earlier may not fully

Table 1   Sections and Tribal Areas

X Square Miles	0	2	4	8	Total
0–250					
250–500		I			1
500–750		I			1
750–1000		1m			1
1000–1250					
1250–1500					
1500–1750	1m	I			2
1750–2000	I				1
2000–2250			I		1
2250–2500					
2500–2750					
2750–3000			I		1
3000–3250					
3250–3500					
3500–3750					
3750–4000			3m		3
4000–4250		I			1
4250–4500					
4500–4750					
4750–5000			I		1
5000–5250			I		1
5250–5500					
5500–5750					
5750–6000				I	1
6000–6250			I		1
6250–6500					
6500–6570					
6750–7000					
7000–7250					
7250–7500				I	1
7500–7570					
7750–8000					
8000–8250					
8250–8500					
8500–8750					
8750–9000					
9000–9250					
9250–9500					
9700–9750					
9750–10000					
10000–10250					
10250–10500					
10500–10750					
10750–11000					
11000–11250					
11250–11500				1m	I
11500–11750					
11750–12000					
12000–over				2	2
Totals	2	5	8	5	20

m = Median

Table 2 Sections and Tribal Size

Population per Tribe	0	2	4	8	Total
50–100		2	1	?	3
100–150	4	3			7
150–200	2	2			4
200–250	1	4	2		7
250–300	1m	14m		2	17
300–350	1	2			3
350–400			2		2
400–450	1	2	1		4
450–500		1			1
500–550	1	1	3		5
550–600		1m			1
600–650	1	2			3
650–700					
700–750			1		1
750–800			1		1
800–850	1		1		2
850–900			2		2
900–950	1		1		2
950–1000			1		1
1000–1050		1	1		2
1050–1100					
1100–1150				1m	1
1150–1200					
1200–1250		2			
1200–1250	1				1
1250–1300				1	1
1300–1350					
1350–1400				1	1
1400–1450			1		1
1450–1500					
1500–1550	1				1
1550–1600					
1600–1700				1	1
1700–1800					
1800–1900					
1900–2000					
2000–2100				1	1
Totals	15	30	24	7	76

m = Median

Table 3 Sections and Tribal Density

1 person per "X" sq. mi.	0	2	4	8	Total
0–1		1			1
1–2		3			3
2–3	1	2m			3
3–4	1m		1		2
4–5			1		1
5–6			2		2
6–7					
7–8			1m		1
8–9					
9–10		1			1
10–12			1		1
12–14				1	1
14–16					
16–18		1			1
18–20					
20–25			1		1
25–30					
30–35				1	1
35–40			1		1
40–45				1m	1
45–50					
50–60					
60–70				1	1
70–80				1	1
80–90			1		1
90–100					
Totals	2	8	9	5	24

m = Median

explain this type. As is expected, the correlation between section systems and population density also patterns in the same direction as the two previous cases.

Figure 1 presents the spatial distribution of section systems in aboriginal Australia. Both Davidson's (1928a) and Radcliffe-Brown's (1930) maps are basically similar, yet in a few particulars there are notable differences. Davidson's information on the Kimberleys and Arnhem Land was practically nil, while Radcliffe-Brown had access to the most recent field work of Elkin, Hart, Stanner, and Warner. Furthermore, Davidson did not distinguish between marriage and descent functions of the section system, a distinction which Radcliffe-Brown fully utilized. However, Radcliffe-Brown designated the Murngin as having a subsection system, yet Warner (1937) noted that although Murngin descent is based on an eight-subsection system, their marriage restrictions are on a four-section basis. Both authorities made systematic errors in certain localities such as the Cairns rain forest of coastal Queensland. For this area, Davidson and Radcliffe-Brown interpreted the tribal social organization as

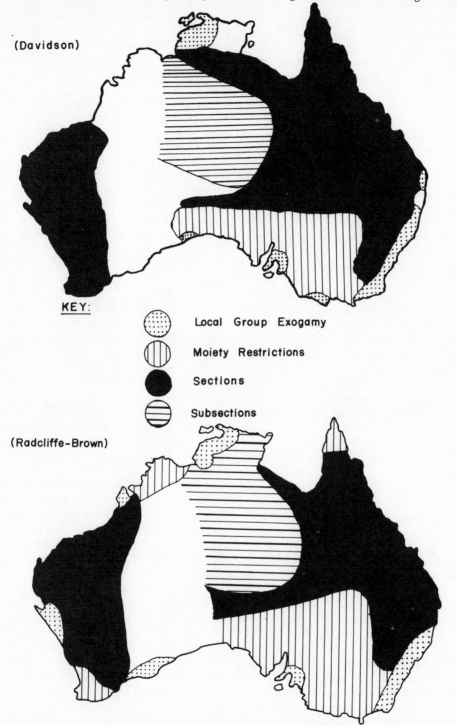

FIGURE 1. GEOGRAPHIC DISTRIBUTION OF SECTION SYSTEMS IN ABORIGINAL AUSTRALIA. UPPER: AFTER DAVIDSON; LOWER: AFTER RADCLIFFE-BROWN.

possessing section marriage restrictions; however, Tindale and Birdsell (1941, p. 6) noted that the Cairns people had only moiety restrictions on the coast and section systems in the interior. A more recent map and discussion on the distribution of section systems is available in Berndt and Berndt's (1964, pp. 53–60) new volume on the Australian aborigines.

From the data in Tables 1, 2, and 3, the following conclusions may be tentatively stated:

1. Those tribes characterized by subsections possess the largest tribal areas and sizes, and the lowest population densities.

2. Following the first point, as the number of sections decrease from eight to four to two, tribal areas and sizes also decrease and population density goes up.

3. Since environmental factors strongly influence the population parameter, and since the latter is related to the number of sections into which a tribe is divided, it may be tentatively concluded that an indirect relation exists between sections, population, and environment. The remainder of this paper is devoted to the investigation of the processes by which section systems are regulated by population size.

DISCUSSION

In this section, population size is explored in terms of its functions and limits on the "ideal" operation of marriage sections. A population pyramid (Fig. 2) is utilized in analyzing the interrelationships between population size and marital unions. The pyramid is based on generalized hunting and gathering groups, and on a few assumptions to be spelled out.

Figure 2 shows the age and sex breakdown of a tribe numbering 100 individuals. First, a balanced sex ratio for each five-year interval is assumed, although specific ethnographic cases may not verify this assumption for all age levels. Second, population equilibrium is assumed. In a population where equilibrium with the carrying capacity is stabilized, each adult must reproduce himself, consequently a married couple must replace themselves with two offspring who reach reproductive age.

Populations control mechanisms include natural infant and child mortality, abortion, infanticide, birth spacing through late weaning, and so forth. For example, infanticide rates among aboriginal Australians may have been as high as 30 per cent (Birdsell, 1958).

The age of first marriage among Australian males varies from the early twenties to the mid-thirties, and the average is between the ages of 25 to 30. Marriage age for females varies from eight to ten years among the Walbiri and some Arnhem Land groups to the late teens among the Pitjandjara. Although age of females at marriage in many groups is relatively early, menarche and conception usually occur later. A young female may not effectively reproduce until 15 or 16, and only after the birth of her first offspring will her economic role become important. Thus, females may become "effective" marital partners—for economic and reproductive purposes —at about 15 or 16 years of age. For convenience, an overall age bracket in which practically all females would be married is 15–19, though one must recognize earlier marriage in some groups.

If all able males over 25 are of marriageable age, then a total of thirteen males in a population of 100 may take a spouse at any one time. Any women over 15 may acquire a spouse at any particular time, thus resulting in 24 eligible females. Older widows are often given to younger men as first spouses and elder males often have primary access to younger females (Rose, Chapter 21, this volume).

To balance the model with ethnographic fact, three alternative stipulations concerning marriage are set forth. The first stipulation is that a male marries only females younger than himself though all males over 40 have access to all eligible females. This results in an average of seventeen eligible females at any one time. The second stipulation, that males marry females younger and up to five years older, results in 19.2 (= 19) eligible females. The third stipulation is males marry females younger and up to ten years older. This yields 20.8 (= 21) eligible females at any one time in a population of 100. The computations for assessing eligible females are in Table 4.

Of the three stipulations, the third one is closest to ethnographic reality. While older

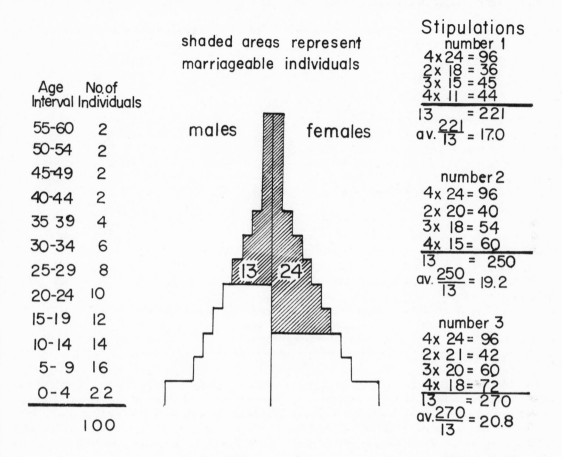

Age Interval / No. of Individuals

Age Interval	No. of Individuals
55-60	2
50-54	2
45-49	2
40-44	2
35 39	4
30-34	6
25-29	8
20-24	10
15-19	12
10-14	14
5- 9	16
0-4	22
	100

shaded areas represent marriageable individuals

males   females

Stipulations

number 1

$$4 \times 24 = 96$$
$$2 \times 18 = 36$$
$$3 \times 15 = 45$$
$$4 \times 11 = 44$$
$$\overline{13 \qquad = 221}$$
$$\text{av.} \frac{221}{13} = 17.0$$

number 2

$$4 \times 24 = 96$$
$$2 \times 20 = 40$$
$$3 \times 18 = 54$$
$$4 \times 15 = 60$$
$$\overline{13 \qquad = 250}$$
$$\text{av.} \frac{250}{13} = 19.2$$

number 3

$$4 \times 24 = 96$$
$$2 \times 21 = 42$$
$$3 \times 20 = 60$$
$$4 \times 18 = 72$$
$$\overline{13 \qquad = 270}$$
$$\text{av.} \frac{270}{13} = 20.8$$

FIGURE 2. POPULATION PYRAMID FOR A HYPOTHETICAL TRIBE NUMBERING 100.

males control the younger women, the younger males are often provided widows as their first spouse. In fact, an estimate such as the third stipulation is still conservative (see Goodale, 1962; Meggitt, 1965; Rose, 1960b). The age difference for the first marriage of either sex to their first spouse is quite marked.

The interrelationship between the population pyramid and different marriage restrictions is found in Table 4. Assuming a hypothetical number of ten local groups and an ideal situation where each group has equal representation as regards females, a local group would then have 2.1 eligible females per male. With only local group exogamy (the "o" condition), a male has a total 18.9 possible mates. When moiety restrictions are imposed the number of potential mates, and possibly potential competitors, is reduced by one-half. Subsequently, with section marriage restrictions, the number of eligible females is reduced to one-fourth of the "o" condition, and with sub-section marriage to one-eighth. Thus, with a tribal size of 100 and the existence of subsections, a male would ideally have only 2.36 possible marriage mates.

Table 4   *Number of Possible Mates under Four Sets of Marriage Restrictions*

1. Local Group Exogamy ("0")

2.1	2.1	2.1	2.1	2.1	18.9 possible
2.1	2.1	2.1	2.1	ego	mates

2. Moiety Restrictions ("2")

1.05	1.05	1.05	1.05	1.05	9.45 possible
1.05	1.05	1.05	1.05	ego	mates

3. Section Restrictions ("4")

.525	.525	.525	.525	.525	4.725 possible
.525	.525	.525	.525	ego	mates

4. Subsection Restrictions ("8")

.2625	.2625	.2625	.2625	.2625	2.3625 possible
.2625	.2625	.2625	.2625	ego	mates

The correlation between number of eligible mates and population size is presented in Figure 3. Extrapolating from the tribal model of 100 to larger, more realistic population sizes, allows us to ascertain the number of eligible mates under varying tribal sizes and section restrictions. A tribe of 500 people with subsection marriage rules yields an ideal figure of nearly twelve eligible females per male at any one time.

When the results of the model are compared with the empirical data in Table 2, a few interesting observations are noted. First, is the occurrence of a tribe of 50–100 individuals with a subsection system (listed in Table 2 as "?"). The reality of this case is doubted since the tribe was occupying approximately 10,500 square miles thus resulting in an extremely low population density of one person per 100–200 square miles. A small population with low densities operating on a set of highly selective marriage restrictions would be most impractical.

Also, the presence of ideally two eligible mates would be improbable since local groups occupy large areas with wide intervening distances.

From Table 2, the medians for tribes with moiety, section, and subsection restrictions are 250–300, 550–600, and 1,100–1,150. When the median figures are plotted on Figure 3, the result is that in each case a figure of 25–27 eligible mates per male is derived. With the existence of 25 eligible mates and only moiety restrictions, an ideal tribal size figure is approximately 262 which falls between the median range of 250 to 300. Twenty-five eligible mates in a section system yields a size of 530 while the empirically derived median is 550 to 600. With subsections and 25 eligible mates, an ideal tribal size of 1,070 is postulated. Once again, the median of 1,100–1,150 is remarkably close to the predicted figure from the model.

If the existence of 25 eligible mates represents an operational number, then it is

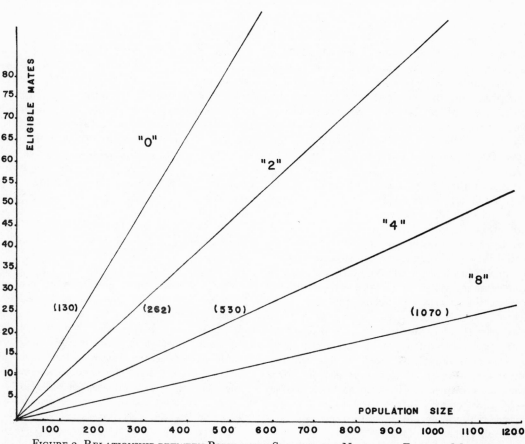

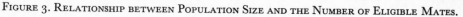

FIGURE 3. RELATIONSHIP BETWEEN POPULATION SIZE AND THE NUMBER OF ELIGIBLE MATES.

suggested that those populations with sections and subsections whose tribal sizes are significantly lower than the predicted range could not statistically confirm ideal marriage rules. Three cases may be briefly discussed to illustrate this point. Walbiri population size in 1954 was approximately 1,400 (Meggitt, 1962, p. 31), a figure well above the predicted range of 1,070 for tribes with subsections. As might be expected, preferred unions with matrilateral second cross-cousins occurred in 91.6 per cent (566/617) of all cases (Meggitt, 1962, p. 86) and thus confirm the stated marriage rule. At

Borroloola near the Gulf of Carpentaria, Reay (1962) discussed subsections and semimoieties among eight small tribal groups of which the Garawa and the Anyula are the largest. The total population of these groups in 1958–59 was 268, a figure well below the predicted range of 1,070. Consequently, out of 88 unions only 51 (57.95 per cent) marriages were regular. Furthermore, the natives were fully conscious that appropriate subsection partners were not always available and that highly frequent irregular unions did not follow the ideal marriage pattern (Reay, 1962, pp. 109–110).

Among the Lunga, Djaru, Kunian, Punaba, and Wolmeri of the Kimberleys, Kaberry (1939, p. 115) noted a range of 47.2 per cent to 73.1 per cent for all regular marriages. However, the tribal population of these groups is not listed, though detribalization was in process.

It may be concluded that population size sets definite limitations on the operation of section systems. Thus when tribal size significantly decreases from the predicted range, certain compensating factors such as increasing intertribal and theft unions with consequent destructive conflicts, become prominent. However, it must recognized that subsection systems in all probability have never operated entirely according to the ideal pattern.

Intertribal exchanges, theft unions, and wrong and alternative marriages may occur as adaptive factors when ideal marriage partners are infrequent through decreasing tribal size and other factors. However, all intertribal marriages can not be attributed to the unavailability of designated mates. Tribes such as the Pitjandjara and Ngadadjara regard intertribal marriages as usual events which fit into existing marriage patterns (Tindale, 1953, p. 173).

Marriages with alternative and prohibited mates vary in frequency and may be utilized as an index of population decline. The attitude towards marriages of this type differs from group to group, and in some cases, a wrong marriage is "corrected" after the union through partial realignment of kinship relations and terminology.

Another form of adjustment to population size is the fusion of two or more groups whose tribal identities are diminishing. In the coastal areas of the Kimberleys, one finds small tribes who socially recognize the acquiring of marriage mates from adjacent populations.

CONCLUSIONS

Population size is a critical factor in the ideal operation of section systems. When tribal numbers significantly decrease and the number of eligible mates is few and spatially dispersed, certain adaptive changes may arise to provide marriage mates. Since population size is regulated by ecological factors, the environmental influences on marriage patterns are important variables, though indirect. Furthermore, tribal units with exceedingly small and fragmented populations and subsections have been recorded, but statistically it is highly improbable that these groups could conform to stated marriage rules.

Many tribes with subsections occupy vast areas in the central arid regions of the continent. As Elkin has repeatedly noted, subsection groupings are simplified combinations of kin relations, and class terms are employed primarily among individuals and groups who are not in close association and whose interaction with one another is sporadic. Among the Pitjandjara and the Jankuntjatara for example, section terms are used in referring to individuals whose kin relationships are either ambiguous or non-existent. Among immediate and genealogically "close" kinsmen, kin terms are always employed. Strehlow also noted similar use of class terms among the Aranda when he stated:

> Since the use of these kinship terms accurately indicated the social obligations that existed between persons who use them toward each other, the class-names or *anbanerintja* were of prime importance when first contacts were being established between members of a local group and new arrivals who had come as guests, also between men belonging to a number of different local groups who had assembled on one ground for a ceremonial gathering (1965, p. 135).

Service's analysis of egocentric and sociocentric relationship terms in Australia concludes with the following statement:

> Where meetings are less frequent and the people are relative strangers to each other, the need for sociocentric terminology is greater—a stimulus is present. This would mean that in inland Australia social conditions exist which make the naming of the sections more likely there than in more productive areas (1960, p. 431).

One of the characteristics of section systems is the extension of section terms to distant kinsmen and non-kinsmen, who may occupy adjacent and distant areas of exploitation. The expansion of section terms not only combines spatially distant groups into meaningful units for marriage and ceremonial functions, but also permits reciprocal movements of related groups into larger territorial domains. For the Aranda, Fry (1934, p. 20) stated that "marriage with a distant kin not only minimizes the danger of infringing the tabu on parents-in-law, but also gives a certain right of entry to other districts in addition to that of the mother."

Since sections and subsections commonly occur in tribal units with large areas, the degree of spatial distribution of one's relations is greater than in small tribal areas. This network of related individuals and groups permits local groups to move into different areas of exploitation, especially during severe droughts and periods of economic hardship. The extension of kin relations via section groupings thus "insures" for each local group the ability of movement into adjacent areas, as well as reducing the possibility of non-tribal members crossing traditional boundaries.[3]

It is thus suggested that the ability of local populations to survive under rigorous environmental conditions requires a certain flexibility in local organization which allows for maximum mobility of exploiting groups, and a means of linking vast numbers of individuals

and groups through sections and subsections into a network which permits small mobile units to spatially expand and contract under varying environmental conditions. Consequently, one of the functions of sections and subsections may have been an economic factor in allowing populations to "insure" a vast territorial domain from non-tribal groups, as well as "insuring" each local group's future against economic hardship by permitting access into more favorable environments. On the coastal regions of Australia, subsections were not necessary, but in the central arid areas, sections and subsections linked spatially and socially distant groups together for mutual interaction and mobility. A somewhat analogous situation is reported by Sahlins (1958, p. 236) for the Polynesian atolls. The main problem on the atolls is the survival of a dense population in an area of sporadic or limited surplus production. Since economic specialization can not be sustained, every individual is interconnected by some alignment principle—descent, age grades, residence—to every other type of socioeconomic group. Thus, everyone shares in the distribution and consumption of what is produced. Sahlins (1958, p. 245) postulates that the development of a number of interlocking social groups, each dedicated to exploitation of different resources, may be expected on atolls as adaptations to selective pressures limiting surplus production. In aboriginal Australia, one may regard the interlocking of kinsmen through section and subsection groupings as allowing for greater interaction and mobility over exploitable lands and thus "insuring" utilizable resources.

3. It should not be assumed that all non-tribal members were excluded from crossing tribal boundaries. Section and subsection terms in central Australia typically run across tribal areas, thus permitting local groups access to the territory of neighboring tribes. However ceremonial and totemic factors might have partially limited intertribal mobility.

21.

Australian Marriage,
Land-Owning Groups, and Initiations

FREDERICK G. G. ROSE

Introduction

At the symposium on Man the Hunter we discussed the Australian land-owning groups and marriage arrangements. Except indirectly, initiation found no place in the discussion, let alone its relevance to the relations between social groups, marriage, and resource use. The purpose of the present contribution is to show that marriage, initiation, and the relations between the land-owning groups are mutually interdependent and that an appreciation of the reciprocal relations between them takes one a considerable way to understanding the organization of aboriginal society as a whole.

Marriage and the Land-Owning Group

Because our views are conditioned by our own experience, we tend to think of marriage arrangements among, for instance, the Australian aborigines as essentially a means of regulating biological relations between men and women necessary for the propagation of the species. This notion has little relevance to the Australian aborigines because they do not or did not know the connection between sexual relations and the birth of children. It is not in-

tended to argue here for or against the evidence on the aborigines' ignorance of the facts of life reported by various field workers. It is merely intended to cite a piece of indirect evidence in support of this alleged ignorance of the aborigines.

An ever-recurring theme of cult life and of art throughout Australia, north, central, and south, is the fertility of nature and of man. In the north of Australia, however, probably through the contact with the Indonesians, and possibly other Asians before them, the aborigines learned of the connection between the birth of children and sexual intercourse, although they retained in the background as a kind of theology the usual Australian concept of spirit children. Anyone who compares the fertility cult life and concepts of the north with those of the center and the south will immediately be struck with the erotic form the cults and beliefs of the north have taken. A presupposition to the development of the erotic in the fertility beliefs is clearly a knowledge of the significance of the sexual act for the birth of children. We are convinced that this knowledge was lacking in the south and center and until a few centuries ago was probably also lacking in the north.

For the aborigines, therefore, a woman was a being who throughout the period of her life from puberty to the menopause regularly produced children, and in the eyes of the aborigines the man with whom she was living had no relevance to the biological facts. A woman who did not produce children was an anomaly in the aborigines' scheme of things.

The relation between the man and the woman in marriage, from the viewpoint of aboriginal society, was essentially a reciprocal economic one, the man primarily providing the meat and the woman the vegetable foodstuffs for themselves and her children.

If this economic element is the essential one in aboriginal marriage, to understand its dynamics it is necessary to consider two other aspects of their life which reciprocally influence one another and, in their different ways, have a bearing on marriage. These two aspects or institutions are, first, the relationships between the land-owning (i.e., the political) groups or clans and, second, the initiation of the males: both are the obverse of the coin to the marriage arrangements or, perhaps better expressed, the other two sides of the triangle.

A generation ago it was considered almost as axiomatic that marriage arrangements were determined by kinship relationships, perhaps reinforced—in a somewhat obscure way—by the so-called "marriage classes," where these existed. Thus we were told that the Aranda-type of kinship system was the most prevalent in Australia, in which a man married his mother's mother's brother's daughter's daughter (who at the same time was the other three second cousins), and if he married anyone else, then it was considered an "exceptional" marriage. This all made for excellent "modeling" and kinship algebra but got us little nearer to understanding why aboriginal society was integrated the way it was.

However, the main determinant of aboriginal marriage is not the kinship system or the "marriage classes." Rather, each individual marriage is determined ultimately by the reciprocal rights and obligations existing between the actual political land-owning groups and to a less extent the reciprocal rights and obligations between members of these different land-owning groups. These reciprocal rights and obligations aggregate into an extraordinarily complicated network linking groups and individuals throughout the society.

The kinship terminology—at least as far as the Australian aborigines are concerned and whatever might be true of other societies—is primarily an expression of these rights and obligations between individuals as members of groups, and do not express blood relationship (real or fictive) which we social anthropologists in our superior wisdom and in our categories of thought have arbitrarily imposed on them.

What is more, the network of which we have spoken is continually changing in the temporal dimension. The lasting service of Hart and Pilling (1960) is that they were able to show just how complicated this network was, and what factors ultimately determine a marriage.

It is, of course, much simpler to determine the kinship structure of an aboriginal society than to determine what are the economic, diplomatic, political (or call them what one will) relations between groups and individuals. As far as we know, Hart and Pilling's work is, of its kind, unique, while there are scores of accounts of Australian kinship systems. As a consequence it has become almost a dogma that kinship was the ultimate determinant of marriage.

If it is ultimately the economic relations between land-owning groups that determine what marriages take place, how are these relations manifested? Here again we have to clear away another dogma. The land-owning group in the drier, near-desert areas (perhaps it would be better to speak of the waterhole-owning group) is an abstraction, for it never comes together except, almost incidentally, when very large numbers of aborigines meet. Although an abstraction in the sense mentioned, it is nonetheless real. In Australia it is the fundamental political unit, deriving its power from the common ownership of the land[1] (or more exactly the game that lives on it, and the vegetable foods which grow in or on it) which is the most important means of production. It was early recognized that the land-owning group was exogamous and that the men of the group received their wives from other groups and, in

1. Chrustov (1959) has discussed the evidence for and against the common ownership of land in Australia. He puts a cogent case for land ownership in Australia being in common.

their turn, the women born into a land-owning group went to other groups at marriage. However, it was assumed that the men of a land-owning group worked together as a foraging group, horde, or band on their own land, except on rare occasions when they visited other land-owning groups. In other words, we had a virtual identification of the foraging group with the land-owning group.[2] This is an incorrect conception and one that can easily be shown to be incorrect when the members of foraging groups are classified according to membership in land-owing groups (Hiatt, 1962, Chapter 10 and 18, this volume). The foraging group is an extremely variable entity not only in respect to size but also in respect to land-owning group membership.

It is variable in respect to size mainly because the availability of food in any area is extremely changeable, not only between seasons but also from year to year. At a particular time of year, when food resources are scattered, the foraging group breaks down even to the individual family; at other times, when food is abundant in a small area, the groups come together to form aggregations of two hundred or more aborigines at a single camp. These large groups persist sometimes for weeks or even months at a time (Meggitt, 1962; Strehlow, 1967). Abundant food in a limited area was clearly a prerequisite for the carrying out of large-scale initiation and increase rituals.

The foraging group is variable in respect to male membership of land-owning groups because, given low population density, an estate belonging to a particular land-owning group simply cannot provide continuously for twelve months of the year, year in and year out, sufficient foodstuffs for its members. The land of one group may provide an abundance of food during the spring, for example, while another may provide an abundance of food during the winter. This leads to reciprocity between the land-owning groups. Inevitably, there are seasonal movements of population from one area to another. The reason for this is ecological and is determined essentially by distribution of resources.

A man can hunt on his own land. He also has certain rights to hunt on the group-land of his mother and of his wife, but in order to hunt on the land of other land-owning groups, he has to be invited or to obtain permission.[3] It is the sum of the obligations a man incurs by being allowed to hunt on another group's territory, and the rights that he possesses to allow men of other groups to hunt on his territory, that constitutes the network of obligations and rights mentioned earlier as being the essential factors in determining marriage arrangements. The land-owning group does not, in fact cannot, live by itself; it usually has some kind of economic, political, or social relationship with some ten to fifteen other land-owning groups. This would appear to be the mean radius, under Australian hunting-collecting nomadism, that a man can extend his contacts. Because of the social contacts existing within this radius, a certain language and cultural homogeneity develops, and the sum total of land-owning groups existing within this radius is often spoken of as a "tribe," although there is in Australia no political organization at a "tribal" level. The "tribe" numbers some 400 or so aborigines on the basis of a mean

2. Another reason for erroneously identifying the males of the land-owning group (clan) and their wives and children with the foraging group (horde or band) is that although the size of the land-owning group varies greatly between "tribes," and as well as within "tribes," the normal size (say thirty men, women, and children) is not greatly different from the size of the normal foraging group, although, as noted this also varies greatly. Some examples of the constitution of foraging groups for Groote Eylandt in 1941 are recorded (Rose, 1960b, pp. 77 and 81). Tindale (1925, pp. 74 and 94) reproduces photographs of groups of male aborigines taken in 1922 and refers to them as men of particular land-owning groups. The aborigines in the photographs were identified in 1948 and their land-owning group affiliations obtained (Rose, 1960b, pp. 207–208). Instead of belonging in each case to one land-owning group, they belonged to several.

3. The question of being invited by another land-owning group and the despatch of emissaries for this purpose is frequently mentioned in the older literature. Morgan in the old classic *The Life and Adventures of William Buckley* (Hobart, 1852), mentions on several occasions the "diplomatic" relations between the land-owning groups. Morgan's work is now virtually unobtainable and a new edition in German translation with annotations has recently been published (Reim, 1964). Little information on the actual relations between either the land-owning or the foraging groups has been obtained by trained ethnographers. The reason for this has been discussed by Barnes (1963, p. 200).

membership of thirty for the land-owning group.[4]

One often reads in the literature of exchange of wives between individuals or between groups. While this occurs, of course, the actual exchange of wives is only one manifestation of a much wider reciprocity between land-owning groups. However, because it is a phenomenon that can easily be observed—or logically, although not necessarily correctly, deduced from observation (cf. Rose, 1960b, p. 119)—it is reported as if it were independent of the wider reciprocity.

Sahlins' Original Affluent Society: A Comment

At this point a digression will be made to follow a train of thought stimulated by Marshall Sahlins' "Notes on the Original Affluent Society" (Chapter 9b, this volume). If Sahlins is right and those like Tokarev (1961, p. 683) who conceive of the hunter-collectors as living continuously on the borderline of starvation are wrong, why are the Australian aborigines so preoccupied with the fertility of man and nature? There seems to be a contradiction here. If they need to spend only three or four hours a day hunting or collecting, there is obviously plenty of foodstuffs available and increase rituals for kangaroos (or other foodstuffs) just do not make sense. Why was there also a preoccupation with human fertility? Were the women peculiarly sterile?

Quantitative records such as we have of remnants of tribes on the fringes of civilization, where the aborigines were riddled with disease and were living under bad sanitational conditions and with inadequate diet, show that the women were indeed peculiarly sterile. But such detribalized aborigines were in the process of dying out. What was the situation under tribal conditions unaffected by the deleterious influences of civilization? Were the women peculiarly sterile here, so that it was necessary to invoke magical or religious means to increase the population and so prevent the society dying out? Records of aboriginal (or other hunter-gatherers for that matter) birth rates under traditional conditions are almost nonexistent. Although the birth rate, as such, is not recorded, the writer's data (1960b) on a tribe that was still living under traditional conditions indicate how high the birth rate must have been. Far from being peculiarly sterile, the women were quite the reverse. If a woman lived the full span from puberty to the menopause, she had at least eighteen children. Surely this stands in logical contradiction to the aborigines' apparent obsession with human fertility? One might expect a greater interest in birth control! But on Groote Eylandt, where the writer worked, there was no birth control and little infanticide was practiced.

Sahlins is, nevertheless, right for Groote Eylandt subsistence: for the greater part of their time they only needed to work three or four hours a day. There was an abundance of meat and an abundance of vegetable foodstuffs, and the population certainly did not starve in spite of the women's high fertility.

Let us examine more closely the second aspect—the maintenance of the population. It was stable and an extraordinarily high birth rate implies in these circumstances a very high death rate among infants and small children so that only a fraction reached the reproductive age. This was, indeed, the situation among the Groote Eylandt people. The writer estimated that at least 60 per cent of infants died before they reached their first birthday and there was a correspondingly high death rate among young children. In these circumstances the aborigines' concern with the fertility of women was well founded.[5]

4. See note 2 on the size of the land-owning group. Likewise the size of the "tribe" shows great variations. The Groote Eylandt people were a "tribe" in 1941, numbering between 300 and 350. The Pitjandjara originally probably numbered over a thousand.

5. On Groote Eylandt the introduction of antibiotics and infant care by missionaries and the government during the later years of the war and following has led to a marked drop in the infant and young child mortality rate, with the result that a virtual population explosion has taken place. In 1941 there were between 300 to 350 aborigines on the island; in 1965 the population had increased to over 600. At the symposium it was argued that infanticide must have been a feature of all hunting-collecting communities. Undoubtedly infanticide occurred, but only under duress. It is this writer's view that the "normal" wastage owing to high infant and young children mortality rates would render infanticide unnecessary in ordinary circumstances. We are inclined to think of our own infant mortality rate of

But why the concern with the fertility of nature if there was plenty of game and vegetable foods? The aborigines know from their own experience, if they are older men, or from what they have been told if they are not, that in the past there have been times when the land was gripped by drought so that the kangaroos became scarce and thin and the yams were not to be found. The people then were truly faced by starvation. The aborigines' prime interest in the fertility of nature is to maintain the status quo where there is an abundance of kangaroos and yams, and above all to avoid a recurrence of the situation when the land was gripped by drought. They also know that in spite of all the magical and religious means they employ in their increase rituals and no matter how beneficently nature may be smiling on them today, perhaps next year, the year after, or in five or ten years the land will again be visited by drought and once again they will face starvation.

At the low technical level of hunting and gathering, man is a parasite on nature. Apart from his meager equipment, the attribute he possesses which prevents his own population numbers being subjected to the violent fluctuations of the other fauna in his environment is his social organization and the reciprocity and co-operation it implies. Most of the time the need for cooperation and reciprocity, specifically of the political land-owning groups, is not immediately apparent; but when drought or other natural catastrophe occurs, cooperation and reciprocity in the division of the few available food resources on the tracts of land owned by the various groups is a matter of life and death for the community as a whole. It is only at these times of food shortage that infanticide has the sanction of the society. It is better to

destroy an infant or young child whose chances of survival are small anyway than to hinder the mother unnecessarily in her task of food collecting. When times are better, she will breed again. The belief in spirit-children gives her the solace that her dead child's spirit will return to the store of spirit-children awaiting to be reborn.

We have digressed somewhat from the main theme of this contribution to resolve the apparent contradictions implied by Sahlins' paper. By doing so we have underlined how cooperation and reciprocity is a matter of life and death for aboriginal society.

Before dealing with the question of male initiation—the third side of the triangle—we shall discuss what we have called "marriage gerontocracy" in Australia. This was the limited subject of the writer's paper read at the Chicago symposium and the following with suitable additions and comments arising from the discussion largely follows what was presented to the symposium.

MARRIAGE GERONTOCRACY IN AUSTRALIA

What do we understand by Australian marriage gerontocracy?[6] Eylmann in a few words gave a good description.[7] He wrote that "marriage relations of the Australian Aborigines are remarkable in that an eighteen to twenty-five year old man often has no wife, or if he does she is old enough to be his grandmother, while the oldest, most influential men in the community, on the average have most wives, amongst them not infrequently very old women and girls in their early teens" (1902, p. 131).

6. The use of the expression "gerontocracy," which literally means "government by the old people" in the sense of marriage of older men with young girls, was criticized at the symposium. This criticism is, of course, valid. Is there a better expression?

7. Eylmann's (1902, p. 131) original read as follows: "im Binnenlande und vielleicht auch im nördlichen Küstengebiet sind die ehelichen Verhältnisse insofern recht sonderbar, als die achtzehn bis fünfundzwanzigjährigen Manner oft ganz unbeweibt sind, oder eine Ehegenossin besitzen, die dem Alter nach ihre Grossmutter sein könnte, und die Ältesten, die Einflussreichsten des Gemeinwesens, durchgängig die meisten Frauen haben, und sich unter diesen nicht selten Greisinnen und noch in Backfischalter stehende Personen befinden."

---

about 2 per cent as normal. This low figure is in fact a relatively new phenomenon. For instance, in 1880 the infant mortality rate in Germany was about 25 per cent. A "normal" infant mortality rate of at least 60 per cent for a hunting-collecting society—as the writer estimated for Groote Eylandt in 1941—should not be considered as excessive. It is the writer's opinion that under traditional conditions the fertility of Australian aboriginal women throughout the continent was not greatly different from that of the Groote Eylandt women and that bearing an average of eighteen children between puberty and the menopause would not be excessive. At the symposium a figure of 4 was mentioned: this seems much too low.

Although probably the best brief statement of the matter, we would not entirely agree with Eylmann's description. For instance, we would not say that in traditional conditions it was the *oldest* men who had most wives. Rather, it was the *older* men in their forties or fifties. Eylmann's statement that it was the "most influential" men who had most wives would support this viewpoint.

From what he wrote, one could draw the conclusion that girls were married at puberty. It is our observation that under traditional or near traditional conditions a girl went to live with her first husband when she was considerably younger—about 9 years old, with intercourse delayed until she had reached puberty. Going to live with her first husband should not be confused with the fact that a girl was promised to a man when she was much younger or even before she was born.

With these minor strictures the situation that Eylmann describes has some important consequences. We see that the young girls go as wives to the older men while the old women can be wives of men of any age. One can say that the older men have a monopoly of the younger women, while also having some of the old or older women. The normal population pyramid of an aboriginal society—as, of course, in our own society—shows that there are considerably more females in their teens and twenties than men in their forties or fifties. As an obvious consequence these older men are married polygynously. This frequently reported fact deserved mention here since polygyny is a corollary of gerontocracy and it would perhaps be better to speak of "polygyny-gerontocracy" and not merely of "gerontocracy."

Another logical consequence of the situation described by Eylmann, but one which is more rarely reported, is that a woman in the course of her lifetime has several husbands. Hart wrote for the Tiwi of Melville and Bathurst Islands that "while a woman goes to live with her husband at about thirteen, a man is lucky to get his first wife under the age of 35. It follows that in the great majority of cases the father of children dies long before the mother. There-fore . . . a woman passes through the possession of quite a number of different men during her lifetime" (1930, p. 282). On Groote Eylandt a woman had at least four husbands in the course

of a full lifetime. This number is quite apart from clandestine sex relations. By the same token a man had at least four wives—for the most part polygynously—in the course of his lifetime. Marriage in Australia is thus seen to be an extraordinarily fluid institution. Although at any one time polygynous unions are in the minority, most men who lived to old age would spend part of their lives married polygynously. Similarly a woman lived at least part of her lifetime inside a collective of co-wives. In this sense we can say that polygyny is the rule and monogamy the exception.

Before discussing the attempts made to interpret this fluidity of Australian marriage, something can be said on the distribution of marriage gerontocracy inside Australia. The evidence is at times contradictory; nevertheless it would appear that gerontocracy was a feature of marriage throughout Australia and Tasmania (Rose, 1960b, pp. 91–99, 234–36, 482). It is a remarkable fact that some observers with wide experience of aborigines under traditional conditions did not report gerontocracy in areas where it is known definitely to have existed. For instance, in his monograph *Economic Structure and the Ceremonial Exchange Cycle in Arnhem Land* (1949), Thomson does not once mention gerontocracy although it clearly would have had considerable bearing on the subject with which he was dealing. Similarly Sir Baldwin Spencer (1914) does not mention it among the Tiwi. One can explain these omissions by the assumption that these particular observers had become so used to gerontocracy as part of the fabric of aboriginal society that they simply ignored it. In the writer's own case it was not until he examined the actual ages of man and wife in the Groote Eylandt family units that he realized how pronounced it was. Without the actual age data he would also probably have ignored it, although, of course, in general terms he was quite aware that in Australian societies a man tended to marry a woman considerably younger than himself.

The evidence for polygyny-gerontocracy is further complicated by the fact that it can disappear very rapidly under contact situations. A report of its absence, or the fact that the aborigines married monogamously, by no means disproves the existence of polygyny-gerontocracy under traditional conditions.

Elkin (1954, p. 127 note) has noted its disappearance under contact situations, and the writer has shown that it is particularly the change in the economic activity of the women under such conditions that leads to its disappearance (Rose, 1965b, pp. 75–83 *passim*). As a consequence, in evaluating the older writers it is necessary to determine under what contact situation the observations were made. Taking the reports at their face value is unsatisfactory; a certain historical research is also necessary.

In spite of the popular opinion that Australia is virtually a land of near deserts and steppes, the ecological conditions are, in fact, extremely varied. The universality of polygyny-gerontocracy is surprising and would indicate an extremely low degree of specialization in the social organization to meet the particular ecological situations.

INTERPRETATION OF
MARRIAGE GERONTOCRACY

Let us now return to the question mentioned earlier, the fluidity of the marriage relation as the result of polygyny-gerontocracy. A problem which has occupied the writer since he first described in statistical terms the polygyny-gerontocracy of the Groote Eylandt people and its universality in Australia has been finding an interpretation of the custom.

A perfectly rational explanation is, of course, that it is "natural" for the older, most influential men to monopolize the younger and more desirable women to the exclusion of their younger clansmen (Fison and Howitt, 1880, p. 355). But a more objective explanation was sought; that is to say, a reason that was independent of the will or wishes of the individual. The explanation mentioned appeared to stand the issue on its head. To explain the power of the older men to monopolize the women in terms of its being "natural" for them to do so, was, in fact, no explanation. It was unsatisfactory, first, because it did not explain how the older men obtained this power and secondly, because, as had frequently been observed, polygyny-gerontocracy disappears extremely quickly once the economic basis of the society changes, apparently without any effective resistance from the older men. This latter consideration would seem to point to a material, possibly ultimately a relatively simple economic explanation of polygyny-gerontocracy.

On the basis of his own data, the writer propounded an hypothesis which ran generally as follows. The women tended to aggregate themselves in collectives of co-wives around the men at the peak of their productive capacity and this tendency reached its maximum when the women had their greatest child-bearing and child-rearing burdens.[8] It will be immediately noted that in this explanation it was the women and not the men who took the active role to establish polygynous units, and that this type of family provided the optimum conditions for the rearing of the younger generation inside the collectives of co-wives of the polygynous families.

The writer went further and suggested that the men were at the peak of their productive capacity when they were in their early forties and the women had their greatest burdens to bear when they were about 24 (Rose, 1960a; 1963).

Unfortunately for this neat theory, Ashley-Montagu (1957) has provided certain biological facts that showed that the women's maximum burden in caring for children must have occurred when they were considerably older than 24. Then Meggitt (1965b) produced comparative figures on polygyny-gerontocracy for the Walbiri. On this particular point his results did not confirm the original hypothesis, and Meggitt sought a "multifactoral" explanation of maximum polygyny: Nevertheless, it would seem that the difference between the writer's and Meggitt's conclusions on this point are more apparent than real. While the explanation of maximum polygyny may, as Meggitt expressed it, be multifactoral, the writer is not convinced that the essential explanation of polygyny-gerontocracy in Australia cannot be

---

8. It was suggested at the symposium that productive capacity should be taken in a wider sense to include the organizing ability of current activities by these older men, and that in this sense the peak of their productive capacity is reached in their early forties. This suggestion has much to commend it.

given in the general terms originally formulated.[9]

INITIATION

We can now return to the question of male initiation and its relation to marriage and to the cooperation between the land-owning groups.

The discussion above on marriage gerontocracy has shown that the Australian aboriginal society is on the horns of a dilemma. On the one side there is the tendency for the women to aggregate themselves around men at the peak of their productive activity with this tendency reaching a maximum when the women have their greatest maternal burdens to bear. This situation leads to the older men—past their physical and sexual peak—monopolizing the women in polygynous units. On the other hand, the younger men—at their physical and sexual peak—are virtually without women, or at most with a woman old enough to be their grandmother. Economic necessity, expressed as a need to provide collectives of co-wives in which to raise the infants and young children, comes into conflict with the sexual drive of the younger men who are denied women. This contradiction in Australian society has been resolved by the older men controlling the younger through the elaborate system of male initiation found in Australia.

It would take us too far to consider the various forms initiation takes, but even though the forms vary considerably, they all have certain features in common. The first is that the full series of initiation covers a span of a young man's lifetime from before puberty until his middle or late twenties.

The second feature is that the initiate cannot form an economic alliance for the foundation of a family with a woman (i.e., marry her), until he has completed his initiation.

Third, the initiate is instructed by didactic methods both in the ecology of the country in which he lives and in the art of obtaining the wherewithal of life. He absorbs this knowledge by learning the tribal myths and by witnessing the cult ceremonies centered on the wanderings and creative feats of the heroes of the Dreamtime.

Fourth, the initiation of a youth is not simply a domestic matter of his own land-owning group, but is an issue of intergroup importance. Relatives who can and frequently do play an important role in a youth's initiation are his mother's brother, his male patrilateral cross-cousin (who is sometimes his sister's husband), his sister's husband when he is not the initiate's patrilateral cross-cousin, and a representative of the land-owning group from which he will later obtain a wife. All of these relatives belong to land-owning groups other than the initiate's own, and each of these groups in its own way has a vested interest in the youth's initiation.

Fifth, during part of his initiation extending over some years, a youth is attached to, and is under the strict control and tutelate of, a guardian, a considerably older man. This guardian is frequently the youth's sister's husband. This relationship has definite advantages for the guardian. He not only has the responsibility of continuing by practical example the instruction of the initiate in the hunting of game and the other manly arts, but he also has rights to dispose of what foodstuffs the initiate brings back to camp. The guardian's interest in controlling an initiate is not greatly dissimilar to his interest in controlling the initiate's sister as wife. It is indicative of the relationship existing between initiate and guardian that on Groote Eylandt the missionaries frequently referred to the initiate as a "boy slave" or alternatively as a "boy wife." Stealing of young wives from their husbands was a feature of traditional life on Groote Eylandt, and it is significant that initiates were stolen in the same way and as frequently from their guardians (Rose, 1960b, p. 73).

9. At the symposium it was pointed out that there was a high correlation between the incidence of polygyny and age difference between man and wife. From the population pyramid this is a rational conclusion and the positive correlation is what one would expect. It was suggested that polygyny-gerontocracy in Australia was merely an extreme case of a world-wide phenomenon. Viewing the Australian data as purely one of a world-wide sample, that conclusion is, of course, correct. But the difference between polygyny-gerontocracy in Australia and, for example, in black Africa or among Muslim Arabs is not just one of degree. There is a difference of kind which is fundamental. The reasons for polygyny in Australia are quite different from the reasons for polygyny in black Africa or among Muslim Arabs.

Sixth, the initiate is secluded for long periods in the bush, during which time he has to fend for himself. Moreover, he is obliged to travel over and live on the country of several land-owning groups other than his own.

Conclusion

We have seen how the preoccupation of the aborigines with maintaining human fertility has a real material basis. In order that adequate population replacements survive the dangerous first decade of life, women with infants and young children to care for, tend to live in collectives of co-wives (i.e., in polygynous units) centered around experienced men at the peak of their economic production. This economic necessity is in conflict with the fact that the younger men at the peak of their physical strength and sexual activity have virtually no women available to them. The contradiction is resolved socially by the control exerted through initiation of the young men. To this extent marriage and initiation are complementary.

We have also seen how the preoccupation of the aborigines with maintaining the fertility of nature has a real material basis. The very survival of the society depends on the reciprocity and cooperation between the political units—the land-owning groups—in the sphere of food resource utilization. Similarly, the survival of the society depends on the maintenance of the type of marriage and initiation described, and the reciprocity and cooperation of the land-owning groups are also manifested in this sphere.

These two spheres of reciprocity and cooperation are not two separate categories for the aborigines as they may appear to be to the ethnologist; they form an integrated unity. This is achieved by the marked sexual division of labor found generally throughout Australia —the woman normally collecting the vegetable foodstuffs while the man is responsible for providing meat. The giving and receiving of females in marriage is not merely the reallocation of a person who will produce babies that will eventually help to maintain the group's numbers, but it is also the reallocation of a gatherer of vegetable foodstuffs who plays an important part in food resource utilization.

The giving of a girl in marriage implies that her husband and her children have a virtual right to utilize the resources of her natal group's land. It is therefore natural that the girl's fellow clansmen have a great interest in her future husband and thus assume certain responsibilities in his initiation.

It is on the above basis, with all the contradictions it involves, that the whole superstructure of aboriginal cult and religious life has been logically erected by the aborigines. A discussion of this superstructure and its connection with the basis was, however, not the purpose of this contribution.

The method used here at first glance may appear to be a functional, nonhistorical interpretation of various institutions of aboriginal society in the classical sense that they are described as a functioning whole. What, in fact, has been described is the interconnection between certain relations of production, in the historical materialists' sense of the expression. The historical materialists' view is that the relations of production—and essentially, as we have dealt with them here, marriage, initiation and the land-owning group relations as such—are determined by the forces of production. The development of these forces of production is the motor of human history. Although it was not the purpose of this contribution to examine the development of these forces of production, it can be remarked that, in so far as the Australian aborigines are the least developed of any known people, they occupy a key position in our understanding of earliest human social development. To elaborate on this theme would take us far afield. However, it has been dealt with cursorily elsewhere (Rose, 1960a).

22.

Discussions, Part IV

22a. Gerontocracy and Polygyny

Speakers: *Bicchieri, Bulmer, Gardner, Isaac, Pilling, Rose, Slobodin, Whiting, Woodburn*

Rose: I would like to make one point about the possible significance of gerontocracy. It is interesting that gerontocracy is found throughout Australia and in Tasmania, and I think the question must be asked whether gerontocracy/polygyny was not also possibly a characteristic of the Paleolithic.

Woodburn: I think it is essential that we look for a term to replace "gerontocracy." This has been with us for some time, but I do not think it is too late to make a change. The term literally means "government by old men." Now, in the first place, we are dealing with men aged 30 and up. The second objection is to the connotation of political power. In fact, we are dealing with differential age at marriage and not necessarily with the implication that political power is involved.

Slobodin: To respond to Woodburn— gerontocracy may or may not be applicable to an ethnographic situation on empirical grounds, but the word does not necessarily, or even usually, mean "rule by the aged." The morpheme -*cracy* is from Greek *kratein*, which means "to rule," but also it more generally means "to exert power," from *kratos*, "strength." Surely those Australian 42-year-olds exert power!

Whiting: In a cross-cultural study of polygyny and its correlates, I found that wherever polygyny occurs the ages at marriage are about 25 for men and 15 for women; while the averages in monogamous societies are 19 for men and 17 for women. Now, these statistics hold fairly constant irrespective of the presence or absence of gerontocracy; polygyny alone is the variable that accounts for some of the difference in ages.

Although polygyny is not directly related to hunting and gathering, it does seem to be related chiefly to nomadism, where the task of carrying children makes child spacing necessary. And it is most frequent when postpartum sex taboo is the means of child spacing. If the postpartum sex taboo is two or three years, the man takes a second wife to help carry the burden of the child and for purposes of sexual access. This leads to enforced bachelorhood for the younger men, thereby giving rise to the idea that polygyny and gerontocracy are correlated.

Gardner: However one can have *gerontogamy* without *gerontocracy*. The Paliyans had gerontogamy of both sorts with both older males and older females. Very frequently this evolved without ceremony out of adoptive parent-child relationships. The child, when attaining freedom from the authority of anyone else (at about 9 years of age), quickly slips into the spouse's role. The point is that there is no authority difference between spouses nor any use of marriage as a device for obtaining authority, and the suffix "-ocracy" would be most inappropriate. In reply to Whiting's point I might add that the combined incidence of polygyny and polyandry is under 5 per cent, while 10 per cent of the Paliyan marriages (and a different 10 per cent) are gerontogamous. It would be impossible in this case, and perhaps in others, to call gerontogamy a simple result of polygamy.

ISAAC: I would like to ask whether it is normal for a man's food-productive capacity to reach a maximum as late as 42 years of age among hunting people.

ROSE: I did not have any direct evidence for the specific age of 42, but I found that there was tendency for a woman to marry a man of 42 (or 41, or 39) in Australia, quite independently of her own age. (There is a correlation coefficient approaching zero between the ages of husband and wife in Australia, while, of course, in our own society it approaches one.) And I assumed that the reason for this was that the man was at his peak of production. I did not try to measure production, however.

PILLING: I think it would be fruitful to review Dr. Rose's material with this question in mind: Are the figures the same when a woman is marrying a man who already has a wife as when she is marrying a single man? I suspect that the motivation for polygyny may be less the sexual gratification of the male than the carrying of co-wife's burden during intensive nursing or late pregnancy, when a man's wife is less productive as a gatherer.

ROSE: My data on that is available and can be examined from that viewpoint (Rose, 1960b). Strehlow gives some data on this particular issue and makes the point that a man often takes another wife when his first wife is in an advanced stage of pregnancy.

BULMER: I am a little puzzled by our new mystical number for peak production in a man's early forties. I can easily understand that he might be at the peak of his political capacity at that age, but it would be hard in any society to demonstrate that his economic capacity was greatest at such an age. If, in fact, political or social influence is at stake, this would seem to hinge back upon marriage arrangements and create a rather circular system.

BICCHIERI: I would like to pursue Dr. Bulmer's reaction to Dr. Rose's idea that man is at peak production in his early forties. This is a case in which it is not desirable to separate economic from political and social factors. Social organization can be regarded as a technological mechanism, so a man of 45— while not in his physical prime—may be able to manipulate other people and add a share of their production to his own, gained by physical manipulation of the environment. So 45 may be an ideal age in the sense of peak ability to coordinate productive activities.

22b. GIDJINGALI MARRIAGE ARRANGEMENTS: COMMENTS AND REJOINDER

[Note: This exchange of correspondence between Lévi-Strauss and Hiatt was received by the editors after the symposium on Man the Hunter.]

LÉVI-STRAUSS: It is quite natural that an Australian scholar should ignore that in the French anthropological usage, the word *realia* (Lévi-Strauss 1966, p. 115) faked after the Latin, does not mean "what really happens" as he believes, but material objects of the kind unearthed by archeologists such as buildings, statues, coins, tools, and weapons. Besides, when I suggested that new techniques such as pollen analysis and carbon-14 may improve what Radcliffe-Brown once called "conjectural history" I was certainly not referring to kinship systems. Thus in two instances Hiatt's poisonous darts fall widely off the mark and I am afraid that the same can be said for the rest of his paper.

I have not made any claim to interpret the kinship system and marriage rules of the Gidjingali of which I had never heard before and I do not know either how they themselves explain their marriage rules. I know, however, in which terms informants from other tribes have explained their system to men such as Spencer and Gillen, Strehlow, Radcliffe-Brown, Sharp, Stanner, Elkin, Warner, and many others and I have tried to articulate these scattered testimonies in a meaningful whole. If Hiatt's recent observation of what is left of a collapsing Australian tribe should carry more weight than the bulk of the older literature, then let us burn the books. It would probably be more sensible to seek in demographic and other factors why the Gidjingali cannot adhere to their own norms. I agree that it is important to find out what really happens in any society, notwithstanding its proclaimed rules. However, my past work on kinship has been mostly concerned with a different problem: to ascertain what was the meaning of the rules, whether they be applied or not. For rules have their own life if only in the mind of the people who are able to state them and to translate them back and forth at will in the language of preferred degrees or in that of sections and subsections. This should suffice to convince us that these two languages are not as wholly disconnected as it has become fashionable to pretend. Finally, it takes more than mere naiveté to believe that since *the theoretical model* of an Aranda system requires only four patrilines, the system itself could not ensure marriage exchange between 28 clans or many more. This empirical complexity has become commonplace at least since the time of Strehlow, and the Gidjingali case teaches nothing new in this respect. For the network can be woven on a shifting basis where the four lines do not need to remain the same ones. Unless the Gidjingali marry their daughters or sisters, which apparently is not the case, my statement that "in human society a man must obtain a woman from another man who gives him a daughter or a sister" (the French wording was more elaborate: "*qui la lui cède sous forme fille ou de soeur*") holds true for them too. I never claimed that this was happening without intermediaries and I even took pains to show that a delayed exchange remains an exchange none the less.

HIATT: If Lévi-Strauss is putting forward a general theory of Australian kinship (as I have always supposed), then the fact that he has never heard of the Gidjingali until now is of as little account as the fact that Newton was never hit on the head by a falling paw-paw. His insinuation that the Gidjingali do not count because they are the remnants of a collapsing Australian tribe must also be rejected. I have already dealt with a similar objection made by Birdsell to my criticisms of

Radcliffe-Brown's generalizations about aboriginal local organization (Chapter 17a, this volume). Lévi-Strauss supposes that some observers were in a better position to describe traditional aboriginal social life simply because they were earlier on the scene. This ignores the fact that European settlement has advanced slowly over the continent and that anthropologists have regularly worked on the frontiers, never beyond them. The Gidjingali system of kinship and marriage was, at the time of my observations, in no worse state of dislocation than those studied by the investigators Lévi-Strauss mentions.

Lévi-Strauss suggests that it would be more sensible to seek in demographic and other factors an answer to the question why the Gidjingali cannot adhere to their own norms. This is a distressing statement. It indicates the great difficulty I shall have in conveying the distinction that exists among the Gidjingali between marriage rules stated in terms of broad kin categories and rules that specify in narrow genealogical terms particular women within these categories to whom a man has marriage rights. Anthropologists in the past have concentrated upon rules of the former type, and it is upon their material that Lévi-Strauss has based his analysis. I must insist that in this respect the Gidjingali are not aberrant, and I repeat that roughly 90 per cent of their marriages are in accordance with the rules. The nonconformity referred to by Lévi-Strauss occurs in relation to rules of the second type, and I have already spent a good deal of time trying to explain it in precisely the terms Lévi-Strauss recommends. I regret that my effort to do so was unsuccessful.

Lévi-Strauss says that it has become fashionable to deny that rules stated in the language of preferred degrees and in the language of sections or subsections can be translated back and forth by the aborigines at will. If by "preferred degrees" he means categories of kin with whom a marriage would be morally proper, then it is clear from my paper that I do not subscribe to the fashion. What I deny is that a marriage rule stated in terms of kin categories or subsections is equivalent to a rule defining a man's right to only certain women within these categories or subsections.

I apologize for failing to grasp the meaning

of Lévi-Strauss's fake Latin and for assuming that he had actually said that one cannot study social rules independently of what really happens. The fact remains, as his final remarks indicate, that he does believe that his analytical models have empirical counterparts; in particular, that when he describes kinship systems as systems of communication in which women are mediators, he means that actual women are being exchanged by actual social groups. I have argued that there is little evidence of either a statistical or ideological kind to support such a view in relation to the Gidjingali. In my paper at this conference I have compared the facts with a hypothetical model of four patriclans; elsewhere I have tried to demonstrate that there is even less evidence for an extended network of exchange (Hiatt, 1965, p. 133).

I am baffled by Lévi-Strauss's final point. I said that Gidjingali men exchange their sister's daughters but do not have rights to bestow their own daughters or sisters. Lévi-Strauss insists that they do exchange daughters or sisters, not directly but through intermediaries. Suppose for the sake of argument that we were able to discover cycles of the postulated kind. We might then say: "Gidjingali men exchange their sister's daughters. They also exchange their daughters or sisters, but they are quite unaware of it." The question is whether this would be a meaningful use of the word "exchange."

22c. The Use and Misuse of Models

Speakers: *Alland, Helm, Lathrap, Laughlin, Lévi-Strauss, Meggitt, Pilling, Schieffelin, Sharp, Whiting.*

ALLAND: I would like to address myself to marriage and residence rules. We find rules that do not work or are misapplied, rules that do not exist, and variations on rules that might work in some way or other. In short, a model is not a model. It is possible, I suppose, that mechanical models could be completely false—a joint creation of the anthropologist and a zealous informant. It is more likely, however, that the models which some anthropologists have extracted from informants do exist, but the researcher's application of the models may be based on a misunderstanding of what they stand for.

What of the existing variation, for which we now have a good deal of empirical evidence? Is it capricious, or does it reflect scientific laws? I prefer the latter interpretation. First, we must consider those cases in which the demographic facts of life make it impossible for a people to follow their rules, and so they do the best they can. Lounsbury (1962) in his review of Needham's *Structure and Sentiment*, suggests that "the best they can do" may, indeed, be good enough to maintain an ongoing system. Computer simulation study—particularly that published by Kunstadter on cross-cousin marriage (Kunstadter *et al.*, 1963) indicates that "the best they can do" certainly is not a replication of the model.

It seems to me that it is, at least, possible that some of the variations in residence and marriage reflect adaptations to changing conditions and are, therefore, only short-term fluctuations. Meggitt has, I think, suggested this in another context. These variations may reflect the operation of supporting variables acting to maintain a state of some system. The statistical model, then, may reflect a certain degree of resource management, including the allocation of men and women. Thus, a diachronic analysis of variation in relation to ecological variables becomes a vital area for research.

In my own analysis of residence patterns among the Abron of the Ivory Coast, I stated that a mechanical model of residence told me more about social structure than did a statistical analysis of residence frequency, in which irregular forms of residence (i.e., those that did not fit the model) would be counted along with predictable types. How might this view be reconciled with my suggestion above that statistical rules might reveal ecological relationships? I think there are two answers to this, either of which might apply in the proper circumstances. The two models reflect different aspects of the system. One is more emic, and the other more etic (if one likes those terms).

1. Traditional categories are imprecise and show no regularity, because they do not reflect an actual, ordered situation. But there may be some undiscovered order in the data. Thus, in the Abron material, I was forced to consider—

as Fortes had done for the Ashanti (1949)—residence rules against domestic cycles. Martial residence alone was inadequate. Unlike Fortes, I then extracted rules that I considered to be significant for the social structure. Deviations from these rules were seen as accidental or temporary aberrations due to such minor factors as housing shortages.

2. A statistical model may be linked into self-regulating systems, in which statistical variations can be predicted on the basis of changing values of some other variables, such as population size, age- and sex-pyramids, allocation of resources, etc. The mechanical model may, as other conferees have noted, support an ideology that may or may not be related to marriage and residence—even if informants say that it is—or it may support partial adherence to marriage rules that are enough to sustain a social system.

I would suggest offhand, as a hypothesis, that as technology grows in complexity (with the concomitant complexities in social systems), strategies of maximization related to direct confrontation between man and environment are complicated by strategies related to property relationships and other social aspects that flow from these. Stated rules then, may be violated less frequently among peoples with higher technologies than among hunter-gatherers, whose pragmatism is closely linked with the vagaries of the base environment.

Lévi-Strauss: There are a few remarks that I would like to make on the papers by Messrs. Hiatt and Meggitt. I do not feel that I have written anything original about the Aranda system; I utilized the existing literature and reasserted the interpretation given years ago by Durkheim, on the one hand, and van Gennep on the other. This is, namely, that the entire set-up of the system can be explained by a series of commutative operations between residence and clan names, so that a satisfactory interlocking of all units concerned will be assured, generation after generation.

I view with great interest Mr. Meggitt's statistical correlations, but there is something that I could not find in his accounts; i.e., what the natives themselves say about their subsection system and its relation to marriage. Trying to explain such things merely by making statistical runs and trying to build up correla-

tions seems to me to amount to very much the same situation as that of a man who, wishing to understand the rules of the game of chess, eschewed a treatise on chess in favor of statistical runs on hundreds of thousands of games played by clumsy players. Of course, the clumsy players would have made mistakes, and the analyst would have no way of distinguishing these from moves made in accordance with the rules.

My acquaintance with Australian studies comes by way of the literature, and I have been very much impressed by the fact that whenever there are verbatim accounts of what native informants say, it is perfectly clear that they can express their marriage rules in terms of sections and subsections. I do not mean that sections and subsections are nothing other than marriage classes. But the natives are able, if need be, to translate the marriage rules in terms of these categories. And it seems to me that the great originality of the Australian native thinkers is shown by their ability to devise a coherent system in which there is the possibility of translation at every level between the social organization, the marriage rules, and the terminology.

Now, I am also aware that Elkin discovered that there is not a close correspondence between the subsection system and the marriage rules and, further, that the subsection system expresses a great number of things other than marriage rules. Mr. Meggitt has said that the system expresses primarily the order of the universe and only incidentally expresses the marriage rules. I question this. Do the natives say this? Is it necessary that we establish a hierarchy of importance and exclude the possibility that in this case cosmology and marriage rules may be on a par with one another? Even if the section and subsection system expresses in some way the order of the universe, as conceptualized by the natives, and even if the marriage rules normally can be used to maintain and perpetuate the social order, it nevertheless seems quite obvious that if—for demographic or other reasons—the marriage rules do not work, it will seem more important to the people concerned to maintain the set-up than to follow the rules. This, I take it, is what Elkin has pointed out. Yet there is nothing extraordinary about this. Every society, including our own, would do exactly the same. What is important for us, as for the Australian, is the moral order and the representation that we have of the universe. And if the rules do not succeed in maintaining that order, then they may be ignored. This does not mean, however—speaking of our own society—that law, institutions, and constitutions are entirely negligible because we violate them every time it is useful to do so.

MEGGITT: For better or worse, the Australian aborigines are in many matters far more sophisticated than anthropologists. By their own reports, they have a hierarchical view of the universe and give primacy to the rules (such as subsection rules) that structure the universe. This is one model. This model is unchanging, as is the universe. Where they differ from us is in the fact that they distinguish a second model for marriage arrangements, while we keep trying to impose the universal model on the marriage realm. Moreover, they point out that their marriage model is in general accord with what actually happens; and they take care to see to this, insofar as demographic and other factors allow them to. For them, *mating* is material (hence, a part of the universal model), but *marriage* is not. So they are able to maintain their marriage rules; even though they may be mating against these rules.

LÉVI-STRAUSS: I would like to make a distinction here, borrowing an illustration from the natural sciences. There are shapeless mollusks living in the sea that secrete marvelous shells, which have mathematical properties. Now, it is a problem to discover how a certain type of mollusk secretes a certain type of shell. That is, if you like, a problem of what happens in the field, and it is a very important kind of problem. But it is perfectly legitimate never even to look at the mollusk, and to try to learn the mathematical transformations involved in passage from one type of shell to another. Either type of investigation is worthwhile, and they are entirely distinct from one another. So we may make use of both, but it is a mistake to mix the two operations or to suppose that we are doing one type when, in fact, we are doing the other.

HELM: I cannot see, in the case either of a mollusk or of a human community, the legitimacy of separating the pattern or map and the actual behavior. I should think that it is not only permissible but altogether necessary that we keep our attention on the relations of the two. The manipulation of models in the abstract or the refusal to test them against events "on the ground" will never tell us to what degree, if any, societies are systems.

ALLAND: Ashby (1960) has said that "a system is anything that the investigator cares to define as one," but I would add that the investigator has the responsibility of proving that the system is at least interesting. Some events which the anthropologist rather arbitrarily fits into a class of behavior, like residence, may be more significant than others, at least for some system that he has in mind. This is what I tried to do with the Abron data, and I think that in my treatment of it I went beyond Fortes' treatment of his data on the Ashanti (1949). He wound up with a range of residence rules that showed that the Ashanti were not just matrilocal or dual-local, but that there was matrilocality, dual-locality, etc. I tried to relate this to a system of social relationships having to do with lineal stresses in the society.

Now, there are two things that interest me in rule systems when the rules systems are related to a single set of phenomena: (1) the question whether the natives try to approximate the rule system as *we* think that they might approximate it; and (2) the variations, which may be very significant—and not just capricious. So both rules and variations may be related to culture.

WHITING: It seems to me that the structure in the native's mind that corresponds to what, in the anthropologists' mind, we might call a model, is really better described as a cognitive view of the universe that serves him as a mnemonic device and an aid to communication with other members of his own society. Now, it is no more an empirical matter to find out who marries whom than it is to try to discover how much consensus there is in a society in the cognitive systems that they espouse. However the latter question is one which we have failed to investigate.

ALLAND: We have had a blush of success from componential analysis, but it has tended to go back to the single informant approach of earlier anthropology. This is unfortunate in many cases, although it seems to work pretty well with kinship systems, since most people know their systems pretty well and agree on them. But I think Whiting's point is a good one. I remember Sapir's story about the time when he had completely worked out a system and then presented it to one of the Indians, Two Crows, who told him that the system simply was not like that. There is this sort of variation in system, even ideal ones, within a single society; and it is significant to know how many "Two Crows" there are in any particular society.

LAUGHLIN: I recall an early paper by Steve Hart, published in the *American Anthropologist* (Hart, 1943) in the 1940's, in which he analyzed the marriage rules for the Natchez Indians. As I recall, they had an exotic system that differentiated Suns, Honors, Nobles, and Stinkards. And by purely arithmetical means he demonstrated that the system could not work. Some years later, the mathematician Robert Busch demonstrated again, this time by means of matrix algebra, that the system could not work. This might make us wonder how well other systems would stand a test of internal consistency—quite apart from the question as to the conformity of the people to the systems.

LATHRAP: I think that the demonstrations just mentioned were made on the assumption that the system was intended to function as a closed one, while the Natchez and other groups with somewhat similar systems, such as the Mbaya of the Gran Chaco, were continually adding to their lower class through conquest. The details of the setting and the operation of such a system must be taken into account.

ALLAND: It seems significant that this should be a model that cannot work unless something unusual happens, which seems especially important if we are studying, say, gene flow.

SHARP: There may be different models and different kinds of models that should have been considered here. The Australian aboriginal, however abstract his thinking may become, is not really concerned to distinguish between Dr. Birdsell's linguistic community and Dr. Alland's breeding one, which might include two to three linguistic communities. It is up to us not to be taken in by stereotyped constructs—either the natives' or our own—or to apply them to the wrong group or the wrong activities.

SCHIEFFELIN: While there seems to be agreement on the fact that the scientist's model is not identical to that in the native's mind, it has not yet been seriously asked whether the native's construct is even the same sort of thing as the anthropologist's model. We appear to assume that the native does live in accordance with some sort of system of explicit and implicit beliefs to be brought out by careful questioning; while it may well be that, in fact, the native synthesizes and systematizes his beliefs for the very first time in the act of explaining them to the anthropologist. It might be useful to look at the "model" in the native's mind in the same way that Thomas Kuhn (1962) looks at paradigms in scientific theory. Instead of being strict models, according to which scientific theories are elaborated, they are bodies of assumptions that are more or less consistent with one another and include exemplary examples, so to speak.

PILLING: In view of the monographs published on Australia, I might stress the importance of graphic representations of "models," which the aborigines often make in the sand (in circumstances which suggest that such graphic representations are not a new, acculturative phenomenon). In studying some of these, I found that they were of a very different nature from the anthropologist's presentation of the same material. As ethnographers, we ought to be certain that we do not overlook the aid to be had from these graphic representations as supplements to the verbal explanations.

LÉVI-STRAUSS: I would like to cite an example of the clarity of the model that sometimes is to be found in the mind of the native. One of my students has just returned from Africa, where she studied a Voltaic people with a kinship system of the Crow-Omaha type (but with bilateral descent and, accordingly, numerous clan interdictions). Now, the use of the terms is extremely complicated, and in order to explain why in describing a certain degree of kinship they use one term rather than another, the natives expounded a set of rules resembling very much those developed by Lounsbury in his analysis of the Crow-Omaha system (Lounsbury, 1964). Is it not striking that Lounsbury, by sophisticated techniques of analysis, should have actually rediscovered rules that do exist in the mind of a native in a quite different part of the world?

22d. STATISTICS OF KIN MARRIAGE: A NON-AUSTRALIAN EXAMPLE

Speaker: *Helm*

HELM: The bulk of our discussion today has concerned marriage among Australian aborigines. It hardly needs saying that the Australians are not the only hunter-gatherers who marry, nor are they the only ones who exhibit cross-cousin marriage. To broaden the perspective it may be useful to consider marriage data from other areas.

I present part of the results of an effort to identify kin-pattern in marriages among the Hare Indians. The Athapaskan Hare live near the Arctic circle in western Canada and have numbered around 300 for the last several generations. In my few weeks with the Hare in 1957, I found Iroquois cousin terms, terminological equivalence of father's sister and mother's brother with mother-in-law and father-in-law, and the apparent fact that terms for cross-cousins of opposite sex derive from husband and wife terms. These forms suggested that, at least in the past, cross-cousin marriage might be practiced (MacNeish, 1960a). In a subsequent study of the Hare, Hiroko Sue (1964, p. 424) indicates that first cross-cousin marriage was formerly the preferred type and that "more distant cross-cousins do marry each other."

In considering the Hare material, the marriage patterns and terminology systems of Northern Algonkians (Cree, Northern Ojibwa, Naskapi) came to mind as immediate models (see Eggan, 1955, pp. 519 ff.). Hallowell and Dunning, for example, have given us quantified data on kin-connected marriages in two Northern Ojibwa groups (with populations comparable in size to the Hare). Although at pains to point out that persons falling in the "marriageable" class may be distant relatives of Ego, Hallowell and Dunning demonstrate that consanguineal first and second cross-cousin marriages are high. Such marriages comprised 40.8 per cent of three generations of marriages among the Island Lake Salteaux

(Hallowell, 1937, pp. 98, 101) and 50.0 per cent of the marriages taking place among the Pekangekum Ojibwa in a five-year interval in the 1950's (Dunning, 1959, p. 154). The kinship terminology system of the Hare differs from the cited Northern Ojibwa groups only in that sibling-in-law categories are identified by distinct terms. In his comparative analysis of Algonkian terminology systems, Eggan (1955, p. 529) argues that "separation of siblings-in-law from cross-cousins is an important marker in the breakdown of cross-cousin marriage" and for several cases suggests "white acculturation" as a critical factor. If the distinct sibling-in-law terms in the Hare system represent an acculturative shift, then a reasonable expectation, by analogy from the Algonkian material, is that marriages in earlier generations at least would show a fair incidence of consanguine cross-cousin marriage of first and second degree.

Data on Hare genealogies and all marriages from the beginning of the Mission Period (that is, 1860) were available to me through the records of the Oblate missionaries. The marriages of almost 1,000 individuals were recorded. The genealogical and marital data were subjected to computer processing. Given sufficient data, the computer yields a print-out of all chains of primary consanguineal and/or affinal links to the tenth remove that may obtain between spouses.[1] For 457 Hare marriages falling within the interval between 1890 and 1956, there was sufficient genealogical background to demonstrate all linkages between the spouses.

The computer print-out revealed that almost every Hare was linked, within ten or less removes, to his partner in several or many ways (maximum: 148) *if* affinal connections are included. But the surprising result was that only 35 or 7.6 per cent of the marriages were between consanguines. Out of these there were twelve cases—2.4 per cent of all marriages—of consanguineal cousin marriage, all between second cousins. Eleven of the twelve were terminologically "cross-cousins." Compare this with the 40 to 50 per cent of first and second

1. I am indebted to Allan Coult (then at the University of California at Davis) and his associates, who developed the computer program and ran the Hare data for me.

cross-cousin marriages in the two Ojibwa populations cited above.

The rates of consanguineal marriages through six and a half decades (1890 to 1956) remain remarkably constant for the Hare. However, half of the second-cousin marriages (six) occurred in the first two decades. In sum, it appears that the Hare suppress marriage between consanguines, and did so at a period when it is very unlikely that white accultura-tive press would have had much effect. Specifically, if it were simply a matter of choosing among a number of kin-types, including consanguineal cross-cousins, that fall within the class of "marriageable relative," distant or near, the Hare should come considerably closer to approaching the proportions of first and second cross-cousin marriages found among the Ojibwa groups reported by Hallowell and Dunning.

PART V

Demography and Population Ecology

23.

Epidemiological Factors:
Health and Disease in Hunter-Gatherers

FREDERICK L. DUNN

INTRODUCTION

A series of generalizations concerning health, disease, and mortality in hunter-gatherers are reviewed and discussed in this paper. Some are long-established and widely accepted; others are proposed in the light of certain considerations of ecological diversity and complexity. I shall refer particularly to the published record for health and disease in the Bushman, the Australian aborigine, the Eskimo, the African Pygmy, and the Semang (Malayan Negrito). In the course of the discussion some epidemiological or "medical ecological" issues will be raised which pertain to the study of diseases: (1) as agents of natural selection, and (2) as dependent or independent variables influencing size and stability of human populations. I shall emphasize the role of disease in population regulation rather than in selection, but much that will be said relates to both areas of inquiry. Disease—particularly parasitic and infectious disease—has attracted considerable attention from human geneticists and anthropologists in recent years (Livingstone, 1960; Motulsky, 1960; Neel et al., 1964; World Health Organization, 1964) but the role of disease in population regulation has been somewhat neglected.

Whether one's concern may be the destiny of the modern hunter-gatherer or the reconstruction of prehistoric hunting and gathering conditions, hunter-gatherer studies are really urgent today. This urgency is emphasized in a succinct World Health Organization report, "Research in population genetics of primitive groups" (1964), which also outlines research needs, procedures, and the kinds of demographic, ethnographic, genetic, and biomedical data whose collection is so essential. These procedural matters need not be discussed here, but a brief review of the means available for gathering data and developing a picture of disease patterns in prehistoric hunter-gatherers may be useful. Only four approaches come to mind:

1. We may study health and disease in modern hunter-gatherers and project these findings into the past. This approach assumes that disease patterns in populations still removed from substantial contact with outsiders are to some extent similar to ancient disease patterns. The extensive pilot study of the Xavante Indians of the Brazilian Mato Grosso by Neel and his colleagues (1964) is a good example. Their report provides some tentative hypotheses of human genetic and evolutionary interest; many indications exist that additional studies along the same lines may also provide data of value in the interpretation of prehistoric

populations and demographic conditions.

2. We may review first-contact records—historical and ethnographic within this century—for information about specific diseases and conditions of health. Much of our knowledge of aboriginal health conditions in the Americas has been built up in this way (Cook, 1955, for example).

3. We may make use of increasing refinement of archeological technique and extensive multidisciplinary collaboration in archeological investigations, which are beginning to provide extraordinary dividends in knowledge of the prehistoric environment. Paleoecological studies now make it possible to assess prehistoric environmental potentials for transmission of infectious and parastic agents of disease. Paleopathological investigations are becoming increasingly sophisticated, and coprolite studies, which also provide valuable dietary and ecological information, have opened the way to epidemiological assessment of intestinal helminthiases in prehistoric populations (Callen and Cameron, 1960; Samuels, 1965). Recently, in collaboration with Dr. Robert Heizer of the University of California I have had the opportunity to study a series of more than fifty coprolites from Lovelock Cave in Nevada. We found no eggs or larvae of parasitic helminths, but because of the extraordinary state of preservation of certain pseudoparasites—mites and nematodes—we were able to conclude, with a fair degree of certainty, that the ancient people represented by these specimens were in fact free of a whole series of intestinal helminths, including flukes, tapeworms, and important nematodes such as hookworm and *Ascaris*. This conclusion was not altogether surprising in the light of our knowledge of helminthiasis in modern Bushmen and other hunter-gatherers of arid regions.

4. We may finally approach the study of prehistoric patterns of disease in man through the study of disease patterns in non-human primates today in a variety of ecological settings, some of which are shared with modern hunter-gatherers (Dunn MS-1, MS-2). In this relatively unexplored field we can only expect to discern broad patterns of similarity for man and other primates. I shall return briefly to this approach when I discuss ecological complexity and diversity.

DISEASE IN THE POPULATION EQUATION

To examine the role of disease in a human population, we may refer to the "equation of recruitment and loss" of Wynne-Edwards (1962), defining the variables contributing to the condition of population stability:

Recruit- + Immi- = Uncon- + Emi- + Social
ment   gration   trollable   gration   Mortality
Arising   Losses
from Re-
production

In this equation, "uncontrollable losses" are identified as the independent variable and include losses due to predation, parasitism (infectious and parasitic diseases), accidents, starvation and old age (chronic diseases, diseases associated with aging). Social mortality comprises that mortality arising from "social stress": strife, stress diseases, cannibalism, infanticide, war, homicide, suicide, etc. Wynne-Edwards, with an acknowledgement to Carr-Saunders (1922), discusses population stability in hunter-gatherer and subsistence agriculturalist societies in terms of this equation. Births and immigration are balanced by emigration and two kinds of mortality, the socially controllable (social mortality) and the socially uncontrollable (losses due to independent variables). Within the realm of controllable (sometimes even "acceptable") mortality is population regulation by abortion and infanticide, by reduction in numbers (sacrifice, cannibalism, head-hunting and other forms of warfare, geronticide, and even homicide and suicide), and by territoriality (rules regulating the utilization of space and resources, land tenure, marriage regulations, etc.). In a brief discussion of mortality due to predation and disease, Wynne-Edwards points out that neither of these variables can be considered wholly density-dependent or density-independent. Predation not only contributes to uncontrollable loss but is also density-dependent insofar as the prey may "cooperate" in making its surplus members available to predators. Similarly, infectious and parastic diseases may be either uncontrollable or density-dependent, as socially stressed individuals are selected out by disease because of their "depressed" physiological state. Thus, as variables contributing to mortality, predation and disease due to parasitism are to some extent controllable and density-dependent, to some extent uncontrollable and independent. The disease variable is obviously important in the regulation of human population but its impact is constantly modified by sociocultural and ecological factors. Other variables in the demographic equation—notably accidents, predation, and certain forms of social mortality—may affect population size more profoundly than disease in certain settings.

MORTALITY AND DISEASE IN HUNTER-GATHERERS

Some of the characteristics of the hunting and gathering way of life (as seen today, and in historic times) that may influence the prevalence and distribution of various diseases and other causes of mortality are these: the size of the social group is small, and contact between groups is limited, in part because of the relatively large area needed to support each small population unit; the group utilizes environmental resources intensively but with minimal permanent disturbance of the environment; the individuals are well adapted to the conditions of the ecosystem in which they belong; the individual lives in intimate contact with his fellows and the environment; the group is characteristically mobile, within certain territorial limits; dwellings are often rudimentary or temporary; the dietary range is relatively wide, at least potentially—less desirable foods are available as a reserve for times of hardship; in general the diet may be said to be well balanced in the sense that minimal nutritional requirements are apparently met; in the tropics and subtropics the vegetable component of the diet normally exceeds the animal component in quantity if not in quality; in the arctic and in certain maritime and riverine settings the animal component may bulk larger than the vegetable; occupational specialization except along lines of age and sex is relatively slight.

With these characteristics in mind we may consider some generalizations about health, disease, and mortality in hunting and gathering peoples (prehistoric, precontact, or isolated modern population).

1. *Patent (and perhaps even borderline) mal-*
nutrition is rare. We should expect this in stable, well-adapted hunter-gatherer populations, modern or prehistoric. Dietary resources, even in arid environments, are diverse: typical sampling of these resources by modern hunter-gatherers in ecosystems relatively undisturbed by outsiders seems to provide at least the minimal protein, carbohydrate, fat, mineral, and vitamin requirements. Many workers have commented on the relatively good nutritional status of hunter-gatherers in comparison with neighboring agriculturalists or urban dwellers (for example: Ackerknecht, 1948; Maingard, 1937; Turnbull, 1965b; Woodburn, 1959). Neel (1962) postulated a dramatic gorging-and-fasting way of life for hunter-gatherers through "99 percent of hominid existence" in developing his hypotheses of the "thrifty" diabetic genotype. In the light of recent studies of the Bushman (Lee, 1965), this portrayal of major fluctuations in the quantity and quality of the hunter-gatherer diet is probably somewhat exaggerated.

2. *Starvation occurs infrequently.* While hunter-gatherers are rarely exposed to *relative* dietary deficiencies leading to malnutrition, they may, exceptionally, be faced with *gross* deficits. In tropical and temperate regions of moderate to heavy rainfall, starvation has undoubtedly been the exception, occurring only in individuals incapacitated for other reasons (Turnbull, 1965b). In the arid tropics only an unusually prolonged drought may be expected to imperil the food supply, but failure of the water supply may select out the aged and sick before gross food shortages can have their effect. In the arctic and subarctic winter, on the other hand, starvation has probably always been a relatively important cause of death (Ackerknecht, 1948). In general it seems that agriculturalists, more or less dependent on one or several staple crops, are more liable to food supply failure and famine than are hunters and gatherers. Famine risk may even be increased as the effects of dry seasons are exaggerated through agricultural modification of the natural vegetational cover.

3. *Chronic diseases, especially those associated with old age, are relatively infrequent.* Birth rates are high, but the population pyramid for hunter-gatherers is broad only at the base because life-expectancy at birth is low for

males and even lower for females (Ackerknecht, 1948; Krogman, 1939; Krzwicki, 1934; Neel *et al.*, 1964; Polunin, 1953; Roney, 1959). Shorter female life expectancies presumably reflect maternal losses in childbirth, stresses associated with multiple pregnancies and deliveries, and in certain cultures male-female dietary disparities. Although life expectancies of hunter-gatherers are low by modern European or American standards, they compare favourably with expectancies for displaced hunter-gatherers, many subsistence agriculturalists, and impoverished urbanized people of the tropics today (Ackerknecht, 1948; Billington, 1960; Duguid, 1963; Dunn, MS-1; Maingard, 1937; Polunin, 1953). Few hunter-gatherers survive long enough to develop clinical cardiovascular disease or cancer, major causes of mortality in America and Europe today. These diseases do occur infrequently, however, and preclinical manifestations of cardiovascular disorder may be detected in such populations (Mann *et al.*, 1962). Occasional writers have claimed that certain primitive populations are "cancer-free" or "heart disease-free," but sound evidence to support such contentions is lacking, and evidence to the contrary has been steadily accumulating. Chronic diseases of early onset, including genetic disorders, do of course occur regularly in all human populations; upon survey the more severe of these appear less frequent in hunter-gatherers, probably because prolonged survival of incapacitated individuals is less likely in mobile than in settled situations. Such persons have sometimes been abandoned or killed, particularly in the Arctic (Ackerknecht, 1948).

4. *Accidental and traumatic death rates vary greatly among hunter-gatherer populations.* It is sometimes said that accidents constitute a major cause of death in hunting and gathering societies. Although this is indeed the case for certain peoples, it is not universally true for all hunter-gatherers, past and present. Deaths due to drowning, burns, suffocation, exposure, and hunting accidents have probably always weighed heavily in the population equation for Eskimos and other peoples of polar and subpolar regions (Ackerknecht, 1948; Hughes, 1965; World Health Organization, 1963). The Australian aborigines and Bushmen, on the other hand, cannot often drown or suffocate or fall from trees, and are physiologically tolerant of an environment that is climatically "constant" compared to that of the Eskimo. Turnbull (1965b) has recently commented on the low incidence of accidental injuries and deaths among the Mbuti Pygmies. He recorded falls from trees, falls into campfires, attacks by animals, falling on a spear, bee stings, and snakebites as Congo forest hazards. Similarly, Billington (1960) noted the infrequent occurrence of trauma among "settled" aborigines in Arnhem Land. Paleopathologists have nevertheless demonstrated abundant traumatic pathology in skeletal series for certain hunters and agriculturalists; most of these series have been recovered from archeological sites outside the tropics.

5. *Predation, excluding snakebite, is a minor cause of death in modern hunter-gatherers; predation may have been relatively more important in the past.* Haldane (1957) and Motulsky (1960) suggest that through much of hominid evolution predation and other selective agencies were far more important than infectious and parasitic diseases, which became major agents of natural selection only after the introduction of agriculture with its concomitant increases in population density, community size, and community contact. Livingstone (1958) has provided an interpretation of sickle cell gene distribution in West Africa that supports such an hypothesis, but little other evidence is available at this time to assist us in evaluating Haldane's suggestion. We cannot rule out the possibility (a strong probability, in my opinion) that some infectious and parasitic diseases were important selective agencies in prehistoric hunting and gathering populations, as they undoubtedly are and have been in modern hunter-gatherer societies. Other parasites and microorganisms have undoubtedly become important in selection only in recent millenia in response to culturally induced environmental change. We do not know the relative importance of predators at various points in human evolution, although common sense suggests that predators constituted a greater hazard for early man than for modern hunter-gatherers. Accurate predation data for the great apes would be of interest in this connection, but it would be rash to utilize these data in generalizing about predation in early hominid life. In reviewing

some of the literature on health in hunter-gatherers, I have come upon occasional references to snakebite fatalities, which were apparently particularly frequent in Australia (Cleland, 1928), but references to animal attacks have been few, even for the Arctic (Ackerknecht, 1948; Turnbull, 1965b).

6. *Mental disorders of hunting and gathering peoples have been so little investigated that no generalizations about incidence can be justified.* Descriptions I have encountered of presumed mental disorder have been presented in terms of the psychological norms of the observer-recorder (for example, Cleland, 1928; Basedow, 1932). Ackerknecht (1948) and others have suggested that the rates for phobias and hysteria were higher for the precontact Eskimo than for other societies; discussions of mental disorder in other hunter-gatherers usually emphasize that mental health was good, at least in the aboriginal state. Facts to support such statements are essentially non-existent. Cawte and his colleagues in Australia are pioneering in their ethnopsychiatric investigations of acculturated and unacculturated aborigines. A few limited psychological investigations of Bushmen and Pygmies have been cited by Doob (1965).

7. *Ample evidence is available that "social mortality" has been and is significant in the population equation for any hunting and gathering society.* Cannibalism, infanticide, sacrifice, geronticide, head-hunting, and other forms of warfare have largely disappeared today, but the early contact records provide abundant evidence of the importance of these practices in many societies (for example, Ackerknecht, 1948; Krzwicki, 1934; Neel *et al.*, 1964; Radcliffe-Brown, 1933). Other forms of social mortality, such as homicide, suicide, and stress diseases, were apparently less frequent prior to contact; today they are replacing the old forms and increasing in frequency in displaced and acculturated hunter-gatherers as in so many other human societies (Doob, 1965; Duguid, 1963; Hughes, 1965; Polunin, 1953; World Health Organization, 1963).

8. *Parasitic and infectious disease rates of prevalence and incidence are related to ecosystem diversity and complexity. Although many of these diseases contribute substantially to mortality, no simple, single generalization is possible for all hunter-gatherers.*

A. *Introductory comments: Infection.* Infections by microorganisms and parasites[1] may be classified for epidemiological purposes in two primary subdivisions: *asexual infections* (organisms reproducing asexually) and *sexual infections* (organisms with some form of sexual reproduction; Macdonald, 1965). Each subdivision may be further divided into *direct* and *indirect* categories. An indirect infection requires some development outside the definitive host in normal transmission. This type of infection is therefore partially dependent upon conditions of environmental temperature and humidity; many but not all are specifically tropical.

Asexual infections may be introduced into a population by a single dose in a single individual. Multiplication in the community occurs most readily if the agent is *rare* in that community, and particularly if that agent has not circulated in the community previously. Malaria and yellow fever, whose agents are arthropod vector-transmitted, are good examples of indirect asexual infections. Direct asexual infections are numerous; they include many of the common viral and bacterial infections of mankind (measles, smallpox, diphtheria, etc.). Asexual infections often produce partial and sometimes complete acquired immunity to repeated infection.

Sexual infections cannot normally be introduced into new populations by single doses. The agents multiply and maintain themselves in the population more readily if they occur in large numbers in a high proportion of available hosts—that is, if the prevalence rate is high in the community and if the intensity of infection in the individual is great. Indirect sexual infections include many of the helminthiases: schistosomiasis, filariasis, hookworm infection, etc. Direct sexual infections are not numerous, but include such well-known parasitic helminths as the pinworm. Sexual infections stimulate poor to partial acquired immunity at best.

B. *Introductory comments: Ecological diversity and complexity.* The concepts of ecological

---

1. Parasites, in the strict sense used here, comprise the protozoa, helminths, and ectoparasites of biomedical importance. Microorganisms (or infectious organisms) include the viruses, bacteria, rickettsia, and fungi.

diversity and complexity are well known to ecologists (Holdridge, 1965; Odum, 1959) but little attention has been paid to their epidemiological implications until recently. The starting point for discussion is the climax tropical rainforest, which is characterized by many species of plants and animals per unit area and by few individuals per species in the same unit area. A one-hectare plot in the Brazilian tropical rainforest, for example, contained 564 trees (greater than 10 cm. diameter at chest height) belonging to 60 species. Even the commonest species was represented by only 49 individuals, and 33 species were represented by single individuals (Dobzhansky, 1950). I I need not stress the contrast with the tree species/individual relationships in boreal forest. As Dobzhansky (1950) has said, where diversity of inhabitants is great, the environment is rich in adaptive opportunities. This diversity in climax rain forest applies not only to trees, and to other plants, but of course also to birds, snakes, insects, mammals, and many other forms of life, not omitting potential or actual vectors, intermediate hosts, and alternative hosts for infective organisms. We are now beginning to see that this diversity also extends to parasites and microorganisms.

The ratio between the number of species and the number of individuals per species has been called the *diversity index* (Odum, 1959). In the tropical rain forest the diversity index is high; wherever man disturbs this forest the index is lower; wherever physical factors are severe and limiting, as in the Arctic, the desert, or at high altitude, the diversity index is very low—few species but large numbers of individuals per species. At an "edge," that is, the line of contact between a forest and a field, the diversity index may be somewhat higher than on either side of the line. Wherever man has substantially altered the environment, and the diversity is accordingly low, some of the species represented by large numbers of individuals are commonly called "weeds." Actually all plants and animals (including man) are weeds in such circumstances.

The *complexity index* recently developed by

Complex Ecosystem	Simple Ecosystem
(example: tropical rain forest)	(examples: subpolar tundra, desert bush, thorn woodland)
—*Many* species of plants and animals	—*Few* species of plants and animals
—*Few* individuals per species	—*Many* individuals per species
—*Many* species of parasitic and infectious organisms (in man and in other animals)	—*Few* species of parasitic and infectious organisms (in man and in other animals)
—*Many* species of potential vectors, intermediate hosts, and alternative hosts (to man) for parasitic and infectious organisms	—*Few* species of potential vectors, intermediate hosts, and alternative hosts (to man) for parasitic and infectious organisms
—*Low* potential transmission efficiency for indirect infections	—*High* potential transmission efficiency for those few indirect infections occurring in this ecosystem
—Sexual infections: *many* kinds due to many species of organisms	—Sexual infections: *few* kinds
—Sexual infections: *low* intensities of infection—*low* worm burdens—light infections	—Sexual infections: *greater* intensity of infection—*heavier* worm burdens
—Asexual infections: *many* kinds due to many species of organisms	—Asexual infections: *few* kinds
—Direc tasexual infections producing good partial or permanent immunity: appearing in human popuation units at long intervals	—Direct asexual infections producing good partial or permanent immunity: appearing in human population units at long intervals
—Direclt asexual infections producing little or no immunity: *low* prevalence	—Direct asexual infections producing little or no immunity: *high* prevalence
—Indirect asexual infections (except those producing substantial immunity): *low* prevalence	—Indirect asexual infections (except those producing substantial immunity): *high* prevalence
—(Also: many species but few individuals of venomous and noxious arthropods and reptiles = *low* incidence of bites)	—(Also: many individuals of a few species of venomous and noxious arthropods and reptiles = *high* incidence of bites)

Table 1 Parasitic Helminths and Protozoa in Four Hunting and Gathering Peoples (summarizing all available records)

	Bushman Africa	Australian Aborigine Entire Continent	Australian Aborigine Central Australia	Semang Malaya	Pygmy Africa
PLANT FORMATION	Desert Desert Bush Thorn Woodland	Primarily: Desert Desert Bush Thorn Woodland	Desert Desert Bush	Tropical, Premontane & Lower Montane Rain-Forest	Tropical & Premontane Rain-Forest
Complexity Index (Holdridge)	5.6 or less	primarily less than 5.6	5.6 or less	270–405	270–405
No. Species Helminths	2	6	1	10	11
No. Species Intestinal Protozoa	—	1	—	9	6
No. Species Blood Protozoa	1	2	—	3	3
Total No. Species	3	9	1	22	20

Holdridge (1965) provides a measure of vegetation complexity (and secondarily of other biological complexity), but should not be confused with the diversity index. The complexity index is based on height of forest stand, basal area of stand, number of trees, and number of tree species, but it does not take into account the number of trees per species. Holdridge has recently published a useful classification of world plant formations; it provides complexity indices for many of these formations (Holdridge 1965).

C. *Infection and ecological diversity and complexity: hypothetical conditions.* We may now contrast two "ideal" and undisturbed ecosystems including human populations of similar group sizes, similarly dispersed. One is complex—with high diversity and complexity indices; the other is simple—with low indices.

D. *Generalizations: infectious and parasitic disease in hunter-gatherers.* The ideal conditions outlined for a *complex* ecosystem are believed applicable in any consideration of infection in unacculturated, undisplaced Congo forest Pygmies or Malayan Negritos (Semang). The conditions for a *simple ecosystem* are presumably applicable to the Eskimo, the Bushman, or the Australian aborigine. These conditions should also be relevant in any epidemiological study of infection in non-human primates: in the more or less arboreal rain-forest species on the one hand, and in the more or less terrestrial open-country species on the other. I have recently reviewed records for parasitism in African primates, setting the findings against the conditions outlined above. The results are consistent with these conditions (Dunn, MS-2). The epidemiological record for infection in hunter-gatherers is of course considerably "contaminated" by contact with outsiders, introductions of infections, environmental disturbances, and displacements. Careful study of historical and ethnographic records will probably provide additional data for examination against the hypothesized conditions. At the moment, however, I can offer only limited supporting data on helminthic and protozoan parasite species numbers in four hunting and gathering peoples (Table 1). Records for the Bushmen, Australians, and Pygmies have been extracted from the literature (primarily: Billington, 1960; Black, 1959; Bronte-Stewart *et al.*, 1960; Casley-Smith, 1959; Cleland, 1928; Crotty and Webb, 1960; Heinz, 1961; Maingard, 1937; Mann *et al.*, 1962; Price *et al.*, 1963). Records for intestinal protozoa are probably incomplete; in other respects the records appear adequate. All available records for the Australian continent, representing a variety of habitats (mainly arid), are shown in one column; findings for one nomadic and isolated population in Central Australia are also shown separately. Semang data are based primarily upon my own surveys in 1962–64 (Dunn and Bolton, 1963), and on the work of Wharton *et al.* (1963) and Polunin (1953). A few species of helminths and intestinal protozoa in modern acculturated, semiurbanized Eskimos have been recorded, but I have not so far encountered any records of parasitological survey for truly isolated Eskimo populations.

E. *Summary*. The complexity and diversity of the ecosystem must influence—perhaps profoundly—the patterning of infection and disease in hunter-gatherer populations. Prevalence, incidence, intensity, distribution, transmission efficiency, vector abundance, intermediate or alternative host variety and abundance are all affected by these ecological factors. For some hunter-gatherers many kinds of parasitic and infectious diseases may be responsible for moderate rates of morbidity and mortality; for others only a few kinds of disease may be responsible for much morbidity, and even mortality; some diseases appear at long intervals, causing high mortality; others are ever present, causing more or less morbidity and mortality depending on a complex array of ecological and cultural factors. If diseases caused by parasites and microorganisms serve as agents of natural selection and population regulation, then any patterning of these diseases will mirror, or be mirrored by, similar patterning of disease-related selection pressures and population-regulating mechanisms.

Conclusion

The hunter-gatherer is an element in an ecosystem and cannot isolate himself from his environment. Little or no buffering stands between him and the other components of the system. His relationship to the land, to its flora and fauna, and to his fellow man is intimate. Although he is never perfectly adapted to the conditions in his environment, there is a degree of adaptive stability—of ecological conservatism—which does not exist in a modern urban setting. When forces of change appear, how-

ever, rapid and profound destabilization may follow. The medical sphere today provides many examples of this destabilization among the surviving hunting peoples as they encounter outsiders, lose their lands to agricultural and pastoral encroachment, and even suffer permanent displacement from these lands. "New" diseases and disorders appear, endemic diseases either disappear or become more prevalent and more damaging as social and ecological change enhances their transmissibility, and former causes of mortality are displaced by new causes.

Hunters today do not live in wholly aboriginal or "prehistoric" states of health, and historic or ethnographic records offer little data upon which to base speculations about prehistoric conditions of health. We can, however, take note of the *patterning* of present-day health problems among the surviving hunters. This patterning is inevitably affected by the ecological setting of the hunting group, for, as I have previously noted, the hunter lives in a truly intimate relationship with his surroundings. If we can determine and understand the factors that contribute to patterning of diseases and causes of death in modern peoples who live in an unbuffered relationship to their environment, we can apply this understanding to the interpretation of the prehistoric and evolutionary record, even in the absence of knowledge about which (specific) diseases may or may not have been present in an ancient population.

A discussion of epidemiological patterning for the infectious and parasitic diseases has been presented; this patterning is linked to ecological factors, including diversity and complexity. Elsewhere in this review I have mentioned striking differences in incidence for predation, accidents, and other causes of death for hunter-gatherers in various geographical settings. A few ecologically linked patterns of morbidity and mortality have emerged; others will no doubt be added as old information is screened and new data become available. The findings already emphasize the fallacy in generalizing about "hunter-gatherers" as though they were some kind of homogeneous cultural-genetic-ecological unity. They are *diverse*, their hunting territories are diverse, and so are their diseases and ways of death.

24.

Some Predictions for the Pleistocene Based on Equilibrium Systems among Recent Hunter-Gatherers

JOSEPH B. BIRDSELL

INTRODUCTION

The conceptual use of equilibrium systems is ancient and honorable in the social sciences. But in practice such systems have usually remained at the level of diagramatic models. A stable equilibrium system provides a suitable basis for prediction from a number of points of view. It ordinarily remains in a steady state, or if displaced returns to it. An analysis of those forces which contribute to its balanced state allows for the quantification of the forces and encourages the exploration of the inter-relations between them. Especially suitable for predictive projections are equilibrium systems whose mean values show a high degree of correlation with one or more external variables. In the brief outline below, a series of equilibrium systems are discussed which will assist directly, or with further elaboration, in reconstructing the dynamics and attributes of prehistoric populations, both socially and biologically, and in defining the ecological niche occupied by hunters in the Pleistocene period.

THE DENSITY EQUILIBRIUM SYSTEM

The System

Density is a ratio expressing the relationship between people and space. Among hunters it is usually expressed in terms of the number of square miles or square kilometers needed to support one individual. It contains the implicit assumption that the population is representative in numbers, in sex ratio, and in age distributions. To be meaningful, it further presumes an essential constancy in population numbers; that is, neither rapid expansion nor decline is involved. For our purposes it always refers to precontact conditions, and some systematic form of reconstruction of numbers and territorial usage will necessarily be involved.

A density equilibrium system is based upon the broad biological assumption of a balanced condition in nature for all life, including man at a hunting and collecting level of economy. Short-term oscillations are not precluded, but are a necessary part of the system, and reflect various forces applying corrective measures after the equilibrium system is disturbed. The system is usually visualized as representing a population approaching the carrying capacity of a given environment at their given level of extractive efficiency and pattern of social behavior. Among even the simplest of peoples, social factors seem to operate to stabilize population numbers below the absolute level of saturation. Where food resources are scattered and generalized, and methods of food preservation limited or absent, the equilibrium system can be expressed in rather simple and direct terms. Where concentrations of food allow specialization, together with its preservation, cultural deviations in behavior are to be expected.

The primary force toward an expansion of population numbers is no more complicated than the inherent excessive fertility which characterizes all successful species. For simple hunters, the intrinsic rate of increase has been calculated as a doubling of numbers per generation (Birdsell, 1957) but this should be raised to a tripling in numbers per generation, with the mean generational interval extended to about thirty years. The depressant forces of the system which balance the fertility force are highly varied and include all of the climatic, biotic, and social factors which directly or indirectly limit human numbers. They may exist both as short term seasonal forms, involving stochastic variations, as well as those of a long trend nature. While the real depressant system represents a complex multifactorial series of forces, reasonable approximations in some regions may be simple in nature.

The Evidence

The general nature of the system of density equilibrium has long been known to zoologists, geographers, and anthropologists. But as expressed in purely qualitative terms, this knowledge resulted in few useful predictions. The first detailed quantification was based upon Australian aboriginal tribal distributions (Tindale, 1940) as analyzed by Birdsell (1953). A series of 123 ecologically uniform tribal territories yielded a logarithmic relationship with mean annual rainfall. The coefficient of curvilinear correlation reached the very high value

of 0.8. The remarkable functional relationship between rainfall and tribal area (1) demonstrated the existence of an equilibrium density system, (2) validated the previously necessary assumption that these hunters existed at the approximate carrying capacity of the environment, and (3) with further analysis, showed that the size of the dialectical tribe statistically tended toward a constant value which was estimated as approaching 500 persons. The nature of this density system allowed statistically accurate predictions for aboriginal Australia. But it was pointed out explicitly that the constants for this equation would change markedly in terms of differences in biota, environmental variables, and methods of extractive efficiency for hunters in other regions.

Two of my students have made similar analyses. M. Vorkapich (unpublished) found among the Great Basin Shoshoni tribes a density equilibrium system comparable to the Australian one, with an equivalent coefficient of correlation for the restricted rainfall values involved. J. Hainline (1965) investigated data in Micronesia and found that population numbers were a direct and highly correlated function of the land area in that region. It is to be hoped that someone will undertake a similar analysis based on the scanty remaining African data.

Some evidence exists to show how the system operates when densities have been reduced well below carrying capacity. Four populations which serve as models under these circumstances have been quoted by Birdsell (1957) and are the basis for calculating the intrinsic rate of increase in economically simple populations. These empirical data reveal that where unoccupied ecological space exists, the expanding population may begin to bud off when values from 60 to 70 per cent of carrying capacity are realized. Since man is a long-lived mammal, the extrapolation from other sources suggests that his population numbers may overshoot carrying capacity before being depressed back to the long-term equilibrium value.

Predictions for the Pleistocene

1. Pleistocene men everywhere belonged in a long-term density equilibrium systems for

which the constants would change with biotic, climactic, and technological variables.

2. Oscillations in such an equilibrium system would quickly be restored upward to normal values by human fertility factors on the one hand, or depressed when necessary by the complex of forces existing in the environment.

3. The intrinsic rate of increase in man is sufficiently high to assure that depleted numbers would be completely restored within a few decades. In Pleistocene time perspectives, the recovery was instantaneous.

4. The thrust of the fertility force is sufficient so that human populations would tend to overshoot carrying capacity as they restore their numbers from a depressed condition.

5. While ecologically available empty space was present, whether due to colonizing of new areas, or due to the loss of previous occupants, it is predicted that budding-off of colonizing groups would occur well below the density equilibrium value.

Areas of Needed Research

Starting with a basic territorial unit, in which both food and water resources are locally earned, densities have a constant meaning. But as one proceeds to ecologically more variable regions, added factors begin to complicate the basic concept. Densities at the mouth of the Murray River were forty times greater in fact than would be predicted from the rainfall regression curve. This is a dramatic manifestation of the influence of locally unearned water. Marine resources, ranging all the way from sedentary shellfish to free-ranging fish and pelagic mammals, represent a locally unearned food resource. Since they directly affect human density, where they are technologically available, a system must be devised to translate these marine energy sources into terms that are consonant with purely basic terrestrial densities. Among the Kaiadilt of Bentinck Island, in the Gulf of Carpentaria (Tindale, 1962b), high population densities prevail, when measured in terrestrial area, but almost all of their food resources were derived from tidal waters around the island. Neither the statement that one square mile of tidal reef will support eight Kaiadilt, nor the figures that are based upon one square mile of island sur-

face can be meaningfully translated into the density system based upon inland tribes living upon locally earned resources. Where broad regional deviations from the basic ecological conditions occur, as with the seasonal availability of salmon, whether it be among the Ainu, or with the Indians of the British Columbia Coast, ecological density systems no doubt prevail, but they need redefining to be equated with terrestrial ratios.

Archeologically, sites based upon local concentrations of food resources will systematically be better represented in the recovered data than will scattered occupancies based upon generalized sources of food. The Pleistocene record will be biased heavily in favor of the former. *A priori*, it would be difficult to predict the number of elephant bog-trap sites on the one hand, or the migratory pathways that channeled big game herds, such as that at Solutré, on the other hand. Their existence may be determined empirically, but there remains the difficult problem of translating their ecological impact into broad regional density values.

Numerous studies of subhuman mammals have shown that food resources are not the sole determinant of population densities. Behavioral factors influence the equilibrium densities, and under some conditions become the critical factor (Calhoun, 1962). Even in aboriginal Australia the densities attained reflect some behavioral influences. Research is urgently needed among high-density hunters, especially those living upon locally unearned food resources, to determine the impact of social factors upon equilibrium population densities.

COMMUNICATION EQUILIBRIUM SYSTEM

The System

Density is an expression for the distribution of people in space. It contains no implications as to the nature of their social or cultural aggregations in that space. *A priori*, spatial distribution among hunters might be expected to fall into two polar types. Distance alone might act as an isolating mechanism, so that variations in behavior occur as some fairly constant function in space. On the other hand, behavioral patterns might be nucleated so that cultural and social space take on a cellular characteristic. Most of the living hunting and gathering peoples for whom the reasonable precontact reconstructions can be made, show a cellular arrangement in terms of language variations. The Australians, the Andamanese, the Kalahari Bushmen, and even the territorially diffuse Shoshoni reveal a honeycomb pattern, where dialectical homogeneity provides the best form of group identity. Both the natives and the anthropologists have recognized the dialectical tribe as a reality.

In its clearest form, the dialectical tribe lacks all aspects of political authority, and simply consists of an aggregation of local groups in spatial proximity. The Australian data show a useful constancy in size for the dialectical tribe, which statistically approximates 500 persons. This tendency is independent of regional variations in density. Since the data cover mean annual rainfall variations from 4 inches to more than 160 inches, the size of the dialectical tribal unit is insensitive to regional variations in both climatic and biotic factors. Its primary determinants are competence in speech, and mobility on foot.

Dialectical homogeneity at the simple level of hunters may profitably be viewed as a consequence of the pattern of density in face-to-face communications. Involved are (1) frequency of interaction, (2) intensity of interaction, (3) duration of interaction, and (4) facility of communication. The density of communication defines the clustering of groups that will show a dialectical homogeneity. These variables in turn are mediated by the basic geometry of the local groups. It has been shown (Birdsell, 1958) that as the number of local groups increases, greater internal cultural and linguistic homogeneity should be expected, for alien contacts are reduced in a systematic fashion. Thus, there is a positive force acting to increase the number of local groups who speak the same dialect[1] as a consequence of the pattern of communication density. But the effect of isolation by distance opposes this integrating force. It can be shown that given constant limits on personal mobility, in time the dialect unit frequently becomes too large to maintain its tribal homogeneity. Speech differentiation proceeds further, and in time will produce tribal separation through dialectical fragmentation. Since there is a central tendency for the dialect tribe to approximate 500 persons among widely different groups, such as Australians, Shoshoni, and Andamanese, among others, it is tempting to consider that this value is relatively independent of both the local biota and the technology upon which its extractive efficiency is based.

Deviations from the modal value of 500 persons in themselves provide material for investigating those factors which may change the balance point of the communication equilibrium system. In Australia, on parts of the Darling and Murray rivers systems, there were several tribes regionally adjacent to each other in which the size of the dialectical unit greatly exceeded the normal value. Among the Kamilaroi, the Wiradjuri, and the Worgaibon, tribal numbers are estimated to have ranged from 2,000 to 5,000. In this same area, there is a clue as to why dialectical integration may have resulted in these larger groups of people. Unlike most regions of Australia, men in these tribes could and did inherit territorial rights to special food resources in their mothers' territory. The data suggests that this simple modification in jural behavior modified the pattern of the density of communications so as to result in the linguistic integration of unusually large numbers of local groups. In a comparable fashion, among the Kalahari Bushmen, variations in residence have been reported in terms of the universal bride-service (Marshall, 1960). When combined with an incipient tendency toward political authority vested in headsmen, this may have resulted in the development of larger dialect groups there. These examples suggest that the size of the dialect units, and their equilibrium value, may respond sensitively to seemingly minor differences in behavior which they infringe upon the pattern of communication density.

The Evidence

There are a variety of data bearing upon the existence of the dialectical tribe as an expression

---

1. Speech is homogeneous within the dialect tribe only relative to other tribes. Very slight differences can be expected between all of the local groups that comprise the tribe, as a simple function of distance as an isolating mechanism *within* the tribe.

of the communication equilibrium system. Its widespread existence, as in cases mentioned above and others, gives an empirical verification. It is a commonplace in Australia that when tribal numbers expand to 1,000 or more individuals, then dialect fragmentation regularly occurs. At the time of contact the Aranda were visibly differentiated into five dialect subgroups (Strehlow, 1947) with a combined population estimated at 1,500 persons. The Walbiri according to Meggitt (1962), numbered somewhere between 1,000 and 1,400 aborigines, and had differentiated into four dialect subgroups. Those data suggest that isolation by distance begins to produce recognizable dialect fragmentation when tribal size approaches 1,000 persons and that the differentiating dialect subgroups range from about 250 to 375 in numbers, values well below the equilibrium value of 500 persons. In the Kimberleys of Western Australia other large tribal groups, such as the Walmadjari and Njamal, were in the process of linguistic differentiation at the time of contact. The model of band interaction, referred to above, suggests that a pair of main and opposing forces, involving cultural cohesion and isolation by distance, tend to maintain the equilibrium numbers in a fairly rigid manner.

Finally, in an experiment in nature (Birdsell, MS-1), it can be shown that after the size of the Australian tribe has been abruptly reduced in numbers (but with no reduction in density), there follows in time a regular reintegration, presumably in terms of local groups, until the full and normal number of 500 persons is restored for the dialect tribe. The social dislocation in this case involves tribal names and identity rather than dialect differentiation. The form of the restoring curve is heavily damped, with no tendency to overshoot the equilibrium value. This is what one would expect in terms of a system whose values are primarily determined by the overall density of communication.

Predictions for the Pleistocene

1. Pleistocene populations will ordinarily be expected to be arranged in tribal units marked off by dialect differences. If exceptions are to be postulated, they should be based upon some influence which tends to minimize distance as an isolating factor, such as a concentration of food resources.

2. In a statistical sense, the central tendency for the size of the dialect tribe in the Pleistocene can be estimated as 500 persons, although the variance will be considerable. This is based upon the value among a variety of living hunters and gatherers showing a wide range of variations in extractive technology, biota, and other ecological variables. There is no reason why this estimate should not be pushed as far back into the Pleistocene as the development of fully symbolic speech and foot mobility would allow.

3. While much individual variation in the size of the dialect tribe will occur in the Pleistocene, as in the present, those which become too numerous will be subject to linguistic differentiation and division, while those which decline below a critical number will be forced into amalgamation with others, since they would reach a position of instability in the equilibrium system.

Research Needed

A linguistic analysis of the degree of difference between the dialects which form tribal groups is badly needed. While the native informants themselves recognize varying degrees of difference, these will not become materials for further analysis until they are linguistically standardized. There is even some question whether dialect tribal groups are always defined at the same level of difference. Are the much larger groups found among Kalahari Bushmen real, meaning that the linguistic differentiation is at the same level, or has a different measure of language differentation been used there than in Australia and elsewhere? Linguistic controls are obviously needed to answer questions like this. It would be helpful further to determine the degree of linguistic differentiating normal among the local groups which comprise the dialect tribe.

There exist, in the voluminous ethnological data upon Australians, almost no details which can be used to investigate and elaborate the variables which make up the overall density of communication. While most writers report that initiation ceremonies exist, they never report the interval in years between them, the recruitment, composition and origin of the visiting parties, how far they had traveled, or other factors of importance. Models serve as guides for this sort of investigation, but they can only be tested and refined against good empirical data. It is too late to hope for the critical data from the Australia of today, so they must be recorded for other economically simple groups which are still functioning.

LOCAL GROUP EQUILIBRIUM SYSTEMS

The System

Just as most terrestrial vertebrates have evolved patterns of behavior which result in their efficient distribution in space to maximize population survival probabilities, so have men at a hunting and gathering level of economy. Human behavior is both generally adaptive and conveniently flexible so that the composition of the local territorial group and the details of its relations with neighboring groups can be expected to vary. There is no need to consider the rigidly ideal model constructed by Hiatt (1962) and criticized with complete competence by Stanner (1965). Local group functioning and structure have seldom been observed in undisturbed density equilibrium systems, although a few data do exist. In general, their characteristics must be reconstructed through a detailed and conscientious evaluation of precontact food resources, surface water availabilities, and group compositions. This is a most difficult task, for local group structure and function are the first things to disappear in the contact situation.

Using Australian aborigines as models, some general attributes of the modal type of local group can be defined. It will tend to consist of a suitably sized group of genealogically related families. Anthropologists have noted and models confirm (Birdsell, MS-3) that the variety of possible relationships is both great and will change with time. The type of food resources is perhaps the most important single determinant of local group size and composition. Where plant and animal resources are largely raised locally and comprise wide variety of forms, the size of the exploitive groups will

be small, and figures tend to oscillate around an equilibrium value of 25 persons. Such groups are almost universally exogamous, although Tindale (1962b) has found an interesting exception, which is to be explained by the unique circumstances in which it occurs.

Where food resources are more concentrated, the dietary becomes more specialized and local group structure frequently changes. It should be stressed that this is not a consequence of increasing density, but rather a function of concentration. In such circumstances the average size of local groups may range between 50 and 100 individuals, and in some exceptional cases reach several hundred persons. But it is to be noted that the reality of such groups can be reconstructed only where sufficient food and water resources can be systematically demonstrated by detailed data. This has not been done, for example, by either Meggitt (1962) or Elkin (1962) for the Walbiri of central desert Australia. This does not deny that transient groups of several hundred individuals may not congregate where food and water resources are available, for evidence indeed suggests this is an almost universal human impulse. But a temporary aggregation cannot be considered as representing local groups or communities who demonstrate their territoriality in some consistent fashion. Where ecological resources allow these larger groups for some portion of the annual cycle, it is to be expected that both social and genealogical relations, as well as forms of recruitment, will differ from smaller groups. Forms of descent, marital restrictions, and permanence of membership can be expected to vary within the reasonable limits of adaptive human behavior.

The first type of local group, characterized by small numbers supported by a local biota which generally requires greater group mobility for its use, does represent a rather tight equilibrium system. But the system's forces which maintain its central tendencies are not easy to discern. It is tempting, regarding such local groups in Australia, to consider that territorial defense, which occured frequently, set the limit of group size by its demand for a minimal number of competent spearmen. But the same size group prevails among the Kalahari Bushmen, where territorial defense is exceedingly rare. It is also found among the

Birhor of India, where Williams (Chapter 14, this volume) shows that rigid territoriality does not exist. Williams' explanation, that local groups of this size and character have size limits determined primarily by such social arrangements as are involved in the pattern of marital exchanges of women, is attractive and more likely will prove the primary determinant. Stochastic variations in the periodicity and sex of births can be visualized as imposing a minimum size for successful survival on such local groups. The upper limitations on size will be determined by a complex of factors involving human mobility, the nature and concentration of food resources, and the form of the technologies by which the biota is exploited. It is revealing that using netting techniques for the primary pursuit of game, the Birhor consider that three to four families comprise the efficient work group in their environment, whereas Turnbull (1961) indicates that four or five families are too few to constitute a viable netting team among the Bambuti of the Congo rain forests. There can be no doubt that the type of local work group will represent an important determinant in group size, but more data are needed to define its impact. That reconstructions of basic ecology, local residential group, and work groups can be achieved, in some cases long after they have disappeared functionally, has been demonstrated by Watanabe (1964a) in his elegant work upon the Tokapchi Ainu.

The Nature of the Evidence

Local groups dependent upon a generalized dietary have been well censused for three different peoples. In each case the average size approximates 25 individuals and this seems to represent a minimum, modal value for viability for this type of group organization. Among the Birhor, Williams shows that in 25 bands the average group consisted of 26 individuals. Marshall (1960) found that for eighteen bands of !Kung Bushmen, the average size was again 25 persons per group. Unpublished data from Tindale (personal communication) indicates that among ten precontact desert Australian local groups counted by him, the average number is again 25 persons. In the last case, the range is very tight and suggests that the forces

which maintain such an equilibrium of numbers act powerfully. Data detailed by all three authors validates the nature of the equilibrium system by the demonstration that bands that are either unusually small or large in their numbers find an explanation within the forces of the system. Local groups of this type must be large enough to function successfully in a social sense, and small enough to minimize strain on food and water resources.

Local groups of larger size have been widely documented in the ethnological literature and in a general way their occurrence is based upon concentrations of food rather than high population densities *per se*. The nature of such food concentration varies and may be partly regional, as in the cases where acorns and salmon are major food resources, or highly localized as in the case of sago swamps, elephant-bog traps, and the ancient sea mammal resources as at Iputiak. The very availability of large masses of food in a concentrated form, combined with methods of food preservation, suggests that the local groups will be maintained by a much looser system of equilibrium forces and that these will show a wide variety of forms. Behavioral preferences may override energetics. There is no profit in attempting to model such situations until much more detailed data have been provided from field research.

Local group territoriality manifests itself adaptively in a wide range of definitions. These are well discussed by Stanner (1965) where he introduces a terminology involving (1) estate, (2) range, (3) domain, and (4) regime. These terms focus attention upon the ecologically varying nature of territoriality among such generalized hunters as the Australians.

Predictions for Pleistocene Hunters

1. Hunters dependent upon a generalized and locally raised biota should fall into the equilibrium system found among desert Australians, Kalahari Bushmen, and Birhor. Their modal numbers should approximate 25 persons, marriage should be exogamous, and the probabilities are high that the group was patrilineal and patrilocal.

2. Where large food resources are concentrated either regionally or seasonally, local groups take on a very different nature. They

will be larger in size, different manifestations of territoriality can be expected, and their principles of descent, marriage, and recruitment can be expected to show wide variety. Data among living hunters in such situations show such a wide range of adaptive behavior that Pleistocene reconstructions will largely depend upon archeological evidences. While ecology will determine the limiting factors in such cases, it will also permit a wide variety of social solutions.

Required Research for the Future

The most urgent need is to detail or reconstruct the functioning of local groups. How many people, of what ages and sexes, in what specified biological and social relationships, reside or camp together for what defined periods, and for what reasons? Travel distances between camps in terms of seasonal rhythms, and defined in terms of exploitation both of varying food resources and water supplies, are further imperatives. Much of the current confusion in the literature stems from a failure to define the ecological base which makes possible larger groupings. Australian ceremonial gatherings held at intervals of several years in locally favored spots are not comparable to the more or less permanent residential groups of similar size elsewhere which depend upon concentrations of food and some form of food preservation. Although these extremes can be conceived of as existing along a kind of complex continuum, they are near its poles and the ecologically necessary conditions require specification.

EQUILIBRIUM IN FAMILY SIZE

The System

In a population stabilized at the operationally defined carrying capacity of its given environment, some limitation on procreative activities naturally filter down to the level of the biological family. These may be examined most profitably in terms of the requirements which affect the spacing of the natal survivors. Generalized hunters with their requirements of high mobility, present the most exacting

model. Australian data (Birdsell, MS-3) indicate that the inability of a mother to carry more than one child at a time, together with her female baggage, impose the first insurmountable barrier to a large number of children. This factor, strongly reinforced by an equally limiting incapacity to nurse more than one child simultaneously, imposes a minimum of a three-year spacing upon children designed for survival. Since human female reproductive physiology does not reliably prevent conception while still nursing, children who cannot be reared are frequently conceived and born. The solution is systematic infanticide. There is every reason to believe that it would have been present throughout human groups in the Pleistocene period. It seems to represent a dislocation in human reproductive physiology following entrance into the bipedal niche and rapid brain expansion.

The Evidence

Among 194 matings based upon precontact genealogies for desert Australians (126 collected by Birdsell, 68 by Tindale), data show a sex ratio at adulthood of approximately 150 per cent (150 males for 100 females). Other data show that the sex ratio at birth among Australian aborigines is 100 per cent. The discrepancy in the sex ratios among adults indicates that at least 15 per cent of the children born to aboriginal women are eliminated by infanticide. Ethnological evidence for Australia documents that infanticide was preferentially practiced upon female babies. This was true for desert groups, and also for those living in better endowed areas. The value of 15 per cent demonstrated by these data is a minimal one, and the observations of observant, early, postcontact Europeans places the figure as high as 50 per cent. Unfortunately, medical science has not yielded accurate information on the relationships between nursing and ovulation needed to fix the figure more accurately. Overall considerations incline a judgment toward the higher values.

That the Australian evidence is not isolated is provided by data from other groups. Birket-Smith (1929) documented sex ratios equally warped among the Caribou Eskimo, and his values were strikingly consistent among the five groups he censused. But Marshall (1962) found no sex preference in the systematic infanticide practiced by the !Kung Bushmen. There is reason to believe that the limiting forces involved in the necessary spacing of children to be saved would apply broadly to all hunting groups, although sex preferences might vary.

The factors which produce compulsory spacing of the viable children among hunters limits the total number that can be saved and hence affects the variance statistically. Among the 194 sibships contained in the precontact desert genealogies referred to above, the range of children surviving to adulthood extends from 0 to 7 offspring. And 185 of the sibships included between 1 and 5 children each. In a hunting population in which total numbers are remaining essentially constant, the standard deviations for the surviving offsprings approximates 1.4 and this when squared gives a variance of about 2.0. These values not only represent equilibrium figures, but exist in so tightly structured a system that they may be considered a constant for people living under these conditions. Such values should characterize human populations far back into the Pleistocene period.

Predictions for Pleistocene Populations

Systematic infanticide may be assumed to have characterized human populations throughout the Pleistocene. Its probability of being preferential female infanticide is strengthened by data from recent hunters. The variance in surviving adult sibs would approximate the constant value of 2.0, with a standard deviation of 1.4 and a range from 0 to 7.

Research Needed

Demographic and genealogical data extending into precontact situations are urgently needed. Disturbed sex ratios at birth or among adults provide indirect evidence of systematic infanticide. But their absence does not deny the practice. Medical research is urgently needed to define the relationship between the resumption of ovulation in terms of the prolongation of nursing for periods up to three years after birth.

EQUILIBRIUM IN THE SIZE OF THE EFFECTIVE BREEDING POPULATION

The System

In terms of evolutionary processes, one of the most important population factors involves the effective size of the breeding population. Its value is determined from the following equation given by Wright (1938):

$$\tilde{N} = \frac{4\tilde{N} - 2}{\sigma_k{}^2 + 2}$$

The equation states in essence that for evolutionary processes the effective size of the breeding population is a direct function of the number of persons who contribute their genes effectively to the next generation and an inverse function of the variance of the offspring so produced. Offspring to be counted must in their own time reach the midpoint of their reproductive span. Thus, both for parents and children very special types of data are required and these are difficult to obtain in practice.

The actual number of parents who reproduce effectively will be some proportion of the total of adults in the breeding isolate. Since in Australia, and among other hunters generally, the genetic isolate is the equivalent of the dialectical tribe, it becomes clear that the number of effective breeders will be related to tribal size. As shown above, the size of a dialectical tribe is in itself an equilibrium system and it follows that this will hold true for the number of effective breeders as well.

The rate of intertribal marriages acts in such a fashion as to further reinforce the equilibrium system represented by the number of effective breeders. Tindale (1953) showed that over wide stretches of aboriginal Australia the rate of intertribal marriage averaged 14 per cent per generation. But this rate may be expected to vary with the size of the dialectical tribe involved. In tribes which number much fewer than the 500 persons which comprised the modal tribe, more women will be brought in from outside tribes than is customary. This will tend to extend the size of the breeding population and so restore its numbers toward the higher modal value. In contrary circumstances, where the dialectical tribe considerably exceeds 500 persons, there will be less need to go outside of tribal boundaries to obtain the wives so that the rate of intertribal marriage should be less than average. In very large tribes it is to be expected that distance will also operate as an isolating factor within the bands of the tribe. These tendencies will somewhat reduce the number of effective breeders and again act as a restoring force toward the equilibrium values.

The Evidence

In spite of having worked intensively with Australian aboriginal material for a quarter of a century, the author has not yet calculated the effective size of the breeding population. This is not due to any difficulty in calculating the variance of the effective offspring in Wright's equation, but lies in the difficulty of estimating the number of effective breeders in the population. As indicated earlier they can only be included when in turn their children reach ·the midpoint of the reproductive span. For man, the problem is complicated by the fact that generations overlap in real population. Genealogical evidence, as useful as it is for many purposes, contains the built-in artifacts that originate from its origins in the memories of men. The errors contained in genealogies will often be systematic and hence effect the calculation of the size of the breeding population.

As a figure of magnitude, the size of the effective breeding population for aboriginal Australia should approximate 175 persons where the size of the dialectical tribe is 500. As explained above, this figure will rise a little less rapidly than the number of individuals in the dialectical tribe increase; it will diminish a little more slowly than will a comparable decrease in numbers of tribal members. But further data are needed for an accurate estimation of the real value. The size of the effective breeding population is affected by polygamous marriages, and these data for Australia are available. But biological realities require the estimation of biological paternity insofar as it differs from social paternity. This will require the analysis of blood group data to calculate a reasonable rate of illegitimacy and so to correct for the number of males effectively contributing gametes to the next generation.

One of the methods available for refining the estimate of the number of effective breeders depends upon the availability of detailed population pyramids. These have never been published for precontact Australians, but data in two areas will become available in the near future. These will help control the complication introduced by the fact that in a society where males outnumber females in the ratio of 150:100 it is still possible to practice polygamous marriage. The solution, of course, is to be found in the delayed age at which males obtain their wives. The quantitative data provided by Meggitt (1962) and several others will help estimate the effect of a sequence of husbands upon the effective reproduction of a given female.

There is another further loose end to be tied in before proper estimates can be made of the number of effective breeders in a genetic isolate. Given the stringent requirement that parents can only be counted as effective when their own offspring in their proper turn produce effectively, genealogical data do not provide adequate time depth. This can be found in a model of the proper construction. The author (MS-3) has explored the long-range effects of this phenomenon in a patrilineal society. Using the range of effective sibship size determined by the precontact genealogies referred to earlier in a model in which stochastic reproductive processes are assigned by random numbers, an unexpected result was obtained. Patrilineages die out at the rate of approximately 30 per cent per generation. This is of course one of the great sources of errors in genealogical materials. It has not yet been possible to determine what the exact impact of this high rate of patrilineage extinction would be upon the number of effective breeders. It is likely to reduce the size of the effective breeding population well below the value of 175 persons as estimated in an earlier and incomplete analysis.

A final problem involved in calculating the size of the effective breeding population turns upon the occurrence of periodic reductions in isolate numbers due to catastrophes in nature. Neither the spacing nor the effect is determinate, but the result would be to further reduce $\tilde{N}$.

Predictions for Pleistocene Populations

With the exception of those special instances in which concentrated food resources allow for larger human societies, it can be predicted that throughout that portion of the Pleistocene in which man lived as a successful hunter the size of the effective breeding populations will be small in numbers. The equilibrium system will be somewhat tighter than that which structures the dialect tribes through its communication system. The evolutionary processes which are to be associated with small breeding populations should have been operative during the entirety of this period. While random genetic drift has been indicated by the mathematical models to be anticipated under such conditions, empirical data from Australia aboriginal isolates suggest that the processes of evolution are in fact more complicated than have been predicted.

Research Needed

Granted that the effective size of the breeding population does constitute its own equilibrium system, there is a great need for detailed data at a precontact level for the factors which influence its magnitude. This includes not only the overt aspects of marriage sequencing but the covert aspects that may influence procreation outside of marriage. The definition of effective parenthood in terms of evolutionarily effective offspring imposes difficulties which do not promise a direct solution. Even so, empirical values from real populations and detailed genealogies are needed to assist in the modeling of effective estimates bracketing the real values.

CONCLUSIONS

Systematic infanticide has been a necessary procedure for spacing human children, presumably beginning after man's entry into the niche of bipedalism, and lasting until the development of advanced agriculture. It involved between 15 and 50 per cent of the total number of births. Among recent hunters it tends to be preferentially female in character and probably was in the Pleistocene. The variance among effective surviving sibs approaches 2.0 as a constant.

The necessary mechanisms for spacing human societies are primarily invested in local groups. Among generalized hunters, dependent upon local biota for their food sources, the local group averages about 25 persons as a basement figure. Smaller populations would be handicapped socially in a variety of ways, but primarily in those affecting martial exchanges of girls. Larger local groups would be at a disadvantage in terms of food and water resources except in unusually rich environments. Local groups of this character may be projected backward in human evolution to that point which the observer estimates as involving local group exogamy as a source of social regulation.

For generalized hunters and gatherers, the density of communications normally defined by foot mobility and fully developed symbolic speech results in a language community known as the dialect tribe. Its numbers tend to stabilize around a population involving 500 individuals, quite independently of population density, the richness of the biota, and the technological development of extractive efficiency. Since the evidence for competent bipedal mobility, as defined by the structure of the foot, goes back into the beginning of the Pleistocene, the development of dialect tribal groups can be best associated with the evolution of the capacity for a rich oral communication. This would presumably push these linguistic units back into the middle of the Pleistocene period.

The size of the effective breeding population, a parameter of considerable evolutionary significance, has its own equilibrium system, a modification of that based upon the density communication system. For dialect tribes with the modal value of 500, it would be less than 175 in numbers. While its exact determination is not possible, Pleistocene populations were effectively small.

There are numerous situations in which concentrated food resources, such as migrating big game, spawning salmon, or sago swamps provide a different basis for existence. When accompanied by either artificial or natural means of a preservation, these concentrated sources of energy characteristically result in the development of much larger groups involving various kinds of recruitment, descent, marital relations, and seasonal residence. Such local population will reflect the adaptive nature of human behavior in their variety. With man's gregarious tendencies limited largely by food resources, this type of local group should be projected well back into the Pleistocene in localities which are suitable for its development. It will appear in the archeological record with a biased frequency since generalized hunters leave but scanty remains for recovery. Since it can be shown that the size of the dialect tribal group varies sensitively with those factors which alter the pattern of the density of communication, it should be expected that large local groups based upon concentrated food supplies would also increase its size.

Since the intrinsic rate of increase in man allows it, human populations should be considered to reach the culturally effective carrying capacity of a given environment within very short time periods. For most Pleistocene situations, the population density should be considered to approximate that of operational saturation. Regional densities will be determined by variations in biota, climate, and the extractive efficiency of the men who exploit the environment. These can be determined for given zoogeographical regions only from detailed analyses using living hunters and gatherers as analogue types of models. In all cases population attributes must be effectively reconstructed to approximate precontact conditions.

25.

Discussions, Part V

25a. THE DEMOGRAPHY OF HUNTERS: AN ESKIMO EXAMPLE

Speaker: *Laughlin*

LAUGHLIN: I should like to use population reconstruction, primarily of the Aleut and Eskimo stock, as a means of demonstrating one kind of systematic approach to the analysis of a population and its history. To begin with, we ought to appreciate that the concept of the Eskimo is enormously distorted, since their distribution is quite at variance with geographical areas to which we have formerly paid most attention. The distribution of the population makes sense in terms of the history, for which there is a considerable antiquity— some 8,500 years documented in the west— and in terms of resources available in an accessible form. The polar Eskimos, who are most talked about, constituted 250–300 at the time of their discovery. The literature published about them must surely exceed in actual poundage the total body weight of all the polar Eskimos living since the year 1000. Much the same thing applies for the some 7,000 central Eskimos, who are exceeded in number by the single population of Konyang Eskimos living on Kodiak Island. The population distribution very clearly centers in the southwest, where the greatest amount of cultural diversity occurs in language, material culture, art styles,

etc. Another major population center is around the Bering Strait, and a third is found on the west (particularly the southwest) coast of Greenland.

The first ordinate that we can see is the contrast between the zones in which winter ice deprives people of access to the intertidal area, and the open water zones where there is easy access to the intertidal area. If we eschew talking about a community as such and instead break it into components—such as the kinds of people and varieties of habitat present—we find that we can easily chart kinds of people and the particular habitats that they can exploit. This, in turn, makes it clear that there are more habitats available to people in certain areas than in others, which suggests one reason why there are more people living in the former areas.

If we take an Aleutian or Kodiak Island example, we can categorize the population in terms, roughly, of mobility in the following (ascending) order:

1. Old, infirm females, who cannot do much beyond collecting shellfish;

2. Old, infirm males, who can do the same things, and can also go fishing in boats;

3. Pregnant women, who can do a variety of things, subject to local taboos (not touching salmon or whales, not going near streams, etc.) and the advancement of pregnancy;

4. Children, who actually produce a great

percentage of their own food supply in the subarctic zone—including, especially, shellfish;

5. Young and middle-aged females; and
6. Young and middle-aged males. On both of these last groups we have a good deal of data, which in some cases tends to bias our views about subsistence.

We can see immediately that as one moves north of the winter ice line, the proportion of the population actively engaged in procuring food must decline. Since the aged and infirm simply cannot drive a sled over the ice, punch a hole through two feet of ice, harpoon a seal, and bring it home, members of this group are all potential candidates for abandonment and exposure. Overall, we can count some four or more different habitats available to limited segments of the population, which keeps members of these groups from being a burden to the rest. So population density reflects not just the natural resources, but the natural resources keyed to certain kinds of individuals (and to differential technological development).

Another factor in the matter of ecological resources is, of course, the annual distribution of the resources. When bears, walrus, and other exotic forms are not available, the populations of the southwest can get by on fish, shellfish, octopi, and other denizens of the intertidal zone. They eat less well, but they survive. In contrast, people in the central Arctic may undergo final starvation, as witness the Sadlermiut Eskimo skeletons in our collections.

I would like to say something about population "bottlenecks," since these are prominent all over the world. The people anticipate these, and there is a considerable feedback process. They know that they have to adjust to the leanest months of the year and to areas of lesser resources or greater rigor. In such situations there is an increase in intentional and explicit population controls such as prolonged nursing, abortion, infanticide, abstention, and increased adoptions. Infanticide, in particular, involves decisions based on careful consideration of a number of factors. The choice of the child to be left out to die depends upon the sex and health of the child and his siblings, the time of year, and the parents' estimate of the likelihood of having a child of the desired sex. The anticipation of population bottlenecks is as prominent in the thinking of the Aleuts as it is among peoples further north. It influences their movements and, as described, calls forth intentional population controls.

Turning now to the topic of longevity, one of the variables about which we have reliable information is the large contrast in longevity between isolates around the world, and we can demonstrate them most neatly in the Aleut and Eskimo area. One of the two best samples that we have is the collection of 187 skeletons—collected by Dr. Charles Merbs and me—of the now-extinct Sadlermiut Eskimo. In this particular population (treating the collection like one population although this is not actually the case), we find that no one lived to an age greater than 55. Something on the order of 40 per cent died before age 4. Undoubtedly, as with all archeological series, certain ages are underrepresented, and the youngest are most underrepresented. But Eskimos are required to confess stillbirths and miscarriages, and they tend to bury the infant dead, so the series is still pretty good.

In marked contrast to this is a series for the Fox of the eastern Aleutian islands, a series compiled by Bishop Veniaminov, who spent ten years there. Fortunately, he recorded age at death, and here we find a number of people between ages 90–100 and quite a few over age 55. Infant mortality was on the order of 20 per cent, roughly half that in the central Arctic. This situation can be generalized for the area as a whole. Longevity is obviously and considerably greater in an area of good, accessible resources and high technological development.

With an increase in longevity, other changes take place in the composition of the population, some with genetic and some with cultural implications. I will point out that the development of intellectual knowledge depends upon the retention of older people who are, in a sense, libraries. There is actually some feedback in the documented fact that the older people were the sophisticated doctors who intervened in the delivery of offspring and did a substantial amount to reduce infant mortality. So it is not just a question of more people with more food.

Pathology has told us very little about the causes of death. We can learn a certain amount about other things from gross abnormalities in the skeletons. Many of the Arctic peoples periodically suffered from malnutrition, as shown by cases of enamel hypoplasia on the teeth of the Aleuts and the Arctic Eskimos. We also know that in this area the people had a high frequency of spinal disorders—separate neural arches, and spondylitis. Yet these and some other gross pathologies apparently did not affect their behavior as much as one would expect. The frequency of fractures over the entire area is rather low, in spite of the fact that we know that they often fall and occasionally have encounters with animals having ulterior motives.

The pathological or disease load that these people carry is difficult to understand today, because they have been put through several selection filters. After the first smallpox epidemic went through the area, the population was genetically restructured. Apropos of this, one thing that we ought to keep in mind is the fact that a population can maintain its distinctive marker genes—those that deal with the external characteristics by which we identify them—and yet undergo an enormous and significant restructuring as regards certain other genes.

25b. POPULATION CONTROL FACTORS: INFANTICIDE, DISEASE, NUTRITION, AND FOOD SUPPLY

Speakers: *Alland, Birdsell, Deevey, Isaac, Turnbull, Washburn, Williams, Woodburn*

BIRDSELL: I would like to talk briefly about family size and birth spacing—subjects on which we have some very good data. If you arrange precontact genealogies and adult sibships of Australian aborigines according to completed family size, the sex-ratios form a very interesting systematic curve varying from about 130 males per 100 females for the modal families to about 260 males per 100 females for families in which five children have survived. Statistically, this shows an enormous amount of family planning that is not indicated in the ethnology.

Doctors who have done the best work at present on the relationship of ovulation and conception to lactation have still never done

it under optimal circumstances. For example, one team did endometrial biopsies on roughly 200 women for a year; they were able to get good data on ovulation, but since the duration of lactation over this period was not known, it is of little use for our purposes. However, it is clear that in humans lactation only incompletely and/or sporadically suppresses ovulation. That is, I take it, a post-bipedal phenomenon, and I see no reason not to suppose that it characterizes all human groups. On the basis of this, I project the hypothesis that difficulties of nursing and mobility in the Pleistocene may have made necessary the killing of 15–50 per cent of children born, since lactation alone would not have provided sufficient spacing of births to maintain equilibrium.

WOODBURN: In talking about birth control and infanticide, it is important to remember that these decisions appear to be made right within the family, often by the mother alone. This has important implications; chief among these is the simple fact that the making of the choice is relative to the circumstances of a particular mother and not necessarily to the circumstances of the whole population.

DEEVEY: As you know, it is a moot question both in ecology and in evolutionary biology as to how it is possible for the system to exert pressure independently of or in conflict with an individual component of the system. An aspect of the same problem is the question whether there can be group selection in contrast to individual selection.

WOODBURN: I think that the Netsilik are particularly interesting in this respect. It looks as though the female infanticide rate works to the disadvantage of the population in general. I would be interested to know about the effects of infanticide on other populations, taken as wholes.

BIRDSELL: The Caribou Eskimo make a good case in this regard. I think that they do show the individual and the system working together. Birket-Smith (1929) had five groups—subtribes, as we might call them. He only dichotomized the population into children and adults. All five showed an average sex ratio of 145 for children. In the adults, the average ratio had fallen to 80. Those data suggest that infanticide was done as a primary family spacing, and was so programmed in terms of population effects that there were just about enough hunters that could hunt for two families as one would expect in a population of this sort. In other words, I take it that the number of competent hunters in a future context was predicted.

WILLIAMS: Birdsell once suggested in an article that populations of man have fertility such that they can fill up an ecological niche in fairly short order. Is there any evidence that the populations of the Hadza and Mbuti are growing now? And if not, why not?

WOODBURN: There is no evidence that the Hadza population was ever any greater or smaller than at present. I think the population could be a good deal larger than it is without causing hardship for the Hadza or damage to the environment. I really cannot understand the widespread emphasis on the ties between population and physical environment to the exclusion, say, of medical factors. One should not overlook the fact that when good health services are brought to an area, there are likely to be sudden and great population increases in that area, especially if malaria or any equally important disease is eradicated.

DEEVEY: Regarding population size and limits on it, I would like to ask Dr. Woodburn about mineral nutrition, especially salt.

WOODBURN: When I was in the field in 1960 I was visited by pediatricians, from Makerere College Medical School, who examined the children and described them as one of the best-nourished groups they had seen in East Africa. In the ordinary course of things, Hadza do not take any salt as such. A salt lake is nearby, but no one bothers to gather salt except those living right at the lake. They occasionally obtain a little through trade, but they do not consider it as worth much effort or expense. I assume, therefore, that they must get sufficient quantities of minerals from their animal and vegetable foods.

ALLAND: Dubos, in his recent book *Man Adapting* (1965), has suggested that disease does *not* play an important factor in population control. I am not sure that I wholly agree with him, but I do think that disease (excepting, perhaps, malaria and trypanosomiasis) is not a factor in population control among hunters and gatherers, and for the following reasons: (1) Isolated populations are less likely to pick

up epidemic diseases—an epidemic likes large number of people. (2) The parasites themselves tend to accommodate to populations in which they have existed for a long period of time, so that there is a genetic sieve operating both to make humans more resistant to parasites and to make the parasites less noxious to humans. In hunting and gathering groups, the most common infection is helminthic, and helminths accommodate particularly well to their hosts. Furthermore, there is good evidence that many of the helminths may have been in human hosts for a considerable amount of time and may, in fact, have switched from nonhuman primates to humans a long time ago during the evolution of hominids. (3) One of the factors that affects the severity of disease, particularly in agricultural peoples, is the nutritional factor—especially a high-starch, low-protein diet, where the immunochemical system is unbalanced. In hunters and gatherers, where there is an adequate supply of game animal protein of high quality, one expects the nutritional substratum would be good. (4) Density-dependent factors are more likely to be related to large, stable populations than to migratory peoples. (5) Many of the hunter-gatherers that we see now have been pushed into areas that are marginal, not only in terms of productivity, but also in terms of their being unhealthy and uncomfortable.

ISAAC: It seems to me that in discussing population limits and in postulating a mechanism, say, disease, we must look at it in relation to density. That is, if the Hadza are indeed in an equilibrium situation and disease is taken as the mechanism, then clearly the incidence of disease must be in balance as a result of density-dependent factors.

WASHBURN: In discussing population numbers, it is well to have a model in mind, for example, one could check the birth rate and see how fast the population would expand if no one died, and then see how many die of snakebite, how many from disease, etc. One of the reasons for looking at hunting peoples is to throw light on the changes that came with agriculture, when the human population soared. One finds monkeys in areas with plenty of available food, where one has reason to expect rapid population increases—16 per cent per year in the rhesus, for example—and yet the increase does not occur under natural conditions. Yet, if food is put out for them, as has been done on Cayo Santiago Island, then the population increases in accordance with the model; even though the natural food supply seemed not to be holding down the population. So the relation between food supply and birth rate appears to be a tricky matter.

We should note also that the size of these hunter groups relative to their food supply and habits is very small by primate standards. A group of 80 monkeys is not large, and groups of 180 baboons are observed frequently. So I think we must look for social and economic factors that make small hunter groups of 30–50 efficient.

The data that we are now getting on monkeys shows that we have to be very careful in speaking of a species as territorial or as defending a territory. For instance, Steve Gartlan (in press) studied small monkeys on Lolui Island, where they are overcrowded. Here they are territorial and boundaries are sharply marked; hence, this is a territorial species *if* you look at it only on Lolui Island. However, a few miles away in Chobe the same species of monkey is not territorial at all. According to Phyllis Jay's data, rhesus monkeys in the forest are not territorial (Jay, 1965), but in the city—where their ranges are restricted and overlapping—they fight and act territorially. So if a species of subhuman primate can vary so greatly in territorial behavior, we may certainly expect a wide variation in man.

TURNBULL: I am surprised by the assumption that any environment should be filled to its economic capacity. In studying a community, the economic aspect cannot be separated from others; and particularly in thinking of the social unit in relation to the environment, we have to think of political and religious aspects as well. Economically, an area in the Ituri forest could support double the number of Pygmies that hunt there, but they need extra space for political reasons—for example, to avoid conflict with neighboring groups.

Let me add that the only years in which the Ik in northern Uganda and the Sudan starve to death are the years when they are cultivators rather than hunters.

ALLAND: I agree with Turnbull that people need space and that this accounts for fission,

but to say that there is a religious or economic reason for ecological stability is to beg the question. We have to know how they maintain a population size without infanticide, gerontocide, disease, or other biological mechanisms.

BIRDSELL: We have frequently discussed hunters as living in marginal areas, and I would like now to single this out as pseudo-concept. These areas are marginal for agriculturalists, but not for hunters. I think we have had enough data here to show that if you took a density value near the maximum of 1 person in 1 or 2 square miles, such density can be found in almost any environment. In fact, I suggest that these scattered occurences on several continents destroy the notion of an optimum environment, since human hunters do not increase in an environment as we think they should. It may well be that we are facing the problem raised by Turnbull's Pygmy examples, where density controls are invisible and social, rather than economic.

25c. The Magic Numbers "25" and "500": Determinants of Group size in Modern and Pleistocene Hunters

Speakers: *L. Binford, Birdsell, Damas, Freeman, Hiatt, Sahlins, Washburn*

HIATT: There has been some discussion in Dr. Birdsell's paper of the mystical number 25, and the number 500 appears to be another such. We are told that there is an amazing constancy of numbers from the dialect tribe in Australia, centering around 500. However, the range given by Elkin (1954) is about 100 to 1,500 or 2,000. I recorded numbers in nine tribes near the Liverpool River of Arnhem Land. The largest of these—the one I concentrated on and for which I have full genealogies—is about 300. There was a good deal of intermarriage, particularly around the edges of this largest tribe. And it seems to me that in talking about the tribe as a dialectal unit, the important thing is not a mystically determined number but, rather, communication through regular association. The 1,500 or so Walbiri were divided into four communities, and there were dialectal differences among them. Each community lived separately, but there were contacts between them. Contact and separation in these circumstances are obvious factors in the persistence of common language and the formation of dialectal differences.

BIRDSELL: The basic data were published some years ago (Birdsell, 1953). It was explained very carefully at that time that for Australia, 500 was a central tendency, and a rather wide-frequency polygon showing the range of variation was illustrated. The number 500 was derived from taking early observers' estimates and breaking them into three categories (anthropologists, careful amateur observers, and seemingly untrustworthy ones). They scattered about as one might expect, and that diagram was also illustrated in the paper. The sample was too small to justify calling the number 500 anything but an indication of magnitude, and I am now inclined to think that the number is probably a little too high. To show what magic there is in numbers, however, Krzwicki (1934) in his book on primitive vital statistics—using different methods and with erroneous tribal assignments—got exactly the same figure. This, of course, is too good to be true, and I do not press the figure.

The tribe as an isolate is based upon a sliding definition. A genetic isolate consists of a group of people who tend to breed more among themselves than with others. Now, this is a very fluid genetical situation, since 51 per cent endogamy would make an isolate. Actually, the Australian tribe is a much better isolate. Tindale's basic datum for precontact intertribal marriages was 14.7 per cent, greater in some areas and less in others (Tindale, 1953). This is ample semantic assurance that the tribe does act as a genetic unit. On the other hand, as numbers decline—even in precontact situations—one would expect the number of intertribal marriages necessarily to increase. Hiatt's enumerations are postcontact in time.

SAHLINS: Having never lived in Australia, I am somewhat confused by the notion of tribe. Even Radcliffe-Brown, with his Aristotelian mind, admitted that neither he nor the natives could tell where one tribe ended and another began. Perhaps someone would explain how this concept can be used with such statistical rigor.

BIRDSELL: It was pointed out earlier that Radcliffe-Brown never saw a bush native. He was dealing in a very dramatic case of salvage ethnology. The tribal boundaries are a closed system. There are, of course, occasional small errors in the placement of one to the other, and they shift a little. The statistics, however, are good, and in most areas the concept of the tribal boundary is clear.

DAMAS: In regard to the unity of the dialect tribe, I wonder how far that would be congruent with a genealogical pool or marriage universe unit, and just how sharp the edges of these types of units might be in this area.

BIRDSELL: I have tried to generate interest among linguists in doing dialectical transects, but it would be very hard to tell where to find local groups still functioning in a band context. The layman's evidence is not very good. Larger tribes do begin to show dialect differentiation. The largest ones are quite clearly in the process of fragmenting. The Aranda would be one of these, and there are others. So, as you approach 1,000 persons per tribe, distance becomes an isolating factor. Foot mobility and density of communications patterns remain the same, and they simply cannot maintain dialect homogeneity over too large a group. Interestingly enough, this does not seem to be a density-determined function at all. All Australians can walk all the places that they need to walk during the annual cycle.

There are a few cases alleged in which bands on the margins of dialectical groups speak languages that may be intermediate or may indicate bilingualism in some of the older members of these bands. Roger Owen (1965) has pointed out one or two cases reported by Radcliffe-Brown, and I have one or two cases of my own. The natives usually say "These are all-mixed-up ones." But evidence suggests another type of explanation involving changing band territoriality.

Dr. Damas has asked about the genealogical reality of the tribe. I do not know of anyone who has ever covered a complete tribe, although Professor Rose may have something pretty close to this for Groote Eylandt. In any case, genealogies or no, the tribe does function as a genetic isolate. So if you are concerned with relationships, it is *the* biological evolutionary unit.

BINFORD: I think it is interesting in the genetic material that a linear distribution may give slightly different patterns of gene flow, with resultant greater restriction along the linear distribution; while the model used by both Williams and Birdsell is a continuous space model with hexagonal exposure on all sides. During the Pleistocene, if you take a combination of Leibig's law (Odum, 1959) and the law of the optimum (Dansereau, 1957), you find that many kinds of adaptations are those that move from one major environmental zone to another. During the time that people are distributed in any one environmental zone, they tend to be distributed optimally within that zone, so that there is a hexagonal distribution of persons. On the other hand, near the terminal Pleistocene—when you begin to find tremendous exploitation of unearned resources along the coastal regions and of resources that allow sedentism at the edges of major biotic zones—this is, in fact, a linear distribution. So we might expect to find a major change in the size of dialect groups and in the way that genetic changes might occur during the adaptation to linear or edge-oriented adaptations.

To turn to the figure of 25 for local group size, my wife and I have been concerned with minimal population figures, as estimated from size of life space in bounded areas like the caves of the Paleolithic. We have found a correlation between the presence of tools used to make tools and an average floor space of over 250 square meters. According to cross-cultural correlations developed by both Cook and Heizer (1965) and Naroll (1962), an average living space is 10 square meters per person. This suggests that a limiting factor in choosing a cave as a base camp was the size of the cave, which had to have at least 250 square meters of floor space, or about enough for 25 people.

WASHBURN: Binford has mentioned the changes in population that took place at the terminal Pleistocene. Now, looking back towards the non-human primates, I would like to comment on the two mystic numbers. We frequently assume that as man becomes a more efficient tool-user, the density in any particular area goes up. This is certainly not the case. There are many species of monkeys that live at a much higher density than does man right down until the origin of agriculture. Two hundred animals per square mile is a normal figure for many of the forest monkeys. So we

might consider whether, in fact, the hunting way of life may greatly have reduced the density of our ancestors, which is the opposite of the traditional view.

A second point is that the number of human beings estimated for the Pleistocene—ten million is a common estimate—is also much less than for any of the non-human primates. We tried to get an estimate for baboons and came up with something on the order of forty million baboons in the savannah of Africa alone—competing, you see, with only a small part of the estimated ten million human beings. Again, there is the suggestion that for some reason the particular way of life of man leads to many fewer people than is the case with the non-human primates.

As regards local group size, 25 is much less than for many of the non-human primates. So one needs an explanation for why 25—granting a great deal of variation—is a relevant and fairly constant figure. In the non-human primates, there is, of course, no correlate for the number 500 or for the tribe. There really is something new in this.

I suggest that the adaptation of man is such that it determines the number of small groups, determines mobility between them (involving language, which is also really new), and leads to one species living over an area so large as to preclude adaptation to local disease and diet in the sense in which monkeys are adapted to them. Man has moved through areas that are so diverse in diet and disease that he has had to adapt culturally, rather than biologically. In terms of diet especially, I suspect that there are very few areas of the world that will support many human beings unless they cook food, carry water, and use other such cultural devices. So my suggestion, in general, is that the success of the mobile hunting adaptation is paid for in non-adaptation to local disease and diet, if we take the monkeys and apes as standards of efficient local adaptation.

BIRDSELL: I think that if we visualize the bipedal niche as involving essentially a partially carnivorous diet, then we can see that such a relatively expensive diet will cause a reduction in numbers. But it may be that this is a good niche because in a number of critical areas in the Old World tropics a little meat will carry one across an otherwise dangerous period of the year. In other words, man gave up density for plasticity and, consequently, remains a single species.

Mr. Gardner was good enough this morning to give me three more groups of generalized hunters in India whose groups are said to be of the magnitude of 25. I do not know whether to ask Mr. Freeman if he still stands by the idea that his butchering sites suggest groups of 25 in the Mindel, but perhaps he will comment on that later. Nonetheless, there is no reason why this group size should not have very great antiquity, since it is presumably a basic minimum social structure. And I suggest that both this and the dialectical tribe can be projected backward in imagination a long distance. The dialectical tribe depends on speech as well as on feet, so one must limit its projection to the range within which one thinks symbolic communication existed.

FREEMAN: The evidence from the site of Torralba, to which Dr. Birdsell refers, is derived from the analysis of materials from a single occupation level. The figure of 25 people was my tenative estimate of the possible minimum number commensurate with the patterned distribution of materials in that occupation, and of course involves numerous assumptions about duration of occupation and other factors. I would not want to go on record as suggesting that during the Acheulian—or even at Torralba alone—the mean band size was 25 active people. But I would definitely say that figures of that order of magnitude and even larger ones are not excluded by the evidence at hand.

25d. PLEISTOCENE FAMILY PLANNING

Speakers: *Deevey, Whiting*

DEEVEY: Let me note first the previously unsuspected importance to anthropology and archeology of quantitative data on age at death. It is the most easily observed and, in some respects, the most informative single statistic that one can get in studying ancient or primitive demography. My own treatment of this, published in *Scientific American* (Deevey, 1960) some years ago, was not very professional, but it is the kind of calculation that is borne

out by the papers we have heard here. If one is prepared to assume that over long times and wide areas during the Pleistocene human populations were in some sort of equilibrium, and Dr. Birdsell makes this point seem defensible—and if it is also assumed that about half the children died before sexual maturity, then to maintain the population at a steady state requires that the number of children born per parous female be of the order of four—two to maintain the population and two to make up for the infant mortality rate. Now, the available data indicate that for a large population, under any ordinary circumstances, the mean number of children born during a female's lifetime is of the order of eight. So it would appear that over a long period of the Pleistocene there was a degree of population control and family planning that one would not have attributed to primitive man until very recently.

We have heard that female infanticide among particularly disadvantaged hunting' populations like the Arctic Eskimo is, perhaps, the most important mode of limiting family size. I doubt that that is a universal method. There are other devices, including certain drugs that decrease the ovulation rate. And it is not evident on the face of it that, to use Dr. Birdsell's figures, 15–50 per cent limitation by female infanticide would make up the difference between eight and four.

Given this steady-state system, in which the family size is maintained in approximate equilibrium, one may ask what determines this. Here I think anthropologists have been misled by a professional argument within ecology on the dependence of population density upon food supply. Those who make use of Wynne-Edwards' book (Wynne-Edwards, 1962) are, I suspect, unaware that it centers around an argument between British ornithologists and a group of Australian economic entomologists as to whether or not climate is the main control on the population density of insects. Much of this seems irrelevant to anthropology, since insects are not vertebrates. I would recommend that anthropologists looking for comparative information on limitation of population size among vertebrates, especially territorial vertebrates, look at David Lack's books (1954, 1960). The population sizes maintained are not atypical for primates generally.

It certainly looks as though a modal band size of 25 is reasonable, and I might cite Star Carr as an instance (Clark, 1954) in which archeological finds support figure for the Mesolithic. And the common tribal size of 500, mentioned repeatedly in this discussion, matches Livi's data for the mean size of medieval Apennine hill villages (1949). Now, it seems unlikely—in view of what we have heard about the Pygmy, the Hadza, and others—that it was purely the food supply that set these size limits. Social forces (whatever that means) seem to be much more relevant both for man and for other vertebrates. The environment, of course, sets upper limits, but these are, in fact, almost never reached. Instead, the limitation falls at a much lower level through such bottlenecks as social interaction, territoriality, and antagonisms.

After a remarkably long period during which we can assume populations to have been in equilibrium and well below the carrying capacity of the environment, something quite extraordinary happened. Food-producing was invented, and since that time the hunter-gatherers have come to see themselves as disadvantaged relative to others, bringing all sorts of psychological and cultural compensations into existence. This means that it is impossible, strictly speaking, to study Pleistocene ecology by anthropological methods. However, I suspect that most of the anthropologists working with primitive peoples around the world are not working with hunter-gatherers but, rather, with agricultural peoples at various levels of technology. So great opportunities exist for applying much more quantitative thinking to the time and stage of the origin of agriculture.

We *seem* to know a great deal all of a sudden about the amount of land under cultivation at one time in slash-and-burn agriculture. But none of this is published in any form that an ecologist can use. At least I have been unable to find more than a handful of relevant data to indicate, even roughly, the average length of the fallowing cycle in slash-and-burn practice. The reason, of course, is that anthropologists—although they have learned to count and weigh things—have not yet learned to pay attention to land areas and time cycles. So the perfectly elementary question as to how much land is supporting people is a difficult one to answer, even though it is just a first approach to the question of ecology. This applies with even greater force to those studying hunter-gatherers. Regardless of what the people say about their boundaries, the plants and animals that they collect do have an areal distribution. And we can never get very far with input-output economics or estimates of productivity until we can get caloric data on particular land areas.

WHITING: I want to ask Dr. Deevey about the figure of eight children per mother. What assumptions are made about the spacing of children in arriving at this average? I ask this in order to compare it with the average spacing among hunters, which comes to about four years.

DEEVEY: The figure is an empirical finding for French Canada and large segments of the Brazilian population. Both sets of data are from Lorimer's original Unesco publication. This takes into account all women subject to bearing children, multiple births, etc.

WHITING: I understand that the average spacing in sedentary populations is about two years, so I assume that the hunter's average of four years would cut down the total number of children born.

DEEVEY: That was my original point; i.e., that there are spacing devices at work in hunter populations.

PART VI

Prehistoric Hunter-Gatherers

26.

Traces of Pleistocene Hunters :
An East African Example

GLYNN L. ISAAC

Anthropological interest in peoples that subsist solely on hunted and foraged foodstuffs has long been heightened by the notion that these people are in some sense survivors from the primitive condition of all mankind. Today this hypothesis—like the hunting peoples themselves—is so hedged about by reservations and restrictions, that it no longer has much value. However, the conviction remains that comparative anthropological information concerning hunters is of relevance to prehistorians as an aid to the interpretation of archeological evidence. The range of social and economic patterns observed among the "foraging" peoples of historic times certainly provides a valuable source of data for assessing the degree of contrast between this way of life and that of farming peoples (see Whiting, Chapter 35a, this volume). Comparisons of the behavior of modern "foraging" peoples with that of other primates have the advantage that the subsistence base is reduced as nearly as possible to a common factor for all species. Thus, although simple analogies have in the past generally proved more misleading than useful, broad comparative studies certainly have great importance for establishing perspective in prehistory.

It scarcely requires emphasis that neither the behavioral science of primatologists, nor that of anthropologists can replace archeology as a means of discovering the actual evolutionary pathways that human behavior has followed during the course of its development. However, prehistorians have passed through oscillating phases of attachment to, and divorce from, these other disciplines, and there is real need to consider these oscillations, and determine afresh what kind of interrelationship will be most fruitful for all disciplines.

Darwinian evolutionary theory created an initial phase of uncritical exuberance among prehistorians and anthropologists. Contemporary hunter-gatherers were viewed as "living fossils," surviving from more or less remote periods, while Pleistocene archeological evidence was commonly seen as a manifestation of behavior analogous in detail with that of some convenient contemporary "primitive" group. Thus Sollas, writing a general tract in 1911 on "Ancient Hunters," felt it appropriate to intersperse chapters dealing with Tasmanians, Australian aborigines, and Eskimos with the chapters dealing with the Lower, Middle, and Upper Paleolithic respectively. This kind of thinking has resulted in a strong reaction away from oversimplification and misleading analogy. During much of this century, prehistorians have confined their researches to the study of stone tools and the factual content of the Pleistocene prehistory of the "Old World" has come to be expressed almost exclusively in the technical terms of stone-tool morphology (Sackett, 1965, 1966).

Considerations of activities other than tool-making tended to become a minor, semi-disrespectable adjunct to the interpretation of selected artifacts. Clearly the results of highly technical artifact studies have only a limited contribution to make to our understanding of the evolution of human behavior as a whole. Hence there has been in the last decade a revival of interest in obtaining, by rigorous archeological field work, actual evidence to be used as a basis for reconstructing total patterns of human behavior during the Pleistocene. Some of the requirements and problems of such archeological investigations are outlined in J. D. Clark's contribution to this symposium (Chapter 30). Lewis Binford and L. G. Freeman, Jr. (Chapter 28 and 27, this volume), have given valuable comments on the role of ethnographic data in modern behavior-oriented archeological studies.

It appears to me that the contributions of ethnography and primate ethology can be usefully divided into three components: (1) Comparative study helps to establish the terms of reference for an archeological inquiry, i.e., specific hypotheses can be formulated for testing. (2) Ethnographic data often provides inspiration for the interpretation of archeological evidence, the significance of which might otherwise be obscure. (3) The application of archeological methods to ethnographic material can test the validity and limitations of archeological inferences.

Elsewhere in this symposium, L. Binford has stressed the point that archeological deductions must stand on their own merit as verifiable hypotheses, regardless of the existence of close modern analogies. Nonetheless, it remains true that the most useful and economic hypotheses will normally be suggested by a knowledge of situations that are more completely documented than prehistoric ones ever can be. Further, there are certain types of semi-quantitative information obtained by archeological methods which can only be used as a basis for behavioral reconstructions if they are "calibrated" by reference to contemporary observations. Relationships between size of occupation area and size of occupying group are of this kind, but have only rarely been systematically observed.

It must be emphasized that many topics of interest to anthropologists and primatologists are in general not amenable to archeological investigation. Kinship systems and marriage arrangements, which are prominent subject matter in this symposium, can scarcely be considered in relation to the archeological evidence for the Pleistocene. It is necessary in planning archeological investigation to consider what questions it is legitimate to ask from the evidence available and then to attack these questions incisively, while remaining alert to other possibilities that may emerge. Washburn (1965) and DeVore and Washburn (1963) discussed certain questions which arose from observation of apparently consistent differences between primate and human social and ecological patterns. These questions were specifically chosen as being potentially answerable from the archeological record. They included such matters as the existence of "home bases," the size of cohabiting groups, the magnitude of territorial ranges, and population densities. These are all legitimate meaningful questions and their explicit formulation has helped to clarify some of the issues with which contemporary prehistory must concern itself.

The remainder of this contribution is devoted to an outline presentation of some aspects of a specific investigation, given in order (1) to illustrate some of the features of archeological evidence concerning Pleistocene hunters; (2) to provide examples of the use of comparative data in archeological inference; (3) to indicate some of the archeologist's special requirements for ethnographic data of various kinds not generally recorded. The example presented is based on the author's work on the archeological evidence stratified in a "Middle Pleistocene" sedimentary formation at Olorgesailie in Kenya.

PRESERVATION, SAMPLES, AND HYPOTHESES

Detailed investigation of archeological evidence for hominid behavior during the earlier portion of the Pleistocene is only possible in rare localities where favorable geological circumstances have preserved primary patterned associations of fossil artifacts and food remains. Such preservation occurs mainly in relatively moist topographic depressions where continual deposition of fine-grained sediments has occurred. Olduvai Gorge, Kalambo Falls, Isimila, Torralba, and Olorgesailie are all similar in this regard (Howell and Clark, 1963). Thus it can be expected that situations with satisfactory preservation of evidence might constitute a very biased "sample" of the totality which they are used to represent. For the Upper Pleistocene subperiod, cave sites probably constitute an analogously biased sample. It is difficult at present to assess the importance of such environmental bias in the evidence, but it has to be kept in mind. The material which we have at present relates directly only to specific topographic situations. To take an example on a large scale—the prominence of East Africa as a source of evidence concerning early hominids is at least in part a consequence of this selective preservation bias. Numerous suitable Lower and Middle Pleistocene sedimentary formations are exposed there and have yielded a wealth of fossils and artifacts in primary contexts. But the hypothesis that the region was the "center" of hominid evolution remains untested because corresponding opportunities for preservation occurred much more rarely in most other parts of the Old World.

The problem of "sampling" at the locality level of investigation can be illustrated by reference to the Olorgesailie instance. The evidence which is outlined in this contribution was all drawn from study of a stratified series of sediments, the Olorgesailie formation, which were deposited over an area of about fifty square miles in a small basin of internal drainage within the Gregory Rift Valley, latitude 1° 35′S, longitude 36° 26′E (Cole, 1963; Isaac, in press, c). Erosion has exposed the beds and their archeological contents over an area less than five square miles in extent. No archeological material of comparable age has been found on the rocky hills that constitute the dominant topography of the area around the basin. Hence the sites investigated at Olorgesailie represent exclusively a sample of activities within the special environment of the alluvial flats surrounding a small lake, and even the

sample within this restricted situation is drawn from a small, possibly non-representative segment of the lake basin.

The Olorgesailie sedimentary formation attains a maximum thickness of about 200 feet (60 meters), and represents a considerable time span within the East African equivalent of the late Middle, or possibly early Upper, Pleistocene. However, the cultural material appears to fall entirely within a single cultural-stratigraphic unit (see Bishop and Clark, 1967 for terminological discussion) which is a segment of the "Acheulean Industrial Complex." For the purposes of this paper, evidence from all levels is combined to constitute, however unequally, the basis for deducing behavior in the area during part of the Middle Pleistocene.

THE OCCURRENCE OF ARCHEOLOGICAL EVIDENCE

A very diffuse scatter of artifacts and fossil bone occurs throughout the alluvial and sub-aerial deposits of the sedimentary formation, estimated at less than one piece per 1,000 cubic meters. These presumably represent the wanderings and sporadic activities of Acheulean men. Much higher degrees of artifact concentration are assumed to result from localized activities of men; this we may term an occupation. Three types have been recognized (Howell *et al.*, 1962) at Isimila, and these apply equally to Olorgesailie:

1. Horizontally and/or vertically diffuse.
2. Horizontally concentrated, but vertically diffuse (rare at Olorgesailie).
3. Horizontally and vertically concentrated (an occupation floor).

Types (1) and (2) seem likely in many cases to represent sporadic, intermittent occupations of great duration. Such occupation patterns may not in themselves denote patterns of settlement and movement distinct from the casual wanderings of primate troops (DeVore and Washburn, 1963). Type (3) can probably be interpreted as fairly stable "home bases." The most spectacular instance at Olorgesailie is a camp-site with stone and bone debris covering an area of 200 square meters, and weighing more than a ton (1,000 kilograms).

Table 1   Locations

Location in Relation to Major Topographic Features	Number of sites	
	Excavated in Whole or Part	Surface Observation
Scree and alluvial fans at the foot of rocky slopes above the basin	1	3
Rocky "Peninsula" projecting into the alluvial flats	1	—
Possibly near lake margin, as indicated by proximity to contemporary diatomites or "beach sands"	3	3
Alluvial flats remote (more than two miles) from the lake	12	4
Location in Relation to Minor Topographic Features and Substratum. (Only excavated examples, the context of which are known to me, are included here.)	Number of sites	Character
Boulder-strewn rock surface	1	Horizontally diffuse
Flat surfaces with clay soil formation	2	Horizontally diffuse
Sandy patches along the courses of braided seasonal runnels in alluvial flats	6	"Floors"
Related to sand deposits in shallow seasonal channels, context disturbed or obscure	4	3 "Floors," 1 horizontally diffuse

LOCATION AND CHARACTER OF OCCUPATION SITES

Such information is likely to prove a useful basis for deductions about the movements and general natural history of earlier Pleistocene hominids. The Olorgesailie evidence on these points is summarized in Table 1.

The choice of sandy substratum in or near the course of a seasonal braided channel is a strongly recurrent feature of the location of most dense accumulations of occupation debris at Olorgesailie. It has been recorded also for a Lower Acheulean site at Peninj, Tanzania (Isaac in press, a and b), and has been reported

by J. D. Clark at Latumne in Syria (1966). Some of the Isimila and Kalambo Falls camps may also be examples.

The occurrence of prodigious numbers of handaxes from some fluviatile deposits in western Europe may well relate to similar preferences for sand and gravel patches on the flood plains of rivers. Concentrations of several thousand handaxes in the small area of a gravel pit seem more likely to have been brought about by intensive localized occupation than by natural agencies concentrating initially dispersed material.

At Olorgesailie this choice of sites may be partly accounted for in the following ways:

Table 2   Occupation Site Data

Site Grid Ref.	Comments	Average Diameter	Area	Number of large Cutting Tools	Estimated Total No. of Intro- duced stones
DE/89					
Horizon A	Disturbed by stream action	6 m.	28 m.²	72	699
Horizon B	Not significantly disturbed	16 m.	200 m.²	524	5000
Horizon C	Not disturbed	6 m.	28 m.²	21	1000
H/9					
Horizon A	Disturbed by stream action; possibly palimpsest of 2 or more occupations	20 m.	300 m.²	148	6000
KL/67					
"Catwalk"	Aggregate exposed by erosion, but not dispersed. Possibly 2 superimposed occupations	15 m. (or less . . .)	180 m.²	620	—

either the sandy channels were bare patches in otherwise swamp-grass covered plains or the lake was two or more miles distant, and water may have been obtainable by shallow scoops in the sandy runnels. The camps may have been situated away from the actual lake shores to avoid the heavy infestation of mosquitoes common near fresh water, and to avoid disturbing game. Systematic ethnographic observation of the location of camp sites in relation to topography and substratum is urgently needed, together with inquiry into the explicit and implicit factors determining choice in each case.

SIZE OF OCCUPATION SITES

The horizontally diffuse sites may cover considerable areas: for example, approximately 120 × 80 meters for a site at the foot of the mountain; 100 × 100 meters for the thirteen-rock peninsula site; 150 × 120 meters for the LHS scatter on clay soil substratum. These scatters are all assumed to be palimpsests of unknown numbers of occupations, localized only vaguely in a particular area. Their size depends presumably on the interaction of numerous factors—numbers of persons in different occupying groups, number and duration of occupations, extent of overlap with previous occupation areas, etc. At present there is little prospect of getting evidence relating to group size or duration of occupation from such diffuse scatters.

A limited number of "occupation floors" has been excavated, principally on the "Main Site" where eight occur within a strip 120 meters long, 60 meters wide, all stratified within Member 7, a layer of alluvially deposited volcanic silt 2 meters thick. It was found that the "floors" in this complex did not show gradational boundaries, but were discrete patches of stone and bone occupation debris with sharp limits. Such marked site boundaries were not anticipated, and one can only surmise that they coincide with some former natural or artificial limit to the occupation areas. Natural confines might be caused by, for instance, the bank of the sandy runnel in which the occupation was situated, or the edge of the shade afforded by a large tree. A thorn hedge is a possible artificial barrier that would leave no direct archeological traces but would have limited the spread of material. Systematic determination of phosphate concentration patterns over both modern and Pleistocene camp sites may eventually provide the best basis for estimating group size/camp area relationships. The data on the occupation sites are summarized in Table 2.

If we assume that the distribution of stone artifacts, rubble, and cobbles fairly represents the minimum area of a camp site, then it can be surmised that the smaller sized floors (5–6 meters) would result from occupation by a group comprising no more than four or five adults, while the larger ones may have held twenty or more. The problem of the size of prehistoric social aggregates was discussed among the participants of the symposium, and is one that requires more archeological and ethnographic data before firm conclusions are drawn. However, it seems possible that the size range of sites observed at Olorgesailie is consistent with the pattern outlined by Birdsell in his treatment of the demography of precontact Australia: that is, the small, 30-square-meter sites possibly represent occupation places of single family groups, while the larger sites, 200–300 square meters, may represent "home bases" of "local groups" of the predicted order of magnitude, twenty to thirty adults. Lee (personal communication) reports a range of camp sizes from 230 to 790 square meters for groups of !Kung Bushmen between 25 and 30 in number. The mean is 440 square meters ($n = 6$). There are too many variables for precise equivalence to be assumed.

We have no direct evidence for deducing the *duration of occupation* in sites of the kind referred to above. However, it is clear that the accumulation of a ton or more of stone artifacts and manuports, as in the largest examples, requires either a continuous occupation of some length (perhaps not less than two or three months),

or repeated reoccupations amounting to an equivalent period. The sharpness of the margins and the low degree of rearrangement by natural forces favors continuous rather than intermittent occupation. Lee reports that Bushman groups reoccupy the same area, but seldom exactly the same site.

Food Remains

No traces of vegetable foods have survived on any site at Olorgesailie excavated to date. It might be expected that stones used in the preparation of vegetable food could give indirect evidence. Lee and Woodburn have mentioned "nutting stones" and seed-pounding stones. Similar stones are recorded for Australia (D. Thomson, 1964). The Olorgesailie sites commonly contain an abundance of subspherical stones suitable for use as hammers and pounders, but flat preparation platform stones are not usually obvious. More detailed ethnographic information on the morphology of stones in current use would help investigation of this point.

Bone fragments occur on all occupation sites, suggesting that hunting and/or scavenging was generally practised. The density of bone on the sites is generally low, consisting of small scattered splinters and a few teeth. However, experimental observations suggest that dispersal of bone by scavengers and disintegration by weathering proceed at a sufficient rate to account for this. M. Posnansky, who was warden at Olorgesailie 1957–58, laid out part of the skeleton of a goat on the ground and covered it with wire netting to protect it from scavengers and footfalls. By 1965 most of the thinner bones, scapulae, ribs, and parts of the skull had disintegrated. The remaining bones are so friable that only small fragments would have survived if it were not for the protective cover. In addition, during part of my stay in East Africa, bone dispersal was experimentally observed. Domestic bones and bone fragments were recorded and dumped at a peg out in the "bush." Scavenging animals removed most of the bones beyond a radius in which is was possible to search (30–50 yards); only relatively small splinters and a few isolated larger fragments remained near the peg (see also Leakey, 1965).

Thus we are not in a position to assess general level of hunting success by Acheulean men camping at Olorgesailie. We do however have some instances where interesting evidence has been preserved. Specialist reports on the bone assemblages are not yet completed, so that this account can only be in general qualitative terms.

SPECIES REPRESENTED

Most of the excavated sites have yielded identifiable scraps of the teeth of the following:

Hippopotamus sp.

Equus, and/or Stylohipparion.

Bovidae (relatively scarce).

Some sites have yielded fragmentary remains of the following groups:

Simopithecus, an extinct robust baboon (superabundant on one site).

Suidae.

Elephas recki.

Rhinocerotidae.

Rodent bones, bird bones, and reptile bones including crocodile are present on some sites, but are scarce and poorly preserved. Fish and amphibian bones were found on a few sites, but were not in concentrations sufficient to indicate that they formed part of the diet. Even on those sites where bone is comparatively abundant, it mostly consists of finely comminuted splinters. It seems clear either that the occupants had cause to pulverize bones on the camp site, or that scavengers moved in afterwards and did so.

Some examples of sites on which evidence is comparatively well preserved may serve to illustrate the character of the evidence:

A. 13, "Peninsula Site": An excavated area of about 100 square meters yielded forty equid teeth, eighteen bovid teeth, and five hippo teeth, together with about thirty podials and bone fragments which are possibly large enough for anatomical identification. The remainder consisted of 19.2 kilograms of fossilized bone splinters with an average weight per splinter of 1.25 grams. The excavation is a sample of a total area of a diffuse occupation scatter estimated to be nearly 100 times larger. Extrapolation from these figures is unreliable but could indicate that a fair number of carcasses were broken up in the vicinity.

B. "Hippo Banda Site": A former warden, Mr. Andrews, excavated in an area 10×5 meters a portion of a disarticulated hippo carcass and preserved his finds in situ by covering them with a roof. The bones consist of a hind leg, teeth, vertebrae, and rib fragments. Among the bones are a small number of Acheulean artifacts. No records of the excavations are preserved, but there seems no reason to doubt that this exhibition excavation exposed a hippo butchery site.

C. The largest and most completely preserved occupation floor to be excavated was that of DE/89 Horizon B (Land Surface 7 of L. S. B. Leakey, 1952), in Member 7 on the Main Site. The occupation concentration is oval in plan, about 19×13 meters in extent. It has yielded more than 1,000 kilograms of stone artifacts, rubble, and unmodified cobbles. Many of the 500 cleavers and handaxes show signs of chipping and blunting by use. Among the stones comprising the floor there was a large quantity of bone splinters and relatively few intact or identifiable pieces, mainly teeth and podial bones. Most of these belong to numerous individuals of an extinct robust species of baboon, hitherto classified as *Simopithecus oswaldi*. The material is at present being studied under the direction of Dr. Leakey. Field records and a preliminary sorting done by Dr. Leakey and S. Mitchell indicate that more than 800 teeth were recovered in my own and Dr. Leakey's excavations. A preliminary estimate indicates a minimum of fifty adult and subadult baboons, together with at least thirteen juveniles. In addition to more than 150 shaft and articular fragments of long bone and very numerous phalanges, tarsals, and carpals, there were 12.7 kilograms of comminuted bone splinters, most of which is probably *Simopithecus* bone. With the *Simopithecus* bones are a few scattered teeth and bones of equids, bovids, hippos, and an elephant; but these probably constitute much less than 10 per cent of the bones.

This site thus attests either continued extremely successful, specialized hunting of baboons, or perhaps the massacre of a single baboon troop. J. Woodburn (Chapter 11, this volume, and personal communication) reports that the Hadza people of north Tanganyika normally hunt singly but occasionally band together to surround a baboon troop at night, while the animals are asleep. The baboons are dislodged by arrow shots and clubbed to death as they attempt to break out. This record provides a plausible explanation of the special abundance of baboon remains on the site, without involving the postulation of elaborate hunting or trapping techniques; but the hypothesis cannot at present be critically tested. Woodburn and Lee have also gathered valuable observations on the procedures for cutting up carcasses, selection of parts for transport to camp, and the choice of bones broken up for the extraction of marrow, but more quantitative data on these processes would be of great interest.

HUNTING METHODS

There is no direct evidence regarding the nature of hunting methods employed by Acheulean men at Olorgesailie. Recent excavation has revealed nothing definite in support of the hypothesis that the bolas was known to these people. It is hard to imagine how hunters on foot and without bows could kill large numbers of baboons except by surrounding them at night. Drugged waterholes is another possibility that comes to mind.

Positive evidence of fire is absent from the Olorgesailie occupation sites, as it is at all "Middle Pleistocene" sites in East Africa. Microscopic carbon is present in silts of the formation, and it may be that the negative evidence on the excavated sites is not conclusive.

Limited territorial range of the groups occupying sites at Olorgesailie can be guessed from the scarcity of stone exotic to the vicinity. Chert and metamorphic rocks are generally present on the sites only as small worked-out stubs or splinters. The metamorphic rocks do not outcrop closer than twenty miles away.

The absence of any human remains from Acheulean culture occupation sites at Olorgesailie and Olduvai is in contrast to several occurrences on earlier Oldowan culture sites. It can tentatively be concluded that corpses were removed from occupation sites, and that cannibalism was not an important practice.

As the discussions of this symposium have indicated, changes in *demographic patterns* during prehistory are of considerable interest to anthropologists and human biologists. Washburn (1965) has deduced from the evidence of a comparative primatologist that hominid population densities declined from a relatively high number (ten to 400 or more per square mile), characteristic of non-human primates, to the relatively low number characteristic of most non-agricultural human societies for which data exists: for example, 1 per square mile maximum for Australia (Pilling, Chapter 16, this volume). Most prehistorians (for example, J. D. Clark, 1965) conclude that the record shows a gradual increase in hominid population density through the Pleistocene. Both points of view require more factual documentation, but because of the nature of Pleistocene archeological evidence and the bias of samples, archeology is unlikely ever to be able to contribute unambiguous, direct demographic evidence for the Lower and Middle Pleistocene subperiods. However, there are features of the archeological record which may conceivably give indirectly the required indications: artifact assemblages may be found to show patterns of differentiation which are related to demographic factors and population density, in a fashion analogous to linguistic dialects (see Birdsell, Chapter 24, this volume). Preliminary treatment of this problem for some North American archeological occurrences has been given by Binford (1963). Individual campsite assemblages at Olorgesailie show marked stylistic idiosyncrasies, perhaps indicating stability of group composition. When the patterns have been worked out at this and other sites, tentative demographic deductions may become possible.

Archeologists are frequently under pressure to abandon the shelter of the technicalities and indirectness of their evidence and to risk speculative total reconstructions of the behavior of prehistoric peoples; but uncontrolled speculation is of no value, or is even misleading. Therefore, in accepting such challenges, the archeologist should firmly omit aspects of culture for which he can find no prospect of material evidence to use as a test of validity. Yet, a bold outline reconstruction of the situation actually indicated by the evidence may be attempted, to conclude this example:

Acheulean men at Olorgesailie appear to have lived in groups varying in size from approximately four to approximately thirty adults, the smaller groups possibly being the result of temporary splitting of relatively stable "bands" with twenty to thirty adult members. The "bands," or individual specialist members, appear to have shown real, perceptible stylistic variation in their artifacts. This, and other observed variation (Kleindienst, 1961b) might also in part relate to temporary, perhaps seasonal, or sectional task differentiation, which may be reflected in diversity of composition among tool kits.

The people subsisted at least in part on hunted, or scavenged, animal food, but the evidence is consistent with an opportunistic subsistence pattern similar to those observed among the Bushmen, Hadza, and other contemporary "foragers," where meat is a socially important prestige food, but the diet consists predominantly of gathered plant food. In one instance at least, the evidence suggests systematic communal hunting of baboons. Territorial range was quite possibly rather restricted. The general scatter of artifacts indicates that man was present persistently in the area, but ecologically he was probably no more significant than any other predatory species.

Generalizations from such evidence as that of Olorgesailie to wider hypotheses about a "stage" in behavioral evolution should probably not be attempted yet. Other comparable site complexes in Africa have been investigated and are reviewed by Howell and Clark (1963), though none are published in detail. However, the results of each hold out promise that meaningful paleoethological and paleoecological interpretations are possible where sufficient care is taken in the investigations.

The example given should also have shown some of the uses of ethnographic data both at the level of interpreting site features, and for general hypothetical reconstructions. It should also be clear that the prehistorian often needs a specific type of ethnographic information which can only be recorded by a worker with an "inside" knowledge of archeological evidence. Close field collaboration between archeologists and ethnologists is thus urgently needed.[1]

1. Much of the field and laboratory work of this study has been done jointly with my wife. Dr. and Mrs. Leakey kindly gave us the opportunity to work at Olorgesailie, and helped and encouraged us throughout its execution. The Government of Kenya gave permission for excavation, while the National Parks and National Museum provided many facilities during my employment there. Research grants have been generously provided by the following organizations: Wenner-Gren Foundation for Anthropological Research; Boise Fund, Oxford University; British Academy; British Institute for History and Archaeology in East Africa.

27.

A Theoretical Framework
for Interpreting Archeological Materials

L. G. FREEMAN, JR.

This essay discusses the proposition that the most serious failings in present models for interpeting archeological evidence are directly related to the fact that they incorporate numerous analogies with modern groups. This has prevented the development of frameworks of theory which might lead to an understanding of the sociocultural significance of archeological residues based directly on the comparison of those residues. The use of analogy has demanded that prehistorians adopt the frames of reference of anthropologists who study modern populations and attempt to force their data into those frames, a process which will eventually cause serious errors in prehistoric analysis, if it has not done so already. It is unnecessary, because it is possible to develop models for the interpretation of archeological evidence which minimize analogy. It is unscientific, because if we utilize models which are only sensitive to the elucidation of parallels with modern groups, the discovery of parameters of sociocultural structure unique to prehistoric time periods is impossible. Unless we can discover those parameters where they exist, evidence from prehistory will contribute very little to the understanding of ranges of variation in cultural systems, the nature of the interrelationships between elements of culture, or processes of cultural development.

RECENT DEVELOPMENTS

In the last decade, prehistoric research has attained a new level of sophistication in the gathering and interpretation of archeological materials. The revolution that has taken place is a twofold one, involving the development of new methodological approaches to the gathering and simple description of data (most of which owe a great deal to other disciplines such as physics, statistics, paleontology, paleobotany, geomorphology, geography, climatology, and pedology) and the construction of new theoretical approaches to the interpretation of those data.

While all prehistorians agree that the materials with which they deal represent only a small proportion of the materials used in and altered by human behavior, many would now reject the view Hawkes expressed only thirteen years ago, that without the aid of written records little information except that dealing with past economies can be extracted from archeological evidence (Hawkes, 1954). A brief survey of only some of the modern research that illustrates this trend shows studies exploring the ramifications of White's (1959) view of culture as man's extrasomatic means of adaptation and Steward's (1955) concept of cultural ecology by Binford (1962) and Struever (1966);

studies involving consideration of the nature of the socialization process (Deetz, 1960; Whallon, 1965); examination of the process of cultural drift (Binford, 1963); studies concerned with the nature of stylistic differentiation of sociocultural groups and subgroups (Binford and Binford, 1966b; Cronin, 1962; Deetz, 1960; Longacre, 1964b, Whallon, 1965), and attempts at definition of the number and nature of tasks undertaken by prehistoric groups (Binford and Binford, 1966b; Freeman and Brown, 1964; Freeman, in press). The best of these studies have been directed to the isolation and examination of the functional and processual dimensions of cultural systems. Much less effort has been spent in the construction of frameworks for viewing the structure of such systems. Even where attention has been given to this aspect of cultural studies, research has involved attempts to determine the existence, in the prehistoric record, of structural principles observable in (especially "related") modern societies. The method takes for granted that it is possible to derive, from the study of a sample of modern societies, elements of sociocultural structure (including whole institutions and corporate groups) which are homologous with those of the prehistoric period. Although this approach may be an especially fruitful one when applied to recently extinct cultural systems, it is likely to yield misleading results when applied to the study of cultural materials produced by more ancient societies, especially societies more than 40,000 years extinct.

The Use of Analogy

In part, the use of analogy in archeological interpretation has been due to a desire to construct categories of cultural development— "levels" of economic organization or social complexity—under the assumption that such constructs are the goal of evolutionary studies, and that the principles of the classification are derivable from our knowledge of the evolutionary process. However, the construction of such categories, which has been called "general evolution" by Sahlins and Service (1960) is really not "evolution" at all, but taxonomy. Multitudes of classifications of the same items,

be they objects, organisms, or sociocultural systems, are possible (Simpson, 1961). Some of those are "evolutionary" in the sense of being derived from the developmental history of the items classified, and some are not. To establish the relevance of such a classification to the evolution of the items concerned, one must base it on the historical record of development of the items. As yet, studies of the "fossil record" of cultural evolution are inadequate to serve as the basis for any evolutionary classification that is detailed enough to be useful. It is impossible to classify as yet ungathered data.

But are the data really ungathered? It is often assumed that this is not the case. Admittedly, it is said, the "fossil record" is incomplete, but we can substitute for missing elements in the record studies of the behavior of "modern representatives" of those elements. As Service says, "Certainly aboriginal Arunta culture is not younger than western civilization; it is obviously a great deal older, and precisely therein lies one of the virtues of studying that kind of culture" (1962, p. 8). The assumption that modern representatives of past stages of cultural development exist is a major justification for the use of analogy. Curiously, that justification is a derivative of the view that culture is an adaptive system. As Service goes on to say: "the aboriginal culture of the Arunta . . . is . . . a form of adaptation to a particular kind of (total) environment made long, long, ago and preserved into modern times because of its isolation" (1962, p. 8; the parentheses are his). This kind of reasoning is misleading.

It is based, of course, on the hypothesis that like environmental stimuli produce like cultural responses. In a very general way, this is true. (There are a limited number of methods of working stone by percussion. Elements not present in an environment cannot be utilized.) Nevertheless, if the statement is examined in detail, it is false. Each society exercises some degree of control over the influence of its environment by exploiting some aspects of environment at the expense of others. No society utilizes all it could of the offerings of its surroundings. In addition, the differences in the manipulation of the same resource by two distinct cultures are often great. Two "distinct" cultures from exactly similar environments, both of which are affected by exactly the same aspects of those environments, and both of which utilize identical resources in identical ways, would be part of exactly identical ecological systems. This is really the same as saying they would be one and the same culture. The validity of making inferences based upon general principles of adaptation discernible among modern populations is not denied; on the contrary, such inferences are necessary. But that is not the same as the inferential process I am attacking. In fact, it leads to contrary results.

It is known that modern populations of higher animals and their distributions are the result of a complex historical process involving long sequences of changes in adaptation to changing environments, including other animal populations. The present diversity of such animal forms is the end product of a series of developments involving numerous transitions from old to new environmental situations, either by population spread or environmental change, and numerous consequent readaptations. In addition to this process, the complementary development of a variety of new "ways of making a living ... examplified in the phenomenon of adaptive radiation" (Simpson, 1961, pp. 14–15) also played a large part. Competition for resources resulted either in differentiation of forms, often involving increasing specialization in the utilization of specific resources, or in the disappearance of all but one form from the environmental locus of competition (Simpson, 1961, pp. 16–17).

Sociocultural systems, like animal populations, have tended to regional-and-resource specialization during the course of human history. New ways of making a living have occurred at the same time: one can certainly speak of the dispersal of food-production as an example of an adaptive radiation. Any such radiation alters the interaction between members of the invaded natural community in some way (Simpson, 1961, p. 10). In the case of the spread of food-production, the process of clearing land for planting, among other factors, altered the size and nature of animal communities, and thus altered the possibility for hunter-gatherers in competition with agriculturalists to survive. At the present time, hunting and gathering adaptations tend to exist in situations which are undesirable to food-producing peoples. Where hunter-gatherers survive in environments utilized by food producers, they have usually had to specialize in the extraction of kinds of resources least affected by food-production. They must, in fact, be totally unrepresentative of the sorts of hunting-gathering adaptations that existed before the advent of food production.

Another line of reasoning that militates against Service's hypothesis is based simply on the logical limits to prediction from a limited sample. Hunting-gathering adaptations of the present are extremely diverse. From a detailed analysis of Bushman cultural systems, it would be possible to predict very little about the social structure of the Kwakiutl. The cultures do have elements in common, of course, but those elements are of such a general nature that information gleaned from one group is not particularly useful in interpreting the behavior of the other in any detail. (It is true that in another sense a great deal can be learned from the comparison. It illustrates the diversity of forms of structural elements among hunting-gathering peoples of the present, and the dangers inherent in reasoning from one or a few such systems to all.) Now, useful and detailed analyses of sociocultural systems have really only been made among peoples who lived during the last hundred years. The total length of time during which hunting-gathering adaptations have existed, on the other hand, is on the order of two million years or more. It would seem logical that Bushmen are many thousands of times more likely to be representative of all modern hunting-gathering groups than all such groups of the present are to be representative of the total range of hunting-gathering adaptations past and present. This is especially so because most past groups were composed of beings biologically so different from present humanity that we simply cannot assume continuities (other than such broad ones that they are relatively useless in interpretation) between their behavior and our own.

I have not meant to imply that the comparison of past and present sociocultural adaptations can reveal no important similarities or identities. However, such parallels must not be assumed to exist before it has been demonstrated that they do. The use of assumed similarities with modern behavior in the explanation of the behavior of extinct groups is not only fallacious, it is also deleterious to research since it prevents the discovery that the postulated similarities do not exist.

A Model Minimizing Analogy

I have attempted to establish the fact that analogical reasoning from modern behavior must be kept to a minimum in the construction of models of past cultural systems. I intend to show in the remainder of this paper that the construction of a workable model of the structure of culture, for use in interpreting archeological materials in which a minimum of analogical reasoning is involved, is feasible, and that its application avoids the pitfalls I have outlined.

The Nature of Culture

Any model of cultural structure which is to be of utility to the prehistorian must consider the material aspects of culture, since those include the observational data upon which he must base inferences about human behavior. It must be assumed, for the purposes of such a definition, that patterned occurrences of the elements the prehistorian studies can be discovered, and that when they are derived from undisturbed contexts they indicate that patterned human behavior was responsible for their existence. It must also be assumed that patterned behavior due to biological factors can be isolated from culturally conditioned behavior, at least potentially. Last, although ideas and values are important to the prehistorian as they influence behavior, values which do not become observable through some effect on behavior need not be considered part of culture. A definition of culture which satisfies these restrictions is the following: culture consists of both the total configuration of patterned activities (which are not simply referable to the biology of the actors) performed by a society, including the materials used in or produced by those activities, and the social units responsible for activity performance. This definition resembles that of

Malinowski (1960) except that the focus of attention is on the end products of his institutions, and the "charter" of the institutions is equated with their "function."

I stress that the prehistorian cannot reconstruct any activity undertaken by a given society unless that activity produced some preserved material evidence. Binford, on the other hand, has claimed that it is possible to "recover, both from the nature of the populations of artifacts and from their spatial associations, the fossilized structure of the total cultural system" (Binford, 1964, p. 425). This statement would seem at first glance to contradict what I have just said. I do not really think it does. Binford does not mean to imply that we can reconstruct an extinct linguistic system, for example, from prehistoric materials. However, the linguistic system as part of the general system of communication in a given society is also part of the mechanism of socialization, and the nature of the process of socialization certainly cannot be denied to influence the patterning of activities in the society, right down to the form of the tools made and used by social units.

The Nature of Social Units

While it is relatively easy for the prehistorian to discern patterned occurrences of elements and to infer from them some of the parameters of the activities which produced them, and at least some of the norms governing their performance, it is much harder to determine the nature of the social units which performed those activities. In this stage of analysis, prehistorians have tended to refer to the patterned materials they observe as the end products of activities undertaken by corporate groups like those observable in one or another modern society. Once more, caution is necessary. In the first place it is unfortunately fair to say that few significant advances have been made from the study of modern peoples, in the ascertainment of "the extent to which the behavior patterns entailed in exploiting the environment affect other aspects of culture" (Steward, 1955, p. 41) since Steward's formulation of the method of "cultural ecology"; there is really no body of data available in analogy with moderns that can be applied to this problem without numerous intervening assumptions. Were usable data available, even if all extant social groups were found to exhibit a given correlation between social structural type and activity patterns, I am not prepared to admit that it is justifiable to assume that past social groups with many or even most of the same activity patterns necessarily also had the social structural type that is their modern correlate. I would expect to find among extinct cultural systems at least some relations between social structural type and activity pattern that are totally unrepresented among modern societies.

Another criticism of the equation of archeological materials with the activity patterns of corporate groups can be directed at a general confusion about the nature of social groups that is manifest in that equation. Social anthropologists have long recognized that not all social groups are corporate. A corporate group can be defined as one which has a body of collective rights and duties, an "estate," vested in all members and "activated in diverse situations," so that it can be said to be a "multipurposive" group (Fortes, 1953; Nadel, 1951, p. 160). In addition it may have longer existence than the life span of any member. All members of a corporate group may act as a body on occasion for the performance of some activity, or, on the other hand, only some of the members may cooperate as representative of the group as a whole. In contexts where they act as group representatives, they are recognized and recognize themselves as such, and their way of acting and their organization then follow from the rules of organization of membership in the group and its way of acting (Nadel, 1951, p. 161). However, members of a corporate group may cooperate in contexts in which that membership is irrelevant. The structure of a hunting party need not be based upon the same principles as the structure of a composite family, even where all members of the hunting party are members of the same composite family. Some of the dimensions of group organization must vary, at least in the relative intensity with which they are stressed, as the group performs different functions.

Even though social anthropologists have tended to focus their attention on the corporate groups in society, those groups need not be the only important groups, or even the most important ones for the day-to-day survival of society as a whole. Special-purpose groups made up of members of one or more corporate groups, cooperating to perform specific tasks and, perhaps, immediately dissolving after a very brief existence are the basic units of action in society. They are also the units responsible for the accumulation of archeological materials. While such parties may, in fact, frequently coincide with corporate groups, the prehistorian cannot assume that they do; he must prove that they do, where possible, and this involves distinguishing the two conceptually for analytic purposes. To be of utility to the prehistorian, the definition of the "social unit" must include special-purpose groups or "parties" as well as corporate groups. (Since the culturally patterned activites of individuals can be as important to group survival as those of multi-person groups, the most utilitarian definition of the "party" is: any number of individuals [from 1 to n], who contribute to the performance of a given activity.)

A GENERAL ILLUSTRATION OF THE USE OF THE MODEL

The application of this theoretical framework to the study of prehistoric materials does not produce any spectacular insights about their significance. In fact, its results are not nearly as interesting or emotionally satisfying as the probably greatly misleading caricatures of prehistoric life-ways which have often been derived by the misuse of analogy. It necessitates the slow and painstaking isolation of regular types of associations of materials, and their formal equation with activity types. Only much later may an attempt at functional definition of those activities, based on the characteristics of artifacts and contexts, be made. Each activity type must be first be assumed to be the result of the behavior of a distinct party type. Next, detailed examinations of the formal characteristics of the artifacts which indicate the techniques of their manufacture and reflect motor habits involved in that process (Binford and Quimby, 1963), combined with microscopic study of variations in their wear-characteristics (Semenov, 1964), and analysis of the distribution of associated materials in the clusters may aid in the discovery that ranges of variation of these characteristics overlap for some clusters and are distinct for others. This will hopefully permit the identification of parties which are multipurposive, or involved in multiple activities. Perhaps membership characteristics of a party may in future be determinable from the recognition of individual idiosyncracies in artifact manufacture and use. These studies in conjunction with an examination of the configuration of between-cluster spatial relationships and cluster size (the "proxemic" pattern of each occupation [Hall, 1966]) may be expected to lead eventually to the discovery of the boundaries of identity-conscious social groups.

Conclusions

The system just outlined affords a systematic, objective method for the control of selected culturally significant aspects of archeological evidence for the purpose of intra- and inter-occupation comparisons. It makes possible control over activity type, as an example, permitting eventual study of variations in party make-up or size, or of the variation between functionally equivalent units indicative of activity performance by different identity-conscious social groups. Starting with evidence from one site, we may hope to extend these comparisons first to a few other sites, then gradually over the totality of the prehistoric period, as more excavations conducted to recover comparable evidence are completed. This method, an extension of the technique of "controlled comparison" (Eggan, 1954) to archeological evidence, offers the only secure means of acquiring an understanding of the nature of the types of prehistoric institutions and the mechanisms which contributed to their maintenance or transformation (Eggan, 1954, p. 748).

It is certainly desirable for all of us, as anthropologists, to work toward increased communication, and to make our findings as intelligible as possible to each other. But no anthropological subdiscipline has yet elicited the laws governing the structure and operation of cultural systems. The idea that prehistorians must interpret their evidence solely in terms of inferences derived from social and cultural anthropology is as fallacious as the idea that interpretations of the behavior of modern groups must be derived from prehistory. Each of the subdisciplines of anthropology studies but one part of the total spectrum of cultural behavior. No segment of the spectrum is any more important than any other. All must be combined if we ever hope to understand the nature of culture in all its dimensions, and, hopefully, from that understanding to derive general laws regulating the structure of cultural systems, their interrelationships and the processes whereby they are transformed.[1]

1. I am aware that many of the ideas expressed here are the results of the genius of others, especially F. C. Howell, L. R. Binford, J. D. Clark, J. Sackett, R. Klein, and, more recently, J. Deetz and D. Damas. I suspect that the ones I consider original are also secondhand, and that I have simply forgotten where I borrowed them. The total configuration is my own, however. It was helpfully criticized by R. Klein, C. Merbs, and S. Tax, and students at the University of Chicago, while I was writing the drafts. I am grateful for the advice I followed, and apologize for having ignored the rest.

Note: Sackett's unpublished paper entitled "Archaeological Interpretation in the Upper Paleolithic," delivered to the AAA annual meeting in 1965 also incorporates some of the same elements in a model of cultural systems. This paper did not come to my attention until it was circulated for the Man the Hunter Symposium, after my essay was completed.

28.

Methodological Considerations
of the Archeological Use of Ethnographic Data

LEWIS R. BINFORD

Any consideration of the implications for archeological interpretation of new ethnographic data on hunter-gatherers requires an examination of the general relationship between ethnographic observations and archeological reasoning. Only then can the particulars of any new ethnographic data be placed in proper perspective.

It is frequently stated that one of the main tasks of the archeologist is the interpretation of the past and that the primary means available is reconstruction based on analogies to living peoples. Such a view presupposes that our knowledge of the past is only as good as our knowledge of the present and that our reconstructions are valid only insofar as we are justified in projecting knowledge of living peoples into the past. I would like to take exception to the above-stated position and set as the task of the archeologist and the anthropologist the explanation and explication of cultural differences and similarities. Ethnologists may, by virtue of their particular field of observation, explicate certain cultural forms not directly observable in the archeological record. The archeologist, on the other hand, may explicate forms of cultural phenomena not generally discussed by the ethnologist, although these phenomena may be available to the ethnologist for observation. However, some

phenomena, particularly those of a processual nature covering considerable periods of time, may be unavailable for direct observation by the ethnologist.

Adequate explanations are in no way dependent upon the data having been collected within any particular frame of reference; ethnologists can and do use archeological data, and vice versa. Cultural systems function within an ecological field whose structural changes are most frequently not synchronously phased with the life span of an individual. It follows that even if an individual were to devote his life exclusively to observation, he could not be expected to give an accurate or replicable account of the operation of cultural evolutionary processes. We would expect that some explanations for phenomena explicated through ethnographic observation to be found in archeological data, and vice versa. Further, archeological research might be expected to yield explanations for some observations of cultural phenomena made exclusively through archeological data.

If we define an hypothesis as the statement of a relationship between two or more variables, and if both variables are observable in the archeological record, then the hypothesis formulated is testable. It is only through the testing of hypotheses logically related to a series of theoretical propositions that we can increase or decrease the explanatory value of our propositions. The same procedure is the only means available to the ethnologist for generating adequate explanations. Methodologically, then, the archeologist is in no way dependent upon the ethnologist. Archeologists are dependent for building models upon the knowledge currently available on the range of variability in form, structure, and functioning of cultural systems. Much of this information has, of course, been provided by ethnographic investigation. It is this background information which serves the archeologist in offering explanatory propositions for some of the differences and similarities observed in the archeological record, many of which may not necessarily reveal differences or similarities between distinct cultural systems.

For example, some observed differences and similarities may be explained by differences in preservation; others may reveal differences in function between sites occupied by the same social unit; others may document different occupation histories by social units at separate locations. Many adequate and accurate explanations may refer to functional relationships between locations, material items, and classes of human activities, etc. However, as I have argued elsewhere (L. R. Binford, 1967) the "interpretation" of the archeological record by the citation of analogies between archeologically observed phenomena and phenomena from a known behavioral context simply allows one to offer his *postulate* that the behavioral context was the same in both cases. In order to increase the probability that the postulate is accurate, a number of testable hypotheses must be formulated and tested.

Archeologists are not limited to analogies to ethnographic data as the sole basis for offering explanatory postulates; models can be formulated in a theoretical calculus some of which may deal with forms without ethnographic analogs. Archeologists are certainly indebted to ethnographers for providing sources which can be used as inspirations for model-building. The crucial point, however, is that our understanding of the past is not simply a matter of interpreting the archeological record by analogy to living societies as has been commonly asserted (cf. Thompson, 1956, p. 329). Our

knowledge is sound to the degree that we can verify our postulates scientifically, regardless of the source of their inspiration. Scientific verification for archeologists is the same as for other scientists; it involves testing hypotheses systematically.

If archeologists and ethnologists are to overcome the limitations of their observational fields and contribute to the general field of anthropology, they must develop methods which will allow explanatory propositions regarding the operation of cultural systems to be tested by both archeological and ethnographic data. The archeologist, independent of the ethnologist, must search for order in the data available to him. After the recognition of classes of order in the record, the archeologist must then develop models that will allow him to relate the archeologically observed phenomena to variables which, although observable in different form among living peoples, are thought to have explanatory value. The only other alternative is to advertise his findings as indicating a new explanatory variable previously not isolated which might still be operative in the cultural systems of living peoples.

For example, archeologists and ethnologists may observe different phenomena to gain knowledge of a common variable. Ethnologists may interview informants and determine verbally the jural rules regarding postmarital residence. In addition they may take a census to determine the degree of conformity between the stated jural rule and actual decisions. These data may then be descriptively summarized and later treated as a case in testing various hypotheses regarding the conditions determining form of postmarital residence.

For many years it would have been argued that knowledge of postmarital residence rules of prehistoric communities was unobtainable by archeologists since it was not "material culture." A Soviet archeologist, Tretyakov, was the first to my knowledge to suggest that there was evidence for the forms of postmarital residence preserved in the archeological record (Tretyakov, 1934, p. 141). His work was summarized and commented upon favorably by Childe (1943, p. 6). Tretyakov's argument was fairly straightforward: the form of fingerprints on the inside of vessels indicated that it was females who manufactured pottery. In societies where matrilocal residence was the rule, there would be less formal variability expected in the execution of ceramic designs within any single community than under conditions where patrilocality was the rule, since patrilocality brings about a mixed population of female potters. Quimby (1956) suggested a similar argument to account for observed differences in variability between samples of pottery from Huron and Chippewan historic sites in the Great Lakes. The development and refinement of this particular argument and the perfection of reliable analytical methods have been accomplished by several recent workers (Deetz, 1965; Freeman and Brown, 1964; Hill, 1965, 1966; Longacre, 1964a, 1964b; McPherron, 1965; Whallon, 1965). As a result of this work, we can today state within definable confidence limits the postmarital residence patterns of prehistoric communities. Given the discussions at this conference over the nature of the determinants of residence rules and the degree to which patrilocality characterizes "pristine" hunter-gathers, we may find that some of the answers will be found in archeological data.

This case provides a good example of a study in which different forms of information were relevant in the elucidation of a single variable. It also exemplifies another important point—the interpretive model for the archeological data was not based on simple analogy to ethnographically known societies. The model was drawn deductively from several assumptions and propositions:

1. Females were the potters.

2. Homogeneity of cultural expression within a group varies directly with the homogeneity of the group's composition.

3. Many formal characteristics of pottery are stylistic and tend to vary with tradition rather than utilitarian or mechanical factors.

The model developed from these propositions states the nature of the expected relationship between two variables: formal variability in items produced at a given location by females and variability in premarital residence of these females. While the points of premarital residence of females of an archeologically known community are not directly observable, this proposition remains a postulate. However, among contemporary groups, or groups whose residence patterns are known through documents, the proposition may be stated as a testable hypothesis. This illustrates one of the functions of ethnographic data in archeological reasoning. These data may be used for testing hypotheses for which information on one or more of the relevant variables is not obtainable through archeology. While models for the interpretation of archeological data may be tested and verified on other than ethnographic sources, it may often be more impressive or scientifically more efficient in obtaining high levels of confidence to make such tests with ethnographic data.

This latter kind of investigation was strongly advocated by Kleindienst and Watson (1956) in urging a kind of inquiry they termed "action archeology." Watson actually did carry out a study of a living community from the perspective of an archeologist while she was a member of the staff of Braidwood's 1959–60 Iranian project. Since then there have been increasing numbers of workers studying archeologically relevant data among living peoples. Ascher (1962) studied the Seri; Leshnik (1964) lived with village agriculturalists in India; Richard Gould of the American Museum of Natural History is currently engaged in research among the Australian aborigines. Margaret Hardin, a graduate student at the University of Chicago, is currently studying functional variability in ceramic styles among Mexican potters. Longacre and Ayres recently reported their analysis of an abandoned Apache wickiup (1966).

From the preceding discussion, we see that ethnographic data can play two basic roles in archeological investigation: first, they serve as resources for testing hypotheses which seek to relate material and behavioral cultural phenomena; second, they may often (but need not always) serve as the basis for models of particular social relations which are postulated to have been the context for an observed archeological structure. In the former case, "action archeology" studies are relevant; in the latter, model building and testing can be related to ethnographic facts, but verification of propositions would remain a problem to be solved by the formulation of hypotheses testable by archeological data.

Given this relationship between ethnographic data and archeological inquiry, how can cooperation between the two specialists be maximized for the solution of common problems? In the first place, if archeologists and ethnologists are to work with common problems, their observations must be geared toward gathering data on the same variables, despite the obvious differences in their fields of observation. Second, they must work in terms of comparable sociocultural units. Finally, there must be a free exchange of information between archeologists and ethnologists to achieve the first two aims.

The kind of profitable feedback that can occur through such interdisciplinary exchange is nicely illustrated by this conference. Archeologists have worked too long without the benefits of the understandings of ethnology as to the operation of sociocultural systems. Further, some of the work discussed at this conference was directly relevant to the perfecting of techniques for gaining information on identical variables. I am referring to the "action archeology" studies of Richard Lee among the Bushmen and Bob Williams among the Birhor. These two studies add tremendously to our knowledge and are two of the most comprehensive in seeking to document the relationships between behavior and the spatial structure of artifacts which would be observable in the archeological record. Such information will be very useful in testing some of the propositions of Cook and Treganza (1950), Cook and Heizer (1965), and Naroll (1962) as to the relationships between population size and site size as well as population size and amount of enclosed space required. The site maps and structural details illustrating the internal spatial-formal structure of settlements, documented by Lee and Williams, will be valuable in testing a number of propositions regarding spatial disposition and correlates of social status. With the data now available it would be possible to measure the degree to which proximity between living areas in a settlement is correlated with social distance as measured in kinship affiliations. Exceptions to such correlations and the kinds of contingencies which intervene can be more easily spotted with data like Lee's and Williams' available.

On a slightly more critical note, and writing from only a superficial knowledge of the data gathered by Lee, some of the observations made and some of the emphases stressed at this conference bear witness to the need for freer communication between ethnographers and archeologists. For example, Lee's site maps are informative, yet he uses them to illustrate how little of the physical remains of a living people are left for the archeologist to observe. However, it should be noted that Lee made only surface observations and did no excavation. In the discussion of the relative importance of meat versus plant food, Lee's exact measurements of intake of the !Kung Bushmen is good to have, but it does duplicate many of the points raised and resolved fourteen years ago and reported in *An Appraisal of Anthropology Today* (Tax, 1953). Linton discussed many of the points raised here and stated:

> there are very few places in the world where people live entirely by hunting . . . you may remember that the occupation layers of Peking Man at Choukoutien have hackberry seeds (1953).

I suspect that an archeologist actively engaged in research might have made many different observations than those made by Lee. In his site maps Lee does plot hearths and fire areas but treats them all as the same. Detailed descriptive data on the formal differences in discrete and metrical attributes of hearths used in lighting, heating, and cooking of various kinds of food might have contributed greatly to our understanding of the functional variables which must be considered in dealing with archeologically observed hearths. This kind of information might help to prevent the simplistic kind of archeological interpretation recently made by Movius in which the size of the hearth is taken as an index of the size of the social unit occupying the site (Movius, 1966, p. 321).

This critical note is not meant to discourage "action archeology" studies, but it is to be hoped that ethnologists in making such observations might do well to put their observations in the framework of archeological question-asking.

The emphasis by the participants in this symposium on questioning certain propositions which have generally been accepted as truisms has far-reaching implications for archeological research. To my knowledge all archeological theorists who have considered the role of subsistence technology in evolutionary change have used a rather simplistic Malthusian model for population dynamics. The traditional view, superbly dealt with here by Sahlins, has been termed by Boulding (1955, p. 197) the Dismal Theorem. It holds that the ultimate check on population is misery; population will grow until the nutritional level falls and disease brings about population equilibrium. The fresh and challenging viewpoint put forth by Sahlins, and less playfully by Birdsell and Williams certainly brings into question many anthropological cliches about the origins of agriculture and animal domestication.

One of the most encouraging aspects of this conference is that archeologists and ethnologists are moving in the direction of dealing with comparable units. For example, archeologists assume that the size, composition, and spatial structure of an assemblage are jointly determined by: first, the size and composition of the social unit responsible; and second, the form of differential task performance carried out by individuals and segments of the occupying social unit. Such assumptions allow us to analyze in structural terms the contents of sites and permit the definition of the different tasks represented (see Binford and Binford, 1966b). In all his work the archeologist has available information on the behavior of persons making up either task-specific work groups or local residential groups. Any social unit larger than these are known archeologically only through comparative analysis of differences and similarities in form, composition, and distribution in a generally unbounded universe of sites yielding archeological data. Local groups and task forces are the social units about which archeologists can get information without having to work their data through a fairly elaborate body of culture theory.

In view of this, it is very heartening to hear at this conference considerable discussion on form and cyclically varying composition of local groups. The work of Helm and Watanabe is especially useful in this regard and will undoubtedly serve archeologists as a basis for model-building.

But perhaps the major contribution of this conference for me is the stimulation it has provided; the specific data as they were presented were literally food for thought. At the risk of presenting some of these ideas before—to continue the metaphor—they have been properly digested, I would like to offer an argument which is the direct result of on-the-spot linkages made between data presented here and archeological problems. The following observations are drawn largely from archeological data:

1. Judging from the scanty information on settlements and from the inferred functions of recovered tools, man's adaptations during the Pleistocene were accomplished almost exclusively through the use of *implements*. Implements have been defined by Wagner (1960) as tools which serve to translate or enhance energy exchanges; examples would be spears, knives, digging sticks, atlatls, etc.

2. Near the close of the Pleistocene and during the immediately post-Pleistocene period there was increased elaboration in the use of *facilities* (this is Wagner's term also). Facilities are objects which serve to prevent motion and/or energy transfers—that is, fish weirs, nets, pottery.

Let us add to these observations some points made at this meeting. Hunters and gatherers whose subsistence is largely obtained through the use of implements (Bushmen, Hadza, forest Pygmies, and during the winter the Central Eskimo) are said to be somewhat casual about death and nonchalant in their treatment of the dead or dying. An exception was the Birhor discussed by Williams who hunt with facilities—nets.

Let us now add one more archeological observation: Systematic burial of the dead and elaborate mortuary ritual are greatly increased on a worldwide basis at the close of the Pleistocene. True cemeteries appear first in the Mesolithic in the Old World and the Archaic in the New World; the Archaic and the Mesolithic are further characterized by a heavy dependence on facilities in their subsistence activities.

It is tempting to make functional linkages between the structure of technological adjustment, nature of status definition, and hence of attitudinal involvement with persons occupying these statuses as expressed in mortuary ritual. Facilities to be efficient require precise placement in space; their effectiveness is dependent upon energy flow and they must be placed so as to maximize the interruption of this flow. Fish weirs are an excellent example.

Facilities further require cooperative labor for their construction and maintenance.

All of this implies that the responsibility for coordination of effort will be assumed and, more important, that stewardships involving maintenance will be established. There would also be a necessary development of rules governing access to the facility and the distribution of its yields. Many other elements of role content would become part of newly defined status positions arising out of the use of facilities at the close of the Pleistocene. It is also suggested that emotional involvements would thus have been linked to interstatus dependencies of an order unknown in societies in which implements dominated the technology. In this new kind of facility-dependent society the death of an individual occupying a structured status position would necessitate the reallocation of his position to others, the retirement of "debts" to his descendants, and many other kinds of socially defined obligations which may well have been effected through mortuary rites.

If some of the ideas briefly outlined above should prove upon testing to have explanatory value, the coincident appearance of cemeteries in the New and Old Worlds at the close of the Pleistocene (as well as some of the "aberrant" features of the Birhor) might be elucidated simultaneously. The development and refinement of ideas stimulated by this conference will be one of the chief profits of having been in attendance.

29.

Ethnographic Data
and Understanding the Pleistocene

SALLY R. BINFORD

The following quotation is taken from the paper circulated by DeVore and Lee as part of the announcement of this conference:

> It should soon be possible for enthnographers and archeologists to meet together and, as an exercise in the deduction of extinct life patterns, realistically compare the occupation sites of living hunter-gatherers with those of prehistoric hunter-gatherers. It should be clear that this is a "logical exercise," and that there is no assumption that living hunter-gatherers are somehow living relics of the Pleistocene.

At the risk of sounding a discordant note in a harmonious meeting of people working in various subdisciplines, I would like to remark that the pertinence of ethnographic data to prehistoric research involves more than a "logical exercise." All of us are here for more than tightening up our intellectual muscle tone and have some rational belief or irrational faith that what we are saying is relevant to common problems. It is the problem of the translatability of ethnographic data back into earlier Pleistocene times that I would like to discuss briefly.

It is stated in the quotation above that there can be no valid assumption that living hunter-gatherers are relics of the Pleistocene. This is

unquestionably true. However, I would like to issue a corollary *caveat*—that Pleistocene hominids cannot be assumed to be simply earlier representatives of living hunter-gatherers. This means that the use of ethnographic data from the Arunta or the Bushmen to elucidate a Lower or Middle Pleistocene way of life must take into account certain differences in the biological and psychological constitution of the hominids involved which have been suggested by recent work in paleoanthropology.

Our typologies of lithic remains from the entire Pleistocene time range have undergone considerable refinement in recent years (see Bordes, 1953, 1961; Kleindienst, 1961a; deSonneville-Bordes and Perrot, 1954–56), and the use of comparable typological units has allowed comparisons over broad geographical areas. Most of the typologies currently used for Paleolithic assemblages deal with functional classes of tools—for example, scrapers versus points versus handaxes. The further back in time one goes, the fewer clearly recognizable functional classes of tools exist. This might be the result of fewer kinds of tasks or more multipurpose tools in the earlier time ranges, or both.

Besides function, another analytical tool used by archeologists is that of style. Stylistic attributes are those formal qualities of artifacts that are not directly explicable in terms of the nature of the raw material or of the technology of production (L. R. Binford, 1962, p. 220).

In the archeological assemblages associated with anatomically modern man (*Homo sapiens sapiens*) we can discern clearly definable *style zones*—bounded areas in which stylistic attributes are seen to cluster. Such style zones characterize the terminal Pleistocene assemblages of both the New World (Mason, 1962) and the Old World (Sackett, 1966). The function of style is thought to be a means of either group or individual identification with a product or class of products (L. R. Binford, 1963).

No such style zones can be seen in earlier Pleistocene assemblages. It is a truism that handaxes from South Africa, northern France, and southern England are remarkably similar. In the words of an anonymous archeologist, "You've seen one handax, you've seen 'em all"; the absence of stylistic differences within major classes of artifacts during the Acheulian is striking, regardless of the wide variety of raw materials used in their manufacture. It has been suggested (J. D. Clark, 1959; Kleindienst, 1961b) that the selection by an Acheulian group of a subclass of tool within some functional class of tool (for example, limande versus cordiform handaxes) may yield some information on style. However, this is very different from style in later assemblages.

The stylistic differences observable in earlier assemblages would appear to fit the model of cultural drift—the accretion of small changes or variations which give the appearance through time of directional change. Stylistic differences in assemblages from the Upper Paleolithic and later, on the other hand, appear to be the result, at least in part, of self-conscious symbolic behavior.

The point in time and the context in which such self-conscious symbolic behavior appears is a present subject of investigation by the writer and L. R. Binford. It is our present as-yet-undemonstrated hunch that the first evidence of *style clines* appear in the Mousterian. Bordes' type list of Mousterian artifacts, which is essentially a functional one, can be applied broadly—to Mousterian assemblages of the Near and Far East, North Africa, as well as France. But in using this type list in widely separated areas, the investigator is beset by a feeling of unease, since attributes not covered by Bordes' list appear to vary between broad geographical zones. The construction of an attribute list designed to inform about stylistic differences in the Mousterian is a present concern.

The distinction between style zones and clines is important, since a zone is a bounded area formally distinct from adjacent regions. Since Mousterian stylistic variability has not yet been systematically measured, we do not know if the differences we impressionistically perceive cluster in the discrete units which have been demonstrated for later assemblages.

The purpose here of bringing up style and its function, and of differences observable through time, is to raise the question of the implications of new kinds of ethnographic data for archeology. In dealing with pre-*sapiens* populations, observations from living groups cannot be directly used. (The exception would be observations on the function of specific artifact forms in similar environments.) Observations of living groups, to be usable for the early time ranges, must serve as a base line against which we measure differences in the structure of cultural systems and the psychological capacities of the culture-bearers.

30.

Studies of Hunter-Gatherers
as an Aid to the Interpretation of Prehistoric Societies

J. DESMOND CLARK

It has become clear to me while listening to the debates of the two previous days that a better understanding of precontact behavior, social grouping patterns, population density, and distribution in Australia and, probably, also in North America and Africa would be possible by making a closer use of archeological data. A critical evaluation of the archeological evidence that can be obtained from late or historic settlements, supplemented by oral tradition, provides a promising means of resolving some of the problems of conflicting data as between present-day and early-contact times and also for the immediately previous period.

If archeological evidence has hitherto been little used by the ethnographer, the reverse is also true of the archeologist in his use of ethnographic data to help in interpreting the way of life and behavior of prehistoric populations. However, the evident flexibility of the social unit and the lack of any consistent composition or general grouping patterns among hunter-gatherers, as demonstrated at this conference, makes the archeologist's task even more difficult than it already appeared. Whereas the dangers of adducing any direct archeological and ethnographic comparisons are generally recognized and avoided, the basis for reconstructing prehistoric behavior must lie in a systematized use of the whole corpus of information on human behavior at the hunter-gatherer and other subsistence levels, and the selection and critical application of what is relevant in this for archeology.

The more complete the evidence for length and area of occupation and the associations of the full range of cultural remains, the greater the validity for any attempted interpretation of the site and its contents. The older the site, the more complex any reconstruction becomes.

Only during the last ten years or so has systematic excavation and study of artifact distribution on Lower Paleolithic living floors been undertaken in the Old World. Such studies have shown that it is quite possible to find sealed occupation sites that have suffered little or no natural disturbance before or after burial. In such cases it is presumed that the distribution scatter of the artifacts and any other artificial features of the site is as it was when abandoned by the occupants. Theoretically, therefore, it should be possible to go a long way toward reconstructing the activities of the occupants and obtaining some knowledge of their general behavior. In practice, however, what remains unknown and the variables among what is known, make any attempted reconstructions at present highly tenuous.

PREHISTORIC SETTLEMENT SITES AND SURVIVAL PATTERNS

Leaving aside butchery sites, I know of only one (Olorgesailie, Land Surface 8)—perhaps two (Olduvai, FLK I)—excavated Lower Paleolithic occupation areas that can claim to represent complete occupation units. All others comprise excavation of only a part of more extensive units, the exact areal distribution of which remains unknown. In not a few cases this can never be known since it was the natural erosion of the site that revealed it in the first instance. Clearly, therefore, the first requirement is the excavation of complete units of settlement, both those where there are no natural features limiting the spread of occupation debris (open sites) and those where the area of occupation is naturally confined (cave and rock shelter sites).

Once a sufficient number of distribution plots of complete occupation units are available, it will be possible to see the extent to which the association patterns of the components of a site vary or are consistent—the associations between different classes of tools, of certain tools with food debris, hearths, working areas, etc. Such different activities as, for example, required the use of the La Quina scraper, denticulated scrapers, handaxes, cleavers or core-axes, may sometimes all have been carried on contemporaneously on one site, as at the Kalambo Falls during the late Upper Acheulian. At other sites, the range of types is restricted, suggesting a special rather than a general-purpose occupation. At present the interpretation is hampered by the narrow lateral spread of most excavations and permits of more than one explanation for the several limited but distinctive tool kits of Paleolithic times.

In nearly every case, also—and this is most important—it is impossible at present to give an accurate estimate of the duration of time that is represented by one of these concentrations of tools and lithic debris. Since there is rarely, if ever, any accumulated midden waste present, either the sites were occupied for a short time only or their antiquity has resulted in the complete disappearance of organic remains, except bone. There is reason to believe that both explanations are pertinent. It seems probable that a site such as the Upper Acheu-

lian occupation at Broken Hill represents only temporary occupation. The same seems likely for the sand bank sites of similar age at the Kalambo Falls, whereas thirty feet or so of stratified succession at the Cave of Hearths represent interrupted but recurring occupation over a long period of time. We are, however, still without the means of determining whether days, weeks, or years elapsed before most of the sites we have were finally sealed over. In this connection it is heartening to know that Bushmen and Hadza today rarely reoccupy exactly the same camp site unless this be a cave or rock shelter.

Again, at most Paleolithic sites only the stone artifacts survive, though sometimes, especially in temperate latitudes, bone is plentiful. More rarely, wood is preserved, but there are very few sites where stone, bone, and wood all occur together. Only a very small part of the material culture of a Paleolithic group is available, therefore, as a basis of reconstruction of group behavior. However, when this is added to the complete or partial floor patterns, it amounts to considerably more data than were generally available ten years ago.

As a result of coordinating work in a number of different disciplines, it is now possible to reconstruct with some accuracy the paleo-environment of the occupation site and it is only once this has been determined that interpretation of the cultural data becomes at all meaningful.

Obviously, therefore, the living sites selected for investigation need to be very carefully chosen with the reasonably certain knowledge that much of the ecological data will be forthcoming and that the occupation areas are undisturbed and in primary context. Such a combination of prerequisites is not readily come by, and this indicates the necessity for systematic survey of likely regions in the main environments occupied by early man.

With the best possible conditions of preservation, therefore, the prehistorian starts with the same kind of evidence as is preserved on the settlement sites of present-day hunting and gathering groups after these have been abandoned for a sufficient length of time for the more perishable remains to have disappeared. However, if we can reconstruct the environment, we can then build models for the potential food and other resources, vegetable, animal, water, etc., available to the human population. Then, by applying the adaptive data from extant hunter-gatherer groups to the specific archeological occurrences, we can attempt a hypothetical estimate or estimates of behavior, group size and density.

So far as Upper Paleolithic and later sites are concerned, since they represent the living places of *Homo sapiens*, we are in a better position to interpret the behavior of the occupants. For the various "paleoanthropoid" populations, however, meaningful interpretation of the cultural data is dependent also upon a knowledge of the physical and intellectual capabilities of the makers, and these are but imperfectly known.

These are some of the disabilities under which the paleoanthropologist has to work.

For historic and late prehistoric sites, good results can be expected for interpreting social behavior if the excavated evidence can be directly related to oral tradition and to the behavior of an extant population. From this it may prove possible to establish for different habitats a consistency between archeological patterns and behavior. If such consistency exists, attempts will be made to project this back into the more distant past. The validity of such extrapolation for interpreting human behavior at the Paleolithic level will depend on a demonstration of significant consistency in distribution and association patterns. At the same time, there must be a related investigation into the various agencies responsible for the distribution and disappearance of campsite debris. Probably the best way to start is by studying the abandoned settlements of extant populations and observing what happens to these over set periods of years. In some regions such as South-West Africa, where the habitat is dry or semiarid, reasonably good results can be obtained since it has been my experience that in such areas stone is used for many more purposes connected with the construction of the camp and with hunting practices than is the case in tropical regions of higher rainfall where heavier timber is very often used to the exclusion of stone and where, in a few years, organic and inorganic agents will have removed practically every trace of the settlement. Generally, however, evidence of dwel-

ling floors, hearth stones, enclosure walling, pits, etc., is preserved and if, moreover, the population is still a stone-using one, much extremely valuable information must result since the existence of lithic material can provide a direct basis for comparison with the prehistoric settlement.

This emphasizes the urgent need for "ethno-archeological" studies of such extant "Stone Age" groups while they still exist. When studies of the Baines Mountains OvaTjimba groups in South-West Africa or of the Bindibu and other groups in Australia are completed, they should provide a wealth of new data which can be used as a basis for establishing a more precise reconstruction of behavior at prehistoric sites. There cannot be many such groups surviving, but there must still be several in Australia and South America, more than one in Africa and, perhaps, in the Arctic also. Studies of peoples who are known to have used stone until fairly recent times can also be expected to produce not a little data regarding techniques—for example, the method of manufacture of bone-matting needles and arrowheads by the MaKwango Bushmen, or the punch technique behind the gun-flint industry among the Chokwe and Lunda in northeastern Angola.

Where the group studied is no longer using stone, there is so much less permanent debris remaining on an abandoned site that it may be doubted how much direct use the settlement data are going to be to the prehistorian. Personally, I think the fact that most of the evidence disappears after a few years does not matter too greatly if we know the basis of the pattern while the site is in use and the agents and manner of dispersal of what remains after the site is abandoned. The sharply defined limits of the sleeping area, the spread and limits of hearths, of the waste resulting from special activities—the peeling of water lily bulbs, the cracking of *mongongo* nuts, the shaping of a digging stick or a bow stave, for example—will help to give an approximate indication of "spread" of debris which can be compared with the spread of factory waste and tools, hearths, sleeping areas, etc., on a prehistoric living site and with the dispersal of debris by natural agencies. It is most important to have controlled data from observation and experiment here.

There is a large number of questions to which the prehistorian hopes for an answer from such studies as those on the Kalahari Bushmen by Lee and DeVore, on the Hadza by Woodburn, or the Mbuti by Turnbull. Is there a correlation between habitat, the dimensions of the settlement, human activity and season? Can we, for example, distinguish dry-season from wet-season camps? On this basis can one compute the approximate size of the occupying group? What alteration to the habitat results from man's presence at the site over different periods of time? What is the rate of disappearance of perishable occupation debris in different ecosystems and is it possible to obtain any indication of age of an abandoned site from the differential weathering of bone or other materials? Does an abandoned occupation area consistently show an increase in phosphate and calcium content of the soil? If so, how long does this persist? To what extent is artifact and food debris trodden or otherwise carried down into the soil of the occupation area? If settlements are reoccupied, is there any discernable and, however slight, any vertical separation of the artifacts of later and earlier seasons? Is there any consistent pattern of weathering or absence of weathering of bone, ivory, or wood that is quickly buried or suffers long exposure? Is there a consistent pattern behind the different activity areas? Does each family or individual social unit work within the confines of its own habitation area, or are activity areas randomly or sometimes intentionally selected? For example, is bone waste regularly piled and are there regular butchery places? What is the rate of accumulation of debris that can be expected at such sites and what is the rate of dispersal by natural agents, man, and animals? What activities are associated with hearths (stone working, shaft straightening, cooking, sleeping, etc.) and what kind of disturbance or modification of the hearth results? Significant hearth pattern differences must exist as between the cold temperate and subarctic regions and the tropics, so that it is necessary to know these and also the rate of dispersal of charcoal on different kinds of settlement areas under specific conditions.

Some of these queries have been in part or in whole answered at this symposium, but whether it is practicable to obtain answers to others and similar questions will depend, I suggest and would particularly stress this, on the cooperation of ethnographer and archeologist working closely together in the field. It may be that many of these questions cannot be resolved, but until the attempt has been made we are not in a position to know one way or the other. In due course, it should be possible to combine the special knowledge of ethnographer and archeologist in a single individual, but I believe this needs to be tackled as a special training project that has yet to be formulated.

TECHNOLOGY

Much can also be learned regarding the technique of working different raw materials and the reasons behind the selection of some materials to the exclusion of others. Especially valuable are the data from groups still using stone tools. In these cases it is possible to know how many tools are made for a particular purpose, how many individuals cooperate in this, how many of the tools that are made are actually used, what the variation is in shape or form of a single class of tool, and what is the intensity of use. Are the tools left on the site or are they carried away? Are tools made in one year reused on reoccupation in another year? What are the methods of use of different tools —how are they held, what muscles are used, and where and when is the force applied? Are tools used for more than one purpose or in more than one way and, if so, is this a regular or an unusual practice?

Such inquiries inevitably lead on to a study of the wear patterns that result from use of the tools. Tools on prehistoric sites *in primary context* show fracture and damage that is the result of use. Although as yet it is only the more obvious damage that has received investigation, a great deal more is likely to be learned from systematic studies of edge damage —for example, it should be possible to isolate particular patterns of wear. Comparison of these with the wear patterns on stone tools, or even on iron or bone tools, in an ethnographic context and with the damage on specimens resulting from controlled experiment, should throw appreciably more light on the functional nature of Paleolithic tools. After the initial disastrous essays of the late nineteenth century, archeologists have rightly fought shy of functional interpretations, but the time is now ripe for new attempts to be made.

HISTORICAL SOURCES

There are many other matters having a more general bearing on the interpretation of the behavior of prehistoric hunting and gathering populations that the new "ethnoarcheological" studies may clarify. Besides those having to do with the relationship of the human group to the animal and vegetable resources of the habitat, both for food and utilitarian purposes, and the degree to which the human population is independent of the seasonal availability of these, it would be particularly valuable to know what are the changes that can be seen in the technology and the settlement pattern when a hunting and gathering group accepts domesticates, thus changing its economic basis, as some of the Botswana Bushman groups are doing today. What are the factors that bring about permanent settlement at the hunting and gathering level and what is the importance of freshwater and sea foods in this connection?

Most of the hunting and gathering groups existing today are living in some of the least favorable habitats and have for long been in contact with more complex societies and technologies. They can, therefore, no longer be considered "typical" or useful for any direct comparison with prehistoric populations of optimum and favorable, or even of the marginal, ecological zones; yet a knowledge of their technology and behavior is of general significance for an understanding of human behavior at this economic level. Moreover, it should still be possible to supplement the data obtained from direct field studies by searching the historical sources, if these are reexamined with the specific problems in mind that such studies are trying to answer. Much exists in the literature on Indian populations in the New World, and the same can be said also for Africa so far as the Bush, Hottentot, BaTwa, and Pygmy peoples are concerned.

Coordination of the results from fieldwork among hunters and gatherers undertaken by ethnographers and archeologists *working together*, and supplemented also from historical sources as well as from comparative study of edge-damage patterns on tools, should broaden considerably the *basis* for a more precise interpretation of the behavior of prehistoric societies as revealed by the excavation of selected living places. If and when a critical comparison of these results, with the archeological data from undisturbed living places establishes consistencies in patterning and grouping that are common to both, the framework for reconstruction will exist. The operation, as I see it, is twofold: first, to obtain this "ethnoarcheological" data by field work; second, to apply it to the archeological evidence with sufficient precision that a reasonable measure of accuracy in reconstruction is ensured.

31.

Discussions, Part VI

Speaker: *Deetz*

Deetz: This statement probably represents a viewpoint somewhat different from those of the other participants in this symposium, since I am neither a Paleolithic archeologist nor have I had field experience among living hunting peoples. I suppose there are few subjects within anthropology as far removed from the study of hunting and gathering peoples as European Colonial North America, the area in which my major research interests lie. Yet as an archeologist, I feel that there are certain things which I might profitably say that are germane to the subject simply because they are based on archeological and ethnological theory in general, as well as being concerned with hunters in particular. Many of the remarks which follow should be taken as attempts to tighten up our view of hunting peoples; they are not meant to be as critical as they might seem. In many instances the position taken is that of devil's advocate.

The topic of the symposium—Man the Hunter—suggests that there is a utility in the concept of hunting man as opposed to man involved in other activities. While I am certain that all of us use the idea of hunters and gatherers to signify a certain cultural level,

both in archeology and ethnology, I am equally certain that none of us would deny that grouping hunting peoples under one head creates some strange bedfellows. If hunting and gathering is taken to indicate the total absence of any type of productive economy, then we can include Kwakiutl, Asmat, Eskimo, Chumash, and even Arapaho under one heading; certainly these five examples exhibit a great variety of cultural types and share in few characteristics other than a common economic base. The grouping excludes the Wampanoag, who even fertilized their corn but whose social organization is similar to most northeastern hunting peoples; the Gê, who cultivate, but who are more than casually similar to the Australians in many aspects of their society; the Siriono, who are admittedly a refugee group and not exactly typical of anything; and most of the peoples of the Chaco, who cultivate, but place great emphasis on hunting and gathering, and share many aspects of social and ritual culture with those groups usually thought of as hunters.

Since hunting, even among those peoples who we normally think of as hunters, is perhaps of less importance than was earlier thought (see Lee's remarks, Chapter 4, this volume) it really becomes reduced to the status of a single occupational activity, such as gathering, pottery making, or house construction. It might then be equally profitable to consider Man the Gatherer or Man the Potter, and in the latter case, grouping those cultures which possess ceramics just possibly might produce sets with more culture traits in common. Of course, this is an over-literal interpretation of the title of the symposium, since hunting is taken as a convenient label to attach to a group of cultures which *do* share in many things, as can be seen from looking at the program and reading the titles of the various papers. However, I think if we reduce this to a semi-absurdity such as that above, a purpose is served in that we do not tend to let the label over describe the subject. The numerous suggestions for alternate terms for hunters, such as foragers, indicate this concern among many of us for a more descriptive category.

The symposium is divided into a number of sessions devoted to specific problems; I will comment on these from a perspective which is largely archeological, though not entirely so.

The Subsistence Base

Determination of the basis of subsistence from archeological material is perhaps the most satisfying of all of the aspects of society under consideration here. In this case, we can excavate the remains of food, as well as the tools used to obtain it, and make quite specific and quantitative statements about who was eating what, and when.

As a word of caution, however, it has occurred to me, as it probably has to many others, that there is a peculiar difference between the evidence of hunting and the evidence of gathering in terms of what is preserved. Bone and stone are the normal materials which survive from the Paleolithic. These materials also form the bulk of the evidence of game pursuit at that time; combined with the cave paintings of the Upper Paleolithic they give us a clear picture of hunting activities and technology.

If ethnographic example is in any way trustworthy, and in this case I think it is, the tools used in gathering, and the plant foods gathered, are quite perishable, and except for rare cases of carbonization or excellent preservation of organic substances, would not be present in midden deposits of the period. In view of recently gained understandings of the ratio

between hunting and gathering in the subsistence base of living hunters, might we be over-emphasizing the role of hunting during the Paleolithic? Perhaps not, but the caution voiced here may be in order. It can be argued that the cave paintings of the Upper Paleolithic show a great concern for animals, and suggest in some way a high interest in the hunt. But if I were faced with the choice between drawing a stag or a mammoth on the one hand, and a seed or a root on the other, I am certain what decision I would make—a subjective, ethnocentric remark to be sure, but perhaps relevant.

The Social Unit

Until lately, statements regarding the specific nature of prehistoric social units were almost impossible to formulate. There has been recent interest in social reconstruction which has resulted in our ability, or at least potential, to make such specific statements about certain aspects of prehistoric social organization in a way not available earlier. The symposium at the national meeting of the American Anthropological Association in Denver, which addressed itself to problems of social organization in the past, focused attention on these innovations in archeological method.

In a Paleolithic context, where the most pressing and important problems concerning the social organization of hunters probably exist, these new methods hold promise of developing models of the sort discussed by Lewis Binford to detail the structure of Paleolithic societies. The caution which I would suggest in this case is that of making certain that we have very precise chronological control before making too many statements about patterning in assemblages as it reflects social patterning in a synchronic way. As Roger Owen suggested to me in a conversation last fall, it would be most desirable to know that the assemblages which we were comparing were within 25 years of each other in time, since this period represents roughly one generation. If hunting populations were as fluid in the past in terms of membership and sharing of ideas, and the limits of such sharing, more than one generation could well introduce differences which might be seen as a function of synchronic variation but which are in reality a matter of chronological separation. Now I don't think we can ever get 25-year accuracy with regularity, if at all, in the Paleolithic, but we must be careful that we do not compare assemblages which might in fact be hundreds or thousands of years apart in time.

I heartily agree with Binford's emphasis on viewing prehistoric cultures as integrated systems, but such integration automatically assumes a large measure of contemporaneity. Perhaps there are already at our disposal means of determining that a single Paleolithic stratum, for example, represents a short interval of time, or at least that there is some depositional unit which can be seen in such a way. I honestly don't know, but from what we know about trash-deposition rates based on studies such as Lee's and DeVore's of the Bushmen, it takes time for material to accumulate. Of course, caves have a certain built-in "trash container" function which does not prevail in open-air situations.

In this connection, I would suggest that features, especially structures, with their associated artifacts are considerably more dependable in assuring the archeologist of contemporaneity than stratified middens. Deflation, for example, can combine separate midden deposits into a rather homogeneous whole. Structures, on the other hand, such as the spectacular houses at Kostienki and other south Russian Paleolithic sites (Klein, 1965a, 1965b), are behaviorial units with a set of contemporary objects within. Thus in inspecting the contents of a single structure, we can be fairly confident that the associated assemblage was all in use at one time, if not made at the same time.

In any case, all inferences drawn regarding social units in the Paleolithic which are based on comparing patterns from assemblage to assemblage must ultimately rest on the contemporary nature of these assemblages for their accuracy. I do not mean that such an approach is not advisable; quite to the contrary, this method promises exciting advances in the direction of sharpening our understanding of social organization in the Paleolithic. I am only concerned that we are as careful to control the dimension of time as we are in our control of form and space.

The problem addressed in a part of the Binfords' statements (Chapters 28 and 29), that of the validity of using ethnographic data to assist us in our reconstruction of earlier hunters' social units, is a genuine one, and they have made explicit some of the ramifications and possible pitfalls involved. I would like to call attention to another aspect of this same problem which might have implications that go beyond those involved in archeological reconstruction. Even if we were to agree that there was great value in using the Bushman, Eskimo, or Pygmy as typical hunters, and possible survivors from an earlier time, we must ask how typical these people actually are of the type of life which existed before the initial years of the Neolithic revolution. To put it another way, of the hunting peoples in existence today, which might be thought of as most typical of pre-Neolithic society?

I think that there is a possibility that the closest approach to Paleolithic social units which exist in the ethnographic present is to be seen in the Australians, the Gê, and to a somewhat lesser extent, aboriginal Californians. This rather strange selection is based on certain logical considerations. If we consider the hunting peoples of the world in the time immediately before widespread European influence (sixteenth through nineteenth centuries), there are three areas in the world which were almost absolutely immune from influence and pressure from cultures based on a productive economy —areas where hunters had lived for millenia in a stable relationship to their environment. These areas—California, eastern Brazil, and Australia—are the largest such continuous regions where the influence of the Neolithic or formative simply did not penetrate. I can not think of any other comparable area which has had such long isolation, with the possible exception of the Arctic. The Eskimos are a rather specialized case in many ways, however, and in any event, are relative newcomers to their area.

All other hunting peoples of which we have ethnographic knowledge were subject in some way or another to influences from developing Neolithic peoples from as early as the eighth millenium B.C. in many cases. The Bushmen, for example, were under the direct influence of other Africans prior to the arrival of

Europeans, and the marginal and encysted nature of the other enclaves of hunters around the world probably came into being prior to their contact with European culture. It is only in the three areas mentioned above that we can confidently postulate long-term undisturbed development of hunting peoples, free of any disruptions from without. The Californians were cut off by the Basin and deserts; their nearest farming neighbors were encysted themselves. The Gê seem to have been quite free from major influence from tropical forest farmers to the north; while manioc is cultivated by some of the Gê groups, the main cultivated crops include maize, beans, and squash, a very different complex from that found among their nearest neighbors. Furthermore, Gê mythology includes origin myths for these latter three plants, but none for manioc. The additional cultivation of *Cissus* by these people, unique in the world, points to their long isolation, and independent activity in matters pertaining to cultivation. The Australians of course, have been isolated since the end of the Pleistocene.

There are certain similarities seen in all three of these groups in the form of their social units which seem to be more than coincidental. Most striking is the existence and strong development of moiety organization in all three cases. The correspondence of this feature in Gê and Australian culture has often been commented on, and moiety development is marked among many California Indian groups. It is assumed that moieties serve the purpose of providing the individual with a clearly defined sense of social orientation wherever he might find himself over a broad geographic area. Thus in the case of thinly distributed populations, and small social groups, a person can immediately align himself with this or that social unit even when he enters a strange community for the first time. Moieties are also found in more complex cultures, but their function is somewhat different in these cases. But the only instances of strong development of moieties among hunting peoples that I have been able to discover are the Gê, Australian, and Californian cases.

Is this a coincidence? Could it be that these three large isolates have retained a form of social organization which was much more widely distributed before the Neolithic? Hunt-

ing populations living in the same environment for millenia might be expected to evolve such a structure, given a large amount of stability, with no outside influence, since it serves a valuable social integrative purpose among thinly distributed populations. All other hunting groups, having been more or less moved about and influenced by expanding Neolithic culture, might not have been able to retain such a complex structure. In one sense, such an organization is a spatial phenomenon and depends on a rather formal and fixed spatial relationship between the people and the environment. Should frequent movement become common, with some environmental change, such a delicate and complex institution might be expected to weaken and disappear.

If the Gê, Australians, and Californians are indeed more typical of pre-Neolithic social structures than those groups which we conventionally think of as hunters, with some form of "patrilocal band" organization, or some similar type, then we might consider shifting our concept of a modal hunting culture away from the Bushmen, Pygmy, and Eskimo and in the direction of these somewhat more complex societies. While Service suggests that the composite and family-band types defined by Steward are the result of pressures brought to bear by Europeans, perhaps the patrilocal band is also such a contact phenomenon, although the superior cultures would be different in this case. If this is so, most of the hunting peoples of the world are very little like those of the Paleolithic, and only a very few of them retain even a vestige of what may have been a very complex social form in the time before the Neolithic.

POPULATION RECONSTRUCTION

The determination of population density from archeological data is less precise than the reconstruction of at least a portion of prehistoric subsistence bases of early hunters, but is still a relatively productive and valuable approach to understanding these cultures. This is particularly so when one has available archeological information concerning houses, and some idea of household sizes within a community. In many ways, some of the most stimulating results, to me at least, of the recent work by Lee and DeVore among the Bushman are those which indicate just how many people are needed to create a recognizable archeological unit. In this case, it would seem to be more people than the average Bushman band contains.

I was talking to Richard Lee about the problem of "archeological visibility"—that is, how much activity is needed to produce a site which could be found a long time later. We decided that there might be a value in talking about some kind of a threshold value which would represent the amount and type of activity needed to produce a visible pattern on and ultimately in the ground. It seemed that two factors are involved at least. In the first place, a quite large community would make less of an imprint on the archeological record if it were more mobile than a smaller population which maintained occupancy of one location over a longer period, or reused it periodically. The second factor is absolute community size, and the two combine to create an archeological impression which is either above or below this threshold. The threshold would then represent that combination of community size and use of a given locus of sufficient intensity to yield a recognizable effect on the locus after final abandonment. The Bushmen seem well below this threshold, and many other hunters are probably below it as well. If in our studies of known hunters in the ethnographic present we were to consider how they relate to this threshold value, we might be able to come up with some statement of minimal "archeological visibility," which could then be used with advantage in our archeological interpretation. The Californians are certainly very visible, as are the Upper Paleolithic inhabitants of much of Europe. Less visible, except at their kill sites, are the pedestrian hunters of the Plains prior to the coming of the Europeans with their horses, or the Shoshonean peoples of the Great Basin. Presumably these groups are well above the threshold, and the Bushmen are below.

I am concerned about those peoples in the past who are *invisible* in this sense, and whether many modern hunters are more like them, or closer to those cultures who left their imprint on the landscape in a wide and deep way. If they are, then those cultures which have been "invisible" through time could well have been extremely similar to their modern counterparts, but aligning many modern hunters with archeologically visible groups is in part a potential error which could have serious effects. The often asked question, "Are the Bushmen typical of culture in the past?" would then be answered in the affirmative, but with the qualification that we cannot determine how these earlier cultures functioned from the archeological record, since they would be below the "visibility threshold." The Bushmen thus would be typical of some past cultures, but not those which we are able to excavate and study. If the above remarks concerning the Gê and similar cultures have any merit whatsoever, perhaps there are remnants of archeologically visible cultures with us today, but they are few in number.

There is yet another factor contributing to the degree of utility which any archeological configuration might possess for inferential purposes. This factor might be termed "sharpness" or focus; that is, how distinct is the pattern which is visible? A very visible assembly might not be too sharp in the patterning which it exhibits, while a much less *visible* unit might be very clear in its patterning. At least two factors would seem to affect the sharpness in focus of an assemblage.

Groups of the kind we have heard discussed at this session, characterized by very fluid, changing behavioral patterns, might be expected to produce more diffuse patterns in their assemblages than highly structured societies in theirs.

31b. ARCHEOLOGICAL VISIBILITY OF FOOD-GATHERERS

Speakers: *L. Binford, Clark, Deevey, Owen, Pilling, Sackett, Struever, Suttles, Washburn*

WASHBURN: I have two brief points on the matter of visibility in respect to the tremendous problems of reconstructing the vegetative components of an archeological site. I think it is frequently forgotten that animal bones found at a site often give us some rough notion about the plants on which the animals fed. The other point, one that Robert Heizer has made, is that the trace elements in the site are altered by the particular kinds of plants that grew there. It can be proved, for example, that there was corn at a certain site, even though there are no actual plant remains whatsoever. So I do not think that we should think of visibility in an archeological context simply in the usual sense of the word.

STRUEVER: There are other recovery techniques, such as flotation techniques, that archeologists do not yet use. By such techniques, one can recover a remarkable quantity of plant remains invisible to the eye, even though they are macroplant remains. These techniques could be used to extend the record a lot further.

PILLING: I might also stress the importance of minute fragments of charcoal, which normally allow species identification. Also, we have some pretty tricky ecological questions to settle for many grassland areas of the world. If a prehistoric culture participated in fire drives for game, I think this will have a significant effect on the floral remains. The remains may last until the present time in what we would interpret to be a fairly good representation of prehistoric floral remains, and yet not be an accurate representation of this at all.

CLARK: I would like to join the others in emphasizing the importance of studying vegetable foods in the prehistoric context. As Jim Deetz has said, archeologists have grossly underestimated their importance up to now, mainly because the data are not a part of the typed series of artifacts that they have analyzed—or, rather, they have felt that the data were not there. There are certain sites that clearly produce this evidence, such as waterlogged sites, which are well known in New Zealand and in Mesolithic and Paleolithic sites in Europe. At another such site, Kalambo Falls, we have actual seeds and nuts of about half a dozen species, which tell us (besides the fact that they were collected) the time of year at which the site was occupied. Also, there are certain short sticks, pointed at both ends; and I would be interested to know from ethnographers whether anything of this kind is used for digging up vegetable materials.

One of the main pieces of evidence that occur on these sites with shaped artifacts are rough blocks and chunks of stone. These must be looked at very carefully and compared with ethnographic evidence. James Woodburn collected a hammer used for breaking bones among the Hadza. Now this is a perfectly ordinary chunk which has nothing more revealing on it than a few bash marks and blunted edges. So I would like to know from ethnographers what, in addition to shaped tools, is used for breaking up and preparing vegetable foods.

Finally, something further to Dr. Pilling's remarks about minute pieces of charcoal: there is a danger in dealing with them. These occur in certain of the *mushitu*, relict forest patches in central Africa, and it was thought that they might well give an indication of the age of the original, unburned forest patches. But the evidence suggests that burrowing animals have almost certainly complicated the matter of interpretation. So one must be careful in dealing with microscopic particles.

DEEVEY: In view of the high probability that pebble tools of Paleolithic age were almost invariably used for chopping up plant food, and in view of the ease with which gas chromatography extracts microgram and millimicrogram quantities of hydrocarbons from meteorites, I would strongly recommend that archeologists stop washing and handling the pebble tools that they find.

SUTTLES: If I may return to that anomalous area, the Northwest coast, I might say that among the Salish the pattern for exploiting the habitat consisted in their going to favorite places at particular times of the year. For example, at the lowest tides in June people came from several villages to a favorite clam bed, dug clams in great quantities, steamed and dryed them, and took them back—leaving the shells behind. To the archeologist, this might look like long occupation by a small group or, perhaps, seasonal occupation by a much larger group than, in fact, was involved. To cite another example, a professional hunter might go into the hills, spend the summer hunting and process the kills at a campsite, taking the dried meat back and leaving the bones. An archeologist digging into such a site might not even recognize it as belonging to the same culture that had left the pile of shells on the beach.

BINFORD: This very thing has occurred. There are cases that could be documented for eastern North America, where "cultural units" have been defined for sites that actually represent either seasonal or task-specific occupation. I refer particularly to some of the sites along the Tennessee River. However, if one follows an operational procedure based on theoretical considerations of the type outlined by Freeman, one's first concern is to account for the observed variations within a region. This at least gives us a chance of seeing the shell heap and the isolated campsite as task-specific sites within a variable region, rather than as necessarily separate basic units. Hopefully, by anticipating such variability, we may be able to develop means of testing alternative hypotheses and coming out with an approximation of the adaptive system present in the region.

OWEN: I wonder whether someone would elaborate on the techniques that make it possible to tell whether a living floor was occupied for a short or a long period of time.

CLARK: This sort of thing is a problem for the geologists as well as for archeologists, but in any particular case it will be clear whether a horizon has been exposed for a long time or not. If it has been exposed for a long time there will be erosion, formation of soils, differential wearing of the artifacts, artifacts of different ages associated, natural accumulations of rubble, and other such signs.

SACKETT: You can also tell a great deal from maturation evidence in bones. For example, in the Upper Paleolithic of France you find reindeer teeth and antlers showing every stage of growth, and you know that you are dealing with year-round occupation. Likewise, bone material that indicates year-round occupation is usually found in association with strictly local raw materials; while evidence of periodicity in animal bones is often associated with exotic raw materials.

31C. THE USE OF
ETHNOGRAPHY IN
RECONSTRUCTING THE PAST

Speakers: *Clark, DeVore, Howell, Sharp, Turnbull*

HOWELL: I want to direct the attention of anthropologists concerned with existing hunter-gatherers to some of the situations and problems that confront the paleoanthropologist concerned with Quaternary hominids. Until this afternoon, there has been little said about cultural evolution beyond an occasional mention of how unsatisfactory are precontact cultural reconstructions for some of the groups discussed.

Paleoanthropologists seem to fall into two camps—I hesitate to say "bands" or "hordes": (1) those who feel that intensive study and deep understanding of the present may offer guidelines or even solutions to problematic situations of the distant past, and (2) those, less so inclined, who are ever hopeful that new methods, procedures, and formulations will be developed which might provide insights into the adaptation and behavior of hominid populations, often long extinct and biologically, at least in part, quite unlike ourselves. I stand among the latter, and I trust that after the discussions of the past few days, our numbers may increase markedly. To list a number of the points on which we have heard new and/or conflicting data here—all of them used more or less unquestioningly by some paleoanthropologists—I might mention: the importance to be assigned to scavenged meat; the extent and significance of game procurement among so-called "hunters"; the importance of vegetable food sources; the permeability of a well-delineated "territory"; the fluid size and semi-structured character of human groups; the frequency of bilaterality; the variability of and exceptions to fixed-cousin marriage rules; the frequent and perhaps universal lack of immediate environmental determinism of group size, spacing, or mobility; the diversity and significance of subcommunity units, whether dyads, subfactions, etc.; and the low degree of predator-determined mortality. The paleoanthropologist who is still set on reconstructing the past on the basis of existing hunter-gatherer evidence has, obviously, an unusually wide range of choices from which to draw analogies about social structure and human behavior. Therefore, I suggest that reconstruction efforts of this sort be discouraged or very severely curtailed except for very recent time periods.

In secondary sources and in many texts

relating to early man, there is a lot of generalization about stages in the Pleistocene. I think, however, that we may safely disregard *everything* that has been said about Pleistocene stages, because all the new evidence provides exceptions to the existing generalizations. Many sites show a great diversity in local ecological and regional settings. All that one can now say about the earlier range of Pleistocene times is that the sites are immensely diversified; there is no single pattern. They are not always related to water or to open areas. About all that we can say is that, so far as we know, there were no sites in specifically tropical evergreen forests, although some were very close to these areas.

Most of the sites have been characterized in terms of industries—Acheulian, Oldowan, and so on. These terms have generally originated from the *fossiles directeurs* concept mentioned by Sackett. We now have a lot of data for a long period of time to show the variety, diversity, and frequency of occurrence of tool kits or debris, or both in combination. It turns out that most of the *fossiles directeurs* for, say, the Acheulian or Oldowan are among the objects *least* frequently found in occurrences in which there is a scatter pattern. So in the very near future we shall have to revise our terminology completely.

Much has been written about early man in the Pleistocene as a hunter or hunter-gatherer. The more we learn about early occupation sites within the 500,000–2,000,000-year time range, the more diverse the "hunting" behavior appears to be. The early material in Bed I at Olduvai was originally said to represent the remains of small, slow-moving, and easily captured game; as more of the sites are exposed, this no longer appears to be the case. At Vertesszöllös it was also thought that the fauna associated with Oldowan-like artifacts was small, which is true of the south end of the site. But at the north end, they have recently found four new occurrences—all bears!

Isaac (Chapter 26, this volume) has talked a bit about the size of sites, and I might add a few more comments and examples. Some are very large. We have one in Spain, partially preserved, of over 4,000 square meters; and it continues, with interruption, into another area. The mystic figure of 25 persons, which has been correlated with a living space of about 250 square meters is easily derived from certain *abris* in the limestone valleys of southern France, but I know of many exceptions to these figures in southern Germany and Yugoslavia, where one finds just as many tools in a much smaller area—perhaps 10 square meters. Density of material varies, associations vary, the condition of artifacts varies, and there are problematic intrasite patterns that we are only now beginning to study.

From all this varied data we want to derive some ideas about man's activities in the distant past. I think we can do this. But it seems to me that generalizations about the entire Pleistocene or the earlier parts of it concerning hominid extractive efficiency, distribution, ecological adaptation, or group size are all highly premature. Now that we are getting a lot of data from field studies, we find that all of these things are tremendously variable. Perhaps in ten more years, with the analysis of this data, it will be possible to make some new observations and deductions that will be solidly founded, rather than analogically argued.

TURNBULL: I have noticed a great difference in the tone of the presentations by archeologists and those of the social anthropologists. The archeologists have shown a great awareness of the limitations of their data and the interpretations of it, while the rest of us have all spoken as though we knew what we were talking about. I think that both we and the archeologists should be aware of the limitations of our methods, our data, and our interpretations. As social anthropologists, we hear people make noises, and we can try to understand them, but how close do we really get to the concepts that they have in their minds? The intellectual problem of bringing our own personalities into the field, and the physical problem of keeping track of all the activities going on in a tribe of 2,000 people over the period of a year—all such things force us to recognize that our results are necessarily partial and tentative.

SHARP: I second what Colin Turnbull has said and suggest that the ethnologist might be of greater help to the archeologist if the ethnologist were more sophisticated in his knowledge of archeological problems. I would suggest a project in which archeologists might interview some of the ethnologists who have lived with hunter-gatherers, and specify the kinds of information that they could best use. I once wrote a paper on what would be found by the archeologist at a campsite abandoned by a North Australian group, presented copies of it to several archeologists, and then discovered that I simply had not answered the questions they were interested in. So I suggest that they come to us and tell us about the kinds of questions that need to be answered.

CLARK: I should like to differ from Dr. Sharp and say that I think it essential that the archeologist and the ethnographer work together. As things are now set up, it is quite impossible for one man to do both jobs. And, after all, we have been going to ethnographers for a number of years now to get information and we have not obtained it, because they have not been trained well enough in archeology to observe anything of particular interest to us. Indeed, up until a very few years ago, such comparative enterprises were not of interest to anyone.

DEVORE: For years, social anthropologists have been asked to be discussants at archeological symposia, and a few have had the temerity to try this. They sat in mild shock as they looked at slides of multi-colored sections, vast profusions of scatter patterns, and the like . . . and were then asked to comment! It is a pleasure occasionally to reverse the setting, to expose archeologists to the complexity of the ethnographic data. Now that archeologists are finding enough living floors to be able to describe the variation within local areas, it seems appropriate to recall that in social anthropology we have had this method of controlled comparison for some time. And I suspect that it may be at this level of generalization that we may achieve a greater *rapprochement* between the two disciplines.

Some years ago archeologists had to abandon the notion that any one person could encompass all the fields of expertise necessary to extract the information obtainable from a site. So bones, stones, soils, pollen, and charcoal are turned over to the people who are equipped to analyze them. In social anthropology the tradition has run counter to this trend. The stereotype of the ethnographer is still the lone man with "his" people. Yet it is now clear that we cannot possibly train our students to be competent zoologists and botanists, to collect and analyze blood samples, do demographic studies, linguistic analysis, to plot the living floors carefully and analyze the debris left by hunter-gatherers, and so on. It seems perfectly obvious that social anthropologists must also have specialists, if only because—leaving aside the important matter of training—there is not enough time for one man to do all these things in the field. I am not implying that it is possible for us to collect all the data that anyone at any future time will need, but I do share the feeling expressed by Professor Lévi-Strauss that research on hunter-gatherers is of the utmost urgency. And given this urgency, I see no excuse for our not collecting all the data that we *already* know or believe to be significant.

GOOD IDEA !!

PART VII

Hunting and Human Evolution

32.

The Evolution of Hunting

SHERWOOD L. WASHBURN AND C. S. LANCASTER

It is significant that the title of this symposium is Man the Hunter for, in contrast to carnivores, human hunting, if done by males, is based on a division of labor and is a social and technical adaptation quite different from that of other mammals.[1] Human hunting is made possible by tools, but it is far more than a technique or even a variety of techniques. It is a way of life, and the success of this adaptation (in its total social, technical, and psychological dimensions) has dominated the course of human evolution for hundreds of thousands of years. In a very real sense our intellect, interests, emotions, and basic social life—all are evolutionary products of the success of the hunting adaptation. When anthropologists speak of the unity of mankind, they are stating that the selection pressures of the hunting and gathering way of life were so similar and the result so successful that populations of *Homo sapiens* are still fundamentally the same everywhere. In this essay we are concerned with the general characteristics of man that we believe can be attributed to the hunting way of life.

Perhaps the importance of the hunting way of life in producing man is best shown by the length of time hunting has dominated human history. The genus *Homo*[2] has existed for some 600,000 years, and agriculture has been important only during the last few thousand years. Even 6,000 years ago large parts of the world's population were nonagricultural, and the entire evolution of man from the earliest populations of *Homo erectus* to the existing races took place during the period in which man was a hunter. The common factors that dominated human evolution and produced *Homo sapiens* were preagricultural. Agricultural ways of life have dominated less than 1 per cent of human history, and there is no evidence of major biological changes during that period of time. The kind of minor biological changes that occurred and which are used to characterize modern races were not common to *Homo sapiens*. The origin of all common characteristics must be sought in preagricultural times. Probably all experts would agree that hunting was a part of the social adaptation of all populations of the genus *Homo*, and many would regard *Australopithecus*[3] as a still earlier hominid who was already a hunter, although possibly much less efficient than the later forms. If this

1. This paper is part of a program on primate behavior, supported by the United States Public Health Service (Grant No. 8623) and aided by a Research Professorship in the Miller Institute for Basic Research in Science at the University of California at Berkeley. We wish to thank Dr. Phyllis C. Jay for her helpful criticism and suggestions about this paper.

2. The term *Homo* includes Java, Pekin, Mauer, etc., and later forms.

3. Using the term to include both the small *A. africanus* and large *A. robustus* forms. Simpson (1966) briefly and clearly discusses the taxonomy of these forms and of the fragments called *Homo habilis*.

is true and if the Pleistocene period had a duration of three million years, then pre-*Homo erectus* human tool using and hunting lasted for at least four times as long as the duration of the genus *Homo* (Lancaster, MS.). No matter how the earlier times may ultimately be interpreted, the observation of more hunting among apes than was previously suspected (Goodall, 1965) and increasing evidence for hunting by *Australopithecus* strengthens the position that less than 1 per cent of human history has been dominated by agriculture. It is for this reason that the consideration of hunting is so important for the understanding of human evolution.

When hunting and the way of life of successive populations of the genus *Homo* are considered, it is important to remember that there must have been both technical and biological progress during this vast period of time. Although the locomotor system appears to have changed very little in the last 500,000 years, the brain did increase in size and the form of the face changed. But for present purposes it is particularly necessary to direct attention to the cultural changes that occurred in the last ten or fifteen thousand years before agriculture. There is no convenient term for this period of time, traditionally spoken of as the end of the Upper Paleolithic and the Mesolithic, but Binford and Binford (1966a) have rightly emphasized its importance.

During most of human history, water must have been a major physical and psychological barrier and the inability to cope with water is shown in the archeological record by the absence of remains of fish, shellfish, or any object that required going deeply into water or using boats. There is no evidence that the resources of river and sea were utilized until this late preagricultural period, and since the consumption of shellfish in particular leaves huge middens, the negative evidence is impressive. It is likely that the basic problem in utilization of resources from sea or river was that man cannot swim naturally but to do so must learn a difficult skill. In monkeys the normal quadrupedal running motions serve to keep them afloat and moving quite rapidly. A macaque, for example, does not have to learn any new motor habit in order to swim. But the locomotor patterns of gibbons and apes will not keep them above the water surface, and even

a narrow, shallow stream is a barrier for the gorilla (Schaller, 1963). For early man, water was a barrier and a danger, not a resource. (Obviously water was important for drinking, for richer vegetation along rivers and lakeshores, and for concentrating animal life. Here we are referring to water as a barrier prior to swimming and boats, and we stress that, judging from the behavior of contemporary apes, even a small stream may be a major barrier.)

In addition to the conquest of water, there seems to have been great technical progress in this late preagricultural period. Along with a much wider variety of stone tools of earlier kinds, the archeological record shows bows and arrows, grinding stones, boats, houses of much more advanced types and even villages, sledges drawn by animals and used for transport, and the domestic dog. These facts have two special kinds of significance for this symposium. First, the technology of *all* the living hunters belongs to this late Mesolithic era at the earliest, and many have elements borrowed from agricultural and metal-using peoples. Second, the occasional high densities of hunters mentioned as problems and exceptions at the symposium are based on this very late and modified extension of the hunting and gathering way of life. For example, the way of life of the tribes of the Northwest Coast, with polished stone axes for woodworking, boats, and extensive reliance on products of the river and sea, should be seen as a very late adaptation. Goldschmidt's distinction (1959, pp. 185–93) between nomadic and sedentary hunting and gathering societies makes this point in a slightly different way. He shows the social elaboration which comes with the settled groups with larger populations.

The presence of the dog (Zeuner, 1963) is a good index of the late preagricultural period, and domestic dogs were used by hunters in Africa, Australia, and the Americas. Among the Eskimo, dogs were used in hunting, for transportation, as food in time of famine, and as watchdogs. With dogs, sleds, boats, metal, and complex technology, Eskimos may be a better example of the extremes to which human adaptation can go than an example of primitive hunting ways. Although hardly mentioned at the symposium, dogs were of great importance in hunting, for locating, tracking, bringing to bay, and even killing. Lee (1965, p. 131) reports that one Bushman with a trained pack of hunting dogs brought in 75 per cent of the meat of a camp. Six other resident hunters lacked hunting packs and accounted for only 25 per cent of the meat. Dogs may be important in hunting even very large animals; in the Amboseli Game Reserve in Kenya one of us saw two small dogs bring a rhinoceros to bay and dodge repeated charges.

With the acquisition of dogs, bows, and boats it is certain that hunting became much more complex in the last few thousand years before agriculture. The antiquity of traps, snares, and poisons is unknown, but it appears that for thousands of years man was able to kill large game close in with spear or axe. As Brues (1959) has shown, this limits the size of the hunters, and there are no very large or very small fossil men. Pygmoid hunters of large game are probably possible only if hunting is with bows, traps, and poison. It is remarkable that nearly all the estimated statures for fossil men fall between 5 feet 2 inches and 5 feet 10 inches. This suggests that strong selection pressures kept human stature within narrow limits for hundreds of thousands of years and that these pressures relaxed a few thousand years ago, allowing the evolution of a much wider range of statures.

Gathering and the preparation of food also seem to have become more complex during the last few thousand years before agriculture. Obviously gathering by nonhuman primates is limited to things that can be eaten immediately. In constrast, man gathers a wide range of items that he cannot digest without soaking, boiling, grinding, or other special preparation. Seeds may have been a particularly important addition to the human diet because they are abundant and can be stored easily. Since grinding stones appear before agriculture, grinding and boiling may have been the necessary preconditions to the discovery of agriculture. One can easily imagine that people who were grinding seeds would see repeated examples of seeds sprouting or being planted by accident. Grinding and boiling were certainly known to the preagricultural peoples, and this knowledge could spread along an Arctic route, setting the stage for a nearly simultaneous discovery of agriculture in both the New and Old Worlds.

It was not necessary for agriculture itself to spread through the Arctic but only the seed-using technology, which could then lead to the discovery of seed planting. If this analysis is at all correct, then the hunting-gathering adaptation of the Indians of California, for example, should be seen as representing the possibilities of this late preagricultural gathering, making possible much higher population densities than would have been the case in pregrinding and preboiling economy.

Whatever the fate of these speculations, we think that the main conclusion, based on the archeological record, ecological considerations, and the ethnology of the surviving hunter-gatherers, will be sustained. In the last few thousand years before agriculture, both hunting and gathering became much more complex. This final adaptation, including the use of products of river and sea and the grinding and cooking of otherwise inedible seeds and nuts, was worldwide, laid the basis for the discovery of agriculture, and was much more effective and diversified than the previously existing hunting and gathering adaptations.

Hunting by members of the genus *Homo* throughout the 600,000 years that the genus has persisted has included the killing of large numbers of big animals. This implies the efficient use of tools, as Birdsell stressed at the symposium. The adaptive value of hunting large animals has been shown by Bourlière (1963), who demonstrated that 75 per cent of the meat available to human hunters in the eastern Congo was in elephant, buffalo, and hippopotamus. It is some measure of the success of human hunting that when these large species are protected in game reserves (as in the Murchison Falls or Queen Elizabeth Parks in Uganda), they multiply rapidly and destroy the vegetation. Elephants alone can destroy trees more rapidly than they are replaced naturally, as they do in the Masai Amboseli Reserve in Kenya. Since the predators are also protected in reserves, it appears that human hunters have been killing enough large game to maintain the balance of nature for many thousands of years. It is tempting to think that man replaced the saber-toothed tiger as the major predator of large game, both controlling the numbers of the game and causing the extinction of Old World saber-tooths. We think that hunting and butchering large animals put a maximum premium on cooperation among males, a behavior that is at an absolute minimum among the nonhuman primates. It is difficult to imagine the killing of creatures such as cave bears, mastodons, mammoths—or *Dinotherium* at a much earlier time—without highly coordinated, cooperative action among males. It may be that the origin of male-male associations lies in the necessities of cooperation in hunting, butchering, and war. Certainly butchering sites, such as described by F. Clark Howell in Spain, imply that the organization of the community for hunting large animals goes back for many, many thousands of years. From the biological point of view, the development of such organizations would have been paralleled by selection for an ability to plan and cooperate (or reduction of rage). Because females and juveniles may be involved in hunting small creatures, the social organization of big-game hunting would also lead to an intensification of a sexual division of labor.

It is important to stress, as noted before, that human hunting is a set of ways of life. It involves divisions of labor between male and female, sharing according to custom, cooperation among males, planning, knowledge of many species and large areas, and technical skill. Goldschmidt (1966, p. 87 ff.) has stressed the uniqueness and importance of human sharing, both in the family and in the wider society, and Lee (personal communication) emphasizes orderly sharing as fundamental to human hunting society. The importance of seeing human hunting as a whole social pattern is well illustrated by the old idea, recently revived, that the way of life of our ancestors was similar to that of wolves rather than that of apes or monkeys. But this completely misses the special nature of the human adaptation. Human females do not go out and hunt and then regurgitate to their young when they return. Human young do not stay in dens but are carried by mothers. Male wolves do not kill with tools, butcher, and share with females who have been gathering. In an evolutionary sense the whole human pattern is new, and it is the success of this particularly human way that dominated human evolution and determined the relation of biology and culture for thousands of years. Judging from the archeo-

logical record, it is probable that the major features of this human way, possibly even including the beginnings of language, had evolved by the time of *Homo erectus*.[4]

THE WORLD VIEW OF THE HUNTER

Lévi-Strauss urged that we study the world view of hunters, and, perhaps surprisingly, some of the major aspects of world view can be traced from the archeological record. We have already mentioned that boats and the entire complex of fishing, hunting sea mammals, and using shellfish was late. With this new orientation, wide rivers and seas changed from barriers to pathways and sources of food, and the human attitude toward water must have changed completely. But many hundreds of thousands of years earlier, perhaps with *Australopithecus*, the relation of the hunters to the land must also have changed from an earlier relationship which may be inferred from studies of contemporary monkeys and apes. Social groups of nonhuman primates occupy exceedingly small areas, and the vast majority

4. In speculations of this kind, it is well to keep the purpose of the speculation and the limitation of the evidence in mind. Our aim is to understand human evolution. What shaped the course of human evolution was a succession of successful adaptations, both biological and cultural. These may be inferred in part from the direct evidence of the archeological record. But the record is very incomplete. For example, Lee (personal communication) has described, for the Bushmen, how large game may be butchered where it falls and only meat brought back to camp. This kind of behavior means that analysis of bones around living sites is likely to underestimate both the amount and variety of game killed. If there is any evidence that large animals were killed, it is probable that far more were killed than the record shows. Just as the number of human bones gives no indication of the number of human beings, the number of animal bones, although it provides clues to the existence of hunting, gives no direct evidence of how many animals were killed. The Pleistocene way of life can only be known by inference and speculation. Obviously, speculations are based on much surer ground when the last few thousand years are under consideration. Ethnographic information is then directly relevant and the culture bearers are of our own species. As we go farther back in time, there is less evidence and the biological and cultural difference becomes progressively greater. Yet it was in those remote times that the human way took shape, and it is only through speculation that we may gain some insights into what the life of our ancestors may have been.

of animals probably spend their entire lives within less than four or five square miles. Even though they have excellent vision and can see for many miles, especially from tops of trees, they make no effort to explore more than a tiny fraction of the area they see. Even for gorillas the range is only about fifteen square miles (Schaller, 1963), and it is of the same order of magnitude for savanna baboons (DeVore and Hall, 1965). When Hall tried to drive a troop of baboons beyond the end of their range, they refused to be driven and doubled back into familiar territory, although they were easy to drive within the range. The known area is a psychological reality, clear in the minds of the animals. Only a small part of even this limited range is used, and exploration is confined to the canopy, lower branches, and bushes, or ground, depending on the biology of the particular species. Napier (1962) has discussed this highly differential use of a single area by several species. In marked contrast, human hunters are familiar with very large areas. In the area studied by Lee (1965), eleven waterholes and 600 square miles supported 248 Bushmen, a figure less than the number of baboons supported by a single waterhole and a few square miles in the Amboseli Reserve in Kenya. The most minor hunting expedition covers an area larger than most nonhuman primates would cover in a lifetime. Interest in a large area is human. The small ranges of monkeys and apes restrict the opportunities for gathering, hunting, and meeting conspecifics, and limit the kind of predation and the number of diseases. In the wide area, hunters and gatherers can take advantage of seasonal foods, and only man among the primates can migrate long distances seasonally. In the small area, the population must be carried throughout the year on local resources, and natural selection favors biology and behavior that efficiently utilize these limited opportunities. But in the wide area, natural selection favors the knowledge that enables a group to utilize seasonal and occasional food sources. Gathering over a wide and diversified area implies a greater knowledge of flora and fauna, knowledge of the annual cycle, and a different attitude toward group movements. Clearly one of the great advantages of slow maturation is that learning

covers a series of years, and the meaning of events in these years become a part of the individual's knowledge. With rapid maturation and no language, the chances that any member of the group will know the appropriate behavior for rare events is greatly reduced.

Moving over long distances creates problems of carrying food and water. Lee (1965, p. 124) has pointed out that the sharing of food even in one locality implies that food is carried, and there is no use in gathering quantities of fruit or nuts unless they can be moved. If women are to gather while men hunt, the results of the labors of both sexes must be carried back to some agreed upon location. Meat can be carried away easily, but the development of some sort of receptacles for carrying vegetable products may have been one of the most fundamental advances in human evolution. Without a means of carrying, the advantages of a large area are greatly reduced, and sharing implies that a person carries much more than one can use. However that may be, the whole human pattern of gathering and hunting to share— indeed, the whole complex of economic reciprocity that dominates so much of human life —is unique to man. In its small range, a monkey gathers only what it itself needs to eat at that moment. Wherever archeological evidence can suggest the beginnings of movement over large ranges, cooperation, and sharing, it is dating the origin of some of the most fundamental aspects of human behavior—the human world view. We believe that hunting large animals may demand all these aspects of human behavior which separate man so sharply from the other primates. If this is so, then the human way appears to be as old as *Homo erectus*.

The price that man pays for his high mobility is well illustrated by the problems of living in the African savanna. Man is not adapted to this environment in the same sense that baboons or vervet monkeys are. Man needs much more water, and without preparation and cooking he can only eat a limited number of the foods on which the local primates thrive. Unless there have been major physiological changes, the diet of our ancestors must have been far more like that of chimpanzees than like that of a savanna-adapted species. Further, man cannot survive the diseases of the African savanna without lying down and being cared for. Even when sick, the locally adapted animals are usually able to keep moving with their troop; and the importance to their survival of a home base has been stressed elsewhere (DeVore and Washburn, 1963). Also man becomes liable to new diseases and parasites by eating meat, and it is of interest that the products of the sea, which we believe were the last class of foods added to human diet, are widely regarded as indigestible and carry diseases to which man is particularly susceptible. Although many humans die of disease and injury, those who do not, almost without exception, owe their lives to others who cared for them when they were unable to hunt or gather, and this uniquely human caring is one of the patterns that builds social bonds in the group and permits the species to occupy almost every environment in the world.

A large territory not only provides a much wider range of possible foods but also a greater variety of potentially useful materials. With tool use this variety takes on meaning, and even the earliest pebble tools show selection in size, form, and material. When wood ceases to be just something to climb on, hardness, texture, and form become important. Availability of materials is critical to the tool user, and early men must have had a very different interest in their environment from that of monkeys or apes. Thus, the presence of tools in the archeological record is not only an indication of technical progress but also an index of interest in inanimate objects and in a much larger part of the environment than is the case with non-human primates.

The tools of the hunters include the earliest beautiful manmade objects, the symmetrical bifaces, especially those of the Acheulian tradition. Just how they were used is still a matter of debate, but, as contemporary attempts to copy them show, their manufacture is technically difficult, taking much time and practice and a high degree of skill. The symmetry of these tools may indicate that they were swung with great speed and force, presumably attached to some sort of handle. A tool that is moved slowly does not have to be symmetrical, but balance becomes important when an object is swung rapidly or thrown with speed. Irregularities will lead to deviations in the course of the blow or the trajectory of flight.

An axe or spear to be used with speed and power is subject to very different technical limitations from those of scrapers or digging sticks, and it may well be that it was the attempt to produce efficient high-speed weapons that first produced beautiful, symmetrical objects.

When the selective advantage of a finely worked point over an irregular one is considered, it must be remembered that a small difference might give a very large advantage. A population in which hunters hit the game 5 per cent more frequently, more accurately, or at greater distance would bring back much more meat. There must have been strong selection for greater skill in manufacture and use, and it is no accident that the bones of small-brained men (*Australopithecus*) are never found with beautiful, symmetrical tools. If the brains of contemporary apes and men are compared, the areas associated with manual skills (both in cerebellum and cortex) are at least three times as large in man. Clearly, the success of tools has exerted a great influence on the evolution of the brain, and has created the skills that make art possible. The evolution of the capacity to appreciate the product must evolve along with the skills of manufacture and use, and the biological capacities that the individual inherits must be developed in play and practiced in games. In this way, the beautiful, symmetrical tool becomes a symbol of a level of human intellectual achievement, representing far more than just the tool itself.

In a small group like the hunting band, which is devoted to one or two major cooperative activities, the necessity for long practice in developing skills to a very high level restricts the number of useful arts, and social organization is relatively simple. Where there is little division of labor, all men learn the same activities, such as skill in the hunt or in war. In sports (like the decathlon) we take it for granted that no one individual can achieve record levels of performance in more than a limited set of skills. This kind of limitation is partially biological but it is also a matter of culture. In warfare, for example, a wide variety of weapons is useful only if there are enough men to permit a division of labor so that different groups can practice different skills. Handedness, a feature that separates man from ape, is a part of this biology of skill. To be ambidextrous might seem to be ideal, but in fact the highest level of skill is attained by concentrating both biological ability and practice primarily on one hand. The evolution of handedness reflects the importance of skill, rather than mere use.

Hunting changed man's relations to other animals and his view of what is natural. The human notion that it is normal for animals to flee, the whole concept of animals being wild, is the result of man's habit of hunting. In game reserves many different kinds of animals soon learn not to fear man, and they no longer flee. James Woodburn took a Hadza into the Nairobi Park, and the Hadza was amazed and excited, because although he had hunted all his life, he had never seen such a quantity and variety of animals close at hand. His previous view of animals was the result of his having been their enemy, and they had reacted to him as the most destructive carnivore. In the park the Hadza hunter saw for the first time the peace of the herbivorous world. Prior to hunting, the relations of our ancestors to other animals must have been very much like those of the other noncarnivores. They could have moved close among the other species, fed beside them, and shared the same waterholes. But with the origin of human hunting, the peaceful relationship was destroyed, and for at least half a million years man has been the enemy of even the largest mammals. In this way the whole human view of what is normal and natural in the relation of man to animals is a product of hunting, and the world of flight and fear is the result of the efficiency of the hunters.

Behind this human view that the flight of animals from man is natural lie some aspects of human psychology. Men enjoy hunting and killing, and these activities are continued as sports even when they are no longer economically necessary. If a behavior is important to the survival of a species (as hunting was for man throughout most of human history), then it must be both easily learned and pleasurable (Hamburg, 1963). Part of the motivation for hunting is the immediate pleasure it gives the hunter, and the human killer can no more afford to be sorry for the game than a cat can for its intended victim. Evolution builds a relation between biology, psychology, and behavior, and, therefore, the evolutionary success of hunting exerted a profound effect on human psychology. Perhaps, this is most easily shown by the extent of the efforts devoted to maintain killing as a sport. In former times royalty and nobility maintained parks where they could enjoy the sport of killing, and today the United States government spends many millions of dollars to supply game for hunters. Many people dislike the notion that man is naturally aggressive and that he naturally enjoys the destruction of other creatures. Yet we all know people who use the lightest fishing tackle to prolong the fish's futile struggle, in order to maximize the personal sense of mastery and skill. And until recently war was viewed in much the same way as hunting. Other human beings were simply the most dangerous game. War has been far too important in human history for it to be other than pleasurable for the males involved. It is only recently, with the entire change in the nature and conditions of war, that this institution has been challenged, that the wisdom of war as a normal part of national policy or as an approved road to personal social glory has been questioned.

Human killing differs from killing by carnivorous mammals in that the victims are frequently of the same species as the killer. In carnivores there are submission gestures or sounds that normally stop a fatal attack (Lorenz, 1966). But in man there are no effective submission gestures. It was the Roman emperor who might raise his thumb; the victim could make no sound or gesture that might restrain the victor or move the crowd to pity. The lack of biological controls over killing conspecifics is a character of human killing that separates this behavior sharply from that of other carnivorous mammals. This difference may be interpreted in a variety of ways. It may be that human hunting is so recent from an evolutionary point of view that there was not enough time for controls to evolve. Or it may be that killing other humans was a part of the adaptation from the beginning, and our sharp separation of war from hunting is due to the recent development of these institutions. Or it may be simply that in most human behavior stimulus and response are not tightly bound. Whatever the origin of this behavior, it has had profound effects on human evolution, and almost every human society has regarded killing members of certain other human societies as desirable (D. Freeman, 1964). Certainly this has been a major factor in man's view of the world, and every folklore contains tales of culture heroes whose fame is based on the human enemies they destroyed.

The extent to which the biological bases for killing have been incorporated into human psychology may be measured by the ease with which boys can be interested in hunting, fishing, fighting, and games of war. It is not that these behaviors are inevitable, but they are easily learned, satisfying, and have been socially rewarded in most cultures. The skills for killing and the pleasures of killing are normally developed in play, and the patterns of play prepare the children for their adult roles. At the conference Woodburn's excellent motion pictures showed Hadza boys killing small mammals, and Laughlin described how Aleuts train boys from early childhood so that they would be able to throw harpoons with accuracy and power while seated in kayaks. The whole youth of the hunter is dominated by practice and appreciation of the skills of the adult males, and the pleasure of the games motivates the practice that is necessary to develop the skills of weaponry. Even in monkeys, rougher play and play fighting are largely the activities of the males, and the young females explore less and show a greater interest in infants at an early age. These basic biological differences are reinforced in man by a division of labor which makes adult sex roles differ far more in humans than they do in nonhuman primates. Again, hunting must be seen as a whole pattern of activities, a wide variety of ways of life, the psychobiological roots of which are reinforced by play and by a clear identification with adult roles. Hunting is more than a part of the economic system, and the animal bones in Choukoutien are evidence of the patterns of play and pleasure of our ancestors.

THE SOCIAL ORGANIZATION OF HUMAN HUNTING

The success of the human hunting and gathering way of life lay in its adaptability. It permitted a single species to occupy most of the earth with a minimum of biological adaptation to local conditions. The occupation of Australia and the New World was probably late, but even so there is no evidence that any other primate species occupied more than a fraction of the area of *Homo erectus*. Obviously, this adaptability makes any detailed reconstruction impossible, and we are not looking for stages in the traditional evolutionary sense. However, using both the knowledge of the contemporary primates and the archeological record, certain important general conditions of our evolution may be reconstructed. For example, the extent of the distribution of the species noted above is remarkable and gives the strongest sort of indirect evidence for the adaptability of the way of life, even half a million years ago. Likewise all evidence suggests that the local group was small. Twenty to fifty individuals is suggested by Goldschmidt (1959, p. 187). Such a group size is common in nonhuman primates and so we can say with some assurance that the number did not increase greatly until after agriculture. This means that the number of adult males who might cooperate in hunting or war was very limited, and this sets limits to the kinds of social organizations that were possible. Probably one of the great adaptive advantages of language was that it permits the planning of cooperation between local groups, temporary division of groups, and the transmission of information over a much wider area than that occupied by any one group.

Within the group of the nonhuman primates, the mother and her young may form a subgroup that continues even after the young are fully grown (Sade, 1965, 1966; Yamada, 1963). This grouping affects dominance, grooming, and resting patterns, and, along with dominance, is one of the factors giving order to the social relations in the group. The group is not a horde in the nineteenth-century sense, but it is ordered by positive affectionate habits and by the strength of personal dominance. Both these principles continue into human society, and dominance based on personal achievement must have been particularly powerful in small groups living physically dangerous lives. The mother-young group certainly continued and the bonds must have been intensified by the prolongation of infancy.

But in human society, economic reciprocity is added, and this created a wholly new set of interpersonal bonds.

When males hunt and females gather, the results are shared and given to the young, and the habitual sharing between a male, a female, and their offspring becomes the basis for the human family. According to this view, the human family is the result of the reciprocity of hunting, the addition of a male to the mother-plus-young social group of the monkeys and apes.

A clue to the adaptive advantage and evolutionary origin of our psychological taboo on incest is provided by this view of the family. Incest prohibitions are reported universally among humans and these always operate to limit sexual activity involving subadults within the nuclear family. Taking the nuclear family as the unit of account, incest prohibitions tend to keep the birth rate in line with economic productivity. If in creating what we call the family the addition of a male is important in economic terms, then the male who is added must be able to fulfill the role of a socially responsible provider. In the case of the hunter, this necessitates a degree of skill in hunting and a social maturity that is attained some years after puberty. As a young man grows up, this necessary delay in his assumption of the role of provider for a female and her young is paralleled by a taboo which prevents him from prematurely adding unsupported members to the family. Brother-sister mating could result in an infant while the brother was still years away from effective social maturity. Father-daughter incest could also produce a baby without adding a productive male to the family. This would be quite different from the taking of a second wife which, if permitted, occurs only when the male has shown he is already able to provide for and maintain more than one female.

To see how radically hunting changed the economic situation, it is necessary to remember that in monkeys and apes an individual simply eats what it needs. After an infant is weaned, it is on its own economically and is not dependent on adults. This means that adult males never have economic responsibility for any other animal, and adult females do only when they are nursing. In such a system, there is no economic gain in delaying any kind of social relationship. But when hunting makes females and young dependent on the success of male skills, there is a great gain to the family members in establishing behaviors which prevent the addition of infants, unless these can be supported.

These considerations in no way alter the importance of the incest taboo as a deterrent to role conflict in the family and as the necessary precondition to all other rules of exogamy. A set of behaviors is more likely to persist and be widespread, if it serves many uses, and the rule of parsimony is completely wrong when applied to the explanation of social situations. However, these considerations do alter the emphasis and the conditions of the discussion of incest. In the first place, a mother-son sexual avoidance may be present in some species of monkeys (Sade, 1966) and this extremely strong taboo among humans requires a different explanation than the one we have offered for brother-sister and father-daughter incest prohibitions. In this case, the role conflict argument may be paramount. Second, the central consideration is that incest produces pregnancies, and the most fundamental adaptive value of the taboo is the provision of situations in which infants are more likely to survive. In the reviews of the incest taboo by Aberle and others (1963) and Mair (1965), the biological advantages of the taboo in controlling the production of infants are not adequately considered, and we find the treatment by Service (1962) closest to our own. In a society in which the majority of males die young, but a few live on past forty, the probability of incest is increased. By stressing the average length of life rather than the age of the surviving few, Slater (1959) underestimated the probability of mating between close relatives. Vallois (1961, p. 222) has summarized the evidence on length of life in early man and shows that "few individuals passed forty years, and it is only quite exceptionally that any passed fifty."

That family organization may be attributed to the hunting way of life is supported by ethnography. Since the same economic and social problems as those under hunting continue under agriculture, the institution continued. The data on the behavior of contemporary monkeys and apes also show why this institution was not necessary in a society in which each individual gets its own food.[5] Obviously the origin of the custom cannot be dated, and we cannot prove *Homo erectus* had a family organized in the human way. But it can be shown that the conditions that make the family adaptive existed at the time of *Homo erectus*. The evidence of hunting is clear in the archeological record. A further suggestion that the human kind of family is old comes from physiology; the loss of estrus is essential to the human family organization, and it is unlikely that this physiology, which is universal in contemporary mankind, evolved recently.

If the local group is looked upon as a source of male-female pairs (an experienced hunter-provider and a female who gathers and who cares for the young), then it is apparent that a small group cannot produce pairs regularly, since chance determines whether a particular child is a male or female. If the number maturing in a given year or two is small, then there may be too many males or females (either males with no mates or females with no providers). The problem of excess females may not seem serious today or in agricultural societies, but among hunters it was recognized and was regarded as so severe that female infanticide was often practiced. How grave the problem of imbalance can become is shown by the following hypothetical example. In a society of approximately forty individuals there might be nine couples. With infants born at the rate of about one in three years, this would give three infants per year, but only approximately one of these three would survive to become fully adult. The net production in the example would be one child per year in a population of

forty. And because the sex of the child is randomly determined, the odds that all the children would be male for a three-year period are 1 in 8. Likewise the odds for all surviving children being female for a three-year period are 1 in 8. In this example the chances of all surviving children being of one sex are 1 in 4, and smaller departures from a 50/50 sex ratio would be very common.

In monkeys, because the economic unit is the individual (not a pair), a surplus of females causes no problem. Surplus males may increase fighting in the group or males may migrate to other groups.

For humans, the problem of imbalance in sex ratios may be met by exogamy, which permits mates to be obtained from a much wider social field. The orderly pairing of hunter males with females requires a much larger group than can be supported locally by hunting and gathering, and this problem is solved by reciprocal relations among several local groups. It takes something on the order of 100 pairs to produce enough children so that the sex ratio is near enough to 50/50 for social life to proceed smoothly, and this requires a population of approximately 500 people. With smaller numbers there will be constant random fluctuations in the sex ratio large enough to cause social problems. This argument shows the importance of a sizable linguistic community, one large enough to cover an area in which many people may find suitable mates and make alliances of many kinds. It does not mean either that the large community or that exogamy does not have many other functions, as outlined by Mair (1965). As indicated earlier, the more factors that favor a custom, the more likely it is to be geographically widespread and long lasting. What the argument does stress is that the finding of mates and the production of babies under the particular conditions of human hunting and gathering favor both incest taboo and exogamy for basic demographic reasons.

Assumptions behind this argument are that social customs are adaptive, as Tax (1937) has argued, and that nothing is more crucial for evolutionary success than the orderly production of the number of infants that can be supported. This argument also presumes that, at least under extreme conditions, these necessities

5. The advantage of considering both the social group and the facilitating biology is shown by considering the "family" in the gibbon. The social group consists of an adult male, an adult female, and their young. But this group is maintained by extreme territorial behavior in which no adult male tolerates another, by aggressive females with large canine teeth, and by very low sex drive in the males. The male-female group is the whole society (Carpenter 1941; Ellefson, 1966). The gibbon group is based on a different biology from that of the human family and has none of its reciprocal economic functions. Although the kind of social life seen in chimpanzees lacks a family organization, to change it into that of a man would require far less evolution than would be required in the case of the gibbon.

and reasons are obvious to the people involved, as infanticide attests. The impossibility of finding suitable mates must have been a common experience for hunters trying to exist in very small groups, and the initial advantages of exogamy, kinship, and alliance with other such groups may at first have amounted to no more than, as Whiting said at the conference, a mother suggesting to her son that he might find a suitable mate in the group where her brother was located.

If customs are adaptive and if humans are necessarily opportunistic, it might be expected that social rules would be particularly labile under the conditions of small hunting and gathering societies. At the conference, Murdock (Chapter 1, this volume) pointed out the high frequency of bilateral kinship systems among hunters, and the experts on Australia all seemed to believe that the Australian systems had been described in much too static terms. Under hunting conditions, systems that allow for exceptions and local adaptation make sense and surely political dominance and status must have been largely achieved.

Conclusion

While stressing the success of the hunting and gathering way of life with its great diversity of local forms and while emphasizing the way it influenced human evolution, we must also take into account its limitations. There is no indication that this way of life could support large communities of more than a few million people in the whole world. To call the hunters "affluent" (Sahlins, Chapter 9b, this volume) is to give a very special definition to the word. During much of the year, many monkeys can obtain enough food in only three or four hours of gathering each day, and under normal conditions baboons have plenty of time to build the Taj Mahal. The restriction on population, however, is the lean season or the atypical year, and, as Sahlins recognized, building by the hunters and the accumulation of gains was limited by motivation and technical knowledge, not by time. Where monkeys are fed, population rises, and Koford (1966) estimates the rate of increase on an island at 16 per cent per year.

After agriculture, human populations increased dramatically in spite of disease, war, and slowly changing customs. Even with fully human (*Homo sapiens*) biology, language, technical sophistication, cooperation, art, the support of kinship, the control of custom and political power, and the solace of religion—in spite of this whole web of culture and biology—the local group in the Mesolithic was no larger than that of baboons. Regardless of statements made at the symposium on the ease with which hunters obtain food some of the time, it is still true that food was the primary factor in limiting early human populations, as is shown by the events subsequent to agriculture.

The agricultural revolution, continuing into the industrial and scientific revolutions, is now freeing man from the conditions and restraints of 99 per cent of his history, but the biology of our species was created in that long gathering and hunting period. To assert the biological unity of mankind is to affirm the importance of the hunting way of life. It is to claim that, however much conditions and customs may have varied locally, the main selection pressures that forged the species were the same. The biology, psychology, and customs that separate us from the apes—all these we owe to the hunters of time past. And, although the record is incomplete and speculation looms larger than fact, for those who would understand the origin and nature of human behavior there is no choice but to try to understand "Man the Hunter."

33.

Hunting:

An Integrating Biobehavior System
and Its Evolutionary Importance

WILLIAM S. LAUGHLIN

INTRODUCTION

Hunting is the master behavior pattern of the human species. It is the organizing activity which integrated the morphological, physiological, genetic, and intellectual aspects of the individual human organisms and of the population who compose our single species. Hunting is a way of life, not simply a "subsistence technique," which importantly involves commitments, correlates, and consequences spanning the entire biobehavioral continuum of the individual and of the entire species of which he is a member.

That man achieved a worldwide distribution while still a hunter reflects the enormous universality of this kind of behavioral adaptation. The corollary fact that he practiced hunting for 99 per cent of his history indicates the significance of two neglected aspects: (1) hunting is a much more complex organization of behavior than is currently admitted under the traditional "subsistence technique" categorization, and (2) the intellectual and genetic repertoire of the animal developed in this behavioral regime both permitted and enabled the recent acquisition of civilization to be a rapid acquisition and to be developed independently by hunting peoples in different parts of the world.

The total biobehavioral configuration of hunting includes the ethological training of children to be skilled observers of animal behavior, including other humans. The process itself includes five distinguishable components whose combinations and permutations are certainly varied, but with recurrent and widely distributed commonalities.

Hunting is an active process which puts motion and direction into the diagram of man's morphology, technology, social organization, and ecological relations. Hunting involves goals and motivations for which intricate inhibition systems have been developed. Hunting has placed a premium upon inventiveness, upon problem solving, and has imposed a real penalty for failure to solve the problem. Therefore it has contributed as much to advancing the human species as to holding it together within the confines of a single variable species. A study of hunting removes the tedious ambiguity contained in many current discussions of the importance of tools, whether tool use means that tools use humans or that humans use tools.

304

HUNTING AS
AN INTEGRATING
SEQUENCE BEHAVIOR PATTERN

Hunting may profitably be analyzed as a sequence pattern of behavioral complexes. This analysis recognizes the ordered interdependencies of the diverse constituent elements of hunting and it also provides a comparative basis for evaluating the functions and intensities, their similarities and dissimilarities, in radically different cultures. As defined here, hunting consists of five series of patterned activities, beginning early in childhood and extending through the life of the individual engaged in hunting. These five behavior complexes consist of (1) programming the child, (2) scanning or the collection of information, (3) stalking and pursuit of game, (4) immobilization of game, including the killing or capture of game, and (5) retrieval of the game. Although more complexes might be added, such as those concerned with the distribution of game and its various uses, none can be subtracted without impoverishing an appreciation of hunting.

In overall perspective, both for the individual and for the evolution of mankind, this behavior system has had an integrating function. It has served as an integrating schedule for the nervous system. Hunting is obviously an instrumental system in the real sense that something gets done, several ordered behaviors are performed with a crucial result. The technological aspects, the spears, clubs, handaxes, and all the other objects suitable for museum display, are essentially meaningless apart from the context in which they are used. They do not represent a suitable place to begin analysis because their position in the sequence is remote from the several preceding complexes.

Programming Children

Three indispensable parts of the hunting system are programmed into the child beginning early in life. These are the habit of observation, a systematic knowledge of animal behavior, and the interpretation and appropriate action for living with animals and for utilizing them for food and fabricational purposes. Owing to the fact that in many cultures various animals are endowed with souls, that there are animal beings as well as human beings, the killing and eating of animal beings may be fraught with spiritual hazards (Rasmussen, 1929, p. 56). Appropriate behavior toward animals is prominently based upon familiarity with animal behavior and includes ways of living peacefully with animals, of maintaining a discourse with them, as well as the appropriate behaviors, the highly coordinated movements of the hunter proceeding toward a kill, and appropriate social behavior where other hunters are involved. Within a single community it is possible to arrange the hunters in a rank order in terms of their efficiency or productivity. It is sometimes possible to relate lack of success to inadequate training as well as to the other sources of ineptitude. This is especially apparent where the child has been removed from his village during the crucial years, or where the child has been raised by a grandmother or other nonhunter who was not able to provide the necessary tuition.

A general statement embracing the styles, modes, and mechanisms of neurological patterning in childhood has been provided by Gajdusek:

Phylogeny has already patterned the view of the physical world which a child will receive in the structure of the sense receptors: eyes, ears, nose, taste buds; tactile, temperature, and pain receptors; and proprioceptors. The cultural milieu, however, can determine the schemata of thought and the modes of handling of these sense perceptions as well as it determines the quality and quantity in which they impinge upon the infant and child. There is a vast number of neurological functions of the central nervous system which different cultures have programmed in their own specific ways by the unique environment they provide for the growth and development of their children. These include the style of neuromuscular coordination in fine and gross movements, even at the level of speech and eye movements; styles of posture, gait, stance, climbing and swimming, etc.; modes of nonverbal communication including gesture and dance; use of language, at times polylinguality; the form of the body image; sense of time, space, rhythm, and tone; color sense and acuity of smell and taste, hearing and vision; conceptions of quantity and number, methods of counting (some non-verbal), and processes of reconning and computation; styles of symbolic representation in play or drawing; patterns of sexual responsiveness and behavior; mnemonic mechanisms; and even methods and mechanisms of imagery and imagination, reverie, trance, and dream (1963, p. 56).

It is useful to realize, as D. A. Hamburg has noted (1961, p. 281) that even the autonomic nervous system is not autonomous but rather that it is substantially under central nervous control. Unfortunately we do not have the full span of physiological and neurological observations on a longitudinal, or cross-sectional, series of children for a single hunting community. However, we do have a body of observations, variously rich or sparse, on comparatively gross activities, and in these we can see the way in which children are progressively trained to become active hunters. We can see the end products, the overt manifestations of deeper and more subtle maturational alterations of the nervous system. Our major problem here is to determine what programming, what childhood instruction, is essential and indispensable to subsequent hunting behaviors.

In any community of hunters it is possible to find general exercises that prepare the child for active hunting but many fewer that involve a specific commitment. Probably all forms of exercise are of some value, but only a few have demonstrable relevance in the sense that they are a necessary and specific prerequisite. Beginning with the different practices for the two sexes which are maximized in hunting groups, a series can be assembled. Thus, those practices leading to use of spear throwers, boomerangs, bows and arrows, lances, boat handling, sledding, harpooning, etc., are ordinarily restricted to males or males are clearly favored in systematic instruction. Nevertheless, there is little data bearing on the question of how much instruction is necessary in childhood. The best preparation for throwing a spear as an adult hunter is probably throwing one at an earlier age, but how early or how many practice hours are required is not amenable to quantified estimate. The bow and arrow is in common use among many hunters —Pygmies, Bushmen, Eskimos, various Ameri-

can Indians, Andamanese, Chukchee, to name only enough to illustrate considerable diversity in the technology and use, however, most observers agree that these hunters are mediocre or indifferent as archers. They hunt effectively with their equipment, but, they compensate for lack of accuracy at appreciable distances, perhaps more than twenty or thirty yards, by spending their time getting closer to the animal. In brief, these hunters clearly spend more time and attention in utilization of their knowledge of animal behavior than in improvement of their equipment or of its use. This generalization, if well founded, probably constitutes an important aspect of primitive hunting and provides a scale for comparisons between groups.

Children were taught to close the distance between themselves and their quarry by sophisticated stalking methods that depended more upon comprehensive observation, detailed ethological knowledge and an equally detailed system of interpretation and action, than upon the improvement of their equipment and the addition of ten or twenty yards to its effective range. In fact, one may pass from this generalization to another and suggest that the very slow improvement in technology, clubs, spears, throwing boards, bows and arrows, as indicated by the archeological record, was contingent upon success in learning animal behavior. It was easier or more effective to instruct children in ethology, to take up the slack by minimizing their distance from the animal prey, than to invest heavily in equipment improvement. The rapid advances in archery of the last fifteen years reflect an application of technological methods to archery equipment that clearly did not arise from a need to depend upon such equipment for any important portion of the annual food supply.

The difference between specifically programmed and generally programmed prerequisite childhood exercises for hunting in adulthood is epitomized in the tendon lengthening exercises for Aleut children, designed for hunting from the kayak, contrasted with their general exercises. These former focused on the shoulder joint of the throwing arm, on the low back, and on the posterior region of the knee joint.

Very early in childhood, apparently as early

as beginning to walk, the male child was placed in a sitting position on a flat surface or on a stool with his heels on another stool or box. His preceptor, a father, uncle, or grandfather, stood behind or to the side of him and pulled his throwing arm up and over behind his back. This was done gently and intermittently, often with a little song or rhythmic susurration, so that several excursions were made rather than one prolonged excursion. This exercise created greater mobility at the shoulder joint and specifically enabled the arm to move farther backward and to come directly forward in a flat, vertical plane. As a consequence, the arm functioned as a longer lever than in those persons who cannot rotate their arm backward without moving it progressively to the side of the body at the same time. A spear or harpoon could be thrown farther, more easily, and from a greater variety of positions available to the seated kayak hunter.

The second and related exercise stretched the tendons and ligaments of the low back. The seated child, legs extended in front, was pushed forward by a hand applied to the back. This exercise specifically anticipated the considerable strain placed on the low back while paddling or throwing when seated in a kayak.

The third exercise of this series consisted of depressing the knees of the seated child so that the tendons on the posterior of the leg, especially the semimembranosus and the semitendinosus tendons in particular, were stretched. As a consequence the person was enabled to sit with legs extended for long periods of time and to operate efficiently.

These three specific exercises were reinforced with various games. In one, the child sat on the ground, legs extended, and threw a dart at a small wooden model of a whale suspended from a flexible withe. Two boys played this game, each facing the other and with his own whale target.

An example of a non-specific exercise of general value to a kayak hunter but with no specific relevance to kayak hunting, is that of finger-hanging. The young child was suspended from a ceiling beam of the house by his fingers. His preceptor then withdrew and the child hung until he was forced to drop. He dropped to the floor, an earth floor covered with dried grass. The exercise was intended to strengthen the fingers and to teach the child to fall on his feet with ease and agility.

The peculiar monopoly which the Aleuts and Koniags held on sea-otter hunting and the corollary fact that no European ever became a successful kayak sea-otter hunter, may be traced in part to their childhood training, both the physical and the behavioral aspect. Many Europeans have learned to paddle kayaks, and many have learned to hunt sea mammals, but extremely few, possibly five, ever became kayak hunters. Aleuts and Koniags were transported from their homeland to alien waters off California and Japan by their Russian administrators, because of their non-duplicable skills in sea-otter hunting. The point in citing this well-known history is that it reflects some of the consequences of a complex hunting achievement which is demonstrably and specifically related to childhood training. While kayak hunting represents a rare technological achievement, the use of the throwing board enjoyed a much wider distribution about the world. Certainly one factor in the failure of the throwing board to diffuse from Eskimos to contiguous groups of Indians is that an essential portion of the complex rested in child training practices. It was not a trait, like the axe, the bow and arrow, or the rifle, which could be easily used by adults.

A fear of kayaks, as found among the Eskimos of Wainwright (Nelson, in press), must be distinguished from the relatively localized "kayak fear" found in west Greenland. The possible relationship of the disease, "kayak fear," to inadequate child training has not been explored. The inability of adult hunters to perform normally is a generic category for investigation and might well be especially rewarding in revealing defects in childhood programming.

Scanning

Scanning includes the collection of information on where to hunt, what to hunt, and the scheduling of a hunt. The choice of animals to be hunted and the areas which will be searched reflect sophisticated knowledge concerning the behavior of animals, environmental conditions, and other commitments the hunter to partners or to the portion of the community which depends upon him. His need for food and fabricational materials may outweigh several other considerations. The independence of scanning and its role may be seen in the common practices conducted prior to the pursuit or stalking of detected animals.

For several days prior to the actual detection and pursuit of an animal or herd the hunter may search an area for signs. Frequently he gets this information from other hunters. He must first find what animals are in the territory and the actual tracks, feces, and browsed plants may provide him with the information he needs. The presence of one animal may signal the presence of another so that the hunter is encouraged to continue with this inspection even if he has not actually sighted the animal he wants. He may sight the animal, or a herd, but wait for it to move into a better position, perhaps closer to camp or in a valley where more can be killed than in the open.

In scanning, the knowledge of tracks and indications of animals generally is the paramount feature and obviously the complex which utilizes previously learned observational information concerning animal behavior. The time invested in this portion of the hunting sequence is usually far greater than for any other portion except for the childhood programming.

The scanning and identification problem is quite different for the marine mammal hunter. He must proceed to the most likely area and then search for the interrupting profile of the mammal when it comes to that horizon (Laughlin, 1967). He may first proceed to a mummy cave and ask for help from the hunters interred there who still maintain an active part in the affairs of living people, and he certainly utilizes the information provided by watchmen, those who sit on vantage points and scan the sea, and upon the weather prognosticators. A man of meteorological sophistication, an "astronome" may even be included in a party of kayak hunters (Heizer, 1960, p. 133).

Choices of hunting routes may involve various sorts of divining, whose effect is to randomize the routes or areas searched. This is based on the fact, well known to the primitive hunter, that animals learn the habits of humans and adjust their behavior accordingly.

The religious elements which pervade the preparation are multitudinous and need only be called to mind here. Cleansing rites and special clothing are ubiquitous. They importantly reflect the reciprocal nature of the interaction between those beings in the animal world and those in the human, or stated less egocentrically, the contingent relations between animal beings and human beings (Marsh, 1954; Hallowell, 1960).

Stalking

Stalking and pursuit of game ordinarily begins once the animal has been sighted. Attention then shifts to getting as close to the animal as necessary for an effective shot. In much of hunting, however, there is no sharp line of demarcation between these two portions of the sequence pattern. The hunter may commit himself to a particular animal or herd without having actually seen it. There may be ample evidence that a particular animal is being followed, and the animal may be aware of the pursuit without an actual visual sighting. The hunter and the hunted may smell each other, they may hear each other, they may see each other's tracks, and the animal may actually be attracted to its human pursuer by his urine. Following a polar bear for one or two days, running down a horse over a three-day period, and certainly some of the desert hunting in Australia and in the Kalahari involves a long pursuit and relatively short period for killing.

The hunter is concerned with the freshness of the track and the direction in which he is moving. He wants all possible information on his quarry's condition; its age, sex, size, rate of travel, and a working estimate of the distance by which the animal leads him. In the final stages, when he is closing with the animal, the hunter employs his knowledge of animal behavior and situational factors relevant to that behavior in a crucial fashion. For all birds, animals, and fish the hunter must estimate flight distance, the point at which they will take flight or run away. Conversely, with animals that are aggressive, he needs to interpret any signs, raising or lowering of tail, flexing of muscles, blowing, or salivation, etc., that indicate an attack rather than a flight. In many cases the animal is intentionally provoked to attack. The variations are innumerable.

One useful generalization of the problem faced by the hunter is that he wants to get as close as possible for the best possible shot but he would rather have a poor shot than none at all. The enormous labor and skill that is expended in approaching the animal, often hours of lying on the ground waiting for a change in direction of wind or in the position of the animal, testifies to the crucial importance of stalking.

The technological equipment of most primitive hunters is such that their quarry is usually shot at relatively short distances, usually less than thirty feet for harpoons, bows and arrows, and spears. Even the one generalization about the minimum distance for the best shot must be qualified because the hunter may want the maximum distance compatible with his weapon, in order to provide time for a second shot. Some animals tend to continue in the direction they were traveling after they are shot. Other animals have a tendency to simply stand and bleed, if not frightened by sight or smell of the hunter. The point here is simply that the enormous range and complexities of animal behavior; the influence of situational factors depending upon time of day, sex, age, nutritional state, degree of excitation, being in the company of a mate, with or without young, etc., these factors must all be read into the decision-making machinery of the hunter.

Hunting with high-powered rifles and telescopic sights, and to a lesser extent with modern archery equipment, is substantially different from the hunting of primitive man. In a general fashion, the better the technological equipment the less intimate knowledge of animal behavior is required. Getting close to an animal represents the major investment of the primitive hunter and explains the extensive attention given to childhood programming and to the location of game.

Immobilization, Killing, and Capture

The vast majority of animals taken by primitive hunters are not killed outright or are not killed upon initial contact. More often they are wounded, stunned, or immobilized to a degree that renders them incapable of rapid or prolonged flight. Even with the use of poisons the larger mammals may live on, traveling slowly, for one or more days. The Pygmy elephant hunter does not expect his quarry to fall over immediately after the first puncture, but he does expect to be able to induce hemorrhaging that will impair the functioning of the elephant and simplify tracking. In other cases the hunter intentionally avoids killing the animal for very practical reasons. An Eskimo may wound a bear and then drive him down to a stream where he can be killed and boated home. If inland on a small island, the Eskimo may wound the bear and walk him over to the edge of the island, then dispatch him and roll him into the sea where he can be floated and towed away. In many such cases it is practical and highly desirable to save an enormous amount of labor, the backpacking of some 1,200 pounds through difficult country, by wounding the animal and heading him in the preferred direction.

Capture of animals may be an objective and done for many different reasons. One important reason is the need to secure living specimens for study and child instruction, commonly categorized as "pets" in the literature. Live animals may be desired for decoys, and of course live animals may be used for various ritual purposes. Birds may be taken for training in hunting or fishing (cormorants, falcons, etc.), or simply kept as a source of feathers. From the enormous range of methods of taking the quarry it is obvious that immediate and outright killing is only one of many variations. The extensive use of snares, traps, and pitfalls in itself testifies to the concern with capture rather than immediate killing.

Retrieval

Retrieval of game represents the end point of the hunting complex pattern, it is the object of those things which have preceded it. Within the retrieval complex are included the immediate details of retrieving a floating seal or walrus, and of getting it secured to the kayak, or to an umiak, or an ice cake so that it can be cut up. Many items of material culture naturally fall in here and retrieving hooks for securing floating animals before they sink are prominent among them. This complex category broadens out to include the dressing and preparation of the animal for return to the camp or village. Finally, the activities involved in this complex extend ultimately to the distribution and use of the game, and ultimately the return of some of the materials back into earlier portions of the sequence system. A flow

The intellectual requirements for appropriate behavior in this portion of the system still depend in part upon those that were prerequisite to the preceding four portions. However, there is a qualitative difference. An animal must be expertly drawn in accordance with the anatomy of the animal, the various

PROCESS OF HUNTING

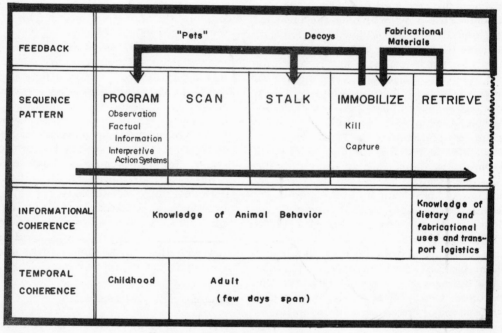

FEEDBACK		"Pets"		Decoys		Fabricational Materials
SEQUENCE PATTERN	PROGRAM Observation Factual Information Interpretive Action Systems	SCAN	STALK	IMMOBILIZE Kill Capture	RETRIEVE	
INFORMATIONAL COHERENCE	Knowledge of Animal Behavior				Knowledge of dietary and fabricational uses and transport logistics	
TEMPORAL COHERENCE	Childhood	Adult (few days span)				

FIGURE 1. THE PROCESS OF HUNTING.

chart shows the routes by which some of the materials return to participate again in the system (Fig. 1). The most ⸱bvious is the capture of an animal to be used for instruction of children in animal behavior. Thus, the entire system is activated in proper sequence and reverts to flow again into the system.

fabricational and nutritional uses of the animal, with attention to size requirements that affect carrying it back to the camp, and to social factors such as some desired portions, horns, tail, forward flipper, or fluke meat, for persons of relevant status. Attention shifts over to anatomy rather than behavior, to material characteristics, to the fabricational and dietary qualities of the animal. Some portions may be eaten immediately, and some may be employed in a ritual observance to insure affability of the animal spirit. Hides are carefully removed if they are intended for fabricational use and their cutting is in accord with a particular use. Thus, if a sealskin is to be used for a line, it must be slipped, in tubular fashion, off the carcass so that a continuous, circumferentially spiral line can be cut. But if the seal is to be fed to dogs, or its skin to be used for clothing, or both, it is drawn quite differently. A worldwide survey indicates great differences in the utilization of animal tissues. Some people use the intestines and pericardium, others discard them or feed them to dogs (Table 1). The same animal has different meanings for different peoples and this extends far beyond its rank order in their list of food preferences.

Women and dogs have been the principal beasts of burden since Paleolithic times and these are not universally available for the reason that women are not always at the site of killing and butchering, and many people did not breed dogs suitable for packing. Where long distances and large amounts of meat are involved, a village may move to the animal. Elephants and whales, unless juvenile or easily floated, usually become community projects. It is interesting that, excepting the sled and dog traction, both comparatively recent, the only

mechanical advantage accessible to primitive man was water transport. The retrieval flow pattern for the Eskimo or Aleut who harpoons a seal, tows it home behind his kayak, and eats all the meat, contrasted with the sledging Eskimo who harpoons a seal, carries it home on a sled, and then shares it with the dogs, is enormous.

The kayak-hunter can tow much greater weights more easily, than can the sledgers. The kayak-hunter can use the hide of his quarry to make the kayak with which he hunts the beast. Marine hunters use more of the products of the animals they hunt than do terrestrial hunters, and they use them more advantageously. Esophagus, intestines, and pericardia are of little use to most hunting groups as fabricational materials, yet they account for an appreciable part of the clothing of some northern peoples.

THE PHYSICAL SUPERIORITIES OF MAN

Pound for pound, man is a tough, durable, strong, and versatile animal. To the extent that comparisons between species have validity, he is superior in overall physical performance to all or most other mammals. This physical superiority is intimately related to his hunting habit.

It has become a common routine to observe that man is born helpless and remains dependent upon others for a long period of time, that

---

| *Table 1* | *Multiple Use of Resources* |

(*Eumetopia jubata* [*Northern or Steller sea lion*])

Part of Animal	Partial List of Uses
1. Hide	Cover for kayak and umiak; line for harpoon
2. Flesh	Food, for humans
3. Blubber	Food: eaten with meat, rendered for oil
4. Organs (heart, liver, spleen, kidney)	Food
5. Bones	Ribs for root diggers, humerus for club, baculum for flaker
6. Teeth	Decorative pendants
7. Whiskers	Decoration of wood hunting hats and visors
8. Sinew	Back sinews used for sewing, lashing, cordage (less desirable than sinew of whale or caribou)
9. Flippers	Soles used for boot soles; contents gelatinized in flipper and eaten
10. Pericardium	Water bottle, general-purpose container
11. Esophagus	Parka, pants, leggings of boots, pouches
12. Stomach	Storage container (especially for dried salmon)
13. Intestines	Parka, pants, pouches

he is a generalized animal lacking the specializations that characterize other species, and this recitation often leads to the observation that man is physically weak and defenseless because he is dependent upon culture. This in turn provides the argument for the implication that evolution took place in the past and that the rapidity and pervasiveness of cultural evolution has supplanted physical evolution. A more realistic and holistic view is the recognition of the biobehavioral continuum that characterizes the development of each individual (Ginsburg and Laughlin, 1966). The dichotomy between biology and culture, between cultural learning and its neurological base, has been historically conducive to the denigration of man's physical abilities.

In fact, human beings are remarkably versatile, durable, and strong in their physical constitution. As Haldane has observed, only man can swim a mile, walk twenty miles, and then climb a tree (Haldane, 1956, p. 5). The full list of man's physical superiorities, when compared with other mammals, must include his ability to run rapidly and to run long distances. One need only cite the conquest of the four-minute mile and the long-distance running of various Indian tribes. Tarahumara endurance runners have been scientifically studied and the results confirm and extend various anecdotal accounts. Participants in kick-ball races may cover up to 100 miles in 24 hours (Balke and Snow, 1965). That Indians can run down horses and deer is well known, by pacing the animal, keeping him moving, and taking advantage of the tendency of many ungulates to move in an arc by traversing the chord. The Indian hunter who is running down an animal makes use of his own physical superiority and his knowledge of the animal's behavior.

In pulling strength, humans compare favorably with adult chimpanzees. In ability to carry loads, humans regularly display abilities superior to the donkey, and this superiority is demonstrated at high altitudes as well. Loads of sixty pounds are commonly carried and the literature abounds with examples of porters carrying loads in excess of their own body weight.

Functional flexibility permitting a wide range of movements and postures, best seen in young children, acrobats, gymnasts, ballet dancers, wrestlers, swimmers, and divers, is unequivocally superior to other mammals. The closest approach to human flexibility as a whole is probably found in the orangutan and in the spider monkeys, the latter having the advantage of a prehensile tail. However, these contenders are lacking in the fine motor control of the hand and of a specialized foot. Nor can they swivel their heads as far or as easily as humans. They do not have the ability to milk a cow, a manual feat requiring a subtle succession of digital closure, and as runners or weight bearers they cannot even be entered in the lists.

Man's sensory apparatus is excellent. His vision is acute and of course includes color vision. It is exceeded only by that of various birds. His auditory acuity compares well with other animals and is a prime factor in his hunting abilities. His olfactory abilities do appear to be more limited than those of some other species, polar bears for example, but it is adequate to facilitate hunting. The external integument of humans is remarkably tough. Many groups live their entire lives without benefit of clothes and this includes groups living in areas as stressful and divergent as Australia, Tierra del Fuego, the Congo, and the Kalahari Desert. The fallacious idea that man lost his body hair as a consequence of wearing clothes, still recited as a demonstrated fact (Glass, 1965, p. 1254), is easily disposed of by the examples of hirsute and naked hunters, the Australian aborigines, and of glabrous and naked hunters, the Bushmen. Human skin tans well and is far more durable than that of many other mammals. One may speculate on the role hair has played in human evolution, but a tough skin has been a distinct advantage in a large variety of recurrent situations to the primitive hunter.

Considerable physiological tolerance, an unsurpassed ability to adapt to environmental stresses of which high altitude is most prominent, is surely one of man's major physical superiorities. Few animals, rats and dogs, to cite undomesticated and domesticated examples, compare with humans in this respect. A review of all the areas in which members of our species live serves to indicate our great physiological plasticity. No other single species lives at high and low altitudes, extremely hot and extremely cold climates and in all the combinations of humidity, light and darkness that compose the panel of human habitats.

Among the many other superiorities enjoyed by the human animal is a dental and alimentary system that permits a truly omnivorous diet. Humans can tolerate a large number of plants and animals and can adapt to diets that are composed totally of flesh or of plant foods. Additionally, they can continue work under conditions of deprivation.

When the superior memory and learning abilities of man is included, and the use of tools, language, and other elements of the biobehavioral matrix in which man operates, the remarkable versatility of the human animal becomes even more apparent. However, this should not obscure the basic fact that viewed solely from the standpoint of anatomy, physiology, and neurology man enjoys many superiorities compared with other species. A man can run down a horse in two or three days, and then decide whether to eat it, ride it, pull a load with it, wear it, or worship it.

SIMPLICITY OF BASIC TECHNOLOGY

The common weapons and related devices used in stalking and in the immobilization of game animals is basically simple and elementary. Over the million or more years in which man has evolved as a hunter, it is probable that the vast majority of mammals, birds, and fish have been killed with clubs, stones, knives, and spears or simply strangled with the hands or in a snare or noose. Examination of the archeological record, even that of Upper Paleolithic big-game hunters, is not impressive except in virtuosity of flaking or in other artistic variations. Diagonal flaking of a spear point has no demonstrable advantage over parallel flaking, and fluting offers no discernible advantage over unfluted points.

As Boas observed, "As soon as a reasonably long shaft allowed an attack from a point beyond the reach of the teeth and paws of the animal, hunting became safer" (Boas, 1938, p. 254). The spear, used as a lance or cast, was certainly a major step forward, and has persisted for some hundreds of thousands of years. Nevertheless, it is basically a simple invention, and the spear-thrower, still in use by some

Eskimos and Australian aborigines, is similarly an uncomplicated device. The bows and arrows in use by most primitive hunters were not impressive for their cast, their distance, nor their accuracy. An examination of the variety of arrow releases and their geographical distribution (Wissler, 1926, pp. 30-40) serves to reinforce the idea that cultural styles in the construction and use of various tools and weapons have only limited relevance to the potential efficiency of the weapon. As previously suggested, the enormous variety of harpoon heads that have been used to harpoon the same species of seal, or the variety of fishhooks that are used to catch the same species of fish, illuminates the basic fact that the hunter invests more heavily in knowledge of the behavior of the animals, in methods for approaching them or attracting them close to him, than in increasing the range or firepower of his weapons.

A substantial amount of hunting reveals the way in which animals can be easily approached under suitable conditions; and then dispatched with a club or a spear. Many animals are killed while asleep. Obviously the most ferocious beast in the world is utterly harmless while asleep, or hibernating. Walrus, who are often victors in combat with polar and brown bears, are frequently taken while asleep. Screening noises are prominently utilized in many forms of hunting. During storms, the sea otter hauls up on shore. The Aleuts approached them with ease at this time owing to the animals' inability to hear the approaching hunters, and simply clubbed them (Elliott, 1886, pp. 142-43). To a significant extent, young animals fall in the same accessible category as sleeping animals. The archeological and ethnographic record is unambiguous on the fact that the vast majority of mammals killed are immature or subadult. This reflects the population profile of many species, but it also represents a preference on the part of the hunter. The largest and oldest animals are more difficult to kill or capture, they do not taste as good as younger ones, their hides are often scarred and therefore less desirable for clothing, and they may even be avoided for frankly conservational and for religious considerations.

Driving animals, whether into a net, a pit, over a cliff, or within range of concealed hunters, is again obviously simple so far as the technology is concerned, but considerably more complex with reference to the coordination required of the persons conducting this part of the hunt. The signalling system used by Aleut and Koniag kayak hunters when employing a surround method reflects the solution of a problem in communication where spoken language would frustrate the combined efforts of the hunters. The position of the paddle of the first man to sight the quarry provided ample cues to the other hunters. The many ways in which group hunting provided an effective means of scanning, stalking, and killing, and at the same time placed a premium upon precisely coordinated social organization, simultaneously reveals the importance of alternate forms of communication between the participants. Brief, silent, inconspicuous, and unambiguous cues are absolutely necessary in such operations.

Though the technological sophistication of many poisons is considerably advanced beyond the handax and club, the use of poisons also illustrates the point that much programming must precede the killing complex (Linné, 1957). The development of effective poisons importantly demonstrates the basic inventiveness of primitive hunters.

Among the great inventory of hunting technology is the ancient and widespread bolas. Its principle, common to the bull-roarer sling and centrifuge alike, is simple enough for women and children to manipulate and helps explain some of their substantial contributions to the hunting economy.

The point of drawing attention to the simplicity of the basic technology is of course to draw attention to the sophistication of the complexes preceding the actual use of the weapons. In a very real sense the hunter is taking a final examination with a mortal demerit for failure. It is the preceding period of learning that enables him to perform adequately.

HUNTER'S SOPHISTICATED KNOWLEDGE OF BEHAVIOR AND ANATOMY

There is ample documentation, though surprisingly few systematic studies, for the postulate that primitive man is sophisticated in his knowledge of the natural world. This sophistication encompasses the entire macroscopic zoological world of mammals, marsupials, reptiles, birds, fish, insects, and plants. Knowledge of tides, meteorological phenomena generally, astronomy, and other aspects of the natural world are also well developed among some primitive peoples. There are genuinely large variations between groups with reference to the sophistication and extent of their knowledge, and to the areas in which they have concentrated. Empiricism is not at all uncommon, and inventiveness similarly recurs in widely separated areas with only remote or no discernible historical connections. Having previously discussed these topics (Laughlin, 1961, 1963), I will here only cite the relevance of this sophistication to the hunting behavior system and to its significance for the evolution of man.

Hunters are extremely knowledgeable concerning animal behavior and anatomy for a variety of reasons. Hunting is their profession and this requires such knowledge. They recite events of hunting, they discuss endlessly the weather and its effects on ice conditions, or on the moss on which caribou feed; they make predictions on the numbers of various animals based on weather conditions and its effects on animals and plants that serve as food for carnivores and grazers. Their conversations often sound like a classroom discussion of ecology, of food chains, and trophic levels.

The accuracy of their information is attested by their success in hunting and by comparisons with scientific studies of behavior and anatomy and systematics. In discussing the species concept of the local naturalist, Ernst Mayr includes the opinion of primitive natives:

> Some 30 years ago I spent several months with a tribe of superb woodsmen and hunters in the Arfak Mountains of New Guinea. They had 136 different vernacular names for the 137 species of birds that occurred in the area, confusing only two species. It is not, of course, pure coincidence that these primitive woodsmen arrive at the same conclusion as the museum taxonomists, but an indication that both groups of observers deal with the same arbitrary discontinuities of nature (1963, p. 17).

The consultation of native hunters by naturalists extends well back into the nineteenth century. The naturalist Chamisso who visited Unalaska as early as 1817 published a detailed study of whales in which he depended upon the local Aleuts who carved wooden models of each of the whales and provided various information about each of them (Chamisso, 1824).

The ubiquity of sophisticated information among hunters is probably of more importance for interpreting the development and consequences of such information than the unusual and rare achievements that may occasionally be associated with such knowledge. The preparation of mummies and intentional autopsy of the dead to find out why they died are expectable developments where there is the appropriate context and concern.

The Tungus, described in detail by Shirokogorov (1935), compare favorably with Eskimos and even with the Aleuts (Marsh and Laughlin, 1956). They are good gross anatomists, their ideas on physiological functions are based on their observations, they are good naturalists, and they are concerned to acquaint themselves with the behavior and the anatomy of animals or birds not well known to them, capturing live specimens for this specific purpose and for pets for the instruction of children. "He [the Tungu] is interested in the comparative study of bones and soft parts of the body and he comes to form a good idea as to the anatomical similarities and dissimilarities in animals and even man" (Shirokogorov, 1935, p. 73).

As previously indicated, the sources of Aleut anatomical knowledge can be partitioned into five categories: (1) the study of anatomical structures; (2) a rational medicine and physical culture; (3) dissection of human bodies; (4) true comparative anatomy, focused on the sea otter; and (5) the manufacture of dried mummies (Laughlin, 1961, pp. 157–60). The first, second, and fourth categories appear most ubiquitous. The daily butchering and drawing of animals leads to knowledge about them, and to the extent that internal tissues are used for food or fabricational purposes, the knowledge may be considerably detailed. Hunters are well aware of the affinity between man and other animals, and they all have relevant exercises designed to condition the hunter. A good deal

of information inevitably obtains for human biology stemming first from the need for assistance or intervention at birth.

If primitive hunters are compared with ethologists, some common procedures are obvious, and though the goals may rapidly diverge, they are neither antipathetic nor wholly dissimilar. Drawing upon an important position paper of the ethologist, G. P. Baerends, the common element is immediately apparent. "Starting from detailed description of behaviour, ethologists study the factors that underlie their causation, their genetic basis and their ontogeny" (Baerends, 1958, p. 466). The Bushmen, Pygmies, or Aleuts have the detailed description of behavior well in hand, with the emphasis probably on motor systems. Their knowledge of physiology, genetics, and allied disciplines is clearly inadequate to sustain their interests in causation. To my knowledge, no one has inquired into primitive definitions of units of behavior, and how behavior elements enter into their taxonomic groupings. Such studies could only be conducted among hunters who are actively engaged in hunting, not upon reservation natives who have access only to memory.

GENETIC MECHANISMS IN HUNTING SOCIETIES

The nature of the hunting behavior system early imposed conditions on mating behavior both within and between groups. These conditions have had important influences on genetic mechanisms at any given time, and on trends in human evolution over long periods of time in the history of our species. In succinct form, the most salient generalizations applicable to contemporary or recent hunting societies with a focus on big-game hunting, and which can be extrapolated into earlier times, are these: (1) They are small in numbers, with low effective population size. The nature of a hunting economy does not ordinarily permit the aggregation of large numbers of people in one place at one time. The high population density of marine hunters such as the Eastern Aleuts was achieved by multiplication of the number of demes, less so of the size of demes. Most bands tend to be genetic units, with the obvious exception of Australian bands which tend to be exogamous, in which case the tribal units are the important genetic units. (2) Their populations are isolated and the constituent demes are isolated in varying degree, the ideal condition for maximum evolutionary opportunity as demonstrated by Sewall Wright. (3) The inbreeding effect is usually present and inbreeding is common. This may contribute to rapid action of selection by increasing the number of homozygotes (that would otherwise be undetected). (4) Differential fertility favors headmen, chiefs, or especially successful hunters. They have more wives and more children in porportion to other hunters. Their reproductive success has been a major factor in the evolution of intelligence and will be discussed in more detail. (5) There is a high frequency of accidental deaths. Though the causes of death are poorly known, it does appear that wild animals, disease, and starvation, in various combinations, are prominent among the causes of death of subadults and adults. The category of wild animals may be matched or exceeded by intertribal fights, cannibalism, and related human disaffections. (6) There is a short life span. Although the data are poor and probably over estimate longevity, twenty years is probably a more accurate estimate for a generation than 25. Outstanding exceptions may be found and the contrast between short-lived Eskimos in the Canadian Arctic and much longer-lived Eastern Aleuts has likely been duplicated in a number of places and times (Laughlin, 1963b, p. 638). (7) There is high infant mortality. This again prominently varies with the richness of the exploitational area and the technological sophistication of the people. Infanticide plays an extremely important role. When stillbirths and miscarriages are considered, the genetic wastage may be extremely high. (8) There are frequent population bottlenecks. Annual fluctuations in food supply are common, especially for people hunting migratory animals. Related to the annual cycles of the animals are those of environmental conditions. Dramatic annual alterations occur in desert areas where increase or decrease in water supply involves multitudinous correlative changes, and in arctic regions where water is replaced with ice. Meager storage facilities make it impossible to utilize the common superabundance, for example of caribou, much later

in the year. Populations appear to adjust to the lower limits of food resources. During periods of privation the practice of abortion, infanticide, exposure of elderly and infirm persons, and "voluntary death" may further reduce the population size. Bottlenecks provide opportunity for inadequate sampling between generations. (9) *Founder's Principle:* New communities or demes are often founded by only a few migrants, and these may be closely related. The genetical importance of such partitioning of the gene pool is recognized in the concept of "founder's principle" (see Mayr, 1963, p. 211). The founders carry a small fraction of the genetical variation of the total population. Some authors identify "founder's principle" with random genetic drift. This kind of migrant sampling has been extremely important in human evolution and may therefore be worth separate itemization. (10) There has been fusion of remnant groups. R. H. Osborne has noted that the fusion of surviving groups following a severe bottleneck has an effect similar to recurrent selection. The resulting recombinations may represent an improvement over either of the parental contributors. (11) Gene flow is predominantly from central to marginal populations. Marginal populations do not ordinarily feed back to central populations.

Two points of special importance to the relationship between the hunting behavior pattern and human evolution are seen in (a) the population characteristics of such hunting groups leading to diversity, and (b) those favoring the evolution of intelligence. The opportunities for random variation and for the development of differences between groups are maximized in these groups. Small, isolated populations, with many subdivisions, frequently strained through genetic bottlenecks, and with migrant sampling ("founder's principle") as a major form of moving into new territories and new continents constitutes the ideal conditions for rapid evolution, when viewed over long time periods, and for the accumulation of many chance differences. In examining the mechanism of human raciation, and especially the role of isolation and migration, G. Lasker provides the relevant comment:

Race formation seems to be a continual process. Although there is no reason to doubt that it has operated on man, natural selection has not been satisfactorily demonstrated as a significant factor in racial differentiation. It is more plausible that small groups would come to differ racially by the purely random process of primarily endogamous mate selection. Subsequent rapid increases in population size based on cultural advantages or historical opportunities could be responsible in the main for the kind of racial pattern manifest today (1960).

High intergroup diversity is a characteristic of the human species which is closely related to the group size, isolation, and generational and migrational sampling inadequacies of hunting groups. To the isolating factors, those of culture as such, of distance and of distributional pattern, the common result of inhibition of gene flow over distance, of dilution of frequencies outward from centers are especially effective. As Shapiro has remarked, "Thus although some cross-cultural miscegenation is an ancient phenomenon and can occur in a variety of ways, the isolating effects of culture are on the whole predominant" (1957, p. 24).

A major function of culture is that of maximizing the welfare of its members and therefore minimizing and screening contacts with nonmembers. The more cultures there are, the more diffusion barriers there are to gene flow. This is especially important over distance. Contemporary racial diversity has been enhanced by the distributional patterns imposed by the hunting system. In fact, viewing the genetic diversity of our species from the question of why it did not break into separate species, we find that our knowledge of what holds the species together is not well studied. Mayr has remarked, "The essential genetic unity of species cannot be doubted. Yet the mechanisms by which this unity is maintained are still largely unexplored. Gene flow is not nearly strong enough to make these species anywhere nearly panmictic. It is far more likely that all the populations share a limited number of highly successful epigenetic systems and homeostatic devices which place a severe restraint on genetic and phenotypic change" (Mayr, 1963, p. 523). The human species fits this problem and deserves the kind of study necessary to elucidate the ways in which its unity has been maintained.

The rewards accruing to superior hunters within a community throw light on the evolution of intelligence. The headmen, chiefs, or leaders are generally excellent hunters. Their excellence in hunting depends in part on intelligence, which, however defined, is a multigenic trait with moderate to high heritability. The headmen have more wives than other members and consequently more children, and thus contribute differentially to the succeeding generation. This process can be demonstrated for contemporary hunters and its projection into earlier times provides a major insight into the way in which the hunting system has favored the evolution of intelligence.

The Xavante Indians of Brazil illustrate this mechanism. "As befits the chief, he had more wives (five) than any other member of the tribe" (Neel *et al.*, 1964, p. 94). This man had 23 surviving offspring and in descending order of wives, one man had four wives and six offspring, four men had three wives and thirteen offspring, ten men had two wives and 23 offspring, and 21 men had one wife and 24 offspring. Thus, the leader has produced over 25 per cent of the surviving offspring.

The Anaktuvuk Eskimos of Alaska, a small inland group of some 78 caribou hunters, illustrate the disproportionate contributions of a superior hunter. One elderly but able hunter, one of the founders of the isolate, had seven children of whom six had the blood group gene B. Five matings from these children produced ten children of whom eight had at least one gene for blood group B. Thus, he had contributed to some 20 per cent of the total living population (Laughlin, 1957).

It is possible to generalize on headmen from the existing literature. As a rule they appear to be well informed, to have better memories, more equipment or material goods, more wives including access to women who may not formally be their wives, to be above average in physical constitution, and—directly as a consequence of their superior hunting abilities—to have a better food supply than those less well endowed. A multitude of consequences follow. The wife, or wives, of a headman are better fed and more likely to carry a pregnancy to full term, and any infants are likely to be better fed and therefore more likely to survive to reproductive age than those infants that are less well fed.

Crow has suggested that it would be easier, by selection, to change the intellectual or other aptitudes of a population than to change the incidence of disabling diseases or sterility. "This is not to say that there has not been some selection for intelligence in the past, but it has surely been much less intense than that for fertility, for example" (Crow, 1961, p. 429). This is certainly true, but I would suggest that there has been a constant selection for intelligence and that it has been sufficient to prepare the species for a relatively rapid shift over to civilization where assortative mating tracks based on culturally defined interests in very large populations take over the role of selecting for intelligence and aptitudes.

EVOLUTIONARY ASPECTS

Hunting played the dominant role in transforming a bipedal ape into a tool-using and tool-making man who communicated by means of speech and expressed a complex culture in the infinite number of ways now known to us. The evolutionary importance of hunting can be demonstrated by a combination of nutritional, psychological, and anatomical (including neurophysiological) aspects of our contemporary behavior, with the fossil and archeological record, and with primate comparisons.

Three things are essential to this thesis. One, that hunting is a complex sequence behavior pattern beginning in childhood. Two, the nutritional advantages of a carnivorous-omnivorous diet extend into several aspects of life ranging from childhood dependency and longer period for learning over to the increased territorial mobility permitting occupation of any place in the world. Three, hunting behavior is prior, psychologically, to the use and manufacture of tools. In brief, what the tools were used for, how they could be made to serve the objectives of the hunter, what the hunter was doing that he needed tools, and what he was doing that developed the mind that conceived the design of tools, that executed their manufacture, and that employed them and revised them, these are the important considerations. Tools provide a thermometer

for measuring intellectual heat generated by the animal, they are not the source of heat. There is of course a constant feedback so that tool use contributes to the patterning of the brain, thus becoming both subject and object in both a neurological and philosophical sense. For these reasons I stress the importance of the behavior first, and the relevance and importance of tools second. Tools did not make the man, man made tools in order to hunt.

The nutritional advantages of a carnivorous-omnivorous diet, its correlates and its consequences are well attested (Oakley, 1961; Spuhler, 1959; Washburn and Avis, 1958). Spuhler has presented the most succinct itemization in a context with six other preconditions for the beginning of culture: accommodative vision, bipedal locomotion, manipulation, carnivorous-omnivorous diet, cortical control of sexual behavior, vocal communication, and expansion of the association areas in the cerebral cortex. A large supply of compact animal proteins, high in caloric values, concentrated and packaged in a container suitable for transport, its own skin, provides a basis for food sharing, for the differentiation of functions in a family unit, for the long dependency of human children, and such a food supply facilitates migration and it provides more time in which to accomplish other things. Plant-eating primates, gorillas for example, must procure a much larger bulk of shoots, leaves, and stems to have an equivalent caloric value, and they must spend a much longer period each day in eating their vegetarian diet (Schaller, 1963, pp. 149–68). They do not share food. One can only remark that if such vegetarians did want to share food they would need baskets or wheelbarrows. The amount of information which must be exchanged between plant eaters is small compared with that needed in group-hunting of large animals, wolves for example. Equally to the point is the lack of challenge or psychological stimulation involved in plant eating. Plants do not run away nor do they turn and attack. They can be approached at any time from any direction, and they do not need to be trapped, speared, clubbed, or pursued on foot until they are exhausted.

The value of plant food in sustaining a hunting population during periods when meat is in short supply, and the value of invertebrates that can be collected by simple methods, for example the crucial use of sea urchins collected in the intertidal zone by Aleuts, cannot be overlooked. It is however the focus on hunting moving game that has organized the structure and functioning of humans, not the casually collected foods.

Washburn has remarked (Washburn and Avis, 1958, p. 433) that hunting has had three important effects on human behavior and nature: psychological, social, and territorial, and he has summarized by indicating that after bipedalism came the use of tools, the hunting habit, increase in intelligence and, finally, the animal we know as man (p. 435). This is a coherent and synoptic view which is well documented. However, the priority of the hunting habit before the use of tools should be considered as a necessary sequence. Bipedalism was a necessary precondition, but at least two apparently well differentiated species, *Australopithecus robustus* and *A. africanus*, and possibly a third, "Homo habilis," to use the names of three groups of uncertain taxonomic status, were bipedal, and only one appears to have continued along the line leading into man. The possibility that desiccation led to a dietary change requiring carnivorism for the Australopithecines is well known, and the possibility that *A. robustus* remained primarily a vegetarian and became extinct is equally well known. The archeological evidence is ambiguous and whether both of these lines used tools and made tools is uncertain. If *A. robustus* was a vegetarian, it is difficult to imagine what he was doing with tools. On the other hand, tools became useful to a bipedal hunter because they do facilitate killing and the reduction of the dead animal for food and fabricational purposes.

Dental morphology is of little help. Gorillas have very large canines and high cusps compared to humans, and they are vegetarian. Humans can and do eat everything from leaves to meat and bones with no detectable correlation between the diet and their dental morphology. In fact, humans the world over promptly remove their cusps and fissural patterns by normal attrition during childhood so that it is difficult to find a readable fissural pattern in an adult male or female primitive. Chipped teeth are found in Eskimos and in Aleuts, in keeping with their extensive chewing on bones

and bone splinters, and the use of their teeth for fabricational purposes. Deducing what humans have eaten with their teeth is comparable to deducing what they have held in their prehensile hand.

At what point in the continuous line leading to man we choose to apply the label *human* is subjective in the extreme. Because of the necessity of childhood instruction for hunting, the overall integration of posture, vision, hand, communication, and brain required for hunting behavior, I would suggest that this was the crucial adaptation and therefore provides a meaningful criterion for so labeling the organism who had achieved this level of organization.

Conclusions and Summary

The overall evolutionary efficacy of hunting as a master integrating pattern of our species is illustrated in many ways. Man successfully evolved with a simple technology over hundreds of thousands of years; he migrated into all the continents and climes; he solved all the local problems of adaptation with ingenuity and inventiveness. These feats are climaxed by the relative rapidity with which he developed civilizations and, equally important, that he as a hunter was converted to civilized man independently in different continents. He was obviously preadapted and even predisposed to civilization.

The inherent ingenuity of primitive hunters, of marginal peoples generally, can be attested by citing inventions and by examining the great heterogeneity of marginal peoples (Lowie, 1952). It is commonplace to cite the inventions of various peoples, but I think it more instructive to assemble them within the context of an historical tradition rather than cut across cultures gleaning exotic examples. Two points of interest result: the inventions listed are confined almost entirely to material devices and particular peoples have been more inventive than is generally appreciated. The kayak with three-piece keelson of the Aleuts, the snow dome house of the Arctic Eskimos, the double-purchase pulley, screw-thread, slit goggle, visor, three-legged stool, etc., of the Aleut-Eskimo stock is matched by their development of human anatomical knowledge, their knowledge of natural phenomena, prominently including animal behavior, and by their systems of navigation on sea and land. Goggles and stools are well known, however; the non-material inventions are not. The material things remain clever devices until the intellectual context of their invention and use is comprehended. Where primitive hunters have not invented material devices that capture the attention of observers, they are less often credited with inventiveness and their knowledge in those areas in which they invested their time and interest is underestimated.

The psychological differences between hunters contrasted with farmers and livestock breeders has properly been emphasized (Clark and Piggott, 1965, pp. 157–59). However, it should be noted that primitive hunters domesticated the dog, probably more than once, and this may have provided a model for the domestication of other animals. As I have suggested previously, hunters capture animals for use as pets and a major use is the instruction of children in animal behavior. Domestication of the dog ranks as a great achievement in the investigation of wolf behavior and subsequently in animal breeding.

The theory of cultural advance offered by Ginsburg and Laughlin (1966), suggesting that crossing the biobehavioral threshold leading to civilization depended upon the important ingredient of assortative mating tracks within large populations, is an explanation of how existing variability can be recombined and repackaged without the addition of new genetic materials or of outside intervention.

Man's life as a hunter supplied all the other ingredients for achieving civilization: the genetic variability, the inventiveness, the systems of vocal communication, the coordination of social life. It could not provide the large and dense population size nor the internal genetic restructuring attendant upon the establishment of assortative mating tracks whereby the frequency of matings between persons sharing culturally defined interests and talents could be maximized. The basic anatomical structure, the neurophysiological processes, and the basic patterns of behavior had been so successfully organized and integrated by the attention given to the lifelong study of behavior and anatomy and the other portions of the total sequence pattern that rapid and extensive changes could take place. While learning to learn, man, the hunter, was learning animal behavior and anatomy, including his own. He domesticated himself first and then turned to other animals and to plants. In this sense, hunting was the school of learning that made the human species self-taught.

In the final analysis we return to the informational requirements of the hunting system for the development of the individual. Hunting must be learned by children and the children must learn by observation and by participation the habit of critical observation, the facts concerning animal behavior, and the appropriate responses. It is insufficient to tell children about animal behavior and anatomy; it must be programmed into them in a far more integrated fashion. A corollary point which applies to hunting groups and their history clearly is that a simple technology does not indicate simplemindedness. We know a good deal about the magnitude of the task accomplished with simple tools, the hundreds of thousands of years of successful human evolution. We know therefore that the major information investment went into the nervous system and the non-material aspects of the highly adaptive hunting cultures.

34.

Causal Factors and Processes in the Evolution of Pre-farming Societies

ULIAN H. STEWARD

METHODOLOGICAL TRENDS

The papers of this conference as well as of the recent conferences on the Great Basin and on bands seem to me notable for the interest in causality that runs through the comparisons of prefarming societies. This interest has led to the scrutiny of concepts and to the reporting of kinds of data that were accorded little attention two or three decades ago. But, as these papers clearly demonstrate, we have not yet perfected a methodology for determining cause-and-effect relationships in the evolution of different kinds of cultures. I wish, therefore, to examine some of the methodological implications of these conferences, especially in the conceptualization of the nature of causes and effects. Specifically, I stress that a distinction needs to be made between causal factors and processes. If any of my comments appear to contradict my earlier statements, it is because I endeavor to sharpen and, if necessary, re-design old tools rather than discard them.

Because cross-cultural comparisons are the essence of the present papers and discussions—although they are not the only means of examining causality—the nature of cultural taxonomies and their use in determining causal factors is of major concern. The ethnographic cases reported in these papers, however, are not holistic descriptions, and such descriptions do not lend themselves to explanatory analyses. This raises the question of which aspects of culture shall constitute diagnostic characteristics of cross-cultural types. The present papers accord major attention to social structures, and they generally start with small aggregates of nuclear families and extend analysis outward through kinship and marriage systems. This emphasis reflects the empirical importance of kinship ties, which are very responsive to the inescapable requirements of subsistence activities within these difficult environments, rather than any theoretical presuppositions according to which certain characteristics are ascribed greater importance than others. Even though structural characteristics have a continuity with past tradition, and in some cases may have been influenced by culture contacts, all must have sufficient adaptability to remain viable.

Cross-cultural comparisons have shown many cases of near similarity of social structure. There is danger, however, of committing a methodological fallacy in assuming that similar structural manifestations or effects are always caused by identical factors. The validity of the reverse hypothesis, that similar causes will have similar effects, does not prove that causes can be deduced unfailingly from effects. The data of these conferences have repeatedly

321

demonstrated that similar effects may be traced back to various combinations of dissimilar causes. One must, of course, start with analysis of structures having similar characteristics. A preliminary taxonomy is inescapable. But thorough empiricism demands that causality be traced in each case.

In this methodology, it is necessary to distinguish causes, processes, and effects or manifestations. Although processes may be considered causes in one sense, I conceptualize them for present purposes as changes set in motion when more ultimate cultural and environmental factors are utilized by human societies. I define these ultimate factors as sets of cultural devices and practices and environmental features, which are no more than inert potentials and which may be classified in separable categories until they are activated and interrelated by human behavior. Thus, fire, carrying baskets, and weapons are merely part of the cultural inventory and fishing resources or edible seeds are features of the natural landscape. These have effects on society only when put to use, whereupon they initiate processes that affect the nature of society. Processes such as demographic trends and seasonal aggregation and dispersal of the population may bring about very similar structures of the social groups even though initiated by use of very dissimilar cultural practices in quite unlike environments. In large measure, these processes among simpler societies consist of cultural ecological adaptations.

At the present stage of investigations, there may be some question of whether we have any cross-cultural types that are truly identical structurally. Detailed analysis discloses tendencies rather than fixed structures. For this reason, the term "model" may be preferable, provided it is understood to indicate a fairly high degree of abstraction, as in the case of Birdsell's models. "Type" perhaps denotes too great a degree of substantive similarity.

A striking illustration of two cases in which very different combinations of causal factors have produced generally similar social structures is provided by a comparison of Lee's !Kung Bushmen and Helm's Dogrib Athapaskans. In each case, the minimum social aggregate consists of a core of consanguinal kin together with affinals from other aggre-

gates. My concept that the nuclear family is structurally the irreducible social unit does not imply that it is the isolated independent social unit. To the contrary, among the Shoshoni, Bushmen, Athapaskans and certain other pre-farming societies, several nuclear families that are consanguinally and affinally related generally comprise the irreducible aggregate, for isolated families would ordinarily not be viable. These basic aggregates vary with circumstances and may range from ten to fifty persons, but usually average between twenty and thirty persons. Such small groups necessarily intermarry with one another.

Owing to their fluctuating composition and size, these minimum groups have been designated local bands, micro-bands, task groups, and camps. Since they have great cohesion, owing to their strong kinship bonds and joint subsistence activities, the term "primary subsistence band" seems to me a useful term for distinguishing them from larger groups or maximum bands.

Because members of primary bands become closely interrelated, kinship ties extend to other such bands. It seems probable, although I am unaware of supporting genealogical evidence, that a network of kinship ties as well as of visiting and cooperation extends to a maximum band—the "regional band" of the Dogrib—of 300 to 400 persons, where they become more diffuse. The equivalent among the Bushmen may be the 350 residents of the Dobe area. These maximum limitations appear to be determined partly by the accessibility of primary bands to one another, partly by distribution of food and water, and partly by bounding deserts or other barriers beyond which contacts are difficult.

Owing to seasonal and often annual changes in the processes that induce nucleation and dispersal, primary bands may associate in varying numbers for varying periods of time, so that intermediate groupings of different sizes and compositions form and dissolve. These processes and their social consequences are similar in an abstract sense among both Bushmen and Athapaskans, although very detailed comparison of marriage patterns and other interband ties discloses special factors and processes that affect particular features. In certain other areas, primary subsistence bands may have strong lineage tendencies.

My basic point is to show that the specific cultural and environmental factors that initiate these processes are very dissimilar. The Bushmen are 80 per cent vegetarians and occupy an environment where plant foods are perennially available, whereas the Dogrib are largely fish and game eaters. Dogrib territories are ten to forty times greater than those of the Bushmen, yet about the same number of primary bands interact in each case. The factors that make this possible are, first, the population density of the Bushmen, which is ten to forty times greater than that of the Dogrib and permits small bands that use only human carriers to maintain contacts with one another over short distances, and, second, the use of canoes and toboggans by the Dogrib, which enables the local bands to traverse enormous distances. In addition, survival in Canada requires clothing, shelters, and devices for taking fish which the Bushmen lack.

In my early efforts to classify and explain band types (1936, 1938), a distinction between causal factors and processes was implied in my stress on the great differences in environmental factors where similar social types, such as the patrilineal band, occurred. As late as 1949, however, the necessary conceptualizations remained unclarified in my paper on the development of early state civilizations, wherein I ventured to call attention to the strikingly similar sequences of social structures and cultural achievements of these states. Because basic research on the development of these civilizations really produced relevant data only after World War II, I inferred that similar cultural manifestations resulted from similar causes, and I took Wittfogel's sweeping generalization about irrigation to be the basic cause in each case. Subsequent research, which Adams (1966) has summarized and interpreted for Mesoamerica and Mesopotamia, has shown that irrigation was definitely an unimportant factor in these two areas, although its role may have been greater elsewhere. In all of these early states, however, similar processes such as those creating interdependencies of local population segments, specialization, stratification, centralization of authority, and others were initiated by a number of factors that have not yet been clearly identified.

In the case of the prefarming societies reported in these conferences, my effort to identify causes has revealed an astonishingly small number of factors. Viewed in terms of their formal and stylistic characteristics, thousands of cultural elements might be listed as causal factors. The provisional list given later is based on function—on whether a society has the means of getting certain kinds of jobs done. It involves such basic categories of activity as food collecting, fishing, hunting, transportation, food preservation and preparation, and, in some areas, clothing and shelter. Some of the categories have been accorded detailed attention in these conferences, but others have been largely ignored. The importance of transportation to interband contacts and activities, which I have suggested in comparing the Bushmen and Dogrib, has been almost wholly neglected, perhaps because it is so obvious. One wonders, however, by what means men got about over the deep snows of glacial age Europe.

The present conference clearly demonstrates that hunting is not a primary diagnostic characteristic of social types. Hunting is not even a single causal factor. Comparison of societies that do some hunting—and only inhabitants of oceanic islands are non-hunters—indicates that there are many kinds of hunting, each involving different cultural means, distinctive kinds of game, and varied social processes that cause different kinds of societies. Hunting cannot be isolated from other factors, but a comparative study of hunting would have enormous value in indicating the subcategories into which it may be divided.

An empirical approach that extends inquiry from cultural manifestations through processes to ultimate causes may theoretically have great value for reconstructing lines of past evolution. If cultural and environmental factors can be reduced to a limited number of basic functional categories, we should be able within the limitations of prehistoric identification of these factors to infer the nature of the society. Thus, the inherent difficulty of using ethnographic models, especially holistic models, to interpret prehistoric materials will be avoided. This matter has properly concerned many persons, such as Freeman, L. R. Binford, S. R. Binford, Sackett, Deetz, and others. Although analysis starts with cultural manifestations, it does not infer causality by correlating such manifestations, as in "factor analysis" (for example, Sawyer and Levine, 1966), and it does not project ethnographic types backward as hypothetical evolutionary stages. So far as my method is distinctive, it might be designated "causal factor identification" or "causal factor determination."

FACTOR DETERMINATION

The effects of the cultural factors listed below are vividly suggested if we can imagine what human societies would be like if any were absent. The comparison of men and apes made subsequently discloses sharp contrasts between cultural and non-cultural beings, but what would human societies be like if they lacked human carrying devices, means of processing or storing food, or devices for obtaining animals that may run, fly, or swim away?

All recent societies have means of collecting vegetable foods, hunting, fishing, transporting and preparing food. So far as these factors are concerned, local differences must be ascribed to environmental variables. But certain environments have entailed additional factors. Imagine, then, the Eskimo without dog sleds, skin boats, and special apparatus for marine hunting and fishing, the Northwest Coast without sea-going canoes and elaborate techniques for fishing and hunting sea mammals, the northern Athapaskans without canoes and toboggans, any peoples of the extreme north without adequate shelter and clothing, or desert dwellers without means of transporting water. (One case of the last has been reported in Mexico.) Food preservation and storage is necessary when there are seasons with no vegetable growth, when game migrates away or fish runs cease. In tropical and subtropical latitudes, preservation and storage may not be necessary if, as Lee has shown for the Bushmen (Chapter 4, this volume) and Woodburn for the Hadza (Chapter 5 and 11, this volume), foraging is possible perennially. This crucial matter, however, has been largely ignored.

A related problem is how much processing is necessary to utilize all possible resources. This involves not only the role of cooking and other processing of vegetable foods, but the very important matter of meat eating. Did man's physiology undergo evolutionary changes as he became a carnivore? Did fire, which apparently appeared after meat eating, help make spoiled meats digestible?

In my list, large game hunting is a single factor because it includes ways of taking large, mobile animals. Closer scrutiny of hunting might warrant several major subcategories based especially on the nature of the game. In the Great Basin, deer were ambushed or pursued by relays of hunters, mountain sheep were taken with the help of dogs in the high peaks, and antelope were driven by men, women, and children into enclosures. Although any of these animals might be taken by a single hunter, each of the more productive hunts involved a different kind of cooperation. An individual lucky enough to wound a deer might have to trail it for hours or days before it died.

Without making a detailed comparative study of hunting, I treat this category with considerable misgivings. Quantification of the yield of hunting in comparison with food collecting (Lee, Chapter 4, this volume) has shown that it is astonishingly small—perhaps 30 per cent of the food—except in higher latitudes. Intimate knowledge of the habits and habitats of game of different kinds—the size, migratory patterns, extent of herding, and reactions to human beings—as well as of the cultural devices available for hunting are also necessary. The lone Hadza hunter armed only with a bow and arrow must have been at some disadvantage in confronting an African buffalo or rhino. What of lower Paleolithic hunters whose artifacts include only hand axes and perhaps bolas? Did they construct pitfalls large enough for elephants, confront rhinos with bolas or throwing sticks, or bring down fleet antelope with untipped wooden spears? Did they hunt mainly the young of these animals or seek smaller species? Did they scavenge?

The cultural ecological factors with which we are concerned obviously cannot be divorced from environmental, historical, and biological factors, which may constitute preconditions for their operation. These other factors are also reducible to a few basic categories, and they require only brief mention.

Biological Factors

Contrary to the culturological assumption that evolution must not be reduced to biological factors, the latter cannot be ignored, first, because certain fundamental characteristics of human beings changed during cultural evolution and, second, because they are preconditions of all modern cultures.

In the course of biological evolution, the early hominids acquired bipedalism, which enormously extended their range as compared with that of their quadrupedal ancestors. At a very early time, they also became meat eaters, which vastly increased their subsistence potentials and may have been a precondition of living in northern climates. The period of dependency of the immature hominid became greatly lengthened, thus strengthening mother-child bonds but also restricting women's activities. In ethnographic cases, where males have the complementary function of hunting, women's roles in the nuclear family became more specialized and restrictive.

Enlargement of the brain and all that this implies have become distinctive human characteristics, but they do not explain any particular features of culture. It might be said that, to the contrary, the vast human adaptability they permit is basic to the increasing range of cultural variations.

Cultural Factors

The subsequent list of cultural factors is drawn from ethnographic cases, and it is intended to explore the possibilities of a functional classification of causal factors. It is remarkable that so many of these factors are present where they are useful. All societies have some means of collecting, hunting, preparing, and transporting foods, and all that occupy regions of seasonal shortages have some means of storing foods. All that live in winter climates have adequate clothing and shelter. Those which occupy areas where water craft expedite fishing and transportation have canoes, skin vessels, or simple balsa rafts. This is not to say that all hunting and gathering societies have achieved maximum efficiency in the exploitation of their environments, but their knowledge of resources and cultural devices is extraordinarily

extensive. Absence of certain factors in marginal areas—Australia and the extreme south of Africa and of South America—is expectable, since some late inventions did not diffuse to all societies. Some absences, therefore, may have made a greater difference than has been noted. But, unless the effect of each factor is carefully analyzed, we could be misled.

Could the Australians have hunted marsupials more effectively with bows and arrows? Even if true, was their hunting success primarily limited by the quantity of game? Are there major fisheries that remained unexploited for lack of canoes and fishing gear? Perhaps, but the Chilean archipelago, which has been cited as backward for want of diffused culture traits, simply had very minor marine resources. Could populations have increased in certain areas had the people stored a maximum amount of food when it was available? This is a complicated question, for it involves factors other than subsistence, but it seems likely that what Birdsell calls the "equilibrium system" rather than nutrition alone controlled the population density.

Another aspect of the question of maximum use of the environment is whether these societies might, without any changes in environment or improved cultural devices, have augmented their subsistence, sustained larger populations, and nucleated in greater aggregates, if they had been more industrious. If food getting required only one third to one half the total time, an increase of food would seem possible. I think, however, that Sahlins' picture of "affluent" hunters and gatherers is very unrealistic. Any abundance during brief periods dwindled until, as in the case of the Shoshoni, it ended in near starvation before new supplies became available. When the necessary food trek began, travel in temperatures over 100° away from water sources while carrying children, gear, and water was a thoroughly unpleasant necessity. Again, one must conclude with Birdsell, that the equilibrium of factors maintained a population at fairly constant levels over periods of time. Any local or temporary abundance of foods could not be laid up to insure more abundant nutrition throughout the whole year or a succession of years to increase the population.

Distinctions made in the following list are

handicapped by the absence of unambiguous subsistence terms. *Foraging* denotes eating foods as they are gathered, and it is an activity that man shares with many other animals. *Food extraction* has been employed to designate utilization of natural resources and *food production* for use of plant and animal domesticates. *Food gathering* or *food collecting* are traditional terms for extraction of vegetable foods, larvae, and other small items, but they do not imply what is done with the food collected. An additional term such as *food storing* could be used to indicate that the foods are transported to another locality, sometimes to a central encampment, where they are stored to provide sustenance for varying lengths of time. *Food scavenging* is a useful concept if delimited to the consumption of animals that have been killed by predators, crippled, accidentally entrapped, or stranded, as in the case of whales. Scavenging does not involve the question of whether hominids, like vultures, ate putrescent meat. There are many ethnographic reports of scavenging, although *hunting* implies the killing of live animals.

1. *Foraging.* If the only foods eaten are those foraged, but not hunted or stored, occupation of areas of cold winters must have been rare or impossible. Subsistence, moreover, would not differ greatly from that of the apes, except in the larger area covered by bipedal animals.

2. *Collecting.* Many foods, such as fruits, nuts, shellfish, eggs, insects, and larvae were eaten as they were gathered, that is, foraged, although they were obtained in greater quantity by means of various cultural devices, for example, containers, digging sticks, climbing rings, poles, and others. All societies carried on this activity by one means or another.

Assembling food at a central point requires transportation, which can be considered a separate factor. If storage involves accumulation of more than enough for immediate needs, and especially enough for long periods, it requires special preparation. Storage is not a universal factor and it is therefore listed separately.

3. *Small game hunting.* This category is distinguished from large game hunting because it does not always require men to absent themselves from their band for arduous and extensive cooperative efforts. Small game such as rodents, rabbits, hares, small species of ungulates, marsupials and mammals, monkeys, various reptiles, and birds are taken by an extraordinary variety of traps, nets, snares, pitfalls, deadfalls, throwing sticks, spears, arrows, blowguns, bird lime, and other devices more often than by methods used for large, far-ranging mammals. To the extent that hunters did not have to leave their bands for long periods, this factor supplemented food collecting.

Because most societies had reasonably effective means of hunting small game, variation in the effects of this factor depended more upon the nature and abundance of game than on culture. It was probably of major importance in northern latitudes where small game could be a major source of food during the winters. Traplines exploited for a commercial market, however, may have very different effects than native trapping and do not fall under "small game hunting."

4. *Large game hunting.* This category is distinguished from the last in its reference to hunting large, herbivorous, fairly mobile, terrestrial animals, whose means of self-protection present serious problems. These animals are either fleet, have tough hides, or make formidable foes. Hunting them by digging pitfalls or preparing ambushes, surrounds, and pursuits required great effort and entailed cooperation as well as endurance. Confrontation of such animals as rhinos and elephants also required caution.

The Upper Paleolithic seems to have marked a climax in hunting. Many animals, including now extinct giant species, were taken with stone-tipped spears and atlatls and probably by other means. How large animals were killed in lower Paleolithic times is perplexing, for use of wooden spears or any other means is inferential. Yet Isaac describes an Acheulian site in East Africa containing bones of elephants, rhinos, and hippos (Chapter 26, this volume). Early Paleolithic stone industries include choppers or fist hatchets, and later traditions include flake tools, that suggest skin working, but nothing indicates weapons for killing or wounding from a distance. The use of bolas by men on foot to entangle large, tough-skinned mammals until they were killed with wooden spears or stones would seem to be a difficult feat. To excavate a pitfall large enough for any of these animals would be a prodigious task. It will be interesting to learn how often a Hadza hunter armed only with a bow could seriously wound a rhino or elephant.

Other possible methods were, as Isaac suggests, poisoning water holes, or, to use ethnographic analogies, drives with fire over cliffs or into bogs. Possibly, like some of the Congo Negritoes, elephants could be induced to impale themselves on spears, although this hardly seems to commend itself as a routine procedure.

A simple method of taking these large species would be to hunt only the young or crippled stragglers. Still simpler would be scavenging.

5. *Aquatic hunting.* In many areas, water mammals such as whales, seals, walrus, otter, dugongs, and others were a fairly important subsistence resource, and the local societies seem always to have possessed some effective means of taking them, such as spears, harpoons, arrows, and various accessories. Since these animals are riverine or marine, some kind of water craft were generally used to hunt and transport them. Their importance to social structures is similar to that of large game hunting in that they required much time, effort, and cooperation between males. Most areas of aquatic hunting, however, were also major fishing areas.

6. *Fishing.* This category is enormously variable, for it includes cases in which fishing was so unimportant as to be a type of food collecting and other cases in which its effect was comparable to aquatic mammal hunting. Except for certain coastal and island areas, most major fisheries were riverine and required traps, weirs, baskets, and nets as well as canoes. Where fishing was of major importance, a high degree of social cooperation was required. Even where fishing was only an important supplement to other subsistence, as in the Amazon, there was considerable cooperation in use of poisons, canoes, and other methods.

There may be areas of rich fisheries that were unexploited for want of canoes, nets, hooks, or other devices, but simple societies seem to have made excellent use of their resources by one means or another. Fish drugs, for example, are very widely distributed, and in South America alone several hundred different plants are used for this purpose.

7. *Transportational devices.* The importance of transportation has been mentioned in connection with accumulating and storing foods at some central point. It is also essential for transporting children and basic gear as a society moves about. Ethnographically, there are four subcategories of transportation.

a. Human carriers. All societies have some means of carrying foods, children, and various impedimenta. These devices, though highly varied, are generally limited in efficiency by human strength.

b. Sleds and toboggans. Where snow provides suitable surfaces, human beings can pull greater loads than they can carry. Dog traction adds further to the transportational potentials. It seems certain that the great territorial range of societies in the far north were a function of such transportation, complemented by water craft in the summer. It should also offset the need for infanticide, in which case Eskimo infanticide was practiced for reasons other than women's limitations on carrying children (see Balikci, 1964).

c. Water craft. Umiaks, kayaks, bark or dugout canoes, and balsa rafts give an enormous advantage in such subsistence activities as fishing, aquatic hunting, and even gathering wild rice, and they also increase transportational potentials. Except for certain marginal areas, such as Tierra del Fuego and parts of Australia, where better use might have been made of water craft, few societies lacked some kind of water transportation adequate to their needs.

The relatively high population density of coastal areas is obviously correlated with the combined land, sea, and littoral resources, but these areas usually have canoes which facilitate subsistence activities and permit concentration in large, permanent communities. In the Amazon, communities increased in size after steel axes enabled the people to range farther from the villages for foods.

d. Dog traction and packing. Use of dogs is probably comparatively recent, and it has limited distribution. The dog sled is certainly a major factor in the enormous range of some of the arctic societies and therefore also a factor in permitting large periodic aggregations. The dog-drawn travois and dog packing of the Plains were also of considerable value. Lowie (1963, p. 42) cites Coronado that dogs could draw 35 to 50 pounds on travois.

8. *Food preparation.* Many methods of treating vegetable and perhaps animal products extend the number of foods beyond that of precultural animals.

a. Mechanical processing. Certain hard-shell seeds and nuts must be opened before eating, but this can be accomplished with crude stones nearly as well as with metates and mortars. Greater efficiency may have increased leisure time rather than the amount of food. Other processing, such as winnowing seeds or cutting raw meat presents no problem, and stone-cutting tools have great antiquity.

b. Poison extraction. Some foods, such as acorns in California and elsewhere and the cycad of Australia, are made edible by extracting harmful ingredients. Domesticated manioc (*Manihot utillisima*) is elaborately treated with the tipití to remove the prussic acid, but Goldman states (1948, p. 772) that the acid readily boils off or disappears with drying or soaking in water. The Great Basin staple, pine nuts (*Pinus edulis* and *P. monophyla*), may be eaten raw, but roasting seems to change if not remove much of the resin.

c. Cooking. Although many fruits, greens, buds, and nuts require no treatment, probably the majority of foods, including roots, seeds, fish, and game, were cooked when necessary, and sometimes when not necessary. In addition to tenderizing foods, cooking may change deleterious chemicals and perhaps kills bacteria in over-ripe meat. If, however, the use of fire was not general until the second interstadial period (Clark and Piggott, 1965, p. 49), perhaps at about the first appearance of *Homo sapiens*, the earlier species of *H. erectus*, avoided poisonous plants and consumed meats raw. In this case, the conversion to a meat diet was accomplished without the aid of cooking.

All ethnographic cases have some means of cooking foods of all kinds—roasting on coals or in earth ovens, boiling in pots or with hot stones in containers of hide, basketry, bark, wood, etc., broiling over coals or on babracots, and others. Cooking, therefore, is another universal or constant factor.

9. *Food preservation and storage.* It has been noted that certain tribes in low latitudes do not preserve or store foods—for example, the Bushmen and Hadza—because vegetable resources can be obtained at any time. Storage is difficult in tropical areas because of heat and humidity, but farming societies were able to preserve certain foods. In higher latitudes, however, where preservation and storage of foods are essential during certain seasons, all societies have appropriate techniques.

This factor has many subcategories: protection of seeds against moisture and marauding animals, drying and smoking flesh, and preservative mixtures such as pemmican in which the meat is protected by adding fat.

10. *Shelter and clothing.* Special factors are necessary to survive in certain environments. These include for cold climates adequate clothing and footgear, which the Clactonian stone flake industry shows were probably made by the second interstadial period of Europe, perhaps fire which appeared about the same time, and possibly means of travel on deep snow of which we have evidence only from ethnographic sources. Clothing and shelters were less imperative in warm climates, although all known societies improvised temporary lean-tos and in some of the tropics protected the body against insects with capes or with grease.

Environmental Factors

Environmental features are significant in terms of their functional importance to ecological adaptations rather than their intrinsic properties such as climate, topography, or biota; for dissimilar environments may support somewhat similar societies if exploited in certain ways.

First, there are environmental potentials which, if exploited by appropriate cultural devices, determine the overall population density.

Second, there are factors which affect the nucleation of social segments. Natural barriers may separate major population groups and sometimes fairly small groups. Distribution of foods, as along shorelines, rivers, or lakes, and localization of water may entail special kinds of nucleation. Transportational devices other than human carriers will profoundly affect nucleation in areas where these can be used.

Third, the nature of the flora and fauna requires various kinds of subsistence activities, including certain patterns of cooperation and sharing.

Fourth, subsistence in some zones necessitates no food storing, whereas in others, especially in hard winter climates, it is impossible without considerable storage and methods of preservation. Accessories, such as clothing, shelters, and possibly fire, are also required by winter climates.

Cultural-Historical Factors

Perhaps 90 per cent of any tribal cultural inventory including subsistence devices is borrowed. Whether borrowed or locally innovated, the important consideration is the function of cultural features of different kinds to varying kinds of social aggregates. Exploitative devices are readily borrowed if they are useful. Restrictive marriage institutions, such as clans and moieties, will ordinarily be impossible among small widely separate primary groups or bands whose choice of marriage partners is already limited. Clans, although highly developed in the Southwest and part of the Plains, did not spread to the sparsely populated Great Basin or the Mackenzie River drainage. Among societies of sparse population, the only institutions pertaining to aggregates larger than the subsistence bands were ceremonialism, including initiation rites in some areas, and games, contests, and dances that became functional only when the larger group was assembled.

On the other hand, large permanent communities or strongly integrated bands or tribes permitted complex social and ritual elaboration, as on the Northwest Coast or the Plains. It is of historical interest but minor importance functionally whether the clans, moieties, social stratification and potlatches of the Northwest Coast and the strong chieftanship, sun dance, war patterns and proliferation of associations of the Plains were borrowed from elsewhere or developed locally. These supra-kin-level institutions were possible only if ecological preconditions existed, although they became functionally intertwined with subsistence activities.

EVOLUTIONARY FACTORS AND PROCESSES

Non-Cultural Adaptations

The effects of cultural ecological factors becomes most readily apparent when projected against the non-cultural adaptations of certain of the primates. The most instructive primates are the chimpanzees, gorillas, and baboons, for they have received greatest attention and are most similar to hominids in several respects. These primates have greatest body size, dimorphism, perennial sexuality, some degree of terrestriality, a varied subsistence basis mainly within the range of plant foods, and high adaptability. Their behavior discloses patterns within the limits of these biological potentials, and it is not therefore a genetically determined archetype from which hominid behavior was necessarily derived. It represents patterns of the ancestors of hominids only to the extent that ecological adaptations may be assumed to have been similar.

1. *Subsistence.* These primates are herbivorous, except that some consume small insects and mammals (DeVore, 1963, p. 32) and the chacma baboons eat shellfish, crabs, birds' eggs, and young birds (Hall, 1963, p. 6–18). Goodall reported only three occasions during eighteen months when chimpanzees scavenged meat (1963, p. 46). Food is found predominantly in trees—90 per cent among the chimpanzees (Goodall, 1963, p. 40)—which limits subsistence areas to stands of appropriate trees. Lacking transportation and storage devices, these foragers do not accumulate surpluses to establish even temporary encampments. There is no food sharing, even between mothers and offspring—which is true of herbivores generally in contrast to carnivores—and consequently no cooperation or dependencies based on subsistence activities.

2. *Territoriality.* Evidence on territoriality is conflicting, partly, I suspect, because of the meaning attached to the term. Habitual use of a delimited territory and familiarity with the members of one's own troop apparently inhibit free association with strangers within the same species. In addition, as Schaller (1963, p. 27) clearly states of gorillas, the territory of each troop is separated from that of other troops by uninhabitable areas. Unequal concentrations of resources, therefore, would predispose any species to a degree of troop isolation. Owing to natural vicissitudes of troop expansion and contraction, however, there would be budding off in some cases and amalgamation in others.

The tendency toward territoriality is

explainable by the ecological adaptations of various types of animals rather than by some genetically determined possessiveness which Ardrey in sensational articles in *Life* (1966a, 1966b) represents as the basis of conflict in man. Grazing herbivores of many species intermingled freely, and their herds are limited only by the extent of fodder. They defend themselves against predators rather than other herbivores. Male competition for estrous females is irrelevant to territoriality. Carnivorous predators, on the other hand, defend their kill and, unlike herbivores, share it. If game is locally scarce, they may come into competition with other groups of their species.

3. *Group and territory size.* Ape troops vary in size with population density, for the home range of these quadrupeds is only a fraction of that of human beings. To travel the length and breadth of a troop's territory would require a minimum trip of about three miles and rarely as much as nine miles.

Baboon troops are reported to occupy two to fifteen square miles (DeVore and Hall, 1965); gorillas, ten to fifteen (Schaller, 1965); and chimpanzees six to twenty (Goodall, 1965).

Gorilla troop size has been reported at two to thirty individuals (Schaller, 1965); chimpanzees at twenty to thirty (Reynolds, 1963); and baboons, thirteen to 185 at Amboseli (DeVore and Washburn, 1963); and twelve to 750 in Ethiopia (Kummer and Kurt, 1963).

4. *Group composition.* Conflicting data on group composition probably reflect differences among troops observed rather than errors of reporting, although distinction between troops may be difficult in densely populated areas and identification of individual members requires familiarity with the group. In addition, troops on game reserves such as that adjoining Nairobi, which is visited by hundreds of tourists daily, are not truly in a state of nature.

There is unanimity that mature males and females do not form permanent attachments, orangs possibly excepted. Male dominance and dimorphism are strong among the more terrestrial primates, which may be a function of sexual competition for the females and of the need to protect the troop against predators rather than against other troops. Whether a troop consists of a single dominant male and

several females and immature animals, whether it includes several "harems," or whether there is a hierarchy of dominance, or pecking order, seems to vary with the troops observed. Comparable male dominance cannot be assumed for all hominid societies, because sexual roles are determined more by cultural functions that by physical strength, and the female reproductive functions preclude some activities women might otherwise carry out.

Effects of Cultural Factors

The general effects of cultural factors added to biological potentials bring cultural ecological adaptations into sharp focus. Human bipeds may range at least twenty to thirty miles, and with certain transportation devices they may cover several hundred miles. Means of collecting, hunting, transporting, and preparing foods vastly augment man's subsistence basis. Primary human subsistence groups are little larger than those of the apes, but specialized functions in subsistence and child rearing have set lower limits on social groups, while exploitation of a wider environment and the kind of transportation have set upper limits. In all ethnographic cases, cultural complementarity is the basis of the nuclear family, and, because this involves marriage proscriptions and preferences, kinship relations extend from one minimal or primary group to another, their nature being determined by ecological adaptations and their limits by the size of the maximum group.

Cultural devices have also permitted occupation of higher latitudes, which non-hominids and early hominids probably could occupy only during warm interstadial periods (see Carpenter, 1942, pp. 303–311).

In analyzing the various social responses to ecological factors, it is convenient to start with the irreducible social unit, the family, although social evolution almost certainly began with such larger aggregates as a pre-hominid troop. Since the nuclear family is the focal point of all kinship analysis, it is important to ascertain the factors that underlie it.

1. *The nuclear family.* Although a nuclear family—a minimal unit of father, mother, and children—is basic to all ethnographic cases, it may not have existed in early periods. The family among hunters and gatherers is based

on strong sexual complementarity, men being primarily hunters and women carriers of wood and water, seed collectors, camp keepers, and child tenders. Unproductive as hunting may be in certain areas, it nonetheless gives men a distinctive and important subsistence role and was presumably the principal factor that created the nuclear family. If the early hominids were not hunters, their family may have been matrifocal in that it consisted of females and immature offspring. Food collecting, as far as we know, does not create a sexual division of labor, for it is carried out by both sexes in the same way.

Hunting of large game is clearly implied by Upper Paleolithic sites in Europe, and it was undoubtedly the special task of men, wherein masculine strength was probably less important than hunting devices and the considerable time spent away from the family. Fishing and aquatic hunting would have similar effects. Whether comparable specialization by the male was required to obtain large game during the lower Paleolithic is wholly conjectural, for hunting methods are unknown. Scavenging, if practiced, probably did not require special masculine activities, while hunting small animals cannot have imposed activities on men similar to those of large game hunting. Net hunting of rabbits among the Great Basin people, for example, involved women and children along with men.

Although it is now impossible to date the appearance of the nuclear family, the assumption that it is based on cultural complementarity rather than on some inherent or "natural" tendency means that it may be weakened. This is happening today, especially in certain economically depressed segments of society where males form such loose and transient unions with females that the stable social unit is the women and children, which has been designated the "matrifocal family." Sexual complementarity has also been decreasing for many reasons in nuclear families of all segments of Western society.

2. *The minimum or primary band.* Completely isolated nuclear families are very exceptional, for clusters of several families provide greater security. This symposium has made it strikingly clear, however, that many of the larger aggregates, which were formerly designated bands, are composed of smaller groups and sometimes of intermediate but very fluid groups. Since relations that begin with the nuclear family are of major importance to the minimum group, even though they extend beyond it, it is convenient to consider these first. Variations are clearly related to the major factors previously discussed, although space prevents adequate analysis of some of the problems raised by comparisons of marriage and kinship systems.

Except for those areas of abundant subsistence, special transportation, and permanent villages, the minimum group as exemplified by Australians, Athapaskans, Bushmen, Hadza, Western Shoshoni and probably many others is very close to Birdsell's model of 25 persons, although there is great seasonal variation and change over periods of years. (The patrilineal band discussed below is, however, somewhat larger.) This approximate size is maintained, despite population densities that range from one person to one or two square miles to one per forty or fifty square miles, because of the effect of transportational devices other than human carriers in some areas and because groups may be restricted in their range in other areas, concentrating, for example, near water or special resources.

I have designated these "primary bands" because they are connected most closely with subsistence, but other terms such as "special task groups" have been used.

Although the kinship structure of primary bands depends upon several factors, all consist of closely related families. Food collecting can rarely be cooperative, but, as Rose points out in the case of Australia, child tending becomes a particularly important function. In the case of hunters, cooperation by a number of men is common, and the kill is ordinarily shared.

Multifamily primary bands. Owing to expectable fluctuations in the size of primary bands, a strongly patterned cultural ideal of band composition would be difficult to maintain, except where factors making for a unilineal tendency become reinforced by myths or other fictions of descent. Composition of the primary band therefore varies, although its core is a number of intermarried families.

Among the Western Shoshoni, the primary group consisted of several families related through multiple marriages—brother and sister to sister and brother or brothers to sisters—and reinforced by the levirate and sororate. Because members of such small clusters of families soon become consanguinally as well as affinally interrelated, these clusters were interlinked through a network of marriages that extended territorially to the limits of natural barriers. These local groups were not, as Service believes (1962), patrilocal bands, a fact supported by unpublished ethnohistorical data (Steward, 1953). In southern Nevada and the Death Valley area, the lower altitudes, great aridity, sparse resources, and widely spaced springs isolated Southern Paiute groups to the degree of restricting the marriage network (Steward, 1938), and the same pattern seems to have prevailed among the Southern Paiute of Utah (Kelly, 1964).

The primary unit or band is very similar in composition among the northern Athapaskans. There has been semantic confusion regarding my statement (1936) that these bands could marry endogamously because they consisted of unrelated families. These bands contrast to patrilineages in that each had some consanguinally unrelated families. This is obviously true of Morice's large bands, which seem to be the same as Helm's "regional bands," and it is also true of Helm's "local bands," according to her genealogies. In the two Dogrib bands described, many families were related consanguinally through parents and children and through siblings, but there were also members related only affinally. After marriage all band members became affinals but not all were consanguines. Presumably, many of the spouses were drawn from other local bands. Unlike the Shoshoni, however, there were few cases of multiple marriage ties between two families.

From Helm's data I gather that trapping and fishing are far more important to the local band than I had previously recognized. In modern times, at least, this apparently affected post-marital residence in unpredictable ways, for siblings of both sexes often remained with their parents' group, although consanguinal barriers would force many to marry elsewhere. Group composition among the Bushmen (Lee, 1965) seems also to be based on multiple marriage between families that extended throughout the maximum band of 430 persons. Further

comparisons of group composition would require extended genealogical comparisons, but Australia has special interest.

If the primary Australian band is only some 25 to 40 persons and these bands are widely separated in arid areas, the imposition of exogamous clans and moieties might restrict the number of potential marriage partners to an impossible extent. Some of the marriage classes or sections may historically be a combination of patrilineal and matrilineal moieties. Viewed in terms of generations, this would place individuals of alternate generations in the same class. If however the tendency toward so-called gerontocracy is included and consanguinity is redefined, enough marriages are possible, especially between widely differing age groups. A possible means of clarifying this situation is the use of algebraic descriptions of marriage systems (for example, Reid, 1967).

Lineage based bands. The primary band has undoubtedly been a lineage when stochastically predictable circumstances have produced only sons or daughters for two generations, but this implies no ideal pattern. In other cases, specific factors may create tendencies toward a lineage, but this too does not become fixed. Woodburn (Chapter 11, this volume) describes the Hadza of Tanzania as matrilineal and matrilocal, with qualifications; the bands, which average eighteen persons and are attached to larger encampments up to a hundred persons, are highly unstable. A dominance of food collecting over hunting, wherein less than half the men hunt and these do so individually and ineffectively, may be a partial explanation.

Patrilineal bands. This is a more clear-cut type, and although my earlier formulation of the factors producing it (1936) have been doubted by some persons; others, including Birdsell, who takes his model from Australia, and Williams, on the basis of the Birhor, have made it the general model of all food hunters and collectors. There are several possible sources of confusion about the patrilineal band.

First, the factor of hunting may have lost importance with the reduction of game in the last four or five decades. Schapera (1926, 1930) and the sources on which he based his description of the Bushmen may have been correct for an earlier period, although, as Lee (1965) notes, the quantity of game in the area has decreased and Bantu have brought herds into a portion of the !Kung Bushman territory. The same is doubtless true of many areas, although assumptions about the game population must be made cautiously. It has recently been estimated that the total deer population of the United States today is greater than in aboriginal times, although its distribution is not the same, whereas bison now number but a fraction of that of pre-Columbian times.

Second, during early periods of ethnographic exploration many writers undoubtedly took structural types found in limited regions to be representative of large areas or continents. This does not necessarily invalidate what they observed, but it is expectable that in a continent as varied as Australia Radcliffe-Brown's "horde" would not occur everywhere.

Third, where the patrilineal band is reported it seems too large for a patrilineage based on known genealogy. If ancestry were not known beyond five generations, a group of twenty-five or thirty persons might continue to practice exogamy but their patrilineal consanguinity would become untraceable. These bands, however, are reported at thirty to 150 persons. In the absence of a strong genealogical sense, the fiction of relationship between all members could be perpetuated by myths of descent, which I believe were present among all the patrilineal bands previously described (Steward, 1936). In this case, we can accept as descriptive of a strong tendency the accounts of Gusinde (1931–39; also, Baer and Schitz, 1965) for the Ona, Radcliffe-Brown (1931) for at least some Australians, Schebesta (1929, 1931) for the Congo and Malayan Negritos, Roth (1890) for the Tasmanians, and Strong (1929a) for the southern California Shoshoneans.

The importance of the hunter's familiarity with his country is questioned by Williams on the basis of the Birhor of India who have patrilineal bands. The Birhor, however, are very distinctive in that they mainly hunt hares by means of nets for trade to neighboring peoples for rice. The Shoshoni hunt rabbits in the same way and need only to know where the animals are abundant. Unlike the Birhor, who were not self-sufficient in subsistence, the Shoshoni had to be familiar with their terrain to obtain other foods.

The factors that explain the patrilineal band are more environmental than technological. Such bands occur where there are large, highly mobile animals that do not migrate long distances, where hunting exceeds collecting in effort and sometimes in quantity, where population is sparse, and where transportation is limited to human carriers. It may have other preconditions and causes. This structure is the result of a strong tendency but, for reasons previously particularized (Steward, 1936), not an unalterable pattern.

The Indians of the Plains exhibit the effects of contrasting factors. The vast bison herds made food collecting secondary, the nature of the animals was such that highly coordinated and even policed hunts were carried out by large numbers of men, and the dog travois and packing supplemented human carriers.

3. *The maximum band.* This is the group of maximum social interaction, which Birdsell (1953) designates the "dialectical tribe" and which rarely exceeds 500 persons. Although such groups may be somewhat integrated through subsistence activities, they are based principally on similar dialect, intermarriage, visiting, and other social interactions and, unlike permanent communities, are not strongly structured and rarely have leaders of any importance. The social, cultural, and dialectical frontiers of such bands may be delimited by distances within which people can associate or by such barriers as deserts, lakes, and mountain ranges. Devices for snow travel in northern latitudes and greater resource density in lower latitudes are factors that permit communications within the bands.

Not all maximum bands, however, conform to the model of the dialectical tribe. Owing to unpredictability of resources, the annual subsistence trek among the Western Shoshoni (Steward, 1938) and the Alacaluf of the Chilean archipelago (Bird, 1946) brings family clusters into association with different clusters from year to year. The larger network of social interaction, therefore, was a series of intermarriages that extended over hundreds of miles.

Territoriality and warfare. There have been many contentions that primitive bands own territories or resources and fight to protect them. Although I cannot assert that this is never the case, it is probably very uncommon. First, the primary groups that comprise the larger maximum bands intermarry, amalgamate if they are too small or split off if too large. Second, in the cases reported here, there is no more than a tendency for primary groups to utilize special areas. Third, most so-called "warfare" among such societies is no more than revenge for alleged witchcraft or continued interfamily feuds. Fourth, collecting is the main resource in most areas, but I know of no reported defense of seed areas. Primary bands did not fight one another, and it is difficult to see how a maximum band could assemble its manpower to defend its territory against another band or why it should do so. It is true that durian trees, eagle nests, and a few other specific resources were sometimes individually claimed, but how they were defended by a person miles away has not been made clear.

Defense of the hunting territories of patrilineal bands has also been claimed, but this too is open to question. Slain animals are owned by the individual or group of hunters. Fishing weirs, dams, and other constructions are always owned by their builders, and the same is doubtless true of pitfalls, blinds, corrals, and the like. Whether a band defended live game within a territory against other bands with which it intermarried deserves reexamination.

Ethnographic and archeological models. An ethnographic model based on dialect, stylistic features, value systems, corporate limits, jural principles, and ritual patterns is quite useless and unnecessary for archeology. The starting point is to compare the special purpose encampment of a primary band with a prehistoric site where the same factors can be inferred. Larger temporary encampments of ethnographic cases are more difficult to equate with archeological sites, for non-ecological factors may have operated. But where the ethnographic and archeological sites are reasonably permanent, factor determination of the preconditions of such sites is possible. Sackett has noted that Upper Paleolithic sites seem generally to represent more permanent, multi-purpose habitations than Mousterian sites which lack evidence of the full hunting complex and has suggested that the functional nature of hunting and fishing in the Upper Paleolithic may have been comparable to that of the Northwest Coast. If the Upper Paleolithic people had some of the transportational devices known among modern Arctic societies, nucleation of populations would have been easier.

As for Sackett's question about the kind of future Paleolithic research needed, I suggest that in addition to information on the locations and on the depth and artifact content of sites, it is important to estimate the relative quantities of fish and game, to speculate about the kinds of social activities that were required in hunting both mature and immature animals of different species with the methods that may have been used, and to attempt to relate the purpose and permanence of the site to micro-environments of different resources.

35.

Discussions, Part VII

35a. Are the Hunter-Gatherers a Cultural Type?

Speakers: *DeVore, Murdock, Whiting*

MURDOCK: I shall confine my remarks to the area of social organization. My interest in hunters is twofold. First, in comparative work, using the cross-cultural method that I employ, we have always had a great deal of difficulty finding enough independent cases of hunters. If you know of the earlier study by Hobhouse, Wheeler, and Ginsburg (1961), you may recall that between 75 and 85 per cent of all their lower hunters were Australians, while a similar precentage of their higher hunters were North American Indians. Of course, this situation, statistically, is entirely improper today. The problem is to add to our cases of hunting peoples, and that has been done here. My second interest in hunters is shared by many of you. We are interested in contemporary hunters because of the light they may shed on the behavior of Pleistocene man. This does not mean that any hunting society today resembles one in the Pleistocene. But to whatever limited extent we are to understand Pleistocene man by evidence other than archeological remains, we need the widest possible range of cultural variations to indicate the possibilities for adjustments that presumably occurred during the Pleistocene.

The new contributions to the literature on hunter-gatherers made at this symposium seem to me to aid in the clarification of a whole super-type of culture that I had not really understood before I came. June Helm's paper comparing Dogrib, !Kung, and Nambikwara shows us the remarkable similarities among the three. Looking back on the 27 hunting societies covered in my conference paper, I come to the conclusion (leaving aside the Australian ones for the moment) that there is a surprisingly narrow range of variation in hunting and gathering cultures with regard to social organization. The two universal human social groupings—nuclear family and local community—stand out clearly in all the hunter-gatherer societies. The nuclear is less frequently swamped by larger types of family organization among hunter-gatherers than is elsewhere the case. There is a strikingly uniform division of labor in hunter-gatherer societies. The women gather; the men hunt. And—something that has not been brought out—when these societies fish, the men manage the more complex techniques; while the women do basketry, fishing, gather shellfish, etc. Now, this neatness of the division of labor is far more uniform than one finds among many other types of societies, say agricultural ones in general.

With the exception of the Australians, there is no case of rigid unilocal rules of residence among hunter-gatherers. There is some type

335

of ambilocal residence, in which often viri- and uxorilocal residence is of about equal occurence. This is a part of the adaptability of hunters that has been pointed out in other contexts. Descent is rarely unilineal. Some of the Athabaskans, some of the California Indians, some of the Northeastern Algonkians, a few of the Apache, and possibly the Vedda are unilineal to a considerable degree. But clearly the general picture is similar to that for residence, as regards flexibility.

Polygyny occurs among hunter-gatherers, but it rarely reaches the extremes reached in some unilineal societies, particularly patrilineal ones. Extended families of one type or another appear quite frequently, but they never cause the nuclear family to lose its distinctive features. Exogamy is particularly universal among hunters-gatherers. So in general there is a rather restricted distribution curve in the main elements of their social organization— except for the Australians!

Now, the Australians are not only unilinear, but they are also largely characterized by double descent. Their residence rules are over- whelmingly patrilocal. They have polygyny in a more developed form than other hunter- gatherers. Without the example of the Aus- tralians, we might agree that Lowie was right when he postulated a bilateral type of society with a prominent nuclear family as necessarily the earliest form of human social organization. The Australian evidence, however, makes this seem dubious. I suggest that we recognize the near uniqueness of Australian social organiza- tion and pay more attention than before to attempts to explain their sharp divergence from similar societies elsewhere in the world.

WHITING: I would like to underline Professor Murdock's comments by presenting some statis- tical data comparing hunters and gatherers with societies whose subsistence economy is either agricultural or pastoral or both. Numer- ous times in this conference similarities have emerged between groups observed in very diff- erent parts of the world. This report will, I hope, confirm most of these strong impressions and at the same time highlight those characteristics that are peculiar to hunters and gatherers and distinguish them as a special cultural type.

The sample upon which this study is based consists of one society from each of the 412 culture clusters defined by Murdock in the *Ethnographic Atlas* (1967). The particular society chosen to represent each cluster was the one with the best ethnographic coverage as judged by the number of categories coded in Tables A and B of the *Atlas*. If two or more societies in a given cluster were equal in coverage the representative was chosen by lot.

The variables coded in the *Ethnographic Atlas* were then converted into unidimensional scalar variables whenever this was possible (Whiting, 1967). One of these codes was an estimate of the relative dependence upon hunting, gather- ing, and fishing. This estimate was obtained by summing the scores in columns 7, 8, and 9 of the *Atlas*. The score was then correlated (Pearson's r.) with each of the remaining 86 scalar variables. Nearly half of the resulting correlations were statistically significant. Since a correlation coefficient is difficult to interpret, it was determined to make a further analysis so that the results could be presented in a more meaningful way.

To do this we chose two subsamples, one of which consisted of more or less pure hunters and gatherers and the other more or less pure agriculturalists and/or pastoralists. This could easily be done on the basis of the scalar score for subsistence described above. If on the basis of the score, 75 per cent of a society's food supply was provided by foraging (for example, hunting, gathering, or fishing), it was placed in the "pure" foraging group. On the other hand, if less than 15 per cent of the food supply was provided by foraging techniques it was placed in the non-foraging category. This procedure yielded 74 "pure" foragers and 99 "pure" non-foragers. The remaining 239 cases were considered mixed and omitted from this analysis.

The geographic distribution of these two groups is shown in Table 1.

The geographic bias in the sample is unfor- tunate but not surprising. It might have been better to draw separate samples for the Old and the New World as Lee has done (Chapter 4, this volume). This was not done, however, and therefore it should be kept in mind that societies from North and South America con- tribute heavily to the foragers in our sample and the Circum-Mediterranean, East Eurasia and Africa are over represented in the non- foraging group.

Table 1   Foragers and Non-Foragers

Distribution by region of the sample of cultures whose subsistence economy is primarily (over 75 per cent) based upon hunting, gathering, and fishing and those in which such techniques are negligible, contributing 15 per cent or less to subsistence.

	Foragers	Non-Foragers
Africa	4	21
Circum-Mediterranean	0	38
East Eurasia	8	23
Insular Pacific	6	9
North America	42	4
South America	14	4

The percentage of societies in each group having certain characteristics was calculated and is listed together with an estimate of the statistical significance of the difference between foragers and non-foragers based upon χ^2 tests. Since, as Professor Murdock pointed out, the hunters and gatherers in Australia seem somewhat atypical, the percentage for each variable for the seven Australian cases coded in the *Atlas* have also been listed whenever sufficient data were available. Only those variables that yielded statistically significant results in the first correlational analysis are reported on this test.

It is worthwhile to comment of the position of the Australian tribes as shown in Table 2. In some respects they are typical foragers. They have small nomadic communities, have a preference for sororal polygyny, and do not have a caste system. In some respects they stand intermediate between the two groups, e.g., bride price, bride service, and initial uxorilocal residence. They are more like the non-foraging group however, in that their final residence is virilocal, descent is unilinear, matrilateral cross-cousin marriage is permitted, and initiation rites with genital operations are performed. Statistical evidence thus confirms in certain respects the observations made by Murdock and others as to the unique position of the Australian tribes among the hunters and gatherers.

In order that one not be misled by Table 2 into thinking that foragers are different from non-foragers in every respect, it should be repeated that only the variables that showed a significant relationship in the initial correlational analysis have been presented. Some of the variables that showed no differences were

the degree of polygyny (rather than the type), extended versus nuclear families, games of chance, and type of succession to local office.

I would also like to comment on differences in child rearing between foragers and non-foragers. The data on child-rearing practices are not available for the sample used above, but some interesting results are reported in a study by Barry, Child, and Bacon (1959) on a similar sample. Judgments were made on the degree to which parents put pressure on their children to be compliant, e.g., achieving, self-reliant, and independent. Of the 22 foraging cultures in their sample, 19, or 86 per cent, stressed assertiveness more than compliance. By contrast, 34 of the 39 cultures whose economy was primarily based on agriculture and/or animal husbandry stressed compliance over assertiveness. They argue that this difference is a consequence of differences in the accumulation of economic goods. Cattle and cultivated fields are part of the establishment which must be cared for responsibly and obediently according to rules set by the older generation. The successful forager, however, with no accumulation to protect, should be assertive and independent and is so trained as a child.

On the basis of a detailed study of child rearing (B. Whiting, 1963), it was noted that in societies with large animals and no fences, children were generally assigned the task of herd boys, which is a task requiring a high degree of both obedience and responsibility. By contrast among hunters and gatherers, there are no tasks that substantially contribute to the economy and are appropriate for young children. I would judge the hunting episode of the two young boys that we saw in Woodburn's Hadza film would be quite typical. The boys were hunting for their own pleasure rather than carrying out a task assigned by their elders. If they failed, they would almost certainly not be punished for it. On the other hand, if a herd boy should let his animals get into the neighbor's garden, he would most certainly be severely punished. Perhaps these differences in child rearing account in part for the reluctance of hunters and gatherers to change their ways and become part of the modern world.

One final comment should be made with respect to the effect of foraging upon children.

Table 2   Characteristics of Societies in Three Groups

	Atlas Column No.	Foragers (n = 74)	Australians (n = 7) (Percentages)	Non-Foragers (n = 99)	P. Value (Foragers vs. Non-foragers)
LOCAL COMMUNITY SIZE	31				
Less than 50		47	87	5	.0001
50–99		29	0	8	.0001
100 or more		24	13	87	.0001
SETTLED COMMUNITIES	30	7	0	84	.0001
HOUSE TYPE:					
Curvilinear floor plan	80	54	—	28	.001
Round or conical roof	83	54	—	35	.02
EXCHANGE AT MARRIAGES	12				
Bride price		30	57	80	.0001
Bride service		23	15	2	.0001
FORM OF MARRIAGE	14–15				
General polygyny		14	15	34	.0001
Sororal polygyny		22	70	0	.0001
Limited polygyny		47	15	39	.0001
Monogamy		18	0	27	.0001
RESIDENCE	16–17				
Initially uxorilocal		27	15	10	.001
Finally uxorilocal		22	0	6	.0001
Finally avunculocal		4	ò	1	.0001
Finally virilocal		56	100	79	.0001
Finally ambilocal		15	0	3	.0001
Finally neolocal		3	0	8	.0001
Finally natolocal		0	0	3	.0001
DESCENT UNILINEAR	20–24	27	100	67	.0001
EXOGAMOUS COMMUNITIES	19	43	85	25	.024
CROSS-COUSIN MARRIAGE PERMITTED	26				
Matrilateral		31	57	54	.005
Patrilateral		26	15	49	.005
PRESENCE OF HIGH GODS	34	37	17	83	.0001
GAMES	35				
Physical skill		98	75	79	.002
Strategy		0	25	62	.0001
INITIATION WITH GENITAL MUTILATION	37–38	6	43	20	.024
CASTE	69	20	0	53	.0001

The number 25–30 has been suggested by several people as the typical size of the micro-band. With such a small group there cannot be enough children of the appropriate age to get up a game of football or baseball even if you let the girls play. Although I know of no data on the subject, I would be very surprised if there were many competitive team sports among the hunters or gatherers—another reason for the emphasis on individual achievement rather than group responsibility.

DeVore: It is banal to say that we have raised more questions than we have answered; yet this is particularly true of this conference and, indeed, was one of our main purposes in organizing it. To the extent that we can still see the forest despite the trees, it is apparent that it is a very lush, variegated, tropical rain-forest. Although synthetic statements concerning hunter-gatherers as a "culture type" may now seem further away than before, I think that it was necessary for us to pass through the stage of critical reexamination represented by this conference. There were overly simple typologies to be amended and unquestioned generalizations to be called into question and exorcised. Many of the older statements are now of no greater value to us than the Pleistocene "stages" are to the contemporary archeologist.

On the other hand, I am not yet willing to abandon the search for generalizations that seem to apply to most hunter-gatherers most of the time. To try, in three days' time, to range over a topic so broad as "man the hunter"—a topic which, merely in terms of geography, took us from the high arctic to the Kalahari Desert and from India, to South America, to Australia—makes it unlikely that any sweeping generalizations will suddenly appear from the data. Indeed, we might well be suspicious of any generalization that was intended to apply to all men who have ever hunted in any place or at any time.

35b. Primate Behavior and the Evolution of Aggression

Speakers: *L. Binford, DeVore, Freeman, Gardner, Hamburg, Schneider, Turnbull, Washburn, Williams, Woodburn*

HAMBURG: Let me start by asking the question: Why should one take an interest in ancient hunting and gathering societies, if one is primarily concerned with the problems of contemporary man (as I am)? It is because this represents such a long period in human evolution. Presumably, during that long period, important adaptive characteristics of *Homo sapiens* evolved. The environment of contemporary man is based on very recent environmental changes. So, much of the genetic equipment of contemporary man is likely to have been shaped by the selective pressures of the hunting and gathering era.

Similarly, it seems to me likely that some prevalent values of hunting and gathering societies may also reflect selection pressures. And I wonder whether some of the values that were useful in solving adaptive problems during the hunting and gathering era may still persist in the face of very recent environmental changes. What conditions would favor the persistence of values that were adaptively useful during the hunting and gathering era? I think these would have a great deal to do with some of the issues that Whiting raised. That is, if the prevalent values have such adaptive utility that they are strongly incorporated into the concept of self by means of reward and punishment, then I should think that these orientations and attitudes would not be easily changed. This is particularly true if one adds that the outcome of the early shaping procedure is ambiguous in its results in later life, which is likely to be the case, given the life span of the human.

If it is true that there are, in contemporary man, both genetic and social characteristics that were once highly adaptive but are no longer so, then man in his present environment might be said to have something of a "carry-over" problem. This consideration was what first led me to an interest in human evolution. After years of examining biochemical and physiological correlates of psychological stress in man and finding it difficult to make biological sense of these responses in terms of the contemporary environment, I began to wonder whether they might make more sense in terms of the earlier human environment. Of course, at this level of analysis one must also consider a large portion of general mammalian evolution. This is along the general lines of the endocrine and autonomic changes associated with sudden apprehension or concern, changes that go in the direction of facilitation of energy metabolism and modifications of circulation such that increased energy expenditure is supported.

Another carry-over problem that may be more important is that having to do with the destructive propensities of *Homo sapiens*, and I often have the feeling that this is a hidden agenda in many discussions of social problems and evolutionary changes. Specifically, the question—which can be a worrisome one—is whether we have carried over aggressive propensities that were highly adaptive in earlier environments but are now highly dangerous. We should understand that this line of study leads us even beyond ancient hunter-gatherers, back to Washburn's baseline at the nonhuman primate level. There are several lines of evidence that show something about the biological mechanisms through which aggressive tendencies may have developed in earlier primates. In the first place, studies of essentially ground-living Old World monkeys (summarized in the volume edited by DeVore, 1965) bring up certain relevant points. There is a great deal of evidence showing rough-and-tumble play over a number of years. This recalls Whiting's point about the development of attitudes and skills in play, since it amounts to the practice of aggressive behavior over a period of several years. They develop complex motor skills that utilize their formidable anatomy—the great canine teeth and the massive temporal muscles. In these species, there is marked sexual dimorphism in both anatomy and behavior. The adult males defend the troop and regulate internal disputes.

In laboratory experiments in recent years, there have been several groups that show something relevant about hormonal influences on brain development. In rodents, for instance, several groups have shown that treatment of the newborn females with testosterone results not only in a shift towards male copulatory behavior, but also increases aggressive behavior. More recently, Young, Goy, and Phoenix have extended these experiments to rhesus macaques and, rather surprisingly, the same sorts of things happened. They gave testosterone to pregnant females during their second quarter of pregnancy, so that it would

influence the brain development in the fetus. And, as with the rodents, this shifted the behavior of female offspring toward male norms, particularly in the matter of aggression. And this is still true now that the females so treated are 3 years old. Of course in the field these females would get badly beaten and might or might not remain so aggressive. In fact, they might turn out to be the most inhibited and surly. The point is simply that the hormonal influence on the brain is by no means independent of the social influences brought to bear upon the developing infant.

In respect to this very long period of hunting and gathering societies, does it seem likely that selection pressure favoring male aggression has eased greatly until very recently? If not, then how dangerous is our present situation. In relation to hunter-gatherers, one point made by Washburn a few years ago and elaborated more recently by Campbell has been the very great differences in the territory utilized in a year's time by present hunter-gatherers, as contrasted with living nonhuman primates. Now, one may wonder what sorts of controls are necessary for the utilization of such large territories, especially if one is hunting large mammals. How much variation on strict territoriality is possible if one is still to accomplish this? It seems to me that the need for some degree of effective control over relatively large areas would lead to tensions between groups, and on this point Turnbull mentioned the need for an excess of space to minimize conflicts between groups. I was surprised to hear that, given the relative unimportance of hunting for these people. Birdsell suggests that the absence of territoriality in some places may be explained as caused by the disruption resulting from contact with Europeans. This seems quite plausible to me; although I suspect that there is still a discernible continuum from the strictest territoriality to the least evident manifestations of it. In-group, out-group distinctions are ubiquitous in modern society, and I wonder whether this tendency may not bear some relation to the problems of the hunting and gathering way of life. In closing, I quote Bill Laughlin's statement:

Hunting is the master behavior pattern for the human species. It is the organizing activity which integrated the morphological, physiological, genetic, and intellectual aspects of the individual human organisms and of the populations that compose our single species. Hunting is a way of life (and not simply a subsistence technique), which importantly involves commitments, correlates, and consequences spanning the entire bio-behavioral continua of the individual and of the entire species of which he is a member. Man evolved as a hunter; he spent over 99 per cent of his species' history as a hunter; and he spread over the entire habitable area of the world as a hunter.

TURNBULL: I am bothered by the assumption that hunters are aggressive. Although I do not know the Bushmen or the Hadza, I feel that what I have to say is probably true of them also. In the two groups known to me, there is an almost total lack of aggression, emotional or physical, and this is borne out by the lack of warfare, feuding, witchcraft, and sorcery.

I am also not convinced that hunting is itself an aggressive activity. This is something that one must see in order to realize; the act of hunting is not carried out in an aggressive spirit at all. Due to the consciousness of depleting natural resources, there is actually a regret at killing life. In some cases, this killing may even bear an element of compassion. My experience with hunters has shown them to be very gentle people, and while it is certainly true that they lead extremely hard lives, this is not the same thing as being aggressive.

WILLIAMS: Although the hunting way of life comprises 99 per cent of human history, we should remember Sahlins' earlier point that throughout this period man has been a hunter among hunters. In this conference however, we have dealt with peoples as they are today and—for very good reasons—have mostly avoided guessing what they would be as hunters in a universe of hunters. The matter of aggression is a case in point. The Birhor of today are not violent; they are more "hapless" than "harmless." But if they were no longer to be an enclave minority I think no one could predict how this would affect the level of aggression.

SCHNEIDER: If Laughlin is correct, then Turnbull must be out of his mind! For if hunting is the master mechanism that Laughlin says it is, then why can't the ethnographer discern any sign of this among the contemporary hunting peoples?

GARDNER: Is it not possible that both are correct? Turnbull cites non-aggression only among refuge area groups. There is, in fact, a pattern of aggression avoidance among hunters and gatherers in refuge areas but there is a contrasting pattern of aggression (war, competitiveness, etc.) among hunters and gatherers in more homogeneous intercultural environments, such as the Australians, Andamanese, and Ona. Laughlin is talking about just such complementary peoples.

All hunting peoples have neighbors, but not all of these peoples are under intercultural pressure of a sort to which they cannot reply. This distinction *is* possible.

TURNBULL: Let me say another word about my contention that the Pygmies are not aggressive, an opinion similar to that of many people who have worked among hunters. I recognize that life in Pygmy camp is far from peaceful; husbands frequently beat up their wives, and *vice versa*. Yet such outlets, as well as the explicit concern shown for avoiding aggression, are insurance policies against aggression of an intended, calculated type—which is what I take to be the definitive component of the sort of aggression that Hamburg mentioned.

SCHNEIDER: The point I keep trying to make is that it is not yet at all clear that hunting is such a distinctive and clearly definable way of life as Laughlin has alleged it to be. It seems to me that the points Washburn and Laughlin are discussing are of such general, diffuse significance that it is hard to see how they can be said to fit specifically into a hunting frame. I fail to see any distinctive set of relationships making up a constellation of aggression or of man-animal relations that are specially centered around hunting peoples. For example, consider the Pueblos. Do we want to call them fundamentally aggressive, generally aggressive, or only slightly aggressive? For after all, Turnbull's descriptions of Pygmy camps sound in some respects like the sort of thing one reads about the Pueblos. Comparisons such as this undermine the delineation of "the hunting way of life" as a clear-cut phenomenon.

Finally, I have noticed that all the exceptional and special cases have been characterized as living in refuge areas. But all of us are in refuge areas in this life, and surely every group has been exposed at some time or another to other peoples. So the idea that we must, unfortunately, look at some peoples as "enclave minorities" seems to recall the myth of the natural man. There are many different kinds of settings, but I do not see any radical dichotomy to be made in them.

WASHBURN: I would like to turn to another matter and question the assumption that scavenging is an easy or necessary stage in human evolution. In the first place, all of the information that we have on primate hunting —Goodall's material on chimpanzees (Goodall, 1965; Goodall and von Lawick, 1965), DeVore's on baboons (DeVore and Hall, 1965; Washburn and DeVore, 1961), Struhasaker's on vervets (Struhsaker, 1967), and Carpenter's on gibbons (Carpenter, 1941)— suggest that these animals will take eggs, young birds, and other small, living creatures, but that they do not scavenge. The evidence shows that hunting small, easily captured prey is far simpler and more nearly universal than is scavenging. Besides, scavenging from large carcasses when carnivores are nearby can be exceedingly difficult. A scavenger must want meat very much to try for it under these circumstances, and he must be able to appraise and cope with the situation. It is said that it is easy to drive a lion from its kill, but this is only true in areas where lions are accustomed to being hunted and are trained to stay away from man.

Finally, scavenged meat is of rare occurrence by comparison with meat that is easy to hunt. In an area in Africa in which there are many lions, there are still hundreds of baboon per lion; so that if the baboons were to try to live on scavenged meat, they would have a hard time getting an ounce of meat per day per baboon. The most minimal hunting of easily killed animals is more rewarding than this.

WOODBURN: I think Professor Washburn may perhaps be understating the importance of scavenging. The Hadza, living in an area at least as rich in both predatory and herbivorous animals as anywhere else in the world where hunters and gatherers survive, often obtain meat by scavenging. The meat is located by watching the movements of vultures flying overhead. The interpretation of the movements of vultures is very skilled; using this method, carcasses of animals can be located up to perhaps three miles away. Very often Hadza camps are built high in the rocks overlooking the plains and, while sitting about in camp, men keep their eyes open both for animals to hunt and for vultures to lead them to dead animals. They eat the meat of animals that have died by themselves as well as those killed by predators.

The Hadza do drive predators off the carcass of an animal without any hesitation. I have myself seen lions, leopards, and wild dogs chased away. Admittedly the Hadza possess powerful bows and arrows which they do not hesitate to use and certainly Paleolithic man may have had more difficulty. But I am inclined to believe that even the simple equipment of at least some types of Paleolithic man may have been enough. The dangers of wild animals have, I believe, been vastly exaggerated particularly by European hunters. The Hadza hunt lion, leopard, rhinoceros, and buffalo, all with bow and arrow. They do not hunt elephant, but they constantly wander through country in which elephant abound. Yet within living memory only one adult Hadza has been killed by any of these animals. Two children have been taken by leopards at night.

DeVORE: I see no necessary contradiction between these two points of view. *Homo sapiens* is clearly capable of scavenging meat as a supplement to his diet, but this not equivalent to the situation confronting the smaller Australopithecines, with their cruder tools. The issue is whether scavenging on a regular basis constituted a stage in the evolution of hunting behavior prior to the skilled hunting of lone prey. I agree with Washburn that the evidence argues strongly against such a stage.

FREEMAN: I am intrigued by one statement in Professor Steward's conference paper in which the subhuman primate family, as an evolutionary stage, is defined as a biologically based matrifocal family. The subhuman primate family, he suggests, might have characterized a phase of primate social organization prior to the development of the nuclear family. It is my understanding that this stage of organization was defined largely on the basis of observations of modern nonhuman primate communities, so I should like to ask Professor DeVore to comment on this formulation. Since we now have studies of groups as diverse in social behavior as say, baboons and gorillas, is there a sense in which it is useful to call the basic unit of nonhuman primate social organization a matrifocal family? Is such an organization important in economic activities or for purposes of defense?

DeVore: With the large number of primate field studies, a wide variety of forms of social organization is beginning to emerge. It would be unfortunate to think of the organization of primate society only in terms, say, of baboons, since we now know that in the Old World primates alone the kinds of social organization range from isolated individuals, mated pairs with offspring, troops, one-male groups, and so on to a very loose aggregation in species like the chimpanzee.

At the same time, however, something else is becoming evident. Many of you have read the work of Jane von Lawick-Goodall (Goodall, 1965) and seen the films by her husband (Goodall and von Lawick, 1965; von Lawick and von Lawick-Goodall, 1966). What strikes me in these—especially in the recent films—is the extraordinary degree to which the offspring continue to be attached to the mother well into young adult life. What one finds, then, is not a band or troop or organized group in any monkey sense, but a great many older females surrounded by immature offspring—up to as many as four, including young adult males. This persistent bond between mother and offspring can also be very important in at least some species of monkeys. As a result of long-term studies at the Japan Monkey Centre (Kawamura, 1958; Washburn *et al.*, 1965) and on Cayo Santiago (e.g. Sade, 1965), we now appreciate that strong ties to the mother extend well into the adult life of her offspring. All this is to say that I agree with Steward's point of view, though I would not call such matrifocal groups "families." Melvin Neville, who has just completed field work on rhesus macaques in India, reports that one of the rhesus troops was entirely organized around adult females. There were no adult males in the troop and males who tried to join were repulsed.

Williams: I want to go back to the statements by the first two gentlemen and to suggest that there is a type of problem other than these raised by ecological considerations. If you conceive of a situation in which there are homogeneously distributed families who are not territorial in any sense, and then imagine them coming into conflict with multifamily groups who *do* defend a territory—who wins? I do not want to oppose an argument to data. Steward says that he has data that show people existing only in families throughout an area; I suggest that it is a problem to understand how this could continue, assuming that they could also have a higher level of organization.

Binford: The use of the term "family" seems to me to imply a segment of social system, rather than simply the form of a set of relationships between individuals. In primate social systems, are we dealing with an internally-segmented system based on units that are *not* simply parallel sets of relationships between individuals classed by sex and age—relationships that go through phases related to the reproductive cycle—or are we seeing an internally-segmented system that goes through annual phases of aggregation and dispersion, where these are regulated by the ecological relationship between the group and the various subsistence resources that the group depends on? In other words, I want to distinguish, in Gearing's sense (1958), a series of structural poses throughout the year adjusted to cycles in the environment from what in primate groups might be more properly viewed in terms of the reproductive cycle and the various roles that go with it. If we view the family in the former context, then speaking of the family with respect to primates is a questionable kind of analytical concept.

Washburn: I would like to underline what Irv DeVore was saying about the female-plus-offspring group in the nonhuman primates, because I think this is a major discovery of the last few years. At least in rhesus monkeys, this can last until the young are fully adult, and Don Sade (Sade, 1965) observed one case in which a mother protected her offspring by diverting an adult male from attacking the offspring, when the offspring himself was fully mature. So this is definitely a continuing group. Furthermore, in marked contrast to what we used to think in anthropology, rhesus monkeys breed only during six months of the year; while the mother-offspring relationships and the whole social system persist throughout the entire year. It is not just sex that is holding these groups together; they are in some sense adaptive groups with more functions and more complex functions than we used to imagine.

35c. FUTURE AGENDA

Speakers: *Bulmer, Condominas, Lévi-Strauss, Posnansky, Tax, Watanabe, Woodburn*

LÉVI-STRAUSS: For three days we have been discussing the cultural category of hunter-gatherers, and it seems to me that this can be taken as either very wide or very narrow. It is very narrow if we insist upon limiting the category to those few tribes who live exclusively by hunting and gathering. But in the course of the discussion it became obvious that this cannot be done; we constantly were drawing data from populations which are far more numerous and are hunter-gatherers only to a certain extent. For example, Dr. Lee discussed the food supply of the Bororo under the headings "hunting," "gathering," and "fishing"; while, in fact, the Bororo are excellent farmers and have been so for a long time—as indicated by an extensive mythology about cultivation, which points towards the eastern slopes of the Andes.

It would be foolish, in my opinion, to leave aside the direct experience we ourselves may have had in our own societies of hunting or gathering behavior. Although my example may not strike home to Americans, I suggest, for example, that we study the psychological experience of people in France, Russia, and elsewhere who are fond of gathering mushrooms. In many parts of Europe this is a full-fledged gathering activity available to our study.

More attention should be given to things which are neither hunted nor gathered in a strict sense but play an important part in the lives of hunter-gatherers. For example, the Guayaki are pure hunter-gatherers and take great care during hunting expeditions to cut down a certain species of wild palm tree from which they can obtain the tasty grubs of a certain butterfly. And, in fact, a substantial portion of their diet is made up of these grubs,

which they both gather and to some extent cultivate in stumps of the palms.

We should also avoid lumping together such tribes as, on the one hand, the Guayaki and Bushmen, who seem always to have plenty to eat and, on the other, the Nambikwara, who really live continually on the verge of starvation.

Some hunter-gatherers practice nomadism while others live in permanent residences. I might mention that in Southern France there was recently discovered a Lower Paleolithic site at which there was a substantial enough house so that there are still conspicuous traces of its existence approximately 200,000 years later. Now, nomadism itself may in some cases consist of wandering over several hundred square miles of territory; while among the Guayaki it consists merely in a daily inspection of a small, bounded territory.

From these and other types of variation—e.g., in social structure and in marriage rules—I conclude that it might be useful to widen the category of hunter-gatherer culture. Instead of defining it in terms of a number of specific groups that can be pointed out on a map, perhaps, the concept should be defined in terms of a certain way of life that may exist in pure, blended, and even highly diluted (but still interesting) forms. Then we see that the object of our studies is not so much individual tribes as it is a certain type of behavior.

I suggest that something has been missing from our discussions of and, indeed, from our research on hunting and gathering peoples. That is, a careful investigation of the type and amount of intellectual knowledge and theory that can be found among hunter-gatherers. We should try to learn in a systematic way what they know and believe about each species of the animal-vegetal world. Nothing would be more interesting than to compare the knowledge, use, and beliefs of different tribes about a botanical species that occurs in several parts of the world. The same could be done with mythology. We should investigate carefully myths pertaining to each type of activity. For example, mythology about honey-gathering is practically identical in South America and Indonesia and is extremely rich in both regions, but in looking into Dr. Turnbull's book (1965) I was struck that the mythology concerning honey-gathering was very poor, with only one myth cited. So I express the hope that in addition to the standard monographs—which are, of course, of the greatest importance—we might envisage putting together a kind of encyclopedia of primitive science the world over, embodying the tremendous body of knowledge that otherwise will eventually die with them.

BULMER: I would like to ask ethnographers about the possibility of getting data on the hunting and gathering sectors of the economies of predominantly horticultural and pastoral peoples. Listening to accounts of hunter-gatherers, I am struck by the way in which some of the horticulturalists in New Guinea seem to exploit a much more comprehensive range of the wild fauna and flora in their environment than do some of the pure hunter-gatherers. There are technological points to be learned and an enormous amount of botanical and zoological knowledge. But this work has to be done quickly, because this seems to be one aspect of both the economy and the traditional knowledge that is very rapidly dwindling since the time of contact. Agriculture may continue with only a few changes, but once the children are in school they no longer learn the very complex and detailed skills required for the hunting and gathering sectors of the economy.

POSNANSKY: My plea is a similar one for Africa. Certainly in East Africa a great deal of hunting and gathering is carried on by agricultural peoples. We have now looked at the primate baseline there, but I think there is still a great deal to be learned from present-day peoples in these same areas. Many settled peoples do have seasons when they collect grubs, flying insects, or certain kinds of roots. And, according to recent work on place-names done in Uganda, it appears that a lot of roots have a complex nomenclature, which seems to indicate that many of them were collected in the past, but not now. This approach would tell us a good deal more about people who are still practicing hunting and gathering in non-retreat circumstances.

CONDOMINAS: I want to say that the same situation is true of Southeast Asia. Last summer I spent time with one of my students, who is an ethnobotanist, in a Cambodian village of rice cultivators. Their knowledge of the forest, especially regarding the plants, is absolutely fantastic. And it is of a high level, perhaps as high as that of the forest peoples themselves.

WOODBURN: I just want to draw attention to a couple of subjects which have not been much discussed.

At the present we have a very inadequate understanding of the way in which authority is exercised in the domestic groupings and the wider residential groupings of hunters and gatherers. The subject would be well worth exploring in the light of the better ethnographic material now becoming available.

I think we should also have a fresh and detailed look at the nature of the various bonds that hold people together in the residential groupings of hunters and gatherers. What transactions occur between a man and the other people in his camp, especially his close kin and affines? To what extent do cooperation and coordination occur in subsistence activities? Do people combine to assert exclusive rights over natural resources? Does inheritance matter? These simple questions of ethnography have profound implications which would bear detailed discussion.

WATANABE: Throughout the conference we have had very little discussion of northern food-gatherers, including hunter-gatherers. If we concentrate primarily on problems of the evolution of Hominidae or hominization only, these northern peoples may be neglected. But if we look at problems concerning the evolution of ourselves, *Homo sapiens*, we cannot neglect them. The evolution of man from the Upper Pleistocene or the Upper Paleolithic onward has proceeded in two quite different habitats. When man entered the arctic-subarctic regions his evolution began to follow different ways.

Another point is the lack of discussion of subsistence technology at the conference. Possible links between prehistoric archeology and ethnography may be found only through technology and/or the material aspects of social life. Promotion of the study of these subjects from a functional-ecological point of view is as urgently needed as the promotion of further field studies of surviving food-gatherers.

TAX: I just want to put one idea in the record, and that is, that we should study the reasons for the persistence of these peoples all over the world in light of all the conditions militating against their persistence. I think that the case of the North American Indians is especially significant. They seem to be waiting for us to go away. I am certain that there is something for us peasant agriculturalists or, if you like, industrialists to learn from the values associated with the tribal life and with the determination of these peoples to preserve this way of life at all costs.

PART VIII

The Concept of Primitiveness

36.

The Concept of Primitiveness

CLAUDE LÉVI-STRAUSS

Like all the conferees, I was tremendously impressed with the wealth, diversity, and quality of the new material brought before us by colleagues recently back from the field. This is the first time in my life that I have attended a conference in which so many names were previously unknown to me. I could understand why as soon as I came into the room: the age bracket has changed! It is indeed comforting to know that anthropology is in such good hands, and to discover that anthropology is back on its feet again, after a period when it could be feared that anthropology would become nothing more than an attempt to work for the betterment of mankind through acculturation studies. It is not that this latter undertaking is unworthy, but anthropology has also another role, that is, to bear testimony to future generations of the ingeniousness, diversity, and imagination of our species—qualities of which evidence would otherwise soon be lost forever.

The problems we have discussed are urgent ones, not only because of the pressing need to study vanishing cultures, but also because the problems occupy a special position in anthropological thinking, making them frought with ambiguity. If I try to grasp the general move-

The Viking Fund Medal and Award was presented to Prof. Lévi-Strauss on April 8, 1966, during the Conference on Man the Hunter at the University of Chicago Center for Continuing Education. This paper is a slightly edited version of his acceptance speech.

ment of our discussion so far, it seems to me that we have been confronted with three different levels of ambiguity. Our main task is to find our way out of them.

The first level of ambiguity comes from the fact that one of the purposes of this conference is to bring about a kind of rehabilitation of hunting and gathering societies; we cannot consider them as belonging to a semi-animal condition of mankind. Yet at the same time, I noticed a strong temptation to call upon recent studies of primates—monkeys and apes—or even studies of lesser mammals such as rodents to explain, for example, the existence of a territorial instinct in Australian aborigines. The appearance of DeVore's magnificent studies makes the consideration of such problems all the more tantalizing. However, we should not forget that the main usefulness of these primate studies is twofold: first, they permit us to make hypotheses about early forms of incipient human cultures—that is to say, what took place about one or two million years ago. Second, they disclose facts which are so fundamental that if they hold true for primates, they also hold true for the whole of mankind. I do not think they can have a special bearing on a certain type of society: whether they refer to the remote past or to the present, their validity should be universal. So, the first point is that hunter-gatherers, different as they may be from our own civilization, belong to such a recent past that there is a much greater difference between them and any kind of animal society than between them and more complex human societies.

Certainly we should not try to use these recent hunter-gatherers to reconstruct events and conditions in the prehistory of mankind. I do not claim that during prehistoric periods small nomadic bands did not exist that were comparable in size and perhaps in mode of life or certain activities to hunters of today. However, prehistoric groups such as these were probably even at that time "leftovers" or devolved descendants of richer contemporary cultures. For example, it has been suggested during this conference that the best ethnographic comparison for the Upper Paleolithic cultures of the Dordogne are the cultures of the Northwest Coast Indians, groups excluded from comparison here on the grounds that they were too different from other hunter-gatherers. We should also recall Lathrap's comment earlier in the conference that in South America, and no doubt, in many other places, hunter-gatherers were not representative of an earlier condition of mankind, but were regressive rather than primitive. I tried to make this point about twenty years ago for the Nambikwara[1] and I even tried to demonstrate it by showing that there were diagnostic symptoms in a regressive society, consisting on the one hand of internal discrepancies within the culture, which on the other hand, when taken one at a time, were in concord with what was happening in one or another neighboring society.

The second level of ambiguity has to do with the discrepancy between the model and empirical reality. It seems strange to me to have heard at this conference that all of a sudden it has been "discovered" that primitive cultures are similar to our own in that they do not follow their own rules closely. Let us elaborate upon this by taking the case in which the reality is faithful to the model in the proportion of, let us say, 20 per cent of the cases. For example, this is what happens in societies that prescribe marriage with a cross-cousin, but where there are actually only about 15 per cent or 20 per cent of such marriages taking place. In these

1. "The Concept of Archaism in Anthropology," in *Structural Anthropology* (New York: Basic Books, 1963).

cases, we cannot say that the model is not conforming to reality, because we know that for many reasons—historical, demographic, and the like—it would be impossible to practice cross-cousin marriage at a higher rate. And even in a case such as this, I maintain that a cross-cousin marriage rate of 20 per cent is amply sufficient to imprint the society with a given structure, to give a definite shape to what we may call the genealogical space, to make this society a member of a sort of species within the taxonomy of human groups. It should not be dismissed as a case in which model and reality do not correspond closely to one another.

The other point, which was aptly made by Schneider, is that a model is not something different from reality; rather, a model has a reality of its own. A model may be different from what takes place in the field, but it is real nonetheless, and it should be studied as perfectly objective. I believe that the reasons for these doubts about the reality of models have to do with the assumption that all models exist only as constructs in the mind of the anthropologist. However, it can be shown that quite frequently models exist in the mind of the native, and possibly, that they are something more: perhaps they are the remote products of an age-old tradition perpetuating itself in the society under study.

We have been trying to compare the data of social anthropology and those of prehistory. But it is worthwhile asking oneself about the ideas of hunter-gatherers themselves have about prehistory. In my studies of mythology, I came across some very remarkable conceptions that are latent in the mind of certain South American tribes. It can be shown that in the mythology we have, so to speak, an embedded theory of kinship. Let me quickly give you an example. In South America, the myths dealing with the origin of culture (that is, the invention of fire, the cooking of meat, and the first implements) call upon protagonists who usually have very precise relationships to one another. They are affines, and moreover, affines of a very special type—either the sister's brother, the wife's brother, or the sister's husband. These are also the kinds of in-laws we feel compelled to represent in our diagrams, for they are needed to express the male and the female part of a lineage; they are the men who exchange women between themselves. The South American myths dealing with the origin of cultivation, however, bring affines of a different type on the scene—that is, the wife's sister and the husband's brother—these being types of people we disregard by virtue of the principle of the equivalence of siblings, well known in the theory of kinship since Radcliffe-Brown. Thus, in these myths we have two different models of kinship relationships: the first, which could be called a "paleolithic" model (without implying any historical connotations), shows the reduction to basic and indispensible elements such that matrimonial exchanges can take place. In the second, or "neolithic," model (since it is found with references to the origins of cultivation), the composition of the family becomes random, and there are too many people to fulfill neatly the requirements of exchange; supernumerary affines appear who are useless in the social structure, their social function being usually limited to that of potential seducer of their sibling's spouse. Here we can see that the distinction between what may be called parallel and cross affines is not just in the anthropologist's mind but rooted very deeply in the principles of myths.

Hiatt has suggested two possible explanations for the discrepancy between model and reality in Australian society; however, there is also a third worth considering—that at one time, all this completed theory was clearly conceived and invented by native sociologists or philosophers. Thus, what we are doing is not building a theory with which to interpret the facts, but rather trying to get back to the older native theory at the origin of the facts we are trying to explain. After all, we know that mankind is about one or two million years old, but while we are ready to grant man this great antiquity, we are not ready to grant him a continuous thinking capacity during this enormous length of time. I see no reason why mankind should have waited until recent times to produce minds of the caliber of a Plato or an Einstein. Already over two or three hundred thousand years ago, there were probably men of a similar capacity, who were of course not applying their intelligence to the solution of the same problems as these more recent thinkers; instead, they were probably more interested in kinship!

The third level of ambiguity crept into our discussions unexpectedly, thanks to our Australian colleagues, who began to question old results about things which unfortunately do not exist any more. The great question that is thus raised refers to the nature of truth in anthropological research. When we are told that fifty-year-old facts (which cannot be restudied) are not exactly like those described by the present-day observer, we are led to wonder whether it is the anthropological objects which have changed or whether it is anthropology itself which has changed and therefore cannot satisfy itself with the same kinds of answers any more. What is really "truth" in anthropology? What is really "proved"? Is anthropological truth factual evidence of the same kind as that sought by the exact sciences, or does it consist in a special kind of relationship between the observed and the observer? As with the study of those objects that are so distant (either because they are far away or because they exist on a scale so small that we will never apprehend them as they actually are), our perception of anthropological entities will be limited to the different manners in which we perceive them. And in that case, the only pretension to truth that we may have will be limited to a set of complementary points of view which leave room for fundamental uncertainties, incapable of final resolution. Thus it could not be said that one type of explanation should or will supersede another type. Instead, a fact which must forever remain unknown will be more and more closely surrounded by different perspectives, but these will be perspectives on a thing which in itself will remain unattainable. This has to do partially with the subject matter: the observer can never coincide with the observed and, despite the fact that in the human sciences what is observed and who observes belong to the same category of things, they can never become the same individual without losing the scientific outlook and perspective. It seems to me that from an epistemological viewpoint, what we have learned about the evolution of the conception of the Australian band or horde raises an extremely important point, not only for Australian anthropological studies but for the fundamental problems before us all.

If I may be permitted to draw a conclusion from these remarks, we should probably be more cautious when tempted to dismiss the work of our great predecessors in the light of new outlooks or recent observations. What they have seen and recorded is gone and we cannot be sure that we are actually observing the same kind of evidence. In anthropology, as elsewhere, progress will never result from destroying what has been previously achieved but rather from incorporating the past of our science into its present and future, enriching the one with the other and turning the whole process into a lasting reality.

References

ABERLE, DAVID F., URIE BRONFENBRENNER, ECKARD H. HESS, DANIEL R. MILLER, DAVID M. SCHNEIDER, and JAMES N. SPUHLER.
1963. The incest taboo and the mating patterns of animals. *American Anthropologist* (n.s.), 65: 253–65.

ACKERKNECHT, ERWIN H.
1948. Medicine and disease among Eskimos. In *The Eskimo, CIBA Symposia*, 10(1): 916–21.

ADAMS, ROBERT MCC.
1966. *The evolution of urban society: early Mesopotamia and prehispanic Mexico.* Chicago: Aldine Publishing Company.

DE ALMEIDA, ANTONIO.
1965. *Bushmen and other non-Bantu peoples of Angola.* Publication of the Institute for the Study of Man in Africa, 1. Johannesburg: Witwatersrand University Press.

ANASTASIO, ANGELO.
1955. *Intergroup relations in the southern plateau.* Unpublished doctoral dissertation, University of Chicago.

ANDERSON, A. J., and E. J. UNDERWOOD.
1959. Trace element deserts. *Scientific American*, 200 (1): 97–106.

ARDREY, ROBERT.
1961. *African genesis.* London: Atheneum.
1966a. The basic drive—for territory. *Life*, 61(9): 40–59.
1966b. Man, the territorial animal. *Life*, 61(10): 50–59.

ASCHER, ROBERT.
1962. Ethnography for archaeology: a case from the Seri Indians. *Ethnology*, 1(3): 360–69.

ASCHMANN, HOMER.
1959. *The central desert of Baja California: demography and ecology.* Ibero-Americana (Berkeley and Los Angeles), 42.

ASHBY, W. R.
1960. *Design for a brain.* (2d ed., rev.) New York: John Wiley.

ASHLEY-MONTAGU, M. F.
1937. *Coming into being among the Australian Aborigines.* London: George Routledge.
1957. *The reproductive development of the female: with especial reference to the period of adolescent sterility.* New York: Julian Press.

353

AUSTRALIA. NATIONAL MAPPING COUNCIL.

1952. *Sydney*. Australian Geographical Series—1:1,000,000. S.I.-56/1. Canberra: Department of National Development.

1954. *Melbourne*. Australian Geographical Series—1:1,000,000. S.J.-55/1. Canberra: Department of National Development.

1957. *Melville Island*. Australian Geographical Series—1:1,000,000. S.C.-52/1.

AUSTRALIA. REGIONAL DEVELOPMENT DIVISION.

1953. *Atlas of Australian resources*. Canberra: Department of National Development.

AUSTRALIA. SCIENTIFIC AND INDUSTRIAL RESEARCH ORGANIZATION.

1960. *The Australian environment*. (3d ed., rev.) Melbourne.

BACK, GEORGE.

1836. *Narrative of the Arctic land expedition to the mouth of the Great Fish River, and along the shores of the Arctic Ocean, in the years 1833, 1834, and 1835*. London: John Murray.

BAER, G., and C. A. SCHITZ.

1965. On the social organization of the Ona (Selk'nam). *Journal de la Société des Américanistes* (Paris) (n.s.), 54: 23–29.

BAERENDS, G. P.

1958. The contribution of ethology to the study of the causation of behaviour. *Acta Physiologica et Pharmacologica Neerlandica*, 7: 466–99.

BAILEY, JOHN.

1863. An account of the wild tribes of the Veddahs of Ceylon; their habits, customs, and superstitions *Transactions of the Ethnological Society of London* (n.s.), 2: 278–320.

BALDUS, HERBERT.

1931. Indianerstudien im nordöstlichen Chaco. *Forschungen zur Völkerpsychologie und Soziologie* (Leipzig), 11: 1–230.

BALIKCI, ASEN.

1960. Quelques cas de suicide parmi les esquimaux Netsilik. *Actes du VIᵉ Congrès International des Sciences Anthropologiques et Ethnologiques* (Paris), 2: 511–16.

1963. Le régime matrimonial des esquimaux Netsilik. *L'Homme*, 3(3): 89–101.

1964. *Development of basic socio-economic units in two Eskimo communities*. Bulletin of the National Museum of Canada, anthropological series, no. 202.

MS. *Infanticide in the Netsilik area*. Paper presented at Seminar on Ecological Systems and Cultural Evolution, Columbia University. Unpublished.

BALKE, BRUNO, and CLYDE SNOW.

1965. Anthropological and physiological observations on Tarahumara endurance runners. *American Journal of Physical Anthropology* (n.s.), 23: 293–301.

BARNES, J. A.

1963. Social organization: limits of contemporary studies. In Helen Sheils (Ed.), *Australian aboriginal studies*. Melbourne: Oxford University Press.

BARNES, VICTOR S. (Ed.).

1964. *The modern encyclopedia of Australia and New Zealand*. Sydney, Melbourne: Horwitz-Grahame.

BARNETT, HOMER G.

1937. Culture element distribution, VII: Oregon coast. *Anthropological Records* (*Berkeley*), 1(3): 155–204.

1938. The nature of the potlatch. *American Anthropologist* (n.s.), 40: 349–58.

BARNS, T. A.

1923. *Across the great craterland to the Congo*. London: Benn.

BARRY, HERBERT, IRVING CHILD, and MARGARET K. BACON.

1959. The relation of child training to subsistence economy. *American Anthropologist* (n.s.), 61: 51–63.

BARTHOLOMEW, GEORGE A., JR., and JOSEPH B. BIRDSELL.

1953. Ecology and the protohominids. *American Anthropologist* (n.s.), 55: 481–98.

BASEDOW, HERBERT.

1925. *The Australian aboriginal*. Adelaide: F. W. Preece.

1932. Diseases of the Australian aborigines. *Journal of Tropical Medicine and Hygiene* (London), 35: 177–85, 193–98, 209–213, 229–33, 247–50, 273–78.

BAUMHOFF, MARTIN A.

1958. Ecological determinants of population. *University of California Archaeological Survey Reports* (Berkeley), 48: 32–65.

1963. Ecological determinants of aboriginal California populations. *University of California Publications in American Archaeology and Ethnology* (Berkeley), 49(2): 155–236.

BEALS, RALPH L.

1933. Ethnology of the Nisenan. *University of California Publications in American Archaeology and Ethnology* (Berkeley), 31(6): 335–414.

BECKETT, JEREMY R.

1958. Marginal men: a study of two half-caste aborigines. *Oceania*, 29: 91–108.

BELL, FRANCIS L. S.

1946–48. The place of food in the social life of the Tanga. *Oceania*. 17: 139–72, 310–26; 18: 36–59, 233–47; 19: 51–74.

BERNATZIK, HUGO ADOLF.

1958. The spirits of the yellow leaves. Trans. by E. W. Dickes. London: Robert Hale. (First published 1938 as *Die Geister der gelben Blätter*. Munich: F. Bruckman.)

BERNDT, RONALD M.

1959. The concept of "the tribe" in the western desert of Australia. *Oceania*, 30: 81–107.

BERNDT, RONALD M., and CATHERINE H. BERNDT.

1942. A preliminary report of field work in the Ooldea region, western South Australia. *Oceania*, 13: 143–69.

1964. *The world of the first Australians*. Chicago: University of Chicago Press.

1965. *Aboriginal man in Australia: essays in honor of Emeritus Professor A. P. Elkin*. Sydney, London, Melbourne: Angus and Robertson.

BERTONI, M. S.

1941. Los Guayakis. *Revista de la Sociedad Científica de Paraguay*, 5: 1–62.

BICCHIERI, MARCO.

1965. *A study of the ecology of food-gathering peoples: a cross-cultural analysis of the relationships of environment, technology, and bio-cultural variability*. Unpublished doctoral dissertation, University of Minnesota.

BILLINGTON, B. P.

1960. The health and nutritional status of the aborigines. In C. P. Mountford (Ed.), *Records of the American-Australian scientific expedition to Arnhem Land: 2. Anthropology and nutrition*. Melbourne: Melbourne University Press.

BINFORD, LEWIS R.

1962. Archaeology as anthropology. *American Antiquity*, 28(2): 217–25.

1963. Red ochre caches from the Michigan area: a possible cases of cultural drift. *Southwestern Journal of Anthropology*, 19(1): 89–108.

1964. A consideration of archaeological research design. *American Antiquity*, 29(4): 425–41.

1967. Smudge pits and hide smoking: the use of analogy in archaeological reasoning. *American Antiquity*, 32(1): 1–12.

BINFORD, LEWIS R., and SALLY R. BINFORD.

1966a. The predatory revolution: a consideration of the evidence for a new subsistence level. *American Anthropologist* (n.s.), 68(2), pt. 1: 508–512.

1966b. A preliminary analysis of functional variability in the Mousterian of Levallois facies. In J. D. Clarke and F. C. Howell (Eds.), *Recent studies in paleoanthropology. American Anthropologist* (n.s.), 68(2), pt. 2.

BINFORD, LEWIS R., AND G. I. QUIMBY.

1963. Indian sites and chipped stone materials in the northern Lake Michigan area. *Fieldiana Anthropology*, 36(12): 277–307.

BINGHAM, H. C.

1932. *Gorillas in a native habitat*. Publications of the Carnegie Institute of Washington, no. 426.

BIRD, JUNIUS.

1946. The Alacaluf. In J. H. Steward (Ed.), *Handbook of South American Indians*, vol. 1: *The marginal tribes.* Bureau of American Ethnology Bulletin, 143 (1): 55–79.

BIRDSELL, J. B.

1950. Some implications of the genetical concept of race in terms of spatial analysis. *Cold Spring Harbor Symposia in Quantitative Biology*, 15: 259–314.

1953. Some environmental and cultural factors influencing the structure of Australian aboriginal populations. *American Naturalist*, 87(834): 171–207.

1957. Some population problems involving Pleistocene Man. In *Population studies: animal ecology and demography. Cold Spring Harbor Symposia in Quantitative Biology*, 22: 47–69.

1958. On population structure in generalized hunting and collecting populations. *Evolution*, 12(2): 189–205.

MSa. *A basic demographic unit and a scale for measuring some social phenomena.* University of California at Los Angeles.

MSb. *The role of systematic infanticide in human evolution.* University of California at Los Angeles.

MSc. *Population dynamics as revealed in models of patrilineal band structured society.* University of California at Los Angeles.

BIRKET-SMITH, KAJ.

1929. The Caribou Eskimos: material and social life and their cultural position. *Report of the fifth Thule expedition, 1921–24*, 5. Trans. by W. E. Calvert. Copenhagen: Gyldendalske boghandel.

1930. Contributions to Chipewyan ethnology. *Report of the fifth Thule expedition, 1921–24*, 6(3). Copenhagen: Gyldendalske boghandel.

1953. The Chugach Eskimo. *Ethnografisk Raekke*, 6. Copenhagen: Nationalmuseets Skrifter.

BISHOP, W. W., AND J. D. CLARK (Eds.).

1967. *Background of African evolution.* Chicago: University of Chicago Press.

BLACK, ROBERT H.

1959. Haptoglobins and haemoglobins in Australian aborigines. *Medical Journal of Australia* (Sydney), 1959(1): 175–76.

BLEEK, DOROTHEA F.

1928. *The Naron: a Bushman tribe of the central Kalahari.* Cambridge: Cambridge University Press.

1931a. The Hadzapi or Watindega of Tanganyika territory. *Africa*, 4: 273–85.

1931b. Traces of former Bushman occupation in Tanganyika Territory. *South African Journal of Science*, 28.

1956. *A Bushman dictionary.* New Haven, Conn.: American Oriental Series, no. 41.

BOAS, FRANZ.

1888. *The Central Eskimo.* Bureau of American Ethnology, Annual Report no. 6 (for 1884–85): 399–699.

1909. The Jesup North Pacific Expedition (5, pt. 2): The Kwakiutl of Vancouver Island. *Memoirs of the American Museum of Natural History*, 8(2).

1916. *Tsimshian mythology.* Bureau of American Ethnology, Annual Report no. 31 (for 1909–10): 29–1037.

1921. *Ethnology of the Kwakiutl, based on data collected by George Hunt.* Bureau of American Ethnology, Annual Report no. 35 (for 1913–14), pts. 1 and 2.

1935. Kwakiutl culture as reflected in mythology. *American Folklore Society Memoir*, 28.

1938. Invention. In F. Boas *et al.* (Eds.), *General anthropology.* Boston, London: D. C. Heath.

BODES, J. J.

1963. Second expedition to the Mrabri of north Thailand. *Journal of the Siam Society*, 51: 133–60.

BOGGIANI, GUIDO.

1894. *I Ciamacoco.* Rome: Presso la Societa Romana per l'Antropologia.

BOGORAS, W.

1904–09. The Chukchee. *American Museum of Natural History Memoir*, no. 11.

BORDES, FRANÇOIS H.

1953. Essai de classification des industries "Moustériennes." *Bulletin de la Société Préhistorique Française*, 50(7–8): 457–66.

1961. *Typologie du paléolithique ancien et moyen.* Publications de l'Université de Bordeaux, Mémoires de l'Institute Préhistorique, no. 1.

BOSERUP, ESTER.

1965. *The conditions of agricultural growth: the economics of agrarian change under population pressure.* Chicago: Aldine Publishing Company.

BOTSWANA, GOVERNMENT OF.

1966. Republic of Botswana fact sheet. Gabarones, Botswana.

BOULDING, KENNETH E.

1955. The Malthusian model as a general system. *Social and Economic Studies* (Kingston, Jamaica), 4: 195–205.

BOURLIÈRE, FRANÇOIS.

1963. Observations on the ecology of some large African mammals. In F. C. Howell and F. Bourlière (Eds.), *African ecology and human evolution.* Chicago: Aldine Publishing Company.

1964. *The natural history of mammals.* (3d ed., rev.) New York: Alfred Knopf. (First published 1951 as *Vie et moeurs des mammifères.* Paris: Payot.)

BOYS, ROBERT DOUGLASS.

1959. *First years at Port Phillip 1834–1842, preceded by a summary of historical events from 1768.* (2d ed.) Melbourne: Robertson and Mullens.

BRAIDWOOD, ROBERT J.

1959. Archaeology and the evolutionary theory. In *Evolution and anthropology: a centennial appraisal.* Washington, D.C.: Anthropological Society of Washington.

BRAIDWOOD, ROBERT J., and CHARLES A. REED.

1957. The achievement and early consequences of food-production: a consideration of the archaeological and natural-historical evidence. In *Population studies: animal ecology and demography. Cold Spring Harbor Symposia in Quantitative Biology,* 22: 19–31.

BRANDT, J. H.

1961. The Negrito of peninsular Thailand. *Journal of the Siam Society,* 49: 123–60.

1965. The Southeast Asian Negrito: further notes on the Negrito of south Thailand. *Journal of the Siam Society,* 53: 27–43.

BRIDGES, E. LUCAS.

1949. *The uttermost part of the earth.* New York: E. P. Dutton.

BRONTE-STEWART, B., O. E. BUDTZ-OLSEN, JOAN M. HICKLEY, and J. F. BROCK.

1960. The health and nutritional status of the Kung Bushmen of South-West Africa. *South African Journal of Laboratory Clinical Medicine,* 6: 187–216.

BRUES, ALICE.

1959. The spearman and the archer, an essay on selection in body build. *American Anthropologist* (n.s.), 61: 457–69.

BUTZER, KARL W.

1964. *Environment and archeology: an introduction to Pleistocene geography.* Chicago: Aldine Publishing Company.

CALHOUN, JOHN B.

1962. Population density and social pathology. *Scientific American,* 206(2): 139–48.

CALLEN, E. O., and T. W. M. CAMERON.

1960. A prehistoric diet revealed in coprolites. *New Scientist,* 8: 35–40.

CAMPBELL, J. M.

1965. *Settlements and settlement patterns: some lessons from the north.* Paper presented at American Anthropological Association Annual Meeting, Denver.

CAMPBELL, T. D.

1934. Notes on the aborigines of the southeast of South Australia, pt. 1. *Transactions of the Royal Society of South Australia,* 58: 22–32.

1939. Notes on the aborigines of the southeast of South Australia, pt. 2. *Transactions of the Royal Society of South Australia,* 63: 27–38.

CARNEIRO, ROBERT L.

1960. Slash-and-burn agriculture: a closer look at its implications for settlement patterns. *Selected Papers of the Fifth International Congress of Anthropological and Ethnological Sciences* (Philadelphia).

1961. Slash-and-burn cultivation among the Kuikuru and its implications for cultural development in the Amazon basin. In J. Wilbert (Ed.), *The evolution of horticultural systems in native South America, causes and consequences: a symposium. Anthropológica* (Caracas), Supplementary Publication no. 2.

1964. Shifting cultivation among the Amahuaca of eastern Peru. *Völkerkundliche Abhandlungen* (Hanover), 1: 9–18.

CARPENTER, CLARENCE R.

1941. *A field study in Siam of the behavior and social relations of the Gibbon (Hylobates lar)*. Baltimore: Johns Hopkins Press.

1942. Characteristics of social behavior in non-human primates. *Transactions of the New York Academy of Sciences*, series 2, 4: 248–58.

1955. Tentative generalizations on the grouping behavior of non-human primates. In J. A. Gaven (Ed.), *The non-human primates and human evolution*. Detroit: Wayne State University Press.

1964. *Naturalistic behavior of nonhuman primates*. University Park: Pennsylvania State University Press.

CARR-SAUNDERS, A. M.

1922. *The population problem: a study in human evolution*. Oxford: Oxford University Press.

CARULLI, E.

1922. Folk literature of the Galla of southern Abyssinia. *Harvard African Studies 3: Varia Africana, 3*.

CASELEY-SMITH, J. R.

1959. The haemotology of the central Australian aborigine, 11. White and differential counts; eosinophil counts and Casoni-tests. *Australian Journal of Experimental Biology and Medical Science*, 37: 481–88.

CHAMISSO, ADELBERTUS DE.

1824. Cetaceorum maris Kamtschatici imagines, ab Aleutis e ligno fictas, adumbravit recensuitque. *Verhandlungen der Kaiserlichen Leopoldnisch-Carolinischen Akademie der Naturforscher* (Breslau and Bonn), 4(1): 249–62 (Nova Acta, 12, pt. 1).

CHANG, KWANG-CHIH.

1962. A typology of settlement and community patterns in some circumpolar societies. *Arctic Anthropology* 1(1): 28–41.

1967. Major aspects of the interrelationship of archaeology and ethnology. *Current Anthropology*, 8(3): 227–34.

CHEWINGS, CHARLES.

1936. *Back in the stone age: the natives of central Australia*. Sydney: Angus and Robertson.

CHILDE, V. GORDON.

1943. Archaeology in the U.S.S.R.; the forest zone. *Man*, 43: 4–9.

CHRUSTOV, G. F.

1959. K voprosu ob otnoshjenijach sobstvjennosti v pjervob'itnom obshchestvje (On the question of property relations in earliest society) *Sovjetskaja Etnografija*, 1959(6): 16–36.

CLARK, J. DESMOND.

1959. Further excavations at Broken Hill, Northern Rhodesia. *Journal of the Royal Anthropological Institute of Great Britain and Ireland*, 89(2): 201–232.

1965. Culture and ecology in prehistoric Africa. In D. Brokensha (Ed.), *Ecology and economic development in tropical Africa*. Berkeley: University of California Institute of International Studies.

1966. Acheulean occupation sites in the Middle East and Africa: a study in cultural variability. In J. D. Clark and F. C. Howell (Eds.), *Recent studies in paleoanthropology. American Anthropologist* (n.s.), 68(2), pt. 2.

CLARK, J. GRAHAM D.

1954. *Excavations at Star Carr: an early Mesolithic site at Seamer near Scarborough, Yorkshire*. Cambridge: Cambridge University Press.

1960. Comment on J. Desmond Clark's "Human ecology during Pleistocene and later times in Africa south of the Sahara," *Current Anthropology*, 1(4): 321.

CLARK, J. GRAHAM D., and STUART PIGGOTT.

1965. *Prehistoric societies*. New York: Alfred A. Knopf.

CLELAND, J. BURTON.

1928. Disease amongst the Australian aborigines. *Journal of Tropical Medicine and Hygiene*, 31: 53–59, 65–70, 141–45, 157–60, 173–77, 196–98, 232–35, 262–66, 281–82, 290–94, 307–313, 326–30.

CLELAND, J. BURTON, and T. HARVEY JOHNSTON.

1933. The ecology of the aborigines of Central Australia: botanical notes. *Transactions of the Royal Society of South Australia*, 57: 113–24.

1939. Aboriginal names and uses of plants at the Granites, Central Australia. *Transactions of the Royal Society of South Australia*, 63(1): 22–26.

CLELAND, J. BURTON, and NORMAN B. TINDALE.

1959 The native names and uses of plants at Haast Bluff, Central Australia. *Transactions of the Royal Society of South Australia*, 82: 123–40.

CLEMENS, W. A., and G. V. WILBY.

1946. *Fishes of the Pacific coast of Canada*. Fisheries Research Board of Canada (Ottawa) Bulletin no. 68.

CODERE, HELEN.

1951. *Fighting with property: a study of Kwakiutl potlatching and warfare*. Monographs of the American Ethnological Society, no. 18. Seattle: University of Washington Press.

1959. The understanding of the Kwakiutl. In W. Goldschmidt (Ed.), *The anthropology of Franz Boas*. American Anthropological Association Memoir, no. 89.

COHEN, R., and J. W. VAN STONE.

1964. Dependency and self-sufficiency in Chipewyan stories. In *Contributions to Anthropology 1961–62*, pt. 2, *Bulletin of the National Museum of Canada*, 194: 29–55.

COLBACCHINI, ANTONIO, and C. ALBISETTI.

1942. *Os Boróros Orientalis, Orarimogodogue de Planalto Oriental de Mato Grosso*. Saõ Paulo: Companhia Editora Nacional.

COLE, SONIA M.

1963. *The prehistory of East Africa*. (rev.) New York: Macmillan. (First published 1954. Hamondsworth: Penguin).

COLLINS, DAVID.

1804. *An account of the English colony in New South Wales*. (2d ed.) London: T. Cadell and W. Davies.

COLLINS, H. B.

1940. Outline of Eskimo prehistory. *Smithsonian Miscellaneous Collections*, 100: 533–92.

CONKLIN, HAROLD C.

1957. *Hanunóo Agriculture: a report on an integral system of shifting cultivation in the Philippines*, vol. 2. Rome: Food and Agriculture Organization of the United Nations.

COOK, SHERBURNE F.

1955. The epidemic of 1830–1833 in California and Oregon. *University of California Publications in American Archaeology and Ethnology* (Berkeley), 43: 303–326.

COOK, SHERBURNE F., and ROBERT F. HEIZER.

1965. The quantitative approach to the relation between population and settlement size. *Report of the University of California Archaeology Survey*, 64. Berkeley: University of California Press.

COOK, SHERBURNE F., and A. E. TREGANZA.

1950. The quantitative investigation of Indian mounds. *University of California Publications in American Archaeology and Ethnology* (Berkeley), 40(5): 223–61.

COON, CARLETON S.

1948. *Reader in general anthropology*. New York: Henry Holt.

COOPER, B.

1949. The Kindiga. *Tanganyika Notes and Records*, 27: 8–15.

COOPER, J. M.

1946. The culture of the Northeastern Indian hunters; a reconstructive interpretation. In F. Johnson (Ed.), *Man in Northeastern North America*. Papers of the Robert Peabody Foundation for Archaeology (Andover) 3: 272–305.

COWAN, IAN MCTAGGART.

1945. The ecological relationships of the food of the Columbian black-tailed deer, *Odocoileus hemionus columbianus* (Richardson), in the coast forest region of southern Vancouver Island, British Columbia. *Ecological Monographs*, 15(2): 109–139.

COWAN, IAN MCTAGGART, and C. J. GUIGUETA.

1956. *The mammals of British Columbia*. British Columbia Provincial Museum Handbook, no. 11.

CROCKER, CHRISTOPHER.

1967. *The social organization of the eastern Bororo*. Unpublished doctoral dissertation, Harvard University.

CRONIN, CONSTANCE.

1962. An analysis of pottery design elements, indicating possible relationships between three decorated types. In P. S. Martin *et al.* (Eds.), *Chapters in the prehistory of eastern Arizona, Fieldiana Anthropology*, 53: 105–114.

CROTTY, J. M., and R. C. WEBB.

1960. Mortality in Northern Territory aborigines. *Medical Journal of Australia*, 1960(2): 489–92.

CROW, JAMES F.

1961. Mechanisms and trends in human evolution. *Daedalus*, 90(3): 416–31.

CRUXENT, JOSÉ M., and IRVING ROUSE.

1959. *An archaeological chronology of Venezuela*. Pan American Union of Social Science Monographs no. 6, vols. 1 and 2.

CUISINIER, JEANNE.

1948. *Les Muong: Géographie humaine et sociologie*. Paris: Institut d'Ethnologie.

CURR, EDWARD M.

1886–87. *The Australian race* (4 vols.). Melbourne: John Ferres.

CURTIS, E. S.

1928. *The North American Indian, vol. 18: the Chipewyan, the Cree, and Sarsi*. Seattle: Norwood.

DAMAS, DAVID.

1963. *Igluligmiut kinship and local groupings: a structural approach*. Bulletin of the National Museum of Canada, no. 196.

In press a. Characteristics of Central Eskimo band structure. In D. Damas (Ed.), *Ecological essays: proceedings of the conference on cultural ecology, National Museum of Canda, 1966*. Contributions to Anthropology, Ethnology 7, National Museum of Canada, Ottawa.

In press b. *Social anthropology in the Eskimo area*. Proceedings of the 37th International Congress of Americanists, 1966.

DANSEREAU, PIERRE M.

1957. *Biogeography: an ecological perspective*. New York: Ronald Press.

DAVENPORT, WILLIAM.

1959. Nonunilinear descent and descent groups. *American Anthropologist* (n.s.), 61: 557–72.

DAVIDSON, DANIEL S.

1926. The basis of social organization in Australia. *American Anthropologist* (n.s.), 28: 529–48.

1928a. *The chronological aspects of certain Australian social institutions as inferred from geographical distribution*. Philadelphia: University of Pennsylvania Press.

1928b. A preliminary survey of the family hunting territory in Australia. *American Anthropologist* (n.s.), 30: 614–31.

1933. Australian netting and basketry techniques. *Journal of the Polynesian Society*, 42: 257–99.

1934. Australian spear-traits and their derivations. *Journal of the Polynesian Society*, 43: 41–72, 142–62.

1935. The chronology of Australian watercraft. *Journal of the Polynesian Society*, 44: 1–16, 69–84, 137–52, 193–207.

1936. Australian throwing-sticks, throwing-clubs, and boomerangs. *American Anthropologist* (n.s.), 38: 76–100.

1937. Transport and receptacles in aboriginal Australia. *Journal of the Polynesian Society*, 46: 175–205.

1938a. *A preliminary register of Australian tribes and hordes*. Philadelphia: American Philosophical Society.

1938b. Stone axes from western Australia. *American Anthropologist* (n.s.), 40: 38–48.

1947. Fire-making in Australia. *American Anthropologist* (n.s.), 49: 426–37.

1949a. Disposal of the dead in western Australia. *Proceedings of the American Philosophical Society*, 93: 71–97.

1949b. Mourning-caps of the Australian aborigines. *Proceedings of the American Philosophical Society*, 93: 57–70.

1952. Notes on the pictographs and petroglyphs of western Australia and a discussion of their affinities with appearances elsewhere on the continent. *Proceedings of the American Philosophical Society*, 96: 76–117.

1953. The possible source and antiquity of the slate *Churingas* of western Australia. *Proceedings of the American Philosophical Society*, 97: 194–213.

DAVIDSON, DANIEL S., and FREDERICK D. McCARTHY.

1957. The distribution and chronology of some important types of stone implements in western Australia. *Anthropos*, 52: 390–458.

DAWSON, JAMES.

1881. *Australian aborigines, the languages and customs of several tribes of aborigines in the western district of Victoria, Australia.* Melbourne: G. Robertson.

DEETZ, JAMES J. F.

1960. *An archaeological approach to kinship change in eighteenth-century Arikara culture.* Unpublished doctoral dissertation, Harvard University.

1965. *The dynamics of stylistic change in Arikara ceramics.* Illinois Studies in Anthropology, no. 4. Urbana: University of Illinois Press.

DEEVEY, EDWARD S.

1956. The human crop. *Scientific American*, 194(4): 105–112.

1960. The human population. *Scientific American*, 203(3): 194–204.

DEVORE, IRVEN.

1963. A comparison of the ecology and behavior of monkeys and apes. In S. L. Washburn (Ed.), *Classification and human evolution.* Chicago: Aldine Publishing Company.

1965. *Primate behavior* (Ed.). New York: Holt, Rinehart, and Winston.

DEVORE, IRVEN, and K. R. L. HALL.

1965. Baboon ecology. In I. DeVore (Ed.), *Primate behavior.* New York: Holt, Rinehart, and Winston.

DEVORE, IRVEN, and SHERWOOD L. WASHBURN.

1963. Baboon ecology and human evolution. In F. C. Howell and F. Bourlière (Eds.), *African ecology and human evolution.* Chicago: Aldine Publishing Company.

DOBZHANSKY, THEODOSIUS.

1950. Evolution in the tropics. *American Scientist*, 38: 209–221.

DOLE, GERTRUDE E.

1960. The classification of Yankee nomenclature in the light of evolution in kinship. In Gertrude E. Dole and Robert L. Carneiro (Eds.), *Essays in the science of culture in honor of Leslie A. White.* New York: Thomas Y. Crowell.

DOOB, LEONARD W.

1965. Psychology. In R. A. Lystad (Ed.), *The African world.* New York: Praeger.

DORNAN, SAMUEL S.

1925. *Pygmies and Bushmen of the Kalahari.* London: Seeley.

DRIVER, HAROLD E.

1939. Culture element distributions, 10: Northwest California. *Anthropological Records* (Berkeley), 1(6): 297–433.

1961. *Indians of North America.* Chicago: University of Chicago Press.

DRIVER, HAROLD E., and WILHELMINE DRIVER.

1963. *Ethnography and acculturation of the Chichimeca-Jonaz of northeast Mexico.* Bloomington: Indiana University Press.

DRUCKER, PHILIP.

1937. The Tolowa and their southwestern Oregon kin. *University of California Publications in American Archaeology and Ethnology* (Berkeley), 36(4): 221–300.

1939. Rank, wealth and kinship in Northwest Coast society. *American Anthropologist* (n.s.), 41: 55–65.

1950. Culture element distribution, 26: Northwest Coast. *Anthropological Records* (Berkeley), 9(3): 157–294.

1951. *The northern and central Nootkan tribes.* Bureau of American Ethnology Bulletin no. 144.

1955. *Indians of the Northwest Coast.* American Museum of Natural History, Anthropological Handbook, no. 10. (Reprinted 1963: American Museum Science Books. Garden City: Natural History Press.)

1965. *Cultures of the North Pacific Coast.* San Francisco: Chandler.

DUBOIS, CORA A.

1936. The wealth concept as an integrative factor in Tolowa-Tututni culture. In R. H. Lowie (Ed.), *Essays in anthropology presented to A. L. Kroeber.* Berkeley: University of California Press.

DUBOS, RENÉ.

1965. *Man adapting.* Yale University Silliman memorial lectures, 39. New Haven: Yale University Press.

DUFF, WILSON.

1952. The Upper Stalo Indians of the Fraser Valley, British Columbia. In *Anthropology in British Columbia.* British Columbia Provincial Museum, Memoir no. 1.

1964. *The Indian history of British Columbia, vol. 1: The impact of the white man.* In *Anthropology in British Columbia.* British Columbia Provincial Museum, Memoir no. 5.

DUGUID, CHARLES.

1963. *No dying race.* Adelaide: Rigby Ltd.

DUNN, F. L.

Ms1. *Ecology, acculturation, and parasitism in the Orang Asli of Malaya.* Paper presented at meetings of Southwestern Anthropological Association, UCLA, Los Angeles, 1965. Unpublished.

Ms2. *Ecological simplification, parasitism, and primate evolution.* Paper presented at American Association for the Advancement of Science Meetings, Berkeley. Unpublished.

DUNN, F. L., and J. M. BOLTON.

1963. The MIF direct smear (DS) method in the study of intestinal parasitism in Malay aborigines. *Singapore Medical Journal*, 4: 175–76.

DUNNING, R. W.

1959. *Social and economic change among the Northern Ojibwa.* Toronto: University of Toronto Press.

1960. Differentiation of status in subsistence level societies. *Proceedings and Transactions of the Royal Society of Canada*, 54, 2: 25–32.

EDWARDS, E. L.

1952. *Ethnohistory of the Mackenzie Valley from Providence to Aklavik.* Unpublished master's thesis, New York University.

EGGAN, FRED.

1954. Social anthropology and the method of controlled comparison. *American Anthropologist* (n.s.), 56: 743–63.

1955. Social anthropology: methods and results. In F. Eggan (Ed.), *Social anthropology of North American tribes.* (2d ed.) Chicago: University of Chicago Press.

EISELEY, LOREN C.

1947. Land tenure in the Northeast: a note on the history of the concept. *American Anthropologist* (n.s.), 49: 680–81.

EKBLAW, W. ELMER.

1948. Significance of movement among the Polar Eskimo. *Bulletin of the Massachusetts Archaeological Society*, 10: 1–4.

ELKIN, A. P.

1931. The social organization of South Australian tribes. *Oceania*, 2: 44–73.

1932. Social organization in the Kimberley Division, northwestern Australia. *Oceania*, 2: 296–333.

1933. Studies in Australian totemism. *Oceania Monographs*, no. 2.

1938. *The Australian aborigines: how to understand them.* (1st. ed.) Sydney: Angus and Robertson.

1938-40. Kinship in South Australia. *Oceania*, 8: 419–52; 9: 41–78; 10: 196–234, 295–349, 369–88.

1945. *Aboriginal men of high degree.* Sydney: Australasian Publishing Co.

1950. The complexity of social organization in Arnhem Land. *Southwestern Journal of Anthropology*, 6: 1–20.

1953. Murngin kinship re-examined and remarks on some generalizations. *American Anthropologist* (n.s.), 55: 412–19.

1954. *The Australian aborigines: how to understand them.* (3d ed.) Sydney: Angus and Robertson.

1962. Introduction. In M. J. Meggitt, *Desert people: a study of the Walbiri aborigines of Central Australia.* Sydney: Angus and Robertson.

1964. *The Australian aborigines: how to understand them.* (4th ed.) Sydney: Angus and Robertson.

ELLEFSON, J. O.

1966. *A natural history of gibbons in the Malay Peninsula.* Unpublished doctoral dissertation, University of California, Berkeley.

ELLIOTT, HENRY W.

1886. *Our Arctic province: Alaska and the Seal islands.* New York: Scribner's.

ELMENDORF, W. W.

1960. *The structure of Twana culture.* Washington State University Research Studies, Monograph Supplement no. 2. Pullman: Washington State University.

EVANS, IVOR H. N.

1937. *The Negritos of Malaya.* Cambridge: Cambridge University Press.

EYLMANN, E.

1902. Das Feuermachen der Eingeborenen der Colonie Süd-Australien. *Zeitschrift für Ethnologie* (Berlin), 34: 89–94.

EYRE, EDWARD JOHN.

1845. *Journals of expeditions of discovery into Central Australia and overland from Adelaide to King George's Sound, in the years 1840–1.* London: T. and W. Boone.

FALKENBERG, JOHANNES.

1962. *Kin and totem.* London: George Allen and Unwin.

FARABEE, WILLIAM C.

1918. *The Central Arawakis.* University Museum Anthropological Publications, no. 9. Philadelphia University of Pennsylvania.

1924. *The Central Caribs.* University Museum Anthropological Publications, no. 10. Philadelphia: University of Pennsylvania.

FIDLER, PETER.

1934. Journal of a journey with the Chipewyans or Northern Indians, to the Slave Lake, & to the east & west of the Slave River, in 1791 & 2. In J. B. Tyrrell (Ed.), *Journals of Samuel Hearne and Philip Turner between the years 1774 and 1792, Publication of the Champlain Society,* 21: 493–555. Toronto: Champlain Society.

FIRTH, RAYMOND W.

1954. Social organization and social change. *Journal of the Royal Anthropological Institute of Great Britain and Ireland,* 84: 1–20.

1966. Twins, birds and vegetables: problems of identification in primitive religious thought. *Man* (n.s.), 1: 1–17.

FISON, LORIMER.

1870a. Comparative table on the Tongan and Fijian system of relationships made by Rev. Lorimer Fison, Rawa, Fiji, December, 1869. In L. H. Morgan, *Systems of consanguinity and affinity of the human family.* Smithsonian Contributions to Knowledge, 17: 573–77.

1870b. Remarks of Mr. Fison on the Fijian system. In L. H. Morgan, *Systems of consanguinity and affinity of the human family.* Smithsonian Contributions to Knowledge, 17: 580–83.

1870c. Remarks of Mr. Fison on the Tongan system. In L. H. Morgan, *Systems of consanguinity and affinity of the human family.* Smithsonian Contributions to Knowledge, 17: 578–80.

FISON, LORIMER, and A. W. HOWITT.

1880. *Kamilaròi and Kurnai.* Melbourne: George Robertson.

FLANAGAN, RODERICK J.

1888. *The aborigines of Australia.* Sydney: Edward F. Flanagan and George Robertson.

FLANNERY, REGINA.

1946. The culture of the northeastern Indian hunters: a descriptive survey. In F. Johnson (Ed.), *Man in northeastern North America*. Papers of the Robert Peabody Foundation for Archaeology (Andover), 3: 263–71.

FLATZ, GEBHARD.

1963. The Mrabri. *Journal of the Siam Society*, 51: 161–78.

1964. Die Geister der gelben Blätter: medizinische, anthrometrische und genetische Untersuchung der Mrabri in Nordthailand. *Zeitschrift für Ethnologie* (Braunschewig), 89: 23–34.

FOCK, NELS.

1963. Waiwai: religion and society of an Amazonian tribe. *Nationalmuseets Skrifter* (Copenhagen), 8.

FORDE, C. DARYLL.

1934. *Habitat, economy, and society: a geographical introduction to ethnology*. London: Methuen.

1954. Foraging, hunting and fishing. In Charles Singer, E. J. Holmyard, and A. R. Hall (Eds.), *A history of technology* (vol. 1). Oxford: Clarendon Press.

FORTES, MEYER.

1949. Time and social structure: an Ashanti case study. In M. Fortes (Ed.), *Social structure: essays presented to A. R. Radcliffe-Brown*. London: Clarendon Press.

1950. Kinship and marriage among the Ashanti. In A. R. Radcliffe-Brown and C. Daryll Forde (Eds.), *African systems of kinship and marriage*. London: Oxford University Press.

1953. The structure of unilineal descent groups. *American Anthropologist* (n.s.), 55: 17–41.

FOX, J. R.

1965. Demography and social anthropology. *Man*, 65: 86–87.

FRAKE, CHARLES O.

1962. Cultural ecology and ethnography. *American Anthropologist* (n.s.), 64(1): 53–59.

FRANKLIN, JOHN.

1823. *Narrative of a journey to the shore of the Polar Sea in the years 1819–20–21–22*. London: John Murray.

1828. *Narrative of a second expedition to the shores of the Polar Sea in the years 1825, 1826, and 1827*. London: John Murray.

FREEMAN, DEREK.

1964. Human aggression in anthropological perspective. In J. D. Carthy and F. J. Ebling (Eds.), *The natural history of aggression*. New York: Academic Press.

FREEMAN, LESLIE G.

1966. The nature of the Mousterian facies in Cantabrian Spain. *American Anthropologist* (n.s.), 68(2), pt. 2: 230–37.

FREEMAN, LESLIE G., and JAMES A. BROWN.

1964. Statistical analysis of Carter Ranch pottery. In P. S. Martin *et al.* (Eds.), *Chapters in the prehistory of eastern Arizona II, Fieldiana Anthropology*, 55: 126–54.

FREEMAN, LESLIE G., AND KARL W. BUTZER.

In press. The Acheulean Station of Torralba, Spain: a progress report. *Quaternaria*, 8.

FRIED, JACOB.

1955. *A survey of the aboriginal populations of Quebec and Labrador*. Eastern Canadian Anthropological Series, no. 1.

FRY, H. KENNETH.

1934. Kinship and descent among the Australian aborigines. *Transactions of the Royal Society of South Australia*, 58: 14–21.

FÜRER-HAIMENDORF, C. VON.

1943. *The Chenchus*. London: Macmillan.

FURNESS, W. H.

1902. *The home-life of Borneo Head-Hunters*. Philadelphia: J. B. Lippincott.

GABUS, JEAN.

1951–52. Contribution à l'étude des Nemadi, chasseurs archaïques du Djouf. *Bulletin der Schweizerischen Gesellschaft für Anthropologie und Ethnologie*, 28: 49–83.

GAJDUSEK, D. CARLETON.

1963. Ethnopediatrics as a study of cybernetics of human development. *American Journal of Diseases of Children*, 105: 554–59.

GALLUS, ALEXANDER.

1966. Comments on L. Pradel's "Transition from Mousterian to Perigordian: skeletal and industrial." *Current Anthropology*, 7(1): 39.

GARFIELD, VIOLA E.

1945. A research problem in northwest Indian economics. *American Anthropologist* (n.s.), 47: 626–30.

1951. *The Tsimshian and their neighbors. The Tsimshian: their arts and music.* American Ethnological Society Publication no. 18. New York: Augustin.

GARTLAN, J. S.

In press. *Social dominance in primate societies.*

GEARING, FRED.

1958. The structural poses of eighteenth-century Cherokee villages. *American Anthropologist* (n.s.), 60: 1148–58.

1962. Priests and warriors: social structures for Cherokee politics in the 18th century. *American Anthropologist* (n.s.), 64(5), pt. 2.

GIDDINGS, JAMES L., JR.

1952. Observations on the "Eskimo type" of kinship and social structure. *Anthropological Papers of the University of Alaska*, 1(1): 5–10.

1960. The archaeology of Bering Strait. *Current Anthropology*, 1(2): 121–38.

GIFFORD, EDWARD W.

1926. Miwok lineages and the political unit in aboriginal California. *American Anthropologist* (n.s.), 28: 389–401.

GILMORE, RAYMOND M.

1950. Fauna and ethnozoology of South America. In J. H. Steward (Ed.), *Handbook of South American Indians*, vol. 6: *Physical anthropology, linguistics, and cultural geography of South American Indians*. Bureau of American Ethnology Bulletin, 143(6): 345–464.

GINSBERG, BENSON E., AND WILLIAM S. LAUGHLIN.

1966. The multiple bases of human adaptability and achievement: a species point of view. *Eugenics Quarterly*, 13(3): 240–57.

GJESSING, GUTORM.

1944. Circum-Polar stone age. *Acta Arctica*, 2.

GLASS, BENTLEY.

1965. The ethical basis of science. *Science*, 150(3701): 1254–61.

GODDARD, P. E.

1961. The Beaver Indians. *Anthropological Papers of the American Museum of Natural History*, 10(4): 201–293.

GOGGIN, JOHN M., and W. C. STURTEVANT.

1964. The Calusa: a stratified, nonagricultural society (with notes on sibling marriage). In W. H. Goodenough (Ed.), *Explorations in cultural anthropology: essays in honor of George Peter Murdock*. New York: McGraw-Hill.

GOLDMAN, IRVING.

1948. Tribes of the Uaupes-Caueta region. In J. H. Steward (Ed.), *Handbook of South American Indians*, vol. 3: *The tropical forest tribes*. Bureau of American Ethnology Bulletin 143(3): 763–98.

1963. *The Cubeo: Indians of the northwest Amazon*. Illinois Studies in Anthropology, no. 2. Urbana: University of Illinois Press.

GOLDSCHMIDT, WALTER R.

1948. Social organization in native California and the origin of clans. *American Anthropologist* (n.s.), 50: 444–56.

1959. *Man's way: a preface to the understanding of human society.* New York: Henry Holt.

1966. *Comparative functionalism: an essay in anthropological theory.* Berkeley and Los Angeles: University of California Press.

GOODALE, JANE.

1957. Alonga bush: a Tiwi hunt. *University Museum Bulletin*, 21: 3–35. Philadelphia: University of Pennsylvania.

1962. Marriage contracts among the Tiwi. *Ethnology*, 1(4): 452–65.

GOODALL, JANE.

1963. Feeding behavior of wild chimpanzees: a preliminary report. In *The primates: proceedings of the symposium held on 12th–14th April 1962.* Zoological Society of London, *Symposia*, 10.

1965. Chimpanzees on the Gombe Stream reserve. In I. DeVore (Ed.), *Primate behavior.* New York: Holt, Rinehart and Winston.

GOODALL, JANE, and HUGO VON LAWICK.

1965. My life with wild chimpanzees. (16mm film). Washington, D.C.: National Geographic Society.

GOODE, J. PAUL.

1957. *Goode's world atlas.* (10th ed.) Ed. by Edward B. Espenshade. Chicago: Rand McNally.

GOODENOUGH, WARD H.

1962. Kindred and hamlet in Lakalai, New Britain. *Ethnology*, 1(1): 5–12.

GOULD, RICHARD A.

1966. The wealth quest among the Tolowa Indians of northwestern California. *Proceedings of the American Philosophical Society*, 110(1): 67–89.

GREENBERG, J. H.

1950. Studies in African linguistic classification: 6. the click languages. *Southwestern Journal of Anthropology*, 6(3): 223–37.

GREY, GEORGE.

1841. *Journals of two expeditions of discovery in north-western and western Australia, during the years 1837, '38, and '39.* London: T. and W. Boone.

GUBSER, N. J.

1965. *The Nunamiut Eskimos: hunters of caribou.* New Haven: Yale University Press.

GUEMPLE, D. L.

1965. Savnik: name sharing as a factor governing Eskimo kinship terms. *Ethnology*, 4(3): 323–35.

GULLIVER, PAMELA, and PHILIP H. GULLIVER.

1953. *The Central Nilo-Hamites.* London: International African Institute.

GUNTHER, E.

1927. Klallam ethnography. *University of Washington Publications in Anthropology* (Seattle), 1: 171–314.

GUSINDE, MARTIN (Ed.).

1931–39. *Die Feuerland Indianer* (3 vols.). St. Gabriel-Mödling bei Wein: Verlag der internationalen Zeitschrift Anthropos.

1961. *The Yamans: the life and thought of the water nomads of Cape Horn.* Trans. by Frieda Schultze. New Haven, Conn.: Human Relations Area Files.

HAGEN, BERNHARD.

1908. Die Orang Kubu auf Sumatra. *Veröffentlichungen des Städtischen Volker-Museum, Frankfurt am Main*, 2.

HAINLINE, JANE.

1965. Culture and biological adaptation. *American Anthropologist* (n.s.), 67(5): 1174–97.

HAJNAL, J.

1963. Concepts of random mating and the frequency of consanguineous marriages. *Proceedings of the Royal Society* (London), Series B, 159: 125–77.

HALDANE, J. B. S.

1956. The argument from animals to men: an examination of its validity for anthropology. *Journal of the Royal Anthropological Institute of Great Britain and Ireland*, 86: 1–14.

1957. Natural selection in man. *Acta Genetica et Statistica Medica* (Basel), 6: 321–32.

HALL, EDWARD T.

1966. *The hidden dimension.* Garden City, N.Y.: Doubleday.

HALL, K. R. L.

1963. Variations in the ecology of the Chacma baboon, *Papio ursinus.* In *The primates: proceedings of the symposium held on 12th–14th April 1962.* Zoological Society of London, *Symposia,* 10.

HALL, K. R. L., AND IRVEN DEVORE.

1965. Baboon social behavior. In I. DeVore (Ed.), *Primate behavior.* New York: Holt, Rinehart, and Winston.

HALLOWELL, A. IRVING.

1937. Cross-cousin marriage in the Lake Winnipeg area. *Publications of the Philadelphia Anthropological Society,* 1: 95–110.

1946. Some psychological characteristics of the northeastern Indians. In F. Johnson (Ed.), *Man in northeastern North America.* Papers of the Robert Peabody Foundation for Archaeology (Andover), 3: 195–225.

1949. The size of Algonkian hunting territories: a function of ecological adjustment. *American Anthropologist* (n.s.), 51: 35–45.

1960. Ojibwa ontology, behavior, and world view. In Stanley Diamond (Ed.), *Culture in history: essays in honor of Paul Radin.* New York: Columbia University Press.

HAMBURG, DAVID A.

1961. The relevance of recent evolutionary changes to human stress biology. In S. L. Washburn (Ed.), *Social life of early man.* Chicago: Aldine Publishing Company.

1963. Emotions in the perspective of human evolution. In P. H. Knapp (Ed.), *Expression of the emotions in man.* New York: International Universities Press.

HART, CHARLES W. M.

1930a. Personal names amongst the Tiwi. *Oceania,* 1: 280–90.

1930b. The Tiwi of Melville and Bathurst Islands. *Oceania,* 1: 167–80.

1943. A reconsideration of the Natchez social structure. *American Anthropologist* (n.s.), 45: 374–86.

HART, CHARLES W. M., and ARNOLD R. PILLING.

1960. *The Tiwi of northern Australia.* New York: Holt, Rinehart and Winston.,

HAWKES, CHRISTOPHER.

1954. Archeological theory and method: some suggestions from the Old World. *American Anthropologist* (n.s.), 56: 155–68.

HEARNE, SAMUEL.

1911. *A journey from Prince of Wales Fort in Hudson's Bay to the Northern Ocean in the years 1769, 1770, 1771, and 1772.* Publications of the Champlain Society (Toronto), no. 6, J. B. Tyrrell (Ed.). (First published 1795; London: A. Strahan and T. Cadell.)

HEINZ, H. J.

1961. Factors governing the survival of Bushmen worm parasites in the Kalahari. *South African Journal of Science,* 57: 207–213.

HEIZER, ROBERT F.

1960. The Aleut sea otter hunt in the late nineteenth century. *Anthropological Papers of the University of Alaska,* 8(2): 131–35.

HELM, JUNE.

1961. *The Lynx Point people: the dynamics of a northern Athapaskan band.* Bulletin of the National Museum of Canada, no. 176.

1965a. Bilaterality in the socio-territorial organization of the Arctic drainage Déné. *Ethnology,* 4(4): 361–85.

1965b. Patterns of allocation among the Arctic drainage Déné. In June Helm (Ed.), *Essays in economic anthropology.* Annual Proceedings of the American Ethnological Society. Seattle: University of Washington Press.

In press a. Methodology of band composition analysis. In D. Damas (Ed.), *Ecological essays: proceedings of the conference on cultural ecology, National Museum of Canada, 1966.* Contributions to Anthropology, Ethnology 7, National Museum of Canada, Ottawa.

In press b. The structure of bands among the Arctic drainage Déné. *Papers of the VII International Congress of Ethnological and Anthropological Sciences,* Moscow, 1964.

HELM, JUNE, and DAVID DAMAS.

1963. The contact-traditional all-native community of the Canadian north: the upper Mackenzie "bush" Athapaskans and the Igluligmiut. *Anthropologica* (n.s.), 5: 9–21.

HELM, JUNE, G. A. DeVos, and TERESA CARTERETTE.

1963. Variations in personality and ego identification in a Slave Indian kin-community. *Bulletin of the National Museum of Canada*, 180(2): 94–138.

HELM, JUNE, and NANCY O. LURIE.

1961. *The subsistence economy of the Dogrib Indians of Lac la Martre in the Mackenzie District of the Northwest Territories*. Ottawa: Northern Coordination and Research Center, Department of Northern Affairs and National Resources, Canada.

1966. *The Dogrib hand game*. Bulletin of the National Museum of Canada, no. 205.

HELM, JUNE, AND VITAL THOMAS.

In press. Tales from the Dogribs. *The Beaver* (Winnipeg).

HENRY, JULES.

1941. *Jungle people: a Kaingang tribe of the Highlands of Brazil*. New York: J. J. Augustin. (Reprinted New York: Vintage, 1964.)

HERNANDEZ, THEODORE.

1941. Social organization of the Drysdale River tribes, northwest Australia. *Oceania*, 11: 211–32.

HIATT, L. R.

1962. Local organization among the Australian aborigines. *Oceania*, 32: 267–86.

1965. *Kinship and conflict: a study of an aboriginal community in northern Arnhem Land*. Canberra: Australian National University.

1966. The lost horde. *Oceania*, 37: 81–92.

HICKERSON, HAROLD.

1960. The feast of the dead among the seventeenth century Algonkins of the upper Great Lakes. *American Anthropologist* (n.s.), 62: 81–107.

1962. *The southwestern Chippewa: an ethnohistorical study*. American Anthropological Association Memoir, no. 92.

HILBERT, PETER PAUL.

1962a. Preliminary results of archaeological research of the Japurá River, middle Amazon. *Akten des 34 Internationalen Amerikanistenkongresses, Wien 1960:* 465–70.

1962b. New stratigraphic evidence of culture change on the middle Amazon (Solimões). *Akten des 34 Internationalen Amerikanistenkongresses, Wien 1960:* 471–76.

HILL, JAMES N.

1965. *Broken K: a prehistoric community in eastern Arizona*. Unpublished doctoral dissertation, University of Chicago.

1966. A prehistoric community in eastern Arizona. *Southwestern Journal of Anthropology*, 22(1): 9–30.

HOBHOUSE, LEONARD TRELAWNY, G. C. WHEELER, AND M. GINSBERG.

1961. The material culture and social institutions of the simpler peoples: an essay in correlation. In F. W. Moore (Ed.), *Readings in cross-cultural methodology*. New Haven, Conn.: Human Relations Area Files Press.

HOCKETT, CHARLES F., AND ROBERT ASCHER.

1964. The human revolution. *Current Anthropology* 5(3): 135–52.

HOIJER, HARRY.

1656. Athapaskan kinship systems. *American Anthropologist* (n.s.), 58: 309–333.

HOIJER, HARRY, et al.

1963. *Studies in the Athapaskan languages*. University of California Publications in Linguistics, no. 29.

HOLDRIDGE, L. R.

1965. The tropics, a misunderstood ecosystem. *Association for Tropical Biology Bulletin*, 5: 21–30.

HOLM, G.

1914. Ethnological sketch of the Angmagssalik Eskimos. *Meddelelser om Grønland*, 39: 1–147.

HOLMBERG, ALLAN R.

1950. *Nomads of the long bow: the Siriono of eastern Bolivia*. Smithsonian Institution, Publications of the Institute of Social Anthropology, no. 10.

HONERY, THOMAS.

1878. Wailwun languages and traditions. *Journal of the Royal Anthropological Institute of Great Britain and Ireland*, 7: 246–54.

HONIGMANN, JOHN J.

1946. *Ethnography and acculturation of the Fort Nelson Slave.* Yale University Publications in Anthropology, no. 33. New Haven: Yale University Press.

1949. *Culture and ethos of Kaska society.* Yale University Publications in Anthropology, no. 40. New Haven: Yale University Press.

1954. *The Kaska Indians: an ethnographic reconstruction.* Yale University Publications in Anthropology, no. 51. New Haven: Yale University Press.

1956. The Attawapiskat Swampy Cree: an ethnographic reconstruction. *Anthropological Papers of the University of Alaska*, 5: 23–82.

1962a. *Foodways in a Muskeg community: an anthropological report on the Attawapiskat Indians.* Northern Coordination and Research Centre Report, no. 62. Ottawa: Department of Northern Affairs and Natural Resources.

1962b. *Social networks in Great Whale River: notes on an Eskimo, Montagnais-Naskapi, and Euro-Canadian community.* Bulletin of the National Museum of Canada, no. 178.

HOSE, C., and W. McDOUGALL.

1911. *The pagan tribes of Borneo I: a description of their physical, moral, and intellectual condition with some discussion of their ethic relations.* London: Macmillan.

HOWELL, F. C., G. H. COLE, and MAXINE R. KLEINDIENST.

1962. Ismila: an Acheulian occupation site on the Iringa highlands, Southern Highlands Province, Tanganyika. *Actes du IVᵉ Congrès Panafricain de Préhistoire*, 1959 (Tervuren), 2:43–80.

HOWELL, F. C., and J. DESMOND CLARK.

1963. Acheulean hunter-gatherers of sub-Saharan Africa. In F. C. Howell and F. Bourlière (Eds.) *African ecology and human evolution.* Chicago: Aldine Publishing Company.

HOWELLS, W. W.

1965. Some present aspects of physical anthropology. In A. Rose (Ed.), *The Negro protest. Annals of the American Academy of Political and Social Science*, 357: 127–33.

HOWITT, A. W.

1880. The Kurnai: their customs in peace and war. In Lorimer Fison and A. W. Howitt, *Kamilaroi and Kurnai.* Melbourne: G. Robertson.

1884. On some Australian ceremonies of initiation. *Journal of the Royal Anthropological Institute of Great Britain and Ireland*, 13: 432–59.

1885. Australian group relations. *Annual Report of the Smithsonian Institution for the year 1883:* 797–824.

1889a. Further notes on the Australian class systems. *Journal of the Royal Anthropological Institute of Great Britain and Ireland*, 18: 31–68.

1889b. Notes on Australian message sticks and messengers. *Journal of the Royal Anthropological Institute of Great Britain and Ireland*, 18: 314–32.

1891. The Dieri and other kindred tribes of central Australia. *Journal of the Royal Anthropological Institute of Great Britain and Ireland*, 20: 30–104.

1904. *The native tribes of South-East Australia.* Gondon, New York: Macmillan.

HUGHES, CHARLES C.

1960. *An Eskimo village in the modern world.* Ithaca: Cornell University Press.

1965. Under four flags: recent culture change among the Eskimo. *Current Anthropology*, 6(1): 3–69.

HUNTINGFORD, G. W. B.

1929. Modern hunters: some account of the Kamelilo-Kapchepkendi Dorobo (Oriek) of Kenya Colony. *Journal of the Royal Anthropological Institute of Great Britain and Ireland*, 69: 333–78.

1942. The social organization of the Dorobo. *African Studies*, 1: 183–200.

1951. The social institutions of the Dorobo. *Anthropos*, 46: 1–48.

1954. The political organization of the Dorobo. *Anthropos*, 49: 123–48.

1955. The economic life of the Dorobo. *Anthropos*, 50: 602–634.

HURLBURT, JANICE.

1962. *Age as a factor in the social organization of the Hare Indians of Fort Good Hope, N. W. T.* Northern Coordination and Research Centre Report, no. 5. Ottawa: Department of Northern Affairs and National Resources.

IMMENROTH, WILHELM.

1933. Kultur und Umwelt der Kleinwüchsigen in Afrika. *Werkgemeinschaft Studien zur Völkerkunde.* (Leipzig), 6.

IRVINE, F. R.

1957. Wild and emergency foods of Australian and Tasmanian aborigines. *Oceania*, 28: 113–42.

IRVING, WILLIAM N.

1953. Evidence of early Tundra cultures in northern Alaska. *Anthropological Papers of the University of Alaska*, 1(2): 55–85.

ISAAC, GLYNN L.

In press a. Geological history of the Olorgesailie area. In L. D. Cuscoy (Ed.), *Actas del V Congreso Pan-Africano de Prehistoria*, 1963 (Tenerife).

In press b. New evidence from Olorgesailie relating to the character of Acheulean occupation sites. In L. D. Cuscoy (Ed.), *Actas del V Congreso Pan-Africano de Prehistorica*, 1963 (Tenerife).

1967. Stratigraphy of the Peninj group. (rev.) In W. Bishop and J. D. Clark (Eds.), *Background of African evolution.* Chicago: University of Chicago Press.

JACKSON, ROY I.

1953. Sockeye from the Fraser. *The Beaver* (Winnipeg), March: 18–25.

JAY, PHYLLIS.

1965. Field studies. In Allan Schrier, Harry F. Harlow, and Fred Stollnitz (Eds.), *Behavior of non-human primates* (vol. 2). New York, London: Academic Press.

JENNESS, DIAMOND.

1922. *The life of the Copper Eskimo. Reports of the Canadian Arctic Expeditions, 1913–18*, 12. Ottawa: F. A. Acland.

1934. Tribes of the Mackenzie and Yukon basins. In *The Indians of Canada.* Bulletin of the National Museum of Canada, no. 65: 377–422.

JENNESS, DIAMOND (Ed.).

1956. The Chipewyan Indians: an account by an early explorer. *Anthropologica*, 3: 15–33.

JEWETT, S. G., et al.

1953. *Birds of Washington state.* Seattle: University of Washington Press.

JOCHELSON, W.

1905–1908. *The Koryak.* American Museum of Natural History, Memoir 10, pt. 2.

1926. *The Yukaghir and Yukaghirized Tungas.* American Museum of Natural History, Memoir 13.

JOHNSON, FREDERICK (Ed.).

1946. *Man in northeastern North America.* Papers of the Robert S. Peabody Foundation for Archaeology (Andover), no. 3.

JOHNSTON, T. HARVEY.

1940. Some aboriginal routes in the western portion of South Australia. *Proceedings of the Royal Geographical Society of Australasia: South Australian Branch*, 41: 33–65.

JONES, ERNEST.

1925. Mother-right and sexual ignorance of savages. *International Journal of Psychoanalysis*, 6(2): 109–130.

JONES, FRANK L.

1963. *A demographic survey of the aboriginal population of the Northern Territory, with special reference to Bathurst Island Mission. Australian Institute of Aboriginal Studies, Occasional Papers in Aboriginal Studies* (Canberra), no. 1.

1965. The demography of the Australian aborigines. *International Social Science Journal*, 17(2): 232–45

KABERRY, PHYLLIS MARY.

1937. Subsections in east and south Kimberley tribes of northwest Australia. *Oceania*, 7: 436–58.

1939. *Aboriginal woman.* London: George Routledge.

KARSTEN, RAFAEL.

1932. Indian tribes of the Argentine and Bolivian Chaco. *Commentationes Humanarum Litterarum*, 4. Helsinki: Societas Scientarum Fennica.

1935. *The head hunters of the western Amazonas*. Helsinki: Societas Scientarum Fennica.

KAWAMURA, SYUNZO.

1958. The matriarchal social order in the Minoo-B group: a study on the rank system of Japanese macaque. *Primates (Journal of Primatology)* 1(2): 149–56 (Text in Japanese; English summary, pp. 149–50).

KEAST, A., R. L. CROCKER, and C. S. CHRISTIAN.

1959. *Biogeography and ecology in Australia*. The Hague: W. Junk

KEITH, GEORGE.

1890. Letters to Mr. Roderick McKenzie, 1807–1817. In L. R. Masson (Ed.), *Les bourgeois de la compagnie du nord-ouest: récits de voyages, lettres, et rapports inédits relatifs au nord-ouest canadien*, Série 2: 61–132. Quebec: A. Coté.

KELLY, ISABEL T.

1964. *Southern Paiute ethnography*. University of Utah Anthropological Papers, no. 69.

KENDREW, W. G., and D. KERR.

1955. *The climate of British Columbia and the Yukon Territory*. Ottawa: The Queen's Printer.

KENTON, EDNA (Ed.).

1927. The Indians of North America. In *The Jesuit relations and allied documents: travels and explorations of the Jesuit missionaries in New France, 1610–1791*. New York: Harcourt Brace. (First published Burrows, 1896.)

KING, RICHARD.

1836. *Narrative of a journey to the shores of the Arctic Ocean in 1833, 1834, and 1835, under the command of Capt. Back, R.N.* 2 vols. London: R. Bentley.

KLEIN, RICHARD G.

1965a. The middle palaeolithic of the Crimea. *Arctic Anthropology*, 3(1): 34–68.

1965b. *Dwelling-types and settlement patterns of the upper Pleistocene of European Russia*. Paper presented at American Anthropological Association, Annual Meetings, Denver.

KLEINDIENST, MAXINE R.

1961a. *The composition of Late Acheulian assemblages from east Africa*. Unpublished doctoral dissertation, University of Chicago.

1961b. Variability within the Late Acheulean assemblage in eastern Africa. *South African Archaeological Bulletin*, 16(62): 35–52.

KLEINDIENST, MAXINE R., and PATTY JO WATSON.

1956. Action archaeology: the archaeological inventory of a living community. *Anthropology Tomorrow*, 5(1): 75–78.

KNIGHT, ROLF.

1965. A re-examination of hunting, trapping, and territoriality among the northeastern Algonkian Indians. In Anthony Leeds and A. P. Vayda (Eds.), *Man, culture, and animals*. Washington, D.C.: American Association for the Advancement of Science, no. 78.

KOFORD, CARL B.

1966. Population changes in rhesus monkeys: Cayo Santiago, 1960–1964. *Tulane Studies in Zoology*, 13: 1–7.

KOHL-LARSEN, LUDWIG.

1958. *Wildbeuter in Ostafrika, die Tindiga, ein Jägerund Sammlervolk*. Berlin: Dietrich Reimer.

KRAISRI, NIMMANAHAEMINDA, AND J. HARTLAND-SWANN.

1962. Expedition to the "Khon Pa." *Journal of the Siam Society*, 50: 165–86.

KROEBER, A. L.

1925. *Handbook of the Indians of California*. Bureau of American Ethnology, Bulletin no. 78.

1931. *The Seri*. Southwest Museum Papers, no. 6.

1938. Basic and secondary patterns of social structure. *Journal of the Royal Anthropological Institute of Great Britain and Ireland*, 68: 299–309. (Also in *The nature of culture*. Chicago: University of Chicago Press, 1952.)

1939. *Cultural and natural areas of native North America.* University of California Publications in American Archaeology and Ethnology (Berkeley), 38.

1945. The ancient Oikeumene as a historic culture aggregate. *Journal of the Royal Anthropological Institute of Great Britain and Ireland*, 75: 9–20. (Also in *The nature of culture.* Chicago: University of Chicago Press, 1952.)

1955. The nature of the land-holding group. *Ethnohistory*, 2: 303–314.

KROEBER, A. L., and S. A. BARRETT.

1960. Fishing among the Indians of northwestern California. *Anthropological Records* (Berkeley), 21(1).

KROGMAN, W. M.

1939. Medical practices and diseases of the aboriginal American Indians. *CIBA Symposia*, 1: 11–18.

KRZWICKI, LUDWIK.

1934. *Primitive society and its vital statistics.* Trans. by H. E. Kennedy and A. Truszkowski. London: Macmillan.

KUHN, THOMAS S.

1962. *The structure of scientific revolutions.* Chicago: University of Chicago Press.

KUMMER, H., and F. KURT.

1963. Social units of a free-living population of Hamadryas baboons. *Folia Primatologica*, 1: 4–19.

KUNSTADTER, PETER, ROALD BUHLER, FREDERICK STAPHAN, AND CHARLES WESTOFF.

1963. Demographic variability and preferential marriage patterns. *American Journal of Physical Anthropology* (n.s.), 21: 511–19.

LACK, DAVID.

1954. *The natural regulation of animal numbers.* Cambridge: Cambridge University Press.

1966. *Population studies of birds.* Oxford: Clarendon Press.

LANCASTER, JANE B.

MS. The evolution of tool-using behavior: primate field studies, fossil apes and the archaeological record.

LANDES, RUTH.

1937a. *Ojibwa sociology.* New York: Columbia University Press.

1937b. The Ojibwa of Canada. In Margaret Mead (Ed.), *Cooperation and competition among primitive peoples.* New York, London: McGraw-Hill.

LANE, BARBARA S.

1961. Structural contrasts between symmetric and asymmetric marriage systems: a fallacy. *Southwestern Journal of Anthropology*, 17: 49–55.

1962 Jural authority and affinal exchange. *Southwestern Journal of Anthropology*, 18: 184–97.

LANNING, EDWARD P., and EUGENE A. HAMMEL.

1961. Early lithic industries of western South America. *American Antiquity*, 27(2): 139–54.

LANTIS, MARGARET.

1946. The social culture of the Nunivak Eskimo. *Transactions of the American Philosophical Society* (n.s.), 35(3): 151–323.

LARSEN, HELGE, and FROELICH RAINEY.

1948. *Ipiutak and the Arctic whale hunting culture.* Anthropological Papers of the American Museum of Natural History, no. 42.

LASKER, G. W. (Ed.).

1960. *The processes of ongoing human evolution.* Detroit: Wayne State University Press.

LATHRAP, DONALD W.

1958. The cultural sequence at Yarinacocha eastern, Peru. *American Antiquity*, 23(4): 379–88.

1962. *Yarinacocha: stratigraphic excavations in the Peruvian Montaña.* Unpublished doctoral dissertation, Harvard University.

1963. Possible affiliations of the Macalilla complex of coastal Ecuador. *American Antiquity*, 29(2): 239–41.

1965a. Origins of central Andean civilization: new evidence (review of *Andes 2: Excavations at Kotosh, Peru, 1960*, by Uzumi and Sono). *Science*, 148(3671): 796–98.

1965b. Investigaciones en la Selva Peruana, 1964–1965. *Boletín del Museo Nacional de Antropología y Arqueología* (Lima), 4: 9–12.

LAUGHLIN, WILLIAM S.

1957. Blood groups of the Anaktuvuk Eskimos, Alaska. *Anthropological Papers of the University of Alaska,* 6(1): 2–15.

1961. Acquisition of anatomical knowledge by ancient man. In S. L. Washburn (Ed.), *Social life of early man.* Chicago: Aldine Publishing Company.

1963a. Primitive theory of medicine: empirical knowledge. In Iago Galdston (Ed.), *Man's image in medicine and anthropology.* Institute of Social and Historic Medicine, Monograph 4: 116–40. New York: The New Academy of Medicine.

1963b. Eskimos and Aleuts: their origins and evolution. *Science,* 142(3593): 633–45.

1966. *Essential scientific activities preliminary to full term biological studies of isolate groups.* Paper presented at Wenner-Gren Burg Wartenstein Conference. (Unpublished).

1967. Human migration and permanent occupation in the Bering Sea area. In D. M. Hopkins (Ed.), *The Bering land bridge.* Stanford: Stanford University Press.

LAWICK, HUGO VON, and JANE VON LAWICK-GOODALL.

1966. *Family life in chimpland* (16mm film). Washington D.C.: National Geographic Society.

LAWRENCE, WILLIAM.

1937. Alternating generations in Australia. In G. P. Murdock (Ed.), *Studies in the science of society: presented to Albert Galloway Keller.* New Haven: Yale University Press.

LEACH, E. R.

1951. The structural implications of matrilateral cross-cousin marriage. *Journal of the Royal Anthropological Institute of Great Britain and Ireland,* 81: 23–55.

1954. *Political systems of Highland Burma: a study of Kachin social structure.* London: G. Bell and Sons, Ltd.

1961. *Pul Eliya, a village in Ceylon: a study of land tenure and kinship.* Cambridge: Cambridge University Press.

1965a. Unilateral cross-cousin marriage. *Man,* 65: 25.

1965b. Claude Lévi-Strauss—anthropologist and philosopher. *New Left Review,* 34.

LEACOCK, ELEANOR B.

1954. *The Montagnais "hunting territory" and fur trade.* American Anthropological Association Memoir, no. 78.

1955. Matrilocality in a simple hunting economy (Montagnais-Naskapi). *Southwestern Journal of Anthropology,* 11: 31–47.

LEAKEY, L. S. B.

1952. The Olorgesailie prehistoric site. *First Pan-African congress on prehistory* (Nairobi), 1947: 209.

1960. *Adam's ancestors.* (4th ed.) New York: Harper Torchbooks.

1965. Comment in symposium. In Paul DeVore (Ed.), *The origin of man.* Transcript of a symposium sponsored by Wenner-Gren Foundation for Anthropological Research.

LeBAR, FRANK M., GERALD C. HICKEY, and JOHN K. MUSGRAVE.

1964. *Ethnic groups of mainland Southeast Asia.* New Haven, Conn.: Human Relations Area Files Press.

LEE, RICHARD B.

1963. The population ecology of man in the early Upper Pleistocene of southern Africa. *Proceedings of the Prehistoric Society* (n.s.), 29: 235–57.

1965. *Subsistence ecology of !Kung Bushmen.* Unpublished doctoral dissertation, University of California, Berkeley.

1967. The sociology of Bushman trance performances. In Raymond Prince (Ed.), *Trance and possession states.* Montreal: McGill University Press.

In press. !Kung Bushman subsistence: input-output analysis. In A. P. Vayda (Ed.), *Human ecology: an anthropological reader.* New York: Natural History Press.

LEHMAN, F. K.

1963. *The structure of Chin society: a tribal people of Burma adapted to a non-Western civilization.* Illinois Studies in Anthropology, no. 3. Urbana: University of Illinois Press.

LENSKI, GERHARD.

1966. *Power and privilege: a theory of social stratification.* New York: McGraw-Hill.

374   *References*

LESHNIK, LORENZ S.

1964. *Sociological interpretation in archaeology: some examples from a village study in central India.* Unpublished doctoral dissertation, University of Chicago.

LE SOUËF, ALBERT A. C.

1878. Notes on the natives of Australia. In R. B. Smyth (Ed.), *The aborigines of Victoria: with notes relating to the habits of the natives of other parts of Australia and Tasmania,* 2: 289–99. Melbourne: J. Ferres.

LÉVI-STRAUSS, CLAUDE.

1936. Contribution à l'étude de l'organisation sociale des Indiens Bororo. *Journal de la Société des Américanistes* (Paris) (n.s.), 28: 269–304.

1940. Le vie familiale et sociale des Indiens Nambikwara. *Journal de la Société des Américanistes* (Paris) (n.s.), 38: 1–131.

1949. *Les structures elémentaires de la parenté.* Paris: Presses Universitaires de France.

1952. La notion de'archaïsme en ethnologie. *Cahiers Internationaux de Sociologie,* 12: 32–35.

1958. *Anthropologie structurale.* Paris: Plon. (Also *Structural Anthropology.* Trans. by Claire Jacobson and Brooke Schoepf. New York, London: Basic Books, 1963.)

1960. On manipulated sociological models. *Bijdragen tot de Taal- Land- en Volkenkunde,* 116(1): 45–54.

1966. The scope of anthropology. *Current Anthropology,* 7(2): 112–23.

LEVINE, MORTON H.

1957. Prehistoric art and ideology. *American Anthropologist* (n.s.), 59(6): 949–64.

LINNÉ, SIGVALD.

1957. Technical secrets of American Indians. *Journal of the Royal Anthropological Institute of Great Britain and Ireland,* 87(2): 149–64.

LINTON, RALPH.

1936. *The study of man.* New York: Appleton-Century-Crofts.

1953. Comments in symposium. In Sol Tax *et al.* (Eds.), *An appraisal of anthropology today.* Chicago: University of Chicago Press.

LIPS, JULIUS E.

1939. Naskapi trade: a study in legal acculturation. *Journal de la Société des Américanistes* (Paris) (n.s.), 31: 129–95.

1947a. Naskapi law. *Transactions of the American Philosophical Society* (n.s.), 37(4): 379–492.

1947b. *Zelte in der Wildnis: Indianerleben in Labrador.* Vienna: Danubia.

LIVI, LIVIO.

1949. Considerations theoriques et pratiques sur le concept de "minimum de population." *Population* (Paris), 4: 754–56.

LIVINGSTONE, FRANK B.

1958. Anthropological implications of sickle cell gene distribution in West Africa. *American Anthropologist* (n.s.), 60: 533–62.

1960. Natural selection, disease, and ongoing evolution, as illustrated by the ABO blood groups. In G.W. Lasker (Ed.), *The processes of ongoing human evolution.* Detroit: Wayne State University Press.

LONGACRE, WILLIAM A.

1963. *Archaeology as anthropology: a case study.* Unpublished doctoral dissertation, University of Chicago.

1964a. Archaeology as anthropology: a case study. *Science,* 144(3625): 1454–55.

1964b. Sociological implications of the ceramic analysis. In P. S. Martin *et al.* (Eds.), *Chapters in the prehistory of eastern Arizona,* 2, *Fieldiana Anthropology,* 55: 155–70.

1966. Changing patterns of social integration: a prehistoric example from the American Southwest. *American Anthropologist* (n.s.), 68(1): 94–102.

LONGACRE, WILLIAM A., and JAMES E. AYRES.

1966. *Archaeological theory: some lessons from an Apache wickiup.* Paper presented at 31st Annual Meeting of the Society for American Archaeology, Reno, Nevada.

LORENZ, KONRAD Z.

1966. *On aggression.* Trans. by Marjorie K. Wilson. New York: Harcourt, Brace and World.

LORIMER, FRANK.

1954. *Culture and human fertility; a study of the relation of cultural conditions to fertility in non-industrial and transitional societies.* Paris: Unesco.

LOTHROP, S. K.

1928. *The Indians of Tierra del Fuego.* Contributions of the Museum of the American Indian, Heye Foundation. New York: Heye Foundation.

LOUNSBURY, FLOYD G.

1962. (Review of) *Structure and sentiment:* a test case in social anthropology. *American Anthropologist* (n.s.), 64(6): 1302–1310.

1964. A formal account of the Crow- and Omaha-type kinship terminologies. In Ward H. Goodenough (Ed.), *Explorations in cultural anthropology: essays in honor of George Peter Murdock.* New York: McGraw-Hill.

LOWIE, ROBERT H.

1948. The tropical forests, an introduction. In J. H. Steward (Ed.), *Handbook of South American Indians,* vol. 3: *the tropical forest tribes.* Bureau of American Ethnology Bulletin, 143(3): 1–56.

1952. The heterogeneity of marginal cultures. In Sol Tax (Ed.), *Selected papers of the 29th international congress of Americanists,* 3: 1–7. Chicago: University of Chicago Press.

1963. *Indians of the Plains.* New York: American Museum Science Books. (First published as *American Museum of Natural History Anthropological Handbook,* no. 1. New York: McGraw-Hill, 1954.)

LUMHOLZ, CARL.

1889. *Among cannibals: an account of four years' travels in Australia and of camp life with the aborigines of Queensland.* Trans. by R. B. Anderson. New York: Scribner's.

McCARTHY, FREDERICK D.

1945. Catalogue of the aboriginal relics of New South Wales, pt. 3: carved trees or dendroglyphs. *Mankind,* 3: 199–206.

1957a. *Australia's aborigines: their life and culture.* Melbourne: Cologravure.

1957b. Distributional notes on Northern Australian point industries. *Mankind,* 5: 163–68.

1957c. Habitat, economy and equipment of the Australian aborigines. *Australian Journal of Science,* 19: 88–97.

McCARTHY, FREDERICK D., and MARGARET McARTHUR.

1960. The food quest and the time factor in aboriginal economic life. In Charles P. Mountford (Ed.), *Records of the American-Australian scientific expedition to Arnhem Land, vol. 2: anthropology and nutrition.* Melbourne: Melbourne University Press.

McCONNELL, URSULA H.

1930–34. The Wik-Munkan and allied tribes of Cape York Peninsula. *Oceania,* 1: 97–104, 181–205; 4: 310–67.

MacDONALD, GEORGE.

1965. On the scientific basis of tropical hygiene. *Transactions of the Royal Society of Tropical Medicine and Hygiene,* 59: 611–20.

McGEE, W. J.

1898. *The Seri Indians.* Annual Report of the Bureau of American Ethnology, vol. 17 (for 1895–96): 1–128, 129–344.

McILWRAITH, THOMAS F.

1948. *The Bella Coola Indians.* Toronto: University of Toronto Press.

McKENNAN, ROBERT A.

1959. *The Upper Tanana Indians.* Yale University Publications in Anthropology, no. 55. New Haven: Yale University Press.

1965. *The Chandalar Kutchin.* Arctic Institute of North America Technical Paper, no. 17.

McKENZIE, ALEXANDER.

1801. *Voyages from Montreal, on the River St. Lawrence, through the continent of North America, to the Frozen and Pacific Oceans: in the years 1789 and 1793.* London: T. Cadell, jun., and W. Davies.

McKENZIE, RODERIC.

1795. An account of the Athabasca Indians by a partner of the North West Company. In *Some account of the North West Company containing analogy of nations ancient and modern,* Athabasca, 1795, pt. 3. Massen

Collection, MS Group 19, *Fur trade and Indians, 1763–1867*. MS Division, Public Archives of Canada.

1889. Reminiscences. In L. R. Masson (Ed.), *Les bourgeois de la compagnie du nord-ouest: récits de voyages, lettres et rapports inédits relatifs au nord-ouest canadien*, Série 1: 7–66. Quebec: A. Coté.

McLEAN, JOHN.

1932. *John McLean's notes of a twenty-five years' service in the Hudson's Bay Territory*. Ed. by W. S. Wallace. Toronto: Champlain Society.

MacNEISH, JUNE HELM.

1954. Contemporary folk beliefs of a Slave Indian band. *Journal of American Folklore*, 67: 185–98.

1955. Folktales of the Slave Indians. *Anthropologica*, 1: 37–44.

1956a. (Ed.). "Field notes on Tahltan and Kaska Indians: 1912–1915" by J. A. Teit. *Anthropologica*, 3: 39–171.

1956b. Leadership among the northeastern Athapaskans. *Anthropologica*, 2: 131–63.

1956c. Problems of acculturation and livelihood in a northern Indian band. *Contributions a l'Etude des Sciences de l'Homme* (Montreal), 3: 169–81.

1957. (Ed.). The Poole Field letters. *Anthropologica*, 4: 47–60.

1960a. Kin terms of arctic drainage Déné: Hare, Slavey, Chipewyan. *American Anthropologist* (n.s.), 62: 279–95.

1960b. Les Indiens Déné de la forêt subarctique. *Science et Nature*, 41: 31–37.

MacNEISH, RICHARD STOCKTON.

1964. The food gathering and incipient agriculture stage of prehistoric Middle America. In Robert C. West (Ed.), *Natural environment and early cultures*. Austin: University of Texas Press.

MACQUARIE, C.

1940. Water gypsies of the Malagarasi. *Tanganyika Notes and Records*, 9: 61–67.

McPHERRON, ALAN.

1965. Ionic removal of corrosion from copper. *Michigan Archaeologist*, 11(2): 53–56.

MAINGARD, J. F.

1937. Somes notes on health and disease among the Bushmen of the southern Kalahari. In J. D. Jones *et al.* (Eds.), *Bushmen of the southern Kalahari*. Johannesburg: University of Witwaterstrand Press.

MAIR, LUCY.

1965. *An introduction to social anthropology*. Oxford: Clarendon Press.

MAJUMDAR, DHIRENDRA NATH.

1944. *The fortunes of primitive tribes*. Lucknow: Universal Publishers.

MALINOWSKI, BRONISLAW.

1960. *A scientific theory of culture*. New York: Oxford University Press. (First published Chapel Hill: University of North Carolina Press, 1944.)

1955. *Sex and repression in savage society*. New York: Meridian Books.

MAN, EDWARD HORACE.

1883. *On the aboriginal inhabitants of the Andaman Islands*. London: Anthropological Institute of Great Britain and Ireland, Trubner.

MANN, G. V., O. A. ROELS, D. L. PRICE, and J. M. MERRILL.

1962. Cardiovascular disease in African Pygmies. A survey of the health status, serum lipids, and diet of Pygmies in Congo. *Journal of Chronic Diseases*, 15: 341–71.

MANNING, T. H.

1943. Notes on the coastal district of the eastern Barren Grounds and Melville Peninsular from Igloolik to Cape Fullerton. *Canadian Geographical Journal*, 26: 84–105.

MARCOY, PAUL (pseud. Laurent Saint-Cricq).

1873. *A journey across South America from the Pacific Ocean to the Atlantic Ocean* (2 vols.). Trans. by Elihu Rich. London: Bladkie and Son.

MARSH, GORDON H.

1954. A comparative survey of Eskimo-Aleut religion. *Anthropological Papers of the University of Alaska*, 3(1): 21–36.

MARSH, GORDON H., and WILLIAM S. LAUGHLIN.

1956. Human anatomical knowledge among the Aleutian Islanders. *Southwestern Journal of Anthropology*, 12(1): 38–78.

MARSHALL, JOHN.

1956. *The hunters*. (16mm film.) Cambridge: Film Study Center of the Peabody Museum, Harvard University.

MARSHALL, LORNA K.

1957. The kin terminology system of the !Kung Bushmen. *Africa*, 27: 1–25.

1959. Marriage among !Kung Bushmen. *Africa*, 29: 335–65.

1960. !Kung Bushmen bands. *Africa*, 30: 325–55.

1961. Sharing, talking and giving: relief of social tensions among !Kung Bushmen. *Africa*, 31: 231–49.

1962. !Kung Bushmen religious beliefs. *Africa*, 32: 221–52.

1965. The !Kung Bushmen of the Kalahari Desert. In James Gibbs (Ed.), *Peoples of Africa*. New York: Holt, Rinehart, and Winston.

MASON, J. ALDEN.

1946. *Notes on the Indians of the Great Slave Lake area*. Yale University Publications in Anthropology, no. 34. New Haven: Yale University Press.

MASON, RONALD J.

1962. The Paleo-Indian tradition in eastern North America. *Current Anthropology*, 3(3): 227–78.

MASSOLA, ALDO.

1956a. Australian fishhooks and their distribution. *Memoirs of the National Museum of Victoria*, 22(1): 1–16.

1956b. Victorian aboriginal strangling cords. *Memoirs of the National Museum of Victoria*, 22(3): 1–4.

MATHEWS, ROBERT H.

1894. Aboriginal Bora held at Gundabloui in 1894. *Journal and Proceedings of the Royal Society of New South Wales*, 28: 98–129.

1895. The Bora, or initiation ceremonies of the Kamilaroi tribe. *Journal of the Royal Anthropological Institute of Great Britain and Ireland*, 24: 411–27.

1896a. Australian class systems. *American Anthropologist* (o.s.), 9: 411–16.

1896b. Australian ground and tree drawings. *American Anthropologist* (o.s.), 9: 33–49.

1896c. The Bora, or initiation ceremonies of the Kamilaroi tribe, pt. 2. *Journal of the Royal Anthropological Institute of Great Britain and Ireland*, 25: 318–39.

1896d. The Burbung of the Wiradthuri tribes. *Journal of the Royal Anthropological Institute of Great Britain and Ireland*, 25: 295–318.

1897a. Australian class systems. *American Anthropologist* (o.s.), 10: 345–47.

1897b. The Bora of the Kamilaroi tribes. *Proceedings of the Royal Society of Victoria* (n.s.), 9: 137–73.

1897c. The Burbung of the Wiradthuri tribes, pt. 2. *Journal of the Royal Anthropological Institute of Great Britain and Ireland*, 26: 272–85.

1897d. The Burbung, or initiation ceremonies of the Murrumbidgee tribes. *Journal and Proceedings of the Royal Society of New South Wales*, 31: 111–53.

1897e. The totemic division of Australian tribes. *Journal and Proceedings of the Royal Society of New South Wales*, 31: 154–76.

1905. Ethnological notes on the aboriginal tribes of New South Wales and Victoria. *Journal and Proceedings of the Royal Society of New South Wales*, 38: 203–381.

MATHIASSEN, THERKEL.

1928. Material culture of the Iglulik Eskimos. *Report of the Fifth Thule Expedition 1921–24*, 6(1). Copenhagen: Gyldendalske boghandel.

MAUSS, MARCEL.

1906. Essai sur les variations saisonniéres des sociétés eskimos: étude de morphologie sociale. *L'Année Sociologique*, 9: 39–132.

MAYBURY-LEWIS, DAVID.

1967. *Akwe-Shavante society*. Oxford: Clarendon Press.

MAYR, ERNST.

1963. *Animal species and evolution*. Cambridge: Belknap Press (Harvard University Press).

MEGGERS, BETTY J.

1954. Environmental limitation on the development of culture. *American Anthropologist* (n.s.), 56: 801–824.

1957a. Environment and culture in the Amazon Basin: an appraisal of the theory of environmental determinism. In Angel Palerm *et al.* (Eds.), *Studies in human ecology*. Pan American Union of Social Sciences, Monograph 3: 71–89.

1957b. Environmental limitation on Maya culture: a reply to Coe. *American Anthropologist* (n.s.), 59: 888–90.

MEGGERS, BETTY J., and CLIFFORD EVANS, Jr.

1956. The reconstruction of settlement pattern in the South American tropical forest. In Gordon R. Willey (Ed.), *Prehistoric settlement patterns in the New World*. Viking Fund Publications in Anthropology no. 23.

1961. An experimental formulation of horizon styles in the tropical forest area of South America. In S. K. Lothrop *et al.* (Eds.), *Essays in pre-Columbian art and archaeology*. Cambridge: Harvard University Press.

MEGGITT, M. J.

1957. Notes on the vegetable foods of the Walbiri of central Australia. *Oceania*, 28: 143–45.

1958. The Enga of the New Guinea highlands. *Oceania*, 28: 253–330.

1962. *Desert people: a study of the Walbiri aborigines of central Australia*. Sydney: Angus and Robertson.

1964a. Indigenous forms of government among the Australian aborigines. *Bijdragen tot de Taal-, Land-, en Volkenkunde*, 120: 163–80.

1964b. Pre-industrial man in the tropical environment: aboriginal food-gatherers of tropical Australia. *Proceedings and Papers of the Ninth Technical Meeting I.U.C.N., Nairobi, Kenya, 1963*. Morges (Vaud), Switzerland: International Union for the Conservation of Nature and Natural Resources.

1965a. The association between Australian aborigines and dingoes. In A. Leeds and A. P. Vayda (Eds.). *Man, culture, and animals: the role of animals in human ecological adjustments*. Washington, D.C.: American Association for the Advancement of Science.

1965b. Marriage among the Walbiri of central Australia: a statistical examination. In R. M. Berndt and C. H. Berndt (Eds.), *Aboriginal man in Australia: essays in honor of Emeritus Professor A. P. Elkin*. Sydney: Angus and Robertson.

MENOVSHCHIKOV, G. A.

1956. Eskimosi (The Eskimos). In M. G. Levin and L. P. Potov (Eds.), *Narody Sibiri (Peoples of Siberia)*. Moscow: Russian Academy of Sciences. (Also trans. by C. C. Hughes. *Anthropological Papers of the University of Alaska* [1964], 12: 1–13.)

MERBS, CHARLES F., and W. H. WILSON.

1962. Anomalies and pathologies of the Sadlermiut Eskimo vertebral column. In *Contributions to Anthropology, 1960*, pt. 1. Bulletin of the National Museum of Canada, 180: 154–80.

MERKER, M.

1904. *Die Masai*. Berlin: Dietrich Reimer.

MÉTRAUX, ALFRED.

1937. Études d'ethnographie Toba-Pilaga (Gran Chaco). *Anthropos*, 32: 171–94, 378–401.

1948a. Tribes of the middle and upper Amazon River. In J. H. Steward (Ed.), *Handbook of South American Indians*, vol. 3: *the tropical forest tribes*. Bureau of American Ethnology Bulletin, 143(3): 687–712.

1948b. The hunting and gathering tribes of the Rio Negro Basin. In J. H. Steward (Ed.), *Handbook of South American Indians*, vol. 3: *the tropical forest tribes*. Bureau of American Ethnology Bulletin, 143(3): 861–67.

MICHEA, JEAN.

1963. Les Chitra-Gottinéké: essaie de monographie d'un groupe Athapascan des montagnes Rocheuses. In *Contributions to anthropology 1960*, pt. 2. Bulletin of the National Museum of Canada, 190: 49–93.

MIGLIAZZA, E.

1964. Notas sobre a organização social dos Xiriâna do Rio Uraricaá. *Boletim do Museu Paraense Emilio Goeldi* (Belem, Brazil) (n.s.), 22: 1–22.

MOMSEN, RICHARD P., Jr.

1964. The Isconahua Indians: a study of change and diversity in the Peruvian Amazon. *Revista Geográfica,*
32(60): 59–81.

MOODIE, DONALD (Ed.).

1838–42. *The record; or a series of official papers relative to the condition and treatment of the native tribes of South
Africa,* pts. 1, 3, 5. Cape Town: A. S. Robertson. (Also phototastic reprint of 1860 edition. Amsterdam:
Balkema, and Cape Town: A. S. Robertson, 1960.)

MOONEY, JAMES.

1928. *The aboriginal population of America north of Mexico.* Smithsonian Miscellaneous Collections, 80(7):

MOORE, OMAR K.

1957. Divination—a new perspective. *American Anthropologist* (n.s.), 59: 69–74.

MOREY, ROBERT.

1967. Unpublished field notes on the Guahibo. University of Pittsburgh.

MORGAN, JOHN.

1852. *The life and adventures of William Buckley, thirty-two years a wanderer amongst the aborigines of the then
unexplored country round Port Phillip, now the Province of Victoria.* Hobart, Tasmania: A. Macdougall.

MORGAN, LEWIS HENRY.

1870. *Systems of consanguinity and affinity of the human family.* Smithsonian Contributions to Knowledge,
no. 17.

1880. Prefatory note. In Lorimer Fison and A. W. Howitt (Eds.), *Kamilaroi and Kurnai.* Melbourne:
G. Robertson.

MORICE, ADRIEN G.

1906–10. The great Déné race. *Anthropos,* 1: 229–77, 483–508, 695–730; 2: 1–34, 181–96; 4: 582–606;
5: 113–42, 419–43, 643–53, 969–90.

MOTULSKY, ARNO G.

1960. Metabolic polymorphisms and the role of infectious diseases in human evolution. In G. W. Lasker
(Ed.), *The processes of ongoing human evolution.* Detroit: Wayne State University Press.

MOVIUS, HALLAM L., Jr.

1966. The hearths of the Upper Périgordian and Aurignacian horizons at the Abri Pataud, Les Eyzies
(Dordogne), and their possible significance. In J. D. Clark and F. C. Howell (Eds.), *Recent studies in
paleoanthropology. American Anthropologist* (n.s.), 68(2), pt. 2.

MUNRO, J. A., and IAN McTAGGART COWAN.

1947. *A review of the bird fauna of British Columbia.* British Columbia Provincial Museum Special
Publication, no. 2.

MURDOCH, J.

1892. *Ethnological results of the Point Barrow expedition.* Bureau of American Ethnology, Annual Report 9
(for 1887–88).

MURDOCK, GEORGE PETER.

1949. *Social structure.* New York: Macmillan.

1960. *Ethnographic bibliography of North America.* (3d ed.) New Haven, Conn.: Human Relations Area
Files Press.

1967. The ethnographic atlas: a summary. *Ethnology,* 6(2).

MURPHY, ROBERT F.

1960. *Headhunter's heritage: social and economic change among the Mundurucu Indians.* Berkeley: University of
California Press.

MURPHY, ROBERT F., and BUELL QUAIN.

1955. *The Trumai Indians of Central Brazil.* American Ethnological Society Monograph no. 24. Seattle:
University of Washington Press.

MURPHY, ROBERT F., and JULIAN H. STEWARD.

1955. Tappers and trappers: parallel process in acculturation. *Economic Development and Cultural Change,*
4: 335–55.

NADEL, S. F.

1951. *The foundations of social anthropology.* Glencoe, Ill.: The Free Press.

NAPIER, JOHN R.

1962. Monkeys and their habitats. *New Scientist,* 15: 88–92.

NAROLL, RAOUL S.

1962. Floor area and settlement population. *American Antiquity,* 27(4): 587–89.

NEEDHAM, RODNEY.

1954. Siriono and Penan: a test of some hypotheses. *Southwestern Journal of Anthropology,* 10(3): 228–32.

1961. An analytical note on the structure of Siriono society. *Southwestern Journal of Anthropology,* 17(3): 239–55.

NEEL, JAMES V.

1962. Diabetes Mellitus: a "thrifty" genotype rendered detrimental by progress? *American Journal of Human Genetics,* 14(4): 353–62.

NEEL, JAMES V., F. M. SALZANO, P. C. JUNQUEIRA, F. KEITER, and D. MAYBURY-LEWIS.

1964. Studies on the Xavante Indians of the Brazilian Mato Grosso. *American Journal of Human Genetics,* 16(1): 52–140.

NELSON, EDWARD W.

1899. *The Eskimo about the Bering Strait.* Bureau of American Ethnology, Annual Report 18 (for 1896–97).

NELSON, RICHARD KING.

In press. *Alaskan Eskimo exploitation of the sea ice environment.* Technical Notes of the U.S. Arctic Aeromedical Laboratory (Fort Wainwright, Alaska).

NIBLACK, ALBERT P.

1890. *The coast Indians of southern Alaska and northern British Columbia.* Annual Report of the U.S. National Museum for 1888: 225–386.

NIMUENDAJÚ, CURT.

1939. *The Apinaye.* Trans. by Robert Lowie. Washington, D.C.: Catholic University of America Press.

1942. *The Serente.* Trans. by Robert Lowie. Los Angeles: Southwest Museum.

1946. *The Eastern Timbira.* Trans. and ed. by Robert Lowie. Berkeley: University of California Press.

1952a. *The Tapajo.* Trans. and ed. by J. H. Rowe. Kroeber Anthropological Society Papers, no. 6.

1952b. *The Tukuna.* Trans. by W. D. Hohenthal and ed. by Robert Lowie. University of California Publications in American Archaeology and Ethnology (Berkeley), 45.

NOBLE, G. KINGSLEY.

1965. *Proto-Arawakan and its descendants.* Indiana University Publications in Anthropology and Linguistics, no. 38.

NOONE, HERBERT D.

1936. Report on the settlements and welfare of the Ple-Temiar Senoi of the Perak-Kelantan watershed. *Journal of the Federal Malay States Museum,* 19(1).

NORDENSKIÖLD, ERLAND.

1919. *An ethno-geographical analysis of the material culture of two Indian tribes in the Gran Chaco.* Trans. by G. E. Fuhrken. Comparative Ethnological Studies (Göteborg), no. 1.

OAKLEY, KENNETH P.

1958. *Man the tool-maker.* (4th ed.) London: British Museum. (First published 1949.)

1961. On man's use of fire, with comments on tool-making and hunting. In S. L. Washburn (Ed.), *Social life of early man.* Chicago: Aldine Publishing Company.

OBLATE CENSUS.

1911. Residence habituelle des sauvages de Fort Rae, avec leurs familles. Holograph list, St. Michael's Mission, Fort Rae, N.W.T., Canada.

ODUM, EUGENE P.

1959. *Fundamentals of ecology.* (2d ed.) Philadelphia, London: Saunders.

OSGOOD, CORNELIUS B.

1932. The ethnography of the Great Bear Lake Indians. *Bulletin of the National Museum of Canada,* 70: 31–97.

1936a. *Contributions to the ethnography of the Kutchin.* Yale University Publications in Anthropology, no. 14. New Haven: Yale University Press.

1936b. *The distribution of the northern Athapaskan Indians.* Yale University Publications in Anthropology, no. 7. New Haven: Yale University Press.

1937. *The enthography of the Tanaina.* Yale University Publications in Anthropology, no. 16. New Haven: Yale University Press.

1940. *Ingalik material culture.* Yale University Publications in Anthropology, no. 22. New Haven: Yale University Press.

1958. *Ingalik social culture.* Yale University Publications in Anthropology, no. 53. New Haven: Yale University Press.

1959. *Ingalik mental culture.* Yale University Publications in Anthropology, no. 56. New Haven: Yale University Press.

OUTRAM, D. N.

1956. *Amount of herring spawn deposited in British Columbia coastal waters in 1956.* Fisheries Research Board of Canada: Pacific Biological Station, Nanaimo, B.C., Circular no. 42.

1957. *Extent of herring spawn in British Columbia in 1957.* Fisheries Research Board of Canada: Pacific Biological Station, Nanaimo, B.C., Circular no. 46.

1958. *The 1958 herring spawn deposition in British Columbia coastal waters.* Fisheries Research Board of Canada: Pacific Biological Station, Nanaimo, B.C., Circular no. 50.

OWEN, ROGER C.

1965. The patrilocal band: a linguistically and culturally hybrid social unit. *American Anthropologist,* (n.s.), 67: 675–90.

PALMATARY, HELEN CONSTANCE.

1960. *The archaeology of the Lower Tapajos Valley, Brazil.* Transactions of the American Philosophical Society (n.s.), 50(3).

1965. *The river of the Amazons.* New York: Carlton Press.

PEHRSON, ROBERT N.

1957. The bilateral network of social relations in Könkämä Lapp District. *International Journal of American Linguistics,* 23(1), pt. 2.

PETITOT, EMILE.

1876. *Monographie des Déné-Dindjie.* Paris: E. Leroux.

1887. *En route pour la Mer Glaciale.* (3d ed.) Paris: Letouzey et Ané.

1891. *Autour du grand lac des esclaves.* Paris: Albert Savine.

PIDDINGTON, RALPH, and MARJORIE PIDDINGTON.

1932. Report on fieldwork in northwestern Australia. *Oceania,* 2: 342–58.

PIDDOCKE, STUART.

1965. The potlatch system of the southern Kwakiutl: a new perspective. *Southwestern Journal of Anthropology,* 21: 244–64.

PIKE, GORDON C., and B. E. MAXWELL.

1958. The abundance and distribution of the northern sea lion (*Eumetopias jubata*) on the coast of British Columbia. *Journal of the Fisheries Research Board of Canada,* 15: 5–17.

PILLING, ARNOLD R.

1958. *Law and feud in an aboriginal society of North Australia.* Unpublished doctoral dissertation, University of California, Berkeley.

1961. Micro-evolution among the Tiwi of north Australia. Proceedings of the 10th Pacific Science Congress (Honolulu). *Abstracts of Symposium Papers,* 87.

PLOMLEY, N. J. B. (Ed.).

1966. *Friendly mission; the Tasmanian journals and papers of George Augustus Robinson, 1829–1834.* Hobart: Tasmanian Historical Research Association.

POLUNIN, IVAN.

1953. The medical natural history of Malayan aborigines and their medical investigation. *Medical Journal of Malaya,* 8: 55–174.

POSPISIL, LEOPOLD.

1964. Law and societal structure among the Nunamiut Eskimo. In Ward H. Goodenough (Ed)., *Explorations in cultural anthropology: essays in honor of George Peter Murdock*. New York: McGraw-Hill.

PRICE, D. L., G. V. MANN, O. A. ROELS, and J. M. MERRILL.

1963. Parasitism in Congo Pygmies. *American Journal of Tropical Medicine and Hygiene*, 12: 383–87.

PUTNAM, PATRICK.

1948. The Pygmies of the Ituri forest. In Carleton S. Coon (Ed.), *A reader in general anthropology*. New York: Henry Holt.

RADCLIFFE-BROWN, A. R.

1930. Former numbers and distribution of the Australian aborigines. *Official Yearbook of the Commonwealth of Australia*, 23: 671–96.

1931. Social organization of Australian tribes. *Oceania Monographs*, 1.

1933. *The Andaman Islanders*. (2d ed.) Cambridge: Cambridge University Press.

1951. Murngin social organization. *American Anthropologist* (n.s.), 53: 37–55.

1952. Patrilineal and matrilineal succession. In A. R. Radcliffe-Brown, *Structure and function in primitive society*. Glencoe, Ill.: The Free Press. (First published 1935 in *The Iowa Law Review*, 20[2].)

1956. On Australian local organization. *American Anthropologist* (n.s.), 58: 363–67.

RAPPAPORT, ROY A.

1966. *Ritual in the ecology of a New Guinea people*. Unpublished doctoral dissertation, Columbia University.

RASMUSSEN, KNUD.

1929. Intellectual culture of the Hudson Bay Eskimo, I: intellectual culture of the Iglulik Eskimos. *Report of the fifth Thule expedition, 1921–24*, 7(1). Copenhagen: Gyldendalske Boghandel.

1931. The Netsilik Eskimos: social life and spiritual culture. *Report of the fifth Thule expedition, 1921–1924*, 8(1, 2). Copenhagen. Gyldendalske Boghandel.

1932. Intellectual culture of the Copper Eskimos. *Report of the fifth Thule expedition, 1921–1924*, 9. Copenhagen: Gyldendalske Boghandel.

RAY, VERNE.

1938. Lower Chinook ethnographic notes. *University of Washington Publications in Anthropology*, 7(2): 29–165.

REAY, MARIE.

1962. Subsections at Borroloola. *Oceania*, 33: 90–115.

REED, WILLIAM ALLEN.

1904. *Negritos of Zambales*. Department of the Interior, Ethnological Survey Publications 2(1). Manila: Bureau of Printing.

REID, RUSSELL M.

1967. Marriage systems and algebraic group theory. *American Anthropologist* (n.s.), 69: 171–78.

REIM, HELMUT.

1964. *Ein australischer Robinson*. Leipzig: Brockhaus Verlag.

REYNOLDS, VERNON.

1963. An outline of the behavior and social organization of forest-living chimpanzees. *Folia Primatologica* (Basel and New York), 1(2): 95–102.

REYNOLDS, VERNON, and FRANCES REYNOLDS.

1965. Chimpanzees of the Budongo forest. In I. DeVore (Ed.), *Primate behavior*. New York: Holt, Rinehart and Winston.

RICHARDS, AUDREY I.

1939. *Land, labour and diet in Northern Rhodesia*. London: Oxford University Press.

1950. Some types of family structure amongst the central Bantu. In A. R. Radcliffe-Brown and Daryll Forde (Eds.), *African systems of kinship and marriage*. London: Oxford University Press.

RICHARDSON, JOHN.

1851. *Arctic searching expedition: a journal of a boat voyage through Rupert's Land and the Arctic Sea in search of the discovery ships under command of Sir John Franklin*. London: Longmans, Brown, Green, and Longmans.

RIVERA, TRINITA.
   1949. Diet of a food-gathering people, with chemical analysis of salmon and saskatoons. In Marian
   Smith (Ed.), *Indians of the urban northwest*. Columbia University Contributions to Anthropology, 36.
RODRIQUES, ARIYON DALL'IGNA.
   1958. Die Klassifikation des Tupí-Sprachstammes. *Proceedings of the 32d International Congress of Americanists*
   (Copenhagen): 679–84.
ROGERS, EDWARD S.
   1962. *The Round Lake Ojibwa*. Royal Ontario Museum, Division of Art and Archaeology, Occasional
   Paper no. 5.
   1963a. Changing settlement patterns of the Cree-Ojibwa of northern Ontario. *Southwestern Journal of
   Anthropology*, 19: 64–88.
   1963b. *The hunting group-hunting territory complex among the Mistassini Indians*. Bulletin of the National
   Museum of Canada, no. 195.
   1965. Leadership among the Indians of eastern sub-arctic Canada. *Anthropologica* (n.s.), 7: 263–84.
ROGERS, EDWARD S., and JEAN ROGERS.
   1960. *The individual in Mistassini society from birth to death*. Bulletin of the National Museum of Canada,
   no. 190.
RONEY, JAMES G., Jr.
   1959. Paleopathology of a California archaeological site. *Bulletin of the History of Medicine*, 33: 97–109.
ROSE, FREDERICK G. G.
   1960a. The Australian aboriginal family: some theoretical considerations. *Forschen and Wirken* (Berlin),
   3: 415–37.
   1960b. *Classification of kin, age structure and marriage amongst the Groote Eylandt aborigines: a study in method and
   a theory of Australian kinship*. Berlin: Akademie-Verlag. (London: Pergamon).
   1963. On the structure of the Australian family. *VIe Congrès International des Sciences Anthropologiques et
   Ethnologiques: Paris—30 Juillet—6 Août, 1960*, 2(1): 247–51.
   1965a. Unilateral cross-cousin marriage. *Man*, 65: 24–25.
   1965b. *The winds of change in central Australia: the aborigines at Angas Downs, 1962*. Berlin: Akademie-
   Verlag.
ROSTLUND, ERHARD.
   1952. *Freshwater fish and fishing in native North America*. University of California Publications in Geography,
   no. 9. (Berkeley).
ROTH, H. LING.
   1890. *The aborigines of Tasmania*. London: Kegan Paul, Trench, Trübner.
   1896. *The natives of Sarawak and British North Borneo, based chiefly on the MSS. of the late Hugh Brooke Low,
   Sarawak government service*. (2 vols.) London: Truslove and Hanson.
ROTH, WALTER E.
   1897. *Ethnological studies among the north-west central Queensland aborigines*. Brisbane: E. Gregory.
   1901. *Food: its search, capture and preparation*. North Queensland Bulletin of Ethnography, no. 3.
ROUNSEFELL, GEORGE A., and GEORGE B. KELEZ.
   1938. *The salmon and salmon fisheries of Swiftsure Bank, Puget Sound, and the Fraser River*. U.S. Department of
   Commerce, Bureau of Fisheries, Bulletin no. 27.
ROUSE, IRVING, and JOSÉ M. CRUXENT.
   1963a. Some recent radiocarbon dates for western Venezuela. *American Antiquity*, 28(4): 537–40.
   1963b. *Venezuelan archaeology*. Yale Caribbean Series, no. 6. New Haven: Yale University Press.
ROWE, JOHN HOWLAND.
   1952. Introduction. In Curt Nimuendajú, *The Tapajo*. Kroeber Anthropological Society Papers, 6: 1–25.
ROY, SARAT CHANDRA.
   1925. *The Birhors: a little-known jungle tribe of Chota Nagpur*. Ranchi: Loudon, Probsthain.
ROYAL ANTHROPOLOGICAL INSTITUTE.
   1951. *Notes and queries in anthropology*. (6th ed.) London: Routledge and Kegan Paul.

RUSSELL, FRANK.

1898. *Explorations in the far north: being the report of an expedition under the auspices of the University of Iowa, 1892–94.* Iowa City: University of Iowa Press.

SACKETT, J. R.

1965. *Archaeological interpretation in the Upper Paleolithic.* Paper presented at American Anthropological Association annual meetings, Denver.

1966. Quantitative analysis of Upper Palaeolithic stone tools. In J. D. Clark and F. C. Howell (Eds.), *Recent studies in paleoanthropology. American Anthropologist* (n.s.), 68(2), pt. 2: 356–94.

SADE, DONALD S.

1965. Some aspects of parent-offspring and sibling relations in a group of rhesus monkeys, with a discussion of grooming. *American Journal of Physical Anthropology* (n.s.), 23(1): 1–17.

1966. *Ontogeny of social relations in a group of free ranging Rhesus monkeys (Macaca mulatta* Zimmerman). Unpublished doctoral dissertation, University of California, Berkeley.

SAHLINS, MARSHALL D.

1958. *Social stratification in Polynesia.* American Ethnological Society Monographs, no. 29. Seattle: University of Washington Press.

1960. Political power and the economy in primitive society. In Gertrude E. Dole and Robert L. Carneiro (Eds.), *Essays in the science of culture in honor of Leslie A. White.* New York: Thomas Y. Crowell.

1965. On the ideology and composition of descent groups. *Man,* 65: 105–107.

1966. On the Delphic writings of Claude Lévi-Strauss. *Scientific American,* 214(6): 131–36.

SAHLINS, MARSHALL D., and ELMAN R. SERVICE (Eds.).

1960. *Evolution and culture.* Ann Arbor: University of Michigan Press.

SAMUELS, ROBERT.

1965. Parasitological study of long-dried fecal samples. In H. D. Osborne (comp.), *Contributions of the Weatherill Mesa archaeological project.* Memoirs of the Society of American Archaeology, no. 19.

SAUER, CARL O.

1950. Geography of South America. In J. H. Steward (Ed.), *Handbook of South American Indians,* vol. 6: *physical anthropology, linguistics and cultural geography of South American Indians.* Bureau of American Ethnology, Bulletin no. 143(6): 319–44.

1952. *Agricultural origins and dispersals.* New York: American Geographical Society.

SAWYER, JACK, and ROBERT A. LEVINE.

1966. Cultural dimension: a factor analysis of the World Ethnographic Sample. *American Anthropologist* (n.s.), 68: 708–731.

SCHALLER, GEORGE B.

1963. *The mountain gorilla: ecology and behavior.* Chicago: University of Chicago Press.

1965. The behavior of the mountain gorilla. In I. DeVore (Ed.), *Primate behavior.* New York: Holt, Rinehart and Winston.

SCHAPERA, ISAAC.

1926. A preliminary consideration of the relationship between the Hottentots and Bushmen. *South African Journal of Science,* 23: 833–36.

1930. *The Khoisan peoples of South Africa: Bushmen and Hottentots.* London: Routledge and Kegan Paul.

SCHEBESTA, PAUL.

1928. *Orang-Utan: Bei den Urwaldmenschen Malayas und Samatras.* Leipzig: F. A. Brockhaus.

1929. *Among the forest dwarfs of Malaya.* Trans. by A. Chambers. London: Hutchinson.

1931. Erste Mitteilungen über die Ergebnisse meiner Forschungsreise bei den Pygmäen in Belgisch-Kongo. *Anthropos,* 26: 1–27.

1938–50. Die Bambute-Pygmäen vom Ituri. *Memoires de l'Institut Royal Colonial Belge, Section des Sciences Morales et Politiques,* 1, 2, 4.

1952. Die Negrito Asiens, 1: Geschichte, Geographie. Umwelt, Demographie, und Anthropologie der Negrito. *Studia Instituti Anthropos,* no. 6. Wien-Mödling: St. Gabriel Verlag.

1954. Die Negrito Asiens, 2: Ethnographie der Negrito, part 1: Wirtschaft und Soziologie. *Studia Instituti Anthropos,* no. 12. Wien-Mödling: St. Gabriel Verlag.

1957. Die Negrito Asiens, 2: Ethnographie der Negrito, part 2: Religion and Mythologie. *Studia Instituti Anthropos*, no. 13. Wien-Mödling: St. Gabriel Verlag.

SCHMIDT, MAX.

1905. *Indianerstudien in Zentralbrasilien*. Berlin: Dietrich Reimer.

1942. Resultados de mi Tercera Expedición a los Guatos. *Revista de la Sociedad Científica del Paraguay*. 5(6): 41–75.

SCHNEIDER, D. M.

1965. Some muddles in the models: or, how the system really works. In *The relevance of models for social anthropology*. Association of Social Anthropologists Monographs, 1: 25–85.

SCHRENCK, LEOPOLD VON.

1881–91. *Die Völker des Amur-Landes, Reisen und Forschungen in Amur-Lande in den Jahren 1854–56*. St. Petersburg.

SELIGMANN, CHARLES G., and BRENDA Z. SELIGMANN.

1911. *The Veddas*. Cambridge: Cambridge University Press.

SELTZER, LEON E. (Ed.).

1952. *The Columbia Lippincott gazetteer of the world*. New York: Columbia University Press.

SEMENOV, S. A.

1964. *Prehistoric technology*. London: Barnes and Noble.

SEMON, RICHARD.

1899. *In the Australian bush and on the coast of the Coral Sea; being the experiences and observations of a naturalist in Australia, New Guinea, and the Moluccas*. London, New York: Macmillan

SEN, BIJAY K., and JYOTI SEN.

1955. Notes on the Birhors. *Man in India*, 35(3): 169–76.

SERVICE, ELMAN R.

1960. Sociocentric relationship terms and the Australian class system. In Gertrude E. Dole and Robert L. Carneiro (Eds.), *Essays in the science of culture in honor of Leslie A. White*. New York: Thomas Y. Crowell.

1962. *Primitive social organization: an evolutionary perspective*. New York: Random House.

1966. *The hunters*. Englewood Cliffs, N. J.: Prentice-Hall.

SHACK, WILLIAM A.

1964. Notes on occupational castes among the Gurage. *Man*, 64: 50–54.

1966. *The Gurage: a people of the Ensete culture*. Oxford: Oxford University Press.

SHAPIRO, HARRY L.

1957. Impact of culture on genetic mechanisms. In *The nature and transmission of the genetic and cultural characteristics of human populations*. New York: Milbank Memorial Fund.

SHARP, RICHARD LAURISTON.

1934. The social organization of the Yir-Yiront tribes, Cape York Peninsula, pt. 2: ritual life and economics. *Oceania*, 5(1): 19–42.

1940. An Australian aboriginal population. *Human Biology*, 12: 481–507.

1952. Steel axes for Stone Age Australians. In Edward Spicer (Ed.), *Human problems in technological change*. New York: Russell Sage Foundation.

SHEILS, HELEN.

1963. *Australian aboriginal studies*. Melbourne: Oxford University Press.

SHIMKIN, DEMITRI B.

1940. A sketch of the Ket, or Yenisei "Ostyak." *Ethnos*, 4: 147–76.

SHIROKOGOROV, S. M.

1935. *Psychomental complex of the Tungus*. London: Kegan Paul, Trench, Trübner.

SILBERBAUER, G. B.

1965. *Report to the Government of Bechuanaland on the Bushman survey*. Gaberones, Bechuanaland: Government of Bechuanaland.

SIMMONS, LEO W.

1945. *The role of the aged in primitive society*. New Haven: Yale University Press.

SIMPSON, GEORGE.

1938. *Journal of occurrences in the Athabasca Department, 1820 and 1821.* vol. 1. Ed. by E. E. Rich. Toronto: Publications of the Champlain Society, no. 1, Hudson's Bay Company Series.

SIMPSON, GEORGE GAYLORD.

1956. *Evolution and geography: an essay on historical biogeography, with special reference to mammals.* Condon Lectures, December, 1953. Eugene: Oregon State System of Higher Education.

1961. *Principles of animal taxonomy.* New York: Columbia University Press.

1966. The biological nature of man. *Science,* 152(3721): 472–78.

SKEAT, WALTER W., and C. O. BLAGDEN.

1906. *Pagan races of the Malay Peninsula.* London: Macmillan.

SLATER, MIRIAM K.

1959. Ecological factors in the origin of incest. *American Anthropologist* (n.s.), 61: 1042–59.

SLOBODIN, RICHARD.

1962. *Band organization of the Peel River Kutchin.* Bulletin of the National Museum of Canada, no. 179.

SOLLAS, WILLIAM J.

1911. *Ancient hunters and their modern representatives.* London: Macmillan.

DeSONNEVILLE-BORDES, DENISE, and J. PERROT.

1954–56. Lexique typologique du Paléolithique supérieur. *Bulletin de la Société Préhistorique Française,* 51: 327–55; 52; 76–79; 53: 408–412.

SPECHT, R. L.

1958. An introduction to the ethnobotany of Arnhem Land. *Records of the American-Australian Scientific Expedition to Arnhem Land,* 3: 479–503.

SPECK, FRANK G.

1915. The family hunting band as the basis of the Algonkian social organization. *American Anthropologist* (n.s.) 17(2): 289–305.

1931. Montagnais-Naskapi bands and early Eskimo distribution in the Labrador Peninsula. *American Anthropologist* (n.s.), 33: 557–600.

SPECK, FRANK G., and LOREN C. EISELEY.

1939. The significance of hunting territory systems of the Algonkian in social theory. *American Anthropologist* (n.s.), 41: 269–80.

SPENCER, BALDWIN.

1914. *Native tribes of the Northern Territory of Australia.* London: Macmillan.

SPENCER, BALDWIN, and F. J. GILLEN.

1899. *The native tribes of central Australia.* London: Macmillan.

1904. *The northern tribes of central Australia.* London: Macmillan.

1927. *The Arunta: a study of a Stone-Age people.* London: Macmillan.

SPENCER, ROBERT F.

1959. *The north Alaskan Eskimo: a study in ecology and society.* Bureau of American Ethnology Bulletin no. 171.

1965. The Eskimo of northern Alaska. In R. F. Spencer *et al.* (Eds.), *The native Americans: prehistory and ethnology of the North American Indians.* New York, London: Harper and Row.

SPUHLER, J. N.

1959. Somatic paths to culture. In J. N. Spuhler (Ed.), *The evolution of man's capacity for culture.* Detroit: Wayne State University Press.

STANNER, W. E. H.

1932. The Daly River tribes, a report of field work in north Australia. *Oceania,* 3: 377–405.

1936. Murinbata kinship and totemism. *Oceania,* 7: 186–216.

1965. Aboriginal territorial organization: estate, range, domain and regime. *Oceania,* 36(1): 1–26.

STEFANSSON, VILHJALMUR.

1914. *The Stefansson-Anderson Arctic expedition of the American Museum: preliminary ethnological report.* Anthropological Papers of the American Museum of Natural History, no. 24.

STERNBERG, HILGARD O'REILLY.

1964. Land and man in the tropics. *Proceedings of the Academy of Political Science,* 27(4): 319–29.

STEWARD, JULIAN H.

1936. The economic and social basis of primitive bands. In R. H. Lowie (Ed.), *Essays in anthropology presented to A. L. Kroeber*. Berkeley: University of California Press.

1937. Linguistic distributions and political groups of the Great Basin Shoshoneans. *American Anthropologist* (n.s.), 39: 625–34.

1938. *Basin-plateau aboriginal socio-political groups*. Bureau of American Ethnology Bulletin no. 120.

1941. Determinism in primitive society? *Scientific Monthly*, 53: 491–501.

1943. Northern and Gosiute Shoshoni. Culture Element Distributions 23. *Anthropological Records* (Berkeley), 8: 263–392.

1946. The marginal tribes. In J. H. Steward (Ed.), *Handbook of South American Indians*, vol. 1: *the marginal tribes*. Bureau of American Ethnology Bulletin 143(1).

1948a. Tribes of the Montaña. In J. H. Steward (Ed.), *Handbook of South American Indians*, vol. 3: *the tropical forest tribes*. Bureau of American Ethnology Bulletin 143(3): 507–533.

1948b. Culture areas of the tropical forest. In J. H. Steward (Ed.), *Handbook of South American Indians*, vol. 3: *the tropical forest tribes*. Bureau of American Ethnology Bulletin 143(3): 883–99.

1953. Aboriginal and historic groups of the Ute Indians of Utah: an analysis. Paper presented before the Indian Claims Commission for the U.S. Department of Justice. (Mimeo.)

1955. *Theory of culture change: the methodology of multilinear evolution*. Urbana: University of Illinois Press.

1960. Carrier acculturation: the direct historical approach. In Stanley Diamond (Ed.), *Culture in history, essays in honor of Paul Radin*. New York: Columbia University Press.

1965. Some problems raised by Roger C. Owen's "The patrilocal band." *American Anthropologist* (n.s.), 67: 732–33.

1966. Toward understanding cultural evolution. (Review of Robert McC. Adam's *The evolution of urban society*.) *Science*, 153(3737): 729–30.

1967. Comments on Chang's "Major aspects of the interrelationship of archaeology and ethnology." *Current Anthropology*, 8(3): 239–40.

In press a. Cultural ecology. In *International Encyclopedia of the Social Sciences*.

In press b. Perspectives of modernization. In J. H. Steward (Ed.), *Contemporary change in traditional societies, I*. Urbana: University of Illinois Press.

STEWARD, JULIAN H., and ERMINE WHEELER-VOGELIN.

1953. *Aboriginal and historic groups of northern Paiute Indians of Oregon, Nevada, and California*. Paper presented before the Indian Claims Commission for the U.S. Department of Justice.

STOW, GEORGE W.

1905. *The native races of South Africa; a history of the intrusion of the Hottentots and Bantu into the hunting grounds of the Bushmen, the aborigines of the country*. London: Swan Sonnenschein.

STREHLOW, THEODOR G. H.

1947. *Aranda traditions*. Melbourne: Melbourne University Press.

1965. Culture, social structure, and environment in aboriginal Australia. In R. M. Berndt and C. H. Berndt (Eds.), *Aboriginal man in Australia: essays in honour of Emeritus Professor A. P. Elkin*. Sydney, London, Melbourne: Angus and Robertson.

STRONG, WILLIAM D.

1929a. *Aboriginal society in Southern California*: University of California Publications in American Archaeology and Ethnology (Berkeley) no. 26.

1929b. Cross-cousin marriage and the culture of the northeastern Algonkian. *American Anthropologist* (n.s.), 31: 277–88.

STRUEVER, STUART.

1966. Middle Woodland culture history in the Great Lakes riverine area. *American Antiquity*, 31: 211–23.

STRUHSAKER, THOMAS T.

1967. Auditory communication among vervet monkeys (Cercopithecus aethiops). In S. A. Altmann (Ed.), *Social communication among primates*. Chicago: University of Chicago Press.

SUE, HIROKO.

1964. *Hare Indians and their world*. Unpublished doctoral dissertation, Bryn Mawr College.

SUTTLES, WAYNE.

1960. Affinal ties, subsistence, and prestige among the Coast Salish. *American Anthropologist* (n.s.), 62: 296–305.

1962. Variation in habitat and culture in the northwest coast. *Akten des 34 Internationalen Amerikanistenkongresses, Wein, 1960:* 522–37.

SWAN, JAMES G.

1870. The Indians of Cape Flattery. *Smithsonian Contributions to Knowledge,* no. 16.

SWEENEY, G.

1947. Food supplies of a desert tribe. *Oceania,* 17: 289–99.

TAX, SOL.

1937. Some problems of social organization. In Fred Eggan (Ed.), *Social anthropology of North American tribes.* Chicago: University of Chicago Press.

TAX, SOL (Ed.).

1953. *An appraisal of anthropology today.* Chicago: University of Chicago Press.

TAYLOR, CLARA M., and ORREA F. PYE.

1966. *Foundations of nutrition.* (6th ed.) New York: Macmillan.

TAYLOR, GARTH J.

1965. *Social organization of the eighteenth century Labrador Eskimo.* Unpublished doctoral dissertation, University of Toronto.

TAYLOR, GRIFFITH.

1943. *Australia.* (2d ed., rev.) New York: E. P. Dutton.

TAYLOR, HERBERT C.

1963. Aboriginal populations of the lower northwest coast. *Pacific Northwest Quarterly,* 54: 158–65.

TEICHER, MORTON I.

1960. Windigo psychosis. *Proceedings,* 1960 Annual Spring Meeting, American Philosophical Society.

THALBITZER, WILLIAM (Ed.).

1914. The Ammassalik Eskimo. *Meddelelser om Grønland* (Copenhagen), 40.

THOMAS, ELIZABETH MARSHALL.

1959. *The harmless people.* New York: Alfred A. Knopf.

THOMAS, NORTHCOTE W.

1906. *Kinship organization and group marriage in Australia.* Cambridge: Cambridge University Press.

THOMAS, WILLIAM.

1878. Succinct sketch of the aboriginal language. In R. Brough Smyth (Ed.), *The aborigines of Victoria,* vol. 2. Melbourne: J. Ferres.

THOMPSON, RAYMOND H.

1956. The subjective element in archaeological inference. *Southwestern Journal of Anthropology,* 12: 327–32.

1958. Modern Yucatecan May pottery making. *Memoirs of the Society for American Archaeology,* 15. (Also: *American Antiquity,* 23[4], pt. 2.)

THOMSON, DONALD F.

1933. The hero cult, initiation and totemism on Cape York. *Journal of the Royal Anthropological Institute of Great Britain and Ireland,* 63: 543–538.

1934a. Notes on a hero cult from the Gulf of Carpentaria, North Queensland. *Journal of the Royal Anthropological Institute of Great Britain and Ireland,* 64: 217–36.

1934b. The dugong hunters of Cape York. *Journal of the Royal Anthropological Institute of Great Britain and Ireland,* 64: 237–63.

1939. The seasonal factor in human culture. *Proceedings of the Prehistoric Society* (n.s.), 10: 209–221.

1948–49. Arnhem Land: explorations among an unknown people. *Geographical Journal,* 112: 146–64; 113: 1–8; 114; 53–67.

1949. *Economic structure and the ceremonial exchange cycle in Arnhem Land.* Melbourne: Macmillan.

1964. Some wood and stone implements of the Bindibu tribe of central West Australia. *Proceedings of the Prehistoric Society* (n.s.), 30: 400–422.

TINDALE, NORMAN B.

1925. Natives of Groote Eylandt and of the west coast of the Gulf of Carpentaria. *Records of the South Australia Museum*, 3(1–2): 61–134.

1940. Results of the Harvard-Adelaide Universities anthropological expedition, 1938–1939: dis ribution of Australian aboriginal tribes: a field survey. *Transactions of the Royal Society of South Australia*, 64: 140–231.

1953. Tribal and intertribal marriage among the Australian aborigines. *Human Biology*, 25: 169–90.

1957. Culture succession in south eastern Australia from late Pleistocene to the present. *Records of the South Australian Museum*, 13: 1–49.

1962a. Geographical knowledge of the Kaiadilt people of Bentinck Island, Queensland. *Records of the South Australian Museum*, 14: 259–96.

1962b. Some population changes among the Kaiadilt people of Bentinck Island, Queensland. *Records of the South Australian Museum*, 14: 297–336.

TINDALE, NORMAN B., and J. B. BIRDSELL.

1941. Results of the Harvard-Adelaide Universities anthropological expedition, 1938–1939: Tasmanoid tribes in north Queensland. *Records of the South Australian Museum*, 7: 1–9.

TINDALE, NORMAN B., and H. V. V. NOONE.

1941. Results of the Harvard-Adelaide Universities anthropological expedition, 1938–1939: analysis of an Australian aboriginal's hoard of knapped flint. *Transactions of the Royal Society of South Australia*, 65: 116–22.

TOBIAS, P. V.

1956. On the survival of the Bushmen, with an estimate of the problem facing anthropologists. *Africa*, 26: 174–86.

1964. Bushman hunter-gatherers: a study in human ecology. In D. H. S. Davis (Ed.), *Ecological studies in southern Africa*. The Hague: W. Junk.

TOKAREV, S. A.

1961. Zur Bedeutung der Frauendarstellungen im Paläolithikum. *Veröffentlichungen des Museums für Völkerkunde* (Leipzig), 11: 682–92.

TREIDE, DIETRICH.

1965. Die Organisierung des indianischen Lachsfangs in westlichen Nordamerika. *Veröffentlichungen des Museums für Völkerkunde* (Leipzig), 14.

TRETYAKOV, P. N.

1934. K Istorii doklassovogo obsh 'chestva verkhnego Povolzhya (On the history of pre-class society in the area of the Upper Volga). In *Iz Istorii Rodovogo Obsh' chestva na Territorii SSSR, Gosudarstavannaia Akademiia Istorii Material'noi Kul'tury* (Moscow), 106: 97–180.

TREWARTHA, GLENN T.

1954. *An introduction to climate*. (3d ed.) New York: McGraw-Hill.

TURNBULL, COLIN M.

1961. *The forest people: a study of the Pygmies of the Congo*. New York: Simon & Schuster.

1965a. The Mbuti Pygmies: an ethnographic survey. *Anthropological Papers of the American Museum of Natural History*, 50(3): 139–282.

1965b. *Wayward servants: the two worlds of the African Pygmies*. Garden City: Natural History Press.

1965c. The Mbuti Pygmies of the Congo. In James L. Gibbs (Ed.), *Peoples of Africa*. New York, London: Holt, Rinehart, and Winston.

TURNER, TERENCE S.

1965. *Social structure and political organization among the northern Cayapo*. Unpublished doctoral dissertation, Harvard University.

UNDERHILL, RUTH.

1945. *Indians of the Pacific Northwest*. Sherman Pamphlets on Indian Life and Customs, no. 5. Lawrence, Kansas: Educational Division, U.S. Office of Indian Affairs.

UNITED NATIONS. DEPARTMENT OF ECONOMIC AND SOCIAL AFFAIRS, Statistical Office.

1958. *Demographic yearbook*. (10th ed.) New York: Author.

VALLOIS, HENRI V.

1961. The social life of early man: the evidence of skeletons. In S. L. Washburn (Ed.), *Social life of early man*. Chicago: Aldine Publishing Company.

VAN DE VELDE, FRANS.

1956. Les règles du partage des phoques pris par la chasse aux aglus. *Anthropologica*, 3: 5–14.

VAN STONE, JAMES W.

1961. *The economy of a frontier community: a preliminary statement*. Canada, Department of Northern Affairs and National Resources, Northern Coordination and Research Centre, Report, no. 4 (for 1961).

1962. *Point Hope: an Eskimo village in transition*. American Ethnological Society Monograph, no. 35. Seattle: University of Washington Press.

VAYDA, ANDREW P.

1961a. A re-examination of Northwest Coast economic systems. *Transactions of the New York Academy of Sciences*, Series 2, 23: 618–24.

1961b. Expansion and warfare among swidden agriculturalists. *American Anthropologist* (n.s.), 63(2), pt. 1: 346–58.

VELDER, C. M.

1963. A description of the Mrabi camp. *Journal of the Siam Society*, 51: 185–88.

1964. Review of H. A. Bernatzik's "Die Geister der Gelben Blätter." *Zeitschrift für Ethnologie*, 89(1): 10–23.

VELLARD, J.

1939. *Une civilisation du miel: les Indiens Guayakis du Paraguay*. (7th ed.) Paris: Gallimard.

VERHOEVEN, L. A., and E. B. DAVIDOFF.

1962. *Marine tagging of Fraser River sockeye salmon*. International Pacific Salmon Fisheries Commission, *Bulletin* (New Westminster, B.C.), 13.

VORKAPICH, MYRA.

MS. *Ecology as a factor in Great Basin aboriginal population density*.

WAGLEY, CHARLES, and E. GALVAO.

1949. *The Tenetehara Indians of Brazil: a culture in transition*. Columbia University Contributions to Anthropology, no. 35.

WAGNER, PHILIP L.

1960. *The human use of the earth*. Glencoe, Ill.: The Free Press.

WARNER, WILLIAM LLOYD.

1937. *A black civilization: a study of an Australian tribe*. New York: Harper.

WASHBURN, SHERWOOD L.

1965. An ape's eye view of evolution. In Paul DeVore (Ed.), *The origin of man* (symposium transcript). New York: Wenner-Gren Foundation for Anthropological Research.

WASHBURN, SHERWOOD L., and VIRGINIA AVIS.

1958. Evolution of human behavior. In Anne Roe and G. G. Simpson (Eds.), *Behavior and evolution*. New Haven: Yale University Press.

WASHBURN, SHERWOOD L., and IRVEN DEVORE.

1961a. Social behavior of baboons and early man. In S. L. Washburn (Ed.), *Social life of early man*. Chicago: Aldine Publishing Company.

1961b. The social life of baboons. *Scientific American*, 204(6): 62–71.

WASHBURN, SHERWOOD L., PHYLLIS C. JAY, and JANE F. B. LANCASTER.

1965. Field studies of Old World monkeys and apes. *Science*, 150(3703): 1541–47.

WATANABE, HITOSHI.

1964a. The Ainu: a study of ecology and the system of social solidarity between man and nature in relation to group structure. *Journal of the Faculty of Science* (Tokyo), Section 5, 2(6). (In Japanese).

1964b. Ecology of the Ainu and problems in prehistory in Japan. *Journal of the Anthropological Society of Nippon*, 72(740): 9–23. (In Japanese)

1966. Ecology of the Jomon people: stability of habitation and its biological and ethnohistorical implications. *Journal of the Anthropological Society of Nippon*, 74(749): 73–84. (In Japanese)

In press. Stability of habitation and food surplus among the Ainu. *Papers of the VII International Congress of Anthropological and Ethnological Sciences*, Moscow, 1964.

WATT, BERNICE K., and ANNABEL L. MERRILL.

1963. *Composition of foods: raw, processed, prepared.* Agricultural Handbook no. 8. U.S. Department of Agriculture, Agricultural Research Service.

WAYLAND, E. J.

1931. Preliminary studies of the tribes of Karamoja. *Journal of the Royal Anthropological Institute of Great Britain and Ireland*, 61: 187–230.

WEBB, T. THEODOR.

1933. Tribal organization in eastern Arnhem Land. *Oceania*, 3: 406–411.

WEINBERG, D.

1965. Models of southern Kwakiutl social organization: general systems. *Yearbook of the Society for General Systems Research*, 10: 169–81.

WENTZEL, W. F.

1889. Letters to the Honorable Roderic McKenzie, 1807–1824. In L. R. Masson (Ed.), *Les bouregois de la compagnie du nord ouest: récits de voyages, lettres et rapports inédits relatifs au nord-ouest canadien, Série 1.* Quebec: A. Coté.

WESTPHAL, E. O. J.

1956. The non-Bantu languages of southern Africa. In A. N. Tucker and M. A. Bryan (Eds.), *Handbook of African languages, 3: the non-Bantu languages of north-eastern Africa.* London: Oxford University Press.

WHALLON, ROBERT.

1965. *The Owasco period: a reanalysis.* Unpublished doctoral dissertation, University of Chicago.

WHARTON, R. H., A. B. G. LAING, and W. H. CHEONG.

1963. Studies on the distribution and transmission of malaria and filariasis among aborigines in Malaya. *Annals of Tropical Medicine and Parasitology*, 57: 235–54.

WHEELER, DAVID E.

1914. The Dogrib Indian and his home. *Bulletin of the Geographic Society of Philadelphia*, 12(2): 47–60.

WHEELER, GERALD C.

1910. *The tribe, and inter-tribal relations in Australia.* London: John Murray.

WHITE, LESLIE A.

1959. *The evolution of culture.* New York: McGraw-Hill.

WHITING, BEATRICE B. (Ed.).

1963. *Six cultures: studies of child-rearing.* New York: John Wiley and Sons.

WHITING, J. W. M.

1967. *Rearrangement of certain Ethnographic Atlas codes.* Unpublished.

WHITON, LOUIS C., H. BRUCE GREENE, and RICHARD P. MOMSEN, Jr.

1964. The Isconahua of the Remo. *Journal de la Société des Américanistes* (Paris), 53: 85–124.

WILBERT, JOHANNES.

1958a. Die soziale und politische Organisation der Warrau. *Kölner Zeitschrift für Soziologie und Sozialpsychologie* (n.s.), 10: 272–91.

1958b. Datos antropologicos de los Indios Piaroa. *Memorias de la Sociedad de Ciencias Naturales La Salle* (Caracas), 18: 155–83.

1966. *Indios de la region Orinoco-Venturi.* Monografias de la Fundacíon La Salle de Ciencias Naturales no. 8. Caracas: Instituto Caribe de Antropología y Sociología y Fundacíon La Salle de Ciencias Naturales.

WILLIAMS, B. J.

In press. Paper presented at Conference on Band Organization, Ottawa. In D. Damas (Ed.), *Ecological essays: proceedings of the conference on cultural ecology, National Museum of Canada, 1966.* Contributions to Anthropology, Ethnology, 7, National Museum of Canada, Ottawa.

WILLIAMS-HUNT, PETER D. R.

1952. *An introduction to the Malayan aborigines.* Kuala Lumpur: Government Printer.

WINTER, EDWARD H.

1956. *Bwamba: a structural-functional analysis of a patrilineal society.* Cambridge: W. Heffer.

WISSLER, CLARK.

1926. *The relation of nature to man in aboriginal America.* New York: Oxford University Press.

WOODBURN, J. C.

1959. Hadza conceptions of health and disease. In *One day symposium on attitudes to health and disease among some East African tribes.* Kampala, Uganda: East African Institute of Social Research, Makerere College.

1962. The future of the Tindiga: a short account of the present position and possibilities for the future of a hunting tribe in Tanganyika. *Tanganyika Notes and Records*, 58–59: 268–73.,

1964. *The social organization of the Hadza of north Tanganyika.* Unpublished doctoral dissertation, Cambridge University.

WOODBURN, J. C., and SEAN HUDSON.

1966. *The Hadza: the food quest of a hunting and gathering tribe of Tanzania.* (16mm film.) London: London School of Economics.

WORLD HEALTH ORGANIZATION.

1963. Conference on medicine and public health in the Arctic and Antarctic. Geneva, 28 August–1 September, 1962. Technical Report Series, no. 253.

1964. *Research in population genetics of primitive groups.* Technical Report Series, no. 279.

WORSELEY, PETER M.

1961. The utilization of natural food resources by an Australian aboriginal tribe. *Acta Ethnographica*, 10(1–2): 153–90.

WRIGHT, SEWALL.

1938. Size of population and breeding structure in relation to evolution. *Science*, 87(2263): 430–31.

WYNNE-EDWARDS, V. C.

1962. *Animal dispersion in relation to social behavior.* Edinburgh: Oliver and Boyd.

YAMADA, MUNEMI.

1963. A study of blood-relationship in the natural society of the Japanese macaque. *Primates (Journal of Primatology)*, 4: 43–66.

YOUNG, R. B.

1954. British Columbia Pilot (Canadian Edition), II: northern portion of the Coast of British Columbia. (3d ed.) Ottawa: Queen's Printer.

ZEUNER, F. E.

1963. *A history of domesticated animals.* New York: Harper and Row.

ZUCKERMANN, SOLLY.

1933. *Functional affinities of man, monkeys, and apes.* New York: Harcourt, Brace.

Index